Corporate Responsibility

Corporate Responsibility

THIRD EDITION

Michael Blowfield

Alan Murray

OXFORD
UNIVERSITY PRESS

OXFORD

UNIVERSITY PRESS

Great Clarendon Street, Oxford OX2 6DP,
United Kingdom

Oxford University Press is a department of the University of Oxford.
It furthers the University's objective of excellence in research, scholarship,
and education by publishing worldwide. Oxford is a registered trade mark of
Oxford University Press in the UK and in certain other countries

© Oxford University Press 2014

The moral rights of the authors have been asserted

First edition 2008
Second edition 2011

Impression: 1

Published in the United States of America by Oxford University Press
198 Madison Avenue, New York, NY 10016, United States of America

British Library Cataloguing in Publication Data
Data available

Library of Congress Control Number: 2014938541

ISBN 978-0-19-967832-7

Printed in Italy by L.E.G.O. S.p.A.

Links to third party websites are provided by Oxford in good faith and
for information only. Oxford disclaims any responsibility for the materials
contained in any third party website referenced in this work.

Preface

The subject of 'corporate responsibility' is at a stage at which it needs a text that introduces the key ideas and practices in the field, and places them in wider contexts. Since we wrote the second edition, corporate taxation, financial mis-selling, and damaged economies have all occupied public attention. The record fines that we wrote about last time are no longer the record-holders in this third edition. By the time this book is published there will be new stories of both negligence and innovation. What links the old and the new is that they are all the result of how the role of business in society is defined, negotiated, and managed. That is the domain of corporate responsibility, and explaining that domain is the purpose of this book.

The book is intended for students and tutors of corporate responsibility at both undergraduate and graduate levels, but we are proud that it has also been taken up by other disciplines concerned about the role of business in modern society. The text provides a strong framework for studying corporate responsibility, which links a wealth of theoretical analysis with more practitioner-oriented materials. Its 14 chapters are divided into three broad themes: the origins and meaning of corporate responsibility; how it is being managed and implemented; its impact to date and its likely future directions. Under these themes, we examine such topics as the social and historical context of corporate responsibility and its business case, key areas of management practice including stakeholder engagement, partnership, ethical supply chains, social auditing, and corporate governance, and the role of responsible investment, as well as that of government and civil society.

We provide an international dimension in that the theories and examples are drawn from around the world. We provide a critical perspective in that we do not advocate any particular ideas about corporate responsibility, preferring instead to compare and contrast a host of differing perspectives. Our aim above all is to assist in building an understanding of the potential and limitations of the private sector in areas of extra-financial performance.

Michael Blowfield
Alan Murray

Acknowledgements

MEB

This book reflects our experiences as academics, practitioners, and consultants working in the field of corporate responsibility for companies, civil societies, and government organizations. I am grateful to the many friends and colleagues who have knowingly, or unknowingly, contributed to that experience. I am grateful also to the University of Wolverhampton Business School for granting me the time to revise the third edition. It would be unfair to single out anyone in particular, but this in no way diminishes my accumulated gratitude over the years, and I trust that those involved will understand why the only people mentioned by name are John MacLean, Catherine, Ieuan, Lucy, and Terry.

AM

I would like to acknowledge the work of the Centre for Social and Environmental Accounting Research at the University of St Andrews—particularly the efforts of Rob and Sue Gray, and all the researchers who have attended the annual summer schools over the last decade or so, whose scholarship and rigour has helped to develop and inform my views and opinions. I would also like to acknowledge the love of Kathryn, Rosie, Ellie, and Florence in supporting me in this endeavour.

We are grateful to the anonymous reviewers whose comments have added immensely to the text, and to Cary Krosinsky, William Frederick, the Center for Corporate Citizenship at Boston College, CANOPUS, and the Ethical Trading Initiative, each of which has granted us permission to use some of their materials. Crown copyright is reproduced under Class License Number C20060110631 with the permission of OPSI and the Queen's printer for Scotland.

Contents

List of Figures	xi
List of Boxes	xii
List of Case Studies	xiii
List of Snapshots	xiv
List of Abbreviations	xv
How to use this Book	xviii
How to use the Online Resource Centre	xx

PART 1 The meaning and origins of corporate responsibility

1	**Introducing corporate responsibility**	**3**
	Why corporate responsibility?	3
	Definitions of corporate responsibility	6
	Corporate governance	9
	A framework for understanding corporate responsibility	10
	Values motivation	12
	Limitations of corporate responsibility frameworks	24
2	**The origins of corporate responsibility**	**31**
	Introduction	31
	Three eras of responsibility	32
	Theories of corporate responsibility	40
3	**Sustainable development**	**53**
	Introduction	54
	Meanings of 'sustainability' and 'sustainable development'	56
	Climate change and global warming	61
	The challenge to business	64
	New models of sustainable business	65
	Capital markets and sustainable development	66
	Signals to the market	67
	Rewarding financial intermediaries	69
4	**Corporate responsibility in developing economies**	**75**
	Introduction	75
	Development agent or development tool?	76

A brief history of business as development agent   77

Theories of development   78

The business–poverty framework   81

Business as a cause of poverty   82

Business as poverty's victim   85

Business as a solution   86

Assessing the business response   89

5   Globalization and corporate responsibility   98

Globalization and corporate responsibility   99

The meaning of 'globalization'   99

Influence of globalization on business   104

Corporate responsibility as a response to globalization   109

Unmet challenges   117

PART 2 **Managing and implementing corporate responsibility**

6   How corporate responsibility is managed   129

Understanding what companies want from corporate responsibility 129

Qualities of good corporate responsibility management   136

Structuring the corporate responsibility function   138

Corporate responsibility as strategy   141

The business case for corporate responsibility   144

7   Corporate responsibility and governance   160

Introduction   161

Theories of corporate governance   162

The 'drivers' of corporate governance reform   163

The development of the UK corporate governance framework   166

International developments in corporate governance   171

Commentary from a corporate responsibility perspective   172

8   Corporate responsibility reporting   179

What is corporate responsibility reporting?   180

The nature of CR reporting   182

The challenges of CR reporting   184

The emergence of CR reporting   185

The upsurge in CR reporting since the early 1990s   186

Researching the practice of CR–KPMG surveys   188

Conventional financial reporting and CR reporting   192
Reporting issues for corporate management   193

9   Stakeholder management and engagement   **201**
Meaning and origins of stakeholder   201
Corporate responsibility standards   208
Stakeholder consensus: deviance and uniformity   215
Government and governance   217

10   Socially responsible investment   **225**
The origins and development of socially responsible investment 226
Sustainable investing   230
Types of SRI analysis and practice   231
Engagement   235
Other SRI approaches   238
SRI performance   244
SRI index performance   244
SRI fund performance   246
Market growth   247
Trends in SRI   248

11   Corporate responsibility in smaller enterprises   **254**
The small business 'problem'   255
The meaning and significance of smaller business   255
Local, national, and regional differences between SMEs   258
SMEs as society members   260
SME perspectives on corporate responsibility   261
Responsibility issues for SMEs   263
SMEs and corporate responsibility management   265
Social enterprise   268
Meanings of social enterprise   269
Why now?   272

PART 3   Impact, critics, and future of corporate responsibility

12   The impact of corporate responsibility   **281**
Understanding impact   281
Different dimensions of the impact of corporate responsibility 287
The challenges of determining impact   303

13   Criticisms of corporate responsibility   **312**

Introducing critiques of corporate responsibility   312

'Corporate responsibility is anti-business'   314

'Corporate responsibility is pro-business'   317

'The scope of corporate responsibility is too narrow'   322

'Corporate responsibility fails to achieve its goals'   325

14   The future of corporate responsibility   **334**

Where is corporate responsibility heading?   334

Mega-trends affecting corporate responsibility   337

Embedding and integrating corporate responsibility   339

Transition and transformation   345

The role of business in society   349

Appendix   360

Glossary   362

Bibliography   369

Index   407

List of Figures

1.1   Relationship between corporate responsibility motivations and outcomes   13

1.2   Carroll's typology of corporate responsibilities   17

2.1   Levels of public confidence in business over the years   33

2.2   Timeline of corporate responsibility   43

4.1   Business's relationships to poverty   81

6.1   Stages of corporate responsibility   135

6.2   Sustainability matrix   150

6.3   Plan A headline commitments   154

6.4   Corporate responsibility management structure at Marks & Spencer   155

9.1   How stakeholders' influence and interests affect corporate prioritization   206

10.1   SRI returns compared with mainstream indices until 2007   245

10.2   Sustainable investing—updated performance analysis   245

10.3   Growth of funds under SRI management—comparison of USA and Europe   247

11.1   Types of social and environmental impact that SMEs can have   259

11.2   Areas of SME management where corporate responsibility issues are relevant   267

14.1   A framework for understanding corporate responsibility trends   337

List of Boxes

1.1	Definitions of corporate responsibility	7
1.2	Published standards of corporate responsibility	8
1.3	How the value of corporate responsibility depends on your viewpoint	18
1.4	Prominent areas of corporate responsibility activity today	24
4.1	The three conditions of business's engagement in poverty	90
5.1	Examples and types of partnership	114
5.2	Partnership outcomes for different stakeholders—examples from mining	116
5.3	The ten principles of the Global Compact	120
6.1	Common advice on introducing corporate responsibility into management	137
6.2	Dimensions of corporate responsibility	146
6.3	Measures of business performance	146
7.1	Summary of share ownership in the UK, 1963–2012	164
9.1	Commonly cited phases and factors in engaging with stakeholders	205
9.2	Underlying principles of business codes	208
9.3	Johnson & Johnson's credo	209
9.4	Examples of corporate responsibility standards	210
9.5	Comparison of priority social and environmental issues across selected countries and regions	216
10.1	Different styles of socially responsible investment	226
10.2	The 'London Principles' on the financial sector's role in sustainable development	229
10.3	UN Principles for Responsible Investment	230
10.4	Resources on voting guidelines	237
11.1	SME objections to corporate responsibility	261
11.2	Reasons for SMEs to adopt corporate responsibility management practices	262
11.3	SME vantage points on corporate responsibility	263
12.1	Surveys and reports on corporate responsibility performance	284
12.2	Strong and weak areas of corporate responsibility reports	285
12.3	Country variations in ratings of brand reputation	301
13.1	The four myths of corporate responsibility	326
14.1	World demographics at a glance	338
14.2	Initiatives aimed at professionalizing corporate responsibility—examples	341
14.3	Principles of the redesigned corporation	353

List of Case Studies

1	What are the limits to responsibility? The case of pharmaceuticals	26
2	Corporate responsibility in different eras: Cadbury	48
3	Interface Inc.	70
4	Poverty as a business opportunity: M-PESA	94
5	The United Nations Global Compact	120
6	Marks & Spencer's Plan A—The evolution of a corporate responsibility strategy	152
7	The CORE network	176
8	Environmental reporting at PUMA	196
9	Roundtable on Sustainable Palm Oil—international multi-stakeholder partnerships across the value chain	220
10	China—SRI's rising star or nemesis?	249
11	SELCO-India—bringing energy to the rural poor	274
12	Can corporate responsibility guarantee an impact?—Fairtrade	305
13	Can corporate responsibility be blamed for a financial crisis?	328
14	Google—global struggles and responsibilities	354

List of Snapshots

1.1   147 'species' of corporate responsibility   10
1.2   What responsibilities do companies have?   25

2.1   Is big business desirable, inevitable, or irredeemable?   36
2.2   Trafigura takes on global civil society   41

3.1   Oil price and supply fluctuations   55
3.2   Aviation and climate change   63
3.3   Individual freedom and the common good   67

4.1   Clean water for poor communities—P&G PuR   80
4.2   Fairtrade: an approach to market redistribution   84

5.1   Globalization and Kenya's rose-growing industry   100
5.2   Water—privatizing basic rights or giving access to basic needs?   105

6.1   General Electric—integrating corporate responsibility as a business driver   143
6.2   Catalytic converters—governments creating the business case   148

7.1   The legacy of Robert Maxwell   165
7.2   Company law reform—the Companies Act 2006   173

8.1   Sustainability at Fujitsu   187
8.2   Is social information of use to investors?   189

9.1   The Global Reporting Initiative   212
9.2   Multi-stakeholder governance—Extractive Industries Transparency Initiative   218

10.1 CalPERS in Japan: shareholder activism to change corporate governance   238
10.2 CANOPUS Foundation—European venture philanthropy   241

11.1 SMEs in Russia—unique challenges and common ground   259
11.2 Zippos—a responsible circus?   264

12.1 The impact of ethical trading on workers   297
12.2 Levi's and China   299

13.1 The Church takes on Caterpillar over Palestine—giving corporate responsibility muscle   316
13.2 Tobacco—can bad industries produce responsible companies?   320

14.1 UN Principles for Responsible Investment   345
14.2 Tree-huggers at the gate—collaboration of private equity and NGOs over coal-fired power   352

List of Abbreviations

ACCA	Association of Chartered Certified Accountants
BAU	business-as-usual
BCCI	Bank of Credit and Commerce International
BITC	Business in the Community
BOP	bottom of the pyramid
BSE	bovine spongiform encephalopathy
BSR	Business for Social Responsibility
CCAB	Consultative Committee of Accountancy Bodies
CC	Center for Corporate Citizenship
CDO	collateralized debt obligation
CEFIC	European Chemical Industry Council
CEO	chief executive officer
CERES	Coalition for Environmentally Responsible Economies
CFA	chartered financial analyst
CPI	University of Cambridge Programme for Industry
CR	corporate responsibility
CSEAR	Centre for Social and Environmental Accounting Research
CSO	civil society organization
CSP	corporate social performance
CSR	corporate social responsibility
DJSI	Dow Jones Sustainability Index
DSI	Domini 400 Social Index
EAI	Enhanced Analytics Initiative
EBITDA	earnings before interest, taxes, depreciation, and amortization
EIL	Environmental Impairment Liability Centre for Competence
EIRIS	Ethical Investment Research Service
EITI	Extractive Industries Transparency Initiative
EIU	Economist Intelligence Unit
EMAS	Eco-Management and Audit System
EPA	Environmental Protection Agency
EPZ	export processing zone
ESG	environmental, social, and governance
ETF	exchange traded fund
ETI	Ethical Trading Initiative

EU	European Union
EurepGAP	European Retailers Group Guidelines on Good Agricultural Practice
Eurosif	European Sustainable and Responsible Investment Forum
FASB	Financial Accounting Standards Board
FDI	foreign direct investment
FEE	Fédération des Experts Compatibles Européens
FLA	Fair Labor Association
FRC	Financial Reporting Council
FSC	Forest Stewardship Council
FWF	Fair Wear Foundation
GAAP	generally accepted accounting principles
GEMI	Global Environmental Management Initiative
GeSI	Global e-Sustainability Initiative
GHG	greenhouse gas
GRI	Global Reporting Initiative
IBLF	International Business Leaders' Forum
ICAEW	Institute of Chartered Accountants in England and Wales
ICCA	International Council of Chemical Associations
ICGN	International Corporate Governance Network
ICT	information and communications technology
IFA	International Federation of Accountants
IFRS	International Financial Reporting Standard
IIRC	International Integrated Reporting Committee
ILO	International Labour Organization
IMF	infant milk formula
IPCC	United Nations Intergovernmental Panel on Climate Change
ISC	Institutional Shareholders' Committee
ISO	International Organization for Standardization
LEAF	Linking Environment and Farming
LSE	London Stock Exchange
MDGs	Millennium Development Goals
MFA	Multi-Fibre Agreement
MIC	methyl isocyanate
MIMCO	Mattel Independent Monitoring Council for Global Manufacturing Principles
MNC	multinational company
MSC	Marine Stewardship Council
NGO	non-government organization
NPV	net present value

OECD	Organisation for Economic Co-operation and Development
OFR	Operating and Financial Review
ONS	Office for National Statistics
OPEC	Organization of Petroleum Exporting Countries
PETA	People for the Ethical Treatment of Animals
PPP	public–private sector partnership
PRI	United Nations Principles for Responsible Investing
RAN	Rainforest Action Network
RSPA	Roundtable on Sustainable Palm Oil
SAI	Social Accountability International
SCP	sustainable consumption and production
SIF	Social Investment Forum
SIV	structured investment vehicle
SME	small and medium-sized enterprise
SRI	socially responsible investing/investment
SSE	social stock exchange
UN	United Nations
UNCED	United Nations Conference on Environment and Development
UNCTAD	United Nations Conference on Trade and Development
UNDP	United Nations Development Programme
UNEP	United Nations Environment Programme
UNIDO	United Nations Industrial Development Organization
UNFCC	United Nations Framework Convention on Climate Change
UNGC	United Nations Global Compact
UNRISD	United Nations Research Institute for Social Development
VBLI	Vietnam Business Links Initiative
WBCSD	World Business Council for Sustainable Development
WCED	World Commission on Economic Development
WEF	World Economic Forum
WMO	World Meteorological Organization
WRAP	Worldwide Responsible Apparel Production
WRI	World Resources Institute
WTO	World Trade Organization
WWF	World Wildlife Fund

How to use this Book

Chapter overview

In this chapter, we introduce the idea of corporate responsibility: its meanings, and why it is a significant part of the business agenda. In parti...

- set out the context within which contemporary corporate responsi... flourished;
- examine the different perspectives on and definitions of corporate ... responsibility;
- discuss the values that companies are being asked to uphold;

Chapter overview

Each chapter opens with an overview that provides a route map through the material and summarizes the goals of the chapter.

Main topics

Why corporate responsibility?

Definitions of corporate responsibility

Corporate governance

A framework for understanding corporate responsibility

Values motivation

Limitations of corporate responsibility frameworks

Main topic boxes

Each chapter has a list of the main topics it covers, acting as a helpful signpost to what you can expect to learn.

Key terms

Business and society	Legal responsibility
Business ethics and values	Economic responsibilit...
Corporate philanthropy	Sustainability

Key terms and concepts

Key terms are presented in boxes at the start of each chapter; they are also defined in the glossary at the end of the book. Key concept boxes introduce and discuss seminal concepts within the chapters.

Key concept: Business ethics

Business ethics is a subset of corporate responsibility offering a crucial analyti... conceptualizing, and legitimizing whether the actions and behaviour of com... wrong. The field comprises two broad areas: (a) normative business ethics wi... philosophy, and a focus on understanding what is moral or immoral in a part... (b) descriptive business ethics rooted in a wider range of disciplines (e.g. psyc... behaviour, anthropology), and a focus on ethical decisions, how they are ma... the process and outcomes (Visser et al. 2007).

Online resources

- Case study of a multinational company's worker welfare scandal... consequences for the company
- Teaching notes on the chapter's main case study
- More detailed overview of business ethics and political theory
- Films, books, and other resources
- Links to other web-based resources

Online resource box

Each chapter contains a helpful list of the resources available in the Online Resource Centre to support the topics discussed.

Snapshot 1.1   147 'species' of corporate responsibili

'*Explorers discover at least 147 species of CSR*': so was headed an article in *Ethical*
a 2005 Ashridge Business School study of corporate responsibility activities. Bas
Denmark, the study identified seven main areas of corporate responsibility activi
divided into 31 classes of activity as follows.

Area 1 Leadership, vision, and values

(a) Defining and setting the corporate purpose, values, and vision

Snapshot cases

The book is packed with case examples designed
to place the content of the chapter into a practical
context. The snapshot cases are followed by quick
questions.

Discussion points

Historically, many companies interpret corporate responsibility as 'giving bac
through philanthropy and community affairs, yet in the following sections w
types of responsibility are considered more important.

● Why do you think that 'giving back' is increasingly less acceptable as a defi
responsibility?

● When some executives say that their companies do not give back to comr
have 'already given', what do they mean?

Discussion points

These points, dispersed throughout the chapters, invite
you to reflect on the various aspects of corporate
responsibility.

**Case study 1   What are the limits to responsibili
of pharmaceuticals**

Some industries seem to have a responsibility advantage just because of wh
it is much easier to imagine a responsible pharmaceutical company than a r
Like other segments of the health sector, the pharmaceutical industry is pop
investors because of the social good that its products bring. Many of its emp
because of the good they can do. On top of this, the industry is renowned fc
long donated drugs to poor countries to treat tropical diseases such as elepl

End-of-chapter case study

A longer case study at the end of each chapter provides
an opportunity to apply what you have learnt and
analyse further examples; these are followed by
extended questions to promote deeper thinking.

Further Reading

online
resource
centre

www.oxfordtextbooks.co.uk/orc/blowfield_murray3e/
Visit the Online Resource Centre that accompanies this
ing of this chapter. Among the resources available are w
case studies.
Anderson, R.C. 1998, *Mid-course correction : toward a sustaina*
Peregrinzilla Press, Atlanta, GA.
Theoretical analysis of the significance of environmental manag

Further reading

An annotated list of recommended reading on each
subject will help guide you through the literature and
provide sources of information for writing essays and
researching projects.

How to use the Online Resource Centre

www.oxfordtextbooks.co.uk/orc/blowfield_murray3e/

For students

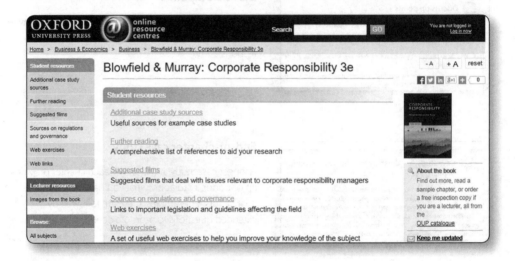

Business and poverty

The following websites offer useful information and li[nks]
business has with poverty, especially in developing c[...]

ELDIS – www.eldis.org
A rich resource of materials about social and econo[...]

An Inconvenient Truth – Al Gore's documentary a[...]
http://www.climatecrisis.net/an_inconvenient_truth/ab[...]

Blood Diamond – Action drama about the links bet[ween]
Africa.
http://blooddiamondmovie.warnerbros.com/

Web exercises

The internet can be a powerful research tool and is a popular medium for today's students. These ready-made online activities are designed to help further your knowledge and understanding of corporate responsibility topics in an interactive way. For each chapter, you are asked to find out information and answer questions based on web links to relevant articles and websites.

Suggested films

A list of suggested films is provided to reinforce your learning and act as a great practical exercise to see what you have learnt put into practice.

Browse the links below for additional cases, informat┊
responsibility:

ASRIA: A site dedicated to transforming Asia through
http://www.asria.org/

Business and Human Rights Resource Center
coverage of discrimination, environment, poverty an┊

Annotated web links

Links to relevant websites direct you towards valuable sources of information, as well as professional associations.

Additional reading
────────────────────

Look at the bibliography at the end of the book and yo┊
material relevant to corporate responsibility. Some of ┊
can be difficult to get hold of. Here is a list of 100 corp┊
available from high street bookstores or online.

Further reading

A list of recommended reading on each subject will help guide you through the literature, providing additional information for writing essays, preparing for exams, and researching projects.

Case Place (www.caseplace.org) specializes in cas┊
responsibility and sustainability. **The Center for Cor**
offers a variety of reports suitable for case studies (w┊
contain a variety of case study material, including the ┊

CRANE, A. and MATTEN, D., 2007. Business ethics:
sustainability in the age of globalization. 2nd edn. Oxf┊

Additional case study sources

A suite of case study sources allows you to delve deeper into the topics discussed and improve your knowledge of this subject area.

UK Combined Code on Corporate Governance - 📄 w┊
/frc/Combined%20Code%20June%202006.pdf

Public Interest Disclosure Act - www.hmso.gov.uk/ac┊

Department of Trade and Industry Guide to Public Inte┊
www.dti.gov.uk/employment/employment-legislation/e┊

Sources on regulations and governance

A selection of web links to key sources of legislation, rules, and guidelines that shape and reflect the development of corporate governance.

For registered adopters of the book

Images from the book

The images from the textbook have been uploaded to the Online Resource Centre and can be added to your lecture materials or virtual learning environment.

Part 1

···

The meaning and origins of corporate responsibility

···

1. Introducing corporate responsibility   3

2. The origins of corporate sustainability   31

3. Sustainable development   53

4. Corporate responsibility in developing economies   75

5. Globalization and corporate responsibility   98

Introducing corporate responsibility

Chapter overview

In this chapter, we introduce the idea of corporate responsibility: its concerns, its meanings, and why it is a significant part of the business agenda. In particular, we will:

- set out the context within which contemporary corporate responsibility has flourished;
- examine the different perspectives on and definitions of corporate responsibility;
- discuss the values that companies are being asked to uphold;
- look at the main issues with which contemporary corporate responsibility is wrestling.

Main topics

Why corporate responsibility?   3
Definitions of corporate responsibility   6
Corporate governance   9
A framework for understanding corporate responsibility   10
Values motivation   12
Limitations of corporate responsibility frameworks   24

Key terms

Business and society	Legal responsibility
Business ethics and values	Economic responsibility
Corporate philanthropy	Sustainability

Why corporate responsibility?

In 2005, *The Economist* published a series of articles castigating corporate responsibility and the folly of managers who thought it would benefit their companies. Corporate-responsibility-conscious managers were accused of taking their eye off shareholder interests. Accusations were made that corporate responsibility and bad governance went hand in hand. In an accompanying survey, the Economist Intelligence Unit found only 35 per cent of managers felt corporate responsibility was a priority.

Fast forward to 2008, and *The Economist* again runs a feature on corporate responsibility. But this time the tone is different. Now it says that 96 per cent of managers believe that corporate responsibility offers value for money, and 56 per cent of managers surveyed by the Economist Intelligence Unit say that it is a high priority. Three years after dismissing it, *The Economist* was now professing that few big companies could ignore corporate responsibility. The same message appears elsewhere despite speculation that interest in corporate responsibility would wane during economic recessions. KPMG's biennial report on the state of corporate responsibility reporting shows a continuing worldwide increase; the second Accenture–UN Global Compact *CEO Study on Sustainability*, published in 2013, shows further executive interest in the impact of business on society as a management issue.

We live in a world in which the richest 20 per cent of people possess 86 per cent of gross national product, in which one country accounts for 23 per cent of worldwide energy consumption, and in which the USA and Europe account for 65 per cent of annual wealth creation.[1] It is a highly unequal world in which over a billion people live on under $ 1.25 a day, and a woman is 100 times more likely to die during pregnancy in Africa than she is in Scandinavia. Yet it is a world in which emerging economies such as China and India are outperforming developed ones in many respects, and in which so-called advanced economies often rely on poorer countries to buy their vast debts.

In this world, prosperity is nearly always measured in terms of economic growth, made possible by greater productivity and cost reduction. The drive for growth increases the demand for natural resources, cheap labour, and new markets. Often these three trends come together in what was once called the Third World, but which is now divided between emerging and developing nations. One can celebrate this growth because it creates new jobs, stimulates local economies, and raises living standards. One can also criticize it because it has been linked to human rights abuses, environmental disasters, and poverty.

Moreover, the concept of growth itself has become problematic. The latest report by the International Panel on Climate Change concludes that there is 95 per cent certainty amongst scientists worldwide that climate change caused by humans is a real phenomenon. That is a high degree of certainty, exceeding for instance the certainty about the benefits of many approved drugs and far more sure than the economic predictions that rule government policy-making. To prevent uncertain, perhaps catastrophic, climate change, energy use in society will have to change by altering the energy mix and/or reducing energy consumption. Yet, historically, economic growth and rising energy consumption have always gone hand in hand, begging the questions: How can society decouple economic growth from increased climate change? Is it possible to maintain growth without jeopardizing the Earth's sustainability?

Business sits in the midst of these complex and vital questions. There are many examples over several decades of business leaders pushing for greater globalization and the interconnected free-flowing world we now inhabit. But even if that were not the case, it is impossible for companies, large or small, to ignore the changing nature of the world they inhabit and the roles they play within it. The fish restaurant on the high street is affected by overfishing and sustainable fisheries—both corporate responsibility issues. The fresh fruit importer is affected by campaigns for healthier food and fair treatment of labourers. The small manufacturer is concerned about how its multinational competitor can avoid taxes. The multinational company, be it in mining, retail, fast-moving consumer goods, or whatever industry, knows that issues such as water scarcity, responsible investment, carbon emissions, and child labour are not just potential PR problems; they are central to company performance.

The private sector creates wealth, generates employment, utilizes natural resources, and attracts investment at unprecedented levels. Consumption plays a pivotal role in our social lives and our personal identities. Brands have a significance that is not dissimilar to that of religion and ideology in previous eras. Companies play important roles in public policy, not least in countries where the standard of governance is low, or in situations in which international governance mechanisms are inadequate.

In today's world it is impossible to imagine the absence of the private sector. Despite the financial collapse starting in 2007, alternatives to a freemarket economy are scarce and have garnered little popular support. In contrast with the 1920s or 1960s, for instance, protest movements in the wake of the financial crisis have focused on reforming not replacing private sector capitalism. Governments around the world have stepped in to save business—from investment banking to manufacturing—from its own failings. In the UK, the government has consistently put the blame for the nation's debt at the feet of politicians, despite the fact that corporate and financial industry debt is 300 per cent of GDP compared with government debt of about 100 per cent.[2] Despite the ethical, financial, and management failings of companies from Lehman Brothers to A4e, JP Morgan and HSBC to G4S and Juventus FC, the private sector is still widely admired as the exemplar of efficiency and prosperity. Goldman Sachs' Lloyd Blankfein might be overstating the case when he says he is *'doing God's work'*, but many believe the statement by Wholefood's John Mackey that *'Great companies have great purposes'*. Allowing widespread business failure is unthinkable, because we seem unable to imagine an alternative to the free market economy.

People in business are often vexed that the contribution of private enterprise to society is not better understood. Yet as we write, senior managers from News International are in court for hacking the phone of a murdered child, JP Morgan has paid the biggest fine in corporate history for misleading investors, and the football industry is in disarray about the treatment of migrant workers building the infrastructure for the 2022 World Cup. In the UK, to add to the long list of recent banking scandals, the Cooperative Bank, a leader in ethical finance, has had to be bailed out by hedge funds following a period of mismanagement that ended up with its Chairman on drugs charges.

Not surprisingly, therefore, for all the private sector's importance to the global economy, company behaviour is often a cause for concern. Firms are being subjected to new levels of transparency, whether in terms of the demands that the largest stock markets make for greater disclosure and changes to corporate governance, or in terms of public outcry on issues as diverse as environmental pollution, consumer rights, child labour, corruption, and support for military regimes. Adverse disclosure threatens shareholder confidence, brand reputation, production stability, employee trust, and other corporate assets, both tangible and intangible.

What is more, the conditions that leave companies open to charges of irresponsibility, when looked at differently, can become business opportunities. Public opinion is becoming less tolerant of corporate excess and malfeasance, but there are also increasing expectations that business will come up with solutions to some of the twenty-first century's main social and environmental challenges, such as water accessibility, global warming, and affordable health care. These are the twin hemispheres that corporate responsibility is charged to embrace: on the one hand, it must deal with what Baker (2005) calls 'capitalism's Achilles heel', within which capital, poverty, and inequality are intertwined; on the other, it must promote capitalism as a solution to the key social and environmental issues of the age.

Discussion points

Surveys of executives and the public repeatedly show that business is distrusted as a member of society.

- Why do you think there is a high degree of distrust?
- Is corporate responsibility a good way to restore business's reputation?
- How would you factor distrust into a company's business plan?

Definitions of corporate responsibility

The above is the context within which corporate responsibility has come to the fore—but what does the term itself actually mean? There never has been a straightforward answer to this, and growing interest in the field—whether from companies, governments, the general public, academics, or civil society organizations—has only served to extend the array of definitions.

Long before there was a name for corporate responsibility, there were ideas about what it meant for business to make a positive contribution to the rest of society. Owen, Rowntree, and Lever were among the many individuals who utilized company assets to improve the conditions of nineteenth-century workers. Throughout the twentieth century, companies such as Norsk Hydro would take responsibility for social conditions in their, often isolated, company towns; many logging, mining, plantation, and oil operations throughout the world set up housing schools, clinics, and other social amenities. Just as importantly, many more were criticized for failing to take on such responsibilities.[3]

The positive and negative impacts that business had on society generated public, political, and academic debate. While it was quite clear that business sought a profit from providing goods and services in response to society's demands, it was much less obvious what constraints should be put on its activities and who should impose them. Was all profit legitimate? Was all profit legitimate provided that the company stayed within the law? What was a fair distribution of the wealth business created between shareholders, employees, and wider society? Should companies give part of their wealth back to the communities within which they operated? Could markets be relied upon to set a fair price, whether for labour, products, or natural resources? Could governments reliably decide what was in the public interest?

Questions such as these gave rise to different notions of corporate responsibility. The field called 'corporate social responsibility' (CSR) began with a focus on the role of business leaders, particularly on how they managed their companies with a view to society and how they gave back to their local communities. In the 1950s, the focus of CSR shifted to the behaviour of companies rather than that of individuals. This generated a fair degree of academic debate about what companies should be responsible for; it also spawned the concepts of 'corporate social responsiveness' and then 'corporate social performance' which, in the

1980s, put less stress on the philosophical meaning of responsibility and more on the act of being responsible.

Other terms were introduced. 'Corporate sustainability', for example, was used in the 1990s to emphasize how environmental concerns were increasingly an area in which companies were expected to exhibit responsibility. More recently still, 'corporate citizenship' (originally used to refer to the types of corporate philanthropy common in the USA) has been used as a development of CSR that emphasizes the role of business as a citizen in global society and its function in delivering the citizenship rights of individuals.[4]

Changes in the focus of corporate responsibility inevitably affect the way it is defined. For Davis (1973), corporate responsibility begins where the law ends. In other words, it is about what companies do to make a positive contribution to society above and beyond that which constitutes their legal obligations. This simple parameter gets to the heart of much of the debate about corporate responsibility in recent years, i.e. the desirability and effectiveness of market-based solutions to social and environmental challenges, and, in particular, their voluntary and self-regulatory nature.

The different definitions of corporate responsibility shown in Box 1.1 share in common the belief that companies have a responsibility for the public good—but they emphasize different elements of this. The definitions used by the *Financial Times* and Chiquita, for example, highlight that responsibility is gauged by how companies listen and respond to stakeholders' concerns. PricewaterhouseCoopers' definition sets out the kinds of stakeholder groups to whom companies are responsible. It also stresses that responsibility involves balancing profit maximization and stakeholders' needs. The Confederation of British Industry's definition sheds light on what some of the responsibilities to stakeholders are, while that of the European Commission stresses that actions under the corporate responsibility umbrella are voluntary in nature. Finally, the ISO 26000 draft refers to what companies are responsible for, reiterates the importance of stakeholder involvement and accountability, and adds that responsibility should be integrated into organizational practices.

Box 1.1   Definitions of corporate responsibility

Corporations have a responsibility to those groups and individuals that they can affect, i.e. its stakeholders, and to society at large. Stakeholders are usually defined as customers, suppliers, employees, communities and shareholders or other financiers.

Financial Times Lexicon, lexicon.ft.com

CSR commits us to operate in a socially responsible way everywhere we do business, fairly balancing the needs and concerns of our various stakeholders—all those who impact, are impacted by, or have a legitimate interest in the Company's actions and performance.

Chiquita, www.chiquita.com

CSR [is] the proposition that companies are responsible not only for maximising profits, but also for recognising the needs of such stakeholders as employees, customers, demographic groups and even the regions they serve.

PricewaterhouseCoopers, www.pwcglobal.com

(continued...)

CSR requires companies to acknowledge that they should be publicly accountable not only for their financial performance but also for their social and environmental record.
Confederation of British Industry, 2001

[CSR is] a concept whereby companies integrate social and environmental concerns in their business operations and in their interactions with their stakeholders on a voluntary basis.
European Commission, Directorate General for Employment and Social Affairs

[Corporate responsibility is the] responsibility of an organization for the impacts of its decisions and activities on society and the environment, through transparent and ethical behaviour that (a) contributes to sustainable development, health and the welfare of society; (b) takes into account the expectations of stakeholders; (c) is in compliance with applicable law and consistent with international norms of behaviour; and (d) is integrated through the organization and practised in its relationships.
Draft of ISO 26000, International Guidance Standard on Social Responsibility, 4 September 2009

These broad definitions reflect claims about the values that companies wish to uphold, such as honesty, fairness, and integrity, and these may be set out in standards or codes of practice (see Box 1.2). The values can be quite diverse, and Paine et al. (2005) have tried to categorize them, differentiating, for example, between management's responsibility to investors (fiduciary responsibilities), respecting human rights (dignity principle), and a duty to honour commitments (reliability principle).

Box 1.2   Published standards of corporate responsibility

The following is a selection of standards, guidelines, and declarations that set out some of the rights that companies are being asked to uphold.

Agenda 21

A far-reaching plan of action for governments, companies, and civil society to address human impacts on society.
www.un.org/esa/sustdev/documents/agenda21

Beijing Declaration

An international United Nations declaration on the rights of women.
www.wolfsberg-principles.com

CERES principles

A ten-point code of corporate environmental conduct, for use as an environmental mission statement or ethic.
www.ceres.org/coalitionandcompanies

Global Reporting Initiative

A framework for reporting on social, environmental, and economic performance.
www.globalreporting.org

Marine Stewardship Council

Standards for sustainable fishing and seafood traceability.
www.msc.org

(continued...)

Organisation for Economic Co-operation and Development (OECD) guidelines for multinational enterprises

Government recommendations on responsible business conduct.
www.oecd.org

Principles for Responsible Investment

Principles on environmental, social, and corporate governance issues pertaining to investors.
www.unpri.org/principles

Social Accountability 8000

Workplace standard against which to assure worker rights and welfare.
www.sa-intl.org

Wolfsberg Anti-Money Laundering Principles

Principles for private banks to counter money laundering.
www.un.org/womenwatch/daw/beijing/platformwww.wolfsberg-principles.com

There are also companies and individuals that define corporate responsibility in terms of its commercial benefits, emphasizing the instrumental value (the business case) that acts of responsibility can bring. Windsor (2001) says that the degree and types of responsibility that individual companies have are a factor of the wealth and power of the company, so that a multinational corporation will have different responsibilities to those of a small or medium-sized enterprise. Equally, separate industries have distinctive social and environmental impacts, so that, for example, good performance in cosmetics will look quite different from that in transportation. Indeed, according to Werther and Chandler (2011), there are so many variables that it is impossible to prescribe what mix of responsibilities any company faces; companies should not look for universal definitions, but should instead build their strategies around the perspectives of their stakeholders (even though that term is itself subject to multiple interpretations—see Chapter 9).

Corporate governance

In the US tradition of corporate responsibility which shaped much of the thinking in the field until fairly recently, corporate governance was not given much consideration. However, as corporate responsibility theory has stopped being the preserve of academe, other thinkers—notably those in socially responsible investing (see Chapter 10)—have argued that it needs to be part of corporate responsibility's scope. Hence, the Certified Financial Analyst Institute's material refers to corporate responsibility as ESG—environmental, social, and governance—as do fund managers such as Jupiter Asset Management.

A valid criticism of corporate responsibility practice is that companies have not taken the governance dimension more seriously, and that it played no discernible part in identifying or addressing the various crises of governance affecting Western markets in the early and late

2000s (see Chapter 13). We explore the evolution of corporate governance and how it relates to corporate responsibility more widely in Chapter 7, and tend to agree that governance is an important (if underdeveloped) aspect of the business–society relationship. In so far as governance is the primary responsibility of boards, and the board's role, as defined by John Harvey Jones (1988), is to 'create tomorrow's company out of today's', corporate responsibility would seem to offer useful frameworks for board-level governance. However, corporate responsibility is also part of the reconstruction of governance: something that is connected to globalization (see Chapter 5) and social accounting (see Chapter 8), and is evident for instance in phenomena such as civil governance when companies are affected as much by the beliefs and actions of groups such as online protest communities, as they are by the interests of investors that conventional governance is intended to protect.

A framework for understanding corporate responsibility

Snapshot 1.1 demonstrates the wide variety of corporate responsibility activities currently being practised by companies. Furthermore, observers such as academics have a multitude of perspectives on the meaning of corporate responsibility (see Chapter 2). Given this array, it is not surprising that no single definition adequately captures the range of issues, policies, processes, and initiatives covered in this book. As we will explore in the coming chapters, the notion of stakeholders, the way issues become recognized, and the role of values are all important elements of corporate responsibility today. Likewise, the tensions that arise because of competing interests, priorities, and goals affect what corporate responsibility means in practice.

 Snapshot 1.1   147 'species' of corporate responsibility

'Explorers discover at least 147 species of CSR': so was headed an article in *Ethical Performance* about a 2005 Ashridge Business School study of corporate responsibility activities. Based on research in Denmark, the study identified seven main areas of corporate responsibility activity, which were then divided into 31 classes of activity as follows.

Area 1 Leadership, vision, and values

(a) Defining and setting the corporate purpose, values, and vision

(b) Translating this into policies and procedures

(c) Putting it into practice, including empowering and embedding

(d) Ethical leadership and championing

Area 2 Marketplace activities

(a) Responsible customer relations, including marketing and advertising

(b) Product responsibility

(c) Using corporate responsibility product labelling

(continued...)

(d) Ethical competition

(e) Making markets work for all

Area 3 Workforce activities

(a) Employee communication and representation

(b) Ensuring employability and skills development

(c) Diversity and equality

(d) Responsible/fair remuneration

(e) Work–life balance

(f) Health, safety, and well-being

(g) Responsible restructuring

Area 4 Supply chain activities

(a) Being a fair customer

(b) Driving social and environmental standards through the supply chain

(c) Promoting social and economic inclusion via the supply chain

Area 5 Stakeholder engagement

(a) Mapping key stakeholders and their main concerns

(b) Stakeholder consultation

(c) Responding to and managing stakeholders

(d) Transparent reporting and communication

Area 6 Community activities

(a) Financial donations

(b) Volunteering employee time

(c) Giving gifts in kind

(d) Being a good neighbour

Area 7 Environmental activities

(a) Resource and energy use

(b) Pollution and waste management

(c) Environmental product responsibility

(d) Transport planning

Sources: Ashridge Centre for Business and Society, 2005; *Ethical Performance*, 2006c

(continued...)

> ....
>
> ## Quick questions
>
> It is sometimes argued that companies are asked to take on too many different types of responsibility and that there are too many corporate responsibility initiatives.
>
> 1 Should companies be allowed to choose which issues to address?
>
> 2 Which of the above activity areas do you think are most important for companies to tackle?
>
> 3 How can companies set about prioritizing the areas of activity in which they should get involved?

However, rather than try to adopt and defend a particular definition, in this book we use corporate responsibility as an umbrella term that captures the variety of ways in which business's relationship with society is being defined, managed, and acted upon. Therefore, for us, corporate responsibility comprises (a) the responsibilities of business in the context of wider society, (b) how those responsibilities are defined and negotiated, and (c) how they are managed and organized. The chapters of this book emphasize one or other of these dimensions, highlighting where the various observers and practitioners share common ground, and where they disagree.

Readers will see soon enough that we do not pretend that there is a unifying vision of corporate responsibility. However, there are two broad motivations for companies to treat corporate responsibility as a management issue: (a) because companies, like people, have values that guide their interactions with other society members (values motivation), and (b) because to succeed companies need to manage their relationship with wider society (materiality motivation) (see Figure 1.1). We tackle these ways of thinking in the following sections.

> **Discussion points**
>
> Historically, many companies interpret corporate responsibility as 'giving back to their communities' through philanthropy and community affairs, yet in the following sections we show that today other types of responsibility are considered more important.
>
> ● Why do you think that 'giving back' is increasingly less acceptable as a definition of corporate responsibility?
>
> ● When some executives say that their companies do not give back to communities because they have 'already given', what do they mean?
>
> ● Why do you think there is a stronger tradition of corporate philanthropy in the USA than in Europe?

Values motivation

When executives talk about corporate responsibility, many stress the importance of their companies' values. Sam Palmisano, IBM's CEO, describes his company's values as innovation that matters for the world as well as the company, trust and personal responsibility in

Values motivation: conscious desire to achieve and be accountable for societally beneficial outcomes by means of operating a profitable business

Corporate responsibility

Materiality motivation: recognition that a successful business can seek out and address societal challenges with resultant material benefits

Outcome:
Profitable enterprises
helping address and redress
societal challenges

Figure 1.1 Relationship between corporate responsibility motivations and outcomes

all relationships, and dedication to client success.[5] Nestlé's core values include favouring long-term development over short-term profit, entering into long-term commitments and relationships, being fair and honest, and showing respect for diverse cultures. According to Waddock (2001), at the core of what she calls 'corporate citizenship' are:

1 a company's adoption of policies, procedures, and processes that are based on integrity (i.e. honesty to oneself and to others), and which allow it to build values-based practices;

2 a company's capacity to perceive and evaluate the long-term consequences of its behaviour, and its willingness to make short-term sacrifices to realize long-term gains.

Others flesh out what those policies, procedures, and processes might embrace (e.g. transparency, empowering stakeholders, managing a triple bottom line of economic, social, and environmental value added, etc.), offering different political and philosophical frameworks for understanding what ethical constructs should be included (e.g. human liberty, social justice, communitarianism, a duty of care).[6]

There is debate about who decides the values to which business should adhere: companies themselves or the societies within which they operate. For those who see corporate responsibility as a choice that business makes, companies face three competing cases that will ultimately determine their corporate responsibility strategy: the moral case (obligations that the company has to society); the rational case (taking proactive steps that will minimize the restrictions society imposes on business); and the economic case (adding financial value to the company by preserving its legitimacy with its stakeholders).[7] For others, however, companies do not choose to practice corporate responsibility; rather, it is an integral part of the free enterprise system, and the issues and problems at the heart of corporate responsibility are:

> a natural consequence of the industrialized quest for profits [and] represent the raw edge of business values rubbing against the social values of human communities and the ecosystems that sustain those communities.

> (Frederick, 2006, p 59)

Underlying these different vantage points is a common acceptance that a legal construct such as a corporation can have values, and that notions of ethics, justice, responsibility, and obligation rooted in human experience can be meaningfully adapted to guide corporate behaviour. As we discuss in Chapter 2, these are debatable assumptions, and an important question is whether corporate responsibility practice today makes companies sufficiently accountable for adhering to society's values in the same way that people are held to account, or whether it, de facto, allows companies to pick and choose those things for which they want to be responsible in a way that would seem preposterous if the choices were to be made by individuals.

Business ethics

Not surprisingly, this pushes us in the direction of the field called 'business ethics', which refers to ethical systems applied in the context of profit-oriented organizations. Some will argue that business ethics should be treated as the overarching framework within which corporate responsibility theories and practices are devised and implemented. For example, under a theory of environmental ethics, humanity may have a duty of care to the planet, and hence corporate responsibility practices should be guided by that duty. If we were concerned only with views on what ideologies should inform corporate behaviour, we might treat corporate responsibility and business ethics as synonymous. However, our interest is something broader which embraces theory, management practice, and the societal context within which business exists. Just as neither politics nor religion can be entirely explained by reference to theoretical principles, neither can corporate responsibility.

There are many fascinating introductions to business ethics, and we are not going to attempt to duplicate them here. Some of these are concerned with the behaviour of individuals as members of the company and wider society, but others concentrate on business as an institution and how a company integrates values, such as honesty, trust, integrity, respect, and fairness, into its policies, practices, and decision-making. This can involve ensuring that employees abide by the law and are not left in a position in which, in order to achieve one set of targets (e.g. earnings), they are necessarily encouraged to bend or break the law. It can also involve going beyond legal requirements and adhering to company, industry, or professional codes of conduct, such as those that have long been adopted in the medical, military, and legal professions.

It might be argued that, before business management can be considered a mature profession, it too needs to develop comprehensive and relevant codes of ethics. Khurana (2007) claims that business schools were originally intended to educate managers in how to lead

Key concept: Business ethics

Business ethics is a subset of corporate responsibility offering a crucial analytical tool for understanding, conceptualizing, and legitimizing whether the actions and behaviour of companies are *morally* right or wrong. The field comprises two broad areas: (a) normative business ethics with its roots in theoretical philosophy, and a focus on understanding what is moral or immoral in a particular situation; and (b) descriptive business ethics rooted in a wider range of disciplines (e.g. psychology, organizational behaviour, anthropology), and a focus on ethical decisions, how they are made, and what influences the process and outcomes (Visser et al. 2007).

One could argue that business ethics underpins the entire field of corporate responsibility theory and practice, but while it is important (and is supported by a vast number of publications), it is not the only lens through which corporate responsibility is being viewed. The influential idea of a 'business case' for corporate responsibility (see Chapter 6) largely relies on societal consensus to set out a moral case which is then addressed by harnessing the capacities of business. Or, if one takes the example of stakeholder theory (see Chapter 9), while it can be used to help understand what is moral or not for business, ethics is not an intrinsic element of it, and it can be (and often is) used just to analyse corporate self-interest. Therefore, even if almost every action involving human beings has an ethical dimension at some level, it can be too regressive and unhelpful to resort to first principles in each discussion of corporate responsibility.

socially responsible institutions, but that these 'higher aims' were sacrificed to a focus on profit maximization so that managers today are simply the hired hands of investors. Certainly, there is now a resurgence of interest in business ethics, both in companies and in business schools, as a result of the corporate corruption scandals of the late 1990s and 2000s. The changing nature of business also presents new ethical challenges in order to resolve issues arising from operating globally and within multiple cultural norms, from new industries such as biotechnology and information technology, and from increasing public scrutiny of business behaviour. Some companies and industries have invested in internal mechanisms to manage the ethical dimensions of their operations, such as the medical company Baxter International's overarching set of bioethics principles, and defence and aircraft manufacturer Raytheon's appointment of a corporate director for ethics compliance and ethics officers in its major business segments.

There are, however, two readily identifiable difficulties with how companies currently implement business ethics. First, there are many examples of even companies with strong ethical policies and processes being found in breach of the law. This was the case with Boeing, which, despite its extensive ethical guidelines on procurement, corruption, and marketing, used confidential materials stolen from rival Lockheed Martin to win nearly $2 billion worth of defence procurement contracts with the US government in 1998, an action that later led the company to be suspended from bidding for defence contracts.[8]

The second difficulty is that, as Davies (1997) points out, company codes and guidelines mostly take the form of usable algorithms that are intended to guide managers through ethically contentious situations, rather than help them to develop a coherent ethical theory that will inform overall business practice. Consequently, ethics is often described as something that is necessary to achieve business imperatives such as profitability, growth, and shareholder value, rather than as something that is at the heart of business behaviour and a prime determinant of what that behaviour should be, especially if there is conflict between instrumental and moral imperatives.

This may seem odd given that much of business ethics seeks to apply ethical theory to the business context. Thus, we find a variety of texts seeking to adapt the ideas of Aristotle, Kant, Mill, Locke, Heidegger, and others to the needs of business.[9] Scherer and Palazzo (2007) argue that companies should not expect to act in accordance with a specific ethical theory but rather, in line with Habermas's view of contemporary ethics, they should adopt the values that emerge from an informed and inclusive negotiation with different sections of society. In what has been characterized as part of a distinct European as opposed to American school of business ethics, companies are seen as uniquely placed organizations in relation to issues with distinct ethical dimensions. For example, Crane and Matten (2004) focus on three core themes that influence the ethical dimension to business behaviour—globalization, sustainability, and citizenship—and, in doing so, refer as much to sociology, political economy, and international relations as they do to philosophy. They highlight, for example, how the Rhenish model of capitalism, found in Italy, Germany, Spain, France, and elsewhere, creates different expectations and challenges to those of the Anglo-Saxon model that is typical of the UK and USA. They also describe how factors such as age, gender, national identity and culture, level of education, personal integrity, and moral imagination all affect individuals' ethical decisions. And they make clear that the concerns of business ethics are affected by the role, capacity, and responsibilities of government and other social institutions.

The Online Resource Centre contains a more detailed overview of business ethics in relation to corporate responsibility. But what the new European school of business ethics highlights is that ethics itself is a social construct—not an absolute value that business should adopt or be judged against, but something that companies as institutions or collectives of individuals both shape and are shaped by. It is insufficient to apply values to business. Rather, values should be seen as an element of what business needs to be cognizant of in building its societal relationships.

Materiality motivation—managing business and society

Central to this European school of business ethics is the idea that the relationship between business and society is subject to continual renegotiation. This counters a criticism of some other forms of business ethics which encourage the idea that responsibility is an end state, or a goal to be strived for, rather than a way of thinking about the role of business in wider society. According to Jonkers, it is confusing to managers to portray responsibility as something that can be accomplished, rather:

> [Corporate responsibility] is a 'sensitising concept': a term that draws attention to a complex range of issues and elements that are all related to the position and function of the business enterprise in contemporary society.

(Jonkers 2005, p 20)

There is a strong belief that corporate responsibility means something different in the USA than in most of Europe because of the different social contracts that business is a part of in these regions. Equally, various authors discuss the fundamental difference in corporate responsibility between developed and developing economies.[10] Concepts such as sensitizing help discussions of corporate responsibility steer clear of national relativism, but we should be aware that in countries such as the USA and the UK, where the welfare state is relatively weak by Western standards, the responsibilities of corporations will be different than in Germany or Denmark where government provides greater workplace protection and social security. However, we should also steer clear of convenient stereotypes, and recognize, for example, that the USA has stronger legal protections in areas such as consumer protection than in most of the world.

There is a long tradition of business and society as an area of academic study and public policy, but its primary concern has been how to regulate and motivate business so as to contribute more to the public good. Thus, for example, governments have passed legislation on issues ranging from working hours to maternity leave and equal pay so as to enhance workers' well-being. Business and government are depicted as having separate concerns: the former, to do with creating wealth; the latter, to do with social cohesion and security, which has often required intervening in the world of business through both regulation and redistribution.

Since the 1950s, it has become clear that this idea of separate sectors with discrete responsibilities is confusing and, moreover, that different societies around the world have very specific, and often complex, expectations of the role that business should play, which go well beyond paying taxes and abiding by the law. These became apparent in the flurry of literature in the 1960s and 1970s, which provided the theoretical context for contemporary corporate responsibility (see Chapter 2). In 1979, Carroll offered what is perhaps the most widely cited framework for understanding the different aspects of social responsibility that had emerged (see Figure 1.2). He identified four types of responsibility under which the various actions taken to manage business's relationship with society should fall, and we examine these individually now.

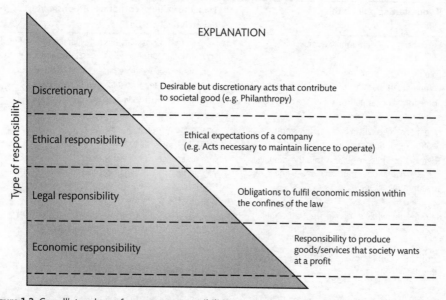

Figure 1.2 Carroll's typology of corporate responsibilities

Source: Reprinted from Carroll, A.B. 1979, 'A three-dimensional conceptual model of corporate performance,' *Academy of Management Review*, vol. 4, no. 4, pp 497–505, with permission from Elsevier.

Economic responsibility

Economic responsibility refers to the fundamental responsibility of business to produce goods and services that society wants, and which it sells at a profit. Many eminent theorists and business leaders would argue that this is the limit of a company's responsibilities, and to attempt any more is at best folly, and at worst a misuse of owners' capital (see Snapshot 1.2). They argue that under the free enterprise system, creating jobs, shareholder value, and goods and services—and doing this in a law-abiding manner—are all inherent ways in which business contributes to society. Managers as agents of the company's owners do not need to worry about the different outcomes because ultimately the company's value will reflect its utility. Indeed, as soon as managers do anything more than focus on profit they risk creating an enterprise with multiple objective functions that ends up having no clear accountability or definition of good performance.[11]

As we shall see in other chapters of this book, there are various counter-arguments to this view. But the idea that companies have a purpose other than simply to make money—that, at the very least, they should consider not only profitability, but also the way in which profits are made—is central to understanding corporate responsibility in terms of business's relationship to society. Indeed, where you stand on this argument can significantly influence what you see as the value of corporate responsibility (see Box 1.3).

Box 1.3   How the value of corporate responsibility depends on your viewpoint

If your starting point is this ...	Then the value of corporate responsibility to you is likely to be this ...
Capitalism is fundamentally wrong	Corporate responsibility has little if anything to offer you, although it might help you to criticize capitalism
Free markets are self-regulating and successful companies inherently contribute to the social good	Corporate responsibility has nothing to offer you, and may appear a threat to your beliefs
Some forms of capitalism are worse than others	Corporate responsibility theory offers some insight: see for instance Reich, 2007 and Vogel, 2005
Free market capitalism is essentially good but needs controlling or moderating	Corporate responsibility theory has a lot to offer in areas from strategy to social accounting
There are business models within the capitalist framework that offer particular social and environmental benefits	Certain aspects under corporate responsibility help you understand and manage these models, such as fairtrade, social enterprise, and socially responsible investment
Responsible behaviour is a driver for business success	Corporate responsibility can provide a framework for identifying behaviour that will deliver value to the financial bottom line
Companies can choose to behave more or less ethically	Business ethics as a subset of corporate responsibility can help to understand and manage ethical behaviour
Individuals within companies can be unethical	Individual ethics in the workplace is a subset of corporate responsibility

Legal responsibility

Legal responsibility refers to the obligation of business to fulfil its economic mission within the confines of the law. Most people who believe corporate responsibility is synonymous with economic responsibility would add the caveat that companies must abide by the law. Equally, those who think that corporate responsibility is much more than profit maximization would accept that companies need to be lawful, at least in so far as the laws are legitimate and just. Local, national, and international law sets out the rules by which corporations play, and, over time, has prescribed what companies can and cannot do with regard to areas such as employment, environmental protection, corruption, human rights, and product safety. One only needs to think of pornography, arms sales, and narcotics to realize how the law defines what is legitimate business activity; one need only consider corporate law to appreciate how it spells out the purpose of the company.

Public outrage about the financial crisis since 2007 and the fact that heads of financial institutions have not been put on trial highlights that in many areas of corporate life the law may not be fit for purpose. On top of this, there is growing public and political consternation that it is legal—indeed, by some definitions responsible—to avoid paying corporation taxes in countries where a company does business. But even without these examples, there are good reasons for saying that corporate responsibility is concerned with more than legal compliance. Forceful arguments have been made that corporate responsibility refers to the actions companies take without legal compulsion. In other words, corporate responsibility as a field is about voluntary not mandatory actions.

The distinction between voluntary and compulsory behaviour may be useful for demarcating a particular subset of corporate responsibility theory and practice. Legislation is not comprehensive, and is often the final resort to address a major issue when neither societal norms nor other means of resolution prove adequate. This means that the law by itself will never define everything that society expects companies to take responsibility for. Moreover, companies can have significant influence on what is passed as law, and spend large sums of money persuading law-makers about how to apply their powers. For example, in the 2009 debate over health-care reform in the USA, pharmaceutical companies spent over $80 million on lobbying.[12] In 2013, GSK saw at least 30 staff arrested in a scandal about bribing doctors to prescribe its drugs. Indeed, company wealth can be used to influence the meaning of acceptable or unacceptable influence, while some companies, as part of their corporate responsibility strategies, have said that they will simply not engage in political debate.

The use of company wealth to influence politicians has been linked to wider debates about the diminishing power of government. Globalization, including the increased international flows of capital, goods, and services (see Chapter 2) has in some respects increased the scope of corporate influence. Headlines along the lines of 'Tesco: Richer than Peru',[13] raise fears about unfettered corporate power and the lack of regulation, especially once one looks beyond national borders. Such information should be treated with caution. For example, to say that a company is richer than a country is a bit like saying a short person standing up is taller than a fat person lying down: it is not an accurate, or even useful, comparison.

Despite arguments that if governments are too harsh on companies, business will invest elsewhere, by some measures governments have become stricter on business. For instance, the European Union's Pollution Prevention and Control Directive has raised the bar on con-trolling industrial pollution, the EU fined Microsoft €899 million because of anti-competitive practices, and in 2013 HSBC had to pay over $6 billion in fines for mis-selling and money laundering. Nonetheless, fears that business wields too much power are widespread and not totally without foundation. For example, in 2006 the British government refused to enforce anti-corruption laws against BAE, the defence company, following what were later described as 'blatant threats',[14] and Total successfully prevented a case about human rights abuse in Burma from going to court in Belgium.

But, even if it is true that governments find it harder to regulate business than in the past, it is a mistake to ignore the very real power that legislation has. For example, the Alien Torts Claims Act 1789, despite being a US law, has been used to make companies legally accountable for their behaviour overseas, and laws modelled on the US Foreign Corrupt Practices Act 1977 are starting to find their way onto statute books in other countries. There is also a complex body of international law on issues such as labour rights, slavery, economic rights, and the environment, which, despite being incomplete, unwieldy, and poorly enforced, nonetheless offers the basis for regulating business in the coming years.

However, legal requirements that vary greatly from country to country present (depending on one's perspective) a problem or an opportunity for business. For example, the work week in China is 44 hours, in France it is 35, and in South Korea it is over 50. Will companies choose to invest where the legal work week is longest? Is it immoral for investors to refuse to let a company relocate to a country where environmental management costs are low due to weak environmental laws? If it is legal in Indonesia to use lead paint, why should a retailer there insist that its suppliers use more expensive non-toxic paints? Time and again in the contem-porary world corporations are finding themselves held to account not for abiding by the laws in a particular country of operation, but for upholding the non-legislated norms and values of globally dispersed groups and individuals.

Similar developments are taking place in the corporate governance field. For example, both Harvard University's Kennedy School and the environmental non-government organi-zation (NGO) CERES have, in different ways, put governance to the fore of their work on corporate responsibility. Companies such as Walt Disney, IBM, and Intel include corporate governance as part of their corporate responsibility reports, while pressure groups such as the Interfaith Center on Corporate Responsibility see aspects of governance, such as execu-tive compensation, the independence and inclusivity of boards of directors, and transpar-ency and accountability to shareholders and other stakeholders, as important parts of the corporate responsibility agenda. Transparency and disclosure are recurring themes in debates about good governance and corporate responsibility more broadly.

Another area where the legal requirements of one region are being spread into other coun-tries is corruption. Business has long been criticized from different parts of the ideological spectrum for using bribery and corruption to influence policy, win contracts, and otherwise distort both the functioning of free markets and the political process. Transparency Interna-tional, an international NGO that lobbies against corrupt practices, defines corruption as the abuse of entrusted power for private gain. Although often portrayed as a victimless crime, corruption has been associated with low wages, unsafe counterfeit products, and hazard-ous living and working conditions. It is also blamed for undermining democracy and sound governance, stifling private sector growth, and encouraging inefficient business management (because winning contracts comes down to influence rather than competency).

Industries such as mining, construction, and defence have been especially criticized for paying commissions to win business, not least in countries with limited transparency and accountability. Although in advanced democracies industries from banking to pharmaceuticals to football have all been implicated in corruption scandals, nonetheless the traditional targets have been at the forefront of corporate responsibility initiatives in this area, including the Extractive Industries Transparency Initiative which enables the public to compare company payments with declared government revenues from oil, gas, and mining. Combating corruption has also been added to the principles of the United Nations Global Compact, but, despite these developments, some still downplay its importance, either because it is held to be culturally acceptable in some parts of the world, or because of fears that, by getting too strict with certain governments, companies will lose business to less scrupulous competitors.

Ethical responsibility

Ethical responsibility refers to the responsibilities of companies that go beyond legal compliance, and which are not determined by economic calculations. For some people, this is the most interesting part of corporate responsibility because it is asking what companies can do beyond what is demanded by regulation and economic rationality. Sometimes, companies preempt tougher legislation (e.g. the chemical industry's Responsible Care standard) believing that voluntary agreements will be easier to manage, and perhaps less stringent. But ethical responsibility is not always so pragmatically motivated. In the 1980s, The Body Shop gave a significant boost to campaigners who, since the publication of Harrison's *Animal Machines* in 1964, had wanted the testing of cosmetics on animals outlawed. Today, campaign groups such as People for the Ethical Treatment of Animals (PETA) are successful in getting companies such as McDonald's to improve animal welfare.

The environment is one area where in the past companies relied on government to say what was permissible, but in the face of global challenges from climate change to water availability to deforestation they are, at least to some degree, willing to go beyond legal compliance. This is part of a trend commencing in the 1980s when the effectiveness of command-and-control regulatory solutions started to be questioned, and both companies and regulators began to accept that preventing pollution could be a more effective way forward than simply punishing it. Environmental issues found their way into marketing strategies, and industries focusing on environmental technologies and services emerged. In the 1990s, environmental management standards such as BS 7750, the EU Eco-Management and Audit System (EMAS), and the ISO 14000 series provided new ways for companies to understand and manage their environmental impacts. Companies began to realize that, in certain situations, improved environmental performance could have a positive impact on the financial bottom line. In what came to be called the 'greening revolution', the business–environment relationship became, for some companies, less a costly problem than a strategic opportunity.[15]

The greening revolution was accompanied by a shift in government attitude, notably in Europe, where the legal responsibility of producers for their products began to cover more of the product life cycle, so that factors such as disposal and recycling had to be considered in product design, manufacturing, and marketing. 'Cradle to grave' thinking has become part of design philosophy in industries ranging from electrical goods to footwear to automotives. Major chemical companies have invested heavily in developing more environmentally beneficial substitutes for harmful materials. At the same time, new industries, such as biotechnology, have presented new environmental challenges (e.g. the perceived environmental consequences of genetically modified organisms) and established industries, such as energy, have generated new debates by investing in renewable energy at the same time as they remain dependent on environmentally damaging carbon-based fuels.

With its emphasis on financial and environmental benefits, the greening revolution marked a significant step forward in corporate responsibility and one that most corporate responsibility theorists failed to predict. The term 'eco-efficiency' has become widely used, highlighting that there need not be a trade-off between business and environmental performance. As McDonough and Braungart (2002) point out, however, there is a significant difference between being eco-efficient and eco-effective: it is the distinction between being *less bad* and consciously striving to do *more good*. If the greening revolution helped companies to think about making their products less harmful, eco-effectiveness (what has been called 'beyond greening') requires companies to rethink their technologies, their products, and their whole vision of the contribution that business makes to society.

The importance of beyond greening has grown as sustainability has become a major public concern. Sustainability—the ability to sustain a high quality of life for current and future generations—requires companies to rethink what they produce and how they do so. It also involves society rethinking what it wants from commercial enterprise—a question that is capturing widespread attention, as the potentially catastrophic consequences of global climate change become more widely believed.

Although 'sustainability' is still used in some corporate responsibility literature to refer to an eco-efficiency agenda, in its fullest sense it refers to something that cannot be captured only by reference to an environmental or a business rationale.[16] The triple bottom line was developed to address this by encouraging companies to think in terms of adding economic, social, and environmental value.[17] This provides the framework for some companies' sustainability reports, but merging these three dimensions of value in a way that shows the company's relationship to sustainable development has proved difficult and there is a marked tendency to treat each topic in isolation.

The distinction between doing less harm compared with doing more good is also evident amongst entrepreneurs whose motivation for going into business is measured by their social or environmental success. In the 1950s, faith-based and other organizations began responding to their members' concerns about unequal distribution of the wealth created by trade by establishing alternative trade organizations. Oxfam Trading, Traidcraft, and others invested in building the capacity of producers in poor countries, and sold their handicrafts and other products in Western markets. Later, beginning in the Netherlands, fairtrade labelling organizations were formed, guaranteeing to the consumer that certified producers and traders, in commodities such as coffee, tea, and cocoa, met specified fairtrade standards which include a minimum price to growers that exceeds the cost of production and payment of a social development premium. Today, companies such as Starbucks, Virgin Atlantic, and J Sainsbury offer fairtrade-certified products.

The same principle of harnessing the power of the markets for the benefit of the poor is found in initiatives popularized under the headings 'bottom of the pyramid' and 'corporate social opportunity'.[18] A well-known example of this is the microfinance model, originally developed in Bangladesh, but now found throughout the world. Microfinance provides poor people with financial capital without the need for collateral, helping them to avoid high usury charges and providing them with a safe place to keep their money. Initially, it was promoted by NGOs and aid organizations, but more recently major banks such as Citigroup and Deutsche Bank have started to offer microfinance services. A variety of models have evolved, such as the pioneering Grameen Bank, BRI in Indonesia with 30 million savers, and ProCredit with banks throughout Eastern Europe (see Chapter 10).

Discretionary responsibilities

Discretionary responsibilities are ones, such as philanthropy, which a company can assume even if there are no clear-cut societal expectations. As noted, for some, corporate responsibility is what lies beyond the law, and an important area of discretionary responsibility has been the idea of 'giving back' to society through philanthropic donations. Business leaders such as Carnegie, Rowntree, and Ford gave back large amounts of their individual wealth to establish foundations or to invest in favoured projects. Companies such as Hitachi, ExxonMobil, and Tata, often encouraged by tax regimes, gave as much as 5 per cent of their pre-tax income to the arts, community development, education, and other valued causes. Even though it no longer defines corporate responsibility, philanthropy remains important, as the multi-billion-dollar endowments by Bill Gates and Warren Buffet show. In the USA, where 2,600 companies have charitable foundations, corporate giving by firms of all sizes was estimated to be $18.5 billion in 2012.[19] In the UK, corporate donations are reckoned to be less than £800 million, and unlike the USA are in decline.[20]

In the 1990s, companies increasingly began to take a more strategic view of philanthropy, seeking out causes that were aligned with their business goals. For example, AT&T's foundation used its funding of education projects to win the ear of government policy advisers and this gave it an inside track in subsequent policy-making about the information superhighway. Companies such as Taiwan's King Car Food and Japan's Sony and Toyota have shown this to be a worldwide trend, and Muirhead (2006) reckons nearly half of companies align their community investment programmes with business objectives.

This has led some companies to adopt cause-related or affinity marketing, under which companies invest in social causes that complement their brands. But companies are wary of criticism that anything they do to give back is perceived as a public relations exercise and have sought to emphasize the win–win nature of investing in communities, while also taking a more critical view of staff volunteering and product gifting. Company-backed initiatives, such as the Partnership for Quality Medical Product Donation and LBG (formerly the London Benchmarking Group), have helped focus attention on what constitutes good practice and the impact that philanthropy can have.

Discussion points

We have set out two ways of thinking about corporate responsibility: company values and materiality.

- Which of these do you find most useful as a way of starting to think about the meaning of 'corporate responsibility'?
- Which of these do you think would resonate most with business managers?
- Do you think the type and size of a company and its industry affect how it approaches corporate responsibility?

Limitations of corporate responsibility frameworks

There are now more sophisticated frameworks for comprehending corporate responsibility than that of Carroll (1979), as we explore in Chapter 6, and some of these put much greater emphasis on the process of managing the relationship with wider society. Interestingly, although Carroll denied that his was a hierarchical framework under which some types of responsibility were more important than others, many of these subsequent theories have perpetuated and expanded on the idea that there are qualitatively different tiers of responsibility. This, in turn, has encouraged the idea that companies undergo different evolutionary stages within which their responsibilities and the nature of their relationship with other elements of society discernibly change (see Box 1.4).

Box 1.4   Prominent areas of corporate responsibility activity today

Business ethics	Human rights
Legal compliance	Worker rights and welfare
Philanthropy and community investment	Market relations
Environmental management	Corruption
Sustainability	Corporate governance
Animal rights	

Demonstrating that these transitions are beneficial either to business or society is an important part of the debate about corporate responsibility, as we discuss in Chapters 6 and 13. Transitions comprise new issues that business is having to address (e.g. climate change and shifts to a low-carbon economy), and also new concepts (e.g. responsibility to stakeholders). But when thinking about such changes, one should be as alert to the responsibilities that are seldom mentioned as one is to the those highlighted in corporate responsibility reports or at conferences. Moreover, one should be prepared to ask why issue A has been included whereas issue B has not. For example, companies such as IBM and Barclays celebrate their commitment to corporate responsibility, but do not include the closing of their company pension schemes or its consequences for workers as a responsibility issue. Likewise, accounting firms such as KPMG and PWC provide corporate responsibility consulting services, but are not especially vociferous on corporate taxation as a dimension of corporate responsibility.

Issues such as tax and pensions draw attention to the importance of long-term corporate performance. In considering how companies negotiate their responsibilities to society, an important test is whether they use their power and resources for the long-term benefit of society, even if there are short-term costs to the company. In its 2005 *Citizenship Report*, multinational conglomerate GE stressed that good citizenship has a more positive and enduring purpose than tackling the ills of the moment: it is about delivering high performance with high integrity over a sustained period of time, so as to create benefits for the long-term health of society and the enterprise. Commentators on business and society have pointed to a number of situations in which private enterprise is most at odds with society's interests, such as when monopolies replace competitive markets, or when companies become so powerful that they unduly influence public policy. These threats exist today, but to these has been added a situation in which the short-term interests of investors prevent companies from taking a long-term view of the well-being of either the enterprise or society.

It is interesting to note that economist Milton Friedman, who made probably the most forceful statement that companies are responsible only to shareholders (see Snapshot 1.2), introduced his theory of corporate responsibility at a time when investors were more inclined to hold shares for the longer term. Nowadays, notably in the Anglo-Saxon model that has become the norm against which other business systems are examined, many of Friedman's unspoken assumptions about what underpins the business–society relationship no longer hold, because investors look for higher and speedier returns, employees are more mobile, and senior managers are rewarded for pushing up the price of shares and increasing productivity, regardless of the human cost.

It is these types of change that some feel corporate responsibility should redress, either by putting limits on what is acceptable behaviour in the short run, or by encouraging companies to pay more attention to long-term performance. As one group of managers within the World Business Council for Sustainable Development (WBCSD) has concluded, corporate responsibility (specifically sustainability) becomes a logical element of profit maximization as soon as one insists that shareholder value equates with long-term shareholder value.[21] The reality for many companies, however, is that they have to straddle the demands of both the short and the long term. In the words of an oil industry CEO who had to contend with pressure from both the financial markets and civil society:

> On the one hand, you've got Wall Street squeezing you harder and harder for shorter and shorter term performance. On the other hand, you have a broader constituent base that wants more than financial results ... Most CEOs will tell you, 'This is damn hard work'.[22]

 Snapshot 1.2 What responsibilities do companies have?

The only social responsibility a law-abiding business has is to maximize profits for its shareholders.

This, in short, is economist Milton Friedman's theory of free market corporate responsibility. It is a controversial viewpoint among corporate responsibility theorists because it appears to say that what's good for investors is good for everyone. That is a difficult position to defend because profit maximization can drive companies to bend or break the law to the point of self-destruction (e.g. Enron

(continued...)

and Arthur Andersen). But Friedman isn't saying that everything is justified by the share price: he believes that government sets the rules of the game, and companies have to operate within them. An important question, therefore, is whether governments do a good job at regulating business behaviour, and the answer to that might be very different in today's globalized economy than it was when many companies primarily operated within national boundaries.

Another important question is what do we mean by shareholder. In the 1960s, it was common for individuals and institutions to hold shares for many years, and people's wealth was closely related to the long-term well-being of the firm. That has changed with the emergence of day-traders, the high turnover in shares even amongst institutional investors, the emphasis put on publicly traded companies' quarterly earnings, and the way success is defined by private equity firms. The shareholder is not the long-term owner that he or she once was.

Even amongst libertarian entrepreneurs, who would typically favour markets over governments as arbiters of the social good, Friedman's view of the firm has been criticized as outdated. For example, John Mackey, CEO of US retailer Whole Foods and a self-proclaimed libertarian, has said: '*The enlightened corporation should try to create value for* all *of its constituencies*'. In a dialogue with Friedman, he argued that shareholders are one group with an interest in the company and that they want the firm to maximize profits. According to Mackey, it is too narrow to say that shareholder interests are paramount: the entrepreneur defines the company's purpose, and if he says from the outset that part of that purpose is, for example, to give a stated percentage of net profits to philanthropy, then subsequent investors have no right to dispute that—they know what they are buying into.

(*Sources:* Friedman, 1962; *Wall Street Journal*, 2005; *Rethinking the Social Responsibility of Business*, www.reason.org)

Quick questions

Corporate responsibility is often depicted as a 'left-wing' intervention to disrupt market capitalism, yet people on 'the right' also disagree about its value and importance.

1 What changes have taken place in society since the 1960s that might make Friedman's notion of corporate responsibility outdated?

2 How convincing is Mackey's argument that profits are not the purpose, but a means to realizing social and environmental ends?

3 Which companies would you hold up as examples of Friedman's view of the responsible company? Which ones represent Mackey's view?

 Case study 1   What are the limits to responsibility? The case of pharmaceuticals

Some industries seem to have a responsibility advantage just because of what they do. For instance, it is much easier to imagine a responsible pharmaceutical company than a reponsible tobacco firm. Like other segments of the health sector, the pharmaceutical industry is popular among ethical investors because of the social good that its products bring. Many of its employees enter the industry because of the good they can do. On top of this, the industry is renowned for giving back, and has long donated drugs to poor countries to treat tropical diseases such as elephantiasis, river blindness, and leprosy.

(continued...)

Yet pharmaceutical companies are also highly controversial. While Johnson & Johnson enhanced its reputation when it swiftly removed contaminated Tylenol-brand capsules from the shelves in the early 1980s, other firms have fought expensive and damaging legal campaigns associated with similar pain-relief products. Merck, for example, faced thousands of personal-injury lawsuits brought by people who claimed its Vioxx brand had caused heart attacks or strokes. The company promised to fight every suit, but between 2007 and 2009 agreed to settlements worth over $5 billion. In 2009, Pfizer, a competitor, had to pay a $2.3 billion fine for promoting a similar drug, Bextra, for unapproved uses.

Around the world, the pharmaceutical salesforce has been criticized for persuading doctors to prescribe inappropriate or ineffective drugs, while prestigious medical journals such as *The New England Journal of Medicine* have spoken out about the way the pharmaceutical industry can undermine the integrity of research. Companies have been accused of over-zealously protecting their patents, and for focusing on developing drugs for the rich rather than the poor. In 1998, a consortium of drug companies filed suit against the South African government, naming Nelson Mandela as a defendant. The case revolved around the companies' attempt to block the distribution of generic drugs used in treating HIV/AIDS—drugs that 39 major companies had patented, but which were 98 per cent cheaper in their generic form. The industry said it was simply protecting its intellectual property rights, but it came under repeated assault for price fixing and for denying the poor access to medicine.

In the same year, a Canadian drug-maker applied to manufacture a generic form of the popular antidepressant Paxil. With its original patent about to expire, GlaxoSmithKline (GSK), the drug's original inventor, filed four patent infringement lawsuits that effectively stopped the generic drug entering the US market.

The drug industry dropped the case in South Africa in 2001 and GSK was among the companies that proceeded to sell HIV/AIDS treatments at heavily discounted prices in developing countries. Jean-Pierre Garnier, the GSK CEO, famously stated that he did not want to head a company that catered only to the rich and said that the company's primary objective must always be public health. Since then, other pharmaceutical companies, such as Abbott Laboratories, have backed initiatives to make HIV/AIDS treatments available and affordable in developing countries, and have become less aggressive in restricting generic brands.

However, elsewhere the industry is still portrayed as very defensive. The Paxil case was continued and 46 US states accused GSK of filing frivolous patent infringement lawsuits that drove up the cost of medicine for the poor. Again, the company was accused of denying access to the most needy in order to maximize its profits. It settled the suit with a $14 million payment to the states in 2006, but admitted no wrongdoing. More recently, pharmaceutical firms contributed some of the $380 million spent in 2008–2009 by the health-care sector on lobbying US politicians about health-care reform.

Yet the industry claims that it is only participating in a democratic process where it is in a unique position to educate politicians. Furthermore, it says that without the profits it generates in wealthier markets, it would be unable to develop the drugs that people are crying out for, from cancer treatments to combating Alzheimer's disease to defeating malaria. And while one judge has ordered a former executive of a drug company to write a book to teach others about his firm's anti-competitive practices, there are still well-respected companies in the industry such as Novo Nordisk which has the corporate purpose of curing diabetes.

(*Sources:* Smith, 2003; Barmann, 2006; McGreal, 2009; Rockoff and Kendall, 2009; Loftus, 2009; Singer, 2009)

....

Questions

1 Headlines about miracle cures from swine flu to erectile dysfunction show the thirst modern society has for ever-improved drugs. But the furore over drug costs, lobbying, and biased research is evidence that many are deeply suspicious about how the pharmaceutical industry behaves.

(continued...)

> **a** What are the advantages and disadvantages of making the private sector responsible for this aspect of health care?
>
> **b** Do you think that the profit motive of pharmaceutical companies helps or harms their ethical mission?
>
> **c** What are the main corporate responsibility issues that the pharmaceutical industry needs to address?
>
> **2** Health care is typically depicted as a human right, something that puts pharmaceutical companies in a very different position to most industries.
>
> **a** Is GlaxoSmithKline justified in making drugs available on a not-for-profit basis in Africa, but not in the USA?
>
> **b** Why do you think various pharmaceutical companies have agreed to provide drugs at lower costs in developing countries?
>
> **c** Would it be responsible for a pharmaceutical company to use profits from a drug used in cosmetic surgery to provide lower-cost cancer treatments to poor communities?

Summary

Corporate responsibility is the newest 'old' thing in business management. What we mean by 'corporate responsibility' is constantly changing as society itself evolves, affecting our expectations of business and the way in which its relationship with society is handled. The discussion about what corporate responsibility means can be entered into from several doors. We can think of the company as an entity with its own values, or at least as a vessel that has to accommodate the competing values and moral principles of different people. We can also think of it as a member of society that has to uphold certain duties and obligations in order to be a good citizen.

Each doorway has its advantages and disadvantages from an analytical standpoint, but it would be a mistake to conclude that corporate responsibility is diminished because there is no universal definition or overarching theory. Instead, what these different perspectives reveal are a multitude of ways in which business impacts upon, and is affected by, the rest of society and hence a multiplicity of reasons why companies might want to manage that relationship. They will do this differently, depending on such variables as the type of company, the moment in history, the nature of the industry, and the geopolitical context. Similar variables will also determine the benefits of addressing the relationship. But the constant and central concern of corporate responsibility is how the relationship between business and wider society is defined and acted upon, whether by business as a whole, through collective action, or by single corporate actors.

Further reading

online
resource
centre

www.oxfordtextbooks.co.uk/orc/blowfield_murray3e/

Visit the Online Resource Centre that accompanies this book to enrich your understanding of this chapter. Among the resources available are web links, exercises, and additional case studies.

Barrett, R. 1998, *Liberating the corporate soul: building a visionary organization*, Butterworth-Heinemann, Boston, MA.

An interesting approach to blending and aligning personal and organizational values.

Crane, A. & Matten, D. 2004, *Business ethics*, Oxford University Press, Oxford.

Comprehensive introduction to business ethics, with an interesting focus on the company as a member of society.

Davis, I. 2005, 'Ian Davis on business and society', *The Economist*, 26 May, online at www.economist.com.

Provocative take on the need to rethink the role of business, from the head of McKinsey's management consultancy.

Frederick, W.C. 2006, *Corporation be good!: the story of corporate social responsibility*, Dog Ear Publishing, Indianapolis, IN.

Several decades of corporate responsibility thinking collected together by an American academic.

Jenkins, R.O., Pearson, R., & Seyfang, G. (eds) 2002, *Corporate responsibility and labour rights: codes of conduct in the global economy*, Earthscan, London.

Good collection of articles on issues to do with voluntary codes of labour conduct in supply chains.

Roddick, A. 2000, *Business as unusual*, Thorsons, London.

The Body Shop founder's take on her own experiences of creating a successful company rooted in ethical principles.

Vogel, D. 2005, *The market for virtue: the potential and limits of corporate social responsibility*, Brookings Institution Press, Washington, DC.

Concise overview of the main drivers and hurdles affecting corporate responsibility today.

Online resources

- Case study of a multinational company's worker welfare scandal: the problem and the consequences for the company
- Teaching notes on the chapter's main case study
- More detailed overview of business ethics and political theory
- Films, books, and other resources
- Links to other web-based resources

Endnotes

1. Mattar, 2001.
2. http://www.economicshelp.org/blog/4060/economics/total-uk-debt/, accessed 7 October 2013.
3. May et al., 2007.
4. For overviews of CSR, see Carroll, 1999; Birch, 2001; Basu and Palazzo, 2005. For a discussion of corporate social responsiveness and performance, see Wartick and Cochran, 1985. Bennett et al., 1999, contains essays on the progress of corporate sustainability. Wood and Logsdon, 2001, 2002 and Moon et al., 2005; Matten & Moon, 2008 provide different viewpoints on corporate citizenship.
5. Hemp and Stewart, 2004.

6.   See e.g. Birch, 2001; Woods and Logsdon, 2001; Dion, 2001.

7.   Werther and Chandler, 2011.

8.   Anderson, 2003; 2005.

9.   See e.g. Sorell and Hendry, 1994; Chryssides and Kaler, 1993; Donaldson and Dunfee, 1999; Ladkin, 2006.

10. Jamali and Mirshak, 2007; Visserand Tolhurst 2010.

11. Jensen and Meckling, 1976; for a fuller discussion, see Chapter 8.

12. www.npr.org/templates/story/story.php?storyId=106899074.

13. www.guardian.co.uk/business/2007/apr/15/supermarkets.uknews.

14. www.news.bbc.co.uk/1/hi/business/7339231.stm.

15. Freeman et al., 2000; Schaltegger et al., 2003.

16. Renn, 1995, cited bySchaltegger et al., 2003.

17. Elkington, 1998.

18. Prahalad, 2005; Grayson and Hodges, 2004.

19. philanthropy.com/article/Big-Businesses-Expect-Modest/140341/, accessed 7 October 2013.

20. www.thirdsector.co.uk/Fundraising/article/1187212/corporate-donations-fell-almost-third-past-two-years/, accessed 7 October 2013.

21. WBCSD, 2006.

22. Blowfield and Googins, 2007, p 22.

2

The origins of corporate responsibility

 ## Chapter overview

In this chapter, we set out the theoretical and historical origins of modern-day corporate responsibility. In particular, we will:

- plot the evolution of the modern corporation and its relevance for the business–society relationship;
- explore how corporate responsibility has evolved from the Industrial Revolution to the current era of globalization;
- trace the development of theories of corporate responsibility.

 ## Main topics

Introduction   31
Three eras of responsibility   32
Theories of corporate responsibility   40

Key terms

Capitalism	Licence to operate
Corporate philanthropy	Limited liability
Industrial Revolution	New Deal
Welfare state	Social contract
Globalization	

Introduction

In 1909, George Cadbury found himself in court because the company bearing his name had been buying cocoa produced by slaves in Africa.[1] In 2000, the company found itself accused once more of the same offence. These incidents demonstrate that issues such as slavery do not go away. More to the point, when corporate behaviour clashes with people's sense of justice and permissibility, companies are held responsible even if there is no legal liability and despite the absence or presence of shareholder interest.

The issues that matter, why they come to the fore, and what a company does to address them vary according to the company, the industry, the location, and the time. Cadbury's response in 1909 was very different to what it was in 2000 (see Case Study 2), even if slavery was always more likely to be more of an issue for the chocolate manufacturer than for its Birmingham neighbour, the car-maker Rover, which in 2000, faced with bankruptcy and allegations of pension fund fraud, had its own corporate responsibility headaches to deal with.

Corporate responsibility is constant, yet variable and dynamic. In this chapter, we examine how society has consistently held expectations of business that go beyond the narrow sphere of wealth creation. We begin by exploring the relationship that business has had with society during different historical periods and in different countries. Then we examine how various theories of corporate responsibility have emerged to help understand and manage that relationship.

What the following sections reveal is that private enterprise has always been the subject of public scrutiny. What we mean by 'corporate responsibility' today has been influenced enormously by our economic systems, the evolution of the modern corporation, and the emergence of theories of corporate responsibility itself. This chapter is a discussion of that heritage.

The *Cadbury* case is a useful starting point for putting corporate responsibility in context. The issues in 1909 were, in many ways, the same as those today. First, companies were then, and are now, felt by many to have a duty to uphold certain human rights, even when there is no legal liability. Second, companies that purchase commodities or manufactured goods are held to have influence over, and responsibility for, the behaviour of their producers. These principles were apparent in the 1909 court case and are central to areas of modern corporate responsibility, such as ethical trade.

Echoes of the Cadbury experience can be heard throughout this chapter as we explore the origins of corporate responsibility. The company's experiences are not unique; stick a pin anywhere in the timeline of corporate evolution and the issues of what a company should be responsible for, who decides, and where accountability lies are recurring themes. Responses can vary, as do the levels of trust in corporations (see Figure 2.1), but what this chapter shows is that the issues of corporate responsibility and the role of commercial endeavour in society are constants throughout human history.

Three eras of responsibility

The Cadbury experience straddles three historical periods, during which the nature of business's relationship with society has changed significantly:

1   the Industrial Revolution;

2   the mid-twentieth-century welfare state;

3   the Globalization era.

Each period has raised new issues about what business should be responsible for, but, as we shall see, many of the issues remain relevant from one era to the next.

The Industrial Revolution

Throughout much of Europe, the biggest change in human demographics and human working life came with the Industrial Revolution, as the poor from the countryside headed towards

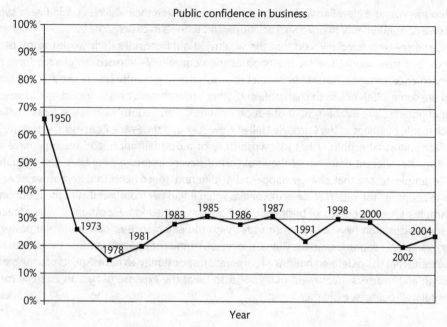

Figure 2.1 Levels of public confidence in business over the years

(*Source:* Based on data from Frederick, 2006)

the cities in search of work. In the UK, the first industrial power, the proportion of the population engaged in manufacturing increased from one fifth to nearly two-thirds between 1801 and 1871.[2]

But this massive increase in urban living brought with it problems of overcrowding and disease. Children were employed in sweeping chimneys, domestic service, and manufacturing, as depicted in the popular novels of Dickens and Kingsley. Factories and mines were responsible for a large number of injuries and fatalities. Slave labour on the African and American continents produced many of the raw materials that industrialization required. In some industries, women became important components of the workforce, not out of choice, but due to poverty.

Industrialization provoked civil unrest. From the late 1770s, there were numerous popular, and frequently violent, protests aimed at resisting industrialization or improving the lives of those affected by it. Information about human exploitation spurred various reform movements, such as Wilberforce's anti-slavery society, while the UK's first Factory Acts were passed in 1819 and laws to control conditions in mines were passed in 1842.

In addition to government intervention, it was around this time that writers such as Carlyle and Arnold began to suggest how heads of industry might behave, marking the start of the era of Victorian philanthropy. Robert Owen had already set up his mills at New Lanark and was an instigator of the early Factory Acts. He strove to establish a new model of industrial development in Scotland and the USA, based on the belief that a man's character was formed by his surroundings and the conditions under which he worked and lived. This vision was developed later in the century by the likes of Cadbury and Rowntree, who established villages at Bourneville and New Earswick, respectively, within which their workers could live in supportive communities with open spaces, shops, and schools in easy reach.

Carnegie—who famously said that the wealthy should consider their wealth to be trust funds that they should use for the good of the community—pursued a different form of benevolence, using his fortune from steel to embark on a philanthropic quest that saw him donate some $350 million to charitable and other philanthropic causes, including the building of libraries, the establishment of educational trusts, and contributions towards creating such iconic buildings as the Carnegie Hall in New York and the Peace Palace in The Hague.

Each industrial economy has its own history of industrialization, and we only have to look at the different timelines of the abolition of slavery in the UK, the USA, and Belgium, for example, to see that change happened at different speeds and in different ways. And some countries' toleration of slavery overseas when it had been outlawed at home is but one example of how standards of business behaviour were affected by location. Similar aspects of industrialization have arisen again today with the emergence of new industrial powers. For example, in countries such as China, the massive influx of rural people into urban areas is one trend that has redefined notions of corporate responsibility, as have aspects of economic growth and overseas investment that appear to be at the expense of human and environmental well-being (see Chapter 5).

The evolution and rise of the modern corporation

In the mind's eye, the first Industrial Revolution in Europe and the USA conjures up images of technological innovation: steam engines, mills, belching factory chimneys, and the like. But this was as much an institutional as an industrial revolution. Work life changed, governed by clocks and machines rather than by seasons. But the idea of business itself changed as well. As important as technology was institutional innovation, not least the emergence of the 'limited liability company' and changes in the meaning of 'incorporation'. These legal constructs were to have a profound effect on the business–society relationship, not only on where liability fell, but what the rights and responsibilities of the company were. Today, the meaning of 'business' is either taken for granted, or the subject of typically polarized arguments over whether it is a good or a bad thing. But in capitalism's early days, the advantages and disadvantages of different types of company were widely debated. Limited liability—the construct by which shareholders in a company are not liable for its debts beyond the nominal value of their shares—was a major factor that allowed the modern corporation to emerge. The economist Adam Smith disliked this idea and favoured partnerships over corporations, because he felt that separating the owner from direct control of the company opens the way for professional managers to pursue their own self-interest.[3] But, despite the fact that the limited liability company is only one of several forms of commercial enterprise, it has nonetheless come to dominate the modern business world.

Limited liability encourages entrepreneurship, but has also been singled out as the root cause of problems in the business–society relationship. It has made possible the emergence of multinational corporations, the power of which Korten (1995) views as a threat to society and Henderson (2004) sees as an asset. It also creates the tension between shareholders and corporate officials that is central to arguments about where a company's responsibilities lie. For some, such as Friedman (1962) and Novak (1982), the primacy given to shareholder interests is the genius of capitalism; for others, such as Mitchell (2001) and Ellsworth (2002), it is the reason why managers focus on short-term results and therefore restricts their freedom to serve the interests of others in society. Thus, limited liability is central to the roles that companies play in creating jobs, paying taxes, and generating wealth, but also to aspects of corporate behaviour such as downsizing, bankruptcy, and who has claim to the company's assets. We discuss these issues in other chapters, not least in the context of the socially responsible investment movement which seeks to change the investor–company relationship (see Chapter 10).

The twentieth century—a more mature capitalism

From corporate to government responsibility

By the early twentieth century, changes in the legal definition of the firm led to a huge increase in the number of mergers, and corporations came to be seen by some as huge impersonal monoliths that were beginning to exert political pressure as never before, leading to public calls for greater regulation and supervision (see Snapshot 2.1). Private enterprise had flourished in the late nineteenth century until the period prior to World War I. Yes, it could be highly exploitative of people and nature. Yes, it was often the bedfellow of imperialism and militarism. Yes, it frequently relied on monopoly and oligopoly to the point where John D Rockefeller, who famously stated that 'competition is a sin', owned wealth equivalent to nearly 2 per cent of US GDP (Bill Gates is worth 0.65 per cent).[4] Capitalism took various forms and had many facets, making it difficult to generalize. But for all its weaknesses and failings, capitalist free enterprise, and with it global free trade, flourished before World War I, corporate power grew, and private self-interest was promoted as serving the public good. This triumphalism faded after the war; momentum increased for greater equality and a rethinking of the social order following the leadership failures that had left eight million dead on battlefields around the world, and the image of the capitalist as war profiteer depicted in Shaw's play *Major Barbara* was commonplace. The International Labour Organization (ILO), founded in 1919 as part of the League of Nations, brought together government, business, and trade unions, and explicitly recognized the dangers of an unjust political or economic order. Business leaders were forced to consider the impact that their activities were having on wider society, and some engaged in movements such as 'New Capitalism'[5] promoting the idea that business should voluntarily take steps to portray itself and its activities as beneficial to society at large.

But such ideas gained limited traction, partly because of the greater struggle between managers and organized labour that was a feature of the post-war period, and also because economic growth (particularly increases in share value in some countries) encouraged a belief that markets could be the ultimate guarantors of the public good. This came to a head with the Great Depression, when corporate greed was blamed as one of the possible causes of the 1929 Wall Street Crash that left millions destitute in the USA, with ramifications throughout the world's economy. It was time to rein in corporate and shareholder excess, and where possible government stepped in to rescue the economy. In Germany, the National Socialist Party struck alliances with big business to align private enterprise with the national good. In the USA, President Franklin D Roosevelt initiated the 'New Deal', a series of measures that were, in part, designed to limit the power of corporations. If the

Snapshot 2.1   Is big business desirable, inevitable, or irredeemable?

Ever since the nineteenth century the size of companies has grown and grown. When people think about corporate responsibility, they often think about the giant multinational companies and conglomerates that dominate industries from information and communication technologies to retail to pharmaceuticals. Most private sector workers may work for small firms, but it is large business that attracts attention. Unilever, Tata, BHP Billiton, and Samsung are a handful of the many multinational companies that put corporate responsibility on the front pages of their websites. But are these companies too big to be responsible members of society?

Thomas Quinn called such companies 'monster business'. The monster business was the inevitable end result of business evolution where companies evolved from small enterprising firms to large ones, then into giant corporations, and finally into monsters. Monster companies not only stifle competition—something that has led to antitrust laws around the world—but also affect social and political institutions, and even pose a menace to the democratic way of life.

Although Quinn was writing during the 1930s Depression, his views find echoes in corporate responsibility discussions today. For example, he pointed to big-banker trustees who control voting at the dominant corporations, representing what he called 'the highest degree of concentrated economic power in our history'. Reflecting recent criticisms about board responsibility, he claimed that directors were responsible for setting 'wholly arbitrary, self-serving judgments, compensation and recognition awards'. He also blamed corporate officials for paying themselves excessive salaries, bonuses, pensions, and stock options, and went on to explain why monster business was inherently antisocial.

Quinn was no radical outsider—certainly not the 1930s equivalent of Naomi Klein or Joel Bakan. He was a star executive at that quintessential 'monster business' General Electric—the man who established that company's refrigerator division. In the economic and social upheaval of his time, his views were part of the cauldron of public debate. Now, when executives are typically portrayed as conservatives, his cry to limit the size of business is in marked contrast to right-wing thinkers such as Rand and Hayek who treated a company's growth within the free market as the best way to increase shareholder value, lower prices, and serve the general good.

Quinn's views are more aligned with the political left, but even here things are not clear cut. Canadian economist JK Galbraith did not necessarily favour big business, but saw its growth as inevitable as perfect competition disappeared beneath its shadow. He agreed with Quinn that, by itself, this would have undesirable outcomes across society. However, we should not worry about this because the interests of capital and management, he argued, would be counterbalanced by trade unions and other organized groups. It was what he called this 'countervailing power' that would keep monster business honest and continuing to serve the public good.

(*Sources:* Galbraith, 1952; Quinn, 1962; Rand, 1966)

Quick questions

1 Does the fact that parts of what Quinn observed still resonate today suggest that 'the problem' of big business is nothing new and is something that society adequately controls through conventional political processes?

2 Do you agree with Galbraith that the power of 'business' can be controlled by 'countervailing powers'?

3 Is Rand right to argue that controls on the size of business such as antitrust laws stifle innovation, success, and economic rewards?

1920s view of corporate managers is encapsulated in the phrase of General Motors' President, Alfred Sloan, *'The business of business is business'*, Roosevelt's view can be seen in the quote, *'We consider too much the good luck of the early bird, and not enough the bad luck of the early worm'*. Despite the very different fortunes of countries such as Germany, the USA, and Japan, the idea of social welfare as a safety net for when capitalism wobbled or fell remained a platform of the social order for the rest of the twentieth century, at least in wealthier nations. In countries from Argentina to Indonesia governments have continued to step in to tackle market failure, and the interventions by major economic powers around the world to save the finance industry in 2008 show that in the world of *realpolitik* free markets are not trusted to serve the public good.

Post World War II

Business emerged from World War II with a mixed reputation. Companies such as Mitsubishi and Mercedes had been part of their nations' war machines, while firms from IBM to Coca Cola were to spend years cleansing themselves of associations with fascism. But business had played a key part in winning the war, whether it be through unprecedented levels of production or fast-track innovation. Where the war had hit hardest, there was exhaustion and an appetite for change. In the UK, the post-war Labour government put in place a system of welfare safety nets. It also acted on its belief in state-owned industry by nationalizing major industries such as coal, railways, steel, gas distribution, and power generation. The idea that business best served the public good if it was state-controlled took hold in much of Western Europe and, of course, in the Eastern Bloc of Communist countries, in which private enterprise was outlawed. It also characterized the role of business in newly independent countries such as Indonesia and India which saw the nationalization of industry as essential to the long-held dream of independence.

In West Germany and Italy, new models of governance were put in place to ensure that workers, as well as shareholders, had a say in how companies were run. In the USA, a seemingly spontaneous interplay between business and society emerged, similar to what chaos theory would later term 'complex adaptive systems', but which at the time was seen as a debate over how much of its power business would cede to wider society.[6]

These different approaches to managing the role of business in society all marked a significant change in thinking from that of the days when it was assumed that business best benefited others by being left largely to its own devices. The welfare state was primarily concerned with a more equitable distribution of the benefits of economic prosperity. Distribution was the responsibility of government and the primary role of business was to create jobs, obey the law, and pay taxes. However, the concerns of the welfare state, such as health care, living wages, and education, influence what we think of as 'corporate responsibility' today. Equally, the renewed interest in human rights shown by national governments in the aftermath of the war gave rise to such agreements as the United Nations Universal Declaration of Human Rights, which is now referenced in important corporate responsibility initiatives.

It is easy to idealize the post World War II contract between business and government. In the former colonies, new governments lacked the expertise or wealth to deliver the comprehensive safety nets enjoyed in wealthier countries. Companies such as Zambia

Consolidated Copper Mines found themselves directly involved in community development. Equally, prosperity brought with it new social concerns. In the early 1950s smog
claimed the lives of many citizens in both the UK and USA, with serious instances in London,
New York, and Los Angeles. Pollution became a political issue, resulting in the passing of
the US Air Pollution Control Act in 1955 and the UK Clean Air Act in 1956. A year later,
Scripps Oceanographic Institute scientists were surprised to discover rising carbon dioxide
levels in the world's oceans.

In 1962, Carson's *Silent Spring* was published, detailing the effect of man-made pesticides,
and throughout the decade scientific discovery of the effects of leaded petroleum, water
pollution, and chemical seepage served to make increasing numbers of people aware of the
connection between environmental degradation and corporate activity. In the following decades, regular instances of corporate malfeasance, such as the Love Canal, Bhopal, Chernobyl,
and the *Exxon Valdez*, served to reinforce this connection.

Non-government environmental groups, such as Greenpeace (founded in 1971), began
advocating for change outside the mainstream political process. In terms of organization
and strategy, they set the agenda for a much broader range of rights-focused activists, such
as those protecting the interests of workers, indigenous people, animals, children, bonded
labour, etc.—the advocacy groups that play an important role in contemporary corporate
responsibility today.

The women's rights movement also became more visible in the 1970s and, among other
things, raised issues of equality in the workplace. One aspect of this was equal treatment in
terms of remuneration and working conditions, and another was equality of opportunity.
The movement worldwide has had an enormous impact in a relatively short space of time,
most notably in the area of legislation (e.g. maternity rights, equal pay). In terms of corporate
responsibility, the women's rights movement established the basic principle that companies
shall not discriminate against women. Similar principles have been applied in relation to age,
ethnicity, race, disability, and sexual orientation, and, in the USA especially, racial discrimination has been a significant part of the corporate responsibility agenda.

 Discussion points

There are expectations across the political spectrum that big business has the power and responsibility
to benefit society. There are also fears across the spectrum that big business is a 'monster'.

- Does 'big business' have different responsibilities to those of other types of business?
- How does limited liability influence how companies view their relationships with society?
- Find examples, at the national and provincial levels, of ways in which company law makes
  companies responsible to stakeholders other than shareholders.

The Globalization era

The relationship of business with society has changed again with globalization, the phenomenon that has affected social, political, economic, and business life since the 1980s. Globalization is often portrayed as a new era, bringing changes that are as momentous as those of

the Industrial Revolution. It is certainly an era during which business's place in society is being transformed and, for that reason alone, it is important that we understand its meaning and consequences.

But we can go further than this. Writers such as Wood et al. (2006), Pedersen and Huniche (2006), and Crane and Matten (2004) tie corporate responsibility to the social, political, and environmental challenges of globalization. In fact, to some degree, its success may influence the direction of globalization overall.[7] This is because globalization is associated, on the one hand, with a limited set of global governance mechanisms and weakened national governments, and on the other, with unprecedented private sector wealth, power, and impact. Thus corporate responsibility has become an important means for addressing what Stiglitz (2002) sees as the fundamental problem with contemporary globalization—a system of global governance without global government.

However, there is a lot of confusion about what is meant by globalization. In corporate responsibility literature, the term is often used in its narrowest sense to mean the worldwide flows of data, capital, goods, and services. Indeed, some aspects of globalization highlighted by certain corporate observers were already features of previous eras. For example, globalization critic Naomi Klein (1999) talks about global colonization by brands—what she calls 'McDonaldization'—and a wider process as part of which Western norms and values wipe out diversity and local cultures. Yet generations earlier in his travels between South Africa, England, and India, Mahatma Gandhi would have found it as easy to buy a packet of Player's cigarettes as we would find it to buy a Big Mac today.

Many economists use globalization to mean the global spread of liberal economic ideas, notably the creation of a global market built on free trade. This kind of liberal globalization is essentially the realization of the economic relations explained by economists such as Smith, Ricardo, or Marx, and the socio-economic system described by Mises and Hayek. Some political economists, on the other hand, argue that we should think more broadly than just economics—that we should see globalization as a social condition that also includes politics, culture, ethics, ecology, and all the other facets that affect human life. What separates globalization today from any previous historical period is that a combination of technological innovation, policy shifts, power relations, and values has meant that physical space and time have become much less important determinants of economic and social activity and of social identity. Alluding to Fukuyama's (1989) idea that globalization marks the end of history, Virilio (2000) concludes that globalization is really the end of geography.

Understandably, the economic dimension to globalization is attractive to many in business, but it is worthwhile understanding the perspective of political economists—what has been called 'globalization as deterritorialization'.[8] In our business lives, we witness many symptoms of globalization, such as the offshoring of jobs, rapid growth in international trade, and international capital flows. Deterritorialization theorists say that all of this reflects more fundamental changes in our social condition (e.g. new social orders transcending traditional political and geographical boundaries; powerful companies and other organizations not strongly linked to a specific place; intense rapid interaction between groups allowing events in one region to trigger reactions anywhere in the world), and is part of a growing consciousness of our interconnectedness and interdependence.[9] This is important for companies to understand because on the one hand they are often criticized for exerting excessive power in this new global order, and on the other they can fall victims to it such as when people connected through cyberspace form an alliance to hold a company to account for its behaviour. This is what the chocolate industry experienced when journalists found slave labour on cocoa farms in West Africa (see Case Study 2), or what Monsanto still experiences because of some people's objections to genetically modified organisms. Moreover, while not all such alliances survive for long, some do, as Nestlé will vouch for after three decades of fighting allegations about its infant milk formula.

Business in the modern globalization era is fundamental to understanding contemporary corporate responsibility, and we discuss it in far more depth in Chapter 4. It accounts for many of the issues companies are being held responsible for, the growth in wealth, poverty, and inequality that has accompanied unprecedented private sector activity, and the recognition of the values and materiality dimensions of issues such as global poverty and sustainability that business is being asked to address. It also accounts for the changing nature of corporate governance, investment, public scrutiny, and social expectation that affect companies' licence to operate and the very definition of success. However, before we flesh out these statements, let us explore the evolution of corporate responsibility theory that shapes some of our thinking today.

Theories of corporate responsibility

The preceding sections describe the historical landscape that has influenced corporate responsibility theory and practice. It feels at times that there is an archaeological quest to discover the earliest instance of corporate responsibility, with examples reported as long ago as Mesopotamian and Roman times.[10] If by theory we mean something that is written down, corporate responsibility theory is relatively new, but if we mean the ideas that underpin business practice, then any enterprise at any moment in history has had to establish what Donaldson and Dunfee (1999) call its 'licence to operate' because without the support of those in power or the wider public it cannot prosper. The different histories and cultures of corporate responsibility are a fascinating area of enquiry, but for purely practical reasons the following discussion of corporate responsibility theory's evolution takes as its starting point business in the West (see Snapshot 2.2).

Evolution of corporate responsibility theory

Before corporate responsibility had a name, philosophy and theology were already informing the thinking of entrepreneurs. Carnegie's *Gospel of Wealth* (1889) sets out the duties wealthy capitalists have to society. The Lever Brothers, the Clarks, and the Cadburys were not only successful industrialists but also Quakers who found it contrary to their faith to ignore worker well-being, or to leave people's fates to the market. They differed from Carnegie in their belief that responsibility was not just about how one used one's wealth, but how that wealth was created in the first place. Early academic writers on corporate responsibility such as Berle and Means (1932) focused on the responsibilities of the individual business leader rather than the company, reflecting a widely held view in the USA that success and responsibility go hand in hand. Davis called this the 'Iron Law of Responsibility' which states that the social responsibilities of business leaders need to be commensurate with their social power[11] (Figure 2.2).

Snapshot 2.2   Trafigura takes on global civil society

Trafigura is a Dutch commodity trading company. Dealing in base metals and energy, it is not the kind of company that gets much public attention. However, search on the web for Trafigura and one will typically find the word 'scandal' come up alongside the company's name. In countries such as Malta, Zambia, Nigeria, Jamaica, and Thailand it has been involved in high-level corruption, smuggling, and collusion that has brought down government ministers and led to international enquiries and legal proceedings. During the Saddam Hussein era, the company was accused of sanctions busting and smuggling 500,000 barrels of oil out of Iraq, according to a UN report. It pleaded guilty in the USA and forfeited $20 million.

However, its highest-profile scandal occurred off the waters of Côte d'Ivoire, and came to public attention not because of government officials or the traditional media, but due to a concerted campaign that is typical of the kinds of pressures companies can find themselves under today. In 2006, Trafigura chartered the *Probo Koala* to transport its toxic waste. Its first port of call was the Netherlands which had the facilities to dispose of the waste safely. However, the costs were high, and instead the *Probo Koala* sailed towards Africa. Shipping this waste outside of Europe was illegal because few countries have the facilities to process it properly; but the company made a deal with another company for $15,000 that would lead to the waste being put in landfill sites in Côte d'Ivoire. Within a month, the people of Abidjan were finding foul-smelling toxic waste that had been dumped in numerous places around their city. According to an NGO report:

> Tens of thousands of people suffered from nausea, headaches, breathing difficulties, stinging eyes and burning skin. They did not know what was happening; they were terrified. Health centres and hospitals were soon overwhelmed. International agencies were drafted in to help overstretched local medical staff. More than 100,000 people were treated, according to official records, but it is likely that the number affected was higher as records are incomplete. The authorities reported that between 15 and 17 people died.

Trafigura vigorously denied any wrongdoing, claimed it was not responsible for its subcontractor's behaviour, and won a high court injunction in the UK to stifle coverage of the story by the media. However, if it thought that the story would go away, it was wrong. Human rights and environmental organizations were outraged at the impact the waste had had in Côte d'Ivoire. Newspapers were angry about the use of a court order to stop what they saw as coverage of a legitimate news story. Together they whipped up a worldwide storm amongst concerned citizens linked by social media. A thousand Ivorians filed suit against the company. The network of politicians that the company seems to have nurtured to ensure local support were powerless when it came to the global onslaught. Legal teams found that the loopholes the company was accused of exploiting in its global operations were now working in favour of the company's critics.

As the story snowballed, the company was forced into various agreements, although it always denied liability. It was found guilty of illegal exports in the Dutch courts and fined €1 million, while its CEO had to pay a €67,000 fine. In Côte d'Ivoire, although the case never went to court, the company paid $160 million to the government and $50 million in individual settlements. The head of the subcontractors was given a 20-year jail term. Trafigura employee Naeem Ahmed, who was involved in the ship's operation in Amsterdam, was fined €25,000 and the captain of the *Probo Koala* was sentenced to a five-year suspended jail term. Trafigura denies responsibility for the dumping of the waste and any deaths or injuries caused.

(*Sources:* jamaica-gleaner.com, 5 December 2012; Onzivu, 2013; www.bbc.co.uk/news/world-africa-10735255; www.timesofmalta.com, 8 February 2013; www.trafigura.com: all accessed October 2013)

(continued...)

Quick questions

1 Are companies more susceptible now than in the past to worldwide campaigns criticizing their behaviour?

2 What could Trafigura have done differently?

3 What other examples can you think of where companies have had trouble protecting their reputations against community and NGO attacks?

 Key concept: Licence to operate

Licence to operate refers to the public's acceptance of a company's impact on wider society. It is an idea rooted in theories of the social contract that exists between a government and the people proposed by philosophers such as Hobbes and Locke. Just as in a democracy the electorate can grant and remove a government's permission to govern, so a company's constituents (e.g. consumers, investors, customers, communities) grant tacit or explicit approval to companies to conduct their business.

The right to extract profit from commercial activities is one part of the licence to operate, but the company's constituents can dictate what is a legitimate profit-seeking activity. For example, human trafficking might be profitable, but the criminal networks that are involved cannot claim to have a licence to operate. The tobacco industry is an example of where companies have had their licence to operate severely restricted, not least because of their role in hiding the connection between smoking and cancer. An alternative energy company such as Vestas can claim to have a strong licence to operate because of the positive relationship it seems to have with tackling climate change, whereas a company such as EDF may have to invest more in building its licence because of its association with coal-fired and nuclear power.

There are numerous ways companies can strengthen their licence, including stakeholder engagement, transparency, and corporate responsibility reporting. Such approaches may help companies to build better relations with their constituents, but they should not regard the licence as irrevocable as it will be under continual scrutiny and re-evaluation.

However, Davis (1973) was also one of the first corporate responsibility theorists to argue that social responsibility was more than the acts of individuals—that corporate responsibility should refer to the company as an institution. The shift in focus from the individual to the company led to a new discussion of responsibilities. Some saw corporate responsibility as a way of utilizing company resources towards broad social ends rather than to serve only narrow private interests.[12] In addition to linking responsibility to power, Davis himself held that the social responsibility of business demanded that companies should be open to public input and scrutiny, that social costs and benefits should be factored into their business decisions and also priced into products, and that, where it has the necessary competencies, the company as a citizen should be involved in social affairs.[13] He also noted that there might be long-term economic gain from behaving responsibly.

All of these issues are relevant to corporate responsibility today. So too are some of the dilemmas raised. Should companies take actions beyond what is legally required? (see Chapter 1)? Should a company's assets be used for purposes other than maximizing shareholder value (see Chapter 13)? Are the fiduciary duties of executives and directors too narrowly defined

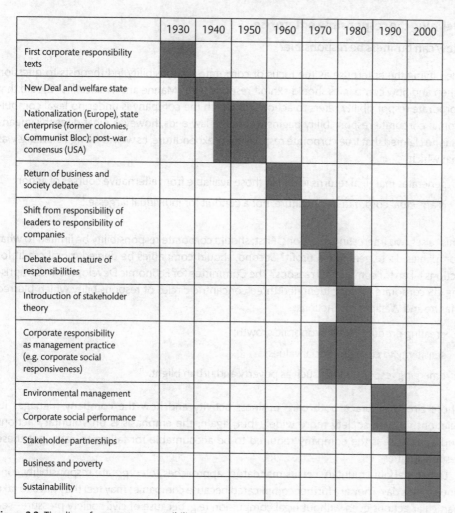

Figure 2.2 Timeline of corporate responsibility

(see Chapter 7)? However, since the 1990s, the theory and practice of corporate responsibility has evolved more rapidly than ever before, raising questions and possibilities that Davis could not have imagined. Corporate responsibility in the 1990s and beyond dominates most of the discussion in this book; but it is interesting and worthwhile to look at its earlier forms because Davis and his peers spurred thinking about how companies could demonstrate their contribution to social goals such as economic justice, stability, and freedom,[14] and the ways in which this can be accomplished, asking three questions that are still as pertinent today.

1 How can business be responsible?
2 For what is it responsible?
3 To whom is it responsible?

It is to these questions that we now turn.

Defining the responsible enterprise

How can business be responsible?

Identifying the enterprise as the focus of corporate responsibility led theorists to question when and how companies should exhibit responsibility. Manne and Wallich (1972) said that corporate responsibility refers to actions for which the company is under no legal compulsion. If corporate responsibility begins where the law ends, however, what does this mean? Manne claimed that true corporate responsibility expenditure, as well as being voluntary, was that which:

1   generates marginal returns less than those available from alternative courses of action;
2   is an actual corporate expenditure, not a conduit for individual largesse.[15]

This raises two interesting questions. First, should corporate responsibility be limited to what companies do to generate a profit? Second, should companies be denied moral credit for actions taken for commercial reasons? The Committee for Economic Development, comprising US corporate leaders, identified three concentric circles of responsibility which blurred Manne and Wallich's distinctions:

1   creating products, jobs, economic growth;
2   sensitivity to changing social values;
3   emerging responsibilities such as poverty and urban blight.[16]

These circles embrace both core business activity and how the company manages its relationship with society more widely, but, again, the emphasis is on voluntary actions and in no case is the company required to be accountable for failing to carry out these responsibilities.

Debates about voluntary versus mandatory approaches to corporate responsibility continue to this day. They are further complicated because companies may feel they have to take particular actions even without legal compulsion (e.g. because of civil society pressure—see Chapter 9). We explore these issues elsewhere and so, for now, limit ourselves to flagging voluntarism as a recurring theme in this book.

 Discussion points

George Soros, the American financial speculator, stock investor, philanthropist, and political activist, has said: *'We can have a market economy, but we cannot have a market society.'*[17]

● What distinction is he making between 'economy' and 'society'?

● Does corporate responsibility help the market economy to become a market society?

● Describe how a company from the former Eastern Bloc might use corporate responsibility to establish its licence to operate in the European Union.

For what is business responsible?

Defining corporate responsibility as voluntary action does little to explain for what business should take responsibility. In Chapter 1, we set out various perspectives on this, including Carroll's (1979) multidimensional model of corporate responsibility which has proved one of the most widely referenced frameworks because it makes clear important principles and spheres of responsibility (i.e. economic, legal, ethical, and discretionary responsibilities– see Figure 1.2). Its strength is that it draws together different types of responsibility that had tended to be treated as mutually exclusive or otherwise problematic. It does this by identifying separate categories, and any action that falls under one category or another can be considered part of corporate responsibility. But this, in itself, can cause problems. For example, does a company accept responsibility for any issue that fits into one of the categories? If not, how does it prioritize its response? Equally, how does the company go about deciding what is ethical, or what discretionary actions it should take?[18] Consequently, at least as important as what companies are responsible for is how those responsibilities are defined.

Corporate responsibility, as already noted, is dynamic and changes according to time, industry and location. Much of academic corporate responsibility theory originates from the USA, and therefore reflects social conditions that are different even in similarly advanced capitalist economies. For example, an American employee often has the legal status of 'at-will employment' meaning that worker and employee can break their relationship without liability to either party. In Europe, a worker may have a three-month notice period before their relationship with the company ends; in the USA, as anyone who watches American TV knows, a worker can walk out the same day, taking their box of personal effects with them. Therefore, in Europe severance pay and dismissal may not be spelled out as a corporate responsibility because the responsibilities are set out in legal statute. In the USA, on the other hand, corporate responsibility might offer a counterbalance to relatively limited legal protections.

The nature of the American free enterprise system—its financial and governance systems, its culture, its education and labour systems, the institution of the firm, etc.—is unique, and different in important ways from that in Europe and elsewhere.[19] This may account for the differences in corporate responsibility between the USA and elsewhere, with the USA adopting what has been called 'explicit' corporate responsibility (i.e. the company carries out certain activities with the explicit intent of serving social interests) and Europe concentrating on 'implicit' corporate responsibility (i.e. business is one of many institutions that are expected to serve the social good and must conform with the social consensus about its role).[20] It may also explain why business in the USA has been what Drucker (1946) called 'the representative institution', responsible for representing and upholding American society's basic values and beliefs, whereas in Europe, for example, companies have been viewed more as supplicants to the social good.

The Atlantic Ocean is not the only corporate responsibility fault line; claims about the geographical distinctions in what companies are responsible for have been made about India, Japan, China, Brazil, and Africa and Asia in general. We will touch on these differences, as well as dissimilarities in responsibility between industries in later chapters. But it is important to consider some of the consequences of thinking in terms of disparities in responsibilities. It may be that an area of behaviour has to be spelled out as an explicit responsibility in one region but not in another because of different laws. But to what extent can something be acceptable in one country and not in another? If violence on the factory floor is common-place in one country, should a French multinational such as Carrefour accept that behaviour amongst its suppliers when it would not be able to do so in France?

This is the area of ethical relativism. There may be good reasons to define the responsibili-ties of corporations in the context of where they are being applied, but there is also a risk of turning a blind eye to unacceptable actions on the grounds that something is a cultural con-vention. For example, when abuse of workers in global supply chains first hit the headlines in the late 1980s, companies and politicians argued that European consumers had no right to dictate what was tolerable in developing countries. Relativism is a topic of much discussion in business ethics,[21] reflecting wider philosophical debates about whether or not morals are universal or culturally contingent. And if they are not applicable everywhere, are there value systems originating in one part of the world that are universalizable to all parts in much the same way that the economic system we know as capitalism, originating in Europe, has been introduced throughout much of the world?

Underpinning these debates are quite different philosophical traditions (see Online Resource Centre for a more detailed overview). For example, justice is defined quite differ-ently by the Utilitarian school than it is by non-consequentialists such as Kant. The former believe that justice is whatever benefits the majority; the latter believe that justice is not a popularity contest, and the good of the many cannot be achieved at the expense of the few. These are contradictory schools of thought. Likewise, Aristotle's belief in absolute values is at odds with Habermas's notion of discourse ethics two millennia later whereby values are the result of public consensus. This is not a book on business ethics, and therefore we are not going to unpack how different ethical schools influence ideas of responsibility. That is not to dismiss them as unimportant; on the contrary, business ethics is a vital subset of corporate responsibility with its own body of literature—Oxford University's Bodleian Library alone contains 265 business ethics titles.

There are various management studies texts on how to incorporate the ideas of Mill, Aristotle, Jesus, Kant, and others, and there are many books offering ethical advice to the individual manager. But rather than repeat much of what has already been written, our focus is on filling two gaps that affect the defining of corporate responsibility. First, instead of study-ing what companies ought to do, we want to emphasize what they actually do and why they make some of the choices they make. Second, mirroring Davis's accomplishment in moving the wider debate about corporate responsibility from the role of the individual to the role of the company, we want to explore how companies as entities manage their responsibilities. In doing this, we are not only going beyond the scope of conventional business ethics, we are building a bridge between what Scherer and Palazzo (2007) call positivist and deliberative corporate responsibility—the former concentrating on actual business practice without much reflection on the wider context that affects what companies do and do not do, and the latter concerned primarily with theories of responsibility and not how these are actually enacted.

To whom is business responsible?

For economist Milton Friedman, it was straightforward that companies were responsible to the law and their investors, and nobody else. Some still defend this position, some say it was never accurate, and some say that it may have been right once but not any longer (see Chapter 1). Investors' interests may conflict with those of wider society, especially when they want rapid or high-yield returns on their capital. Irrespective of the behaviour of business, the law is never a comprehensive code, and for every Bernie Madoff or Ernest Saunders who goes to jail there is a Dick Fuld or London Whale who seriously harm their companies with seeming impunity despite public outrage. Moreover, legal responsibilities differ from jurisdiction to jurisdiction, and multinational companies can, to a degree, choose which laws they like or not by relocating their operations. There may be no legal distinction between someone who invests for the short run and one who does so for longer, but their interests and what they would like the company to do may be quite different.

According to IBM CEO Sam Palmisano, the biggest shift in recent business history is that from shareholder to stakeholder companies.[22] The idea that business has responsibility to a variety of stakeholders has been an important element of corporate responsibility theory, at least since Preston and Post's 1975 book on how host environments affect corporate behaviour. As we explore in Chapters 6 and 9, stakeholder theory suggests a way of explaining why and with whom corporations should engage. It is based on the notion that many people (and groups of people) have a stake in any corporation and that, in order for a company to achieve its objectives effectively, it must consider them all, not only the shareholders to whom corporations have long discharged accountability. In this regard it is not only distinct from previous ideas of the responsibility of companies, but echoes the discourse ethics of Habermas (see earlier) and the idea that duties and responsibilities are fluid, defined as part of a social consensus that itself depends on the free and informed participation of the populus in democratic processes.

Stakeholder theory promises a way in which companies can learn what is needed to establish and maintain the aforementioned 'licence to operate', i.e. the idea that business requires the approval of others in society in order to function effectively. It provides a potentially stronger rationale than Carroll's framework for choosing certain courses of action by implying that a company should do whatever is necessary to maintain its legitimacy, but that it is under no obligation to go further than that.

The licence to operate is central to legitimacy theory and posits that an organization can only continue to exist if its core values are aligned with the core values of the society in which it operates. The fate of accounting firm Arthur Andersen, in the wake of the Enron scandal, brought this into stark relief when the company's integrity was so badly damaged that it went out of business. Legitimacy theory offers a method of managing stakeholders in the face of various threats through, for example, educating them about the company's intentions, changing their perceptions of events, diverting their attention, and altering their expectations.[23] Such strategies are evident in the actions taken by Shell in response to Brent Spar or the treatment of the Ogoni people in Nigeria.

Important though theories such as those described above are in their own right, one of their major contributions is that they have made management practice part of corporate responsibility enquiry. Early corporate responsibility theory was primarily concerned with the normative behaviour of companies, but, since the 1970s, there has been at least equal emphasis given to corporate responsibility as management practice.[24] For example, Ackerman and Bauer's (1976) theory of 'corporate social responsiveness' put the emphasis on what companies *can* do to respond to societal expectations (i.e. capacity), in contrast with more theoretical ideas of what they *should* do. Social responsiveness shunned the idea of philosophy in favour of a managerial approach and, in many ways, helped corporate responsibility to get out of academia and into day-to-day business. By the 1990s, managerial approaches to corporate responsibility were evolving rapidly and measurement had become an integral part of this, summed up in MacGillivray and Zadek's phrase: *'If you want it to count, count it.'*[25]

We take a closer look at corporate responsibility as management practice in Chapter 6 and later chapters. But we would not pretend that responsiveness to society is an unproblematic way of resolving what business should take responsibility for; on the contrary, as later discussions of stakeholder theory reveal (see Chapter 9), it can leave companies without clear moral guidance of the kind promised by ethical theory.

 Discussion points

A number of companies publicize the amounts they donate to philanthropic causes. Indeed, it is one of the measures used by some rating agencies when scoring corporate responsibility points.

- To what extent do philanthropic donations act as a measure of corporate responsibility?
- What arguments can you put forward against using this criterion as a measure of corporate responsibility?
- Using other companies as benchmarks, present a case to the board for adopting a particular philanthropic strategy.

 Case study 2   Corporate responsibility in different eras: Cadbury

In 1909, the *London Evening Standard* accused the confectionery company Cadbury of knowingly profiting from the widespread use of slaves on cocoa plantations in the Portuguese colony of São Tomé. The public was shocked: the company was not only one of the most famous brands in the British Empire, but also an exemplar of compassionate capitalism founded in the Quaker religious tradition.

Cadbury sued the *Evening Standard* for libel. The company won the case, but over the course of the trial Charles Cadbury, joint head of the firm and a figurehead of virtuous capitalism, was forced to admit that he not only knew slaves were being used, but actually regarded it as essential to his company's prosperity. Despite the court's ruling in Cadbury's favour, it lost in the court of public opinion, and the reputation of the firm was damaged.

A century later, in 2000, the company found itself once again accused of buying slave-farmed cocoa beans from West Africa in a media assault by the full spectrum of the British press, from the *Daily Mirror* to the *Financial Times*. Acting with others in the industry, Cadbury (by then Cadbury Schweppes) denied the allegations. In contrast with the 1909 case, this time the industry condemned the use of slavery outright, but to no avail because it was unable to prove that it really knew what was happening on cocoa farms. The human rights advocates seemed to know little more; their early allegations of slavery soon switched to ones about child labour as it became apparent that slavery was not prevalent on cocoa farms. But that did not matter—these groups held the moral high ground and the industry could do nothing to displace them.

The news headlines could not have come at a worse time, appearing on the front pages in the run-up to Easter, a peak time for chocolate sales. Schoolchildren around Britain wrote in to Cadbury

(continued...)

saying they would not be buying Easter eggs that year. In the USA, two congressmen persuaded the industry to sign up to the Harkin–Engel Protocol, an industry-wide certification standard to eliminate the worst forms of child labour. Cadbury had once again lost in the court of public opinion. The company's share price was not hurt but its reputation was. The question was whether it needed to take action, and if so what?

Across the industry, companies pondered whether to be defensive and protect their reputations, or to become more proactive and see if there was a value-adding dimension to the cocoa labour problem. Cadbury supported a 2002 study by the International Institute of Tropical Agriculture to investigate the extent of child labour and forced labour. It also joined the International Cocoa Initiative, a partnership of business, NGO, and government representatives committed to getting rid of unacceptable labour practices in cocoa production. In 2006 it asked consultants to map out what sustainable production would mean for the company.

These activities helped the company realize that it had lost touch with its supply base. Not only was it blind to human rights issues in the supply chain, it was ignorant of the production issues affecting the millions of small independent farmers it depended on. If anything, the risk of being out of touch was greater now than in 2000. In 2005, Cadbury had acquired Green & Black's, the organic chocolate company with a loyal ethical consumer base. This was one of Cadbury's fastest growing business areas, a brand built on product quality and ethical credibility. Any criticism of the Cadbury supply chain now would damage Green & Black's reputation as well.

But another problem came to light as Cadbury started to re-acquaint itself with its supply base: various farmers were growing less cocoa, and if the situation continued Cadbury risked not having enough beans to meet demand. Cadbury-commissioned academic research had shown that the average production for smallholder cocoa farmers in Ghana had dropped to just 40 per cent of potential yield, and that cocoa farming was becoming less and less appealing to the next generation of farmers despite rising prices. In January 2008, Cadbury launched its £44 million Cocoa Partnership 'to secure the economic, social and environmental sustainability of around a million cocoa farmers and their communities in Ghana, India, Indonesia and the Caribbean'. Furthermore, in 2009 Cadbury announced that all cocoa used in its top-selling Dairy Milk brand would be sourced from Fairtrade certified farms, with the hope that farmers would benefit from the stable prices and community investment that Fairtrade promises.

(*Sources:* original research; Du Cann, 1993; International Institute of Tropical Agriculture and International Labour Organisation, 2002; Satre, 2005; www.cadbury.com/ourresponsibilities/cadburycocoapartnership/Pages/mappingsustainableproduction.aspx; www.cadbury.com/ourresponsibilities/cadburycocoapartnership/Pages/cadburycocoapartnership.aspx)

Questions

1 The events of 1909 and 2000 had few major commercial ramifications for Cadbury, and until the 2010 takeover by Kraft the company was a long-time member of the Fortune Global 500 list of leading businesses. In fact, Cadbury Schweppes won the 2004 UK 'Most Admired Company' award presented by Nottingham Business School.

   a Did the company overreact by stopping its sourcing of 'slave-produced' cocoa?

   b Why did the company feel the need to act at all?

   c Is it not the role of government to regulate how industries are run and to prevent these practices from recurring?

(continued...)

2 Cadbury faced similar issues in 1909 and 2000, and in both cases had to mount a defence of its reputation and practices.

    a Are companies more responsible today than they were in the past?

    b Are Cadbury's responsibilities different today than they were in the early twentieth century?

    c Why do you think companies' responsibilities have changed in the last hundred years?

3 In corporate responsibility theory, a distinction is sometimes made between actions taken to reduce risks, such as protecting reputation, and those taken to add value, such as using ethical values to promote a brand.

    a Which of Cadbury's actions do you think were done to protect its reputation?

    b Why do you think Cadbury purchased Green & Black's?

    c How would you persuade senior management to support the Cocoa Partnership?

Summary

Corporate responsibility did not spring out of nowhere. What we think of as the responsibilities of business and how these are acted upon reflect some of the main debates about social justice going far back in time. Nowhere is this more apparent than in theories about how private enterprise impacts upon economic well-being and how the economy itself relates to society. In this chapter we have discussed how different types of economy affect what we mean by 'justice' and 'well-being'. We have also compared different theories of how business and free markets can best contribute to the good of society in capitalist societies. What emerges is a set of questions on issues such as the relationship between private self-interest and the public good, and how the rewards of enterprise are distributed—things that lie at the heart of contemporary corporate responsibility.

Tackling these questions has occupied politicians, academics, company managers, and community leaders since the earliest days of capitalism. We have explored how corporate responsibility theory developed as one way of finding answers about what business should be responsible for and to whom. We have also examined the way in which different approaches to thinking about responsibility can lead to quite different conclusions about what companies should be responsible for.

However, the origins of corporate responsibility are not only to be found in theory. The evolution of modern business, and, in particular, the emergence of limited liability and the corporation, have all affected business's relationship with society and expectations about companies' responsibilities. Equally, the specific aspects of business activity that society addresses have, paradoxically, both changed and remained constant over time. What the exploration of aspects of corporate responsibility over three eras does show, however, is how the role of business in resolving these issues has changed. In fact, the unintended consequence of the market liberalization that was central to economic globalization is that business is being expected, as never before, to take action to rectify perceived weaknesses in markets on issues such as social justice and sustainability. It is how globalization has affected corporate responsibility in developing countries to which we turn in the next chapter.

Further reading

www.oxfordtextbooks.co.uk/orc/blowfield_murray3e/

Visit the Online Resource Centre that accompanies this book to enrich your understanding of this chapter. Among the resources available are web links, exercises, and additional case studies.

online
resource
centre

Historical context

Bakan, J. 2004, *The corporation: the pathological pursuit of profit and power*, Free Press, New York.
Readable and provocative critique of the dominance of corporations.

Kenneally, T. 1983, *Schindler's ark*, Coronet, Sevenoaks.
Novel based on the true story of a businessman's struggle to do good in Nazi Germany. The Spielberg film adaptation is called Schindler's List.

Robins, N. 2012, *The corporation that changed the world: how the East India Company shaped the modern multinational*, Pluto Press, London.
A lively look at one of the earliest multinational companies, and what it tells us about modern day business.

Thompson, E.P. 1963, *The making of the English working class*, Victor Gollancz, London.
Comprehensive study of workers, working conditions, and worker protest in nineteenth-century England.

Theoretical context

Carroll, A.B. 1999, 'Corporate social responsibility: evolution of a definitional construct', *Business and Society*, vol. 38, no. 3, pp 268–95.
Widely cited overview of corporate responsibility theory.

Drucker, P.F. 1946, *Concept of the corporation*, John Day, New York.
Early work by leading management thinker on the nature of the corporation.

Mackey, J. & Sisodia, R. 2013, *Conscious capitalism: liberating the heroic spirit of business*, Harvard Business Review Press, Boston, MA.
Prominent US entrepreneur sets out his views on values-driven business.

Marx, K. 1865, *Value, price, and profit: an introduction to the theory of capitalism*, abridged by P. Zarembka, 2000, JAI/Elsevier Science, Amsterdam, New York, online at ourworld. compuserve.com.

Online resources

- A history of globalization and accompanying references
- Exercises and discussion topics for students
- Fordlandia—case study of corporate responsibility in the 1930s
- Links to other web-based resources
- Additional reading

Endnotes

1. Du Cann, 1993.
2. Kennedy, 1987; Evans, 1983.
3. Carney, 1998, p 662.
4. McQuaid, 1977.
5. Fortune undated. http://money.cnn.com/galleries/2007/fortune/0702/gallery.richestamericans.fortune/index.html.
6. Frederick, 2006.
7. See e.g. Demirag, 2005; Blowfield, 2005a.
8. The term comes from Scholte, 2000, but a similar conceptualization of globalization has been set out by many theorists (e.g. Gray, Mittelman, Held) and has evolved from early work on interdependence (e.g. Giddens, 1990; Robertson, 1992).
9. Steger, 2003.
10. Asongu, 2007.
11. Cited in Carroll, 1999, p 271.
12. Frederick, 1960, cited in Carroll, 1999, p 271.
13. Birch, 2003, pp 7–8.
14. See the discussion of the work on corporate social performance by Anshen and Johnson in Birch, 2003.
15. Cited in Carroll, 1999, p 276.
16. Cited in Carroll, 1999, p 278.
17. Soros, undated.
18. Carroll is not unaware of these types of question and revisited his model in Schwartz and Carroll, 2003.
19. Matten and Moon, 2008.
20. Matten and Moon, 2008.
21. See Donaldson, 2003; Beauchamp et al. 2008.
22. Blowfield, 2007.
23. Lindblom, 1994.
24. Tinker, 1985; see also: Sethi, 1975; Wartick and Cochran, 1985.
25. MacGillivray and Zadek, 1995; see also Gray, 1996.

3

Sustainable development

Chapter overview

In this chapter we explore the concept of 'sustainable development', tracking its enduring importance in the business context, made more challenging as evidence that climate change is inexorably linked to industrial activity becomes stronger and more forceful with each report from the Intergovernmental Panel on Climate Change (IPCC). In particular, we will:

- consider what is meant by the term 'sustainable development';
- examine the evolution of sustainability;
- assess the evidence provided by scientific reports into issues of climate change;
- identify the challenges that sustainable development poses for 'business as usual';
- review research into new models of sustainable business;
- examine the capital market implications of sustainable development;
- explore recent thinking about 'social' aspects of sustainability.

Main topics

Introduction	54
Meanings of 'sustainability' and 'sustainable development'	56
Climate change and global warming	61
The challenge to business	64
New models of sustainable business	65
Capital markets and sustainable development	66
Signals to the market	67
Rewarding financial intermediaries	69

Key terms

Brundtland Commission

Climate change

Financing sustainability

Global warming

Sustainable development

Introduction

In the first two chapters of this book we examined the meaning and origins of corporate responsibility, but in practice very little of this is of any relevance unless, as a collection of societies around the world, we protect precious resources to ensure that succeeding generations can also enjoy economic development while at the same time being able to sustain themselves.

This presents business and policy-makers alike with a number of challenges. The neoclassical theory of the firm places the maximization of shareholder returns central to the business model adopted by the overwhelming majority of 'for profit' companies. In addition, this model assumes a pattern of continued growth. Read any corporate annual report and you soon realize how important growth is to the financial stakeholders in the business.

 Key concept: Sustainable development

Sustainable development means 'development that meets the needs of the current generation without compromising the ability of future generations to meet their own needs' (WECD 1987).

Equally, government policy around the world also demands continued economic growth to fund social infrastructure projects and welfare benefits, and governments depend on business to fuel patterns of economic growth. Indeed, much governmental policy is designed to enable business expansion, and many overseas trade missions arranged by dedicated government departments are organized to facilitate corporate and macroeconomic growth.

Of course, we all benefit in some way from this activity, especially in the West. Whether it results from a wider and cheaper range of consumer goods to choose from, a more efficient and effective health-care service, or a generally more comfortable lifestyle, over the last 50 years standards of living in the West have improved immensely.

However, these improvements have not been universal, and in many developing countries large sections of the population continue to live in poverty. Despite successive initiatives and massive amounts of overseas aid over the years, large numbers of people are still living on $1.25 a day or less, the commonly accepted measure of 'extreme poverty'.[1]

Moreover, scientific findings suggest that the resources available to the human species on this planet are being consumed at a rate which is not sustainable. These findings are available from a number of sources and all point to the same trend. Whether you choose to examine UN data contained in the *UNEP Global Environmental Outlook (5th Report)*[2] or in its *Millennium Ecosystem Assessment Report*,[3] the World Wildlife Fund (WWF) *Living Planet Report*,[4] the *'Limits to Growth: The 30 Years update*,[5] or the *4th Assessment Report of the IPCC*,[6] the evidence across all approaches is deeply concerning. In the quest for growth, natural resources are being exploited in an unprecedented manner, leading to an increase in commodity prices (in real terms) beginning around 1950, but increasing particularly in the last decade.[7]

The push for greener fuels has also had negative effects in many parts of the world. The demand for palm oil, for example, has led to a scale of deforestation in Indonesia that has resulted in the loss of indigenous lands, the threat of species extinction, and a pall of pollution extending far beyond its borders, into Singapore and Malaysia, creating a level of greenhouse gas emission third only to the USA and China.[8] In the developed world too, we are witnessing the conversion of agricultural land to the production of alternative fuels for traditionally fuelled power stations, which potentially reduces the food-producing capacity within any given country.

Evidence also suggests that we are approaching the point where the daily rate of oil extraction reaches its maximum, after which point production fails to keep up with demand. 'Peak-oil', as it is called, has been an issue for debate over the last decade or so, but the exact point at which we can say

(continued...)

we have reached peak oil is obfuscated by a number of factors, not least the fluctuating price of oil, which reacts to rises and falls in demand but rarely has the effects on supply that basic economic theory might suggest (see Snapshot 3.1).

Of equal significance is the recent scientific evidence of human influence on climate change caused by global warming. Concurring with the latest analysis of the scientific evidence, a recent paper concluded that '... the wealth of attribution studies ... show that there is an increasingly remote possibility that climate change is dominated by natural rather than anthropogenic factors'.[9]

These findings, which will be augmented with additional evidence later in the chapter, point to a pressing need to respond to the challenges presented by climate change and sustainable development.

 Snapshot 3.1 Oil price and supply fluctuations

An examination of the association between crude oil supply and price since 1980 reveals some interesting, if slightly confusing, information. We can see that fluctuations in price are closely linked to upturns and downturns of the economic cycle, with the most obvious price drop occurring after the financial crash of 2008. Although the price of crude actually peaked at around $150 in mid-2008, and reached a low of just over $40 in January 2009, annual trend data show that we are now seeing higher prices than at any point in history. On the other hand, if we examine levels of supply during the same period we notice that, despite some minor fluctuations, since 1994 production has increased from around 58,000 barrels per day (bpd) to approximately 75,000 bpd in 2012.

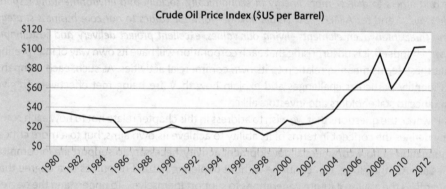

Crude Oil Price Index ($US per Barrel)

(*Source:* International Monetary Fund's International Financial Statistics)

World Crude Oil Production (000's of Barrels per day)

(*Source:* International Monetary Fund's International Financial Statistics)

(continued...)

The price of crude is also affected, on the supply side, by the stance taken by the Organization of Petroleum Exporting Countries (OPEC), by governments of oil-producing states, and by weather, but it is also affected by capital market activity and speculation, exchange rates, and by areas of political unrest and instability. These factors have given rise to predictions that the price of oil may rise to somewhere in the region of $200 by 2020.

Quick questions

1. What steps can companies, and individuals, take to mitigate the effects of higher oil prices?

2. Can higher prices achieve the effect of reducing energy use?

3. Can technology come to the rescue and deliver greater supply? Would that help sustainability?

Meanings of 'sustainability' and 'sustainable development'

A brief examination of how these terms are defined by various organizations offers a bewildering series of options to researchers and students of the subject. For example, for BP sustainability means '*a safety leader in our industry, a world-class operator, a responsible corporate citizen and a good employer*';[10] for Shell, '*... working with governments, partners, communities and others to deliver more energy in economically, socially and environmentally responsible ways*';[11] and for AMEC, '*... a visible linkage from our values to our core business strategy using three interwoven elements—living our values, excellent project delivery and sustainable growth*'.[12] Indeed, it is unsurprising that each corporation will have its own way of interpreting what these terms mean in relation to its own commercial activities. As such, each company can identify particular challenges and explain how they are being met effectively, to give assurance to stakeholders and investors alike.

However, the questions that we wish to address in this chapter relate not to how each company defines the concept in terms of its ability to achieve its own aims, but to a more critical examination of how commercial development activity, necessary to support life in communities around the globe, can continue without depleting natural resources to a degree that jeopardizes the ability of future generations to support themselves. To understand the degree to which this is possible, we must first establish for ourselves what the term means, and to that end we look at the background to the emergence of 'sustainable development' as a concept and the imperatives that led to the definition that was initially ascribed to it. This is because, for many, issues of sustainability lie at the theoretical heart of corporate responsibility: if we ruin our biosphere, as scientific evidence suggests we are in the process of so doing, then all other corporate initiatives, whether responsible or not, become somewhat meaningless.

The UN World Commission on Economic Development

It is now over twenty-five years since the World Commission on Economic Development (WCED), more commonly known as the Brundtland Commission, deliberated on, inter alia, '*environmental strategies for achieving sustainable development by the year 2000 and beyond*'. Having sat for almost three years, the Commission finally agreed a definition of 'sustainable development', which, although intended more as a challenge to governments, is widely referred to in debates about the role of business.

How effective and sufficient the progress has been since the Brundtland Report was published is a matter of continuing debate. The contributors to the report may well be further alarmed by the escalation of the threat to the environment posed by the effect of industrial activity on climate change. Yet in order to appreciate fully the difficulty of linking corporate activity to notions of sustainable development, it is useful to review the processes that led to the Report's publication.

The Commission was established by the United Nations in 1983 as the result of a process that can be traced back to the 1960s, at which time environmental concerns became the focus of various pressure groups. Rachel Carson's *Silent Spring* (1962) had raised popular consciousness about the dangers of excessive pesticide use, and some progress had been made in improving air and water quality in industrialized areas through 'Clean Air' Acts and similar laws. By the early 1970s, NGOs such as Friends of the Earth and Greenpeace had been established in response to the perceived dangers posed to the planet by such phenomena as nuclear testing and the flooding of vast areas as a result of dam building.

However, the calls for a UN conference on the environment originated from the Swedish ambassador to the UN, who was particularly concerned with the effects of 'acid rain' and the general acidification of the water systems in Scandinavia, which was largely due to the emission by coal-fired power stations of excessive quantities of sulphur dioxide. In 1971, a UN-sponsored meeting of experts in pollution in Founex, Switzerland, had, for the first time, made the explicit connection between industrial development—a perceived desire of developing nations—and environmental degradation, which was seen as the price the nation had to pay. By the time the full conference took place in Stockholm in 1972, the issue of pollution had been widened to include the problems being experienced by developing countries. Indeed, environmental protection was seen as one of the limiting factors to development.[13] But, in what some saw as a rather contradictory compromise, this meeting concluded that *'there is no inherent contradiction between environment and development, and that these two concerns should be mutually supportive'.*[14]

This conundrum of whether environmental issues can be tackled without jeopardizing economic growth remains central to sustainable development debates today. For example, the 2007 Stern Review for the UK government argued that not only was there not a contradiction, but that tackling climate change was a prerequisite for long-term prosperity. Certainly, the debate was not settled at Stockholm, but, in many ways, the conference was of greater international significance than is often reported. It involved the participation of not only more than 100 countries, but also of over 400 inter-governmental organizations and NGOs. It ended with the *Stockholm Declaration on Human Environment* and the *Action Plan for the Human Environment*.[15] In sum, it not only raised the environment to national consciousness, but also placed it firmly on the international agenda. Indeed, within twenty years of the end of the conference, over 100 countries had a government department dealing with the environment. Also, the principles of the sovereign right to exploit national resources and the responsibility for transboundary pollution became explicit, and were subsequently ratified in international agreements such as the UN Framework Convention on Climate Change (see later). It also led to the establishment of the United Nations Environment Program (UNEP) a year later.[16]

In addition, throughout the 1970s, there was continuing concern about a number of issues that impacted on notions of justice and fairness. The oil supply crisis in 1973 caused oil prices to rise to their highest ever levels (after inflation adjustment). While the debt of developing countries was already rising, this enormous rise in oil prices brought debt to crisis levels, not only because of the increased costs of oil (from which some developing nations benefited), but because lending institutions, awash with oil money, encouraged such countries to take on more debt than they could afford—something that has only started to be resolved in recent years, with debt relief programmes. Equally, a number of projects designed to aid prosperity in the developing world, particularly huge hydroelectric schemes involving dam building and population relocation, were criticized for their adverse social and environmental ramifications.

In 1982, a special session of UNEP's governing council was convened to discuss Stockholm 'ten years on'. It was here that it was decided that something far more radical and wide-ranging was needed to look much further forward. It was felt that, while the world economy had grown considerably, the least developed countries had made little ground and, in fact, many had seen a fall in per capita production during the 1980s.[17] It was at this point that the UN convened the World Commission on Environment and Development under Gro Harlem Brundtland 'at a time of unprecedented growth in pressures on the global environment, with grave predictions about the human future becoming commonplace'.[18] Its aim was to build a future that would be 'more prosperous, more just, and more secure', resting on ecologically sound policies and practices. Even at the outset, however, there was an overwhelming conviction that, in order to attain this goal, 'significant changes in current approaches' would have to be confronted, which would involve changes in individual attitudes and lifestyles, and, more crucially, 'changes in certain critical policies ... and the nature of co-operation between governments, business, science and people'.[19]

The significantly different approach that this Commission took was to try to conceptualize the relationship between the environment and development, in light of the continuing disparity between levels of prosperity in the northern and southern hemispheres, and the sentiments expressed at Founex in 1971. During its sitting, which lasted two and a half years, a number of unprecedented events occurred.

A major famine in Ethiopia, which led to the death of over a million people, was broadcast to the West in graphic detail. It led to the 'Band Aid' concerts in London and Philadelphia, transmitted on television non-stop for over 16 hours. At a policy level, the role of the government of Ethiopia, in terms of its willingness and ability to help its own peoples, was questioned amid accusations of corruption and ineptitude.[20]

Additionally, Farman, Gardiner, and Shanklin discovered the 'hole' in the ozone layer over Antarctica.[21] The importance of this discovery was not fully understood at the time and was met with some scepticism, because US monitoring satellites did not immediately corroborate the discovery. However, once the monitoring parameters were adjusted to access the data and the phenomenon was confirmed, the implications began to impact on policy-makers.

As these events unfolded, another tragedy struck—this time in Bhopal, India, in 1984. In what has become an iconic study of corporate responsibility or irresponsibility, Union Carbide, which had established a site in Bhopal in 1969 to manufacture pesticides, initially imported one of the key ingredients, methyl isocyanate (MIC), before developing its onsite manufacturing facility in 1979. It seems clear from subsequent investigations that the level of maintenance was seriously short of the required standards. In November 1984, a leak of MIC caused the deaths of some 20,000 people. The health of over 120,000 remains affected by the effects of the gas and the site is still not considered safe.

In late April 1986, a nuclear reactor at Chernobyl in the USSR (now Ukraine) exploded; thirty-one people died within three months and 237 were diagnosed with acute radiation sickness. Again, lack of maintenance was cited as the main cause and, like Bhopal, the legacy remains.[22]

The developed world did not escape either. In November 1986, agricultural chemicals and solvents leaked into the River Rhine following a chemical spill that was the result of a fire at a factory operated by Sandoz, a pharmaceutical conglomerate, in Basel, Switzerland. The Swiss government failed to act quickly enough to contain the spill, and, as a result, the drinking water of millions of people was affected and fish stocks were seriously depleted.

The WCED definition of sustainable development

Some of these events are acknowledged as having had an impact on the Commission,[23] and what emerged was a vision for a sustainable future that was dependent on some fundamental changes to what, in the West, had become an accepted way of life, with standards of living measured in terms of capital accumulation, levels of technological application, travel options, etc. In this new vision, the environment was to be placed at the centre of strategic decision-making. Rather than being seen as a limiting factor in the cause of continued development, the environment was to be seen as an *'aspect of policy'* if growth was to be sustained.[24] It also articulated notions of justice and fairness to the peoples of the developing world, in terms of fair shares of the world's resources and redistribution of wealth to improve the standards of living of the world's worst off.

> Humanity has the ability to make development sustainable—to ensure that it meets the needs of the present generation without compromising the ability of future generations to meet their own needs. The concept of sustainable development does imply limits—not absolute limits, but limitations imposed by the present state of technology and social organization on environmental resources and by the ability of the biosphere to absorb the effect of human activities.
>
> (WCED, 1987, p 8)

This definition of sustainable development—*'meeting the needs of the present generation without compromising the ability of future generations to meet their own needs'*, as it is commonly paraphrased—carries with it a number of implications and a number of challenges to the business world. This definition requires companies to act in *'three time zones'*.

1. Actions will have been taken in the lives of most existing companies that may have created liabilities due to the practice of 'externalizing' costs. This means, for example, that before legislation is passed to prevent companies discharging effluent into rivers and streams, it is clearly in the company's interest to dispose of as much waste as possible, and the more difficult the material is to purify, the greater the benefit. In most developed countries this is now against the law, but there are many companies whose sites are

contaminated with chemicals, oils, and other toxic materials which require remediation. Indeed, there have been recent instances of companies which have gone into liquidation leaving disputes over who picks up the cost for remediation.[25]

2. There is an expectation that companies not only demonstrate an awareness of their environmental responsibilities, but are able to show that they are meeting the benchmarks of today's citizens and consumers, and that the company will be a responsible citizen.

3. There is an expectation that companies consider the interests and rights of future generations.

This challenge is discussed further in the following sections, where we explore the definition further and consider the implications within each part of it. First, we look at the implications of the needs of this generation ('intra-generational' equity), and the needs of this generation together with those of the next generation ('inter-generational' equity).

Intra-generational equity and inter-generational equity

If we break down the definition and look at its component parts, we begin to unravel the complexity of the idea and to understand why it poses such a potential challenge to current commercial activity. *'Development that meets the needs of the present generation'* suggests fair distribution across the present population of the world, in terms of quality of life, measured, perhaps, by comparative standards of living or benefits from sharing the resources of the planet. There is some evidence that this is not happening at the present time. If we reflect on living standards in terms of Western developed societies and think of the comforts that the majority of the population enjoy, we can still observe that there are levels of inequality many find unacceptable and which, in extreme cases, have resulted in civil unrest.[26] If we then reflect on the developing world, we need little reminder that poverty and famine still blight many peoples of the world. For example, more than 40 per cent of Africa's population live in arid, semi-arid, and dry sub-humid areas, meaning that millions in Africa suffer water shortages throughout the year. Perhaps more disturbingly, women bear the overwhelming responsibility for collecting water by a huge proportion.[27] Therefore it can be argued that we are not achieving the first of the tenets of sustainable development and, if that is the case and we are not meeting the needs of the present generation, it is logical to ask if the next generation will fare any better. The balance of evidence from researchers who have looked into this suggests, rather pessimistically, that we are unlikely to perform any better in the future.[28]

The problem that this offers business relates to the tension which arises when the traditional profit-maximizing objective of the company is challenged by the need to reduce inputs, emissions and waste.

We discuss the business case for adopting some of the strategies for sustainability elsewhere (see Chapter 6), but most of that case involves identifying opportunities for business, whether in terms of market niche, efficiencies, or tackling issues of risk and reputation. Putting environmental or social issues at the heart of business strategy is a more challenging proposition, and if these strategies seriously seek to address social justice issues, the challenges become even more profound.

Eco-justice and eco-efficiency

Also wrapped up in the WCED definition are notions of 'eco-justice' and 'eco-efficiency'. By 'eco-justice', we mean that some fairness is applied to the distribution of benefits that accrue from the development of the world's resources. To read the history of the the colonial past of various European nations, for example, is to read how single countries sought to exploit the resources of many other countries without considering the needs of the indigenous peoples. Robins (2012) draws parallels between the companies that led the colonial charge and today's multinationals. He is not alone in believing that commercial exploitation continues to ignore the needs of local communities, and that the profits from such activities are often expatriated from the host country to benefit shareholders and investors who are far removed from the theatres of activity.

Eco-justice is often interpreted as laying the blame at business's door for impacts that may not have been anticipated at the time, or which may not even be substantiated by the evidence. Even when legal decisions, such as those against GE over the Hudson River[29] or those in the case of the *Exxon Valdez*, show that companies are culpable, even punitive damages may not motivate them to be environmentally responsible.[30]

'Eco-efficiency', on the other hand, is a concept that has an appeal to the commercially minded. The idea that one should 'get more from less' is the sort of challenge to which a company can rise, and there is ample evidence that industrial processes are becoming more efficient. As noted in Chapter 6, in the discussion of the business case, it is in this area that we see most innovation. There are good commercial reasons for this, but there are also drivers from outside the economic sphere. Most of these stem from an increasing recognition that industrial activity poses specific threats to the world's environmental health.

However, it is important not to conflate notions of eco-efficiency with those of sustainable development. Eco-efficiency may well become the goal of each commercial entity, but, in itself, this might not prevent overall world resources from becoming depleted. So far, we have reviewed the development and challenges of sustainable development in terms of the Brundtland Commission's remit; we now move on to look at what has now been identified as the greatest threat to modern society—climate change.

 Discussion Points

In the 1970s and 1980s, there were many dire predictions of ecological collapse that did not materialize, and many natural systems have proved to be less fragile and faster to mend than once thought.

● Why are forecasts relating to natural systems so difficult to predict?

● Does the fact that some predictions were not borne out undermine or strengthen current arguments about climate change and other aspects of sustainable development?

● Which industries have most to win, and which have most to lose, from adopting a 'business as usual' attitude to sustainable development?

Climate change and global warming

Climate change created by global warming has now become an accepted fact. A few years ago climate change sceptics argued that there was insufficient evidence to prove a link between human activity and global warming, but following the publication of the Fourth Assessment Report by the IPCC and subsequent scientific studies, only the most stubborn commentator still adheres to that position. The initial working group findings for the fifth assessment, due to be completed in 2014, support earlier conclusions, and put the likelihood of anthropogenic climate change at 95 per cent. Most governments around the world have begun to regulate greenhouse gas (GHG) emissions to some extent and successive annual Climate Change Summits continue to press for stronger action to be taken.

While it is beyond the scope of this book to delve further into the science, or more deeply into the business implications of climate change, there are all manner of questions relating to the types of response required, their timing, and the costs involved that have yet to be answered. But the future of corporate responsibility is likely to be greatly affected by the way in which business and government respond. For many, climate change is the most crucial scientific question of the twenty-first century, although, like many aspects of corporate responsibility, responses to climate change have typically been treated as involving trade-offs in terms of profitability and competitiveness.

The notion that the planet has a finite capability to absorb or to process the results of human (industrial) activity is the underlying theory of sustainable development, yet, even in the mid-1980s, the scientific basis for concern was only just emerging. Indeed, between 1940 and 1970, as the mean worldwide temperature cooled by 0.2°C, so interest in the phenomena of 'greenhouse' effects waned from what had previously been little more than a passing interest. Following the First World Climate Conference in Geneva in 1979—a predominantly scientific gathering, sponsored by the World Meteorological Organization (WMO)—a call was put out to governments to *foresee and prevent potential man-made changes in climate*. The first serious concerns were raised in 1985, when UNEP and WMO jointly organized a scientific conference in Villach, Austria. Here, predictions were made of the possibility of global temperature rises that would be greater than those in all history and of consequent sea level rises of over 1 metre by 2050.[31] In addition, two years later, UNEP published a further report, *Environmental Perspectives to the Year 2000 and Beyond*, which provided a framework within which to operationalize the findings of the Brundtland Commission, and which led the UN General Assembly to convene its Conference on Environment and Development (UNCED), widely known as the 'Earth Summit', held in Rio de Janeiro in June 1992.

Before the Earth Summit, the UN had begun to frame a document for ratification at Rio. The UN Framework Convention on Climate Change (UNFCCC) was adopted by the UN in 1992 and became open for member-country signature at Rio. By June 1993, it had received 166 signatures. It has since been ratified by 189 states and by the European Union as a bloc. But the scepticism held in some quarters on the science of climate change is clear in the wording of the original document, under which a precautionary approach is urged *'in the absence of scientific certainty'*. A tension was developing within governments between appearing to support calls for a cut in emissions, on the one hand, and the political imperative of doing nothing to threaten economic growth within their own economies, on the other.

In response to this political impasse, in 1997 the UNFCCC held a summit in Kyoto to try to bind countries into a legally binding protocol aimed at reducing GHG emissions. The Kyoto Protocol, as it became known, which came into force in 2005, was to be remembered as much for those who refused to ratify the agreement as for the measures that were proposed. Notably, the USA would not ratify, for fear of harming its own economic growth prospects, and this stance was also adopted by Australia, Japan, China, South Korea, and India. This position became entrenched by these countries with the formation of the Asia–Pacific Partnership on Clean Development and Climate, also known as 'AP6'. This non-treaty pact was designed to allow foreign, environment, and energy ministers from partner countries to collaborate to develop technology designed to reduce emissions. Unlike the Kyoto Protocol, which imposes limits on emissions, this agreement allowed the member countries to set their own goals.

Yet, while all of this policy activity was going on, more and more conclusive evidence was emerging about the inevitability and immediacy of the threats from global warming. Throughout 2005 and 2006, there was news, on a regular basis, of successive scientific studies on the likely effects of climate change. Centres of research, such as the Hadley Centre operated by the UK Meteorological Office and the Tyndall Centre for Climate Change Research, have each published numerous reports on the subject and countless articles have been published in scientific journals such as *Science* and *Nature*. In 2007, scientists on the IPCC, in their Fourth Assessment Report (4AR), gave their strongest statement yet that not only is global warming happening, but that it is primarily a result of human activity. The date of the publication of that report (7 February 2007) was heralded by Achim Steiner, the Executive Director of UNEP, as '*the day the question mark was removed from the debate on whether human activities are driving climate change ... the word unequivocal is the key message of this report*', and that '*... (sceptics) can no longer ignore the evidence*'.[32] The report suggested that there was a 90 per cent probability that global warming was being caused by anthropogenic activities. This was up from 66 per cent in 2001 and 50 per cent in 1995. The Fifth Assessment Report (5AR), to be published in sections between September 2013 and October 2014, increases this probability to 95 per cent which, in scientific terms, is about as certain as it gets.[33] 5AR reports cover additional topics in more depth than previously, looking at impact, adaptation, and vulnerability, and at the mitigation of climate change. The full synthesis report is to be published in Copenhagen in October 2014.

 Snapshot 3.2   Aviation and climate change

Most of us who read this book will have benefited from cheap air travel, whether for holiday travel or business trips. Flights from Europe to the USA are frequently on offer for under £500, and from Europe to the Far East and Australasia often at little over £600. Few would have been left wondering, on the one hand, how some airline companies can offer flights so cheaply, and on the other, perhaps tinged with guilt, how this activity contributes to global warming. Indeed, whilst the EU total GHG emissions fell by 3 per cent between 1990 and 2006, emissions from international aviation increased by almost 100 per cent. It may be surprising to learn that it was only in 2009 that aviation was included in the EU Emissions Trading Scheme (ETS); before that it was excluded on the basis that the scheme focused on national boundaries, and aviation was thought to be outside its scope.

(http://ec.europa.eu/environment/climat/aviation/index_en.htm)

(continued...)

> **Quick questions**
>
> 1. What is the purpose of an ETS?
>
> 2. How can an ETS lead to reduced overall emissions
>
> 3. Is it possible to have a sustainable airline industry at the present scale?

The complex science of climate change which is discussed in 5AR is often contrasted with the rather stark statistics released by other agencies. According to NASA scientists, for example, 2012 was the ninth warmest of any year since 1880, continuing a long-term trend of rising global temperatures. With the exception of 1988, the nine warmest years in the 132-year record have all occurred since 2000, with 2010 and 2005 ranking as the hottest years on record.[34] These findings pose issues not just for policy-makers, but for business leaders as well (see Snapshot 3.2).

> **Discussion Points**
>
> Climate change is a very important and high-profile aspect of sustainable development, but it is not the only one.
>
> - What other aspects of sustainable development should business consider?
> - Are there contradictions and dichotomies between some of these aspects?
> - Which of these aspects are beyond the concerns of corporate responsibility at the present time?

The challenge to business

We opened this chapter with examples of how three businesses defined sustainability in the context of their own business operations. To our knowledge, the only business that has openly acknowledged that it is not environmentally sustainable, and has taken positive steps to correct this, is Interface Inc., the global floor coverings company (see Case Study 3). As noted earlier, the weight of evidence suggests that organizations operating under the traditional business model work within a framework where externalizing costs is seen as good practice. Equally, investors expect returns on their investments, and returns are obtained by growing the profits of the business. The challenge is that growth of the business has invariably meant increasing resource usage, which both depletes the Earth's stock of resources and leads to increased emissions.

Traditionally, governments might have attempted to control growth through regulation, but in the Western model of neoliberal capitalism, command-and-control regulation is no longer seen as an option. Governments might consider initiatives such as insuring risk, taxation, or schemes of emissions trading, but business is largely left to manage these challenges itself. Furthermore, it can be argued that business has been proactive in initiatives aimed at avoiding regulation by demonstrating that it is behaving responsibly.[35]

However, as with the business case for adopting a corporate responsibility agenda (see Chapter 6), many perceive that these challenges are bound together with opportunities to engage with new technologies, and with new approaches to deliver alternative products and processes. To the fore in this endeavour is the World Business Council for Sustainable

Development (WBCSD), which stresses that the opportunities to open new markets, develop new businesses, and access new revenue streams mean that companies should not shirk the challenges that sustainable development presents. New initiatives, involving business leaders, are encouraging those most closely involved in the business debate to offer solutions to these challenges. Indeed, in the recent publication by the Tomorrow's Leaders Group of the WBCSD, when considering the *'role of business in tomorrow's society'*, there are a number of objectives for business going forward. These include developing new businesses and new technologies, setting global benchmarks and new strategies, and offering greater opportunity to larger sections of world communities.[36]

The Tomorrow's Leaders Group accepts what, for some, remains a contentious idea—that sustainability can be achieved without compromising economic growth. As noted earlier, the Stern Review goes further and argues that stabilizing climate change is actually essential for economic growth. There are attractive features to sustainability-led growth (e.g. the opportunities for technological innovation and new markets), but, as Stern also recognizes, government may well have to steer business in new directions and towards adopting new business models.

New models of sustainable business

In light of the challenges that sustainable development poses for business, researchers have been working to develop enterprise models that take account of the parameters of sustainable development. Some have looked at the capitalist business model to see if it can be adapted to meet these challenges; others have sought to develop new models. Writing on the theory behind such new models, Birkin[37] calls for managers to adopt a different ontology,[38] recognizing the *'inter-connectedness'* of corporate decision-making. This may be seen as a development of, or an alternative to, the *'systems thinking'*, offered by Gray[39] as his explanation of a similar phenomenon—that of reductionism, under which the focus is on a specific aspect of a system rather than on the system itself.[40]

What both authors call for is a recognition that concentration on specific issues may not be helpful if sustainability is the goal and that wider consequences of specific actions need a much more considered response. Birkin developed his thesis by arguing for the consideration of *'relationships'* within models of business and, in particular, of the relationships among resource flows, resource flow impacts, stakeholder analysis, and carrying capacity assessments. In developing this model of sustainable business, he suggests that only by examining the interaction among these elements will managers fully appreciate the impacts of their actions and the necessary changes that have to be faced to become sustainable. Others have suggested a fundamentally different approach to this form of modelling by thinking outside the conventional financial model. Traditionally, the 'bottom line' refers to the profit that a company makes in financial terms, and 'capital' means financial capital to most people. But if we think of capital in wider terms that encompass the different aspects of resource application, then we can develop different business models. Forum for the Future, the sustainable development NGO, believes that a sustainable future can be achieved, but that:

> We are facing a sustainability crisis because we're consuming our stocks of natural, human and social capital faster than they are being produced. Unless we control the rate of this consumption, we can't sustain these vital stocks in the long-term ... but for this to happen,

it is the responsibility of every organization, business or otherwise, to manage these capital assets sustainably.[41]

Taking this idea of different kinds of capital, some researchers have constructed new models of business that they employ to decide, *ex ante*, whether or not a business is sustainable. Briefly, a sustainability assessment model is applied to assess the social, economic, resource, and environmental impacts of a project over its life cycle, and then to reduce these impacts into a cash–value measurement. These data are then used in the project investment appraisal. This model tracks the internal and external effects of the proposed investment, and allows a much more rounded appraisal to be made than that of traditional accounting techniques such as net present value or internal rate of return, which focus purely on financial issues.[42]

 Discussion Points

One of the most controversial areas is whether economic growth and sustainable development are compatible.

- Is the Stern Review right to say that sustainable development is essential for economic growth?
- Is it possible to run a business that will grow within the limits of the Earth's ecosystem?
- Is it possible to grow a business while shrinking its environmental footprint?

Capital markets and sustainable development

Despite these initiatives to find new models of sustainable business, there are those who believe that the most fundamental challenge to sustainable practices is that posed by the way in which capital markets reward and punish participants. Although the tension between sustainability and the capital market has been acknowledged for some time, the debate was widened in the 1990s with the work of Stephan Schmidheiny (*Changing Course*, 1992), and Schmidheiny with Federico Zorraquin (*Financing Change*, 1996). Both these authors are industrialists who depend upon the capital market system for their business success, yet have tackled problematic questions regarding the role that capital market activity might play in either helping or hindering the development of sustainable practices.

Elsewhere in this book, we look at some of the mechanisms that govern the ways in which companies operate, and equally at the notion of responsible investing which considers social and environmental impacts on a par with financial returns (see Chapter 6.) But it might be useful to review briefly the mechanisms of the capital market system, to illustrate the dilemmas that they reveal.

First and foremost, only in the initial public offering do capital markets transfer funds from those who wish to invest to those who wish to apply these funds to means of producing goods or services. Thereafter investors in the stock market trade on an expectation of either dividend returns or share returns. In most cases success in the market is calculated by rather short-term returns. Bonus schemes for capital market participants, including bankers, are calculated, in the main, on short-term measures of success. The problem, in relation to the connection between capital market investment practices and sustainable development, arises in the way in which companies are rewarded, or punished, by the market (see Snapshot 3.3).

 Snapshot 3.3 Individual freedom and the common good

The Western model of liberal democracy is based on a number of rights which attach to individuals, and a limitation on the role of the state to interfere with an individual as he or she exercises his or her rights. In this economic model there is an overriding right for an individual to make economic decisions to maximize his or her own wealth, and the state should not intervene, except to prevent injustice. The right to trade and own property is intertwined in this philosophy, and these assumptions are largely taken for granted in our daily lives.

The problem arises when actions, in aggregate, pose a threat to the way of life of all of us in the long term. Over-use of resources, as demonstrated in the graph, poses a threat to the way we do business and live our lives, especially if we use more resources than the world can provide in a sustainable context.

(*Source: Living Planet Report*, 2012: WWF. Available at: http://wwf.panda.org/)

Quick questions

1. How do we reconcile private notions of freedom with wider responsibilities to humankind?

2. Who should take responsibility for limiting our use of resources?

3. What can we do, as individuals, to make a difference?

Signals to the market

It is acknowledged in the finance literature that markets respond to 'signals'. These signals are interpreted from information about company activity that is obtained from diverse sources. For example, if a company is thought to be underperforming, a good signal to the market might be an announcement of a change in top management; reducing declared dividends is seen as a bad signal. These signals are interpreted by financial analysts in terms of potential future cash flows and are reflected in patterns of investment, or disinvestment. They contribute to some of the changes that we witness in share price movements over time. Traditionally, the information that tends to move share prices is normally financial, relating to earnings forecasts, dividend policy, investment policy, etc. Indeed, the nature of the investments that a company makes in the course of its operations is central to the way in which the future performance of a company may be assessed. These strategies are disclosed in the course of both formal and informal discussions with analysts, and the concern here is that the fear of communicating the wrong signal may act to inhibit companies from undertaking innovative or experimental investments, which may be necessary if a sustainable development agenda is to be adopted.[43]

Schmidheiny and Zorraquin (1996, p 8) list several 'worrying' assumptions about sustainable development that might convey the wrong signal to markets. They include the following:

- there is a common perception that sustainability requires longer-term investments, where payback times might not fall in the 'good signal' time span;
- a concerted effort to innovate may reduce present earnings;
- for global companies, investment in sustainable development initiatives in developing countries brings with it additional high-risk premiums;
- accounting and reporting systems do not adequately reflect risks and opportunities.

Another issue that companies try to avoid signalling to the market is the threat of regulation. The idea that governments are about to intervene in a particular sector creates uncertainty, which is interpreted as a bad signal. This helps to explain why companies combine to form strong associations aimed at helping to persuade governments that there is no need to regulate. If they can demonstrate that they are handling thorny issues, the hope is that governments will accept that industry is capable of regulating itself. The WBCSD is one such organization, boasting a large number of major corporations worldwide within its membership. The Global Reporting Initiative (GRI) is another example, and adoption of its guidelines (see Chapter 8) has been used to demonstrate that serious efforts are being made to address previously perceived reporting imperfections. These examples and countless others, at professional, industry, national, or supranational levels, are all designed to counter the possibility of the adverse market effect of announcements of regulation.

However, those in favour of a more regulated approach remain sceptical of the motives behind this lobbying process. Their argument is that if regulation only represents the lowest level of acceptable behaviour beyond which it is deemed illegal, and that as corporate responsibility programmes are supposed to go beyond this point in any case, what is the issue with regulation?

As judged by markets, however, operating to the minimum standards allowed by law is usually seen as a positive signal. It also gives rise to the acronyms that are taken as a guide to much commercial activity in the area of environmental management systems, such as BAT-NEEC and CATNIP.[44]

The question is, what will it take for the market to reward behaviour that goes beyond regulation, even if that involves expenditure that might have an adverse impact on short-term earnings? At what stage, for example, might markets see initiatives such as switching away from biomass back to coal in the production of electricity as a bad signal?

Discussion Points

The accountancy profession is seen by some as an essential element in encouraging companies to tackle sustainable development.

- What can the accountancy profession bring to sustainable development that will help companies to change their business models, enabling them to operate with less of an environmental impact?
- To what extent does the accountancy profession lock companies into outdated business models?
- What can the accountancy profession do to remove the barriers to client change?

Rewarding financial intermediaries

Since the global financial crisis in 2008–2009 which led to national governments 'bailing out' many global financial institutions, the award of bonuses to employees by banks has become a discussion about corporate responsibility in itself. Those involved in the investment process as financial intermediaries work within a bonus system, which can represent a large percentage of an individual's salary and which, collectively in the City of London in 2006, amounted to some £8bn, a figure equivalent to the GDP of some developing countries. As the depth of the financial crisis began to emerge and allegations of imprudent trading products and practices emerged, focus turned to those senior executives in the banks at the point of collapse. In a move that further enraged the public, many of those who were accused of being involved in the bad practice that led to the collapse left their posts on very generous terms, a move which seemed to many to epitomize the problems that brought about the crisis in the first place. The global recession which followed the financial meltdown meant that bonuses in 2008 and 2009 were lower than previously, but 2010 saw a return to a figure in the region of £6bn, although some high-profile CEOs of banks declined to take their bonuses and continued pressure on, especially, the UK government has seen continued calls for bonuses to be capped at a salary level, or deferred to a point where recklessness or malpractice can be ruled out.

In Joel Barkan's documentary film *The Corporation* (2004), a Wall Street trader enthuses over the profits made from trading in gold on 11 September 2001 as the twin towers descended to dust. When discussing the possibility of disease affecting the pig population, the trader talks of the opportunities that the news presents: '*It's almost ludicrous not to jump on board*'. Other interviewees talk of the market as '*amoral*', suggesting that issues of morality and ethics should have been negotiated before the trading process began—that is, it is not the trader's job to think about morality. These are important questions that are not fully acknowledged by market participants. There is nothing in corporate governance guidelines that gives companies any direction or reassurance should they consider any such strategy, and shareholder return remains the main driver of market activity.

However, there are attempts to engage analysts in considering social and environmental impacts. The Enhanced Analytics Initiative, the UN Principles for Responsible Investment, the London Accord, and the Marathon Club, which all have the backing of major financial institutions, are working in different ways to get financial intermediaries to take sustainability seriously. The Institute of Chartered Accountants in England and Wales, in association with the WWF, has also launched the Finance Innovation Laboratory, a broad multi-stakeholder initiative that aims to activate solutions for change in financial systems. These emerging trends are discussed further in Chapter 10.

 Discussion Points

Some believe that business can only go so far in addressing sustainable development without the support of other members of society.

- Do markets incentivize short-term and continued-cost externalization of the kind cited as a threat to sustainable development?
- Are consumers motivated as much by encouraging good performance in sustainability as they are by punishing poor performance?
- Would NGOs be likely to criticize a company more or less if it were to take on sustainable development issues?

 Case study 3   Interface Inc.

From modest beginnings in 1973, Interface has risen in stature to become one of the world's leading manufacturers of floor coverings, selling products in 110 countries, with sales approaching $1bn and over 3000 employees. What singles out Interface from other companies in an industry which typically relies on petrochemicals in the manufacturing process is its commitment to become environmentally neutral. Until 1994, like its competitors, Interface used an accepted business model to grow the company, complying with laws and regulations as required.

However, in 1994 Ray Anderson, the founder of the company and then CEO, was asked to make a presentation on the company's environmental plans. In preparation for this he was given a copy of Paul Hawken's book *The Ecology of Commerce*. The effect, in Anderson's words, was like 'a spear to the chest'. From that point Anderson determined to change the way the company interacted with nature and set about its journey to conquer 'Mount Sustainability'.

The journey of Interface towards sustainability has marked a considerable shift in the way the company both operates and designs its products. The company was faced with the considerable challenge of reimagining its business model and then redesigning all of its processes, as well as moving away from its dependency on petrochemicals. It developed a vision to become 'the first company that, by its deeds, shows the entire industrial world what sustainability is in all its dimensions: people, process, product, place and profits—by 2020'.

The journey is characterized by addressing 'the seven fronts of Mount Sustainability':

1   eliminate waste
2   benign emissions
3   renewable energy
4   closing the loop

(continued...)

5 resource-efficient transportation

6 sensitizing stakeholders

7 redesign commerce.

Each of these approaches is developed and explained with practical advice on how to approach the challenges offered.

Equally, the company was open to taking advice and guidance from a number of partners to help it achieve its aims, including the World Resources Institute, the Forum for the Future, the US Environmental Protection Agency, and the National Minority Supplier Development Council. It also has an 'Eco Dream Team' comprising leading thinkers, architects, and engineers to maintain the momentum. Far from costing money, Interface sees its move to a sustainable business model as a positive benefit. As Ray Anderson puts it:

> Costs are down, not up, dispelling a myth and exposing the false choice between the economy and the environment, products are the best they have ever been, because sustainable design has provided an unexpected wellspring of innovation, people are galvanized around a shared higher purpose, better people are applying, the best people are staying and working with a purpose, the goodwill in the marketplace generated by our focus on sustainability far exceeds that which any amount of advertising or marketing expenditure could have generated—this company believes it has found a better way to a bigger and more legitimate profit—a better business model.

(*Source:* www.interfaceglobal.com)

Questions

1. Sustainable development is often seen as an insurmountable objective for many companies.

   a. How might a company approach this challenge, and where might it look for help?

   b. How can companies involve NGO's in this process?

   c. To what extent does collaboration pose a threat to a company's competitive advantage, and how should that threat be managed?

2. Sustainable development, in the Brundtland definition, encompasses notions of social justice across and between generations.

   a. How can notions of social justice be assimilated into the neoclassical theory of the firm which places the emphasis on maximizing shareholder wealth?

   b. What responsibilities do transnational corporations have to their employees in different locations?

   c. To what extent is product re-engineering a viable strategy to address sustainability?

3. Interface embarked on a twenty-five year journey towards 'mission zero', where it will eliminate any negative impact on the environment.

   a. What other sectors might follow this example?

   b. What are the major obstacles to achieving this mission for other companies?

   c. How important is it to have top-level support for this kind of initiative?

Summary

This chapter began and ended with looking at how companies portray their activities in terms of sustainability. In between, we examined how concepts of sustainable development emerged and were defined, how that definition conceals subtle notions of equity and fairness, and how these notions present challenges to the 'business as usual' model of corporate behaviour. Although there are broadly accepted definitions of sustainable development, individual companies still choose to define the concept in their own ways. As will be discussed in relation to the impact of corporate responsibility (see Chapter 13), companies are, at best, only starting to understand that they must take responsibility for some of their most significant sustainability consequences. This is evident in the sustainability reports that many companies are producing and, as we have illustrated, some companies approach this task by redefining sustainable development in ways that can be addressed while leaving out the issues that present the greatest challenges. This also relates to the accountability framework within which reporting sits (see Chapter 8).

If, initially, such reports were dismissed as a public relations exercise, the seriousness with which issues such as climate change and sustainable energy are being taken by both governments and the private sector strongly suggests that sustainability will become an increasingly important part of the business agenda. In some ways, this makes getting the management and reporting frameworks right even more important. This and other aspects of sustainable development, such as demographic change, may also be among the most crucial business questions and with equally significant prizes at stake. Although questions remain about the exact science of climate change (as they do in relation to most areas of scientific enquiry), there is an overwhelming consensus—and one that is increasingly endorsed by business—that it poses a real risk and is related to human activity. As the different dimensions of sustainable development become more apparent in everyday life, so people will turn to major institutions to take a lead in controlling harmful emissions. Business is clearly one such institution and its role is likely to become more prominent, not least because the conventional command-and-control regulatory model of government is being tested by the social and political realities of globalization.

Further Reading

**online
resource
centre**

www.oxfordtextbooks.co.uk/orc/blowfield_murray3e/
    Visit the Online Resource Centre that accompanies this book to enrich your understanding of this chapter. Among the resources available are web links, exercises, and additional case studies.

Anderson, R.C. 1998, *Mid-course correction : toward a sustainable enterprise: the interface model*, Peregrinzilla Press, Atlanta, GA.
    Theoretical analysis of the significance of environmental management and sustainability to corporations.

Elkington, J. 1998, *Cannibals with forks: the triple bottom line of 21st century business*, New Society, Gabriola Island, BC/Stony Creek, CT.
    Influential introduction to the case for considering social, economic, and environmental added value.

Gore, A. 2006, *An inconvenient truth*, Bloomsbury, London.
The book accompanying the Oscar-winning film about the importance of climate change.

Hawken, P. 1993, *The ecology of commerce: a declaration of sustainability*, Harper Business, New York.
Arguments for the importance of sustainability to business.

Henriques, A. & Richardson, J.A. 2004, *The triple bottom line: does it all add up? Assessing the sustainability of business and CSR*, Earthscan, London.
Critical analysis of triple bottom-line theory and practice.

Schmidheiny, S. & Zorraquin, F. 1996, *Financing change: the financial community, eco-efficiency, and sustainable development*, MIT Press, Cambridge, MA.
Influential early book by two business leaders on the role of the finance industry in sustainability.

Online resources

- Suggested additional materials on sustainability-related issues
- Exercises and discussion topics for students
- Emerging sustainability initiatives
- Links to other web-based resources

Endnotes

1. For a detailed analysis, the Oxford Poverty and Human Development Initiative analyses poverty across 104 countries—see www.ophi.org.uk.
2. http://www.unep.org/geo/geo5.asp.
3. The reports are each between 500 and 800 pages long, but summaries can be obtained from: http://www.unep.org/maweb/en/index.aspx.
4. WWF, 2012.
5. Meadows et al., 2004.
6. IPCC, 2007.
7. Jacks, 2013.
8. http://www.worldwatch.org/node/6099.
9. Stott et al., 2010.
10. BP Sustainability Review, 2012, p5, available at http://www.bp.com/.
11. See http://www.shell.com.
12. http://www.amec.com/aboutus/sustainability.htm.
13. Grubb et al., 1993.
14. Engfeldt, 2002; Tobin, 1997.
15. www.unep.org.
16. UNEP was established with its headquarters in Nairobi under the Executive Directorship of Maurice Strong, who had been appointed Secretary-General of the Stockholm Conference in 1972.
17. Tolba and El-Kholy, 1992.
18. WCED, 1987; see http://www.un-documents.net/ocf-a2.htm.

19. WCED, 1987, p 356; see http://www.un-documents.net/ocf-a2.htm.

20. Since then, and despite massive amounts of aid raised in the West for the starving of Africa, famines still occur and continuing allegations of malpractice are laid at the feet of host governments, with new roles being defined for NGOs to administer aid programmes.

21. Farman et al., 1985.

22. Incidences of thyroid cancer in children of up to 15 years old increased tenfold between 1986 and 1997, and it is feared that many others may have died as a consequence of the accident.

23. Tolba and El-Kholy, 1992.

24. Grubb, M., et al 1993.

25. 'Scottish Coal liquidation leads to dispute over clean-ups', *The Herald* http://www.heraldscotland.com/business/company-news/scottish-coal-liquidation-leads-to-dispute-over-clean-ups.21050751.

26. *The Guardian* reported on riots in Sweden in May 2013: 'as inequality and segregation start to rise, the spread of youth disorder has shaken ethnic Swedes and older immigrants alike. These riots follow major disturbances in Paris in 2005, and in other European cities in between'.

27. UNEP 2010.

28. See, for example: Bebbington et al., 2004; Birkin, 2000; Daly, 1996; Elkington, 1998; Gray et al., 1995; Gray, 2006 a, b; Gray and Bebbington, 2000; Hawken, 1993; Suranyi, 2000.

29. http://www.hudsondredging.com/.

30. http://thinkprogress.org/climate/2013/07/15/2301451/25-years-after-exxon-valdez-oil-spill-company-still-hasnt-paid-for-long-term-environmental-damages/.

31. UNEP, 1987.

32. IPCC, 2007.

33. http://ipcc.ch.

34. http://data.giss.nasa.gov/gistemp/.

35. See, for example, http://www.csreurope.org/.

36. Vigar, 2006.

37. Birkin, 2000.

38. Ontology' refers to our perception of reality, the way in which we 'view the world'. Instead of seeing the world as a myriad of discrete issues, each to be managed on its own, Birkin (2000) calls for managers to adopt an 'ontology of interconnected events', within which the consequence of one action will have an effect on others.

39. Gray, 2002.

40. This concept is discussed in more detail in Chapter 8, along with the roots of social and environmental accounting.

41. www.forumforthefuture.org.

42. For more information on this subject, see, for example, Bebbington, 2001 a, b; 2009.

43. Murray et al., 2006.

44. BATNEEC, 'Best Available Technology Not Entailing Excessive Cost'; CATNIP, 'Currently Available Technology Not Involving Prosecution'.

Corporate responsibility in developing economies

Chapter overview

In this chapter, we discuss the role of business in developing economies, and whether and how business can be an agent of poverty reduction.[1] In particular, we will:

- review the role of business in social and economic development;
- what it means for business to be an agent of development;
- examine under what circumstances business takes on a developmental role;
- explore the limitations of business as a force for development.

Main topics

Introduction   75

Development agent or development tool?   76

A brief history of business as development agent   77

Theories of development   78

The business–poverty framework   81

Business as a cause of poverty   82

Business as poverty's victim   85

Business as a solution   86

Assessing the business response   89

Key terms

International development

Poverty

Business as development agent

Bottom of the pyramid

Fairtrade

Microfinance

Introduction

Since the mid-2000s, there has been a flurry of activity around the role of business in advancing social and economic development in what are variously called emerging or developing economies. There are diverse arguments for putting business and development towards the top of theoretical and practical corporate responsibility agendas. Companies have great

wealth; by some measures greater than that of many poor nations. Companies have a significant, sometimes negative, impact on developing economies. Governments cannot always
be trusted to deliver the social and economic benefits that the poor and marginalized have a
right to expect. Business activity is essential to economic growth. Certain types of enterprise
are well suited to meeting the needs of the poor. The gap between rich and poor is a threat to
political and economic stability. According to philosophers such as Singer (1972), it is morally
indefensible to allow suffering on the grounds that it happens in far off places, and, as part of
this ethical debate, it could be argued that companies have a responsibility not just for the
harms they produce but equally for the ones they fail to prevent.

Typically, in considering these perspectives the emphasis is on the role of multinational
companies, and sometimes one can forget that many developing economies have a vibrant
private sector, especially at the level of small and medium-sized enterprises, often located in
the informal rather than formal economy. We examine corporate responsibility in the context
of small and medium-sized companies in Chapter 11, but their role in developing economies
should not be overlooked, as some of the examples in this chapter remind us.

Nonetheless, much more is known about the responsibilities and practices of larger companies, but as we shall see there are many views about when, where, and how they should
act in developing economies. A company's relationship to poverty is a major determinant
of how it behaves in this environment (e.g. whether it is a cause or victim of poverty), and
understanding this relationship is very useful in assessing what a company can and should be
doing. As the following sections reveal, it is possible to build a framework for understanding
what can and cannot be expected of business in the development context.

Development agent or development tool?

The array of viewpoints on why business is important to the prosperity of developing countries, and vice versa, have given rise to quite different ideas about what business should be
doing and why. Liberal economists argue that companies exist to create value for shareholders, subject to legal constraints (see Chapter 2), and by so doing they are a positive force
for development—creating jobs, supplying goods and services, and helping to fund necessary social institutions. This thinking underpinned the so-called 'Washington Consensus', the
set of private-sector-oriented policies that countries around the world had to adopt if they
were to receive assistance from the major international financial institutions in the 1980s and
1990s. The Consensus in its pure form has gone out of fashion, but echoes of it can be heard
in discussions about growth-driven development, and in particular the view that as sustainable poverty alleviation depends on economic growth, then business as the primary creator
of wealth has a central role to play.

But this gives rise to another question. Should business be regarded as a development
agent, consciously striving to deliver and moreover be held to account for developmental
outcomes? Or should it be considered a development tool, no more responsible for positive
or negative outcomes than a hammer is for a carpenter's thumb? When business acts as a
development tool, the outcomes can be positive—creating jobs, generating wealth, meeting
people's needs through the provision of goods and services. Two studies of Unilever's impact
on the poor, and its economic footprint in Indonesia and South Africa, respectively, show the

complex economic outcomes that can result when a multinational produces and markets goods in developing countries.[2]

However, the question is not simply whether business has an impact on poverty, but whether or not it can and should be accountable for causing, preventing, and alleviating poverty. For instance, the development tool might create jobs, but business as development agent takes responsibility for the number of jobs it creates, their location, and the quality. The development tool might make products available in poor countries, but the development agent makes products suited to the needs of and accessible to poor segments of the population. And whereas the business-as-usual approach to development emerges from managerial calculations related to costs, returns, and competition, business as a development agent is also motivated by stakeholder concerns, pressures, and demands.

In this chapter, our main interest is private enterprise as development agent—something that not only affects poverty, but is the subject of conscious actions undertaken because of poverty. The agent can be a company, an industry, an inter-company alliance, a multisector partnership, or any other entity where the actions of the private sector are influenced by an awareness of poverty. Our main focus will be on company actions (e.g. by management or investors), but we will also explore how others, such as international development agencies, have influenced the private sector.

A brief history of business as development agent

There is nothing new about companies being development agents. From the Dutch East India Company in Indonesia to the British South Africa company in 1920s Zambia, private companies have administered vast territories, and performed parallel governmental and commercial functions. The expectations of companies may shift over time, but what these examples and other histories[3] highlight is that while definitions of responsibility change, the idea of companies having responsibility towards society remains constant. Yet despite the evidence that the responsibilities of corporations alter, corporate responsibility theory has failed to produce a substantive theory of change. The analyses that other disciplines bring to the relationship of business with society are not widely used in corporate responsibility theory.[4] For instance, there is a considerable body of scholarship about business and international development, concerning areas such as corporate imperialism and influence over newly independent post-colonial states,[5] but it has not significantly influenced discussion of corporate responsibility and poverty.

There are exceptions such as Ruggie (2003), who draws on Polanyi's theory of embedded and disembedded economies to explain general shifts in the nature of the business–society relationship: *'[Corporate responsibility] may be seen as a voluntary effort to realign the efficiency of markets with the shared value and purposes that societies demand, and that markets themselves require to survive and thrive'* (cited in Nelson, 2007, p 58) But more typically, the responsibilities of companies are presented as ahistorical. Shifts over time are treated as normative, and there is little attempt to explain why, for instance, the radical agendas of the 1930s have been replaced with something much less ambitious in recent times.[6] In other words, the definition of corporate responsibilities is treated as something divorced from the social, political, and historical context of the locations where business is operating. The consequences of this become apparent when we consider the shifting nature of development as a concept.

Discussion points

International development is increasingly emphasized as an important aspect of corporate responsibility.

- Why are social and environmental issues associated with international development important for business?
- Should companies be held to account for the harms they fail to prevent as much as for the ones they cause?
- What can national governments do to encourage companies to be more proactive as development agents?

Theories of development

In the literature on business and development, it is common to concentrate on the type of things that companies are doing, and why they add value to society and the bottom line. However, the potential trap of focusing on a business rationale is that the scope of companies' responsibilities comes to be defined from within the framework of management theory, rather than that of development. Yet what we have labelled the development agent role can be constructed quite differently depending how we think about development. For example, Utting (2007) discusses the relationship between corporate responsibility and an equality/equity approach to development. If such an approach were used to inform business strategy, then the responsibilities of business would include aspects of social protection, rights, empowerment, and redistribution.

 Key concept: International development

International development refers to efforts to improve standards of living in the poorer countries of the world. It is not a new idea; one of the justifications for colonialism, particularly in its later years, was that it would bring about economic growth and better social conditions. But international development as an idea really took off in the post-colonial era as it became clear that independence alone was not going to end the low levels of health, education, household income, infrastructure development, and other features that seemed characteristics of what are variously called less developed countries, emerging economies, and developing nations.

Since the 1960s, international development has been a distinct aspect of social and economic reform, typically referring to the efforts of wealthier countries to help poor ones. Most rich countries have specific government departments dedicated to funding and promoting international development. Often these were set up to deal with emergency aid (e.g. famine relief), but their remit was soon extended to address such emergencies through longer-term development activities based on the principle that if you give someone a fish they will eat for a day, but if you teach them how to fish they will eat forever.

(continued...)

However, international development is not the preserve of donor governments, and indeed there is considerable frustration that so few rich countries have lived up to their agreement in principle to commit 0.7 per cent of GDP to development spending. Oxfam (short for Oxford Famine Relief) was one of the first of what are now an enormous number of development-oriented NGOs with offices around the world. Some of the largest NGOs, such as BRAC in Bangladesh, were founded in developing countries, but there are also numerous development consultancies such as the USA's 'beltway bandits', so called for their location around Washington, DC, where some of the most significant development funding decisions are made.

In earlier development paradigms, such as those of Frank and Wallerstein, the condition of poor countries was held to be a direct consequence of the wealth of others. Today, however, mainstream international development practice has discarded such structural considerations, and development's core aim is to establish the conditions whereby a country is ready to compete in a capitalist world economy. Business's unique position in that economy is the main reason why in recent years attention has been paid to business as a development agent, and how, for instance, it can contribute to measures of that development, exemplified for instance in the targets of the Millennium Development Goals.

Different models of development have been favoured over time, ranging from Streeten's theory of basic human needs to Rostow's take-off model to Sen's work on welfare economics. Each model has its implications for what business might do. However, contemporary corporate responsibility theory in general does not openly acknowledge these different models. Instead, for the most part it adheres to, and tacitly accepts, what Rodrik (1997) calls the augmented Washington Consensus, a model that dominates current development theory.

Current approaches to corporate responsibility as management practice are stronger in some areas than others. For example, for all the widespread adoption of core labour rights into the responsibility discourse, meaningful interventions have proved difficult, especially on issues such as freedom of association and the rights of women. Moreover, the role of business looks different again if one emphasizes the rights-based, empowerment, redistributive, or neoliberal elements of development agendas.[7] However, the distinct responses demanded by such differing ideas of development are often blurred in business–poverty discussions, something that can lead to unwarranted criticism and praise of the private sector's role.[8]

International agencies such as the United Nations Conference on Trade and Development (UNCTAD), the United Nations Development Programme (UNDP), the World Trade Organization (WTO), the World Bank, and the Organisation for Economic Co-operation and Development (OECD) have set out various ways that business can help alleviate poverty.[9] For example, the International Labour Organization (ILO) highlights low wages and vulnerable employment as causes of poverty, OECD stresses the consequences of short-termism amongst multinational corporations, and their abuse of political and economic muscle, while UNCTAD concentrates on the importance of backward linkages and embedding companies into local economies. The United Nations Industrial Development Organization (UNIDO) distinguishes between the substantive dimension to corporate responsibility (i.e. the particular issues that are addressed), and the process dimension (the ways business goes about addressing these issues and identifying the boundaries of accountability) (Nelson, 2007). Various international organizations emphasize the importance of this process dimension as a determinant of the effectiveness of poverty interventions, including support for the self-organization of the poor at community level or workers in factories, a cognizance of local conditions, and cross-sector coordination.[10]

However, there is a mismatch between this kind of aspirational development agenda and what companies are actually doing as development agents (see Snapshot 4.1). The array of substantive issues being addressed is incomplete, but is nonetheless more comprehensive than that of process issues which may not be included at all.[11] Various questions arise from this observation. Is it the case that business has an ad hoc poverty agenda, and if so how has that come about, and what are the likely outcomes? Can business be more effectively integrated into established agendas, and what would this require? Or is it that business is already part of an alternative poverty agenda, and what are the implications of this? We will explore these questions in the coming sections.

 Discussion points

Theorists such as Easterly claim that government aid to developing countries is a failure, and that the private sector offers a better alternative for economic growth.

- Why do you think that the private sector was previously overlooked in some development theories?

- What are the strengths of companies in tackling development issues?

- Are there aspects of development where a private sector response is inappropriate?

 Snapshot 4.1   Clean water for poor communities—P&G PuR

Procter & Gamble is the largest consumer goods manufacturer in the world with a turnover of $79 billion. In 1995, in association with the US Centers for Disease Control and Prevention, it developed PuR packets which purify dirty water. It invested more than $10 million in R&D, and a similar amount in market testing for bottom-of-the-pyramid markets. However, it eventually shifted the product to its charitable foundation because testing in 2000–2003 found the product take-up to be commercially non-viable. This was because PuR required too much investment in public health education to be profitable, despite its undoubted benefits for consumers, employees, and society. Seeing the social returns on investment, the company shelved plans to end the product and chose instead to explore non-conventional marketing approaches.

Instead of using normal outlets, PuR was sold to NGOs for about 3.5 US cents per sachet. Through P&G's Corporate Sustainable Development unit, the company launched its Live, Learn and Thrive programme, and PuR became an important element in partnerships with community development NGOs such as World Vision, Care, and Save the Children. The alliances cost P&G about $3.5 million to fund donations of product, technical expertise, and marketing expertise. Operating around the world, including in disaster zones such as Haiti, P&G aims to provide four billion litres of clean water by 2012, and two billion litres a year by 2020. This would save an estimated 10,000 lives, and prevent about 80 million days lost due to diarrhoea annually. PuR sachet sales have increased as a result of the partnership model. Between 2004 and 2006, 50 million sachets were sold at cost to emergency relief organizations (social model), compared to three million previously.

(continued...)

Quick questions

PuR is a market approach to delivering clean water to poor communities, but it was almost dismissed as a commercial failure.

1 Is the current partnership model a genuine viable business model?

2 Why does P&G continue to market PuR despite selling the product at cost?

3 Are there other bottom-of-the-pyramid situations where this type of marketing approach could work?

The business–poverty framework

Irrespective of whether we consider business to be a development tool or a development agent, to have a bit part or the starring role in tackling poverty, we need to understand that there are multiple facets to the business–poverty relationship. One might argue, in line with Kramer and Kania's (2006) model, that corporate responsibility is either defensive (protecting a company's reputation) or offensive (burnishing the company's reputation), but from society's perspective such a two-dimensional model does not capture the variety of ways that business affects or is affected by poverty. To do this we need to give equal consideration to three dimensions: business as a cause of poverty, its victim, and a solution (see Figure 4.1).

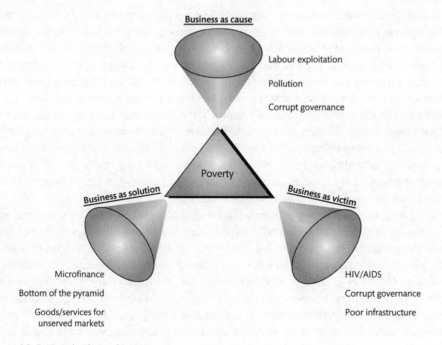

Figure 4.1 Business's relationships to poverty

There is also a fourth dimension which is not explored here, but is worth noting, i.e. that business can be indifferent to poverty, seeing it as neither a threat nor an opportunity, but simply as something that is not factored into decisions. Thus, for instance, decisions about investment are not typically based on their impact on poverty, but what will bring the best return on investment. Sometimes poverty might be appraised as an opportunity in those deliberations (e.g. low labour costs), or it might be a barrier (e.g. weak infrastructure), but in many instances (perhaps in the majority of investment decisions) poverty is not a consideration, and business positions itself as a bystander.

Business as a cause of poverty

In the free market system, an inefficient company has the potential to cause poverty if it fails to generate wealth, create jobs, and provide goods and services (i.e. when it fails as a development tool). However, it is the way in which seemingly efficient companies can cause or exacerbate poverty that is our interest here. The collapse of clothing factories at Bangladesh's Rana Plaza in April 2013, leaving hundreds dead, is just one of many examples over the years of major apparel companies and retailers being linked to unsafe and inhumane working conditions in developing countries. At one level, some argue that the very functioning of international markets may exacerbate poverty, although for reasons too complex to do justice to here. Equally, business and government in developed economies have been accused of protecting parts of their markets from developing economy competition, and also for denying developing economies the kind of protections that some feel are essential for economic development.[12]

Advocates of the assumption that free markets have a singularly important role in economic development make the case that business cannot cause poverty if it acts rationally because the market is the most effective way of determining price and allocating resources. Even if one accepts this, power asymmetries that favour certain business actors mean that there are wide disparities in how the proceeds of trade are distributed, and that poor producers in particular (e.g. marginal smallholder farmers) can find themselves selling their produce for even less than the cost of production.[13] Similarly, the power that some brand-owners hold as gatekeepers to lucrative consumer markets means that some manufacturers have limited bargaining power regarding price or specification, making labour one of the few areas where management can influence profitability. Hence, low wages, long hours, and other abusive labour practices are the norm in places where low-skilled labour is plentiful, the opportunity cost of relocation is low, and law enforcement is lenient.[14]

In the long run, developing economy labour markets may obey the laws of liberal economics, and if so wages will rise with the overall upgrading of a country's economy. But in the short term, wages at less than the cost of survival and reproduction put enormous burdens not only on individual workers, but also on their families and social networks. For example, in a sample of factories in China producing for Wal-Mart, the hourly wage is less than the legal minimum and overtime hours exceed the legal maximum.[15] Only by working excessive overtime can the workers achieve earnings approximating a living wage. Rural to urban migrants often face particularly difficult conditions in terms of stagnating real wages and having to pay for health care and education.[16] Yet, labour continues to migrate, not just within national boundaries but also overseas, where they may also be at risk from exploitation as the September 2013 scandal about migrant labour used to build the facilities for the football World Cup in Qatar demonstrated.

Sudden injections of wealth, and unequal distribution, can have long-term consequences. For example, the promotion of cocoa production in parts of Sulawesi, Indonesia, in the 1990s, together with weak enforcement of traditional land rights, allowed certain migrant ethnic groups to prosper using land alienated from the indigenous population.[17] Other impacts of private sector activity are also experienced differently by different sections of the population. For example, labour markets are gendered institutions that impact differently on women than on men, not least because of the former's need to balance productive and reproductive responsibilities. Poverty as experienced by women is not just a matter of unequal wages, but also relates to issues such as child care, maternity leave, and care of the elderly, aspects that are often neglected in the corporate responsibility initiatives of companies that either do not understand or are not concerned about the connections between reproductive work or care and both business and societal sustainability.[18]

These are examples of the substantive dimension to business's relationship to poverty, and there are more facts and figures in the Online Resource Centre. But we should not forget what we earlier called the process dimension including, for example, the issue of empowerment. Poverty is often associated with disenfranchisement, marginalization, and the lack of capacity or opportunity to advocate for one's own interests. Freedom of association and collective bargaining are amongst the rights business has been accused of interfering with, the absence of which can perpetuate poverty. Companies can also affect the process of poverty alleviation by paying low wages, or avoiding or evading taxes, thereby denying governments essential resources that potentially could be used to invest in the poor.[19] And short-term contracts with suppliers may ultimately limit the opportunity to build up the capacity of poor producers and their communities.[20]

There are other areas where business relates to poverty, if not as the direct cause, then at least as the apparent beneficiary. The poverty that is behind child labour, forced labour, and labour trafficking is something that has benefited business in some circumstances. In an indirect way, business is held responsible for these types of poverty, not just because it is seen as a beneficiary of the global economic system within which such poverty exists, but because it is associated with the changing patterns of governance that are characteristic of that system.

Bad (i.e. corrupt) and weak (i.e. ineffective) government is one cause of poverty, and business has variously supported, tolerated, and resisted such practices. Corporate ambivalence in this regard can be seen from the positions taken by the private sector during the apartheid era in South Africa where parts of the business community both supported and undermined the government.[21] However, generalizations are difficult to make.

While good public governance is generally accepted as essential to alleviating poverty, it remains to be seen if that is true of the alternative models of governance that business is part of. Companies have played a part in the process of deregulation, and the subsequent emergence of an international regulatory system that is highly skewed towards the protection of capital and non-human corporate assets.[22] For Ruggie (2003), companies must help redress the imbalances of the global governance system, and 'the key governance question before us' is how much burden companies, and in particular the kind of voluntary efforts associated with corporate responsibility management, should bear. Wrapped inside that question are issues of regulatory capture by the private sector, and how well self-regulation and voluntary regulation protect the interests of the poor.

The specific relationships between business and poverty are important to understand because they affect how companies behave as development agents. For example, the relocation of factories in contexts of deregulation can have serious impacts in terms of lost employment and downward pressures on wages and working conditions in former host countries. The Multi-Fibre Alliance Forum is one of the few examples of the private sector taking into account the consequences of relocation. It was a response to the lifting in 2005 of the Multi-Fibre Agreement (MFA), which had helped developing countries build up export-oriented garment industries. The end of MFA threatened to have negative consequences for workers, communities, and local and national economies, as competition from China forced factories to close in several countries. The MFA Forum, which at its peak involved over forty organizations, proposed solutions for garment industries in countries such as Bangladesh and Lesotho, but it ended in 2011 and, as with many examples of corporate responsibility in developing countries, its impact is hard to determine.

Another dimension of the business–poverty nexus, namely the bias of markets against the poor, in terms of both the difficulties small producers have in accessing international markets and the unequal distribution of value along the trading chain, is addressed by fairtrade (Snapshot 4.2). Elements of the fairtrade model, which involves the payment of a premium price to small producers and the organization of producers into associations, have found their way into the trading practices of large companies, such as Starbucks' Coffee and Farmer Equity (CAFE) Practices.[23]

To date, when business has been accused of causing poverty, if it has not denied the charge (as has typically been the case with regard to disinvestment, relocation, and corporate tax avoidance and evasion), it has for the most part sought to protect its reputation, notably by adopting new regulatory systems such as company, industry, or multi-stakeholder codes of conduct that promise some form of social accountability. The most significant approach in the development context is the use of multi-stakeholder or non-governmental systems of regulation involving multiple actors in new roles and relationships, and new processes of standard-setting, monitoring, benchmarking, and enforcement. Examples include the Fair Wear Foundation (FWF), the Ethical Trading Initiative (ETI), and the Fair Labor Association (FLA).

 Snapshot 4.2   Fairtrade: an approach to market redistribution

Fairtrade is concerned with the bias of markets against the poor, in terms of both the difficulties small producers have in accessing international markets, and the unequal distribution of value along the trading chain. Although it initially grew as part of a network of alternative trade producers, buyers, processors, and retailers, the term fairtrade today is mostly associated with a product-labelling initiative that ensures a place for the products of marginalized producers in developed economy markets. While there is tension within the fairtrade movement between those who see it as a tool for radically modifying the dominant economic model for the benefit of the poor, and those who see it as an entry point for products from developing economies,[24] fairtrade-labelled products succeed today because they respect many of the rules, norms, behavioural expectations, and cultural assumptions of the wealthiest markets. As Taylor (2005) observes, the challenge for fairtrade is to be in the market but not of it.

(continued...)

Distinguishing features of fairtrade include a focus on the products of small-scale, often family-based, producers (although over time fairtrade buyers have also sourced from plantations and commercial farms), and the organization of producers into politically independent democratic associations such as cooperatives. Fairtrade buyers agree to enter into long-term contracts (more than one harvest cycle) with these organizations, and to pay farmers at least the minimum price that Fairtrade Labelling Organisation International has calculated represents a fair return. Buyers also agree to pre-finance farmers so that they can avoid falling into debt, to pay for producer certification, and to pay a portion of all sales to producer organizations as a social premium to help empower and develop the producer community.

Therefore, from a fairtrade perspective, poverty is not only a factor of financial wealth, but also of impersonal commoditized relationships, power asymmetries within trading chains, lack of institutional capacity amongst poor producers, and the disadvantageous decisions producers make in consequence. Fairtrade challenges liberal economic assumptions that markets are impersonal and fair, and turns trade into a more personal relationship between grower, buyer, retailer, and consumer which requires that a managed distribution of value-added is distributed along the chain (Taylor, 2005). While this model is coming under pressure as mainstream demand for fairtrade products from processors and retailers increases, it is also noticeable that features of the fairtrade system (e.g. long-term contracts, capacity building, and buyer–producer trust) are finding their way into the companies' trading practices of larger companies, such as Starbucks' Coffee and Farmer Equity (CAFE) Practices (Macdonald, 2007).

(*Sources:* Taylor, 2005; Nicholls and Opal, 2005; Macdonald, 2007; Doherty et al., 2013)

Quick questions

1 What weaknesses in conventional trading systems does fairtrade address?

2 Why are consumers attracted to fairtrade?

3 Would the use of fairtrade certified products help defend a multinational brand from accusations that it is a cause of poverty?

Business as poverty's victim

One only needs to look at the facets of poverty set out in the Millennium Development Goals (MDGs) to see how business can be a victim of poverty. The goals are indicators of human development, and failure to achieve them is indicative of the insufficiencies that can hamper business in developing economies. For example, the fact that half the world lives on less than two dollars a day, and 1.1 billion people live in 'extreme poverty'—less than a dollar a day—shows how much greater the market for goods and services could be if only people had more income. The number of children who do not finish primary school is a warning of how difficult it can be for companies to fill even relatively low-skilled positions. Women are less likely to receive education, more likely to work at home, and less likely to obtain full-time salaried positions than men, and gender inequality and disempowerment can harm companies that need educated and independent workers and consumers.

Goals 4, 5, and 6 of the MDGs concern health (child mortality, maternal health, and major diseases such as HIV/AIDS, respectively), and high morbidity, failing health-care systems, malnutrition, and disabling or terminal diseases can all harm business. Companies such as SABMiller in South Africa have invested in programmes to prevent AIDS and provide antiretroviral drugs because of the attrition the disease was causing amongst experienced personnel. Wall (2007) shows how oil companies in Kazakhstan are having to compensate for the declining quality of state health-care provision. Indeed, authors such as Banerjee and Duflo (2011) argue that business is essential to radical solutions for tackling poverty.

Weak public governance and the failure of governments as development agents are underlying themes of the MDGs. They are equally factors in business being a victim of poverty. Though not explicit in the goals themselves, the idea that the private sector can compensate for weak government is evident in crucial agreements and policies surrounding the MDGs. For example, the 2002 Monterrey Consensus, which announced US support for the MDGs, bound the MDG implementation process to the mainstream neoliberal strategic and policy framework.[25] According to Saith (2006), one of the problems with the MDGs is that they are silent on certain important dimensions of global poverty. Rising inequality, for example, is something that poses particular threats for business. This situation creates all manner of uncertainties that risk-averse companies might rather not face, such as mass migration, conflict over natural resources, and political unrest. Moreover, it should not be forgotten that an earlier era of economic globalization in the 1900s came to a halt because of a political backlash against globalization's distributional effects.[26]

There are innumerable examples of companies addressing issues which could affect their long-term prospects, particularly in relation to education. Mining companies in Africa, such as Anglo American, have had to engage seriously with the issue of HIV/AIDS. In addition to investing in human capital, companies respond to other weaknesses in their value chain. The Forest Stewardship Council (FSC), for example, has enabled companies to reduce reputational and supply risks arising from weak governance of forest resources.[27] Cadbury launched its Cocoa Partnership to address the risk of long-term shortages of cocoa should the lack of investment by farmers continue. And one of the UN Global Compact's aims is to increase business's commitment to achieving the MDGs and their successor, the Sustainable Development Goals, due to be launched in 2015.

 Discussion points

Evidence that poverty negatively affects business prospects has attracted many companies to consider corporate responsibility as a management approach.

- Is it more important for companies to tackle issues where they cause poverty or where they are its victims?
- What are some of the main areas where business can justify its investment in tackling poverty on the grounds that it would otherwise be a victim?
- How are small and medium-sized enterprises in developing countries affected by poverty?

Business as a solution

Increasing attention is being paid to the idea of business as a solution to poverty. This is not simply a restatement of the centrality of business to the capitalist economy as the source of employment, goods and services, and wealth. Rather, it is the belief that business can consciously invest in ways that are simultaneously commercially viable and beneficial to the poor. This relates to and overlaps with ideas of social entrepreneurship, a concept with many definitions, but where typically business methods are employed for social development ends (see Chapter 11). In contrast, Hammond, Hart, and Prahalad in their influential work on the 'fortune at the bottom of the pyramid' (BOP) emphasize that there are genuine commercial market-based opportunities to be had by targeting the poor.[28] They argue that whereas the richest 0.8 billion people represent a largely saturated and overserved market, and despite there being significant opportunities to serve the 1.5 billion members of the emerging middle classes, the greatest unexplored opportunity is the five trillion dollar market of four billion people who individually or as households have low incomes, but as a group account for a significant percentage of national income and expenditure.

While these figures are controversial, given the varying income thresholds that have been suggested,[29] the insight that the poor control considerable wealth is important because it suggests that what is considered the untapped purchasing power at the BOP provides an opportunity for companies to profit by selling to these unserved or underserved markets.

If that was the extent of the BOP model's proposition, it would have little direct relevance to the idea that business can be a development agent because all it would imply is that the poor represent a rational, if overlooked, business opportunity. However, BOP advocates say that by meeting the needs of the poor, business can increase their productivity and incomes, and be an engine of empowerment, not least by allowing them to enter the formal economy. In other words, by selling to the poor, companies can help eradicate poverty. Prahalad (2005), in particular, emphasizes the role multinationals can play in this by allowing the poor to benefit from both the quality of their products and the efficiencies of their systems.

A large number of companies invest in building the capacity of local entrepreneurs—for example, in response to government policy such as the Black Economic Empowerment (BEE) programme in South Africa or as a result of business initiatives such as Business Action for Africa—and creating markets for their produce. The Shell Foundation helps link small businesses with buyers, and van Dijk and Trienekens (2012) give examples from across Africa of supply chains giving small producers access to markets. In a different way, the consultancy Accenture is giving the private sector in developing economies access to management and technological expertise through its Accenture Development Partnerships programme.

Microfinance is perhaps the most widespread example of business providing a solution to the problems of the poor. Put simply, it is a system that enables poor people without conventional collateral to access loans at affordable rates of interest, making them less dependent on traditional moneylenders and providing them with a form of savings, insurance, and investment. In recent years, several commercial banks, including Citigroup, Deutsche Bank, and ABN Amro, have offered microfinance services. There are a number of examples such as ICICI Prudential, Hindustan Lever Limited (HLL), and Grameen Phone where the infrastructure developed for microfinance has been used to develop other services such as retail and distribution.

A major criticism of the BOP theory is that it places too much emphasis on integrating the poor into consumer markets and treating them as consumers, when in fact they might be better served if they had better jobs or access to markets as producers.[30] It is inaccurate to say that BOP theory entirely ignores the role of the poor as producers. Indeed, organizations such as the Shell Foundation (e.g. through its collaboration with the retailer Marks & Spencer to promote flower-growing groups on the Agulhas Plain, South Africa) and others involved in Business Action for Africa are focused on the production opportunities for the poor, and especially the promotion of entrepreneurship.

However, within BOP theory and practice the role of the poor as consumers is very important. Many companies that identify with the BOP approach emphasize precisely this aspect. Companies such as Coca Cola and Procter & Gamble have invested in making their products available to the poor, and organizations such as KickStart (capital equipment), D.Light (sustainable energy), and Aravind (health care) specialize in serving poor communities. Vodafone is amongst the telecommunication companies that have recognized the need of migrant workers to remit money home, and has launched its mobile-phone-based M-PESA remittance system in Kenya. Companies as diverse as Philips, Intel, Infosys, and Godrej have also developed new products tailored to the needs of poor communities.

To understand the theory behind this 'consumerist' dimension of BOP, one needs to consider the situation facing many poor people. Not only do they have low incomes, but (a) they have significant unmet needs, (b) they are typically part of an informal or subsistence economy (the ILO estimates that 70 per cent of the workforce in developing economies is in the informal sector), (c) they are part of high-cost microeconomic systems where they pay more for goods and services (e.g. water is more expensive in a Nairobi slum than in central New York), (d) they are often 'prisoners' of local monopolies (e.g. moneylenders), and (e) they lack access to quality products. Therefore, according to Prahalad, if companies compete to serve the poor, the upshot will be lower living costs (e.g. because interest rates will fall), increased productivity (e.g. because if medicines are more affordable, people will be healthier), and new employment opportunities (e.g. from selling the products).

One of the issues in relation to this model as a conscious approach to tackling poverty is the degree to which, having identified the opportunity, the market alone will deliver developmental benefits. The difference between certain proponents and critics of BOP is to a degree a moral one, with the former reluctant to make choices about what the poor should have access to, and the latter arguing that high spending by some poor people on tobacco, alcohol, and gambling suggests that they do not always make 'wise' purchasing decisions. This tension is evident in case studies of the BOP,[31] but if we are thinking of business as a development agent, then it is important to distinguish between companies that serve the poor, and companies that factor poverty alleviation outcomes into their decisions and strategies. This is not straightforward. For example, at first glance it may seem that HLL's supply of shampoo to rural women is less beneficial than Aravind's provision of low-cost cataract surgery, yet this conclusion ignores the increase in rural women's incomes arising from new opportunities to sell shampoo and other household items. However, in the business–poverty context, the key point is that ultimately financial performance should be less important an indicator than social outcomes.

This is not to say that companies should approach poverty as a social enterprise where profits are unimportant,[32] although successful examples of targeting the poor such as Aravind, HealthStore Foundation, and the Grameen Bank have been run on a not-for-profit basis, or involve some form of subsidy or alternative funding. However, to be profitable can require unconventional business models, not only in terms of understanding the market or designing products, but equally in the collaborations that are required. There are various examples of companies collaborating with NGOs to identify needs and deliver products; these include the collaboration of Telenor and Grameen to create Grameen Phone, ICICI

Prudential's collaboration with women's groups in India on insurance products, and Accion International's collaboration with ABN Amro on microfinance. Brugmann and Prahalad (2007) and, more recently, Verhoef et al. (2013) view these collaborations as part of a trend towards 'co-creation' where business and NGOs or grassroots organizations create hybrid business models suited to the very different conditions for commercial and social success when dealing with poverty.

To a degree, these collaborations are about scaling up the success of NGO innovations as witnessed by the entrance of mainstream banks into the world of microfinance. However, companies such as Standard Chartered are bringing new capacities to existing sectors (e.g. raising capital for microfinance on international markets), while partnerships such as that between World Diagnostics and Ugandan NGOs allow existing networks to be used to provide new types of health service. This is not without its problems. For instance, ICICI's collaboration with women's self-help groups in India was criticized by some NGOs for undermining their wider social development goals, and there will be fundamental shifts in relationships as collaborations require NGOs to privilege task-driven partnerships with companies over ideology-driven dialogues.[33] Moreover, such partnerships are becoming a defining (and perhaps legitimating) feature of initiatives affecting the poor's access to, and control over, essential resources such as water privatization, projects associated with the Clean Development Mechanism, and now forest management in the context of voluntary emissions trading. We discuss the implications of this kind of change later, but we should recognize that in stressing partnerships with large companies, we risk further marginalizing the contribution that local small- and medium-sized companies make, and the local partnerships that they have historically been part of.

 Discussion points

Commercial opportunities linked to poverty have attracted a great deal of attention in the business community.

- Are companies justified in saying that they are benefiting the poor when they are pursuing a profit motive?

- Do you agree with Prahalad that the poor benefit as much from being seen as consumers as from becoming producers?

- What advantages do microfinance organizations have compared with conventional banks?

Assessing the business response

The previous discussion of business acting as a development agent provides a framework for the different types of interaction (i.e. based on cause, solution, and victimhood). What it does not reveal is (a) the conditions under which business will actively manage its relationship with poverty, and (b) the effectiveness of its taking on a development role. It is this we turn to now.

Features of managing poverty

The business–poverty relationship can be the focus of different spheres of business activity, such as core business operations, social investment, and philanthropy, as well as policy dialogue and advocacy.[34] As we have also seen, the actions taken may assume a variety of forms. In some instances, such as creating or destroying jobs, or choosing where to locate factories, business clearly impacts economic and social development, but does so as a development tool, not as a development agent consciously negotiating its relationship with poverty. Under what conditions might companies act as development agents?

The examples in the previous section suggest that there are three basic conditions that dictate the circumstances under which business can take on the development agent role. These are set out in Box 4.1.

Box 4.1   The three conditions of business's engagement in poverty

Condition	Examples
Condition 1: Business is more likely to act when poverty is associated with an identifiable risk to a company or industry, including risks to reputation, to the availability of commodities, to production, etc. This condition accounts for genuine innovations with respect to supply chain governance, and responsibility towards producing communities. It also accounts for some of the links created between companies and development organizations.	FWF, ETI, Worldwide Responsible Apparel Production, FLA, CAFE Practices, FSC, Cadbury's Cocoa Partnership.
Condition 2: Business is more likely to act when poverty offers a favourable return on investment (ROI). This accounts for services to underserved markets, new market opportunities for the poor, and in some cases a re-engineering of the benefits of trade in favour of the poor. Initiatives that seek to deliver what might be thought of as a social return on investment (SROI) in addition to ROI can position the poor as producer or consumer.	Fairtrade, microfinance, enterprises such as D.Light, M-PESA, or the Shakti Project, and Merrill Lynch's investment in Ulu Masen.
Condition 3: Business is more likely to act when poverty is associated with inefficiency. This accounts for initiatives to combat corruption, enhance the poor's productive capacity, increase health and safety standards, invest in education, and improve living environments.	Extractive Industry Transparency Initiative, investment in AIDS prevention by firms such as SABMiller and L'Oréal, and the education programmes of companies such as Anglo American and Cisco Systems.

Any of the initiatives undertaken by business as a development agent mentioned in this chapter can be explained by appeal to one or other of those three conditions. Likewise, dimensions to development that lie outside the scope of these conditions are unlikely to be addressed by business overtly. For example, redistributive elements such as corporate taxation, though part of debates about development economics, are not normally incorporated into normative debates about the responsibilities of business. Neither is there any thorough consideration of power and conflict, even though some of the areas where business affects development are historically the sites of dispute and tension (e.g. relations between buyers and small contract farmers or outgrowers). The gender dimensions to poverty are frequently ignored, and this is part of a general pattern of preferencing, where the individual good is preferred to the communal, financial wealth is favoured over non-financial, and issues such as class, ethnicity, sexuality, and other determinants of privilege are discounted or isolated from their wider context. It is not that these dimensions are absent from debates about development; indeed, it is their importance to development theory that makes their absence from corporate responsibility in the development context so noticeable. These and other types of exclusion will be more apparent when we look at the impact of corporate responsibility (see Chapter 12).

 Discussion points

Risk, profitability, and inefficiency are the conditions that underpin any business investment as a development agent.

- Can you imagine a situation where business would make such an investment even though these conditions were not met?
- What sorts of inefficiency in developing countries are significant for business?
- What issues in developing countries will business tackle in 2020 that they are not addressing today?

Business's impact on development

Despite the many examples of business seeking to act as a development agent, there remains criticism that not enough is being done, or that the impact of what is being done is unclear. Blowfield and Dolan (2014) argue that business does not yet fulfil the criteria for being a proper development agent, not least because it does not hold itself up to account for its development impacts. They argue that even though companies are acting voluntarily, there is a case to be made that they are renegotiating their social and environmental responsibilities in ways that meet the requirements of commercial competitiveness rather than societal good. Certainly the three conditions of business acting as a development agent set out in the previous section are all rooted in business self-interest. It is evidence of this kind of shift (e.g. in relation to pensions, labour relations, and taxation) that make some people fearful of companies acting as development agents because ultimately they might pick and choose what constitutes societal good and co-opt the development process. Private sector involvement can be seen as part of a process of neoconstitutionalism whereby those involved in managing the global economy see their rights being secured in law, but are increasingly isolated from popular scrutiny.[35]

There is certainly evidence that business interacts with development in particular ways, and reason to be concerned that it constricts the meaning of development itself.[36] As the business-poverty framework shows, it is something that can lead companies to rethink their relationships, but does not fundamentally alter them. Ponte et al. (2011) and Schwittay (2011) make the case that the standards used to improve social and environmental performance in supply chains or the theory behind BOP have resulted in poverty being reconstructed around a business logic. However, elements of the business response (e.g. the adaptation of conventional management tools and concepts for development purposes, the depoliticization of economic opportunity, and the reduction of complex social, cultural, and economic factors to technical problems) are characteristic of contemporary development itself.[37] Therefore, it may be harder to argue that business co-opts development than to make the case that business as a development agent mirrors the established norms of the predominant development discourse.

Rather than examining business's role as development agent as subversive either to business or to development, we have concentrated on the possibilities and limitations of business's current and likely contribution. In much of the mainstream literature on business and development there is a tendency to stress the generic strengths of private enterprise to explain the significance of the role of business in development (e.g. client focus, ability to raise capital, and specific skills, tools, and competencies). However, the role that any single company or industry can play is greatly affected by the type of relationship it has with poverty (e.g. victim or cause), whether offensive or defensive strategies are pursued (see 'The business–poverty framework'), and the location and context (e.g. whether or not there is a functioning civil society and state regulatory capacity). Too often, in making the case for business to act as a development agent, advocates overlook the context-specific variables and complexities that can ultimately influence outcomes in a given situation as much as flaws in execution can.

Yet even such contextual variables are of secondary importance to the three conditions that predicate any corporate engagement in development, i.e. the association of poverty with risk, opportunity, and inefficiency. The examples of business responses in this chapter demonstrate that at least one of these conditions needs to be met for companies to act as development agents. However, knowledge of how the conditions influence development is far from complete, and to date success has been measured in terms of the instrumental benefit for companies, not the developmental benefit for communities. Various recent studies have raised doubts about the empirical benefits of fairtrade, microfinance, and the bottom of the pyramid.[38] While the poor may participate, they do not have the means to hold others to account for the outcomes. Similarly, while a positive association between poverty and ROI can stimulate companies to deliver a SROI, there can be a tension between developmental outcomes and commercial imperatives, evident, for example, in how the demand for certified timber has been met largely by sourcing from developed rather than developing nations, and concerns that the expansion of fairtrade is weakening the relationships between producers, buyers, and consumers. The emphasis on the financial success of initiatives of this kind, and the limited information on the social impacts, suggest that developmental consequences can be lost or overlooked once ROI attracts more attention than SROI.

Recognizing these conditions is an important step in understanding the parameters of possibility for business as a development agent, and in particular what dimensions of poverty are likely to be included or excluded. However, we should not treat these parameters as static, and it may be too early to pass judgment on what is possible given instances such as the recent change in emphasis from simply expecting suppliers to comply with standards, to major brands working with supplier management and workers to increase local capacity, including creating spaces in oppressive regimes where workers can organize and collaborate. This offers the promise of a more effective way of dealing with reputational issues arising from allegations of exploitation.

At the same time, certain aspects of social development that complement the interests of business are being normalized, and this could explain why they appear less likely to be critiqued. These include, for instance, flexible labour markets in contrast to the emphasis on secure employment in previous eras, private ownership of natural resources, and the free flow of capital. While it is hard to claim that business's role in development exacerbates such trends in a significant way, there are issues of legitimization and delegitimization that need to be addressed. Corporate responsibility plays an important role in framing our understanding of poverty and development. For example, modern management rationalism has been incorporated into the way poverty is understood and approached. Similarly, there are examples where a term such as empowerment has come to be associated with a business quality such as entrepreneurship, thereby imbuing business behaviour with a new moral creditworthiness.[39] This is problematic morally if notions of good come to be reassessed using commercial criteria,[40] but also from a technical developmental perspective where a distinction has to be drawn between very different types of entrepreneurs, some of whom play an essential role in growth and innovation that is conducive to poverty reduction, while others create few jobs and have little security.

Nonetheless, there are examples of issues that are developmentally important being accommodated, even though this means challenging conventional business wisdom as we have seen with the accommodation of practices with their roots in fairtrade. London and Hart (2010) highlight how initiatives are becoming more sophisticated over time, and similar trends are evident in the overview of multinational labour standards by Mosley (2011). As Kolk and Van Tulder (2006) show in the context of voluntary standards, a variety of pressures contribute to what is ultimately legitimized or ignored, and often what emerges is a 'sector-conditioned morality' that reflects a minimum level of expectation from civil society on the one hand, and a ceiling level acceptable to an industry on the other.

The experience of corporate responsibility and business as a development agent suggests that development ends can best be served when there is genuine collaboration whereby different sectors pursue shared or complementary poverty objectives. This conclusion can be challenged on the grounds that it relies on evidence about large companies, and says nothing about the smaller firms and informal sector that are such an important feature of developing economies. It also disregards changes associated with the new influx of foreign direct investment from countries such as China and India, and the different types of relationship that may emerge as a result, just as it ignores the role that large domestic companies played in the development of countries such as Singapore, Taiwan, and South Korea. However, even if consideration of these dimensions to business in developing economies revealed very different features of managing the relationship with society, a significant part of the business community would still be looking to employ collaborative models.

Nevertheless, based on the current pattern of corporate engagement in development, there are reasons to think that increasingly sophisticated models of partnership will be appealing (see Chapter 9). However, a stumbling block could be the unwillingness of companies to be accountable for development objectives in any rigorous way. A test of how far this can be overcome may be the recent wave of socially oriented entrepreneurs claiming a blend of social and commercial vision (see Chapter 11). If these find viable ways to demonstrate social returns, they may influence other companies that recognize a role as development agent, but limit their accountability to internal rationalization.

Case study 4   Poverty as a business opportunity: M-PESA

Mobile telephony is having a huge impact in Africa where the relatively cheap infrastructure is helping to bridge the gap caused by poor transport and communications infrastructure. In Kenya, for example, one in three adults carries a mobile phone, and in five years the number of mobiles in Kenya has grown from one million to 6.5 million, compared with 300,000 landlines. One driver of the boom is the large population of economic migrants eager to stay in touch with their home communities. Migrant workers are a main source of income in many rural areas, but one challenge is how to remit money home given the lack of banks and unsafe roads.

Vodafone is the world's second-largest wireless phone services carrier with more than 200 million customers and sales of $50 billion. Although most of its business is in Europe, it has interests in companies worldwide, including Safaricom in Kenya, and is increasingly looking to penetrate developing markets. In Africa, there are only sixteen mobile phones for every hundred people, compared with Europe where there is more than one phone per head. Recognition of this market potential and the unique contribution that mobile phones could play in meeting consumer needs led to the introduction of M-PESA.

At first glance, there is nothing spectacular about M-PESA. For the user, it is simply an extra line on their mobile phone menu that says 'Send Money'. The subscriber goes to a shop, adds funds to their phone account, and then sends them to friends, family, or anyone else with a mobile. The recipient goes to a similar shop, shows the code on the mobile and some ID, and collects the money.

Yet in Kenya where bank accounts and plastic money are scarce, and carrying cash on journeys can leave you prey to robbers, the M-PESA money transfer system is a genuine innovation. It is not the brainchild of the conventional banking system, but an entirely new product, developed by Vodafone and Safaricom, part-funded by the British government's Department for International Development (DFID), and piloted with the help of the Kenyan microfinance institution Faulu.

M-PESA was launched commercially in March 2007 after a two-year trial period, and Safaricom CEO Michael Joseph says that there are over two million active users: *'We also know that it channels over Kenyan Shillings (KSh) 100 million in a day. ... I see it getting to three or four million customers very soon'*.

According to M-PESA pioneer Nick Hughes, the idea came about at the 2002 World Summit on Sustainable Development in a conversation with someone from DFID about what Vodafone could do to address the Millennium Development Goals. One area where he thought Vodafone could play a role was making it easier to move money around so that entrepreneurs and others had better access to finance. Returns on investment would not be great, and it was likely that, as with many ideas linked to social development, this one would lose out to others in the internal competition to allocate project funding. However, DFID ran a challenge fund offering capital to help ideas that were useful to developing countries circumvent the constraints of company product development processes. With the government offering 50 per cent matching funding, what would otherwise have been seen as a low-yield low-priority project started to look like an interesting idea. However, making the idea a reality presented a variety of challenges ranging from new software to the systems and capabilities of Safaricom, introducing the product to Safaricom's staff and distributors, and working with the Faulu savings groups on product testing.

None of these hurdles has proved insurmountable, and overcoming them may have put M-PESA in a stronger position in the long run because the internal support and external relations are much stronger than before. Soon after its launch, M-PESA was being talked about as a serious competitor to existing money transfer agencies, and Safaricom has started an aggressive campaign to extend the number of subscribers by partnering with established financial institutions such as Equity Bank and Post Bank.

An unintended consequence of M-PESA is how it has spawned new enterprises. M-PESA is no longer just about sending money—the brand has grown organically, taking on a life of its own. Pioneer Nick Hughes, has launched M-KOPA, a solar energy company that allows M-PESA account-holders to buy solar-powered electricity in instalments. Rural customers can use their accounts to buy crop

(continued...)

insurance and their phones to check on the weather and market prices. Such initiatives have created an appetite in rural areas for further innovation that is building the conditions for markets for local entrepreneurs such as KickStart, a manufacturer of low-cost irrigation. The service is also being expanded beyond Kenya. Vodafone has set up M-PAISA in Afghanistan, and its Vodacom subsidiary has launched M-PESA in Tanzania.

(*Sources:* original research; Hughes and Lonie, 2007; Akumu, 2008; Blowfield and Johnson, 2013)

Questions

1 M-PESA was part-funded by the British government which saw its potential to contribute to its goals of poverty alleviation.

   a How does M-PESA contribute towards the Millennium Development Goals?

   b Is M-PESA an example of business acting as a development agent?

   c Do you think expansion of M-PESA will depend on continuing government support?

2 M-PESA is a product aimed at poor and marginalized consumers.

   a Is it a good example of a company identifying commercial opportunities at the 'bottom of the pyramid'?

   b Is it a financially viable business model?

   c What impacts has it had on poor consumers?

3 M-PESA's funding model allowed it to compete for internal resources.

   a Do you think that the service's success will have a significant impact on either Vodafone or Safaricom in the future?

   b How might their behaviour change?

   c How might Safaricom build on this success as it attempts to expand its services in East Africa?

Summary

When we examine the role of business as a development agent today, what we are witnessing is part of a constantly shifting debate about business's contribution to society that plays out differently according to place, time, and culture, but is ultimately about how the norms and values of capitalism, as embodied in modern enterprise, can be accommodated, harnessed, and utilized for societal good. The framework of business's interactions with poverty used in this chapter shows that, even if a company focuses on its financial mission, there can be good reasons to consciously manage the relationship with society. Consequently, there are companies that are mindful of poverty, and are showing a degree of innovation in how they respond. But they have a narrow perspective on what to be accountable for and to whom, and the incentives to be more rigorous about this are lacking. At present, the conditions under which business engages in poverty alleviation are rooted in self-interest, even if responses differ depending on what is meant by that term. What are often called countervailing agents have made some progress in expanding this definition of self-interest, but these government and non-government actors have had more success in getting companies to commit to development objectives than they have in holding them to account for delivering on them. By clarifying how business relates to poverty, and under what conditions it chooses to act as a development agent, it might be easier to hold companies to account and make it in their interests to be more accountable. Without this accountability there is likely to be a randomness and unpredictability to business's interpretation of its responsibilities, leaving open the possibility that for all the justification for business to be a development agent, it will remain a development maverick.

Further reading

online
resource
centre

www.oxfordtextbooks.co.uk/orc/blowfield_murray3e/
    Visit the Online Resource Centre that accompanies this book to enrich your understanding of this chapter. Among the resources available are web links, exercises, and additional case studies.

Banerjee, A.V. & Duflo, E. 2011, *Poor economics*, Public Affairs, New York.
    An engaging look at economics from the poor's perspective.

Clay, J. 2005, *Exploring the links between international business and poverty reduction: a case study of Unilever in Indonesia*, Oxfam, Oxford.
    Innovative study of how a multinational company affects the economy of a country.

Prahalad, C.K. & Hart, S.L. 2002, 'The fortune at the bottom of the pyramid', *Strategy & Business*, no. 26, pp 2–14.
    The initial exposition of an idea of business and poverty that has captured the imagination of people around the world.

Rajak, D. 2011, *In good company: an anatomy of corporate social responsibility*, Stanford, CA, Stanford University Press.
    An anthropologist's take on the role of business in development.

Utting, P. & Marques, J.C. (eds) 2009, *Corporate social responsibility and regulatory governance: towards inclusive development?* Palgrave MacMillan, New York.
    Collection of essays highlighting some of the more troublesome aspects of business's role in development.

WBCSD 2007, *Doing business with the world: the new role of corporate leadership in global development*, World Business Council for Sustainable Development, Geneva.
    Examples of the business case for involvement in development.

Online resources

- Additional case study on private sector alternatives to weak governance
- Facts and figures on global poverty
- Teaching notes on chapter case study
- Exercises and discussion topics for students
- Additional reading and web-based resources

Endnotes

1. This chapter draws heavily on Blowfield, 2010.
2. See, for example, Fig, 2007; Newell and Muro, 2006; Robins, 2007; Glover, 2007.
3. Clay, 2005; Kapstein, 2008.
4. Levy and Newell, 2002; Blowfield, 2005.
5. Newell and Frynas, 2007.
6. Ireland and Pillay, 2009.
7. Utting, 2007.
8. Bond, 2006.
9. Kolk and Van Tulder, 2006.
10. Kolk and Van Tulder, 2006.
11. Kolk and Van Tulder, 2006.
12. Chang, 2002.
13. Raynolds et al., 2004.
14. Graham and Woods, 2006.
15. Chan and Siu, 2007.
16. Pearson, 2007.
17. Blowfield, 2004.
18. Pearson, 2007.
19. Jenkins, 2005.
20. Macdonald, 2007.
21. Fig, 2007.
22. Graham and Woods, 2006.
23. Macdonald, 2007.
24. Raynolds et al., 2004.
25. Bond, 2006.
26. O'Rourke and Williamson, 1999.
27. Taylor, 2005.
28. Prahalad and Hart, 2002; Prahalad, 2005; Hart, 2005; Hammond et al., 2007.
29. Hammond et al., 2007; Karnani, 2007.
30. Karnani, 2007.
31. See, for example, contributions to Rangan et al., 2007.
32. Contrast with Karnani, 2007.
33. Brugmann and Prahalad, 2007.
34. Brainard, 2006.
35. Sum, 2009.
36. Blowfield, 2005.
37. Ferguson, 1990.
38. Elyachar, 2012; Hermes and Lensink, 2011; Ansari et al., 2012.
39. Rajak, 2006.
40. Blowfield and Dolan, 2008.

5

Globalization and corporate responsibility

 Chapter overview

In this chapter, we explore the importance of globalization for corporate responsibility, and how it accounts for some of the ways that corporate responsibility has evolved. In particular, we will:

- discuss different meanings of globalization;
- identify the main areas in which globalization has had an impact;
- discuss the ways in which globalization has altered trade, production, and investment;
- consider how globalization influences governance and the implications of this for corporate responsibility;
- explore corporate responsibility as a business response to the challenges of globalization, identifying what it addresses and examining why some feel it is inadequate;
- examine stakeholder partnerships as a response to the aspects of globalization.

 Main topics

Globalization and corporate responsibility   99
The meaning of 'globalization'   99
Influence of globalization on business   104
Corporate responsibility as a response to globalization   109
Unmet challenges   117

Key terms

Globalization   Civil society

Deterritorialization   International development

Liberal economics   Self-regulation

Global governance   Stakeholder partnerships

Globalization and corporate responsibility

In Chapter 2, we saw how the relationship of business with society has altered during different historical periods. Now we are in a new era—globalization—which is bringing changes
that are as momentous as those of the Industrial Revolution. Writers such as Wood et al.
(2006), Pedersen and Huniche (2006), and Crane et al. (2013) tie corporate responsibility to
the social, political, and environmental challenges of globalization. In fact, to some degree,
its success may influence the direction of globalization overall.[1] This is because globalization is associated, on the one hand, with a limited set of global governance mechanisms
and weakened national governments, and, on the other, with unprecedented private sector
wealth, power, and impact. Corporate responsibility has thus become an important means
for addressing what Stiglitz (2002) sees as the fundamental problem with contemporary globalization—a system of global governance without global government.

In this chapter, we examine the implications of globalization for corporate responsibility, and
how that accounts for particular aspects of corporate responsibility such as stakeholder partnerships. But to put that in context, we need first to reflect on the meaning of globalization itself.

The meaning of 'globalization'

We touched on different meanings of globalization in Chapter 2, in particular the distinction between globalization as an economic construct, and as a social condition called deterritorialization. To clarify this more it can help to think of ice cream. Growing up in the UK,
we remember summers consuming Wall's ice creams, and it was a shock to go to France
and Spain to find that there were brands called Miko and Frigo, with very different ideas
about what an ice cream should be. Travel to far-off Indonesia and one did not find any ice
cream brands, only locally produced, garishly coloured lollies, sold from home-made insu-
lated boxes. Today, Walls, Miko, and Frigo are all part of Unilever: they all market identically
tasting, identically packaged Magnums and Cornettos; the products are developed at a single
Unilever laboratory, and a shop in Toronto will sell the same products as the teams of bicycle-
riding sellers in Indonesian villages.

These changes are emblematic not of the power of brands so much as what some theorists
believe constitutes a fundamental change in our social conditions, particularly:

1 new or intensified social networks, leading to the creation of new social orders that
   transcend traditional political, cultural, economic, and geographical boundaries;

2 stretched and expanded social relations, activities, and interdependencies, leading to the
   emergence of powerful organizations that are not linked to a specific place (e.g. global
   corporations, international NGOs, and international crime syndicates and terrorists);

3 intensified and accelerated interaction between these networks and organizations, so
   that what happens in one area can be shaped by events anywhere in the world;

4 a growing consciousness of our interconnectedness and interdependence, so that
   people do not simply observe globalization—it is something that is shaping who we are
   and how we act in the world.[2]

Instagrams from friends in Thailand, blogging and tweeting, and commercial transactions with people we never meet are all manifestations of this shift. Snapshot 5.1 shows the consequences of these four phenomena and how they have at once allowed an industry to prosper, but also subjected it to unprecedented public scrutiny. It also shows some of the ways in which globalization is interpreted as both beneficial and damaging. It is to the merits and criticisms of globalization that we now turn.

 Snapshot 5.1   Globalization and Kenya's rose growing industry

Non-existent before 1990, the Kenya cut-flower industry is now one of that country's major economic success stories, exporting over $100 million of produce to Europe annually. It is also portrayed as an example of the success and failure of globalization—an industry that has captured significant export earnings, and introduced new technologies and investment to one of the world's poorest nations, but an industry that is blamed for damaging the environment, exploiting women, endangering workers, and damaging local communities.

In part, the industry grew out of Washington Consensus policy reforms that made it easier to invest in Kenya and export to Europe. However, the industry is also a result of technological innovations that accelerated the impact of these policies. The removal of barriers to trade and investment created the opportunity for European entrepreneurs to establish flower farms around Lake Nayvasha to serve the European market. But equally, getting freshly cut flowers to European supermarkets was only made possible by improvements in transport and storage technology, and by a downward trend in transportation costs.

The same industry is also an example of what has been called the 'dark side' of globalization. Environmental experts claim that the water levels of Lake Nayvasha have gone down and that local towns suffer water shortages. There are questions about the environmental cost of airfreighting flowers from one continent to another. The influx of migrant workers has taxed the infrastructure of local towns, while on-farm accommodation is sometimes overcrowded and insanitary. Wages are low by European standards, and the mostly casual workforce can work long hours during peak periods, such as in the run-up to Valentine's Day, and then be left without employment when demand slackens off.

Complaints about the industry have attracted attention from the European media, international NGOs and unions, development agencies, and, not least, the major retailers that have made Kenya Europe's number one source of imported flowers. The industry has adopted a code of labour and environmental practice, and has collaborated with European-based companies, NGOs, and trade unions on a two-year programme to improve working conditions. Despite being an economic success story, by 2005 the industry was being widely portrayed (in the title of one television documentary) as *Costing the Earth*.

(*Sources:* Dolan and Opondo, 2005; ETI, 2005b; O'Reilly, 2005; Kangogo et al., 2013)

Quick questions

1. Do you think that the initial arguments that any such impacts were more than outweighed by the jobs created, the export earnings, the technology transfer, and other economic benefits are valid?

2. Do you feel that Kenya's producers were justified in seeing European protests as protectionism?

3. Should retailers have the right to set social and environmental standards for their suppliers?

Globalization—a tale of the glass half full

Few would deny that globalization is problematic. The free flow of goods, services, and capital has helped to reduce the percentage of people in developing countries living on less than $1.25 from 52 per cent in 1981 to 20 per cent today. Yet, because of population growth, the number of extremely poor people worldwide has only fallen by 0.19 billion in that time.[3] Even globalization's supporters refer to the unavoidable pain involved and the need to have faith that it is ultimately for the good. Some of that good we experience today. Since 1990, the volume of international trade has increased enormously, and even during the recent recession continued to grow by an average 3 per cent a year.[4] This has created jobs in many countries, allowed new industries to emerge, encouraged the transfer of technology, increased the flow of capital, and, for the well-educated at least, has allowed people to pursue opportunities across the world. It has also meant that until the 2000s, at least, international competiveness kept prices stable, and this has been an important factor underlying low inflation in advanced economies.

Moreover, growth has not been confined to the major industrialized countries, as shown by the phenomenal expansion of the Chinese and Indian economies. And while China and India account for a disproportionate amount of foreign direct investment, other developing countries have entered the global economy as suppliers of everything from flipflops to flowers and, increasingly, as consumer markets themselves. Moreover, economic recession in the West has not stopped these trends, in part because inter-regional trade between developing countries is increasing.

What is good for business is meant to be good for society as a whole, and many have benefited from new opportunities, new technology, and the cultural shifts that phenomena such as urbanization have brought. Whether because of class, educational opportunity, or entrepreneurship, many people have seen their life expectations expand by virtue of the new types of skilled employment that have been created. The most fortunate have been able to pursue opportunities in stable prosperous economies as multinational companies increasingly embark on a global war for talent.

Economists and politicians agree that, in a capitalist or free enterprise system, economic growth is essential for long-term prosperity, and international free trade is held to be vital for sustainable growth and equity. Therefore, for many policy-makers and politicians, globalization is nothing short of essential for global prosperity, demanding the removal of government-imposed trade and investment barriers, increased integration of markets across national boundaries, and the spread of market-oriented policies around the world.[5] These elements were characteristics of the first era of liberal globalization that started in the nineteenth century, the end of which is blamed on a revival of government controls and the closing down of economic interdependence which ultimately ushered in decades of conflict and instability in the twentieth century. For Martin Wolf, the significance of liberal globalization is not only that it fosters economic growth: *'Liberalism is ... far more than a purely economic creed. It is the bedrock of democracy at home and peaceful relations abroad'.*[6] As Friedman (2005) has observed, no two countries with McDonald's franchises have ever gone to war.

Wolf's belief, therefore, goes further than those who say globalization is simply about economics. In the traditions of Adam Smith and Hayek, he treats the rights to freedom and property, democratic government, the rule of law, and a supportive values system as being as important as liberalizing markets. Although individual elements may develop at different speeds, ultimately this is the full package that globalization both depends upon and promises. Therefore the benefits of globalization are not simply economic growth, but the particular cultural, political, and ethical model associated with the liberal democracies of Europe, North America, and other 'Western' societies. All of this leads Wolf to conclude that, for all of globalization's shortcomings, *'the world needs more globalization, not less'*.[7]

Globalization—a tale of the glass half empty

Economic globalization has not been an unmitigated success, and corporate responsibility is, to some degree, a response to its excesses. However, it is also one of the methods that companies and others have used to navigate the new terrain associated with globalization that is not necessarily good or bad, but simply different from preceding eras. We look at two areas of globalization criticism, as follows:

1   wealth, poverty, and equity;
2   universalization of norms, values, and culture.

Wealth, poverty, and equity

In 2002, Joseph Stiglitz provided a wake-up call to those who felt that criticism of globalization was misguided. It was one thing for what Wolf labels *'antiglobalization.com'* to protest about injustice, poverty, and environmental degradation; it was quite another when a one-time chief economist of the World Bank appeared to be joining their ranks. Yet Stiglitz's conclusion was that, for millions, globalization is a failure: *'Many have actually been made worse off, as they have seen their jobs destroyed and their lives become more insecure.'*[8]

He argues that the policies that have created the conditions for overseas companies to set up factories, or source from suppliers in countries that hitherto had adopted policies of protectionism and import substitution, have led to the promotion of market solutions to the challenges of welfare and equity. Hardt and Negri (2000), for example, argue that globalization needs to be understood as a 'grid of power', informed by the ways in which capitalism copes with the overproduction, high labour costs, and devaluation that block the capitalist process once markets become saturated. For Stiglitz (2002), however, the issue is not the intractable logic of capitalism, but the way in which globalization is implemented and how rich countries use their power to their advantage in institutions such as the World Bank, the International Monetary Fund, and the World Trade Organization. He counters those opposed to government intervention and restrictions on the free market, arguing that the countries that have benefited most from globalization are those, such as China and India, in which governments have challenged the notion of self-regulating markets and taken charge of their own destiny. As Chang (2010) has argued forcefully, successful developing economies have typically been the ones that have not adopted neoliberal free market prescriptions.

However, globalization affects all countries, not just emerging economies. In developed economies, once major industries such as steel production have shrunk, if not vanished, and the number of manufacturing jobs has declined. The offshoring of certain types of blue-collar job has been followed by that of white-collar jobs, such as data processing, computer programming, and research and development. There is public anxiety as to whether new jobs—and especially well-paying jobs—will be created in their place.[9] As predicted by early globalization theorists such as Beck et al. (1994), the nature of employment is changing. Repeatedly, surveys in the richest countries point to longer working days, stress, job insecurity, and difficulties in balancing working lives with personal lives as causes of public concern. The 2013 *Great British Class Survey*, identified a new class it called the 'precariat', people whose daily lives are the most precarious and insecure, not least because of globalization's impacts.[10] It highlighted that as important as traditional divisions between skilled and unskilled, white collar and blue collar, are the distinctions between those of classes in secure employment and underclasses, such as illegal migrants and 'guest workers', without secure employment. This is not to say, however, that being a migrant is itself a disadvantage; on the contrary, according to Bauman (1998), mobility is a coveted value because it allows people to follow opportunities.

Universalization of norms, values, and culture

Globalization is often portrayed in terms of how it affects society and culture, and, in particular, how some see it as spreading the values, ethics, and institutions of the West. MacLean (1999) argues that a key feature of globalization that distinguishes it from its historical antecedents is that it fosters, legitimizes, and universalizes a transcending form of knowledge, especially in respect to political, economic, ethical, and social ideas. For Wolf (2004), this is one of its benefits; for Klein (1999), it is one of its dangers. Whatever stance one takes, the idea that globalization alters the world in this way is a powerful one.

There are many empirical studies of how particular industries and companies have affected local populations, especially those of indigenous peoples who, by definition, live in non-capitalist societies. Logging, mining, oil and gas drilling and pipelines, and industrial agriculture have all been in the spotlight for the ways in which they affect indigenous people's land, livelihoods, and lifestyles.[11] The impact is not necessarily as simple as appropriating resources or putting people out of work. It can also involve changes in basic social institutions so that, for example, communal land becomes privately owned, or diverse economic livelihoods are replaced with daily-waged labour.[12]

Such examples can be seen as evidence of more fundamental assertions of power. Various authors have argued that, in addition to understanding how organizations and individuals operate in the new networks and alliances that globalization is producing, we need to understand the underlying biases that favour particular norms and values,[13] and how the technologies and techniques that we use to analyse, control, and regulate globalization extend or limit the possibilities for change as much as the actions of any actor.

One of the reasons for considering partnerships in the context of globalization later in this chapter is because what they reveal about this distinction between overt actors and underlying agency has a significant impact on corporate responsibility, and helps to explain some of its successes and failures. It also helps to explain why corporate responsibility is sometimes accused of spreading particular values, or of failing to accommodate others' world views.[14] In terms of understanding the meaning of globalization, it alerts us to the fact that even seemingly neutral views can be charged with norms, values, and meanings that legitimate and advance specific interests. Indeed, building on Gramsci's political theory, Levy and Newell (2005) argue that the moral and intellectual leadership role exhibited by business in areas such as corporate responsibility is a contemporary example of how, throughout history, powerful forces rule through consensus and hegemony.

 Discussion points

Liberal globalization theorists, such as Wolf and Henderson, take umbrage with companies and others that support corporate responsibility.

- What are the main reasons for their hostility?
- Do you think that there are shifts within corporate responsibility thinking that address their concerns?
- Referring to examples such as Unilever's work with Oxfam in Indonesia and theorists such as Stiglitz and Porritt, how would you refute Wolf and Henderson's arguments to a business audience?

Influence of globalization on business

Business is often portrayed as a beneficiary of globalization, but there is truth, falsehood, and myth in such a belief. Under globalization, many of the norms and values suited to private enterprise have been given preferential status, but commerce has prospered under all manner of different political and economic regimes—to say that business benefits from globalization is no more or less true than to say that enterprise flourished under mercantile capitalism or protectionism. However, the nature of business has undoubtedly changed in ways that have special significance for corporate responsibility.

Global capital, production, and trade

For business, the most important outcome of globalization has been the enormous increases in international trade and investment. In the last half of the twentieth century, the value of world trade soared from $57 billion to $6 trillion. This has gone hand in glove with the liberalization of financial transactions, whereby a combination of technological advances and policies to remove credit controls, deregulate interest rates, and privatize banking has created much greater investment opportunities. Today, global business-to-business transactions are worth about $6 trillion, and the world's financial markets are becoming more like networks in cyberspace that can relay billions of trades almost instantaneously.[15]

This does not mean that what happens globally is divorced from the local. The consequence of over-zealous selling of mortgages to poor Americans—while in some ways promoted as a socially beneficial act—ricocheted around the world, and in turn exposed corruption and incompetence from Bear Sterns to BayernLB to Dubai's Sovereign Wealth Fund. Perhaps more important in the long term, the unprecedentedly high levels of household and corporate debt in developed economies are only affordable because of the willingness of emerging economies to buy it, marking a historic shift from when developed economies bailed out poorer countries during economic crises to a new era—not imagined by supporters of the Washington Consensus (see Snapshot 5.1)—when weak economies come to the aid of stronger ones.[16]

Speculative investment has increased due to the ease of conducting fast low-cost transactions. Global investment has also led to industry consolidation and increased foreign ownership, not least of formerly state-owned companies. Indeed, globalization challenges the very idea of an American or European company given how shares are owned around the world. What unites many globalization sceptics is what is viewed as an unhealthy growth in corporate power and alarm at facts such as that a third of world trade occurs between multinational corporations, or that five companies control the global market for consumer durables.[17] At times, the growing presence of multinationals has been highly contentious, as the case of the utilities sector demonstrates (see Snapshot 5.2). It has also provoked fears about security, the global power balance, and other national imperatives. The flood of foreign direct investment from China into Africa to acquire natural resource rights, the rise of sovereign wealth funds buying swathes of land and water resources, and 'foreign ownership' of strategic assets from ports to power plants have all generated controversy. Yet this is just a continuation of a trend started by freeing up trade and capital flows which created the conditions necessary for shifting certain aspects of production to new locations. As countries, such as Malaysia, Indonesia, and, later, China, removed barriers to foreign investment, companies from developed economies rushed to them, either to invest directly or to source from new vendors. Today, we take it for granted that goods and services, from training shoes to banking, can be delivered from around the world, but it is important not to overstate the degree to which poorer countries have succeeded in attracting capital and accessing markets.[18] For all of the focus on multinational firms in India and China, the bulk of investment remains within developed economies and there are still significant barriers in some industries for developing countries to access wealthy markets.[19] Moreover, investment in developing countries is often centred on export processing zones (EPZs) offering financial incentives to investors, and even labour and environmental regulations and enforcement policies that are different to those that are available elsewhere in the country.

Claims about the wealth of corporations being on a par with that of many governments may be exaggerated,[20] and corporate responsibility is full of examples demonstrating that wealth and power are not always synonymous. Nonetheless, the behaviour of multinational companies on a global stage is an important part of corporate responsibility's story and, as we examine later in the chapter ('Corporate responsibility as a response to globalization', p 117), sets important parameters for what corporate responsibility addresses and how.

 Snapshot 5.2 Water—privatizing basic rights or giving access to basic needs?

Water is essential to life, yet the amount of accessible water per person worldwide is falling. This is why water is a global issue, with the private sector at its centre. Over 150 years after John Snow discovered the link between water and cholera, 1.1 billion people are still without access to clean water, 2.4 billion lack proper sanitary provision, and a slum dweller in Nairobi or Accra pays more per litre of water than a resident of Manhattan or Geneva.

The global water crisis is more about management than true scarcity. The current supply of fresh water is a small percentage of our planet's total water, yet it would be more than enough for the world population's current needs if it were more evenly distributed. Unfortunately, that is not the

(continued...)

case. According to the UN Environmental Programme, demand for water will soon exceed availability by 56 per cent and two-thirds of the world's population will face water stress. Major investments in infrastructure and management are needed to amend this problem—challenges that the private sector would seem well suited to tackle.

Yet private sector interventions have met considerable resistance in some regions. Privatization of water utilities in Europe encouraged organizations, such as the World Bank, to promote private sector involvement to reach 2.4 billion new consumers by 2015 in order to meet the Millennium Development Goals. However, the major water companies were accused of privatizing water sources, and have repeatedly been under the media spotlight for cutting off poor consumers and favouring rich customers. In Bolivia, Argentina, and the Philippines, major utilities companies terminated government contracts.

At the heart of the protests is that, for many, water is not simply a human need, but a human right. Some feel that by calling water a 'need', it opens the door to privatization and provision on a for-profit basis, whereas declaring water to be a 'right' might be used to prevent companies from buying up water sources. There are some signs that a middle ground may be reached and that the private sector should be considered neither panacea nor pariah. Talking to fellow business leaders, George Kuper, President of the Council of Great Lakes Industry, said business had a key role to play in making water accessible, but that it had no need to own the resource.

(*Sources:* Gleick, 1999; FAO, 2003; UN, 2003; Rulli et al., 2013)

Quick questions

1 Is the distinction between water as a human need and a human right valid?

2 What are the implications of this distinction for business?

3 Is it accurate to see access to water as a 'management problem', as politicians and business leaders have tended to?

The changing nature of governance and enforcement

Mention of the different, often more lenient, regulatory regimes enjoyed by companies in EPZs is an example of how globalization is connected to changes in how society is governed. In part, this is because liberal globalization depends on the slew of policy changes described earlier. At the same time, deterritorialization creates a new space that cannot readily be governed by existing governance structures, such as national governments, or even the international mechanisms housed within the United Nations. For example, a national government can legislate on toxic emissions, but once those emissions affect the global commons, a multinational solution is required.

There are a few long-established institutions with an international regulatory mandate—notably the International Labour Organization (ILO) which, since the end of World War I, has brought national governments, the business community, and international trade unions together to set and enforce international labour standards. There are also national laws applying to actions overseas, such as the US Alien Tort Claims Act 1789 which has been used to hold US companies to account for human rights violations around the world. More noticeable since the 1970s, however, has been a trend away from seeing government as the sole, or even primary, solution to both regulation and social welfare.

This trend may have reached its peak on 11 September 2001,[21] and in banking in particular light-touch regulation is now being criticized by politicians, investors, and the public alike. But for anyone born before the 1970s, the changes in the roles and expectations of government have already been enormous. They continue to be at the heart of debates about how society responds to globalization and attitudes towards corporate responsibility worldwide.[22]

There are four main interpretations of what has happened.

1 National government has seen its power eroded by globalization

As a condition of joining the global market, national governments surrender much of their power to create policy autonomously, and poor countries, in particular, have had policies forced upon them. Some of those policies have undermined state sovereignty, not only in areas of macroeconomic policy, but also in areas such as taxation, social welfare, and human development. Even in rich countries, governments not only no longer try and control exchange rates, but they are also afraid to raise corporate taxes or the minimum wage, for fear of driving business overseas.

2 There is a governance vacuum at the global level

There is no clear responsibility or accountability for issues such as human rights and poverty, for which the forces of economic globalization may have unacceptable consequences that cannot be resolved by market forces. Equally, there are new challenges, such as the management of the global commons, that cannot be solved through conventional governance mechanisms. As Bell puts it: *'The nation-state is becoming too small for the big problems of life, and too big for the small problems of life'*.[23]

3 Government has deliberately chosen where and where not to exert influence

There are many examples in which national governments have exerted influence on the governance of globalization. For example, the World Trade Organization is a direct result of national government negotiation and agreement, and has been criticized for being too influenced by the interests of the wealthiest economies (e.g. its slowness in tackling agriculture subsidies).[24] As Braithwaite and Drahos (2000) observe, what we are witnessing may not be deregulation but *'re-regulation'*, with state rollback in some areas, such as capital and trade, and a strengthening of regulation to protect other rights. Migration is another issue relating to which governments have been accused of hypocrisy because, while they have removed barriers to trade and investment, they have put up barriers to allowing most people to pursue job opportunities through international migration.

4 Governments still maintain power

As Ward (2003) emphasizes, it is important not to dismiss the regulatory role of government. National laws, such as the US Foreign Corrupt Practices Act 1977 and Alien Tort Claims Act 1789, can affect the behaviour of multinational companies around the world. Bilateral trade agreements, for example, are one way in which the poor in developing nations can benefit from global trade and, in some instances, these agreements have created favourable environments for corporate responsibility.[25]

Key concept: New models of international governance—the World Trade Organization

Establishment of the World Trade Organization in 1995 was one of the most important steps in creating a new model of international governance. Part international negotiating forum, part court of arbitration, it has the power to affect trade rules and to resolve disputes, and its role is to focus on trade. Globalization sceptics point out that, while globalization raises issues about social and environmental justice, the one major international body to come out of globalization so far is an organization that is focused entirely on liberalizing trade. But the WTO's defenders argue that it is not, and should not be, a world court and point, for example, to the International Labour Organization as the competent body for addressing labour rights issues.

(*Sources:* Jones and Pollit, 2004; Narlikar, 2005)

Whatever one's interpretation of governance in this era of globalization, one noticeable change is the prominence of non-government actors in governance processes. From Occupy to the Arab Spring, civil society movements have been at the heart of major issues in recent years. While it would be flying in the face of history to deny the influence that owners and managers of capital or public protest have had on government over time, nonetheless new forms of governance are emerging. There is a growing element of self-regulation by business and, in particular, of business being used by government as the initial enforcer (e.g. in the UK, supermarkets are liable for enforcing food safety standards in their supply chains). There is also widespread outsourcing of the policing of business behaviour, building on approaches originating in financial auditing, and quasi-independent bodies, notably the International Organization for Standardization (ISO), have had a significant impact on environmental management and are developing systems for corporate responsibility more broadly.

Civil society organizations are increasingly involved in both 'street regulation', through campaigns, watchdog activities, and 'naming and shaming' of particular companies, and participation in new regulatory systems, such as international standards and multi-stakeholder partnerships.[26] These different views of public governance are all relevant to the relationship between notions of corporate responsibility and globalization, and the changing nature of governance is especially important in the corporate responsibility context, as we discuss in the next section. Business has gone from dealing with a handful of government regulators to wrestling with innumerable informal regulators.[27]

 Discussion points

Corporate responsibility has been variously described as a 'response' to globalization and as its 'reflection'.

- What distinction is being made here?
- Do companies' policies and programmes appear to reflect one of these views more than the other?
- Selecting the ideological framework of a particular political party, how would you make the case that corporate responsibility complements its policy objectives?

Corporate responsibility as a response to globalization

Understanding the phenomenon of globalization is a necessary part of comprehending the context within which contemporary corporate responsibility has emerged. Ruggie (2003) treats it as a manifestation of Polanyi's notion of the embedded economy (see Chapter 2)—an attempt to contain and share the social adjustment costs that open markets inevitably produce. Criticisms of business, and of big business in particular, as reaping the benefits of globalization without taking responsibility for its negative consequences have become an important driver of contemporary corporate responsibility as a whole. Moreover, specific initiatives, such as codes of labour practice or participation in the environmental agenda that first emerged from the 1992 Rio Earth Summit, address the perceived mismatch of regulatory scope and actual economic structure that is a consequence of expanding global trade. Even if 2012's Rio Plus 20 Summit was downbeat overall about Rio's achievements, business–civil society initiatives that began in 1992, such as the Forest Stewardship Council, continue to flourish.

This does not mean that corporate responsibility is a comprehensive response to business–society issues related to globalization. For example, tax avoidance by companies, though legal, arguably deprives countries of resources that could be used to tackle environmental, social, and governance issues, yet is overlooked in corporate responsibility practice and much of the theory. Equally, it does not mean that the issues that corporate responsibility addresses are necessarily the consequences of globalization. For example, slavery, deforestation, child labour, and over-fishing all took place before globalization. In some cases (e.g. slavery), it may not even be the case that what is happening is worse than that which occurred in the past.[28] But globalization exaggerates and exacerbates by making things quicker, larger, and more visible than before, and this has increased the pressure on companies to act responsibly. For some, corporate responsibility is about making the benefits of globalization accessible to more people, by either limiting the need for government intervention[29] or making new resources available for human development. It can also be seen as a reflection of the interdependence of government and business, under which the former looks to the latter to create wealth in order to retain power, while the latter looks to the former to develop human capital and maintain stability.[30] What is more, reflecting the general widespread growth in self-regulation and voluntary agreements by business, corporate responsibility can be regarded as an element of a new system of global governance that sits alongside the democratic model of national government that is promoted by the most powerful countries.[31]

 Discussion points

If we compare the issues raised in the sections on globalization as 'A tale of the glass half empty' (p 102) and on 'Corporate responsibility as a response to globalization' (p 109), there are clearly gaps between the consequences of globalization and the concerns of corporate responsibility.

● What are the main aspects of globalization that corporate responsibility does not address?

● What are the reasons for these gaps?

● Which of these gaps will corporate responsibility attempt to bridge in the future and why?

How corporate responsibility addresses the challenges of globalization

Some of contemporary corporate responsibility's earliest initiatives were related to globalization. The Rio Earth Summit, for example, brought together different sectors of society to address global environmental challenges. It succeeded in sending the message that business could and should act, and indirectly encouraged business and environmental groups to work together on initiatives such as sustainable forest management. It also lit a flame in the oil industry that influenced Shell's early corporate responsibility reporting and eventually led to BP rebranding itself as Beyond Petroleum, as its then CEO, John Browne, began to speak out on the importance of business addressing greenhouse gases and other threats to the environment.[32]

In a different way, early initiatives intended to rethink the nature of working lives were a response to the ways in which globalization had influenced the workplace. In the UK, Business in the Community was started as a response to urban decay and industrial decline during the 1980s, and the lack of government action. The Prince of Wales Business Leaders' Forum was a tentative step to encourage UK business executives to think about their role in the world. At that stage, these organizations were still firmly rooted in traditions of giving back to communities through, for instance, philanthropy, community investment, and volunteering.

At the same time, the fairtrade movement was establishing itself as a way of dealing with what were seen as inequitable trading relations with poor producers in developing countries. Trade union and NGO campaigns raised public awareness about labour conditions in the apparel and sporting goods industries, which had been early movers in globalizing production. This, in turn, led to a number of companies, primarily in the UK and USA, adopting codes of labour practice and partnering with civil society organizations to implement them. This interest spilled over into parts of agriculture, which was already becoming more global, and which, in Europe, was increasingly interested in improved environmental management and product safety.

Other industries that were, perhaps, more removed from globalization were nonetheless feeling the consequences of rapid information exchange and the power of civil society alliances. Mining companies in Papua, or oil companies in Burma, came under the spotlight because of allegations about human rights, environmental damage, and corruption. Such criticisms, in turn, raised questions about the funding of major private sector projects, such as the Chad–Cameroon oil pipeline, and public and private sector finance bodies, such as the International Finance Corporation and Citigroup, began to pay more attention to the non-financial aspects of their investments. This eventually led, in 2003, to the Equator Principles—a framework promoting environmental and social responsibility in project financing.

In 1999, the UN announced its Global Compact to bring companies together with UN agencies, labour organizations, and civil society to promote responsible corporate practices and to help business be part of the solution to the challenges of globalization. It has paid particular attention to business in developing countries and the private sector's role in meeting the aforementioned Millennium Development Goals (see Chapter 4). The World Economic Forum's (WEF's) Centre for Public–Private Partnership has also stressed that these goals cannot be met by governments, business, or civil society alone. Its mission highlights that, in addition to the role of business in upholding and advancing principles on human rights, labour, environmental, and anti-corruption practices in countries with weak regulatory capacity, business competencies can improve the effectiveness of development programmes (e.g. technology development, providing essential goods and services, and managing large-scale operations).

In Chapter 4, we offered various examples of corporate responsibility as a response to poverty in developing countries. Several of these are partnerships between organizations and groups, reflecting the belief that poverty, global governance, imbalances in power, and other features linked to globalization are best met through collaboration. We turn to this now.

Partnerships

One consequence of economic globalization and the changed nature of governance is that it has created the space where business impacts upon and is influenced by a more geographically dispersed body of stakeholders than ever before. The exact nature of stakeholder is something we explore in Chapter 9, but in terms of globalization, it is not just that business has to manage stakeholders, which is important, but partnering with them has become a significant element of business's relationship with wider society.

Business has long run on networks—the labyrinth of personal relationships and long- or short-term alliances that comprise the web of the day-to-day functioning of business. At various historical moments, collaborations of this kind have met with a political and public backlash when they become the backbone of collusion, oligopoly, and other practices that run against the principles of free market capitalism. As Adam Smith pointed out, '*People of the same trade seldom meet together, even for merriment and diversion, but the conversation ends in a conspiracy against the public, or in some contrivance to raise prices*' (Smith, 1776).

Despite this, alliances and collaborations of one form or another have thrived, especially in recent years, often with the full support of governments. Competitive clusters of complementary businesses in a given geographical area are often seen as essential to competitive advantage,[33] and public–private sector partnerships have gained traction in some countries as a way in which to deliver public services, from schooling to incarceration. Civil society groups which might historically have been expected to be wary of business alliances have come to favour what are called multi-stakeholder partnerships, i.e. alliances between actors from the private, public, and civil society sectors. As we shall see, there are many types of partnership, but the United Nations, which has taken a great deal of interest in alliances with business, offers a broad working definition, describing partnerships as '*voluntary and collaborative relationships between various parties ... in which all participants agree to work together to achieve a common purpose or undertake a specific task, and to share risks, responsibilities, competencies and benefits*' (cited in Mouan, 2010, p 368).

The aims of partnerships range from the broad and grand, to the narrow and specific. For example, the aforementioned Rio Summit on Sustainable Development, which is attributed with stimulating various partnerships between government and civil society, placed business at the centre of international efforts to reduce poverty. In contrast, a partnership might be formed between airport authorities, local government, local community groups, and environmental NGOs, with the specific purpose of negotiating a runway extension. Equally, as we shall discuss further, partnerships involve different levels of participation and involvement, ranging from a company promising to report on social and environmental performance to stakeholders or to fund a specific project, to civil society, business, and government groups

collaborating together to achieve certain ends. It is not that one type of partnership is necessarily better than another—the question is what is fit for purpose—but it must be recognized
that there are different types, each with implications for goals, design, and implementation.

The principle of partnership has been widely lauded both within and outside the business
community. It has been called the 'collaboration paradigm of the twenty-first century' that
allows actors to exceed their individual capabilities, the 'development approach of our time',
and 'the last remedy to the stresses [of] intense globalization.'[34] A large number of companies
have spoken out in favour of partnerships. Hershey acknowledges that 'corporations cannot
address the challenges of ensuring a truly sustainable supply chain without working in partnership with [our] particular industry and, increasingly, without the help of outside nongovernmen-
tal organizations' (cited in Long, 2008, p 317). Accenture sees business–NGO partnerships
as essential to improving the performance of civil society organizations.[35] The International
Commission on Mining and Metals (ICMM) says that a partnership approach is essential in
establishing and strengthening sustainable development approaches in mining areas.[36] As
Warner and Sullivan describe it: 'Tri-sector partnerships are, in essence, a new form of strategic
alliance .... [A] voluntary collaboration to promote sustainable development based on the most
efficient allocation of complementary resources across business, civil society and government'
(Warner and Sullivan, 2004, p 17).

 Discussion points

Managers often want to see the financial value of partnerships.

- Is it possible to demonstrate how a partnership contributes to the bottom line?
- What are the most convincing non-financial arguments for partnerships?
- As the director of an NGO, how would you demonstrate the financial added value of a partnership
  to a South African mineral company?

Partnership as ideology?

There are examples of partnership, particularly of the multi-stakeholder variety, around the
world, and these are being discussed and replicated not just as a methodology, but as an
ideology—what Bendell et al. (2010) term the ideology of 'partnerism.' In the 1990s, partnerships such as the Ethical Trading Initiative were considered radical, but now partnering of
some kind has not only entered into mainstream corporate thinking, it is an indicator of a
company's commitment to good governance, social responsibility, and sustainability, and it
has become an indicator of good performance in these fields in its own right.

There are some widely accepted reasons as to why this has come about. Stakeholders in
their broadest sense are putting pressure on companies to act on environmental, social, and
governance (ESG) issues. Some companies will react to stakeholders as a threat, and seek to
manage them accordingly. However, other companies might see them as groups to engage
with in order to help them navigate the uncertainties that confront modern business.[37] This
reflects a fundamental philosophical difference in stakeholder management theory that
we explore in Chapter 9. However, the role of stakeholders, including how they have been

empowered by the social interconnectedness and opportunities for transparency that are features of contemporary globalization, is an important factor in the evolution of partnerships. Other factors discussed elsewhere in this book also shed light on the emergence of partnerism. There is a sense that governments are less able than before to regulate business, and certain partnerships have arisen to fill this governance vacuum. The perceived diminishing power of governments is often linked to the drop in government overseas development assistance as a percentage of capital flows into developing economies, and partnerships have to a degree been a response to this shift.[38] There are also various instrumental benefits that companies associate with partnership, such as employee satisfaction and morale, effective risk management, and above all brand image, which in one survey was rated as three times more important than other benefits.[39]

A challenge to convention?

Given the enthusiasm for, and proliferation of, partnerships and other variations on collaboration in the broad ESG arena, it is easy to forget that partnering of the kind relevant to corporate responsibility is recent and is a significant change from conventional business models. For example, mainstream management theory still promotes a corporation perspective model of the firm in which the primary goal is to create values for shareholders. An exemplar of this is Porter's 'five forces' framework which seeks to limit the number of competitors by putting one's company in a dominant position and optimizing outcomes for shareholders (and typically executives) over those for suppliers, customers, employees, and regulators.[40] Stakeholder engagement is not precluded by such a model, but its purpose is always to benefit the company (i.e. its shareholders and executives) rather than society as a whole.

The ideological value awarded to partnerships is that they offer an alternative to the corporation perspective model, but, in examining and evaluating partnerships in practice, we should always remember the power of well-established conventions, and therefore be wary of the distinction between collaborations that mark a radical shift away from the status quo and those that are a refurbishment of existing structures. In particular, we should be aware of the differences in sustainability outcome that result from these distinctions. If partnerships that reinforce the aims of the corporation perspective model deliver real benefits from a corporate responsibility perspective, then it would be mistaken to criticize them. However, as the discussion of impact in Chapter 4 shows, demonstrating the benefits is no easy task. The reality is that much of the coverage of partnerships exists in order to promote the ideology of partnering, and there is a dearth of reliable empirical evidence to show the benefits of partnership beyond the many individual case studies that tell interesting stories but do not comprise a comparable analysable data set.[41]

 Discussion points

Partnerships have become one of the ways that companies manage sustainability issues.

- Why do companies think that partnerships are well suited to sustainability challenges?
- What specific advantages do multi-stakeholder partnerships offer?
- Why is the five forces framework at odds with the intentions of partnership approaches?

Types of partnership

There are various ways of categorizing partnerships (Box 5.1). We have already mentioned multi-stakeholder partnerships which, in contrast with business-to-business partnerships, bring together actors from different sectors of society to achieve an agreed set of goals. The Forest Stewardship Council is an example of business partnering with social development and environmental NGOs to further the goal of responsible forest management. It stands out from other partnerships created in the 1990s in that it includes organizations from developing as well as developed economies. It is a voluntary partnership in that there are no legally enforceable elements bringing the organizations together, in contrast with most conventional business-to-business or business-to-other-party relationships. It also does not include government or its agencies, although in common with some other pioneering international collaborations, it has received direct or indirect government funding.

Box 5.1   Examples and types of partnership

	Business-to-business	Multi-stakeholder
Rule-setting partnership	EUREPGAP/GLOBALGAP International Council on Mining and Metals	RSPO FSC MSC
Service/implementation partnership	Sustainable Agriculture Initiative Platform	Better Cotton Initiative Cadbury Cocoa Partnership
Resourcing partnership	Connected Urban Development	Accenture Development Partnership

---

Rule-setting, implementation, and resource partnerships

The FSC operates a certification standard that is applied to well-managed forests, and compliance is recognized by the FSC logo applied to certified products using the output of those forests (e.g. paper, wooden furniture, sawn timber). As such, it is an example of a *rule-setting partnership*, along with the Marine Stewardship Council (MSC), and the IFOAM organic agriculture standard. Not all such partnerships are multi-stakeholder in nature; for example, EUREPGAP is a partnership of retailers and producers that develops certifiable criteria for good agricultural practice.

The WWF, the environmental NGO, played an important part in creating the FSC and the MSC, and that experience was carried over into the creation of the Roundtable on Sustainable Palm Oil (RSPO). The RSPO is a collaboration of companies throughout the palm oil value chain and NGOs, and it oversees a standard for the cultivation of socially and environmentally acceptable oil palm at the plantation and smallholder levels. However, as well as a rule-setting function, the RSPO is involved in creating a market for sustainable palm oil, and in improving cultivation standards. As such, it can also be seen as an *implementation or service partnership* which fulfils not only a governance function, but also a pastoral one with regard to oil palm growers. There are a large number of service partnerships, and they are often found in developing countries where they offer distinct models for increasing the capability of local producers to meet sustainable production best practice.[42] The Cadbury Cocoa Partnership brings NGO and government partners together to improve the livelihoods of cacao farmers and their communities, and the Sustainable Agriculture Initiative Platform is a food-industry-wide initiative to promote sustainable agriculture practices.

Roundtables such as RSPO have become a popular partnership model; there are roundtables on sustainable sugar cane, soy, and biofuels, and such is the momentum behind this approach that the International Cocoa Organization, a traditional industry body, is now imitating it in its industry–government collaboration, the Roundtable for a Sustainable Cocoa Economy. They are examples of 'co-regulation' in which civil society and business representatives jointly regulate business policies and practices.[43]

Another attraction of roundtables is that they offer the potential to provide resources that might otherwise be unavailable. The RSPO generates revenue from the sale of certified palm oil and this is available to build up the capacity of growers, but resources need not just be financial; rule-setting partnerships such as the Fair Labor Association have given companies access to the grassroots-level knowledge of NGOs about working conditions, and a service partnership such as the Better Cotton Initiative has made available the competencies of agriculturalists, manufacturers, and designers for the common goal of more environmentally acceptable cotton cultivation. *Resourcing partnerships* are considered by some a separate type of partnership, especially when their primary aim is to provide particular groups with additional competencies. For example, Accenture Development Partnerships, which makes the skills of management consultants available to NGOs, is a resourcing partnership. This category also includes partnerships to conduct systematic dialogues, i.e. forums that allow business and other stakeholders to come together to discuss particular aspects of sustainability, including sharing best practice.[44] The UN Global Compact and the UN Principles for Responsible Investment (see Case 5) can be seen as resourcing partnerships because although they set out criteria for best practice, these do not constitute rules comparable to the certifiable standards of the FSC or the MSC, and their contribution is probably best measured in terms of the process of dialogue than improved governance.

There are various subtypes of partnership that fall under the preceding three broad headings. Employee volunteering, for example, is a common form of resourcing partnership, as is company sponsorship, and short-term business–NGO consultations. Philanthropy is often dismissed as a lesser form of partnership, in part because it does not imply a substantive change in company behaviour. However, from a company's perspective, philanthropy can be a prized form of partnership because of its demonstrable impact on employee morale, and its measurable effects on reputation and brand value. For example, the Finnish forest products company Stora Enso engages in rule-setting partnerships and systematic dialogues about sustainability, but its support of children's charities is still a key part of its partnership approach.[45]

Box 5.2   Partnership outcomes for different stakeholders—examples from mining

Outcomes for business

Enhanced licence to operate, because communities affected by operations will be satisfied that the business unit is responsive to their concerns	Availability of new social capital for the business
Reduced community dependency on the business unit (e.g. owing to empowerment of communities to manage their own development)	Becoming 'company of choice' in the eyes of governmental authorizing agencies and removing political objections to future ventures
Basis for resolving local disputes that might delay financial approval or operations	Reduced risk to marketing, sales, and share price associated with negative image of social and environmental performance

Outcomes for local communities

Additional resources for community development	Ensuring that those impacted by operations have an equal or greater level of welfare, income, subsistence, and security
Fairer settlement/compensation for community assets	Access to the technology, finance, and markets that are necessary for new assets, and skill sets that can be transformed into sustainable livelihoods
Improved infrastructure and capacity to manage it	

Outcomes for the public sector

Agreed revenue distribution mechanisms before commencing operations	Increased legitimacy with local populations
More equitable distribution of revenues across government, and between government and communities	Exposure to new ways of working and international good practice
Enhanced tax and skills base	Empowerment of local communities

(Adapted from Warner and Sullivan, 2003; Seitanidi, 2010)

Partnerships and globalization

Five different cases can be made for promoting partnering.

1   It is a better way of doing business.

2   It is a new way of regulating business.

3   It is an alternative way of harnessing the power and resources of business, and of redistributing benefits.

4   It is a more effective way of dealing with the realities of global governance.

5   It is an entirely new way of thinking about business.

In each case, the promise of partnership resonates with the challenges of globalization. For instance, we have discussed the changing nature of governance, and partnerships that can harness the respective competencies of different sectors domestically and internationally might provide an effective alternative approach to regulation. We have seen too that business has unique competencies and resources, and partnerships provide a way of leveraging these for the public good, not least in developing countries. The acquisition of TXU by two major private equity firms using a partnership with environmental NGOs, or Unilever's partnership with local women's organizations and microfinance groups for its Shakti programme are just two examples of how new business models are linked to partnering.

However, we should be cautious about uncritical faith in the actual benefits that partnerships deliver. Caplan (2003) claims that the literature on partnerships too often promotes the idea that they are, by their very nature, harmonious and built on trust, common vision, and voluntary commitment. He argues that there are various myths and half-truths behind this belief.

First, in his first-hand experience multi-sector partnerships are rarely built on a common vision because stakeholders have different reference points and, if they focus too much on what they have in common, their aspirations become diluted or masked. The partnership then ends up with a mission statement for which nobody feels ownership. He points out that stakeholders can appear to share values when what is actually happening is that they are using the same words to mean different things. For example, for a company, 'sustainability' has some relationship to cost recovery; for the public sector, it means something that is technically sound that can sustain itself in the future; for a development NGO, it is to do with empowerment and giving communities a voice.

Second, while trust is a much vaunted element of partnerships, it might be more accurate to say that individuals within the partnership build a mutual respect for that which people and organizations can offer. Trust is most likely when organizations can choose with whom to partner, but this rarely happens and most partners are thrust upon each other. Consequently, more important than trust can be creating an understanding of what the various partners can and cannot do. Indeed, more significant than genuine trust can be knowing partners well enough to predict how they will behave within the partnership.

Increasingly, the lessons of partnership seem to be that it is not a panacea for corporate responsibility challenges arising from globalization, and that organizations need to enter into partnerships with their eyes open to both their strengths and their weaknesses. There are many views on why partnerships are important and how to engage in them, and perhaps insufficient information on what is appropriate in different situations. But, overall, there is little argument about the importance attached to partnerships as part of corporate responsibility's armoury.

Unmet challenges

Corporate responsibility faces three main criticisms about how it addresses the challenges and impacts of globalization. The first of these—not least from within the business community itself—is that business can, and should, do more to find new solutions to meet the challenges that globalization presents. There is general consensus that governments cannot meet these challenges alone—hence the formation of alliances with non-state actors, such as the private sector, is essential.[46]

This criticism takes different forms; for example, it underpins the calls for action from Business Action for Africa and WEF's Centre for Public–Private Partnership. It takes a different shape in the concept that Wood et al. (2006) call *global business citizenship*, which seeks to develop a new framework for corporate responsibility within which its boundaries are not prescribed by the competitive pressures of globalization. And it appears again in authors, such as Hart (2005), who recognize business as part of the solution to creating a sustainable environment, but push it to go beyond the business-case-related thinking of the triple bottom line. What is common to all of them, however, is the acceptance of business as a crucial actor, not simply because it does harm, but because it has unique resources, scope, and competencies that need to be harnessed for society's good. As Wettstein (2005) notes, if multinational companies are as powerful as they are portrayed, perhaps they should not be allowed to stay out of political debate or to ignore global problems, but rather should be thought of as quasi-governmental institutions with an inherent responsibility for global well-being.

The second criticism is more accusatory. An Accenture analysis highlights what it calls 'pilot paralysis' referring to the limited replication of seemingly successful initiatives.[47] It acknowledges that business has tried to address society's concerns through certification schemes, adoption of global framework agreements, standard setting and monitoring, and dialogues with other sectors and its critics, but deems all of these approaches to voluntary regulation inadequate. Utting's (2005) analysis concludes the following: too many companies have not participated; there has been limited penetration of corporate responsibility ideas across the corporate structure; compliance procedures are often weak; initiatives, such as codes of conduct, are often top-down and technocratic, and, while focusing on particular named issues, they do not examine the impact of corporate responsibility, especially in developing countries. There are some signs of change,[48] but Reich (2007) concludes that, ultimately, corporate responsibility demonstrates the limitations of self-regulation and the need for government to assert its regulatory role, or, as Utting argues, a more robust approach to *articulated regulation*, under which different regulatory approaches and agents would come together in ways that are complementary, mutually reinforcing, and synergistic.

The final criticism of corporate responsibility as a response to globalization builds on these debates about self-regulation and centres on corporate responsibility's capacity to alter perceptions of corporate self-interest. It holds that many of globalization's shortcomings are exacerbated, or at least overlooked, by companies pursuing their narrow self-interest. For example, lay-offs and plant closures make sense in terms of global competitiveness, but can be devastating for individuals and communities. Indeed, as Visser (2006) has argued in an African context, accepted corporate responsibility frameworks, such as Carroll's pyramid (see Chapter 2), can appear simplistic and static when applied in developing countries, and may not recognize that conflicts and contradictions should be anticipated as the norm rather than treated as the shocking exception. In recent years, companies such as Amazon, Google, and Starbucks have all been ridiculed for their tax avoidance policies. In the USA and the UK, zero-hours contracts, which require workers to be available without paying them, have become the latest in a line of practices that harm rather than improve people's standards of living.

One strand of this critique holds that companies do not try to understand the consequences of their behaviour and focus only on those issues that they feel will affect their reputation, or that will serve their self-interest in other ways (e.g. investing in maintaining a healthy educated workforce and protecting their image).[49] There are indications that companies committed to corporate responsibility are more sensitive to these issues. The collaboration between Unilever and Oxfam to examine ways that the behaviour of a multinational affects poverty in Indonesia is an example of how partnerships are beginning to wrestle with the complexity of international development.[50]

Oxfam's attempts to use what it calls its 'poverty footprint' methodology with other companies has had a limited impact, and only two others (cut flowers in Kenya, and the impact of Coca Cola and SABMiller in Zambia and Ecuador) have been published. A similar approach by other companies has also met with limited success, and PPR (the holding company of Puma), a leader in environmental profit and loss accounting, abandoned its social profit and loss exercise.[51] A critical dimension to this in future will be how far companies can align around a corporate responsibility sensibility so that they are not, for example, claiming improved environmental practices, while at the same time aggressively marketing high-risk products to ill-educated consumers,[52] or not promoting better labour conditions, while using just-in-time contracting that can exacerbate labour exploitation.

The second strand of the same critique argues that aspects of trading and other contractual relationships are inherently unfair and biased towards the interests of the most powerful companies, but mainstream corporate responsibility has done little to address this. For example, as Oxfam's Make Trade Fair campaign asks, to what extent will corporate responsibility push for fairness in trading relations, both between countries and within specific supply chains?[53] And as Jenkins (2005) has noted, there are many areas that might be important for long-term development in which business seems to be silent or hostile (e.g. corporate taxation and tort reform), and corporate responsibility has done little to influence corporate investment in countries with the least foreign direct investment.

Finally, it is argued that the mindset and tools of corporate responsibility are so deeply embedded in the normative frameworks of business that corporate responsibility theory and practice ends up taking for granted, reproducing, and legitimizing, rather than providing an alternative to, the values and priorities associated with free enterprise. We saw earlier how some believe that globalization universalizes certain values; it has been argued that corporate responsibility is one way in which this is done, not only by what is included or excluded from standards of acceptable social and environmental performance, but also by the way in which those tools are used.[54] Current approaches, such as ethical sourcing, have been criticized for ignoring the priorities of workers, and failing to consider the broader impacts of initiatives on other producers and neighbouring communities;[55] as case studies from Newell (2005) and Fig (2005) have shown, initiatives driven from the bottom up run the risk of being ignored or discounted by corporate responsibility. Such case studies reveal how important voices are missing from corporate responsibility partnerships and other initiatives that claim to engage with stakeholders, but often end up doing so on a selective basis.

Discussion points

Since the 1990s, worries about the global environment have been an important driver of corporate responsibility, although some believe that social issues are now more prominent.

- What environmental challenges are most clearly associated with globalization?
- To what extent can, and should, business seek to tackle the major global environmental challenges?
- Over 22 years since the Rio Earth Summit, what are the main overall achievements of the environmental initiatives in which business has been involved?

 Case study 5   The United Nations Global Compact

The United Nations Global Compact is one of the most well-known corporate responsibility partnerships, and has been called 'an excellent source of inspiration' for companies thinking about their relationship with society. It was established in 2000 as a direct result of the call of the then UN Secretary-General, Kofi Annan, for business leaders to partner with UN agencies, and for civil society to support universal environmental and social principles. The partnership was in part a response to the neglect of social and environmental protections in the promotion of economic globalization, and also the failure of UN agencies to engage effectively with the business community. It is based on the premise that the longevity of globalization and the international economic order depends as much on such protections as it does on free markets and economic inclusivity.

   The Compact was never intended to resolve all of global capitalism's deficiencies, but rather to lay a foundation of shared values, as embodied in various UN conventions and declarations, and to attempt to harness the skills and resources of the private sector to uphold those values. Although sometimes mistaken for a certification standard, its main aim is to foster a dialogue among actors from the private, public, and civil society sectors. However, to make that dialogue effective and transparent, companies are expected to report on their progress and actions in implementing the Compact's ten principles (Box 5.3).

Box 5.3   The ten principles of the Global Compact

Businesses should:

1   support and respect the protection of internationally proclaimed human rights within their sphere of influence
2   ensure that their own operations are not complicit in human rights abuses
3   uphold the freedom of association and the effective recognition of the right to collective bargaining
4   uphold the elimination of all forms of forced and compulsory labour
5   uphold the effective abolition of child labour
6   eliminate discrimination in respect of employment and occupation
7   support a precautionary approach to environmental challenges
8   undertake initiatives to promote greater environmental responsibility
9   encourage the development and diffusion of environmentally friendly technologies
10   work against corruption in all its forms, including extortion and bribery

(*Source:* www.unglobalcompact.org)

(continued...)

The ultimate measure of success for the initiative is the degree to which it promotes concrete and sustained action by its varied participants, especially the private sector, in alignment with broad UN objectives, the [Compact's] principles, and the international Millennium Development Goals. It does not substitute for effective action by governments, nor does it present a regulatory framework or code of conduct for companies. Rather the Global Compact is conceived as a value-based platform designed to promote institutional learning with few formalities and no rigid bureaucratic structures.

(Kell and Levin, 2003, p 152)

The Principles mirror the commitments of UN member states under the Universal Declaration of Human Rights, the 1992 Rio Declaration on the Environment and Development, the 1998 ILO Fundamental Principles and Rights at Work, and the 2003 Convention against Corruption. In other words, they already have a degree of legitimacy with national governments. Companies that sign up to the Compact make a clear statement of support for the Principles, signed by the CEO and endorsed by the board, and they agree to report publicly on progress towards meeting commitment. From this stem the Compact's three stated goals:

1 to build consensus and inspire recognition of social and environmental concerns in the global marketplace, especially around problematic areas;

2 to develop a learning bank of corporate best practices, and to integrate the Compact's ten principles into business strategies and operations;

3 to generate concrete sustained implementation of the Millennium Development Goals.

Partnering is an important way of achieving these, and activities include: a) learning forums to analyse case studies and examples of good practice; b) global policy dialogues on the challenges of globalization; c) multi-stakeholder collaborative development projects to further the Millennium Development Goals; d) supporting the creation of new national networks. An important part of the Compact has been local networks that serve as forums within which companies can exchange experiences in a particular region.

The Compact now has about 7000 corporate members in 140 countries, a rapid rise that includes commitments from over 20 per cent of the world's 500 largest companies. There is an under-representation of US companies, partly because they fear litigation based on any alleged failure to comply with the Principles. Equally, 7000 companies divided into about 100 local networks around the world is a less impressive number when one considers that there are 4.8 million companies in the UK alone.[56]

More important, though, are the achievements of the 8000 signatories. Are they leaders in the different areas of corporate responsibility the Principles embrace, or is being part of the Compact an insurance policy against closer scrutiny? The Compact may not be a regulatory body, but it does require that companies engage in continual improvement, and this has grown in emphasis since the launch in 2010 of its Differentiation Framework (to allow companies at different levels of progress to explain their achievements) and its Blueprint for Corporate Sustainability Leadership.

Ultimately, the Compact will be assessed on its contribution to realizing the UN's social and environmental goals, although the Compact and commentators are at pains to stress that it is only one part of the solution and depends heavily on other efforts towards the same end. However, it is natural to want to know more about the direct impact of the Compact itself, and moreover to want to learn about its achievements in the social and environmental spheres. At present, it is much easier to find out about the number of signatories, and the meetings they have had, than to discover whether a company such as G4S, with a well-documented reputation for human rights abuses in prisons and poor employment conditions,[57] has improved its employment practices as a result of Compact membership. Hamann et al. (2009) and Runhaar and Lafferty (2009) argue that there is little evidence on the ground that participating in the Compact improves companies' corporate responsibility efforts, although Woo (2010) states that it has improved the management of initiatives in some companies.

(continued...)

However, even at the broader level for which information about participation is more readily available, the signs of success are hazy. For the Compact's 2013 progress report, less than 25 per cent of companies responded, and of these the majority were only at the stage of defining rather than implementing programmes.

(*Sources:* Kell and Levin, 2003; McIntosh et al., 2004; Runhaar and Lafferty 2008; Hamann et al. 2009; Woo 2010, cited in Rasche and Kell 2010; Kell 2013; Rasche et al. 2013b; *UN Global Compact Corporate Sustainability Report* 2013, http://www.unglobalcompact.org/AboutTheGC/global_corporate_sustainability_report.html)

Questions

For the Compact to be successful, it needs to be a credible partnership tackling important issues.

1 How well aligned are the ten principles to the main issues that business is being asked to address globally by governments and civil society?

2 What are the advantages and disadvantages of striving for a large but less active membership compared with a small but very active one?

3 What can the Compact do to encourage more active involvement from companies?

Summary

Globalization is a specific historical era in which the role of business in the world is being redefined. The human and environmental consequences of globalization are causing us to rethink corporate responsibility. Yet there are competing definitions of globalization and these, in turn, affect what we think the responsibilities of business are, and how we believe companies should approach them.

There are various definitions of globalization that variously emphasize its economic and wider social characteristics. The meaning that we give to 'globalization' affects how we look at its impacts. For some, these impacts are synonymous with 'liberalism', whether we mean by that the benefits of free trade, comparative advantage, and enlightened self-interest, or the exploitation of workers, social inequality, and the externalization of industry's ecological costs. Others may not deny these impacts, but instead highlight that what is distinctive about globalization is how it affects social networks, generates new types of organization, and creates the need for new approaches to governance. These different views are highly evident in debates about corporate responsibility. Some treat it as either a hindrance or a palliative to economic liberalization; others see it as related to the new organizations and alliances that globalization has spawned, and as part of the response to the challenges of global governance.

Further reading

online resource centre

www.oxfordtextbooks.co.uk/orc/blowfield_murray3e/

Visit the Online Resource Centre that accompanies this book to enrich your understanding of this chapter. Among the resources available are web links, exercises, and additional case studies.

Chang, H.-J. 2010, *23 things they don't tell you about capitalism*, Allen Lane, London.
  Lively look at the effects of globalization around the world.

Ghemawat, P. 2011, *World 3.0: global prosperity and how to achieve it*, Harvard Business Review Press, Boston, MA.
  Arguments for continuing but modifying capitalism in the wake of the financial crisis.

Porritt, J. 2005, *Capitalism: as if the world matters*, Earthscan, London.
  An alternative view of capitalism's future from an important sustainability thinker and activist.

Smith, C.N., Bhattacharya, C.B., Vogel, D., & Levine, D.I. (eds) 2010, *Global challenges in responsible business*, Cambridge University Press, Cambridge.
  Overview of the challenges for corporate responsibility as a result of globalization.

Steger, M.B. 2003, *Globalization: a very short introduction*, Oxford University Press, Oxford.
  Accessible overview of theories of globalization.

Stiglitz, J.E. 2005, *Fair trade for all: how trade can promote development*, Oxford University Press, Oxford.
  An influential economist's view on the shortcomings of liberal economic globalization.

Online resources

- Suggested additional material on business and globalization
- Teaching notes on chapter case study
- Additional case study on partnerships between football teams and development organizations
- Links to other web-based resources

Endnotes

1. See, e.g., Demirag, 2005; Blowfield, 2005a.
2. Steger, 2003.
3. World Bank data, accessed 9 October 2013. The number of people living on less than $2 a day was 2.59 billion; the number today is 2.40 billion.
4. WTO data, accessed 9 October 2013.
5. Henderson, 2001; Lindsey, 2002.
6. Wolf, 2004, p 36.
7. Wolf, 2004, p 320.
8. Stiglitz, 2002, p 248.
9. Johnston, 2003; Johnson, 2004.
10. www.bbc.co.uk/science/0/21970879, accessed 9 October 2013.
11. Caufield, 1996.
12. See, e.g., Blowfield, 2004.
13. For example, Germain (2000), MacLean (1999), and Levy and Newell (2005) build on theories of power from writers such as Lukes, Gramsci, and Foucault to examine how exertions of power are not necessarily overt or attributable to recognizable actors.

14. Blowfield and Frynas, 2005.

15. Steger, 2003; Waters, 2001.

16. According to IMF data, household debt in the USA in 2009 was over 90 per cent of GDP, in the UK it was nearly 120 per cent, and in the Eurozone it was over 60 per cent. Corporate debt for the same countries was 80 per cent, 120 per cent, and 100 per cent respectively. In the seven richest economies, government debt guarantees (sovereign debt) are nearly 120 per cent, the same as in the period immediately after World War II.

17. Bendell, 2004a.

18. World Bank, 2005.

19. Wolf, 2004.

20. This is Wolf's position: he says that corporate wealth has been exaggerated by dubious arithmetic. The merits of different claims about the power and influence of multinational companies is examined in Chandler and Mazlish, 2005.

21. Ring et al., 2005.

22. McMurtry, 2002.

23. Cited in Waters, 2001, p 123.

24. See, e.g. Stiglitz, 2002; Wolf, 2004; Watkins and Fowler, 2005.

25. Elliott and Freeman, 2003. Abrami (2003) discusses the US–Cambodia bilateral textile agreement, which was lauded for linking increased market access to the USA to improvements in workers' rights.

26. Utting, 2005.

27. Blowfield and Johnson, 2013.

28. For an overview of modern slavery, see Bales (2004).

29. Block and Barnett, 2005.

30. Stopford et al., 1991.

31. Blowfield, 2005a.

32. Browne, 2004.

33. Porter, 1990.

34. Austin, cited in Kolk 2011; Kjaer et al. and Rochlin et al., cited in Mouan 2010.

35. Bulloch, 2009.

36. McPhail, 2008.

37. Berns et al., 2009.

38. Nelson, 2007.

39. Berns et al., 2009.

40. Harris and Twomey, 2010.

41. Mouan, 2010.

42. Hammann and Boulogne, 2008.

43. Albareda, 2008.

44. Kourula and Halme, 2008.

45. Kourula and Halme, 2008.

46. See, e.g., Nelson, 1996; Pedersen, 2005; Fox and Prescott, 2004.

47. WEF & Accenture 2012.

48. See, e.g., UN, 2005; World Bank, 2005.

49. For example, see the shift from policing suppliers to engaging suppliers and workers in labour monitoring (CCC, 2005a; ETI, 2005a).

50. Maitland, 2005.

51. PPR is now called Kering, which ironically means 'dry' or 'drought' in Indonesian and Malay.

52. Clay, 2005.

53. Christian Aid (2004) and Utting (2005) provide examples of this kind of non-alignment.

54. Materials on Make Trade Fair are available at www.oxfam.org.

55. Blowfield, 2004; Mosley, 2011.

56. www.fsb.org.uk/stats, accessed 25 October 2013.

57. See, for instance, media coverage in 2013 of Mangaung Correctional Centre (Gauteng, South Africa) in which G4S was accused of using unskilled staff who were involved in violence against prisoners. Also, see coverage of G4S's use of unskilled low-wage non-permanent workers at the London Olympics in 2012 which resulted in the police and army having to provide security.

Part 2

Managing and
implementing
corporate
responsibility

6. How corporate responsibility is managed   129

7. Corporate responsibility and governance   160

8. Corporate responsibility reporting   179

9. Stakeholder management and engagement   201

10. Socially responsible investment   225

11. Corporate responsibility in smaller enterprises   254

6

How corporate responsibility is managed

 Chapter overview

In this chapter, we begin to examine the way in which corporate responsibility is being managed within companies, and whether or not there is a business case. In particular, we will:

● discuss the different goals that companies are trying to achieve;

● identify the types and levels of corporate responsibility that companies exhibit;

● examine the shared lessons and common elements of corporate responsibility management;

● look at how corporate responsibility is managed inside companies;

● explore evidence of a business case for corporate responsibility.

 Main topics

Understanding what companies want from corporate responsibility   129

Qualities of good corporate responsibility management   136

Structuring the corporate responsibility function   138

Corporate responsibility as strategy   141

The business case for corporate responsibility   144

Key terms

Change management

Defensive corporate responsibility

Integrated business strategy

Offensive corporate responsibility

Business case

Leadership

Understanding what companies want from corporate responsibility

Corporate responsibility management is typically described in terms of organizational change and transformation, and therefore distinguishes between:

1 the purpose and results (the why and the what);

2 the principles and processes (the how);

3 the leadership (the who).

The next sections broadly follow these distinctions, and therefore we begin with a discussion of the way in which companies decide whether to adopt corporate responsibility. The exception would be companies founded with the specific goal of achieving social or environmental outcomes, and which are discussed in Chapter 11 under 'Social Entrepreneurship'.

The most basic questions that any company thinking about corporate responsibility must answer are as follows.

1   What is our purpose in doing this—i.e. what Holliday et al. (2002) call the 'corporate magnetic north'?

2   What do we need to do to achieve it?

The wide range of definitions, approaches, and issues related to corporate responsibility mean that these basic questions do not necessarily have simple answers (see Chapter 1). Should a company focus on things that affect its financial bottom line? If so, what exactly are those things? Threats to the company's reputation; risks to the supply of materials; attempts to undermine the share price; harm to the company's ability to recruit or retain top quality personnel; acts that expose the firm to costly lawsuits—all of these can affect financial performance and require that significant attention be given to corporate responsibility. But should the company define its corporate responsibility more in terms of addressing social issues, such as access to education, support for the arts, or reducing inequality? Must it try to do both and, if so, is there a point at which the company's social mission overwhelms the conventional business purpose?

Immediately, we see what one study of approaches to corporate responsibility concludes is the distinction between operational responsibilities and citizenship responsibilities.[1] Companies are not limited to focusing on one set of responsibilities to the exclusion of the other, but the resource implications of any decision mean that even the largest corporation has to choose what to prioritize. Yet the same study also makes clear that it is not only the company that decides what responsibilities to act upon. Consumers, for example, have their own priorities, and may reward or punish a company in the marketplace if its values do not concord with their own. For the reasons spelled out in Chapter 5 and elsewhere, the contemporary capitalist has to make sense of a cacophony of voices which have little, if any, acknowledged interest in business's wants or needs,

Defining the company's corporate responsibility purpose is further complicated by the fact that perceptions of responsibility differ from country to country.[2] For example, in Germany, it is a priority that companies provide secure employment; in South Africa, it is a priority that companies improve health, education, and other elements of social welfare; in Australia, the emphasis is on environmental protection. These priorities shift and often reflect recent local crises, so that in Argentina, for example, the main expectation that people have of business is job creation because of the unemployment and financial loss caused by the recent economic collapse. In China, the main expectation is for safe high-quality products because of recent incidents of fire and serious injury caused by shoddy electrical goods. In countries characterized by a strong legally explicit framework defining the social contract within which business operates (e.g. Sweden, Japan, Australia), corporate responsibility issues look quite different from those built on a laissez faire economy (e.g. Australia, USA, UK). Considerable effort has gone into identifying national distinctions about corporate responsibility,[3] and these are particularly valid when thinking about national or regional companies, as van Tilburg et al. (2013)

show in their extensive study of Dutch companies pursuing the goal of becoming sustainable enterprises. What is less explored, however, is whether multinational companies (MNCs) reproduce the social contract from their place of origin. On the admittedly limited evidence available, it seems that while some attention is paid to the national setting, the frameworks used by MNCs to manage corporate responsibility are imported, meaning that while different corporate responsibility issues might receive attention, there is an orthodoxy in how they are managed. Furthermore, that orthodoxy reproduces many of the features of laissez faire economics, even when the company concerned originates from one with different sociopolitical conditions (e.g. IKEA, VW, Toyota).

Other factors and actors also influence the purpose of corporate responsibility. For example, the European Commission has defined corporate responsibility in a way that is intended to reflect what it calls the unique European social model, under which employers and other stakeholders, such as trade unions, function together to shape society and the economy. Reflecting the ideal that companies should not focus solely on profit, but also on the welfare of the workforce, consumers, and the environment, the model sets out the purpose of corporate responsibility in terms of the benefits to workers, customers, communities, and the wider society. Acknowledging the importance of different types of company across Europe, it requires that corporate responsibility be relevant to small and medium-sized enterprises. Reflecting the need to establish European competitive advantage in the global economy, it also requires that corporate responsibility finds ways of demonstrating that responsible business attracts investment and builds a skilled workforce.[4]

Similarly, an industry or a multi-industry collaboration can influence a company's corporate responsibility purpose. For example, the Global Social Compliance Programme, comprising companies such as Wal-Mart, Bata, Carrefour, and the Walt Disney company, aims to improve working and environmental conditions in global supply chains. The programme not only sets out areas in which member companies should take action, but seeks to build a consensus on best practice that would apply across companies by, for example, requiring companies to report their progress against individually determined timelines and goals.[5]

The increase in the range of organizations, individuals, and sectors of society that seek to influence business behaviour is one trend that needs to be understood in terms of thinking about a company's corporate responsibility purpose; how companies consider other trends is also an influencing factor. For example, what significance does the company attach to changing patterns of demand for (and often shrinking supplies of) natural resources, or the challenge of demographic change (see Chapters 4 and 12)? Is the threat of climate change so great that it overwhelms other aspects of the business–society relationship? How will the growing number of tangible and intangible financial factors that might affect the way business is valued and its success measured influence the way in which the company is managed, and in what it invests? Or does the company need to respond to the growing role of international institutions, and the continued acceleration in the speed of policy and behavioural change caused by the global media?[6] Each of these trends has relevance for corporate responsibility, whether in terms of the need to change energy use, or to invest in new building technology because of the natural resource situation, or the financial case for investing in innovative technologies to solve social problems, or the challenges of participating in new models of global governance.

Basic distinctions in corporate responsibility purpose

Given this array of issues, are there common frameworks to help understand a company's corporate responsibility purpose? One way of thinking about what the company aims to achieve through corporate responsibility management is to distinguish between what Kramer and Kania (2006) call 'defensive' and 'offensive' corporate responsibility. In their view, most companies view corporate responsibility in terms of vulnerability, i.e. as an external risk that needs to be managed with minimal investment. Thus, for example, an NGO will raise an issue and the company will seek to find the least costly way to defuse attention, through actions such as lobbying, public relations, and advertising. The defensive approach can also be used to maintain the company's reputation and to avoid legal liabilities, and is generally employed when companies are seeking to resolve problems of their own making.

In contrast, the offensive approach can involve companies offering themselves as the solution even if they had no part in creating the problem. It requires companies to exploit their full capabilities to find and implement solutions, and requires them to do four key things.

1 Pick the right issue—one that is important, timely, and leverages the company's core competencies.
2 Establish concrete goals and report on progress both inside the company and externally.
3 Deploy the company's key assets in addressing the issue including, for example, its products and services, the relevant skills of its employees, industry expertise, and its infrastructure.
4 Work in partnership with other sectors.

BP is a widely cited example of a company deciding to adopt an offensive approach, because the company chose the single issue of global warming, confronted it squarely before others in its industry did so, publicly announced quantitative targets and deadlines, and provided objectively verified reports of its progress.

As Nike's approach to corporate responsibility demonstrates, defensive and offensive approaches are not mutually exclusive, but the two bring different results. For example, a defensive approach allows the company to make short-term gains when it has to respond to specific charges (e.g. child labour in supplier factories), but the gains flatten out as the company meets its critics' expectations. Meanwhile, a company might see little tangible benefit from initial social investments, but, as these become more focused, they can have a significant impact in differentiating the company from its peers.[7] Put simply, as Kramer and Kania conclude:

> offensive [corporate responsibility] can distinguish a company's reputation but cannot protect it; defensive [corporate responsibility] can protect a reputation but cannot distinguish it.

> (Kramer and Kania, 2006, p 25)

This is an instrumental framework that presents a business rationale for acting, but does not provide much guidance on the intrinsic value of those actions. In contrast, Martin (2002) distinguishes between acts that are instrumental because they maintain or enhance shareholder value, and those that are done for their own sake, which are therefore regarded as having an intrinsic value. In what he calls the *'virtue matrix'*, he divides instrumental acts between those that are done because they conform to norms and customs, and those that are necessitated by legal compliance. He divides intrinsically valuable acts between those that create social and shareholder value, and those that benefit society but not shareholders. This distinction between instrumental and intrinsic value brings us back to the discussion of the meaning of corporate responsibility in Chapter 1 (and the debates about impact in Chapters 13 and 14). Is a company's purpose less admirable if the business rationale is strong, or vice versa as some business ethicists maintain? Is a strong business case a signal that a company will remain committed to delivering extra-financial outcomes? What is an acceptable balance between return on investment and social return on investment? People may have strong opinions about which are the right set of questions to ask, but in today's business world each is a valid way to think about purpose, and decisions are highly subjective.

Advocates of corporate responsibility as management reform largely favour the more innovative forward-looking agendas implicit in the concepts of intrinsic value and offensive corporate responsibility. These people see corporate responsibility, to paraphrase Paul Tebo of DuPont, as the right to operate and grow, because products that make lives better and reach more people equate with expanded markets and new customers.[8] But, as we shall see, for many companies the instrumental/defensive approach to corporate responsibility better defines what they want to achieve. Moreover, Waddock (2007) has argued that the defensive–offensive distinction is not comprehensive enough. She accepts that corporate responsibility can be a defensive response to crises and scandals, or a way in which to harness the power of business to meet societal needs. But she adds a third distinction, under which the company's corporate responsibility purpose is to respond to concerns in society that arise from the very success of the company's strategy. This arises when public expectations about the behaviour of business are neither the result of particular abuses, such as forced labour or oil spills, nor linked to demands that companies fill societal needs. Rather, the expectations (or criticisms) are directly related to the consequences of business implementing a system within which success is equated with:

1   continual growth and expansion;
2   a focus on efficiency and externalizing costs wherever possible;
3   corporate control or influence over resources, markets, customer preferences, and employees.

In other words, whether it be outrage at the bonuses paid by Goldman Sachs or disquiet amongst independent booksellers at the competing low-cost volunteer-based business model of Oxfam bookshops,[9] success creates a set of expectations which do not fit comfortably within the two-approach model, but which, as noted earlier, clearly inform public perceptions of responsibility, such as fair competition, job security, workforce prosperity, and aspects of environmental stewardship.

Stages of corporate responsibility

Several theorists use the analogy of a journey when explaining how companies define, and then develop, their corporate responsibility goals. This is a convenient way of exploring why companies' policies, processes, and programmes change, and also of discussing to what companies should aspire. The idea of responsibility as a journey was used by Post and Altman (1992) to describe the evolution of environmental management, and is the subject of numerous case studies of corporate transformation that set out the steps and mis-steps taken by individual companies.[10] Clarkson (1995), building on others, developed the RDAP framework that separates the 'reactive', 'defensive', 'accommodative', and 'proactive' stages of corporate responsibility. Zadek (2000) identified four types of corporate responsibility (defence of reputation, cost–benefit orientation, the strategic business case, and the 'new economy' case, in which corporate responsibility is seen as part of new approaches to learning, innovation, and risk management). He has developed this idea to analyse the experience of Nike in moving from being what he calls a *'stubborn resister'* to the idea it was responsible for the consequences of its products, into what he regards as an active citizen and what Nike itself describes as a stage at which sustainability is a core attribute of Nike product innovation.[11]

Mirvis and Googins (2006) warn that there is no single developmental pathway, but believe that there is a natural progression. Their model builds on ideas of behavioural psychology and posits that companies, like individuals, exhibit distinct patterns of behaviour at different stages of development, with their activities becoming more complex and sophisticated as they mature. We can tell the level of maturity by the company's actions in seven areas of management (see Figure 6.1):

1 how corporate responsibility is defined and the comprehensiveness of the definition (what they call the *'citizenship concept'*);
2 the purpose of the company's corporate responsibility (*'strategic intent'*);
3 the support given by company managers (*'leadership'*);
4 the day-to-day management of corporate responsibility within the firm (*'structure'*);
5 responses to social, environmental, and other relevant issues (*'issues management'*);
6 managing the relationship with key constituencies within and outside the company (*'stakeholder relationships'*);
7 openness, transparency, and disclosure about different aspects of corporate responsibility performance (*'transparency'*).

Thus, for instance, a company at the *'elementary'* stage might define corporate responsibility in terms of the creation of profits and jobs, and payment of corporate taxes (its citizenship concept), it might see its corporate responsibility purpose as complying with the law (strategic intent), and it might adopt a defensive approach to issues management. In contrast, a company at the *'engaged'* stage might in addition conceptualize corporate responsibility in terms of philanthropy or environmental protection, see its purpose as maintaining a licence to operate, and begin to develop policies that allow it to predict what issues it will need to manage. Meanwhile, a company at the *'integrated'* stage might be thinking in terms of the triple bottom line, be using corporate responsibility as a way to inform its product development, and have in place management systems that allow it to predict societal trends (see Figure 6.1).

Both Zadek and Mirvis and Googins feel that companies have yet to reach the most developed stage of corporate responsibility (what they respectively call the 'new economy'

	Stages				
	Stage 1 Elementary	Stage 2 Engaged	Stage 3 Innovative	Stage 4 Integrated	Stage 5 Transforming
Citizenship concept	Jobs; profits; taxes	Philanthropy; environment protection	Stakeholder management	Sustainability/ triple bottom line	Change the game
Strategic intent	Legal compliance	Maintain licence to operate	Make business case	Integration of value and values	Create new markets/social change
Leadership	Minimal	Supportive	On top of the issues	Ahead of the curve	Visionary
Structure	Marginal	Functional ownership	Cross-functional coordination	Organizational alignment	Integrated into mainstream
Issues management	Defensive	Reactive	Responsive	Proactive	Defines the issues
Stakeholder relationships	Unilateral	Interactive	Mutual influence	Alliances and partnerships	Multi-organizational
Transparency	Enough to protect flanks	Public relations	Public reporting	Assurance	Full disclosure

Dimensions (row label, vertical, at left of table)

Figure 6.1 Stages of corporate responsibility

(*Source:* Adapted from Mirvis and Googins, 2006)

and 'transforming' stages). As the overview of criticisms of corporate responsibility in Chapter 13 shows, there are good reasons for doubting whether companies, especially large corporations, can ever have the kind of game-changing purpose some would like them to have. However, authors and business people, such as Mackey, Senge, and McInnes, continue to press the importance of striving for this level of transformation. Their calls for more radical change are in part recognition of the way major external events such as climate change require companies in some industries to leapfrog to an advanced evolutionary stage. Nonetheless, as a whole, the stages provide a framework for understanding the different purposes that companies are pursuing. Equally, as we consider in the next section, they reveal some of the key dimensions to corporate responsibility management.

 Discussion points

Corporate responsibility is often presented as an evolutionary journey.

- Does it help managers to think of corporate responsibility in this way?
- Are the criteria used to measure progression adequate and appropriate?
- What companies would you put at Mirvis and Googins' stages 3 and 4, and which would you say have reached or are approaching stage 5?

Qualities of good corporate responsibility management

Following the three critical areas of organizational change mentioned earlier, we move now from the company's purpose in managing corporate responsibility to a discussion of its implementation (the 'how'). There are an increasing number of books about how to manage corporate responsibility, aimed largely at existing managers. Peters' *Waltzing with the Raptors* (1999) was one of the first of these, promising a practical roadmap to protecting a company's reputation, and since then further titles have concentrated on particular advantages of corporate responsibility (e.g. risk management, the business case, enhanced strategy) and/or the needs of particular business functions (e.g. corporate responsibility for PR professionals; marketing).

A glance at the contents of these books reveals the central elements of corporate responsibility management today. For example, the *Guide to Best Practices in Corporate Social Responsibility*,[12] a book targeted at mid-level PR managers, features chapters on communicating corporate responsibility, building an integrated corporate responsibility strategy, demonstrating its value to senior management, working with stakeholders, managing crises, corporate responsibility reporting, and measuring corporate responsibility performance. Such books reveal a managerial orthodoxy that embraces much of corporate responsibility today and is reflected in various assessments of best practice.[13] This orthodoxy comprises:

1   particular tools and approaches—the ingredients of good corporate responsibility management;

2   advice on execution—the qualities of that management.

We now discuss these two dimensions and also take a more in-depth look at some of the ingredients in coming chapters.

One of the things that distinguishes corporate responsibility today from that of the past is that it is becoming an identifiable area of management expertise. As we discuss later in this chapter ('Structuring the corporate responsibility function', p 138), this expertise is housed in a variety of organizational structures, but there is also a large amount of general advice that is presented as best practice which draws on analysis of diverse corporate experiences and case studies. This ranges from identifying broad areas to which the company should pay attention (e.g. integrating strategies into the corporate culture, adhering to declared values and standards, and communicating what the company is doing, including both achievements and challenges)[14] to more specific steps. Some of the most common advice that can be offered to a company once its purpose is clear is set out in Box 6.1.

Much of this advice relates to the initial stages of adopting corporate responsibility and, as, we discuss in Chapter 9 in relation to stakeholder engagement, for example, some aspects of corporate responsibility management ultimately involve many layers of skill and complexity. This is also true of making the business case for corporate responsibility, which some consultants and theorists stress needs to be established as early as possible within the company (see 'The business case for corporate responsibility, p 144). However, returning to our earlier discussion about instrumental and intrinsic value, Hemingway and MacLagan (2004) argue that the commercial imperative is only part of effective corporate responsibility management and that it should also be linked to the personal values of individual managers. They point out that

> **Box 6.1** Common advice on introducing corporate responsibility into management
>
> - Get started—don't take too long before getting under way with the first activities.
> - Pay attention to terminology—for example, a term such as 'sustainable growth' may have more resonance with company managers than 'sustainability', 'sustainable development', or 'social responsibility', because the latter terms can be interpreted as discarding the idea of economic growth with which managers are most familiar.
> - Be frank and transparent—this is the best way to get staff attention, and winning their attention makes it easier to change the corporate ethos.
> - Instil a company ethic of education and learning around issues of responsibility.
> - Find useful partners and corporate responsibility champions across the company.
> - Get to know the communities within which the company exists, including understanding its norms, values, cultures, traditions, and, of course, applicable laws.
> - Establish dialogues and debates with stakeholders from different sectors and sections of society, and make these transparent and honest, not least in terms of agreeing realistic expectations.
> - Form 'smart partnerships' with stakeholders to achieve genuine corporate responsibility goals, rather than only public relations imperatives.
> - Measure and account for what the company does in areas of corporate responsibility.
> - Report to the public and key constituencies on what the company is doing and make these reports accessible to all who have an interest.
>
> (Adapted from CCC, 2005a; Olsen, 2004; Holliday et al., 2002; SustainAbility/UNEP, 2001; Peters, 1999)

individual discretion allows personnel to introduce their values into corporate responsibility policies, whether through officially sanctioned actions, the unintended consequences of an individual resolving a problem by drawing on personal beliefs, or an individual's entrepreneurship in bringing values into the workplace.

Leaders—or, perhaps more accurately, 'initiators' or what Pinchot (1985) calls 'intrapreneurs'—can come from almost any part of the company and a key ingredient is what Arnold and Hartman (2003) call *'moral imagination'*, a theme that Grayson and Nelson (2013) develop in their overview of corporate partnerships. For example, at BAT, some of the early enthusiasm for corporate responsibility is said to have come from middle managers in corporate affairs, while at The Body Shop and Timberland it stemmed from the moral imagination of CEOs from the outset. Regardless of how it begins, however, there comes a stage at which senior management needs to give legitimacy to the corporate responsibility agenda, so that it is valued across the company. Part of this legitimization is the creation of relevant systems to develop policies, processes, indicators, and targets, so that the full range of corporate-responsibility-related activities are managed. Companies such as Anglo American and the ICT firms involved in the Global e-Sustainability Initiative (GeSI) have made a point of sharing their learning in such areas.[15]

In corporate responsibility literature, there is much more discussion of the aims of these systems (e.g. that they be inclusive, responsive, and engaged with stakeholders),[16] than there is of what they look like in practice. We examine the structuring of the corporate responsibility function in more detail in the next section, but it is typical for systems to evolve and change as the company becomes more familiar with corporate responsibility as a management area. Part of this is the creation of corporate responsibility capacity, and comparative research of company practices shows that systems can include capacity building both within the company (e.g. to understand corporate responsibility issues, or to engage with stakeholders) and among stakeholders themselves, so that they can interact more effectively with firms.[17] For example, through its Leadership Development initiative, 3M has taken the idea of ethics programmes a step further than many companies by having executives give examples of where opportunities for business advantage did not concord with the company's values, and then debating and undertaking role play based on how others would react in that situation. Some companies, such as Levi Strauss and Nike, are investing in building the capacity of suppliers to manage their human resources more effectively so as to avert the need for abusive labour practices, and others, such as Tesco, are training their buyers so that procurement practices do not exacerbate such problems.[18]

However, any single idea of how to manage corporate responsibility reflects received wisdom; it should not be treated as infallible truth. Research with managers from several leading companies has shown that following received wisdom can assist the corporate responsibility effort, but, at the same time, can lay potential traps.[19] For example, making the business case can help to explain why a company should take corporate responsibility seriously and legitimate the topic inside the business—but managers' experiences also show that it can cause companies or individuals to promise more than they can actually deliver or demonstrate, given the available data. In the long run, this makes it more difficult to make a compelling non-financial case. Moreover, the business case tends to be demonstrated using lagging indicators that only explain what happened in the past and do not necessarily help in deciding about future investments.

Structuring the corporate responsibility function

One area in which more detailed information about the actual management of corporate responsibility is starting to emerge is the structuring of corporate responsibility management within companies. Some of this information takes the form of consultancy advice to individual firms and is not in the public domain, but what is available (both officially and unofficially) provides a reasonably detailed picture of actual corporate responsibility management practice.

A relatively early management guide on this topic identified what it considered to be nine essential steps for designing a corporate responsibility structure:[20]

1   understanding the drivers of corporate responsibility within the firm;
2   identifying the key corporate responsibility issues;
3   identifying and evaluating stakeholders;
4   identifying functions within the company that support corporate responsibility efforts;
5   analysing company systems, culture, and impending changes;
6   evaluating structural options;

7 developing a staff plan;

8 creating a structure for cross-functional interaction;

9 assessing the process and framework for budget and resource allocation.

At first glance, this can appear to be an unwieldy list of actions, but the steps can be divided between four main areas of activity:

1 understanding the drivers (step 1);

2 mapping what is already happening inside and outside the company (steps 2, 3, and 4);

3 coming to grips with existing systems (step 5);

4 designing a specific corporate responsibility management structure (steps 6, 7, 8, and 9).

Nobody knows how often this type of methodical approach is followed in real life, but it does highlight aspects of corporate responsibility structuring that have engendered debate within companies. These include the importance, or otherwise, of cross-functional interaction within the firm, decisions about resource allocation, staffing the corporate responsibility function, and, perhaps most significantly, deciding what is the most appropriate structure for a specific company. What has emerged is an array of structures. For example, at Pfizer there is a long-standing tradition of the full board of directors making major decisions rather than specific committees, and as a result, while some firms have brought specialists in at the non-executive director level, the company has sought to diversify the full board with corporate responsibility expertise. Another approach is to place formal responsibility for corporate responsibility issues in the hands of existing executives; for example, at Novartis the heads of legal affairs and human resources have formal responsibility for corporate responsibility issues inside the executive committee. Corporate responsibility can also be placed in other parts of the organization: at IBM, it comes under the executive vice-president for innovation and technology; at Groupe Danone, the head of sustainable development and social responsibility reports to the company general secretary; at Telefónica, a stand-alone department was created, reporting to the head of corporate communications.

A survey of 254 managers and directors, who saw corporate responsibility as part of their role, found that they had 23 job titles.[21] Anecdotally, it seems likely that many companies have renamed their corporate responsibility function as 'sustainability'.[22] Another survey of 580 company structures worldwide found that, in 30 per cent of cases, corporate responsibility was managed by an existing department, such as communications or HR, without staff who have corporate responsibility as their primary function.[23] Ten per cent of companies had set up non-departmental working committees to manage corporate responsibility and 4 per cent had outsourced corporate responsibility activities to an external consultancy. However, in the majority of companies (56 per cent) there were designated corporate responsibility personnel of some kind. The majority of these were either part of a stand-alone corporate responsibility department or team in the corporate centre (22 per cent), or part of another department, such as corporate communications (24 per cent). The remaining companies had several teams dispersed across the organization, either as stand-alone entities (9 per cent), or as part of a number of different departments (10 per cent).

These statistics tell us something about how far companies have moved towards the kind of idealized structure and systems that are depicted as corporate responsibility best practice. The fact that only 10 per cent of companies have dedicated corporate responsibility managers in the regions or business lines suggests that there is a long way to go before the ideal of embedding corporate responsibility into business operations is realized. This is in marked contrast to the areas of knowledge management and quality management, in which specialists are less likely to be located in the corporate centre and more likely to be found in teams dispersed across the business. It also contrasts with the situation in companies acknowledged by their peers as corporate responsibility innovators. In Marks & Spencer and Unilever, for instance, corporate responsibility is embedded throughout the company. This has happened because those firms have evolved from a corporate responsibility focus to a sustainability focus in which issues such as waste, energy, and natural capital management are seen as essential to the future of the business.

There are strong arguments for structuring corporate responsibility in different ways. Some argue that it needs to be at the locus of internal power, so that corporate responsibility factors influence business decisions (e.g. housing it where prices and deadlines are negotiated with suppliers rather than in public affairs). Some believe that it should be at the nodes where key business areas connect, so as to build cross-functional influence. There is a widely felt sentiment that as important as a knowledge of corporate responsibility is an understanding of what affects company performance (e.g. operations, investors, sourcing) and, related to that, there is a desire among many external commentators for corporate responsibility issues to be dealt with in the operational functions to which they belong (e.g. employee issues to be addressed by HR; sourcing issues by buying; customer issues by sales and marketing).

However, as already noted, this kind of integrated corporate responsibility function is a long way from being realized in most firms. Furthermore, some management theorists argue that corporate responsibility managers are unlikely to have the complete range of organizational elements at their disposal (e.g. hierarchy, sanctions, rules), and more typically rely on 'partial' organization in which only sporadic conventional management elements are at the manager's disposal.[24]

Alongside the question of where to situate the corporate responsibility function lies that of how to resource it. Early movers in the field, such as The Body Shop, tended to establish separate well-resourced corporate responsibility departments that were a statement of serious commitment. Now, it is less certain how large a corporate responsibility department should be, or even if there should be such a thing. In a company such as GlaxoSmithKline, a small team is said to have made significant progress because it gained the attention and commitment of multiple departments, encouraging them to deploy their own resources and to incorporate corporate responsibility into their own practices. In other companies, such as Gap Inc., relatively large teams have been created because of the challenges faced in managing global supply chains; procurement is an increasingly important aspect of corporate responsibility management in both private and public sector organizations.[25] Moreover, none of these structures are static, as demonstrated by the evolution of corporate responsibility at Marks & Spencer described in Case Study 6.

Discussion points

The structure of corporate responsibility functions is often seen as an indication of how serious a company is about realizing its corporate responsibility vision.

- Do you think structure is an important indicator of a company's attitude to corporate responsibility?
- Why have some companies rebranded corporate responsibility as sustainability?
- How would you structure the corporate responsibility function in a sports shoe or apparel company?

Corporate responsibility as strategy

Underlying questions about how to locate the corporate responsibility function is the issue of an integrated strategy that makes corporate responsibility part of the corporate DNA.[26] As early as 1973, Andrews recognized that:

> the overriding master problem ... impeding the further progress of corporate responsibility is the difficulty of making credible and effective, throughout a large organization, the social component of a corporate strategy ...

(*Andrews, 1973, p 57*)

There is now widespread agreement with Andrews' subsequent point that a company's social policy should be as much a function of strategic planning as is its choice of products and marketing, or its establishment of profit and growth objectives. Indeed, numerous authors have explored corporate responsibility from the perspective of conventional management disciplines such as marketing and organizational behaviour.[27] As already noted, there is a widely held belief among corporate responsibility thinkers that companies should develop management approaches that establish corporate responsibility as a core driver of business performance, thereby fully aligning it with the firm's strategic operations.

This kind of belief is reflected in the definitions of the more evolved forms of corporate responsibility that we described earlier ('Stages of corporate responsibility', p 133), but there is often frustration among theorists that current corporate responsibility scorecards, standards, reports, and other widely used management tools fail to support strategic alignment or planning.[28] Subsequently, there is a stark contrast between conventional business management excellence and corporate responsibility management excellence. The former involves building a strategy that creates competitive advantage and then reinforcing that strategy with high-quality operational processes that lead to best quality and productivity. In contrast, corporate responsibility often creates programmes to tackle specific issues, and then puts in place systems to enforce and sustain what it considers to be ethical practices, finally producing a report reviewing its commitments and practices. In other words, there is a strong tendency to define excellence as the production of a report about programmes and systems, begging the question: is there any other area of business management in which this would be considered acceptable, let alone 'excellent'?

In contrast, the strategic integration of corporate responsibility means that corporate responsibility is seen as a business driver. It involves corporate responsibility creating value within the company and the company creating value for wider society. An example of this type of integration is when GE began to see spiralling health costs and difficulties in accessing health care as both a social problem and a business opportunity. It responded by investing in products that were tailored to the needs of specific markets around the world, instead of focusing purely on the best technology accessible only to the wealthy.[29] Moreover, as the quote in Snapshot 6.1 shows, serving emerging markets through this kind of approach has become central to the company's strategy for growth.

The GE case is an example of a strategy for offensive corporate responsibility, but strategic integration can also be applied to more defensive objectives. For example, it is already common for companies to use corporate responsibility as part of a strategy to protect their reputations, as was the case when leading IT companies, such as IBM, HP, and Dell, established the Electronics Industry Code of Conduct as a common approach to monitoring the corporate responsibility issues in their suppliers' operations. Similarly, Fedex is applying integrated thinking in its collaboration with the Alliance for Environmental Innovation, which aims to develop trucks that are 50 per cent more fuel-efficient and less harmful to the environment than those it currently operates.

The examples given earlier imply that integrating corporate responsibility into business strategy is another way of making the business case for improved social and environmental performance. But true integration requires that there are processes to ensure that corporate responsibility imperatives are considered on their own merits in strategic planning, regardless of the financial implications. What proponents of integration claim is that the distinction between business imperative and responsibility imperative will become irrelevant, pointing for comparison to quality management, for which poor quality came to be seen as symptomatic of unproductive systems, just as waste, emissions, and environmental impacts are seen today. In this way, corporate responsibility ceases to be a contained entity, and becomes an inseparable part of a larger complex and changing system which, as van Tulder (2006) says, needs to influence different levels (at which it will take different forms) and functions such as marketing, quality control, financial management, and research and development.

 Discussion points

Integration of corporate responsibility into mainstream business strategy is a widely touted ambition among both theorists and practitioners.

- What arguments might managers make to persuade a company of the advantages of the integration of corporate responsibility?
- If integration does not happen more widely than at present, how will this affect future developments in corporate responsibility?
- What examples are there of companies successfully integrating corporate responsibility into business management decisions?

Snapshot 6.1   General Electric—integrating corporate responsibility as a business driver

Edison once said, '*Vision without execution is hallucination*'. Yet much of the information on managing corporate responsibility deals with aims, expectations, and general principles, and not with the detail of its implementation. Part of what is missing is the connection between the why, the what, and the how of transformation management, i.e. the rationale, the expected results, and the way in which these will be achieved.

GE, founded by Edison, which owns businesses in industries as diverse as aviation, transportation, energy, and health care, is trying to make this connection. In developing its 'ecomagination' initiative in the mid-2000s, managers consulted across the company and with what were sometimes hostile external groups, and came up with a list of social and environmental issues in relation to which it could employ its assets to bring about change. They then created a business plan that committed company resources to set output targets which, not least, promised to double company revenues to $2,000m by 2010 by developing products offering environmental advantage to customers. They promised to double the spend on clean technology research and development to $1,500 million, and the same kind of integration is depicted in the company's 2005 *Citizenship Report* (p 42):

> In 2004, GE's revenues from the developing world reached $21 billion, a 37% increase. We now expect to get as much as 60% of our future revenue growth from emerging markets including China, Russia, Eastern Europe, India, and the Middle East. In these markets, GE can provide much-needed infrastructure. We will deliver vital systems for water, power, healthcare, and transportation to improve the quality of life and access to opportunity in these countries ... By providing critical infrastructure needs, GE has the opportunity to lay a foundation for sustainable growth.
>
> *(GE 2005, p 42)*

The achievements over the first five years were encouraging. By 2010, the company had launched 22 ecomagination products. It set itself a target of doubling R&D spend in the area of clean technology, and exceeded it, reaching $1.8 billion. It is now committed to spending $10 billion on ecomagination R&D by 2015. It has also reduced its overall greenhouse gas emissions by 32 per cent and its energy intensity by 32 per cent, and beat its target of cutting freshwater use by 25 per cent. Employees are encouraged to become involved through initiatives such as the Energy Treasure Hunt in which workers identify energy reduction opportunities. Suppliers have to demonstrate their own progress using GE's new Supplier Management Systems Tool.

(Stewart and Immelt, 2006; GE, 2005; Reed and Neubert, 2012; GE Performance Against Commitments[30])

....

Quick questions

Under long-time CEO Jack Welch, GE was widely admired by investors but repeatedly criticized for its environmental performance.

1. What evidence is there that GE has acted on the ecomagination promise of putting corporate responsibility issues at the core of business strategy?

2. Are the reasons that GE gives for integrating corporate responsibility convincing from a shareholder's perspective?

3. What is the business case for ecomagination?

The business case for corporate responsibility

Launching Creating Shared Value, Nestlé's business response to nutrition, water, and rural development challenges, Chairman Peter Brabeck-Letmathe said, 'The financial crisis ... revealed once more a basic business axiom: if you fail to work on behalf of public inter-est and take short cuts that put the public at risk, you will also fail your shareholders'.[31] The term shared value is also used by Porter and Kramer (2011). It refers to a resetting of the boundaries of capitalism by reconceiving products and markets so that they focus on social and environmental impact, redefining productivity, and embedding business activi-ties more in local communities (e.g. through cluster development). The significance of a long-time advocate of business competitiveness and free market capitalism revisiting the purpose of business in this way has meant that shared value has gained attention even if it reflects well-established thinking in the corporate responsibility field. But Porter and Kramer argue that shared value is still driven by the profit motive: the difference is that not all profit is equal, and commercial activities with a social purpose represent a 'higher form of capitalism'.

Pick up any book on corporate responsibility, browse the session themes of conferences, or look at companies' social or environmental reports, and you will soon discern how important the business case has become to contemporary corporate responsibility. For business man-agers, government officials, academics, consultants, to name but a few, making the business case has become the Holy Grail. There is a simple reason for this—demonstrating a posi-tive correlation between corporate responsibility and business performance is seen as giving social and environmental issues legitimacy in the world of mainstream business. In this way, it greatly increases the likelihood that corporate responsibility practices will be adopted. Conse-quently, information, such as that 91 per cent of executives believe that corporate responsibil-ity creates shareholder value, or that 80 per cent say that non-financial indicators are essential to characterize future financial performance, is widely cited as proof positive of corporate responsibility's importance, not as the nice thing to do, but as part of good management practice.[32]

Making the business case has grown in importance as the focus of corporate responsibility has moved from philanthropy and generally giving a proportion of revenues back to society, to the function of corporate responsibility in core business activities, and the role of business in tackling major societal challenges.[33] Showing how corporate responsibility relates to busi-ness performance is intended to help managers to understand why they should be paying attention and to what they should be attending. It is also meant to help companies to explain the importance of social and environmental performance to investors, and vice versa. Mean-while, away from the company-specific level, it provides a basis for corporate responsibility's advocates to demonstrate to mainstream management theorists and economists that corpo-rate responsibility can add to shareholder value, or at least will not damage it.[34]

There are, then, good reasons why the business case has become so important to corpo-rate responsibility. But the *gravitas* that it has accrued gives rise to further questions: What evidence is there of a business case? How does its presence or absence affect corporate responsibility now and in the future? Neither question is easy to answer and there is good reason to consider what the consequences are for corporate responsibility if the business case continues to be brought to the fore. But we will begin with some examples.

Examples of the benefits to business

When BP met its target of reducing greenhouse gas emissions at twice the rate specified in the Kyoto Protocol nine years ahead of schedule, the reductions were the equivalent of 9.6 million tonnes and the company achieved operational savings of $250 million. In 2012, Wal-Mart's investment in fleet efficiency saved it almost $130 million and avoided emitting almost 103,000 tonnes of carbon dioxide, equal to taking 20,000 cars off the road. Dow Chemical estimates that if it could make its water filtration technologies available to the 1.2 billion poorest people in the world, it could generate $300 million in sales. When 3M pre-empted new government regulations by abandoning the use of solvent-based coatings in favour of water-soluble ones, it benefited commercially from having an early mover advantage, and operationally from reductions in downtime, product loss, and waste related to the new technology. Staving off regulation and repairing a severely damaged reputation were key motivations for financial institutions to set up the Equator Principles to combat corruption in overseas projects.[35] Gap Inc. has found that purchasing decisions that negatively impact working conditions also undermine quality, on-time delivery, and cost.[36] Major DIY and furniture stories, such as Home Depot, Ikea, and B&Q, have made sourcing from sustainably managed resources part of their buying policy. Even if there is not a clear financial case, as REWE claims about its commitment to sourcing all of its energy from renewable sources, a strong position can increase the company's leverage with government and civil society.[37]

Different industries; different countries; different dimensions of corporate responsibility—all suggesting that a link can be made between social and environmental performance, and business performance. According to the investment group Innovest, 85 per cent of studies show a positive correlation between environmental governance and financial performance.[38] According to UK-based telecommunications company BT, the benefits of corporate responsibility to a company's reputation, and the money that can be saved through efficient environmental planning and the identification of new market opportunities, *often amount to a convincing financial reason for why business should engage with such issues*.[39] According to one former executive, strategies built around the triple bottom line can yield a 46 per cent increase in profit over five years, fully costed.[40]

Meanings of the 'business case'

Examples such as those in the previous section have generated considerable excitement about the business case, but they also highlight some of the problems in making that case. The case is more than just shareholder value or return on investment; equally, it can be the indirect benefits of creating a favourable business environment (e.g. maintaining reputation, innovation, licence to operate). It is not immediately clear which dimensions of corporate responsibility have the strongest or weakest links to business performance. It is also not always apparent what type of relationship exists between corporate responsibility and business performance, i.e. whether the one causes the other and under what circumstances.

Preston and O'Bannon (1997) divide the business case into three types of relationship:

1 that within which corporate responsibility relates to financial performance;

2 that within which financial performance relates to corporate responsibility;

3 that within which corporate responsibility and financial performance are synergistic.

In all three types, the relationship can be positive, neutral, or negative, so that according to Friedman (1962), for example, there is a negative relationship between corporate responsibility and financial performance because the former misuses company assets (see Chapter 1). According to Cornell and Shapiro (1987), there is a positive relationship because meeting the needs of stakeholders other than shareholders enhances financial performance. Case studies and other analyses exist for each type of relationship; for example, Waddock and Graves (1997) study how the strength of performance affects the amount that a company invests in corporate responsibility.

To make sense of the business performance–corporate responsibility relationship, we need to know what each term refers to. There are many different definitions available,[41] but Boxes 6.2 and 6.3 offer a generic set of possibilities applicable to a variety of industries.

Box 6.2   Dimensions of corporate responsibility

1 The influence of *ethics, values, and principles* on a company's actions, as evident, for example, in business principles, decisions, and legal actions.

2 A company's *accountability and transparency* for its corporate responsibility performance, as evident, for example, in its reporting and management systems.

3 A company's overall commitment and performance in social, economic, and environmental areas (i.e. the *triple bottom line*).

4 A company's record on *eco-efficiency*, evident, for example, in its minimization of adverse environmental impacts associated with product processes.

5 The *environmental product focus* of a company, as seen, for example, in its redesign of products to reduce their environmental impact (e.g. cradle-to-grave product stewardship).

6 The use of a company's resources to support the *social and economic development* of communities.

7 A company's respect for, and protection of, *human rights*.

8 Efforts by a company to foster a high-quality *work environment*, including health and safety issues, but also those such as work–life balance.

9 Involvement of the company's *business stakeholders* (e.g. suppliers, partners, contractors, shareholders) in implementing its corporate responsibility strategy.

10 The quantity and quality of a company's engagement with *external stakeholders* (e.g. civil society organizations, government) in relation to corporate responsibility.[42]

Box 6.3   Measures of business performance

1 **Shareholder value**   Changes in a company's stock price and dividend.

2 **Revenue**   Changes in a company's revenues due to pricing, market share, new markets, etc.

3 **Operational efficiency**   A company's cost-effectiveness in turning inputs into productive outputs.

4 **Access to capital**   A company's access to equity and debt capital.

5 **Customer attraction**   A company's ability to attract and retain customers.

6 **Brand value and reputation**   The value assigned to a company and its brands due to their reputation.

7 **Human capital**   The knowledge and skills of a company's employees, resulting from the ability to attract, develop, and retain a workforce.

(continued...)

8 Risk management   Exposure of a company's assets to short- and long-term risks.

9 Innovation   A company's ability to maintain its competitive advantage through better products, services, and business models.

10 Licence to operate   A company's ability to maintain a level of acceptance among its stakeholders that allows it to operate effectively.

The application of these measures is affected by several variables. First, each audience requires information to meet its specific needs. For example, business managers may want information that will help to convince their superiors or colleagues, while shareholders will want to know if corporate responsibility pays, and governments will want information that will test if corporate responsibility is a viable basis for delivering social and environmental benefits.[43]

Second, the business case differs from industry to industry. For a mining company, such as Placer Dome, corporate responsibility might result in preferred access in future gold-mining projects, whereas for Royal Ahold, the supermarket company, it might help the company to relate better to consumers in fiercely competitive mature markets.[44]

Third, the business case partly depends on how corporate responsibility is viewed within a company and on how developed that company's approach to corporate responsibility is. For example, since disasters such as the Texas refinery explosions and the Deepwater Horizon oil spill, BP has had to shift its focus from blue-sky thinking about a world 'beyond petroleum' (its slogan in the late 1990s) to safety, reputation management, and licence to operate. Shell, by contrast, which was once caught up in scandals about drilling rig decommissioning and its impact on local communities in Nigeria, is now able to exhibit leadership through its energy scenario planning work.[45]

Finally, studies of the business case tend to overlook how the local, national, or regional contexts affect the business case.[46] For example, there might be quite different arguments to be made for eco-efficiency in a country with a tough regulatory regime and a strong utilities infrastructure, compared with that in a country in which environmental regulations are weak, but the cost of energy or clean water is relatively high. Just as corporate responsibility can look different from country to country (see Chapter 5), so, too, can the business case (see Snapshot 6.2).

 Discussion points

One reason for making the business case is that it helps to make corporate responsibility more comprehensible to senior executives and operational managers.

- Choose a particular company or industry with which you are familiar. How would you go about making the business case to the executive team?

- Is there a distinct financial performance case? What do you think are the strongest and weakest areas of that case?

- Pick a company you know that is working on corporate responsibility. Apply conventional marketing and entrepreneurship analysis tools such as Mullins' seven domains (Mullins 2006) or Chan Kim's value curves (Chan Kim and Mauborgne 2005) to understand the business case for one of its products addressing social or environmental issues.

Snapshot 6.2   Catalytic converters—governments creating the business case

The business case is not simply a question of economics; it also depends on the environment within which business operates. Some of the technologies we take for granted originally became viable because of government actions. The catalytic converter is an excellent example of how legislation created a market for an environmental product, and of how major automotive manufacturers overcame their resistance and worked with suppliers to reduce vehicle emissions, even as vehicle use grew.

The market for catalytic converters was a direct consequence of vehicle emissions controls introduced in 1970—notably, amendments to the US Federal Clean Air Act 1963 and the Californian Zero Emission Vehicle Mandate. The legislation was passed even though the technology to achieve the targets they set out was barely proven and not commercialized, and the automakers lobbied aggressively that it would harm their industry. But the strong stance of the Californian government and of the newly established US Environmental Protection Agency (EPA) forced automakers to enter into forward commitment procurement agreements with potential catalytic converter suppliers towards working together to develop the technology that would meet demands for a 90 per cent reduction in carbon dioxide and nitrous oxide.

Engine modifications alone would have been unlikely to meet these much tougher standards, however, and so a real commercial opportunity emerged for companies such as Johnson Matthey, which had relevant experience from working with other industries, to work with the automakers. These companies were encouraged by the EPA's insistence that vehicle manufacturers prove that they were making a determined effort to meet the targets, and in 1972 the EPA held the first of several public hearings to assess progress. Despite the automakers' initial reluctance, catalytic converters have become the norm and emissions from cars are now lower than they were in the 1960s, despite the increase in total car mileage. In terms of government action, the key learnings are that government is able to motivate private industry to deliver better technology for environmental gain at no particular cost to the public purse over the long term.

(*Sources*: www.environmental-expert.com; www.managementtoday.co.uk)

Quick questions

1 What were the main government actions that encouraged automakers to adopt catalytic converters?

2 Why do you think automakers were resistant?

3 Are there other examples in which government has created a new market in this way?

Evidence of a business case

The trouble with the business case is that, apart from individual company case studies that are difficult to compare, the evidence is patchy and confusing. Carroll and Shabana (2010) agree with the earlier findings by Margolis and Walsh (2003) that it is impossible to draw the conclusion that corporate responsibility helps or harms a company. Frustratingly, a decade after Margolis and Walsh, most articles about the business case for corporate responsibility (and more recently sustainability) discuss possible frameworks for analysis rather than attempting a systematic review of the evidence.[47] Alternatively, they try to identify a direct correlation between corporate social performance and financial performance as measured by share price, which is probably too narrow a definition of the business case.[48] It is probably more useful to consider business's justification and rationale for corporate responsibility in terms of the specific benefits to businesses in an economic and financial ('bottom-line') sense that would flow from CSR activities and initiatives.[49]

The consultancy company SustainAbility developed a matrix to review multiple reports, case studies, and academic analyses pertaining to the business case for sustainable development. Although not meeting the criteria of academic rigour required by business studies journals, it is a useful way of comparing the information about the business case found in very diverse sources. The matrix links the business measures of success with the different dimensions of corporate responsibility (see Boxes 6.1 and 6.2). For example, one could look at whether eco-efficiency affects a company's operational efficiency, or if there is a correlation between the firm's licence to operate and its attention to human rights.

The original SustainAbility reports identified 21 areas in which there was strong evidence that corporate responsibility positively affects business performance (see Figure 6.2).[50] The most demonstrable contribution was in the area of eco-efficiency, in which changes in the use of raw materials, recycling and reuse, reductions in emissions, and other new practices had tangible benefits in terms of shareholder value, operational efficiency, access to capital, reputation, risk management, and innovation. Eco-efficiency has become so prevalent in industries such as chemicals, energy, and electrical goods that it could be seen as nothing more than rational profit maximization, i.e. common-sense management practice. But it is relatively recently that pollution has come to be seen not as the inevitable by-product of economic prosperity, but as a form of economic waste,[51] and this change has occurred because of, not despite, the kind of transformation associated with corporate responsibility (see also Chapter 3).

There was also strong evidence that other dimensions of corporate responsibility are linked to better business performance, including protection of human rights, high-quality working conditions, relationships with external stakeholders, and transparency and accountability around corporate responsibility performance. What also stands out is that, whereas eco-efficiency delivers a wide variety of benefits, these other dimensions affect a much narrower selection of business performance measures. By far the greatest impact was on brand value and reputation, for which there is evidence of a strong positive impact from six different dimensions of corporate responsibility, although in emerging and developing economies revenue and operational efficiency are also important. The next most frequent area of impact was risk management, for which dimensions such as eco-efficiency, the development of environmental products, protection of human rights, and a commitment to values and principles all have a strong positive impact. In other words, corporate responsibility is most likely to have a strong positive impact on intangible, rather than tangible, aspects of business performance.

Figure 6.2 also shows that there are as many areas on which corporate responsibility has a neutral or negative impact on business performance, as there are those on which there is a strong positive impact. Notably, the business case for engaging with business stakeholders appears weak, and engaging with non-business stakeholders cannot be justified in terms of financial performance. Important dimensions of corporate responsibility, such as ethics and values, and protecting human rights, also have a neutral or negative relationship to financial performance measures, such as revenue, access to capital, and operational efficiency.

	Dimensions of corporate responsibility									
Business measures	Ethics; values, principles	Accountability and transparency	Adoption of triple bottom line	Eco-efficiency	Environmental products	Social development	Human rights	Working conditions	Business stakeholders	Non-business stakeholders
Shareholder value				■					▨	
Revenue	▨							■		
Operational efficiency				■		▨	▨	■		
Access to capital	▨									
Customer attraction										
Brand value and reputation	■			■		■	■			■
Human capital								■		
Risk management	■			■			■			
Innovation	▨		▨	■						
Licence to operate						■	■	■		■

Key:

■	Strong positive impact of corporate responsibility on business performance
	Some positive impact of corporate responsibility on business performance
▨	Neutral or negative impact of corporate responsibility on business performance

Figure 6.2 Sustainability matrix

(*Source:* SustainAbility, IFC & Ethos, I. 2002)

The SustainAbility research is dated now but many of its findings are borne out by more recent work, and, as subsequent authors have emphasised, in assessing the business case, we are often using data that are difficult to compare, drawn from a mixture of case studies and quantitative surveys covering different industries and countries, and often focused on different dimensions of both corporate responsibility and business performance.[52] Salzmann et al. (2005) conclude that making the business case encounters two stumbling blocks:

1 the complex web of parameters (e.g. technology, regulatory regime, company visibility) and variables (e.g. location, industry, country, time) that can affect outcomes;

2 the difficulty of detecting the impact of corporate responsibility because, except in a small number of areas—notably, eco-efficiency and brand reputation—it tends to be marginal to business practice for most companies and industries.

As Margolis and Walsh (2003) conclude, in their extensive study of corporate social performance, there is little evidence to suggest that paying attention to societal impact damages shareholder value, although companies should not expect to be handsomely rewarded (Margolis et al., 2008). Some argue that, given how little evidence there is of damage to profitability, we should not be asking *'Does corporate responsibility pay?'*, but rather *'Under what conditions does corporate responsibility pay?'*[53] This might mean explaining the specific conditions within a company or industry, but, more broadly, it might mean asking under what market conditions companies will maximize total value by taking account of stakeholder expectations.[54] In relation to the former issue, there are very few studies of how the business case drives corporate responsibility management, and most research concentrates on how corporate responsibility affects business success. Regarding the latter, the relationship between corporate responsibility and the four conditions of perfect competition (i.e. a large number of buyers and sellers, complete information, homogeneity of products, and free entry to and exit from the market), while alluded to by both advocates and critics of corporate responsibility,[55] has not been studied in depth.

It is a weakness in current business case literature that ways in which corporate responsibility might damage business performance are not properly explored. Corporate responsibility's critics like to make the case that it is anti-growth and therefore that it deprives people of the benefits of economic growth which, for example, have raised living standards in successful economies. There is no evidence that corporate responsibility is inherently anti-growth; on the contrary, some advocates of sustainable development say that serious economic growth is needed if we are to meet the needs of current and future generations, and some companies clearly see that addressing social and environmental issues in the future will provide growth opportunities. But some companies, such as low-cost air carriers, would clearly suffer under tougher environmental norms, because air travel results in significantly higher greenhouse gas emissions than does travel by rail or sea.[56] Similarly, despite the instances of increased wages having been offset by productivity gains, it is counter-intuitive (and therefore demands further examination) that increased labour costs due to corporate responsibility will never affect company growth.

As important, though, is that most current studies are unidirectional, focusing on how corporate responsibility affects business performance and ignoring the ways in which business performance may impact on corporate responsibility. For example, few companies have followed Patagonia's lead in disclosing the pros and cons of the social and environmental footprint of its products, and providing the kind of information that consumers would require to make informed decisions about the performance–responsibility relationship.[57] This leaves unanswered questions such as the extent to which successful pursuit of revenue growth has a positive or negative effect on human rights or environmental management. As is explored further later in the text, in relation to criticisms of corporate responsibility (see Chapter 13), the implicit primacy given to the benefits for business is one of the concerns of some observers.

Not surprisingly, therefore, the evidence we have on the business case treats corporate responsibility as an instrumental benefit that can be divided into three types:[58]

1 corporate responsibility as a means of avoiding financial loss (e.g. by defending a company's reputation);

2 corporate responsibility as a driver of tangible financial gains (e.g. by improving the quality of the workforce by driving product innovation);

3   corporate responsibility as an integral element of the company's strategic approach to long-term business performance (e.g. by prompting a move away from dependence on non-renewable natural resources).[59]

Referring back to Martin's virtue matrix ('Basic distinctions in corporate responsibility purpose', p 132), some believe that a fourth type of business case is emerging, within which corporate responsibility is intrinsic to how companies learn, innovate, and manage risk in ever more dynamic and complex business environments (see Chapter 14). However, there is limited evidence of a direct correlation between corporate responsibility and financial performance. In one study, News International had the worst corporate responsibility performance but the best share price, while The Body Shop's good corporate responsibility reputation did not protect its share price when it suffered from poor management and may even have made it more susceptible to public criticism when it was exposed for making false claims about helping developing country suppliers.[60] Furthermore, the quest for a business case could hide the fact that other factors are at least as influential on corporate responsibility management decisions. For example, it has been argued that the widespread adoption of corporate responsibility reporting (see Chapter 12) is because of the readily recognizable analogies it has with financial reporting rather than demonstrable instrumental benefits.[61] Nonetheless, some companies, such as Monsanto, have suffered financially partly because of corporate responsibility failings, while others, such as Shell, have used corporate responsibility to rebuild a damaged image.[62] Perhaps the difficulty again lies in how the problem is framed and, rather than trying to demonstrate that corporate responsibility is a predictor or guarantee of certain outcomes, we should view it, for example, as an approach to strategy and management practice.[63]

 Discussion points

Eco-efficiency is the main area in which a strong business case has been made, while reputation management is an important aspect of business performance.

- Can the success of eco-efficiency be attributed to corporate responsibility, or is it a case of rational profit maximization?
- In which industries do you think reputation is the main management driver of corporate responsibility?
- How would you make the case that corporate responsibility promises benefits to risk management?

 Case study 6   Marks & Spencer's Plan A—The evolution of a corporate responsibility strategy

Marks & Spencer was founded in 1884 in Leeds, England. A long-time fixture of British and Irish high streets, it has over 1000 stores around the world and is the 43rd largest retailer. Its UK stores have 35,000 product lines and it employs 82,000 people, serving 21 million customers weekly. Ninety-nine percent of its products are own-brand, sourced from 2,000 independently owned factories and 20,000 farms which between them employ over a million workers.

(continued...)

CEO Marc Bolland says that the company's 'Plan A is now delivering more for our customers than ever before. It is creating great products with eco and ethical benefits'. His views mirror those of previous chair, Stuart Rose, who in the mid-2000s acknowledged that sustainability 'will shape everything about the way we do business'. However, the commitment to Plan A was not an overnight decision; it was the result of a long journey. In 2000, M&S was experimenting with various ways to restore its company's reputation amongst consumers, investors, and the media after a chain of marketing and reputation failures. Corporate responsibility was not high on the company's must-do list, and few onlookers would have noticed the recruitment of a new environmental manager as Group Finance Director Alison Reid's assistant with responsibility for the environment. But Reid, a long-time M&S employee, knew that the environment was becoming an issue for retailing and had an inkling that it would be a problem the company would need to address.

The new recruit, Mike Barry, had no line manager, and recalls the first two years as being like 'a guerrilla war'. Working alongside two existing heads of technology, Barry soon realized that the company was out of touch with what was happening in its supply chains and amongst its consumers. It found itself caught out by scandals involving genetically modified foods and pesticide residues, and although there was no question of illegality, M&S found it hard to defend itself in the court of public opinion.

But the company's financial position was perilous, and although the need for change was apparent, radical action was out of the question. Instead, in keeping with the spirit of a guerrilla war, a number of low-profile or off-the-radar actions were taken, such as building internal alliances amongst people in the company with shared corporate responsibility concerns. Small initiatives were discovered across the company, and people were corralled in a common sense of purpose—something made possible because the new alliance involved people with an intimate knowledge of the firm and its suppliers. At the same time, M&S began to build external alliances with organizations such as Greenpeace, Friends of the Earth, and WWF.

A formal Head of Corporate Social Responsibility position was created, overseeing two environmental specialists and two philanthropy specialists. But corporate responsibility did not save the company when results went from bad to worse in 2003. Profits which had exceeded £1 billion in 1998 were down to £145 million. However, against a bleak backdrop, corporate responsibility provided some of the few highlights, with M&S winning awards in areas such as pesticides and sustainable timber. When the company became embroiled in a hostile takeover bid in 2004, news that M&S had been chosen as the most responsible company in Britain was met with applause at a shareholder meeting.

In 2006, the company launched its Behind the Label campaign to inform consumers about the way M&S sources its products. This was a response to data showing that a third of shoppers had put clothes back on the rails amid concerns about their origins, and one in five had avoided food items because of concerns about sourcing and processing. In-store publicity and newspaper adverts talked about M&S's commitment to fairtrade and non-GM food, as well as moves to cut salt and fat in foods, promote sustainability, recycle packaging, and protect animal welfare. Publicly, Behind the Label was treated as a toe in the water: 'We'll see how it goes', said Stuart Rose to the BBC, 'Let's test the market'. But inside the company any sense of smugness disappeared when Rose told the corporate responsibility team that Behind the Label was already 'old news'. As Barry recalls it, Rose told the team that they would be out of a job if in three months' time they were still doing Behind the Label—it was time to move on.

That was the spur for Plan A. The alliance of guerrillas that had come together in 2001 had become more formalized, commissioned by the CEO, and containing the directors of technology and communications and the head of marketing. But the members were essentially the same, and

(continued...)

they brainstormed about the social and environmental dimensions to M&S's operations, and what the company could do to have a positive impact. They eventually decided on 100 priority items based on the company's impact, estimates of the cost of taking action, and an assessment of what the competition was doing about these issues. In many instances, nobody knew what the solution would look like, but insiders felt that the risk-taking culture they saw as part of the retail culture meant that it was more important to know what needed to be done than to know if it could be done.

The 100 priorities became the 100 commitments contained in what was called Plan A, launched in January 2007 with enormous media and public attention. In part, this was because in addition to full-page adverts and in-store promotion, Stuart Rose was willing to tell the Plan A story to anyone who would listen—that M&S was committed to becoming —'The greenest—genuinely the greenest—retailer in the UK by 2012'. Timing also played its part, as Rose himself stressed: 'No one had announced a big initiative up until then, and we wanted to be the first. ... I'm not going to deny, if you get it right, [being first gives] you a competitive advantage'. Two days after Plan A's launch, a competitor announced its climate change strategy. It received muted applause, along with criticism for not being up to Plan A.

The 100 commitments of the original Plan A were divided among five pillars (see Figure 6.3). Each had targets to which M&S was willing to be accountable, and each year it revealed its progress. Together, M&S managers believe the pillars cover what the retail industry needs to cover at this time. Says Barry, '[Competitors] will have to take the same pillars and try to better our performance. But the 100 targets are already challenging enough; going beyond them right now would be commercial suicide'.

Climate change	Waste	Sustainable raw materials	Fair partner	Health
Making our operations in the UK and Republic of Ireland carbon neutral and helping customers and suppliers reduce their emissions too	Stop sending waste to landfill from our UK and Irish stores, offices and warehouses; reduce our use of packaging and carrier bags	Ensuring our key raw materials come from the most sustainable sources available to us	Improving the lives of hundreds of thousands of people in our supply chain and local communities	Helping thousands of customers and employees choose a healthier lifestyle

Figure 6.3 Plan A headline commitments

As Plan A evolved, responsibility for it was split between two teams: one, under the Director of Communications and CSR, focused on policy and was responsible for engagement, strategic direction, problem-solving, and communications support; the other, comprising successful M&S line managers, focused on delivery and was responsible for project management, integration, and making the business case (see Figure 6.4). Together, the two teams were tasked with making sure that Plan A was implemented throughout the business lines, not by the team members themselves, but as part of everyday operations so that it became treated not as a sustainability strategy, but as a business plan, part of a five-pronged business strategy that also includes building the M&S brand, international expansion, internet expansion, etc.

(continued...)

Structure of sustainability management

CEO

Director communications & CSR

Director plan A

Head of CSR

Head of plan A delivery

CSR team (8)

Delivery team (4)

Responsible for policy
- Engagement
- Strategic direction
- Problem solving
- Communication support

Responsible for delivery
- Project management
- Integration
- Business case

Figure 6.4 Corporate responsibility management structure at Marks & Spencer

(*Source:* Marks & Spencer plc)

In 2012, Plan A was extended to 2015, and in 2013 a restructuring of Plan A management took place when long-time director Richard Gillies left to join Kingfisher.

(*Sources:* Mesure, 2007; Rose, 2007; Vernon, 2007; www.marksandspencer.com; author interviews)

Questions

1. M&S provides insight into how corporate responsibility evolves within a company.

   a. What were the major changes in the M&S approach between 2000 and 2012?

   b. Why did Rose feel it essential to move beyond Behind the Label?

   c. What does the Plan A management structure indicate about M&S's commitment to embedding corporate responsibility in the company?

2. Plan A has been described as setting the bar on corporate responsibility for retailing.

   a. What evidence is there that Plan A is more than a PR exercise?

   b. Are there responsibility issues in retailing that Plan A does not address?

   c. What evidence is there for a business case for Plan A?

3. Plan A was due to end in 2012 but was extended for three more years. During that time, the company will look at what to do next.

   a. What are the key management lessons to learn from implementing Plan A?

   b. How do you think M&S's commitments are likely to change after 2015?

   c. Using the framework in Figure 6.4 and information on the M&S website, where do you think the different elements of Plan A have benefited aspects of business performance?

Summary

Managing corporate responsibility in companies is a form of change management, and, like other types of corporate transformation, corporate responsibility management activity is divided between identifying the purpose and intended results, establishing the principles and processes to achieve the end goal, and allocating responsibility for its execution.

Companies find themselves at different stages of corporate responsibility which affect what the company wants to achieve and how to go about it. There are important distinctions to be made between *defensive* approaches to corporate responsibility, which are focused on reducing risks, protecting the company's reputation, and ensuring that it stays within the law, and *offensive* approaches, which employ corporate assets in finding solutions to societal problems. These approaches can be broken down further into evolutionary levels of responsibility, beginning with a focus on creating jobs, paying taxes, and abiding by the law, and eventually reaching a stage at which values are clearly at the heart of business decisions, the company is transparent about what it is doing, not doing, and hoping to do, and sees part of its role as standing out as a leader in tackling societal issues.

The further one gets from starting to implement corporate responsibility, the more difficult it becomes to state hard and fast rules for execution. While there is a consensus that good practice involves elements such as consulting internally and externally to decide the purpose, engaging with those upon whom the company impacts or by whom it is influenced as part of the management process, and communicating what the company is trying to achieve and the progress it is making, structuring the management function, building awareness and capacity, and deciding what actions to take will vary according to the company's culture, its industry, the regions it operates in, and the resources available. Another set of challenges emerges when companies take responsibility for the behaviour of their suppliers and others in their value chains, requiring the development of additional management styles and approaches, as companies committed to corporate responsibility seek out ways of improving others' performance, not least by exerting their own power as customers.

Further reading

online resource centre

www.oxfordtextbooks.co.uk/orc/blowfield_murray3e/

Visit the Online Resource Centre that accompanies this book to enrich your understanding of this chapter. Among the resources available are web links, exercises, and additional case studies.

Herrera, M.E. 2012, *Towards strategic CSR: aligning CSR with the business and embedding CSR into the organization (a manual for practitioners)*, Asian Institute of Management, Makati, Philippines.

A recent edition to the handbooks and manuals on implementing corporate responsibility practices in companies.

Holliday, C.O., Schmidheiny, S., & Watts, P. 2002, *Walking the talk: the business case for sustainable development*, Greenleaf, Sheffield.
   Influential argument by European executives emphasizing the importance of sustainable development to business success.

Strand, R. 2013, 'The chief officer of corporate social responsibility: a study of its presence in top management teams', *Journal of Business Ethics*, vol. 112, pp 121–134.
   A comparison of the nature and roles of corporate responsibility officers in top management teams in different companies.

Visser, W. & Tolhurst, N. (eds) 2010, *The world guide to CSR*, Greenleaf, Sheffield.
   A kind of Lonely Planet tour of corporate responsibility around the world.

Werther, W.B. & Chandler, D. 2011, *Strategic corporate social responsibility: stakeholders in a global environment*, Sage, Thousand Oaks, CA.
   Aspects of the business case for stakeholder engagement and other corporate responsibility management practices.

Online resources

- Teaching notes on the chapter case study
- Exercises and discussion topics for students
- Suggestions for additional materials on corporate responsibility management Links to other web-based resources

Endnotes

1.   Maitland, 2006.
2.   For a detailed comparison of country differences in Europe, see www.csreurope.org/pages/en/a_guide_to_csr_in_europe_2009.html.
3.   See, e.g., Visser and Tolhurst, 2010.
4.   European Commission, 2002.
5.   www.gscpnet.com/, accessed 10 October 2013.
6.   PWC, 2006.
7.   Cited in Kramer and Kania, 2006.
8.   Holliday et al., 2002, p 27.
9.   Quinn, 2009; Hale, 2009.
10. See, e.g., Schwartz and Gibb, 1999; Holliday et al., 2002, pp 142–149; Jackson and Nelson, 2004; Werther and Chandler, 2011.
11. Zadek, 2004; www.nike.com/nikebiz.
12. *PR News*, 2006.
13. Ethical Performance, 2008.
14. PWC, 2006.
15. See, for instance, www.angloamerican.co.uk/aa/development/approach/ and www.gesi.org.
16. BSR, 2002.

17. CCC, 2005a.

18. CCC, 2005a.

19. CCC, 2005b.

20. CCC, 2005c.

21. BSR, 2002.

22. See also van Tulder et al., 2013.

23. Melcrum, 2005.

24. Rasche et al., 2013a.

25. Harwood and Humby, 2008.

26. PWC, 2006.

27. Jahdi and Acikdilli, 2009; Bowd et al., 2006; Weybrecht, 2009.

28. This section draws on Holliday et al., 2002; Olsen, 2004; Werther and Chandler, 2011. The authors are also very grateful to Steve Rochlin at AccountAbility for his ideas on this topic.

29. Stewart and Immelt, 2006.

30. www.gecitizenship.com/2012-report/performance-against-commitments/planet/progress, accessed 13 October 2013.

31. Email announcing launch of Creating Shared Value, sent from webmaster@nestle.com, 27 April 2009.

32. *Ethical Corporation* and Nima Hunter Inc., 2003.

33. See, e.g., Pinkse and Kolk, 2009, pp 79–85, on the business case for disclosing information relevant to climate change.

34. See, e.g., Hawkins, 2006.

35. Healy, 2008.

36. Vogel, 2005; www.ford.com/sustainability; Fitzpatrick, 2004; www.corporatewatch.org; ETI, undated; Porter and van der Linde, 1995.

37. REWE, 2012.

38. Innovest and Environment Agency, 2004.

39. www.bt.co.uk.

40. Willard, 2002.

41. See, e.g., Margolis and Walsh, 2003; Salzmann et al., 2005; Schuler and Cording, 2006.

42. Zadek, 2000.

43. Zadek, 2000.

44. Shell, 2011, 2013.

45. Based on categories in Zadek, 2000; SustainAbility and UNEP, 2001; Zadek et al., 2003.

46. Salzmann, et al., 2005.

47. See, e.g., Searcy, 2012; Schalteger et al., 2012; Calabrese et al., 2013.

48. Aguinis and Glavas, 2012; Schreck, 2011; Barnett and Salomon, 2012.

49. Carroll and Shabana, 2010.

50. See SustainAbility and UNEP, 2002, p 31 for specific figures on developing economies.

51. Porter and van der Linde, 1995.

52. Barnett, 2007; Servaes and Tamayo, 2013; Lim and Tsutsui, 2012.

53. Zadek et al., 2005; Amalric and Hauser, 2005.

54. Amalric and Hauser, 2005.

55. See, e.g., Holliday et al., 2002; Henderson, 2001.

56. Holliday et al., 2002.

57. Zadek et al., 2005.
58. Zadek et al., 2003.
59. Zadek, 2000.
60. Zadek, 2000; Hopkins, 2003.
61. Etzion and Ferraro, 2010.
62. Association of British Insurers, 2001.
63. Zadek et al., 2005.

7

Corporate responsibility and governance

 Chapter overview

Following the global financial meltdown in 2007–2008, calls for new structures of governance and greater responsibility were heard in equal measure from governments, policy-makers, the media, and the public. In this chapter, we explore the connection between governance and responsibility by tracing the development of corporate governance frameworks as they evolved, prompted in no small way by reaction to previous scandals.

We consider some of the fundamental tensions that exist between governance frameworks and calls for greater societal accountability by examining traditional approaches to corporate governance which always place the shareholder, as the 'owner' of the business, at the centre of the accountability relationship, and protection of investment as the primary goal. We examine this model and then consider how and whether it might be adapted to offer greater levels of accountability to a wider group of stakeholders, and how corporate responsibility links to wider aspects of governance in a global context. In particular, we will:

- examine what is meant by 'corporate governance';
- explore the theories of corporate governance;
- consider the 'drivers' of corporate governance;
- trace the development of the UK corporate governance framework;
- examine international developments in corporate governance
- discuss the implications for corporate responsibility.

 Main topics

Introduction?	161
Theories of corporate governance	162
The 'drivers' of corporate governance reform	163
The development of the UK corporate governance framework	166
International developments in corporate governance	171
Commentary from a corporate responsibility perspective	172

Key terms

Accountability	Corporate governance framework
Auditing	Corporate malfeasance
Stakeholder engagement	

Introduction

In Chapter 2, we discussed the reasons for the move away from proprietor-run businesses to the limited company form of enterprise. We noted that this practice became the favoured route as businesses became larger and greater capital was required than could be easily raised by an individual or even in a partnership. The issuing of shares made it possible to reach a much wider investment community and therefore easier to raise larger amounts of money. Changes in regulations allowing companies to own shares in other companies or even own other companies outright were made first in the US state of New Jersey in 1896 and in the state of Delaware in 1899. To this day, Delaware continues to be the most liberal state with regard to US laws governing corporations. Equally, capital markets created the means by which new companies could raise finance from a combination of private and institutional investors.

In turn, however, the investor, whether an individual or an institution such as a bank or a pension fund, will expect that their funds are handled with care and invested in such a way that, in due course, they will receive a return on their investment. But this raises some serious issues for an investor. How can they be sure that their investments are going to be handled with the required levels of stewardship? What structures are there in place to ensure that managers do not invest in risky projects, or simply squander the investors' money on generous salaries and perks? Above all, in the context of corporate responsibility, how does corporate govern-ance relate to the behaviour of companies and serve to encourage, restrict, or otherwise shape their relationship with wider society? In a corporate world in which optimum profit is the measure of success and reward, is there room for any notion of social responsibility?

In this chapter, corporate governance will be examined from the perspective of both the shareholders and their *agents* (i.e. company directors and managers). How frameworks of corporate governance have developed will be contrasted with the continuing scandal of cor-porate collapse and fraud. The role of the auditor will also be examined, to see if there is more that the audit process can contribute to good corporate governance in the face of persistent criticism from some quarters.

 Key concept

Corporate governance 'deals with the ways in which suppliers of finance to corporations assure themselves of getting a return on their investment'.

(Shleifer and Vishney, 1997)

Our primary focus initially is on corporate governance as it applies to listed companies, and we have especially highlighted the situation in the UK. We have made this choice because the Anglo-Saxon notion of the firm, with the primacy it grants to investors and the role of capital markets, while not universal, has come to epitomize the efficiency and hazard of the modern company. It is also the case that the UK model of governance structures has been replicated in many other countries. However, we shall examine international guidelines developed to aid countries seeking to bring their own systems in line with international norms.

Thereafter we consider the broader issues of governance in a global context, in light of some of the corporate excesses we have witnessed in the last few years, and the difficulties policy-makers have encountered in formulating structures of governance for multinational companies operating different functions in different countries, particularly in relation to taxation.

Theories of corporate governance

Although there are exceptions, most large companies are not run by their shareholders, as would be the case in smaller enterprises; rather, they are run on behalf of the owners by *agents*, a board of directors and a management structure that is intended to best serve the interests of the owners. Definitions of corporate governance invariably reflect this owner-agent relationship, and focus on issues of control and accountability in this context.

In the corporate governance literature, 'agency theory' articulates some of the conflicts of interest that must exist between an agent and an owner if agents cannot be readily held to account for their actions or are, perhaps, predisposed to act in a self-interested manner. It is easy to imagine how this might manifest itself in actual situations in which a manager might pursue policies that owners may not consider to be in their best interests. What, then, can shareholders do to ensure that managers return some of the profits and manage their investments carefully?

One frequently quoted definition of corporate governance states simply that it '*deals with the ways in which suppliers of finance to corporations assure themselves of getting a return on their investment*'.[1] This very narrow definition predicates a huge volume of research in the field of accounting and finance, and is vigorously defended when the criticism is made that, for example, it omits the interests of all other stakeholder groups.[2] This shareholder emphasis is shared in many other influential definitions and discussions. Even the most recent version of the UK guidelines, *The UK Corporate Governance Code*, published in September 2012, relies on the 1992 Cadbury Commission definition:

> Corporate governance is the system by which companies are directed and controlled. Boards of directors are responsible for the governance of their companies. The shareholders' role in governance is to appoint the directors and the auditors and to satisfy themselves that an appropriate governance structure is in place. The responsibilities of the board include setting the company's strategic aims, providing the leadership to put them into effect, supervising the management of the business and reporting to shareholders on their stewardship. The board's actions are subject to laws, regulations and the shareholders in general meeting.

(Cadbury, 1992, p 4)

In an international context, the OECD, for example, broadens the scope slightly, but still maintains a strong shareholder focus:

> A good corporate governance regime helps to assure that corporations use their capital efficiently ... (and) ... to ensure that corporations take into account the interests of a wide range of constituencies, as well as of the communities within which they operate, and that their boards are accountable to the company and the shareholders.

(OECD, 1999, p 9)

Although some theorists argue that it is enough to recognize and manage stakeholder groups, others believe that companies need to be accountable to them even though they may have no financial interest in the firm. Stakeholder accountability is highly contentious and its position in corporate responsibility is contested, but to understand how it has won a place in the development of governance structures, we need to consider the events that have brought calls for changes in corporate governance during the last two decades.

 Discussion points

Directors of companies owe certain fiduciary duties to the owners of the companies.

- How far should a 'duty of care' include social and environmental responsibilities?
- What steps can directors take to demonstrate that they are taking their fiduciary duties seriously with respect to ethical issues?
- Referring to work such as that of Kent Greenfield (2006) and Corporation 2020, what key features would you want to see in an alternative governance framework?

The 'drivers' of corporate governance reform

Over the last twenty years, a number of interconnecting events have combined to keep up pressure for change in the way in which corporations are managed and regulated. To understand how some of these changes have come about, it is useful first to consider the changing nature of corporate activity in the last few decades. In the next few sections we shall examine the changing nature of share ownership, using UK data as our example, but the trend towards foreign ownership is something which is concerning policy-makers worldwide. Yet, whilst this is one phenomenon which is shifting the emphasis from notions of locally constructed regimes of governance to structures with a global reach, the history of the most radical reforms of governance shows that the most potent driver was corporate wrongdoing of one form or another.

Changing ownership structure

The size and scope of companies has obviously increased over this period, often by merger and acquisition, but, additionally, the mix of ownership has altered. The Office for National Statistics (ONS) has a detailed analysis of classes of owners of equity in UK-listed companies dating back to 1963. The statistics are now updated biannually, and in Box 7.1 we have reproduced the figures for 1963 alongside more up-to-date figures including the most recent set available (from 2012) as this edition goes to press. If we examine the figures over this period, we can clearly see a number of trends. First, there is a significant shift to foreign ownership. From a modest 7 per cent in 1963 there was a gentle upward trend until 1990, when the figure was still only 11.8 per cent, but in the 1990s foreign ownership almost trebled to 32.4 per cent, and by 2012 stood at 53.2 per cent. Public sector share ownership rose from 0.1 per cent in 2000 to 3.1 per cent in 2010, possibly a result of the reduction in interest rates which followed the banking crisis in the autumn of 2008. However, perhaps the most interesting trend is the decline in individual share ownership, which more than halved , from 54 to 20.3 per cent between 1963 and 1990, and halved again to just 10.2 per cent by 2010, although it seems to be maintaining that sort of percentage. It may be that individuals find it easier to buy more convenient investment products from banks and other institutions, rather than be bothered with dealing in equities. These changes in share ownership have a number of implications for the governance of companies. First, it is not always clear who the beneficial owner is, and therefore transparency with regard to ownership of shares may be obfuscated for any number of reasons, most of which have governance implications. Second, we might assume that foreign owners may not be as keen as UK owners to curb activities seen as damaging to the UK, perhaps in terms of social or environmental stewardship. It may also be the case that foreign owners may not be as aware as UK nationals of the potential role for stakeholders in governance structures. What is clear, however, is that the increase in both foreign ownership of UK companies and, we might expect, UK ownership of foreign-based companies casts focus on structures of governance which transcend borders and bring notions of global governance to the fore.

Box 7.1   Summary of share ownership in the UK, 1963–2012

Category of investor	1963	1990	1998	2010	2012
Rest of the world	7.0	11.8	30.7	43.4	53.2
Insurance companies	10.0	20.4	21.6	8.8	6.2
Pension funds	6.4	31.7	21.7	5.6	4.7
Individuals	54.0	20.3	16.7	10.2	10.7
Unit trusts	1.3	6.1	2.0	8.8	9.6
Investment trusts	0.0	1.6	1.3	2.1	1.7
Financial institutions	11.3	1.1	2.7	12.3	6.6
Charities	2.1	2.3	1.4	0.8	0.6
Non-financial institutions	5.1	3.8	1.4	2.3	2.3
Public sector	1.5	2.0	0.1	3.1	2.5
Banks	1.3	0.7	0.6	2.5	1.9

(The Office for National Statistics, http://www.ons.gov.uk/)

Corporate collapse and malfeasance

It seems odd to think, in an era where issues of governance are seen to be so central to the management and accountability of large corporations, that before 1992 there was no formal code of corporate governance. The Companies Act 1985 had consolidated company legislation, and Statements of Standard Accounting Practice (later to become Financial Reporting Standards) prescribed certain accounting procedures. In the field of auditing, the Auditing

Practices Committee had been established in 1976 and issued guidelines relating to the auditing of financial statements, but there was no overarching framework to guide such issues as the separation of the duties of the Chairman and CEO, directors' remuneration, the role of non-executive directors, and so on. This all changed in the late 1980s and early 1990s as two massive frauds revealed failings of corporate governance in two groups of companies, where subsequent investigations found that the organization and structure of the companies contributed to the ability of individuals to steal company assets for their own enrichment.

While it is true to say that there is a long history of corporate failure going back at least as far as the South Sea Bubble of 1718, and a number of high-profile collapses in the 1970s and 1980s, it was the scandals involving media tycoon Robert Maxwell (see Snapshot 7.1) and the Bank of Credit and Commerce International (BCCI) which revealed systematic failure in governance and the use of dubious accounting techniques aimed at hiding liabilities, amplifying assets, and massaging profits.[3] Following the death of Robert Maxwell in November 1991, it soon became clear that similar issues were to be the focus of further damaging publicity for the financial regulators and the corporate governance framework.

 Snapshot 7.1   The legacy of Robert Maxwell

After an eventful military career during World War II, Robert Maxwell became involved in the business of scientific publishing and later founded Pergamon Press, starting an empire that included the Maxwell Communication Company (MCC) and Mirror Group Newspapers (MGN). By the time of his death, Maxwell had additionally built up a myriad of some 400 subsidiary companies owned by a Gibraltar trust company, and another 400 owned by a Charitable Foundation registered in Lichtenstein. The flow of funds between these companies—what became known as the 'public' and the 'private' sides of the business—was at the heart of the governance issue. Despite warning signs, Maxwell continued to form companies and move assets (usually cash) between the public and private sides, depending on where it was needed most.

Following the purchase of MGN, he embarked on a series of business ventures which plunged him into such massive debt that, by 1991, it was being financed by huge movements of cash between companies and day-to-day currency dealings. It was only after his death that the full story began to unravel and the recriminations began. Failures were identified in the abilities of the existing regulatory bodies to draw connections between all of Maxwell's various companies and in the abilities of the regulators to instigate investigations. Non-executive directors were also accused of failing to inform the boards of those cash transfers which they knew about. The pension fund trustees were blamed for inaction, the Stock Exchange was blamed for failing to supervise the conduct of his listed companies, and the Serious Fraud Office was blamed for failing to start an investigation until pressured by a Swiss bank. In addition, each company had received a clean audit report from its auditors.

(Bower, 1988, 1996; Clarke, 1993; Department of Trade and Industry, 1971)

Quick questions

1. Would the separation of the CEO and Chairman roles have prevented this scandal?

2. Would following the Combined Code have prevented this?

3. Could the intervention of institutional investors have prevented this?

The development of the UK corporate governance framework

The ability of Robert Maxwell to appropriate the pension fund assets for his own use, depriving many Maxwell Group pensioners of their savings, caused outrage. If that was not bad enough, the BCCI scandal, relating to a bank that seemed to have been specifically structured to allow money laundering and other financial irregularities to take place,[4] despite ostensibly being regulated by the Bank of England, sent shock waves through the financial communities in the UK and beyond. The result was that the London Stock Exchange, the Financial Reporting Council, and the accountancy profession established a committee to look into corporate governance, and particularly the financial implications of poor governance. The committee was set up under the chairmanship of Sir Adrian Cadbury.

As it turned out, the Cadbury Committee was only the first of a series of committees that have examined and reported on aspects of corporate governance over the last twenty years, and it is now part of an ongoing process that seems set to evolve and continue into the future. What follows is a summary of the steps taken on the initiative of a variety of agencies, each with a sometimes specific, and at other times overlapping, interest in particular aspects of governance. The early initiatives were responses to specific 'shocks' to the financial systems, but later on in the process there appears to have been a much more coordinated approach to the codes of conduct that were developed, and this trend continues.

The Cadbury Report (1992)

In response to the grave concerns about the general sinking confidence in financial reporting, auditing, and corporate governance, the Financial Reporting Council (FRC), the London Stock Exchange (LSE), and the Consultative Committee of Accountancy Bodies (CCAB) convened a committee to consider '*the financial aspects of corporate governance*'. It first met in May 1991 and was charged to consider:

> aspects of corporate governance . . . the way in which boards set financial policy and oversee its implementation, including the use of financial controls, and the processes whereby they report on the activities and progress of the company to the shareholders.

> (*Cadbury, 1992, p 13*)

It took the form of a 'code of conduct' for companies. It recommended that company boardrooms be constituted in such a way that they would feature appropriate sub-committees dealing with matters of remuneration, audit, and nomination, with independent non-executive directors and, more crucially, a separation in the roles and functions of the CEO and the chairman. At the time, there was some debate about whether to make the recommendations compulsory but, in a trend that continues today, companies were eventually asked to comply with the recommendations in a voluntary way. Indeed, the Cadbury Report is widely regarded as the pioneer of the voluntary approach that has become the model for other internationally recognized governance codes.[5]

In the following five years new committees were formed in response to continuing criticism of corporate behaviour. The Greenbury Report (1995) looked into the salaries of directors, especially the senior executives of the recently privatized utility companies who were being labelled 'fat cats'. The recommendation, again voluntary, was that the remuneration committee should comprise non-executive directors, who would report annually on policy and disclose full details of the remuneration packages of the directors. Since the Greenbury Report, a feature of the company annual report has been the detailed level of disclosure on all aspects of directors' remuneration, with valuation of such items as stock options and pension contributions.

This was followed by the Hampel Report (1998) which looked at how such voluntary codes were being implemented. A number of companies had decided not to implement the Cadbury recommendations for various reasons, and, once again, the behaviour of corporate boards choosing this course of action came in for criticism. This theme is discussed further below, when all of the codes of governance are analysed through the lens of corporate responsibility, but other recommendations that had far-reaching implications were that, first, there should be increased dialogue between companies and their institutional investors, and, second, that institutional investors should consider using their votes to influence company policy wherever possible. At the same time as Hampel was reporting, an initiative of the London Stock Exchange, aiming to consolidate the three previous codes, was published. The Combined Code (1998), as its name suggests, tabulates the recommendations of the three previous committees in terms of the responsibilities of companies, on the one hand, and institutional investors, on the other. All of the issues of remuneration, audit, shareholder relations, etc., are covered. It was appended to the Listing Rules of the London Stock Exchange—subsequently the Listing Rules of the Financial Conduct Authority (FCA).[6] The 'comply or explain' principle of reporting, first mentioned by Cadbury, was reinforced in the Combined Code, which laid down, in unusually prescriptive form, the requirement to report any deviation from the code. A year later, The Turnbull Committee was convened by the ICAEW to give guidance specifically on issues of internal control that were highlighted in the Combined Code as being of particular importance. The subsequent report first outlined existing procedures, and then made recommendations for improving internal control systems.

All of this activity led the 1990s to be referred to by commentators, such as Charkham (2005), as 'the decade of corporate governance'. Yet despite this concerted effort on the part of interested parties, from the stock exchanges to the accountancy profession, to improve systems and thus avoid further criticism, corporate scandals continued. The fall of Barings Bank in 1995 had sent further shock waves through the financial world, but it was the collapse of Enron and Worldcom in the USA that, again, led to calls for further attention. The once dormant proposal of two US legislators became the most far-reaching (and hastily passed) piece of governance legislation—the Sarbanes–Oxley Act 2002. It was felt that that the role being played by non-executive directors was not robust enough in terms of ensuring good practice and governance. Additionally, further criticism was levelled at the accountancy profession for what appeared to be a continuing inability to uncover signals of underlying corporate distress or malfeasance. This led to a flurry of activity to try, once again, to develop systems of governance that would be sufficient to prevent further scandals.

Three more committees sat in the UK before a revised Combined Code was published in 2003. The first of these committees was the result of the UK government wishing to extend the remit of its Company Law Review and an acknowledgement of the globalization of financial markets. It was probably the first time that the collapse of a company in one country precipitated such a wide-ranging enquiry in another. The subsequent report of the Higgs Committee (2003) dealt with the responsibilities of non-executive directors, with recommendations that 'at least half the board' should be made up of non-executive directors and that they should be paid at a rate commensurate with the additional responsibility. At the same time as the Higgs Committee was sitting, the government asked the FRC to consider the particular role of audit committees within the governance framework and the relationship that they should have with the company's external auditor.

The committee, under Sir Robert Smith, reported in January 2003 and had a number of specific points to address, mostly to do with the role of the audit committee within the overall board structure. The Smith Report reinforced the belief that accounting firms needed to be careful in deciding which services to offer to a company if they were also conducting its audit. For many, this recommendation did not go far enough, because pressure for more fundamental reforms to the audit industry was resisted.

In 2003, the DTI commissioned a further report into the recruitment of non-executive directors. This Report was in answer to a call made in the Higgs Report that the recruitment and composition of the boards of non-executive directors should be the subject of a separate examination. The Dean of the London Business School, Laura D'Andrea Tyson, chaired the committee. The Tyson (2003) report called for greater diversity but fell short of the idea that lists of qualified individuals should be compiled, from which non-executives could be drawn. One again, the report was in an advisory capacity and attracted little notice. It seemed to call for a similar approach to a US initiative to recruit more women to the boardroom, but appears not to have captured the imagination this side of the Atlantic.

The Combined Code 2003 (revised 2008)

The 1998 Combined Code was revised to take account of the various recommendations and published in July 2003. Companies were expected to implement its recommendations for financial years beginning after November 2003. The Code was to be reviewed and updated on a regular basis and, indeed, a revised Code was published in 2008, based on the notion that all companies *should* wish to be governed in 'the best interests of shareholders', and that good governance 'should facilitate efficient, effective and entrepreneurial management that can deliver shareholder value over the longer term' (Combined Code, 2008, p 1).

In its preamble, the rationale for the Code is explained with an emphasis that it 'is not a rigid set of rules', rather a 'guide to good practice', where it is expected that companies will comply 'wholly or substantially' with its provisions. Significantly, however, Listing Rules for companies listed on the London Stock Exchange require them to describe in their annual reports their corporate governance from two points of view, 'the first dealing generally with their adherence to the Code's main principles, and the second dealing specifically with non-compliance with any of the Code's provisions' (Combined Code, 2008, p 1). What this means is that a listed company is expected to comply with the Code unless it takes the explicit stance of non-compliance, in which case it must explain the reasons to shareholders. This doctrine of 'comply or explain' is now central to the nature of the non-regulatory stance taken towards corporate governance in the UK.

The financial crisis 2007–2008

In the period leading up to publication of the Combined Code in June 2008 the events of the preceding nine months were beginning to impact on the regulatory framework, most especially in the UK and the USA. In the late 1990s and early 2000s banks had rapidly increased their dealings in financial products derived from asset-backed securities. In simple terms, banks bundled investments and sold them on, making commission and profits as they went. The ultimate assets that backed these products were real estate assets, and as long as the value of property continued to rise, there seemed to be no long-term problem. Bank profits continued to rise, and although bonuses paid within the financial services sector drew criticism in some quarters, governments seemed loathe to intervene. However, in the summer of 2007 a train of events began to unfurl which cast doubt on the true values of these products, which included 'structured investment vehicles' (SIVs) and collateralized debt obligations (CDOs). Initially the stress on financial markets began to impact on securities backed by sub-prime mortgage lending, and the inherent difficulty of allocating exact valuations to these products.

On 9 August 2007 BNP Paribas froze three of its funds based on their concerns that they were unable to properly value their CDOs, fearing that they were underwritten by sub-prime loans. That action signalled to global capital markets that the bubble had burst. On 14 September, the British Bank Northern Rock, which had famously offered mortgages at 25 per cent above valuation, needed to sell its securitized debts into international capital markets to maintain its liquidity. However, nervousness in the markets following BNP's actions created problems for Northern Rock, which was then forced to approach the British government to seek assistance. As news of the bank's predicament was made public by the BBC's then Business Editor, Robert Peston,[7] customers began queuing to withdraw their savings. In the months following, unsuccessful attempts were made to sell Northern Rock, finally prompting the UK government to nationalize the bank. House prices in both the USA and the UK fell, creating yet more pressure on these financial derivatives. In March 2008, the investment bank Bear Sterns was bought out by JP Morgan, and in September the US administration had to step in to give financial support to its main sub-prime lenders Fannie Mae and Freddie Mac. The next major shock came when the US merchant bank Lehman Bros filed for bankruptcy on 15 September, and two days later, in the UK, HBOS was rescued by Lloyds TSB.

The autumn of 2008 saw US and UK stock market falls and, in addition to individual banks coming under pressure, the effect began to impact on nation states, initially in Ireland and Iceland. In response, on 8 October 2008, UK, European, and US central banks cut interest rates to 0.5 per cent. On 13 October the UK government took major stakes in RBS and Lloyds TSB where undisclosed liabilities relating to the takeover of HBOS had been unsupportable,

The financial crisis created another shock to the financial system, to date the most serious since the Wall Street Crash in 1929, and like that crash which brought about the Great Depression that lasted for about 10 years, the financial crisis we have endured is likely to have ramifications for about the same length of time, if not longer. The difference now is that governments stepped in to prevent (most) financial institutions from failing, but the borrowing required to do so has resulted in a severe reduction in public sector services, health provision, policing, benefits payments, and public sector pension provision. Wage rises in the public sectors have also generally been lower than inflation since 2008.

More importantly, the reluctance shown by capital markets to support corporate activity, especially in the banking sector, has important implications in discussions about corporate responsibility and governance. Correct valuation of assets and liabilities lies at the heart of sound financial regulation, and the trust we can place on financial statements as a 'fair, balanced, and understandable' view of a company's state of affairs (value) is central to the advice given by the bodies that issue guidance on financial regulation (the FRC in the UK, and the Financial Accounting Standards Board (FASB) in the USA).

The financial crisis and the fragile state in which many banks found themselves prompted yet another review into the governance and stewardship of financial assets, known as 'The Walker Review', which was published in July 2009. In 2010 this review was updated and published along with an updated version of the Combined Code to become the UK Corporate Governance Code.

The UK Corporate Governance Code 2010 (updated September 2012)

This code consolidates the guides to governance and stewardship that have developed since the Cadbury Report. Indeed, they are at pains to stress that the definition of corporate governance is still the 'classic' definition:[8]

> Corporate governance is the system by which companies are directed and controlled. Boards of directors are responsible for the governance of their companies. The shareholders' role in governance is to appoint the directors and the auditors and to satisfy themselves that an appropriate governance structure is in place. The responsibilities of the board include setting the company's strategic aims, providing the leadership to put them into effect, supervising the management of the business and reporting to shareholders on their stewardship. The board's actions are subject to laws, regulations and the shareholders in general meeting.

(UK Corporate Governance Code, 2012, p 1)

What comes through in reading the code is the emphasis that the FRC place on companies abiding by the 'spirit' of the code. They urge boards to 'think deeply, thoroughly, and on a continuing basis' (UK Corporate Governance Code, p 2) on their responsibilities and the implications of their actions. Indeed, the preface to the code is a call to directors to face the challenges of being responsible stewards of investors' funds, and also a reminder that mere compliance with the code 'cannot guarantee' effective governance.

This seems to impact on the 'comply or explain' principle which is described as 'the trademark' of corporate governance in the UK (UK Corporate Governance Code, p 4). This is at the heart of what is, after all, a voluntary code, although most companies abide by its provisions and markets see compliance as an issue of risk reduction and confidence. However, it means that if a company decides not to comply with the provisions of any part of the code, it should fully explain to shareholders the reasons and circumstances which give rise to the non-compliance.

The Code itself is split into five sections, covering leadership, effectiveness, accountability, remuneration, and relations with shareholders. In these sections each of these topics is broken down and guidance is given relating to duties and responsibilities of boards of directors to shareholders. A discussion on wider accountability and stakeholder relations is given in the following sections.

Discussion points

Codes of corporate governance have developed to include supervision of audit procedures.

● How effective can an audit committee be in supervising the audit procedure within a major corporation?

● Can part-time non-executive directors ever be effective?

● Using the example of a FTSE 100 company, how would you modify the workings of the audit committee to incorporate corporate responsibility issues?

International developments in corporate governance

On the international front there has been a convergence of international codes to mirror the needs of companies which are increasingly operating across boundaries and in many different corporate formations. The accounting bodies developed International Financial Reporting Standards (IFRSs), and an examination of some of the international corporate governance guidelines suggests a similar trend. East European countries, which previously conformed to Soviet accounting rules, first established their own 'Accounting Acts' but as time passes so the influence of IFRSs grows, and homogenization of corporate governance rules seems also to be the trend. However, in so far as it is expected that companies will observe the somewhat prescriptive nature of the IFRSs, all corporate governance codes follow the UK model and are explicitly 'guidelines'. Indeed, the preamble to the OECD *Principles of Corporate Governance*, states that:

> The Principles are non-binding and do not aim at detailed prescriptions for national legislation. Rather, they seek to identify objectives and suggest various means for achieving them. Their purpose is to serve as a reference point.

(OECD, 1999, p 13)

In keeping with the discussions we have had on the development of UK guidelines, so the OECD principles are concerned with 'transparent and efficient markets', 'protecting and facilitating the exercise of shareholder rights', 'timely and accurate disclosure', etc. However, the OECD does explicitly recognize the rights of stakeholders when they have been 'established by law or through mutual agreements', and 'encourage active co-operation between corporations and stakeholders in creating wealth, jobs, and the sustainability of financially sound enterprises' (OECD, 1999, p 21).[9]

In 2009, the International Corporate Governance Network (ICGN) revised its *Global Corporate Governance Principles* with a view that they should be of 'general application around the world, irrespective of legislative background or listing rules'.[10] The ICGN is a global membership organization comprising, in the main, institutional investors who clearly have an interest in good governance. Their Principles, whilst in essence espousing similar approaches to corporate governance as the other codes we have described, also provide additional practical help and direction to those wanting to implement best practice.

As emerging economies seek to develop capital markets to encourage inward investment and joint venture arrangements, so corporate governance structures increasingly come under examination. In countries like China, where there is also a conflict between the traditional command economy model and the new free market approach, transition to that model is problematic, and many institutional obstacles still exist.

 Discussion points

Corporate governance frameworks are not drawn up with corporate responsibility as a guiding structure.

- How would they differ if corporate responsibility were to become a major consideration?
- What changes would need to be made to the legal framework to incorporate corporate responsibility issues?
- What examples can you find from around the world (historical and contemporary) of legislative attempts to incorporate corporate responsibility into governance frameworks?

Commentary from a corporate responsibility perspective

Whilst corporate collapses have been a feature of commercial behaviour for centuries, the failure of the regulatory system to require valuations to reflect true values of assets and liabilities, corporate failures due to fraud and misconduct, which have directed criticism at the role of auditors and the accountancy profession, especially following the spectacular collapses of Enron and WorldCom which had received 'clean' audit reports prior to their collapse, the inability to properly value derivative financial instruments, and the subsequent financial crisis that ensued has had worldwide implications for governance frameworks.

In the USA, following Enron, the Sarbanes–Oxley Act was passed taking a prescriptive approach to governance procedures. In Europe, and most other jurisdictions, the voluntary approach prevails. Indeed, the UK and European position has always been that governance should be principle led, with the emphasis being on 'substance over form'.

However, despite being led on the basis of directors taking a 'responsible' attitude towards governance, the focus remains very much with shareholders, and stewardship relates primarily to the stewardship of financial capital. Other forms of capital, whether natural, human, social, or manufactured,[11] are not addressed explicitly, and this highlights the challenges that lie ahead in a world of depleting resources, inequality, and instability. It seems illogical in the face of such strong scientific evidence that rigid adherence to notions of growth and returns on investment take precedence over the fragility we are observing in many natural systems, caused by the very activity that is being promoted. It will be interesting to note whether in the coming years, in the wake of the IPCC 5th Assessment report (see Chapter 3), calls for carbon reduction will eventually be linked with regimes of corporate governance. It is easy to argue that unless that happens, or some other regulatory regime is adopted, there will be little pressure for change and our relentless pursuit of growth will push natural systems to the brink of tolerance and beyond.

Equally, although by virtue of the latest UK Code boards are urged to consider 'diversity', the under-representation of women and those from minority groups still presents a challenge and is a recurring theme with researchers and policy-makers alike. There is ample research surrounding the financial performance of boards and board composition, but far less on the attributes of board members and how these attributes might influence issues of responsibility.[12] Whilst there are suggestions in the research that female contributions to boardroom decision-making may enhance issues of responsibility, the latest study from the Cranfield International Centre for Women Leaders reports that progress has 'stalled' with only 17.3 per cent of appointments being held by women.[13] Significantly, the report highlights the fact that the 'executive pipeline' remains a challenge, with women holding only 5.8 per cent of executive directorships. Indeed, there are only 18 female FTSE 100 executive directors compared with 292 males, and just 32 female FTSE 250 executive directors compared with 558 males. The inability of corporate boards to address diversity in a meaningful way continues to draw calls for quotas to be introduced. It will be interesting to see how this develops[14] (see Snapshot 7.2).

Discussion points

A number of governance initiatives offer companies the opportunity to adopt voluntarily certain standards of conduct.

- How effective can voluntary codes ever be?
- Outline a case for regulation of public companies.
- How can more individuals from minority groups gain representation on company boards?

Snapshot 7.2   Company law reform—the Companies Act 2006

For many who had campaigned for wider changes in company law reform the early signs were encouraging, but on publication there was criticism that social and environmental responsibilities had been relegated to no more than 'a consideration'. Parts of the act are reproduced below.
s.172 Duty to promote the success of the company

(1) A director of a company must act in the way he considers, in good faith, would be most likely to promote the success of the company for the benefit of its members as a whole, and in doing so have regard (amongst other matters) to—

- the need to foster the company's business relationships with suppliers, customers and others,
- the impact of the company's operations on the community and the environment ...

We can note here that the directors owe a duty 'to promote the success of the company' for the benefit of 'its members' (shareholders) and 'have regard' to the company's impact in social and environmental terms. However, a closer examination of s. 417 of the Act, which deals with the 'Directors Report: Business Review', reveals that in the case of quoted companies the following applies:

(5) In the case of a quoted company the business review must, to the extent necessary for an understanding of the development, performance or position of the company's business, include information about—

- environmental matters (including the impact of the company's business on the environment),
- social and community issues, including information about any policies of the company in relation to those matters and the effectiveness of those policies ...

(*Source:* http://www.statutelaw.gov.uk/)

Quick questions

1 How does company law relate to corporate governance structures, and which has precedence?

2 What steps should a company take to demonstrate compliance with s. 172 of the Companies Act 2006?

3 Where can a company find guidance or a framework which would help it to comply with the provisions of s. 417 of the Act?

'Meaningful stakeholder engagement'

As the discussions of stakeholder management and partnerships in Chapters 5 and 9 show, engaging with stakeholders is an important part of how corporate responsibility is managed— but there is an enormous difference between taking the views of shareholders into consideration and being accountable to them in any meaningful way. Writers on the subject of corporate governance, who are prepared to acknowledge the challenges that corporate responsibility poses to the traditional view of corporate governance, still fall short, in most cases, of suggesting that the corporate governance agenda should change. Charkham[15] talks about being accountable to shareholders and '*taking into account*' the views of stakeholders. Even Kiernan,[16] when calling for '*dramatic changes in the thought process and actions of company directors, executives, and institutional investors*', focuses on the '*business case*' for altering course, based on assessments of balance sheet, operational cost, capital cost, and other '*risks*'.

Companies with strong corporate responsibility reputations are by no means immune to charges of abusing governance processes, and, while organizations such as CERES and Corporation 2020 have demonstrated the link between corporate governance and corporate responsibility, for the most part the gaps between what many stakeholders would consider good governance and the priorities of mainstream corporate responsibility practice ultimately pose a threat to the credibility of corporate responsibility as a concept.

 Discussion points

Most codes of corporate governance stress the importance of shareholders over other stakeholders.

- What groups of stakeholders might have particular interests in issues of corporate governance?
- What is the difference between stakeholder engagement and stakeholder management?
- Imagining that you are an activist shareholder, how would you argue for greater stakeholder representation in the company's governance structures?

Summary

Increasingly, the connection between corporate responsibility and corporate governance is being made by commentators and policy-makers who stand outside the rather specialized field of corporate governance itself, which has a firm background in and connection with the accounting profession and those involved in regulating capital markets. This is a sphere of activity largely controlled and influenced by the accounting profession, and the main organ of governance in the UK, the Financial Reporting Council, is largely populated by members of this profession. What seems clear in studying these bodies is that the primacy of the shareholder remains, and whatever pressure is brought to bear to widen the responsibility of corporations to be accountable to a wider range of stakeholders than at present seems remote at the present time.

This might not be surprising. Any move away from this model would have huge implications for markets around the world, and there would be a natural reluctance for any single jurisdiction to make the first move in widening accountability. The fear of a market backlash or actions by companies to move operations in advance of any change would be sufficient to deter policy-makers from pressing for change.

Yet we also know that things are still not ideal. The aftermath of the financial crisis of 2007–2008 has left some banks, to a greater or lesser extent, still in public ownership, and debates about splitting such institutions into 'good' and 'bad banks' continues. The amount of public funds used to support these institutions will continue to impact on the lives of the populations of many countries for years to come, with unemployment rates in several European countries, in particular, creating public unrest. As if that is not bad enough, we know that, in many cases, the manner in which large corporations consume resources is unsustainable, yet there is no place for sustainability to be part of any governance regime to date.

As companies become more flexible in their operations and, owing to a number of factors, more able to move spheres of operations to respond to economic and commercial opportunities, so governance becomes more problematic. In this book we have not looked specifically at taxation as a governance issue, but a case can easily be made that it is an issue of corporate responsibility. On the one hand, it can be argued that companies have a moral obligation to pay taxes where they fall due. On the other, companies who obey national laws and who structure their corporate activities to manufacture in one location, and have marketing, administrative, and sales functions in other locations, will, and do, claim that they are breaking no laws.

As years go by and the scientific evidence strengthens the case for greater regulation in the areas of emissions and consumption, so the governance of companies, in the widest sense, will remain a focus of discussion among many sectors of society. The next potential milestone in this process may be the introduction of 'integrated reporting' by companies. This is an international initiative being developed by the International Integrated Reporting Committee (IIRC) which has already published consultation documents and are piloting the project with 100 global businesses. The basic premise on which integrated reporting is based is related to the need for reports to be forward-looking and to address the complexity that running a group of large companies involves. It will cover

Case study 7   The CORE network

The CORE network is made up of over 60 environmental, development, and human rights NGOs, including the founders Christian Aid, Friends of the Earth, the think tank New Economics Foundation, Amnesty International UK, and the fairtrade organization Traidcraft. The latter two are represented on CORE's Board, along with CAFOD, War on Want, and Leigh Day & Co., the leading UK law firm in cases involving the claims of foreign nationals against British companies. Other supporters include faith groups, trade unions, academics, and parliamentarians. The Corporate Responsibility (CORE) Coalition's members believe that in order to improve how UK companies behave, there is a need for:

1. greater transparency of business operations

2. better accountability of businesses for their impacts on people and the environment

3. improved access to justice for victims of harmful corporate conduct.

They campaign for stronger regulation on corporate governance and company law reform. Present activities include:

1. a UK Commission for Business, Human Rights, and the Environment

2. the Companies Act 2006.

UK Commission for Business, Human Rights, and the Environment

The UK is a key player in the global economy and UK-based companies can have a positive impact in terms of reducing poverty overseas. However, some UK companies have been implicated in human rights abuses and/or significant environmental damage through their overseas operations. Currently there is a lack of both authoritative guidance for companies to avoid such negative impacts, and solutions and accountability when such breaches occur. This void creates greater risk for people, the environment, and businesses—as well as for the UK's reputation as a whole. Better systems need to be introduced to ensure that all UK companies respect human rights and protect the environment when operating abroad.

CORE has proposed the establishment of a new body in the UK to help guide UK companies towards best practice when operating overseas and to prevent harmful impacts to people and the environment. The Commission could also help resolve disputes between companies and those affected by the companies' activities, promoting solutions when harm has been done. This body would have the effect of reducing violations of environmental and human rights standards related to the operations of UK companies abroad, and help those companies improve their corporate conduct globally.

The key objectives of a UK Commission for Business, Human Rights, and the Environment are:

- to provide redress for overseas victims of human rights abuses involving UK companies
- to promote appropriate environmental and human rights standards for UK companies operating overseas and promulgate best practice
- to work with other human rights commissions and relevant bodies to share learning and build their collective capacity to strengthen the effectiveness of redress in developing countries.

The Companies Act 2006

The CORE Coalition was instrumental in securing changes to company law, helping to improve the impacts of UK companies on people and the environment. The CORE Coalition helped to ensure that the Companies Act 2006 now means that:

(continued...)

- company directors must consider the environmental and social impacts of their decisions
- the largest public companies have to report annually on their environmental and social impacts.

However, these requirements only oblige the company to consider the environmental and social issues it considers are material. The CORE Coalition believes that these obligations would be much more effective if further changes were made.

(*Source:* http://corporate-responsibility.org/recent-news/)

Questions

1. Company law has traditionally been the preserve of policy-makers and parliamentarians, yet active lobbying by NGOs like CORE seems to have influenced policy in this case.

   a. What role should NGOs have in shaping company law reform?

   b. What other NGOs are concerned with changes to company regulation and governance?

   c. How might NGOs collaborate more effectively to achieve specific reforms?

2. Company law decrees the minimum reporting requirements by companies.

   a. Where do corporate governance rules fit with company law?

   b. Why is The Combined Code not law?

   c. What sanctions can be taken against companies which do not comply with the Combined Code?

3. The CORE coalition is campaigning for a UK Commission for Business, Human Rights, and the Environment.

   a. What are the main areas where companies are criticized on human rights issues?

   b. What other issues might be covered by such a commission?

   c. What would the likely outcomes of such a commission be?

issues of organization, operations, strategic objectives, performance, future outlook, and governance.[17]

Further reading

www.oxfordtextbooks.co.uk/orc/blowfield_murray3e/

online resource centre

Visit the Online Resource Centre that accompanies this book to enrich your understanding of this chapter. Among the resources available are web links, exercises, and additional case studies.

Charkham, J. 2008, *Keeping better company*, Oxford University Press, Oxford.
   Comparison of governance strategies in five different countries.

Dallas, G. 2005, *Governance and risk: an analytical handbook for investors, managers, directors and stakeholders*, McGraw-Hill, New York.
   Analysis of the problems of governance from multiple perspectives.

Mallin, C.A. 2012, *Corporate governance*, Oxford University Press, New York.
Internationally focused textbook on corporate governance.

Solomon, J. 2013, *Corporate governance and accountability*, John Wiley, Chichester.
Latest edition of an overview of governance and accountability issues.

Online resources

- Suggested additional information on corporate governance worldwide
- Discussion topics for students
- Case studies and exercises on corporate governance
- Links to other web-based resources

Endnotes

1. Shleifer and Vishney, 1997.
2. See, e.g., Jensen, 2001; Sternberg, 1996.
3. Sikka, 2001; Sikka et al., 1998; Sikka and Willmott, 1995a, b; Mitchell et al., 1991; Mitchell and Sikka, 2004; Mitchell et al., 2001.
4. http://www.fas.org/irp/congress/1992_rpt/bcci.
5. www.icgn.org.
6. This change took effect on 1 May 2000 because criticism had also been levelled at the system of supervision within the financial services sector.
7. Now Economics Editor for BBC News.
8. UK Corporate Governance Code, 2012.
9. An updated version was published in 2004.
10. http://www.icgn.org/.
11. Porritt, 2005; see also http://www.forumforthefuture.org/project/five-capitals/overview.
12. Carter et al., 2003; Rose, 2007.
13. Available at http://www.som.cranfield.ac.uk/som/dinamic-content/media/Research/Research per cent20Centres/CICWL/FTSEReport2013.pdf.
14. For a fuller review, see Rao and Tilt, 2013.
15. Charkham, 2005.
16. Kiernan, 2005, p 16.
17. For more information see http://www.theiirc.org/ and http://www.icaew.com/.

8

Corporate responsibility reporting

Chapter overview

For many years companies have been issuing corporate responsibility (CR) reports—not that they were called CR reports in the early days, any more than the activities that we now count as CR were thought of as such. The first reports that appeared were normally included as a section in the annual report. Only latterly have companies begun to issue 'free-standing' environmental, sustainability, or other types of report, now grouped under the term 'corporate responsibility'. In this chapter we look at the development of CR reporting through an examination of social reporting practice dating back to the 1980s and before—an activity which has invariably involved companies making voluntary disclosures about their activities, only very rarely driven by a statutory requirement. We examine some of the enduring issues that have created difficulties for companies who take the decision to make such reports, such as:

- Who is the intended audience?
- What do we include or leave out?
- How do we account for the contents?
- Who should write the report?
- Is there a PR element to all of this?

We question the subtleties that exist between the reasons why companies might wish to develop CR initiatives, and the (sometimes very different) reasons why they might wish to report on these practices. We look at the focus of such practices on issues such as accountability, transparency, and also sustainability, as many reports now encompass a company's engagement with the sustainable development agenda. This aspect has been given greater impetus, first, in the wake of suggested failures in conventional financial reporting practice in the financial crisis of 2008–2009 and, secondly, in the scientific evidence relating to resource depletion and climate change in the same period.[1] We also plot the rise in the practice of surveying such reporting activity and review longitudinally some of the better-known initiatives that have continued since the early 1990s, most easily illustrated by examining the KPMG surveys which have been conducted since 1993, initially focusing on environmental reports,[2] then on sustainability reports,[3] and latterly on corporate responsibility reports.[4] Thereafter, we look at how CR reporting is likely to develop in the coming decade as the world recovers from the recessions resulting from the financial meltdown, and as new evidence is presented on environmental degradation and climate destabilization. In particular, we will:

- trace the emergence and development of CR (social) reporting;
- discuss the voluntary nature of the reports and the issues that surround this feature;
- examine the theories which might help explain the practice of CR and CR reporting;
- explore surveys of CR reporting and discuss their findings;
- look forward to new forms of reporting in the coming decade.

Main topics

What is corporate responsibility reporting?   180

The nature of CR reporting   182

The challenges of CR reporting   184

The emergence of CR reporting   185

The upsurge in CR reporting since the early 1990s   186

Researching the practice of CR reporting—KPMG surveys   188

Conventional financial reporting and CR reporting   192

Reporting issues for corporate management   193

Key terms

Corporate responsibility reporting

Social accounting

Social reporting

Third-party verification statements

What is corporate responsibility reporting?

Financial reporting is acknowledged to be central to the corporate function. There are many reasons for this, not least the statutory requirement in most countries for directors to report to their shareholders. However, over the last 40 years or so, an increasing proportion of companies in most countries have chosen to report on a range of activities that go beyond imparting purely financial information and include disclosures relating to issues about the wider business environment in which they operate. Systematic research on this phenomenon can be traced back to the 1970s, and a series of studies[5] used a database of social disclosure identifying categories of disclosure typically reported upon under the general headings of 'community', 'product', employees', and 'environment'. Later in this chapter we look at how this form of reporting has increased in terms of volume, geographic coverage, and industry sector, and how the topics covered have developed in equal measure. For example, reporting on the environment may now include reporting on sustainability issues, resource scarcity, and climate change, and in some cases at some depth. So, when researchers look for measures of corporate responsibility (or social performance as it is often referred to in research papers), a company disclosure under these categories is still examined and is often used as a proxy in academic studies.[6]

 Key concept: Social accounting

Accounting for the non-financial aspects of a company's performance; extending accountability to a wider range of stakeholders within society.

Since the reporting of a company's activities traditionally falls to the accounting depart-ment within an organization, it is not surprising that reporting of the non-financial aspects of the organization's activities creates some conceptual problems. Conventional definitions of accounting emphasize that its purpose is to provide financial information that should be useful for decision-makers. This is the starting point for most academic courses in account-ing, and throughout their training accountants are directed to concentrate their focus on 'the entity'—the business for which they are preparing the accounts. This means that accounting information tends to be built on data of relevance only to that entity, ignoring external events if they do not explicitly affect the entity.

Financial accounting and reporting are, essentially, for external stakeholders. Reports of past activity and measures of historic performance are produced both as a legal obligation and as an exercise of accountability to the owners of the business—the shareholders. They are produced using accounting conventions, policies, and standards that have developed over time and which are referred to as the generally accepted accounting principles (GAAP). Recent developments in the internationalization of accounting standards are aimed at bring-ing consistency across national boundaries as companies adopt global perspectives in their operations. These are the results against which analysts' forecasts are measured, and against which anticipated company performance is compared and management competence assessed in terms of market performance.

Traditionally, these measures of performance have focused exclusively on financial issues. Implicitly, as discussed elsewhere in the book, profit maximization is the goal against which per-formance is assessed, and the only items that are applied to this equation are those to which, in the past, accountants have ascribed this privileged status. Thus, measures of profit omit to take account of the by-products of commercial activity for which others have to pay, such as pollu-tion, emissions, road use, etc., which economists refer to as 'externalities'. Therefore for compa-nies it is logical to externalize as much of their activities as possible, as this will help keep profits higher and prices more competitive. Yet it seems equally illogical that taxpayers who have no interest in a particular company's products or activities have to pay the cost of cleaning up after it. This might be serious enough where an externality can be identified and a company called to account—for example, where it is found that a river has been polluted or a site contaminated with some substance or other. But now that we are aware of the damaging effects of greenhouse gas emissions, and know that the solution is extremely expensive and there are calls for world-wide cooperation to find a solution, dealing with externalities is an issue of some importance. In the past, it has been suggested that the reason why externalities have never been included in financial statements is to do with difficulties in putting a value on them in financial terms because these issues are 'intangible'; but that argument is losing support in many quarters. If it is possible to assess the value of other 'intangibles', as accountants have been doing for years, this argument seems difficult to sustain. It is more that taking note of externalities is seen as an obstacle to commercial activity, affecting profits and competitiveness.

We have already mentioned that CR reporting created challenges for those charged with creating the reports. One of the problems is with the language traditionally used in financial reports. Indeed, those used to reading financial reports expect to find 'accounting language' in the text. In many respects accounting provides the accepted language of business—a lan-guage that even non-accountants are keen to adopt to instil elements of what are perceived as essential components of strategic arguments in a business framework. This language and the underlying notions that drive corporate activity, such as year-on-year growth and market positioning, shape the context of corporate activity and help to explain both the power of accounting generally, and how easily thereby it might act against longer-term initiatives that have been designed to take account of sets of more responsible objectives.

Additionally, there is an implicit assumption about the nature of accounting that is shared by the public as well as by many accountants, i.e. that it is a 'neutral' or 'objective' activity. We have already explained that accounting is subject to GAAP and some other conventions that have been agreed by particular interest groups. Thus accountants apply their subjective judgements to the application of such principles—judgements that are values-based, and which often have social and environmental consequences that do not appear in subsequent financial statements. A number of studies have examined the complicity of accounting in such issues as environmental pollution, foreign exploitation,[7] plant closures,[8] and social conflict.[9] The perceived partisan nature of accounting informs a more critical approach that motivates much of the research output in such journals as *Critical Perspectives on Accounting*, *Accounting, Organizations and Society*, and the *Accounting, Auditing and Accountability Journal*. It can also be said that it is in this context that social accounting acts as a critique of conventional accounting practices.

The nature of CR reporting

We have already explained that financial reporting is traditionally understood as the reporting of the financial results of a company's past activities to external stakeholders. The requirement for such reports is now part of company law in most countries, but, as in the UK and USA, the requirements almost invariably cover only the financial activities and commonly call for the directors' report, the profit and loss account, and the balance sheet to be reported to the members of the company. These reports are often augmented by various other requirements of GAAP but, with the exception of a few European countries, all of these requirements—either by law or quasi-law—relate to financial aspects of performance. Reporting of the non-financial aspects of a company's performance is largely voluntary (although changes in corporate governance guidelines have led to increased disclosures relating to directors' contractual details in recent decades).[10] It is the voluntary nature of this form of reporting that has attracted the interest of a growing subset of accounting researchers since the genesis of social accounting. But before we look back at the emergence of social reporting, we should be clear about what it means. The social accounting project in the UK dates back to the mid-1980s, and one of the earliest definitions of corporate social reporting, which still stands up today, states that it is:

> the process of communicating the social and environmental effects of the organisations' economic actions to particular interest groups within society, and society at large. As such, it involves extending the accountability of organisations (particularly companies) beyond the traditional role of providing a financial account to the owners of capital, in particular, shareholders. Such an extension is predicated upon the assumption that companies do have wider responsibilities than to simply make money for their shareholders.
>
> *(Gray et al., 1987)*[11]

Immediately, this definition challenges the taken-for-granted objectives of financial reporting which are to discharge accountability to the members of the company—the shareholders. In this sense, social accounting research may be regarded as offering a critique of mainstream accounting practice, and social accounting researchers have long called for reforms to company law and corporate governance frameworks to broaden the accountability framework to include a wider range of stakeholders.

What is immediately obvious from the statement above, and unavoidable in any subsequent discussion, is the debate about what is meant by 'accountability'. We examined this issue in the previous chapter in the context of corporate governance, but, at this stage, it might be useful to consider how 'accountability' can be interpreted differently by different constituents, and how, within its meaning, there is an implicit relationship of unequal power between the person or body requiring an account and that which is giving the account. This unequal power relationship is evident in the use of phrases such as being *called to account* or being asked to *account for one's actions*. Of course, the word 'account' is not always related to finance, but in the corporate context it invariably has this financial emphasis, and the power relationship here lies in the requirement laid down in law and custom for the directors of a company (the agents) to supply (financial) accounts to the owners (principals).[12] However, the same legal obligation to be called to account for responsibilities that go beyond the financial is largely absent from the corporate responsibility sphere and any such reporting is undertaken largely as a voluntary act, and it is this aspect which is the focus of much social accounting research. Social accounting theorists both challenge the primacy of the shareholder group and recognize an explicit obligation for companies to be accountable to wider society.

In the context of this book, the connection between a company's social performance and social reporting is obvious. In many ways, social reporting is the first insight into the social performance of the company, and certainly it is the easiest way in which a company can explain its approach and operationalization of its corporate responsibility strategy to interested parties external to the company. Indeed, in research studies, social disclosures have frequently been used as a proxy for social performance.[13] However, the information a company reports will largely depend on how it defines its activities in terms of corporate responsibility, and the activities upon which it chooses *not* to report are often as significant as the activities on which it does report. Indeed, many studies looking into the reporting activities of corporations comment on the way in which some companies appear to 'cherry pick' the activities on which they can report favourably, while ignoring those issues towards which criticism may be directed. Equally, many companies report on various issues that come within a broad corporate responsibility remit, while failing to address major issues at the core of the business activity. Thus, banks may extol the virtues of CR within the corporate framework in the same period as being fined by regulators for malpractice in core activities such as fixing LIBOR rates etc. Equally, an energy company may stress how it promotes its staff development to improve leadership qualities in its employees, but may not detail how it aims to tackle the challenges of climate change. Indeed, the inability of boards of directors to join up what they hold out to be responsible conduct throughout the organization remains a real challenge for many companies.

The challenges of CR reporting

In the introduction to this chapter, we mentioned that CR reporting presented challenges to those compiling the reports. One of the challenges mentioned above is in the fact that traditional accounting terminology is not always either appropriate or sufficient to describe some CR issues. But there is an even more fundamental problem facing companies, and that relates to the perceived audience for CR reports. Company directors know who the audience for quarterly and annual financial reports is, and this audience sits squarely in the 'investor/analyst' category. They know the information that this audience wants, and prepare financial ratios and further information to anticipate their needs. The disclosures are guided by GAAP and companies, largely, disclose the same sets of financial information.

However, there is no shortage of guidelines for companies who wish to report. Indeed, there is the Global Reporting Initiative (GRI), which emerged from the earlier activities of the Coalition for Environmentally Responsible Economies (CERES) and the CERES Principles. The initiative was founded in Boston in 1997 and the first version of the Guidelines was published in 2000; since then it has developed through three further 'generations', providing us now with version G4.[14] The GRI guidelines feature elsewhere in this volume, but in terms of offering an approach to CR reporting they warrant a special mention in this chapter, and we shall return to them later to see how they have become the predominant model for reporting by the major corporations of the world.

However, despite this and other initiatives, there is still a degree of uncertainty about who the reports are aimed at. Indeed, it could be conjectured that the potential audience is so wide that it would be impossible to supply sufficient information to satisfy all potential readers. This means that compilers of the reports have to make judgements not only about who the report is to be aimed at, but also about what should be included or left out. Additionally, unlike financial reports, there is no accepted format in which the information should be presented. Because the whole procedure is voluntary, companies can disclose whatever they want. Equally, if the company is actually a group of companies, as most listed companies tend to be, the question arises about which sets of activities in which locations should be reported on. All of these variables suggest that companies are faced with a vast array of possibilities, helping to explain why it is so difficult to compare social performance among similar companies. Equally, it makes it difficult to gauge the actual CR performance of the company in question since the information disclosed is always likely to be partial and, whether consciously or unconsciously, likely to reflect the positive rather than the negative aspects of a company's performance.

This raises the question of how we might judge not just the veracity of the reports, given the complex nature of the reporting process, but also the veracity of the CR performance of the company in question. We know that the technology exists for communication between companies and stakeholders to take place in a meaningful way. Social media is already extensively used by companies seeking to attract customers and in their advertising. Maybe there is scope to rethink how accountability might be demonstrated and discharged. It may take time to reconsider the relationship that business has with society, but many believe that that process is already under way.

If we accept the notion that society assigns control of its economic assets to business for its ultimate benefit, how can it hold corporate management accountable for the use of these assets? In discussing this issue, Dillard and Murray (2012) suggest that an *'ethic of account-ability'* which would ideally be possessed by members of boards of public companies, would impart the responsibility on corporate boards to *'provide relevant, timely, and understandable information adequate for being held accountable through rendering actions transparent'*. They continue:

> Conceptually, an ethic of accountability requires an ongoing conversation among all affected parties. Instantiating an ethic of accountability does not seek 'the good' in a utilitarian sense or 'the right' in a deontological sense, though both are consistent with the ideal. The good and the right are delineated as part of the process of determining the appropriate action within the context of the ongoing community. Fitting action as well as the act of holding, and being held, accountable depends upon open and trustworthy communication between the actor and the community members as well as among the community members themselves.
>
> (Dillard and Murray, 2012, p 15)

What is being discussed, and suggested, here is that to be accountable, companies need to envision their reporting as a more engaged practice based on accountability and transparency. Some of the more innovative and forward-looking companies may already suggest that they are doing this, but, for the others, we still rely largely on NGOs to call major corporations to account.

 Discussion points

In attempting to assess a company's commitment to a corporate responsibility, the volume and content of company disclosures play an important part.

1 To what extent can a company's CR performance be judged from the various reports that it publishes throughout the year?

2 Where can independent evidence of behaviour be found?

3 How can we gauge whether NGO reports, which are often critical of company activity, are objective and verifiable?

The emergence of CR reporting

Research in the 1980s demonstrated that some US and Australian companies were report-ing on social issues before World War I.[15] Likewise, in the European context, a similar pat-tern was observed in the early days of Shell.[16] These studies suggest that company managers have always been concerned, to some degree, with considering non-financial issues that are relevant.

Hogner (1982) suggests that US Steel's disclosures were motivated by the need to respond to perceived societal pressures of the period. But it was, perhaps, as societal awareness of environmental issues grew in the 1960s, and as concerns over corporate behaviour were prompted by various company collapses and scandals in the 1970s, that companies responded by including more non-financial information in their annual reports. It was also in the 1970s that, in various countries, new laws required companies to report on aspects of performance relating to, inter alia, employment practices, pollution expenditure, and the like.[17]

There was also interest in the subject in the UK accounting profession and, in 1975, the publication of *The Corporate Report* represented a radical rethink of the role of reporting to external stakeholders.[18] It emphasized how the traditional role of the annual report could be made more relevant by the inclusion of social and environmental information. In the USA, the American Institute of Certified Public Accountants entered the debate, offering guidance on the measurement of social performance in a 1977 publication,[19] and the atmosphere was one of examining the role of reporting, in general, and the purpose of reports, in particular. The traditional reason that companies report an account of their activities is for the benefit of the 'users' of accounts. This would normally be thought to be the shareholders, but, in the case of social reporting, traditional theory (i.e. that this information is useful for the purpose of decision-making) does not seem to stand up.

As interesting as its emergence in the 1970s might have been, however, so too was the decline in social reporting in the 1980s and its subsequent re-emergence in the 1990s. The decline is largely attributed to the political shifts in the USA and UK that came with the elections of Ronald Reagan and Margaret Thatcher, respectively, and the renewed focus on free market economics. *The Corporate Report* largely failed to bring about any major changes and disappeared from the accounting agenda until memories of its recommendations were stirred, in the 1990s, with the initiatives pioneered by such organizations as the Institute of Social and Ethical Accountability, the Council on Economic Priorities, and the World Business Council for Sustainable Development.[20]

The upsurge in CR reporting since the early 1990s

Despite the varying pattern of corporate reporting of social and environmental issues, a very clear upward trend in CR reporting began to emerge in the 1990s and this can be readily observed from the triennial surveys conducted by the accountancy firm KPMG. Apart from minor changes in corporate governance recommendations, a number of factors began to influence change within companies. These included action at a number of levels, from initiatives within professions and industries to UN and EU initiatives, all encouraging greater detail in the reporting of social and environmental issues.

For example, the UNEP/SustainAbility 'Engaging Stakeholders' programme was launched in 1994. Initially, it served to raise awareness among companies of environmental reporting and it continues to stress the business case for wider reporting. The programme has clearly encouraged participation by widely publicizing the results of the survey and the benefits of participation. The series of surveys continues to the present, and the latest report saw Standard & Poors join the research team and the report taking on even more of a market orientation (UNEP/SustainAbility/Standard&Poors, 2006). The EU Eco-Management and Audit Scheme also promoted the introduction and reporting of environmental management systems, following the introduction of BS 7750 in 1992 and, thereafter, the ISO 14000 series.

At a national level, the UK government's DEFRA/DTI Environmental Reporting Guidelines were published in 2001, and France has followed Denmark, Norway, Sweden, and The Netherlands in introducing mandatory reporting requirements, although the focus here continues to display a financial emphasis. At a business-to-business level, the International Chamber of Commerce published its *Business Charter for Sustainable Development* in 1991, featuring a 16-point guide to environmental reporting. In 1995, the World Business Council for Sustainable Development (WBCSD) was established through a merger of the Business Council for Sustainable Development and the World Industry Council for the Environment, the two organizations that responded on behalf of business to the challenges arising from the Rio Summit in 1992. The WBCSD maintains an influential voice for business and boasts a membership comprising major corporations worldwide.[21]

Around the same time, various industries began to look at how environmental issues affected the perceptions of activities within their sectors. A good example of this is the initiative by the European Chemical Industry Council (CEFIC). Founded in 1972, it has, over the years, expanded and developed its approaches to various aspects of concern within the industry. It is now closely allied to the International Council of Chemical Associations (ICCA) which, in 2006, launched its Responsible Care Global Charter, a development of CEFIC's Responsible Care Programme's reporting guidelines.

At the level of the professions, the Fédération des Experts Compatibles Européens (FEE)—the coordinating organization for the European accounting professions—has been involved in developing reporting guidelines and making representations to the European Parliament on connected issues. In the UK, the initiative taken by the ACCA in 1991 in establishing the Environmental Reporting Awards has done much to encourage and improve social reporting over the years (see below). It broadened its remit in 2002, and until 2005 ran a European Sustainability Reporting Award Scheme. The ACCA still runs award schemes in the USA (in collaboration with CERES) and in several other countries around the world.[22]

Each of these initiatives, or a combination of more than one, served to increase the incidence and volume of environmental reporting (see Snapshot 8.1). In the early stages of this development, the reports bore little resemblance to the best reports we see today. In general, reporting on environmental issues comprised a section in the annual report and was largely qualitative in nature. Even when the first stand-alone reports began to appear, they seemed to be, as Owen (2003) suggested, *'rather crude exercises in public relations'*.

 Snapshot 8.1   Sustainability at Fujitsu

Fujitsu has long been aware of the environmental impacts created by multinational firms. For many years it has taken steps to examine its ecological footprint and today is an exemplar in both the understanding and reporting of its sustainability strategies.

It was in 1993 that Fujitsu established its first Environmental Protection Program, which outlined the company's approach to environmental activities around four key areas—products, factories, solutions, and people. It was one of the first companies to consider the environmental impacts of its products throughout their life cycle, from the acquisition of materials used in manufacture, to their disposal at end of life. It now sets goals and monitors its performance in each successive report.

(continued...)

Their 2013 Sustainability Report clearly outlines their approach to sustainability by arranging sections of the report to mirror their analysis of the priorities in this area: global environmental challenges, food and energy demand, social impacts of urbanization, global population aging, the digital divide, and cyber attacks and cyber crime.

It is interesting to reflect on these categories and how, in comparison with some other sustainability reports, their first four categories do not intuitively relate to their products yet are seen to be the most important, and where their products may have positive impacts. Against each heading the company suggests how ICT can meet the challenges presented.

For example, acknowledging that in a world with a growing population and depleting resources our planet is probably already operating beyond its carrying capacity, Fujitsu sees the power of computing as an essential part of any solution to greenhouse gas (GHG) reduction. In the case of food shortage they see innovative ICT in fields of supply/demand management in areas lacking in this approach to date as an essential part of the solution.

Quick questions

1. Why is it important to be 3 clear about global issues?

2. Why is it essential to measure performance against indicators?

3. In what respect can non-financial information inform the business case?

Researching the practice of CR reporting—KPMG surveys

In 1993, KPMG Peat Marwick Thorne, as it then was known, conducted its first 'International Survey of Environmental Reporting', where it notes that there was '...*a growing need for more and superior environmental information*'. It sent questionnaires to the top 100 companies in the UK, Canada, The Netherlands, France, and Belgium, together with a smaller sample of the largest companies in Germany, Denmark, Portugal, and Ireland—690 companies responded. From this modest beginning has grown an enduring and expanding survey of CR reporting practice around the world. Over the years it has evolved and developed in scope and geographical coverage, and continues to do so, announcing that future additional reports will report specifically on '*water, supply chain, and regulatory optimization*' (KPMG, 2011, p 3). It is interesting to note that an examination of the trail of surveys mirrors the development of the field in general. The 1993 survey was entitled 'An International Survey of Environmental Reporting', reflecting the nature of the first 'stand-alone' environmental reports that had begun to appear in the late 1980s. In 2002 the title was changed to a survey of 'Corporate Sustainability Reporting', and since 2005 there have been surveys of 'Corporate Responsibility Reporting', the last one in 2011 analysing some 3,400 reports from around the world. During this period a number of different approaches have been taken, including the involvement of faculty at the University of Amsterdam in the surveys of 1999 and 2002 (see also Kolk, 2003, 2004).

Because of the nature of the changes made in the focus and methodologies used in constructing the reports it is not so easy to compare results, but the last three have adopted an almost uniform approach, highlighting the fact that CR reporting is now an almost universal corporate activity among large corporations, with 95 per cent of the 250 largest companies in the world reporting on their CR activities (KPMG, 2011, p 6). In the last three reports KPMG have also surveyed the potential reasons why companies choose to report, and the 2011 results are more in line with previous academic research in the area, with companies citing reputation (67 per cent), ethical considerations (58 per cent), employee motivation (44 per cent), and innovation and learning (44 per cent) as the four leading drivers (KPMG, 2011, p 19).

A similar survey was conducted by the Economist Intelligence Unit (EIU) in 2010 acknowledging that the practice '... *had shifted from the voluntary to the vital*' (EIU, 2010, p 3). They conducted their own survey on '*key drivers of sustainability reporting*', and found that regulation, customer pressure, NGO activity, employee pressure, peer pressure, and internal factors were the main drivers. Interestingly, and out of line with research in the past, investors are showing interest in the reports, though the focus is still on issues of risk, and governance.

Whilst these surveys are of some interest to researchers they should be viewed with some circumspection, as it seems clear that the respondents were able to choose a number of drivers from which the table was constructed. The fact that over the three surveys there was such a shift in responses—for example, respondents citing economic considerations at 68 per cent in 2008 and only 32 per cent in 2011—suggests that many companies still do not really understand the reasons why they are publishing this information. Equally, since the survey looks at the biggest companies in the world, it is hardly surprising that they find that the biggest companies disclose most —that phenomenon was identified some years ago (Gray et al., 2001; Trotman and Bradley, 1981; Cowen et al., 1987) and is one of the factors that has to be considered whenever approaching research in this area.

What is clear and irrevocable, however, is that the practice shows no sign of reversing the trend, and it is likely that within a decade CR reporting will be almost universal among listed companies in most developed countries.

 Snapshot 8.2   Is social information of use to investors?

The Association of Chartered Certified Accountants (ACCA), who ran an award scheme for environmental reports in the UK and elsewhere from 1991 to 2008 with the overall aim of improving the quality of non-financial reporting, have recently published a report in response to the European Commission's proposed new requirements that all large EU companies report on the environmental, social, and governance (ESG) aspects of their businesses, with investors as the primary focus.

It has been a feature of most research to date that investors take an ambivalent view of non-financial information, and therefore it is a timely intervention that an organization with the reach of the ACCA should collaborate with the European Sustainable Investment Forum (Eurosif) to examine the sort of information that might be of interest to investors.

To do this, the authors conducted a survey of analysts and investors in 18 countries and based the report on the responses of 94 participants. They examined the sources of information used by investors and scrutinized its adequacy, content, and form; they also looked at what accountability mechanisms might be applied to ensure the veracity of the information contained in the reports. They also considered what sorts of company should have to report and the implications for policy-makers.

The key findings suggest that investors:

i)   do refer to the CSR/Sustainability reports;

ii)   do not believe that sufficient information is supplied to assess financial materiality;

(continued...)

iii) find that reporting is not comparable across companies;

iv) find a lack of quantitative key performance indicators;

v) believe that third-party assurance statements are important.

(*Source:* ACCA 2013)

Quick questions

1. Is there a case for statutory standards to cover sustainability reporting, in the same way as there are standards for financial reporting?

2. If a voluntary approach is to continue, how might companies be persuaded to take note of the criticisms levelled at current reporting practice?

3. What are the main reasons for non-financial information to be integrated with financial information?

Trends in social reporting

Two other trends emerged in the 1990s that, to some extent, still continue today. First, there was the separation of the 'environmental' from the 'social'. Whereas the reports in the 1970s had, in many ways, a shared focus, the trend in the 1990s was to separate the two and to place a greater emphasis on the environmental aspects of company performance. This is significant because CR, as a field, is not concerned solely with issues of environmental management; indeed, at the core of the Brundtland definition of sustainability (see Chapter 3) is the notion of social justice. Secondly, criticism started to be levelled at companies for failing to embed social and environmental policies into the strategy and 'real' purpose of the business (see Chapter 6).

We can conjecture over the reasons for both trends. In the case of the environmental focus, it is worth remembering that there had been a spate of very significant environmental disasters in the mid- and late-1980s including, for example, Bhopal in 1984, Chernobyl in 1986, *Piper Alpha* in 1988, and *Exxon Valdez* in 1989. For obvious reasons, media coverage of these events was concentrated and prolonged, and the events themselves led to many changes in the way in which companies operated and reported. Indeed, each of these events had a lasting impact within their respective industries that is felt even today. Therefore it is probably unsurprising that companies opted for more of an environmental focus in their activities and reports. If we examine the response of BP to the Gulf of Mexico incident we see a similar pattern. In many ways, if this conclusion is correct, it also explains why the strategy may be easily criticized as an 'add-on', because, at least initially, that is what it was. It would have been a reaction, most likely of companies within the affected industry sectors, to how they perceived they should act.

Research into social reporting

Although there is evidence of companies reporting non-financial aspects of their businesses going back over a hundred years, a genuine body of research only really began to emerge in the 1970s.[23] During the period 1970–1980, this mainly consisted of empirical (statistical) studies which, while focusing on some aspects of social and environmental information, still had a clear instrumental rationale aimed at discovering the usefulness of this information to investors.[24] Some discursive work began to appear towards the end of the 1970s,[25] however, and this widened the debate to include more philosophical issues, with the phrase 'social responsibility' appearing in many studies.[26]

Research gained momentum from the mid-1980s, at which time a number of authors, principally in the UK and Australia, began to explore the social dimensions of corporate activity. Influential journals, sympathetic to this subject matter, were also founded in this period; *Critical Perspectives on Accounting* (established 1990), *Accounting, Auditing and Accountability Journal* (1988), and *Journal of Accounting and Public Policy* (1982), joined *Accounting, Organizations and Society* (1975) to provide a wide forum through which to engage academics and broaden the terms of the debate.

These works presaged the increase in social reporting of the early 1990s, and heralded a social and environmental accounting project that has continued, and grown in strength, scope, and reach, ever since. Indeed, from modest beginnings, with only a handful of researchers worldwide, social and environmental accounting research is now conducted by hundreds of researchers in many countries and features in many international accounting conferences each year, as well as having a number of its own dedicated conferences.[27]

Such evidence as there is from research studies looking at the value that investors place on such information is no more than suggestive of 'possible' relevance to investment decisions.[28] Indeed, despite the huge amount of research in the late 1970s and early 1980s into the link between social performance and financial performance, the results tend to be contradictory, largely owing to the variety of measures used to determine both financial and social performance. Taking a moment to consider all the different possible measures of 'financial performance', we are left with choices among profit (whatever that might look like), returns on earning, investment, assets, capital employed, and so on, or market measures relating to share returns, earnings per share, etc., and we soon realize that it is difficult to compare studies. Researchers continuing to seek definitive proof one way or the other might like first to refer to the review by Griffin and Mahon (1997) encompassing *'twenty-five years of incomparable research'*. For a comprehensive summary, others may refer to Margolis and Walsh (2001) to explore the complexities.

 Discussion points

In attempting to assess a company's commitment to corporate responsibility, the volume and content of company disclosures play an important part.

1 To what extent can a company's social performance be judged from the various reports that it publishes throughout the year?

2 What other sources of evidence may be found?

3 How much notice should we take of those NGO reports that are often critical of company activity?

Theories of social reporting

Researchers responded to Ullmann's (1985) call for new theories to be explored to explain the phenomenon of increasing voluntary reporting and a number of studies followed. Roberts (1992) discussed stakeholder theory in an empirical context and, subsequently, Gray et al. (1996a), also prompted by evidence of increasing volumes of social disclosure, reviewed theories of disclosure that might explain the phenomenon. Traditional accounting theories of disclosure aimed at informing market participants were largely discounted and alternative theories focusing on political economy were considered. One of the theories identified— 'legitimacy theory'—has since become one of the most discussed in the literature. The notion of a company existing only with the sanction of society, with connotations of a 'public interest' element to its continued existence, may have seemed somewhat fanciful, but the events surrounding Enron and the collapse of Arthur Andersen, one of the world's largest and, at the time, most respected firms of accountants, demonstrated that it is indeed possible to lose the licence to operate if one's actions are seen to go beyond what society deems acceptable. That companies might choose a strategy to support or enhance their legitimacy in these terms is something that has formed a strand of research since 1990. Indeed, many researchers suggest that rather than exercising the discharge of accountability in reporting their social activities, they are actually engaged in a process of legitimation of their operations. Legitimacy theory suggests that company disclosures may be a reaction to the perception that companies have of how they are viewed by different stakeholder groups within society. Therefore the company needs to disclose details about its activities to achieve this objective and to reassure society about its activities. Lindblom (1994) sparked a long-running debate on legitimacy theory by positing four alternative strategies which might be employed by companies when deciding whether and why to publish. She suggests that companies may seek to 'align activities with expectations', 'educate and inform', 'change perceptions', or 'alter expectations'. We may surmise that each and all of these strategies are connected with the way that the company wishes to communicate with stakeholders, and that they *may* also be connected to its actual performance.

A related theory relating to disclosure strategy concerns the manner in which a company manages its reputation. There is an increasing literature on management of reputation and the risks attaching to events which can damage it.[29] The relationship between social disclosure and social performance seems critical if we are to do anything but discount social reports as some form of public relations exercise. Unless we are able to align reports with performance, we are always likely to be left with this dilemma.

Conventional financial reporting and CR reporting

The major difference between conventional financial reporting and social reporting hinges on the approach taken to the use of the information reported upon. Traditionally, financial reports contain both aggregated data, which may conceal much of the underlying activity, and analyses that focus on very narrow performance measures. We can only imagine the range of activity that is represented by the income statements of BP or Wal-Mart and, in looking at the earning per share figure or other performance ratios, no consideration is given to the wider implications of the plethora of undertakings that led to the derivation of that measure. Indeed, in the application of many accounting techniques, little attention is paid to any factors outside the concern of the entity, and ratios of liquidity, profitability, and solvency, for example, are often used only to compare performance against historic or other data. The same figures are also often used to compare performance of one company with another (this type of comparison is frequently requested in degree and professional accounting courses dealing with 'financial statement analysis'). Equally, what Chua (1986) calls 'mainstream accounting research' tends to have a similar narrow focus, and research questions regularly focus around issues of market efficiency and the usefulness of certain categories of information to investors. It is little wonder, therefore, that the bigger picture is often overlooked in an effort to examine the minutiae of procedure or practice.

On the other hand, CR reporting, at a theoretical level, is concerned with how commercial activity links into other social systems and presents an alternative ontological approach to how one views the role of corporations. 'Systems theory', explained in more detail in Gray et al. (1996b), is an approach that is *designed to reverse the tendency in scientific thought towards reductionist reasoning*. Systems theory has its origins in the natural sciences and can be explained as follows.

1 An attempt to study a part without understanding the whole from which the part comes (reductionism) was bound to lead to misunderstandings. The part can only be understood in its context.
2 Understanding tends to be directed by and limited to one's own discipline. Natural phenomena are complex and cannot be successfully studied by artificially bounded modes of thought.

(Gray et al., 1996b, p 13)

The essence of systems thinking demands that we think about all our activities in the context of how they affect other systems, with what Birkin (2000) calls, *'an ontology of interconnected events'*. This concept is particularly relevant when considering sustainability, and is discussed in more detail in Chapter 3.

Reporting issues for corporate management

From the management perspective, there are a number of problems in making the decision to disclose non-financial information. First, who is the intended audience? Traditionally, as we have mentioned already, corporate reports are released for the benefit of the analyst/investor group. That constituency is relatively homogenous and easy to define; their needs have been the focus of investor relations departments and boardroom discussions for decades, and are backed by numerous research studies. However, the audience for reports on CR issues is much more diverse. These users do not form a homogenous group and are likely to have widely diverging interests. Equally, their desire for information may not always have the company's best interests at heart. Indeed, it is easy to make an argument that few investors take any interest in the non-financial aspects of corporate activity, except if it impinges on issues of risk or governance. Certainly, there is little evidence from research that investors are swayed by social and environmental disclosures. Thus, management must form an opinion on the purpose and scope of the report, and this may pose many challenges.

It is relatively straightforward to make statements along the lines of *'within this company we make every effort to maintain the highest standards of social and environmental practice'*. Indeed, statements such as this peppered annual reports throughout the late 1990s as companies became aware that they were expected to address additional non-financial issues, but were unsure how to position themselves in that regard. What is more difficult to do is to explain how any particular programme is to be rolled out and the effect that it might have on profit figures. At that point, conflict will almost inevitably arise within organizations, and one can see the kind of compromises that are reached by examining such reports, many of which fill the list of criticisms by awards judges (see Snapshot 8.2).

If one looks at it from the outside the company, the picture is entirely different. As a member of society, concerned about aspects of corporate activity that affect you, you may view the issue as one of accountability. Companies and policy-makers often talk about 'transparency', but on close examination it is sometimes difficult to uncover the level of detail that we require in order to be satisfied on any particular issue. On the other hand, how does the company know the level of detail that any single individual or group might want? These issues reveal that company managers involved in the reporting process are better placed to report effectively if they have knowledge of the theories and functions of social reporting which enables them to position the company effectively in terms of its corporate responsibility profile and reputation management.

 Key concept: External verification statement

An external verification statement is an opinion regarding the quality and verifiability of the social reports. Unlike financial audits, which are carried out by registered auditors following comprehensive auditing standards, external verification statements on social reports have no such authority.

The trend towards external verification

We know that the initial choice of whether to report at all is made by the company as part of a strategy by the management and motivated for any number of reasons. It is a largely voluntary act and may have much to do with the activity of competitors, perceptions of stakeholder expectation, or other strategies to obtain *'managerial advantage'*.[30] As companies embrace a global perspective, many will view both the mandatory requirements of some countries and the recommendations under the Global Reporting Initiative sustainability reporting guidelines, which make specific reference to verification as an opportunity to review and to implement external assurance practices. The trend has been observed to be growing steadily and, in its most recent international survey, KPMG (2011) found that the number of companies in the Global 250 with a formal assurance statement had increased to 46 per cent (from 40 per cent in 2008); for the top 100 national companies, it had slightly dipped to 38 per cent (from 39 per cent). The overriding motivation is probably to build trust between company management and external stakeholders over the implementation and maintenance of corporate responsibility strategies. In an ideal world, the verification process should achieve this and reassure the relevant audience, thereby adding value for the company.

However, this motivation is easily contrasted with the theoretical purpose of such accounts—the idea that with transparency comes accountability. There is a real concern, expressed by a number of researchers, that the upsurge in reporting is part of a process whereby the accountability agenda is 'captured' by corporate management, who react to calls for greater accountability and transparency by artefacts aimed at taking control of the agenda, and at taking equal control of the nature and extent of the information reported upon.[31] The idea that such reports only contain information that management wants released adds to criticisms that reports lack completeness and credibility.[32] This notion continues to motivate social accounting researchers to examine the verification process, and to press for the imposition of strict and robust assurance processes.[33]

The KPMG (2011) Report devotes a full chapter to the question of assurance statements. Not too surprisingly it notes that:

> '...of the assurance providers, the market continues to be dominated by major accountancy organizations that currently hold 71 percent of the G250 market and 64 percent of the N100. Market shares of other provider types appear to have grown slightly at the expense of the technical expert firms who lost market share.

(KPMG, 2011, p 30)

 Discussion points

There is now strong evidence from recent surveys that an increasing number of companies in all sectors in all countries are reporting on CR issues.

1 What theories can you suggest that might help to explain this trend?

2 What theories lie behind the notion that statements should be independently verified by third parties?

3 Given that there are no statutory standards against which to audit third-party verification statements, how is it possible to compare their value between companies?

Summary

In this chapter, we have examined how companies report CR to audiences outside the company. This, we discovered, encompasses a complex series of issues that pose some serious challenges for management, especially if the process is designed to be more than an exercise in corporate communication, marketing, or public relations. This process developed through extending the financial reporting function, and, until relatively recently, the annual report was the usual medium through which such disclosures were made.

This posed a number of problems for companies as it became clear that stakeholder groups were scrutinizing the information contained in these social and environmental accounts with different intentions than those of the traditional audience of annual reports, i.e. the shareholders. Academics also began scrutinizing these social disclosures, offering varying levels of critique and, as the reporting medium moved to the internet, so pressure groups were now using the same medium to counter some of the claims made in corporate releases. Even when companies enter reporting award schemes, they rarely emerge without criticism.

There are various reasons for the dramatic increase in the incidence and volume of CR reporting, and a large number of contributory factors, a combination of which is most likely to offer explanation. But with this increase has come criticism from certain quarters that the reports are more akin to public relations initiatives. Indeed, even as the incidence and volume of corporate responsibility reports has increased, criticism of corporate behaviour does not seem to have abated, not least because the material is accused of being incomplete or inadequate, as attested to by successive judging panels of environmental and similar awards. For example, the banking sector, initially ambivalent to issues of CR as it saw itself as having less environmental impact than like-sized corporations, became very active in the 1990s and 2000s, with many banks branding themselves as model corporate citizens whilst their core activities were undermining trust in the financial system worldwide. Even after the financial crash of 2008–2009 and all the stinging criticism levelled against their irresponsible behaviour, new scandals of interest rate fixing and mis-selling of financial products still proliferate.

We noted that accounting plays an important part in this process of improving the credibility of CR performance. Accounting for an activity is the essence of discharging accountability to the appropriate body. Impacts and effects need to be measured in order to gauge accurately whether particular strategies are worthwhile and effective. The design and implementation of appropriate information systems and reporting structures play an essential part of this process. Therefore there are strong arguments to be made that accountants become aware of the social, environmental, and sustainability issues that are challenging the 'business as usual' approach. These professionals will then be better placed to devise accounting systems that can capture non-financial activity in a more meaningful way. Equally, there are new forms of accounting that might be developed, looking to measure different things than those that are traditionally associated with accounting systems.

What this chapter sets out to demonstrate is that accounting plays a central role in the CR process and has the potential to play an even greater role. Social, environmental, corporate responsibility, and sustainability reports have emerged from the financial reporting function within companies. But, whereas financial reporting procedures are highly regulated and controlled, there seems to be appetite to impose such controls on non-financial reporting. If that situation continues, despite continued criticism over the format and content of such reports, then these reports will continue to require careful analysis and critical judgement.

Case study 8   Environmental reporting at PUMA

Traditionally, accounting information has concentrated exclusively on the valuation of assets and liabilities judged by the accounting bodies, which set the standards, as having an impact on the financial standing of the entity in question. Researchers in social and environmental accounting have always criticized this partial view of corporate activity which excludes the valuation of 'externalities'— the damaging effects of pollution, emissions, and waste which are passed to external agencies to remedy, and the cost of which ultimately falls to the taxpayer. Logically, the larger the company and the longer the supply chains feeding into the product ranges of large companies, the greater the impact will be and the more complex the measurement of such impact becomes. Most corporations have avoided such investigations.

(continued...)

However, in 2011, luxury and sports lifestyle company Kering (formerly PPR), the parent company of PUMA, announced that it was to implement a group environmental profit and loss (P&L) account by 2016, and set out on a mission to place values on the GHG emissions, water use, land use, air pollution, and waste caused by their operations worldwide.

The initiative is designed as a three-stage process which seeks to address some of the issues relating to externalities mentioned above, and which may act as a catalyst for other companies with complex supply chains to adopt similar approaches when the full costs are better understood. It is being conducted in consultation with PricewaterhouseCoopers (see http://www.pwc.co.uk/sustainability-climate-change/) and Trucost (see http://www.trucost.com/published-research/79/puma-environmental-profit-and-loss-account).

Stage 1   To gather data on 'GHG emissions, water consumption, air pollution, waste, and impacts on land-use'.

Stage 2   It is envisaged that measurement of some of the more problematic elements of sustainability will be included to gauge social impacts and could include *'decent/fair wages, health and safety, working conditions, standard of living, security and stability, empowerment, community cohesion, human capital, diversity and gender equality, health and well-being, and cultural heritage'*. It is worth noting that PUMA acknowledges that, *'... the development of this stage requires the collaboration with other corporate and civil society stakeholders in tackling the complexities of the social issues'*.

Stage 3   This stage will complete the other side of the equation, focusing on some of the beneficiaries of the economic impacts from PUMA's operations. This could include *'... the creation of jobs, wages, total tax contributions, indirect tax payments, indirect and induced employment, indirect and induced output, productivity and efficiency gains, and business creation and growth'*.

To date, only data relating to stage 1 have been published, but they reveal that:

following an economic valuation of €94 million of GHG emissions and water consumption in May 2011, PUMA has finalised its 2010 E P&L by adding €51 million caused by land use change for the production of raw materials, air pollution and waste along its value chain. Only €8 million of the €145 million total derive from PUMA's core operations such as offices, warehouses, stores and logistics while the remaining €137 million fall upon PUMA's supply chain.

They further report:

- Over half (57 per cent or €83 million) of all environmental impacts are associated with the production of raw materials (including leather, cotton and rubber) in Tier 4 of PUMA's supply chain.

- Only 6 per cent or €8 million derive from PUMA's core operations such as offices, warehouses, stores and logistics; a further 9 per cent (€13 million) occur in Tier 1, with the remaining 85 per cent (€124 million) in Tiers 2–4.

- GHGs make up 90 per cent of the total impact of PUMA's offices, stores and warehouses.

These costs, which will not affect PUMA's net earnings, will serve as an initial metric for the company when aiming to mitigate the footprint of PUMA's operations and all supply chain levels.

This initiative represents an ambitious commitment to reveal the impact that the company is making in terms not only of the cost to the environment, but also of the benefits to society. It also represents a challenge to traditional accounting approaches and seems to encompass the two tenets of social and environmental accounting: to use proven accounting techniques to measure different things, and to develop new techniques to measure non-traditional costs and benefits.

(*Sources:* http://about.puma.com/puma-completes-first-environmental-profit-and-loss-account-which-values-impacts-at-e-145-million/ (a number of PDFs which explain valuation methodology etc. are also available on this page) and http://www.kering.com/en/sustainability)

(continued...)

Questions

1 PUMA has received much attention for its environmental P&L initiative.

    a. What features of their reporting practice put PUMA ahead of its rivals?

    b. To what extent does PUMA use targets to monitor emissions reductions?

    c. What does PUMA identify as the major issue relating to supply chains?

2 Social and environmental reports are often used by researchers as a proxy for actual social performance.

    a. What indicators can we use from PUMA's environmental reports to measure its actual social performance?

    b. What are the main elements of PUMA's environmental profit and loss calculations?

    c. What does PUMA see as the main benefit for the company in preparing an environmental P&L?

3 PUMA has identified that much of the negative environmental impacts relate to supply chains operating in many countries in the developing world.

    a. What difficulties are PUMA likely to face when trying to gather data for stages 2 and 3 of the environmental P&L programme?

    b. What benefits to developing nations can environmental P&L data provide?

    c. How effectively does PUMA presently cover sustainability issues in its annual reports?

Further reading

online resource centre

www.oxfordtextbooks.co.uk/orc/blowfield_murray3e/

Visit the Online Resource Centre that accompanies this book to enrich your understanding of this chapter. Among the resources available are web links, exercises, and additional case studies.

Exploration of theories of social disclosure

Gray, R.H., Owen, D., & Adams, C. 1996, *Accounting and accountability: changes and challenges in corporate social and environmental reporting*, Prentice Hall, London.
Making the case for social and environmental reporting.

Gray, R.H. 2006b 'Social, environmental and sustainability reporting and organizational value creation? Whose value? Whose creation?', *Accounting, Auditing and Accountability Journal*, vol. 19, no. 6, pp 793–819.
Revisiting and updating the debate on reporting on the social and environmental dimensions of business.

Gray, R.H., Dillard, J., & Spence, C. 2009, 'Social accounting as if the world matters: towards absurdia and a new postalgia', *Public Management Review*, vol. 11, no. 5, pp 545–573.
Discusses social accounting in the context of a sustainable world.

Gray, R.H., Owen, D., & Adams, C. 2010, 'Some theories for social accounting? A review essay and a tentative pedagogic categorization of theorizations around social accounting', in Freedman, M. & Jaggi, B. (eds), *Sustainability, environmental performance and disclosures*, Emerald Group, Bingley.
A review of reporting theories in the fields of CR reporting.

Hasseldine, J., Salama, A.I., & Toms, J.S., 2005, 'Quantity versus quality: the impact of environmental disclosures on the reputations of UK PLCs', *British Accounting Review*, vol. 37, no. 2, pp 231–248.
Evaluation of reporting's impact.

Online resources

- Suggested additional information on social and environmental reporting
- Discussion topics for students
- Company and industry case studies
- Links to other web-based resources

Endnotes

1. IPCC, 2007; WWF, 2012.
2. KPMG, 1993, 1996, 1999.
3. KPMG, 2002.
4. KPMG, 2005, 2008, 2011.
5. Beresford, 1973, 1975, 1976.
6. Gray et al. 1995a,b, 2001b; Murray et al., 2006.
7. Tinker, 1985.
8. Berry et al., 1985.
9. Lehman, 1992.
10. Changing corporate governance guidelines have increased the amount of recommended disclosure, categorized as social disclosure, relating to the remuneration of directors following the Cadbury and Greenbury Reports in the mid-1990s (see Chapter 7).
11. For a more recent discussion of the definition, see Gray et al., 1996.
12. This 'agency' relationship lies at the heart of modern corporate activity and is further explored in Chapter 9.
13. There are a number of examples in which disclosure is used when no other measure of performance is available (see, e.g., Belkaoui 1976; Ingram, 1978b; Mahapatra, 1984; Belkaoui and Karpic, 1989).
14. www.globalreporting.org.
15. Lewis et al., 1984; Hogner, 1982; Guthrie and Parker, 1989.
16. Unerman, 2003.
17. Gray, 2002a, b.
18. ASSC, 1975.
19. AICPA, 1977.

20. Deegan, 2002.

21. It also has an extensive website covering issues of climate change, international development, ecosystems, and the business role. There is a section on projects in progress and there are a large number of case studies for reference. See www.wbcsd.org.

22. For a full list of awards schemes around the world, see www.enviroreporting.com.

23. See Mathews (1996) for a detailed discussion of the development of social accounting research in different time periods.

24. See, e.g., Bowman, 1973; Bowman and Haire, 1976; Belkaoui, 1976.

25. See, e.g., R.W. Estes, 1975, 1976; Ramanathan, 1976.

26. See, e.g., Jacoby, 1973; Browne and Haas,1974; Feldberg, 1974; Parket and Eilbert, 1975; J. Estes, 1976.

27. The Centre for Social and Environmental Accounting Research (CSEAR) at the University of St Andrews boasts a membership in excess of 500 people from over 30 countries and holds an annual conference for researchers each September (see http://www.st-andrews.ac.uk/csear).

28. Bowman, 1973; Chenall and Juchau, 1977; Ingram, 1978a; Stewart & Konieczny, 1996; Chan and Milne, 1999; Milne and Chan, 1999; Friedman and Miles, 2001.

29. Friedman and Miles, 2001; Toms, 2002; Hasseldine et al., 2005.

30. Owen et al., 2000.

31. See, e.g., Owen et al., 2000; O'Dwyer and Owen, 2005.

32. Dando and Swift, 2003; Adams,2004; Adams and Evans, 2004.

33. O'Dwyer and Owen, 2005.

Stakeholder management and engagement

 Chapter overview

In this chapter, we explore the significance of stakeholders and how they relate to the way in which corporate responsibility is perceived and managed through partnerships, alliances, and voluntary standards. In particular, we will:

- examine stakeholders as a managerial concept;
- identify the different types of stakeholder and difficulties with the 'stakeholder' construct;
- explore the role of stakeholders in defining and implementing voluntary codes of corporate responsibility practice and standards;
- review experiences of stakeholder management.

 Main topics

Meaning and origins of stakeholder   201
Corporate responsibility standards   208
Stakeholder consensus: deviance and uniformity   215
Government and governance   217

Key terms	
Stakeholder	Voluntary standard
Code of conduct	Engagement
Partnership	Developing countries

Meaning and origins of stakeholder

The theme of this chapter is stakeholders: what they are, how they can be managed, how they influence the management of the company, and the validity of the very concept. We have raised the idea of stakeholders in Chapter 5 when we discussed the partnerships companies are creating with stakeholders as a feature of the business–society relationship that has come to the fore during the current era of globalization. As we touched on then, partnerships are not always straightforward affairs, and one of the reasons for this is the complexity of the stakeholder concept. Prominent CEOs such as IBM's Sam Palmisano have called the shift in business from shareholder companies to stakeholder companies as a defining element of the modern corporation,[1] but there is plenty of disagreement about what this implies in terms of definition, management practice, and consequences.

It might seem obvious but, while the term stakeholder has gained popularity fairly recently, companies have always had stakeholders of one kind or another. There have always been investors, employees, business customers, consumers, and local communities that are affected by and have an influence on the organization called the company. They can be sub-divided so that, for instance, employees comprise managers, supervisors, skilled workers, labourers, and so on, all with their own vested interests. Indeed, although much of corporate responsibility literature uses the term company to refer to a homogenous entity (reflecting common practice in the mass media and day-to-day parlance), companies often need to be understood as the locus of multiple, frequently competing, contracts between individuals and their alliances. There is a long history of viewing companies in this way, but it is no longer commonplace. In fact, critics of stakeholder theory might argue that replacing unsympathetic terms such as worker–management relations with the seemingly more neutral inclusive 'stakeholder' is a victory for normative modern management theory. We shall return to the ideational nature of stakeholder theory later, but first it is worth considering, if stakeholders have always been part of the business landscape, why we need a special term now, and why that term has gained particular popularity in corporate responsibility literature.

 Key concept: Stakeholder

A stakeholder is any person or organization affected by or with the power to influence a company's decisions and actions. Because of the company's impact or their influence, stakeholders are deemed to have a stake in the company. In the shareholder theory of the firm which began to dominate the Anglo-Saxon debate about the purpose of business in the 1960s, the outcome that executives are accountable for is shareholder value. Stakeholder theory of the firm offers an alternative to this by making it explicit that the firm has material and/or moral reasons to consider its relationship with more than just investors. In countries such as Austria, stakeholder participation in corporate governance is enshrined in law, but elsewhere, such as the USA and Australia, it is a voluntary aspect of management that is being accepted as at worst prudent and better still performance-enhancing.

In Chapter 5, we talked about contemporary corporate responsibility practice as the product of a particular sociopolitical discourse—one where companies are responding to certain features of globalization such as the changing nature of governance and the multi-tiered values framework that shapes expectations of business. Stakeholder, in part, has gained its prominence because of such changes. A company might legally have a primary duty to its shareholders, and senior managers might feel more comfortable exercising that responsibility rather than a more loosely defined one to society, but examples throughout this book demonstrate how companies are affected in a material sense by a range of organizations, individuals, and alliances built around common interests that typically position the company's behaviour as something they want to influence. Equally, there have been numerous examples of how the company affects others, such as workers in supplier factories, consumers reliant on product safety for their well-being, communities dependent on a company for employment creation, former employees living off of company pensions, and so on. Into an already tangled web, rising concern about sustainable development (see Chapter 3) has added non-human stakeholders such as the natural environment, the global commons, and climate.

As awareness of the social and political consequences of globalization increased from the 1970s onwards, stakeholder as an analytical construct became widely used, for example in the influential work of Giddens (1991, 1994) and Ackerman and Alstott (1999). The term had been used in business literature since the 1930s[2] as a way of distinguishing between the main groups towards which companies have different kinds of duty—in particular, shareholders, customers, consumers, and employees. In 1984, however, Freeman's *Strategic Management: A Stakeholder Approach* presented stakeholders as something more extensive, complex, and nuanced than this. What is more, they were not simply to be viewed as a convenient taxonomic device; for Freeman, managing stakeholders effectively was essential to the very survival and prosperity of the enterprise. In what he calls *'radical externalism'*, Freeman proposes that managers pay attention to stakeholders as a matter of course by adopting integrative strategic management processes.

In light of the very significant impact that Freeman's book has had on management theory, there are two points to note. First, as Walsh (2005) observes, Freeman wrote at a time when business was seen as weak and *'on the ropes'*. As discussed in Chapters 2 and 5, stagflation was undermining major capitalist economies, US business, in particular, was under threat from Japanese competitors, there were unprecedented levels of mergers and acquisitions, and companies were increasingly targets of consumer and environmentalist advocacy. Ironically, given how, today, stakeholder engagement is portrayed by some as a way of harnessing or reducing the power of corporations, the business world that Freeman sought to help was something fragile and troubled.

Secondly, in contrast with some later authors, Freeman is not positing stakeholder theory as an attack on the shareholder-centric theory of the firm that is central to liberal economics. On the contrary, he adopts a very instrumental approach to stakeholder theory, under which companies choose who their stakeholders are, based on the potential of those stakeholders to jeopardize the firm's survival. This is an important point to note because, subsequently, others have presented the shareholder and stakeholder theories of the firm as something mutually opposed. But as Walsh notes, Freeman only raises this possibility right at the end of his book when he asks (and leaves unanswered):

> Can the notion that managers bear a fiduciary relationship to stockholders ... be replaced by a concept of management whereby they must act in the interests of the stakeholders of the organization?
>
> *(Freeman, 1984; cited in Walsh, 2005, p 249)*

Freeman is not alone in subsuming stakeholder management to the purpose of wealth creation,[3] but his work is widely cited by those who have a quite different view of stakeholder engagement. Rather than sets of discrete, typically bilateral, relationships upon which the company chooses to embark with stakeholder groups, more recent stakeholder theory treats the firm as an organism that is embedded in a complex web of relationships, and requires the company to see these other organisms not as objects of managerial action, as was often the case hitherto, but as subjects with their own objectives and purposes. Therefore the stakeholder management model involves the company being aware of, and responsive to, the demands of its constituents, including employees, customers, investors, suppliers, and local communities. In contrast with Freeman, an important consequence of this is that shareholders are no longer regarded as the most important constituents, and shareholder value is not the sole criterion for assessing the company's performance.

This pluralist notion of the company's responsibilities clearly runs counter to the liberal economic model of the firm which postulates that business contributes to the public good by pursuing its narrow economic goals and, hence, that managers should concentrate on maximizing the market value of their companies. It is predicated on the belief that, in real life, the distinction between economic and social ends is seldom as clear as liberal economists pretend, because economic decisions have social consequences and vice versa, and the very idea of separate social and economic worlds is seen by some as mistaken.[4] Although perhaps not what Freeman intended, the stakeholder model has become the dominant framework for seeing companies as integrated in, rather than separated from, the rest of society.

 Discussion points

Stakeholder has become a common term in corporate and government parlance.

- What is attractive about the term?
- Is Freeman right to emphasize the importance of knowing one's stakeholders?
- Think of a company. Who are its stakeholders?

Management or engagement?

According to authors such as Lindgreen et al. (2012), stakeholder thinking today concerns the interactive, mutually engaged, and responsive relationships that establish the very context of doing business and create the groundwork for transparency and accountability.[5] From this perspective, Freeman's stakeholder management is one that is too business-centric, but one reason that managers have accepted the stakeholder concept may be that it complements management thinking. In Chapters 1 and 2, we discuss the difficulty of defining what the responsibilities of business are, and often managers are faced with sets of issues that beg the questions: *'What am I responsible for?'* and *'To whom am I responsible?'* For managers who have been trained to manage processes such as marketing, production, or finance, it can be easier to understand responsibility in the context of such functional disciplines, and therefore responsibilities to defined constituencies may have more resonance than long, seemingly ad hoc, lists of normative social and environmental issues.[6]

In other words, for stakeholder theorists at least, the value of an issue for a manager derives from the fact that a stakeholder has legitimized it. As Rasche and Esser (2006) point out, this is in line with social theorist Habermas's notion of discourse ethics, wherein ethical norms are justified not by reference to a priori principles, but because all members of society can reach a consensus around them. In contrast with ethicists such as Mill, Kant, Nozick, or Rawls, who offer universal ethical principles (see Chapter 2), Habermas claims that ethical norms can vary according to differences in context. Thus, what is ethical in one situation can change, provided that it is tested and justified through a context-specific discourse involving members of society. Moreover, although the norms can change, what must remain constant and universal are the rules under which the discourse itself is carried out.

Corporate responsibility theory offers a great deal of advice on how to conduct a consistent, robust, and credible discourse with stakeholders (see Box 9.1). For example, the AA1000 Series is, in some ways, an attempt to spell out the universal rules for reaching an ethical consensus through stakeholder participation, comprising four main elements that are underpinned by the principle of stakeholder engagement: (a) company commitment to social and ethical accounting, auditing, and reporting, with stakeholders playing a key role; (b) defining and accounting for the company's actions through stakeholder consultation that identifies issues relating to social and ethical performance, the scope of the social audit, relevant indicators, and the collection and analyses of information; (c) preparation of a corporate responsibility report to be audited by an external group, and subjected to external feedback; and (d) embedding social accountability systems into mainstream management practice.[7]

However, there are a number of problems involved in applying stakeholder theory in everyday management. First, it can be difficult to identify who stakeholders are. At the broadest level, they are individuals, groups, or entities (including, some would argue, the natural environment) that claim rights or interests in a company and in its past, present, and future activities. To narrow this down, Freeman (1984) drew a distinction between 'primary' and 'secondary' stakeholders. Primary stakeholders are those without whose participation a company cannot survive (e.g. investors, employees, suppliers, customers, and the governments and communities that provide infrastructure and markets). Secondary stakeholders are those that influence the company or are affected by it, but are not essential to its survival, although

Box 9.1 Commonly cited phases and factors in engaging with stakeholders

Phases of managing stakeholder dialogue

1. Selection of stakeholders

2. Stakeholder dialogue

3. Interpretation of information from dialogue

4. Decisions about company actions

5. Response to the dialogue through activities

Key factors in acting on stakeholder dialogue

1. Awareness that an issue exists

2. Commitment to prioritize and resource an issue

3. Capacity/availability of resources to tackle an issue

4. Consensus amongst the company and its stakeholders over the issues and relevance of stakeholder dialogue in general

(*Sources:* Andriof et al., 2002; adapted from Pedersen, 2006)

they may be able to help or harm the company (e.g. the media, terrorists). Therefore the manager's duty is to create sufficient wealth, value, or satisfaction for primary stakeholders to ensure that they remain part of the stakeholder system. He/she may pay attention to secondary stakeholders as well, but there may often be circumstances under which the interests of primary stakeholders are pursued at the expense of those who are secondary (e.g. taking a money-losing product sold to poor communities off the market).

Stakeholders include groups with quite different expectations. One common distinction made is that between those who are influenced by the company's actions and those who have an interest in what the company does. In order to understand the nature of a particular stakeholder and to assess what priority to give its expectations, managers are often advised to make judgements about which they have significant or insignificant degrees of interest, and about those over whom the company has high or low degrees of influence (see Figure 9.1). However, this type of approach does little to help managers to make decisions based on a stakeholder's moral claim and has led to a situation in which companies are accused of responding to stakeholders with the loudest voices or most power, rather than to those with the greatest need or strongest entitlement. Phillips (2003) criticizes stakeholder theory for failing to distinguish between, and prioritize, stakeholders based on a moral rather than a business obligation. For Goodpaster (2002), stakeholder analysis is incomplete if it does not weigh the significance of the identified options for the different stakeholder groups and make a normative judgement that integrates this information into a decision. As Gibson (2000) argues, if we do not accept this ethical dimension to the notion of stakeholder, the term itself becomes meaningless, with its use limited to a form of shorthand for referring to a, possibly ad hoc, group of individuals.

Partly because of this, Freeman abandoned the primary–secondary stakeholder distinction, although it remains widely used by corporate responsibility practitioners. One outcome he saw was that stakeholders were being treated as the means to corporate ends, rather than as entities whose interests should be served by the company.[8] This is certainly evident in much of what is called 'stakeholder engagement' today, in which consultation and dialogue are carried

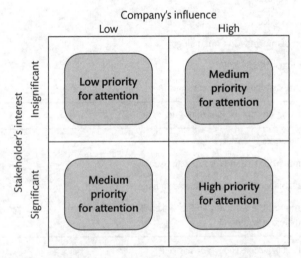

Figure 9.1 How stakeholders' influence and interests affect corporate prioritization

out with the aim of gathering important input and ideas, anticipating and managing conflicts, improving decision-making, building consensus among diverse views, and strengthening the company's relationships and reputation. There can be a strong business case for stakeholder engagement, including reduced costs, opening new markets, and protecting the company against activism. But this leaves companies open to criticism that they are picking and choosing who to call a stakeholder, and hence whom to listen to, and some managers feel that they are under pressure to respond to some stakeholders rather than others, based on who corporate headquarters regards as important rather than who the company affects.[9]

These tensions are highlighted in some of the examples of partnership discussed in Chapter 5, but it is worth reiterating that there is an important distinction to be made between the promise of the stakeholder model, as described by some corporate responsibility theorists, and the way in which it is actually being used by companies at the present time. In theory, stakeholder dialogue, engagement, and participation are at the heart of a more democratic form of corporate accountability. As an early advocate of stakeholder approaches to corporate responsibility described it:

> Corporate accountability, especially when based on stakeholder engagement … is all about learning and change: learning about the organization itself, about those who have a relationship with it, and learning about its place in the larger scheme of things.

> *(AccountAbility, 2002, p 5)*

In practice, the stakeholder model is more typically applied so that a company can manage its stakeholders in the sense of influence and control. It is noticeable, for instance, that many recent studies approach stakeholder engagement from a marketing perspective, and there has been much less interest in applying stakeholder theory in terms of worker or investor relations.[10] This is not to say that stakeholders are taken advantage of, or experience no benefit from this approach; at the very least, companies that participate in extensive stakeholder dialogue have become more sensitized and sensitive to stakeholder concerns. But it is also becoming clear that, if the stakeholder model is to become part of a new way of managing the business–society relationship, companies will need to give up some of their power and influence in order to become accountable to, rather than simply in discussion with, the wider stakeholder community.[11] One arena of corporate responsibility management where this would need to be evident is in the partnerships between a company and other organizations. We have discussed these in general in Chapter 5; now we turn to the particular type of partnership created through voluntary corporate responsibility standards.

 Discussion points

The list of a company's stakeholders is potentially enormous.

- Is the distinction between primary and secondary stakeholders valid and useful?
- What are the strengths and weaknesses of using stakeholders to decide the responsibilities of a company?
- Should companies be accountable to stakeholders?

Corporate responsibility standards

Corporate responsibility standards are an area of collaboration in a world of harsh corporate competitiveness. The Ethical Trading Initiative (ETI), the Forest Stewardship Council (FSC), the Roundtable on Sustainable Palm Oil (RSPA), the Extractive Industries Transparency Initiative (EITI), and the UN Principles for Responsible Investment are some of the standards, guidelines, and codes that bring together companies from a host of industries. Stakeholder partnerships are frequently presented as an approach to corporate responsibility well-suited to companies wrestling with the challenges of globalization. Advocates often cite them as a way to hold companies to account in an era when the limits of traditional governance structures are being tested (see Chapter 5). This is taken a step further in the idea of voluntary multi-stakeholder standards or codes of practice. Voluntary standards are a particular approach to managing the effects of business on stakeholders. We begin by discussing this approach in general, but will then highlight the stakeholder dimension to it.

Features of standards

Standards, guidelines, and codes of conduct or practice are largely synonymous terms for an important tool in the management of corporate responsibility. The terms might be interchangeable, but there are many types and to say that a company has adopted a standard says little, in itself, about the performance, policies, or strategies of that company. Over half of the 200 largest companies have business codes of some fashion, yet there are enormous differences between businesses in terms of what aspects of corporate behaviour are covered and the extent to which they influence what the company does.[12] Paine et al. (2005) have tried to make sense of this by identifying eight principles that cover the statements, commitments, and requirements found in business codes (see Box 9.2). These show that the codes

---

Box 9.2   Underlying principles of business codes

1. Fiduciary principle—aspects of a code that define the responsibilities of directors and management to the company and its investors

2. Property principle—concerning respect for the property rights and assets of the company and its competitors

3. Reliability principle—concerning the honouring of commitments

4. Transparency principle—concerning the conduct of business in a truthful and open manner

5. Dignity principle—concerning respect for people's dignity, including health and safety, human rights, freedom from coercion, and human development

6. Fairness principle—aspects to do with engaging in free and fair competition

7. Citizenship principle—aspects requiring the company to act as a responsible citizen of the community, including legal compliance, environmental responsibility, and non-involvement in politics

8. Responsiveness principle—aspects requiring the company to be responsive to parties with legitimate claims and concerns about its activities

(*Sources:* Adapted from Paine et al., 2005; Carroll and Buckholtz, 2006; Rasche, 2010)

go beyond much of what is included in corporate responsibility today. Many of the issues in contemporary corporate responsibility fall under their principles of 'dignity' (e.g. labour rights, workplace health and safety), 'citizenship' (e.g. environmental management, community involvement), and 'responsiveness' (e.g. stakeholder engagement). As is evident in the discussion of corporate responsibility in the global value chain (see Chapter 5), there are some who would like corporate responsibility to do more to address the principles of transparency and fairness (e.g. treating suppliers fairly and ensuring fair competition). There are also those in the business community who argue that it is hypocritical for companies to talk about corporate responsibility if they disregard the principles of property and reliability.

Broad business codes can provide a context for managing corporate responsibility, as is the case, for example, with Johnson & Johnson's statement of principles (see Box 9.3). For the

---

Box 9.3   Johnson & Johnson's credo

We believe our first responsibility is to the doctors, nurses and patients, to mothers and fathers and others who use our products and services. In meeting their needs everything we do must be of high quality. We must constantly strive to reduce our costs in order to maintain reasonable prices. Customers' orders must be serviced promptly and accurately. Our suppliers and distributors must have an opportunity to make a fair profit.

We are responsible to our employees, the men and women who work with us throughout the world. Everyone must be considered as an individual. We must respect their dignity and recognize their merit. They must have a sense of security in their jobs. Compensation must be fair and adequate, and working conditions clean, orderly and safe. We must be mindful of ways to help our employees fulfil their family responsibilities. Employees must feel free to make suggestions and complaints. There must be equal opportunity for employment, development and advancement for those qualified. We must provide competent management, and their actions must be just and ethical.

We are responsible to the communities in which we live and work and to the world community as well. We must be good citizens, support good works and charities and bear our fair share of taxes. We must encourage civic improvements and better health and education. We must maintain in good order the property we are privileged to use, protecting the environment and natural resources.

Our final responsibility is to our stockholders. Business must make a sound profit. We must experiment with new ideas. Research must be carried on, innovative programs developed and mistakes paid for. New equipment must be purchased, new facilities provided and new products launched. Reserves must be created to provide for adverse times. When we operate according to these principles, the stockholders should realize a fair return.

(*Source:* www.jnj.com/connect/about-jnj/?flash=true)

---

most part, however, modern corporate responsibility has more narrowly defined concerns. Typical broad issues covered in codes are:[13]

1 the natural environment;

2 labour;

3 corporate governance;

4 money laundering;

5 bribery and corruption;

6 human rights;

7 corporate responsibility reporting principles (see Box 9.4).

In some instances, these issues are addressed in individual company standards which, despite sometimes involving a degree of stakeholder consultation, fall short of what might be considered a stakeholder partnership. However, they can also form part of comprehensive industry-specific or general business standards, such as the FSC's principles of sustainable forest management and the Equator Principles for the financial industry.

The distinctions between standards have become important as interest has grown in assessing the effectiveness of so-called 'voluntary' standards.[14] Particular attention has been

---

Box 9.4 Examples of corporate responsibility standards

Issue covered	Examples of standards
Environmental	CERES principles ISO14000 environmental management series Kyoto Protocol
Labour	Fair Labor Association workplace code of conduct ETI base code Fair Wear Foundation
Corporate governance	OECD principles of corporate governance Principles for corporate governance in the Commonwealth Toronto Stock Exchange guidelines for improved corporate governance
Money laundering	Wolfsberg anti-money laundering principles Basel Committee on banking supervision
Bribery and corruption	OECD convention combating bribery of foreign public officials in international business transactions International Chamber of Commerce rules of conduct to combat extortion and bribery Extractive Industry Transparency Initiative
Human rights	Amnesty International human rights principles for companies UN draft norms on the responsibilities of transnational corporations and other business enterprises with regard to human rights Voluntary principles on security and human rights
Corporate reporting	AA1000 series Global Reporting Initiative guidelines on social, economic, and environmental reporting
Comprehensive	UN Global Compact principles OECD guidelines for multinational enterprises ISO 26000 corporate responsibility standard

paid to the way in which standards are developed, as a determinant of their robustness, effectiveness, and credibility, and the following types are common.

1 Company standards developed within a company for its own use, perhaps with some external consultation, and with reference to relevant international norms and standards (e.g. on human rights, emissions, or corruption).

2 Company standards built on consultation with relevant stakeholders and making explicit reference to international standards.

3 Industry standards developed by a peer group of companies, perhaps with external consultation, and with differing degrees of reference to international norms and standards.

4 Multi-stakeholder standards developed for an industry, or a wider range of companies, built on a consensus among business, non-government, and trade union organizations.

5 Independent standards made available to an industry, or wider range of companies, but developed by non-business groups, such as trade unions and NGOs.

6 Framework agreements between a company and trade unions.

Some argue that standards developed by companies, separately or with their peers, are more likely to reflect the concerns of Northern consumers than the full breadth of social or environmental issues relevant to a company, and that standards developed independently of business are more comprehensive.[15] Kolk et al. (1999) claim that certain types of standard are likely to have a greater impact than others; for example, those developed by international organizations, such as the OECD and the ILO, or those developed by civil society organizations, such as the Clean Clothes Campaign and Social Accountability International, will be more rigorous than those developed by individual companies or industries, such as Levi Strauss, Nike, and the Apparel Industry Partnership. However, there is less difference in content between company and independent standards today than there was a few years ago, and Sethi (2003) argues that company standards can be more effective provided that they are subject to external scrutiny (see later).

Ranganathan (1998) says that a standard should meet the '3 Cs' used in financial auditing; that is, they must be:

1 *comprehensive*, or complete enough to cover the issues that are most pertinent or material to the company;

2 *comparable*, to allow inter-company assessment of performance;

3 *credible* enough to allow business and other stakeholders to trust their integrity and to use them in making informed judgements.

This last requirement is also sometimes called 'materiality'. Various additional characteristics of a credible standard have been identified, as follows.[16]

1 Content that is relevant to the industry, but not simply a reflection of the most publicized problems.

2 Clarity and conciseness in terms of language, style, and format.

3 Explicit reference made to relevant international standards and conventions.

4 Inclusivity, requiring the participation of all key stakeholders who have a legitimate interest in what the standard is measuring.

5 Continual improvement of the criteria against which performance is assessed.

6 A commitment regarding to whom the results of any assessment will be disclosed.

7 Suitability of the standard for implementation, including setting out indicators that are measurable and trackable over time.

8 Availability of the standard in the main languages of the locations within which it will be used.

 Discussion points

Stakeholder standards are often portrayed as the most robust way of implementing voluntary regulation.

● What roles do you think stakeholders can play in implementing standards?

● Should stakeholders ignore the law when deciding standards?

● How can it be ensured that all stakeholder voices are heard?

Multi-stakeholder standards

There are many standards, and a common complaint heard from managers is that they are required to comply with too many standards, many of which address the same issues (see Snapshot 9.1). The Wal-Mart-backed Global Social Compliance initiative and the earlier Joint Initiative on Corporate Accountability and Workers' Rights (JOINT) have sought to har-monize the implementation of labour and environmental standards, and are attempts to address this concern through a process called 'equivalence.' However, it remains an issue, especially amongst suppliers of Western retailers and brands which at times have received up to 40 audits in a month. Only a relatively small number of standards can show extensive stakeholder participation in their development, implementation, and accountability. But even those that can have their distinct characteristics, as the following three examples show.

 Snapshot 9.1 The Global Reporting Initiative

The Global Reporting Initiative (GRI) guidelines serve as a framework for reporting on social, economic, and environmental performance. Launched in 2000, they are now in their fourth iteration (G4) based on input from thousands of people in many parts of the world. They are neither a performance standard nor a management system, although they can be useful to the development of both. Their primary purpose is to provide a common benchmark to encourage companies to communicate what actions they are taking to improve non-financial performance, the outcomes of these actions, and the future strategies for improving performance.

(continued...)

The guidelines, which are freely available at www.globalreporting.org, represent what GRI has identified as the most relevant reporting content. There are also supplements for industries, such as mining and banking, and technical protocols on specific indicators, such as child labour and energy. Companies can choose whether to produce reports 'in accordance with' or more loosely 'with reference to' the guidelines, and 90 per cent of those that cite the guidelines choose the latter. This figure may change as GRI introduces more levels of reporting, but questions about how many and how fast new levels should be introduced are indicative of a wider issue that GRI faces in balancing prescription and flexibility.

Despite any shortcomings, proponents say that the guidelines have provided the signposts that have led many companies away from producing reports consisting of, what critics call, photos of happy smiling children and not much else, to those that at least begin to recognize the array of social, economic, and environmental issues with which the company is involved. Furthermore, by retaining the support of business and non-business constituencies while undertaking two major revisions, the guidelines have become a testing ground for global stakeholder engagement.

(*Sources:* Baker, 2002; GRI, 2002; Leipziger, 2010; www.globalreporting.org)

Quick questions

The GRI guidelines are intended to provide a common framework for company reporting on sustainability issues.

1 Why is this kind of common framework necessary?

2 Why has the GRI focused on guidelines rather than on a certifiable standard?

3 What are the strengths and weaknesses of this kind of approach?

SA8000—the independent code[17]

In 1998, the Council on Economic Priorities, now Social Accountability International (SAI), created SA8000 with advice from representatives of business, trade unions, and NGOs. It is a verifiable standard, focusing on labour rights and worker welfare, and is intended to be applicable to any industry and in any country. It combines elements of ILO labour conventions with ISO management systems, and has been revised and extended to include more detailed provisions for specific industries, such as agriculture. SAI and its panel of companies, civil society organizations, and academics certify companies that comply with its provisions. This means that conditions in their facilities have been verified by independent accredited SA8000 auditors, and that the auditors' findings have been ratified by SAI.

SA8000 is different from many standards in that it has both performance and process elements, prescribing not only the labour criteria with which a company must comply, but also acceptable systems for embedding the standard into daily management practice. Over 1,000 facilities in 55 countries have been certified to date. A bone of contention is that these facilities bear the cost of auditing, even though certification is typically a buyer's requirement. But this is not fundamentally different from other costs relating to management systems, such as ISO certification.

Forest Stewardship Council—a stakeholder-owned standard[18]

The Forest Stewardship Council (FSC) was first mooted as an idea in 1990 in response to the failure of traditional approaches to arrest the decline of the world's forest resources. The organization, which is managed by a secretariat and overseen by a partnership comprising business, indigenous rights organizations, community groups, and environmental NGOs, acts as custodian to a certification standard that sets out key principles and criteria for forest stewardship. The standard provides a basis for assessing if a forest is being responsibly managed in relation to silviculture practices, environmental impact, working conditions, workers' and community rights, and indigenous people's rights. Certification of a forest involves a fairly extensive four-stage auditing process, including pre-assessments, field visits, peer review, and ratification. A certificate is valid for five years, although there may be interim inspections.

A feature of the FSC is that it is not only a standard, but also a partnership. As an organization, it draws support from a wide membership base around the world. Moreover, its governance structure is designed to limit the influence of any single member, or category of member. The FSC board features representatives of those with a commercial interest, those with an environmental interest, and those with a social interest in forests, and these groups all have a say in major decisions at the general assembly. This structure is an interesting example of global democracy in action and, although it has been criticized for being slow and unwieldy, the FSC standard is widely regarded as the benchmark for forest certification.

The Equator Principles—an industry-wide stakeholder code[19]

The Equator Principles stipulate how financial institutions should consider environmental and social issues in their project finance operations. The signatories are primarily European and North American banks, and the standard clearly reflects reputational concerns about their portfolios of lending to developing countries. These arise from the potentially high risk of adverse social and environmental impacts that are attached to the infrastructure, energy, extractive, and other projects financed in this way (e.g. relocation, ecological damage, impact on communities). The Principles commit banks to formulating environmental and social policies and processes against which individual projects can be assessed for compliance. Their provisions are based on the social and environmental policies and procedures of the International Finance Corporation, and, among other things, require banks to screen proposed projects according to their potential social and environmental impacts. The outcome of the screening process, in turn, triggers a range of follow-up activities, and the most dangerous projects are subjected to more rigorous assessment, public consultation, and information disclosure requirements.

While signatory banks agree to adopt these policies and procedures, implementation is left to the individual bank and, in contrast with the FSC or SA8000, there is no requirement that companies independently verify how they are implementing the standard. Indeed, the Principles explicitly state that they are a benchmark for use in the development of each member company's policies. However, there is an implicit assumption that, by involving large project finance banks, the Principles will create an environment within which good social and environmental policies are the norm, and will encourage industry-wide improvements. The standard is too new to say whether this will happen and, at present, success is being measured in terms of the number and size of the signatory companies, with about forty banks signing up to the most recent revision of the Principles in 2006.

Stakeholder consensus: deviance and uniformity

A promise of stakeholder engagement is that it will allow companies to better understand and respond to the expectations of society. Standards are a way of establishing a widely applicable benchmark for measuring corporate responsibilities, but one should be careful not to overestimate the feasibility or desirability of universal norms and practices. It is possible to portray the stakeholder role in applying standards as a mere embellishment of the uniformity and standardization found in conventional quality or financial management. But the additionality of stakeholder engagement is if it helps to meet the specific challenges of non-conventional performance management. An example of this is the defining and securing of good performance in diverse locations. Cannon (1994) identifies five types of community in which business might have a role to play to ameliorate the effect of economic downturns. The first is high-stress environments, in which the community has endured a long period of economic disadvantage, and has consequently suffered economically and psychologically. The second is structurally disadvantaged areas, such as remote islands or towns, which have lost their physical competitive advantage, as, for example, happened in Liverpool when UK trade shifted from having a transatlantic to a more European focus. Another type is the crisis zone, within which a dominant company or industry in a region collapses, as has happened with the automotive industry in the UK's Midlands. A different type of community is that of the transitional area, within which the important industries for the local economy are changing, as has happened in the German Ruhr. Finally, there are communities in which powerhouse industries that have been the catalyst for local growth (e.g. California's software industry) find themselves buffeted by competition from elsewhere and have to adjust accordingly.

A comparison of regional studies of corporate responsibility by authors such as Adegbite et al. (2013), Muthuri (2013), and Kuada and Hinsen (2012) show the importance of understanding corporate responsibility in a local context. Hamann et al. (2005) have pointed out, in the South African context, that corporate responsibility needs to take into account five realities specific to that country. First, there is the historical legacy of poverty and inequality that is reflected today in the 55 per cent of the population living in poverty, in over 30 per cent unemployment, in chronic housing and sanitation shortages, and in high HIV prevalence. Second, corporate responsibility needs to recognize, and be rigorous enough to combat, the distrust of certain companies and industries arising from their complicity in exploitation and the apartheid regime. Third, there are established traditions of corporate responsibility in South Africa, particularly community social investment, and now black economic empowerment, through which black entrepreneurship is being encouraged. Fourth, the struggle against apartheid and the consequent emphasis put on legislation to ensure social justice, fundamental human rights, and democracy mean that government has a crucial role to play in corporate responsibility. Finally, small and medium-sized companies in the formal and informal sectors make up 95 per cent of South African business and their role, capacity, and needs are all relevant for corporate responsibility.

These issues are not only pertinent to South Africa, or even Africa more widely. The particular issues that are high on the African corporate responsibility agenda may not be identical to those of other regions (see Box 9.5), but, more significantly, they are often different to, or at least more nuanced than, the corporate responsibility agendas that many multinational companies think of as globally relevant. Often these agendas are built on what Western-based multinationals and, more significantly, Western-oriented stakeholders think should be the priorities of Africa or elsewhere. Thus, for example, Western stakeholder priorities for Africa might be to combat corruption, improve governance and transparency, and improve infrastructure, while local priorities might be to improve the terms of trading, create good jobs, and transfer technology. Such issues may not be mutually exclusive, but it can be questioned how far corporate responsibility can progress if both sets of priorities are not recognized, and

Box 9.5   Comparison of priority social and environmental issues across selected countries and regions

Country/region	Social and environmental issue
European Union	Decoupling growth from consumption
	Sustaining welfare, health, and labour standards in a global economy
	Clean air and emissions trading
	Marine environment and fisheries
USA	Energy security, including renewed calls for nuclear power
	Climate change policy
	Public health accessibility
	Social security
	Corporate governance
Latin America	Rich–poor divide
	Basic environmental management
	Good public governance and fighting corruption
	Infrastructure
	Competitiveness and security of small farmers
Africa	Good public governance and fighting corruption
	Terms of trading
	Infrastructure
	Conflict
	Managerial capacity
Japan	Nuclear power
	Air pollution
	Exploitation of offshore fisheries and foreign tropical forests
	Urban environment
	Foreign workers

(*Sources:* Ethical Corporation, 2006; PWC, 2006)

there remain serious questions about the effectiveness of stakeholder participation in getting multinationals, in particular, to tackle local priorities. As Rajak's work on corporate responsibility in the mining industry shows (Rajak, 2006), companies may not deliberately seek to rule out local priorities, but their decisions about what to support have the effect of legitimizing or delegitimizing particular issues.

Different perspectives on what corporate responsibility's priorities are have also been noted in Latin America, where advocates in the West may focus on rainforest conservation and biodiversity, while local people may be more concerned about poverty, poor education, bad housing, and scarce health care.[20] According to Schmidheiny:

> the key [corporate responsibility] challenges for these regions ... have to do not so much with the number of companies talking about [corporate responsibility], but with creating a home-grown, meaningful form of [corporate responsibility] that addresses local issues and improves society, while also strengthening government's capacity.

(*Schmidheiny 2006, p 22*)

 Discussion points

The responsibilities of companies can vary according to location and circumstance.

● Why do some stakeholders misunderstand local priorities?

● Is it useful for a company to have a universal vision of its responsibilities of the kind developed by Johnson & Johnson (see Box 9.3)?

● What are the difficulties companies face in recognizing regional differences?

Government and governance

As Visser and Tolhurst (2010) point out, what makes corporate responsibility important in the context of any developing country is that it embodies many of the dilemmas that business faces in trying to be responsible, sustainable, and ethical (see Snapshot 9.2). For example, it raises questions about when local traditions take precedence over international standards, about how far a company's responsibilities extend in providing public services, and about when business's involvement in local governance enhances a weak governance infrastructure and when it constitutes an unhealthy intrusion into the political process. Are, for instance, multinationals culpable for the deaths of over 200 workers in factories producing clothes for export, or should responsibility rest with the local government and Bangladeshi factory-owners? This last question reflects a wider theme that marks out discussions about corporate responsibility in developing economies, i.e. the role of government. While the European Union, for example, has chosen to emphasize corporate responsibility as a voluntary approach that places no extra legislative burden on business, the role of government and the links between corporate responsibility and regulation are central to debates in developing nations.

There are various explanations for this. For example, in China, the government has defined corporate responsibility in terms of its own priority of ensuring social stability and uses

Snapshot 9.2 Multi-stakeholder governance—Extractive Industries Transparency Initiative

EITI is an example of a strategic multi-stakeholder partnership with an explicit governance function. It was launched by the British government at the 2002 Johannesburg Summit, and although it is primarily an inter-firm partnership, it has always enjoyed strong political support from OECD governments. Furthermore, its successful implementation depends on active civil society organizations, not least at the national level.

EITI is based on the idea that greater transparency and accountability in countries that depend on revenues from oil, gas, and mining will help those countries avoid the 'resource curse' which in the past has been blamed for the mismanagement of finances and corruption in resource-rich but economically poor countries. Relief of the resource curse, it is argued, will enable the revenues from extractive industries to become an engine for sustainable development. EITI tackles this in three ways. It provides a universal standard for companies to promote revenue transparency by getting companies to publish what they pay.

At the international level, EITI is based on a set of twelve principles that were developed under the stewardship of the British government through discussions involving multinational extractive companies, NGOs, institutional investors, and international institutions such as the World Bank Group. At this level, companies agree to disclose what they pay to governments in resource-rich countries. At the national level, the EITI is a government-led initiative, and governments agree to publish the revenues they receive from extractive industries. But it is also recognized that for this information to be used effectively, there has to be a formal role for other stakeholders from the private sector and civil society. In this way, not only is the information on payments and revenues disclosed in a transparent, accessible, and comprehensible manner, but it can be acted upon, for instance by exploring whether the revenues are being used for development programmes.

The initiative has earned itself a mix of praise and criticism, often for the same reasons. For example, its narrow focus on financial transparency means that it does nothing about many other sustainability issues in the extractive industry value chain, and depending on one's point of view this is a strength or a weakness. It has also been accused of omitting stakeholders that have historically helped local people tackle the resource curse (e.g. trade unions), and of shifting power to community-level government officials regardless of whether they have local people's trust or not.

A recurring criticism is that EITI is a Western-led initiative that not only has failed to gain the support of the increasingly important extractive industries from emerging economies, but may promote values that are not aligned with the culture, philosophy, and business interests of those economies. For example, China's national oil companies have not supported EITI even though they have pursued a programme of rapid international expansion since 2002. This expansion is paid for through the 'Angola' mode of investment in which development aid, debt relief, low-interest loans, and infrastructure development are given to the host country in return for access to its resources. This type of barter relationship is not suited to the EITI system, which assumes a much more Western capitalist model of exchange.

(*Sources:* EITI 2005; Bracking 2009; Mouan 2010)

Quick questions

EITI is a widely acknowledged example of an international multi-stakeholder partnership.

1 What category of partnership does it represent?

2 Is its narrow focus a strength or a weakness?

3 Are extractive companies from emerging economies right not to join EITI?

the term to mean government regulation.[21] In parts of Latin America, Asia, and Africa, an important element of the corporate responsibility agenda concerns fighting corruption and improving public governance, and therefore includes activities to build government capacity and the rule of law. Also, companies do not want to be saddled with an unsustainable burden of providing public goods, and therefore would prefer to partner with government and others. In general, it seems to come down to the fact that the business community is reasonably satisfied that, in countries with developed economies and democracies, government is able to maintain social stability; it is more concerned that business will be over-regulated. In developing economies, however, especially those in which governments are either weak or dictatorial, the business community is more concerned about the rule of law, and the creation of social stability and a favourable business environment, and therefore under- rather than over-regulation is the issue.

Authors such as Reich (2007) and Vogel (2012) are critical of the dumbing down of regulation that they believe corporate self-regulation permits. It is certainly true that some companies have, over the years, thrived in oppressive regimes, and many are prepared to do business in countries, such as Burma and China, that are openly resistant to Western ideals of public governance. But there is evidence that companies operating in such countries at times use corporate responsibility not simply as a substitute for good public governance, but as a way of introducing good governance norms in the hope that they will shape public institutions in the future.[22] This, in turn, reflects a belief that if ever there was a business case for taking advantage of unstable oppressive political conditions, for multinational companies and industries in a global economy these conditions represent an undesirable risk—one that, if it cannot be avoided entirely (e.g. because of the physical location of natural resources, or the competitive advantage of low-waged labour), must be reduced, and corporate responsibility offers a means of achieving that end.

These are compelling arguments, especially if one believes that Western prosperity is a consequence of democracy as much as of capitalism.[23] It is also worth noting that, in countries such as Morocco, governments have used corporate responsibility as a framework within which to promote a renewed commitment to better labour practices, controlling child labour, and new legislation to combat corruption, and to improve workplace rights of women and the disabled, and the rights of trade unions. Indeed, seeing this as a way of complying with trade agreements and attracting businesses in competition with lower-waged competitors, the government has made corporate responsibility part of its strategy to win foreign investment.

Yet many still resent or resist corporate responsibility and see it as an outsiders' imposition. This is not simply a case of the status quo resisting reform. Developing countries can be victims of the subsidies and protections that the USA, European, and other countries give to industries such as agriculture and defence—policies that, in turn, are related to poverty and lack of economic opportunity. Moreover, poverty and exploitation are seen by some as the hallmark of colonial and post-war entrepreneurs, and this sudden conversion to responsibility is seen as hypocrisy, at best, and commercial gamesmanship, at worst.[24] As multinationals headquartered in countries such as India, China, Brazil, and Mexico gain prominence, and foreign direct investment from such countries grows (see Chapter 4), so speculation has mounted that this will undermine the efforts of Western multinationals to raise standards. Such views reflect a somewhat rose-tinted view of Western corporate behaviour in developing countries over the years, and may at times be inflected with racial prejudice. At the very least, such assumptions need more sophisticated analysis than they have received to date. In countries such as India, where some conglomerates date back to the nineteenth century, there is resentment of the implication that they are irresponsible, or have not built a relationship with the society. Tata, for example, has established various institutes that invest in social and environmental innovation, and has a long tradition of giving back to communities. In 1998, it formalized the Tata Code of Conduct, which includes areas such as involvement with communities, ethical conduct for company officers, and a commitment not to support any political party or political activity. This, in turn, is backed up with whistle-blower protections, and sanctions such as demotion and dismissal for anyone breaching the code. Conversely, Scandinavian countries are often admired for their strong worker rights and environmental standards, but the voluntary standards that Scandinavian companies promote in developing countries seems little different from those of multinational companies headquartered elsewhere.

 Discussion points

Stakeholder participation has been described as more inclusive than the conventional government system.

- Is stakeholder participation democratic?
- Is the role of companies in tackling governance issues in developing and developed economies different?
- Will companies headquartered in emerging economies have different ideas of responsibility to their Western counterparts?

One response to disquiet at the imposition of corporate responsibility from overseas has been the creation of local corporate responsibility organizations. While many individual companies have started to produce corporate responsibility reports, these are often aimed at overseas audiences, not least the US or European stock markets, on which some of these companies are now listed. Corporate responsibility organizations, however, have more flexibility in terms of developing a locally relevant corporate responsibility agenda. They include the Malawi-based African Institute for Corporate Citizenship and the Forum EMPRESA network of corporate responsibility organizations in sixteen Latin American countries. However, they are not always successful, and the Chinese Association for Corporate Social Responsibility, established by foreign and domestic companies in 2006, seems to have disappeared without a trace.

 Case study 9   Roundtable on Sustainable Palm Oil—international multi-stakeholder partnerships across the value chain

The Roundtable on Sustainable Palm Oil (RSPO) was formed in 2002, one of several partnerships fostered by the environmental NGO, WWF. Building on its experience with the Forest Stewardship Council and then the Marine Stewardship Council, WWF mobilized an array of industry actors. Palm oil is a major global commodity used in foodstuffs, soaps, cosmetics, and now biofuels. It is produced from the fruit of oil palms that grow in tropical regions on plantations and smallholdings. Production

(continued...)

has escalated rapidly since the 1980s, most notably in Malaysia and Indonesia. This expansion has often resulted in the deforestation of tropical forests. This has negative consequences for biodiversity, and conservationists were amongst the loudest early protesters against oil palm; but when it also involves deforestation of forests in areas of peat, it results in the release of large amounts of what was previously sequestered CO_2.

RSPO was launched as a joint initiative of NGOs, palm oil processors and traders, financiers, retailers, food manufacturers, and industry bodies such as the Malaysian Palm Oil Association. After two years of negotiation, it was formally established as a not-for-profit association in Switzerland, although its secretariat is located in Kuala Lumpur. It was intended to be a demand-side coalition creating a demand for sustainable palm oil, much as the FSC had created a market for certified timber. Unilever and Migros had already set standards for sustainable palm oil, but it was felt that retailers and manufacturers working together would be able to put more pressure on producers to conform to the new standards. Moreover, by involving NGOs, it was felt that the demand side could build consumer awareness and support, and reduce what sometimes felt like ill-informed campaigns by advocacy groups.

Not all NGOs accepted this offer and some, such as Greenpeace, have continued to mount anti-palm-oil campaigns since RSPO's launch. There was also disagreement between companies and the participating NGOs, notably on how much the supply side should be involved, and whether the primary focus should be on oil palms as a cause of deforestation. For example, Unilever, which was the most influential of the initial companies, did not think that the causal link between oil palms and deforestation was as strong as NGOs claimed, and moreover did not believe that simply using buyer strength was sufficient to bring about substantial changes in producer practices. Disagreement about this latter point was keeping producers away from the initiative, but after the first roundtable meeting in 2003 it was agreed that producers, NGOs, and buyers would all have equal representation.

Achieving an acceptable balance between different sectors, and different parts of the value chain, was a major step in RSPO's evolution, and while there continued to be disagreements, there was also a sense of common ownership. In 2005, RSPO members adopted the 'principles and criteria for sustainable palm oil production', comprising eight principles and 39 criteria on economic, environmental, and social aspects of palm oil production. Thus, RSPO had evolved from being a partnership for systematic dialogue to one that included rule-setting as a central focus. However, in doing so, it developed standards that its multiple stakeholders could agree on, and the elaborate governance structures and procedures emphasized consensus rather than coercion—common positions rather than differences.

This approach, which was also time-consuming, was frustrating for some outside the process who wanted rapid change and interpreted the symptoms of consensus-building as evidence of failure. Greenpeace published a report, *Cooking the Climate*, and sent people in orang-utan costumes up the outside of Unilever's HQ. Nonetheless, certification began in 2008 with 106,000 hectares of productive area, and by March 2012 had increased to over 1.2 million hectares. Over 5.1 million metric tonnes of certified palm oil has been sold on the international market, accounting for almost 10 per cent of global production. Despite this significant rise, and the support of some of the largest palm oil producers such as Sime Darby and Wilmar, there are major energy and food markets where non-certified oil can be sold (e.g. China and India), and the European market represents no more than 20 per cent of world demand. Because growing units, not companies, are certified, plantation owners can benefit from the certified and non-certified markets, and continue deforestation. At present, certified palm oil attracts a premium, but this is likely to drop as supply increases, and because RSPO was pioneered largely by technical experts, the marketing side of sustainable palm oil has only recently started to receive any serious attention.

(continued...)

Nonetheless, RSPO has demonstrated the adaptability of its partnership model over time. Early on, its challenge was to bring together powerful organizations to create an immediate legitimacy, but this led to problems in engaging with some parts of the value chain, not least the smaller producers who saw RSPO as a threat, a cost, or an irrelevance. RSPO changed from a demand-based to a supply–demand orientation, and also accepted a role for NGOs. It achieved consensus around a sustainable production standard, but members found that the standard itself, rather than protecting their image, became a target for civil society criticism. Producer unease has been partly offset by the growth in the market for certified oil, but the challenge now is to get yet more of the cultivated area certified even if global demand is uncertain.

(*Sources:* Nikoloyuk et al., 2010; Schouten and Glasbergen, 2011; www.rspo.org) (Originally published in Blowfield 2012)

Quick questions

1. RSPO is an example of a rule-setting partnership and what has been called private or partnered governance.

   a How does this approach to governance differ from conventional governance mechanisms?

   b What are the key elements of its governance system?

   c What are the strengths and weaknesses of multi-stakeholder partnerships as an approach to governance?

2. The partnership challenges of RSPO have evolved over time.

   a Why were NGOs attracted to a demand-side led approach to begin with?

   b Why did retailers and manufacturers doubt that this would work?

   c Should NGO partners protect the palm oil industry from criticism by other civil society organizations?

3. RSPO has created a market for certified sustainable palm oil.

   a How can it expand this market in emerging economies?

   b Can it expand the area under cultivation for certified oil to more than 20 per cent of total production?

   c What role can the different stakeholders play in increasing RSPO's legitimacy?

Summary

The notion of stakeholder and the evolution of stakeholder management and engagement are pivotal in contemporary corporate responsibility practice. While stakeholder management theory regards stakeholders as entities to be recognized but ultimately controlled, stakeholder engagement views companies as parts of complex interdependent webs, within which many groups claim a stake (i.e. a right) in the company by virtue of the impact that the company has on them, or their power to influence the company in some way. Voluntary standards, codes of conduct, and guidelines are one concrete outcome of stakeholder engagement. However, there are many examples of standards being designed and implemented without any real stakeholder engagement, and some advocates of stakeholder management, such as Phillips et al. (2003), believe that normative instruments such as standards run counter to the emphasis of stakeholder theory on continual dialogue and responsiveness.

There are many kinds of standard and a variety of institutional arrangements for developing them. It is in the area of implementation that stakeholder engagement is widely seen as good practice, although, in reality, many companies remain reluctant about how far to go in involving others in what are seen as management decisions. Nonetheless, the stakeholder model has clearly affected the way in which many companies see the world and their role within it, and there is widespread acceptance that, in addition to any responsibility to shareholders, there are also responsibilities to employees, consumers, customers and suppliers, and communities. The location from which a company is engaging with stakeholders has a significant effect on how these processes are managed. In fact, one of the features of corporate responsibility that distinguishes it from many other areas of management, such as quality control, is that good practice can vary by country or region. And herein lies the challenge of managing corporate responsibility—not only the balancing of the expectations and values of diverse, often globally dispersed, stakeholders, and the demonstration of one's accomplishments in concrete terms, but also the accommodation of the fact that these expectations and values are subject to continual change.

Further reading

online
resource
centre

www.oxfordtextbooks.co.uk/orc/blowfield_murray3e/
   Visit the Online Resource Centre that accompanies this book to enrich your understanding of this chapter. Among the resources available are web links, exercises, and additional case studies.

Freeman, R.E. 2010, *Strategic management: a stakeholder approach*, Cambridge University Press, Cambridge.
   A reprint and update of Freeman's seminal book that introduced stakeholder theory to business.

Husted, B. 2011, *Corporate social strategy: stakeholder engagement and competitive advantage*, Cambridge University Press, Cambridge.
   An exploration of the business reasons to adopt a stakeholder approach to strategic thinking.

Parmar, B.L., Freeman, R.E., Harrison, J.S., Wicks, A.C., Purnell, L., & De Colle, S. 2010, 'Stakeholder theory: the state of the art', *Academy of Management Annals*, vol. 4, no. 1, pp 403–445.
   An overview of current thinking about stakeholder management theory.

Seitanidi, M.M. 2010, *The politics of partnerships: a critical examination of nonprofit–business partnerships*, Springer, Dordrecht.
   A discussion of the nature of stakeholder partnerships based on in-depth studies of two major business-NGO collaborations.

Steger, U. 2009, *Sustainability partnerships: the manager's handbook*, Palgrave Macmillan, Basingstoke.
   Guidance on how to implement partnerships.

Zakhem, A.J., Palmer, D.E., & Stoll, M.L. 2007, *Stakeholder theory : essential readings in ethical leadership and management*, Prometheus, Amherst, NY.
   A collection of articles on stakeholder management theory.

Online resources

- Suggested additional materials on real-life partnerships
- Additional case study of multi-stakeholder engagement
- Further discussion and materials on the challenges of implementing voluntary standards
- Links to other web-based resources

Endnotes

1. Blowfield and Googins, 2007.
2. Preston and Sapienza, 1990.
3. See, e.g., Post et al., 2002; Phillips, 2003.
4. See, e.g., the discussion of the work of Karl Polanyi in Chapter 2.
5. Andriof et al., 2002, 29.
6. Clarkson, 1995.
7. Leipziger, 2010; AccountAbility, 2006.
8. Evan and Freeman, 1988.
9. CCC, 2005a.
10. See, e.g., Grappi et al. 2013; Nielsen and Thomsen 2012; Papista and Dimitriadis 2012.
11. CCC, 2005a; Rasche and Esser, 2006.
12. Kaptein, 2004.
13. Cragg and McKague 2003.
14. Utting and Marques 2010.
15. See, e.g. Varley et al., 1998; Kolk et al., 1999; Seyfang, 1999; Ascoly et al., 2001.
16. See, e.g., MacGillivray and Zadek, 1995; ISEA, 1999; Leipziger, 2010; Mamic, 2004.
17. Leipziger, 2001.
18. Bartley, 2003.
19. Wright and Rwabizambuga, 2006.
20. Svendsen and Laberge, 2005.
21. CCC, 2005c. Mitchell et al. (2003) seem to agree with this. Out of six benefits that they cite in their case study, four are given as intangible, i.e. with no assigned monetary value.
22. Sabapathy et al., undated.
23. For a counter-argument to this viewpoint, see Chang 2007, 2010.
24. Svendsen and Laberge, 2005.

10

Socially responsible investment[1]

 ## Chapter overview

In this chapter, we examine socially responsible investment (SRI). We outline the origins and development of SRI and recent developments such as impacting investing and blended value, and address the impact that these investment strategies can have. In particular, we will:

- review the evolution of SRI;
- describe the main approaches used in SRI decision-making;
- examine the performance of SRI funds;
- provide an overview of the international market for SRI and its development in different regional contexts;
- examine emerging trends in SRI.

 ## Main topics

The origins and development of socially responsible investment 226

Sustainable investing 230

Types of SRI analysis and practice 231

Engagement 235

Other SRI approaches 238

SRI performance 244

SRI index performance 244

SRI fund performance 246

Market growth 247

Trends in SRI 248

Key terms

Socially responsible investment (SRI)

Negative screening

Positive screening

Sustainable investing

Engagement

Cleantech

Venture capital

The origins and development of socially responsible investment

In Chapter 7, we addressed the place of corporate responsibility in the corporate governance framework and how companies shape their relationships with a wider society. That discussion included consideration of the structures that are in place to ensure that managers do not invest in risky projects. This chapter looks at the structures in place to ensure that investors—individual investors, institutional investors, and fund managers—consider carefully the social, environmental, and ethical consequences of their investments. This kind of investment is known as 'socially responsible investment' (SRI). Yet, as we shall see, SRI encompasses different styles of investment decisions and investor behaviour such as 'ethical investing', 'values-based investing', 'cleantech investing', 'impact investing', 'sustainable investing', and simply 'responsible investing' (see Box 10.1). These styles share a degree of overlap, but are not semantic synonyms; in fact, the points of differentiation can be hotly contested. However,

Box 10.1   Different styles of socially responsible investment

Style	Overview
Negative screening—ethical	Avoiding companies/industries on moral grounds
Negative screening—environmental or social	Avoiding companies/industries because of their social or environmental practices
Norms-based screening	Avoiding companies because of non-compliance with international standards
Positive screening	Active inclusion of companies because of social and environmental factors
Extra-financial best in class	Active inclusion of companies that lead their sectors in social/environmental performance
Financially weighted best in class	Active inclusion of companies that outperform their sector peers on financially material social/environmental criteria
Community investing	Allocating capital directly to enterprises and projects based on their societal contributions
Sustainability themes	Selecting companies on the basis of sustainability factors (e.g. renewable energy)
Impact investing	Investments made in order to generate measurable social and environmental impact
Blended value investing	Active allocation based on a blend of financial and social/environmental return on investment
Engagement	Dialogue between investors and company management to improve management of environmental, social, and governance issues
Shareholder activism	Using shareholder rights to pressure companies to change environmental, social and governance practices
Integrated analysis	Active inclusion of environmental and social factors within conventional fund management

(Adapted from Krosinsky, 2008; Lydenberg, 2005; Sparkes, 2002; Bugg-Levine and Emerson, 2011)

Key concept: Performance

Performance is a major aspect of an investment decision. But what is the real meaning of performance? The word 'performance' comes from the English 'to perform' which itself comes from the French *'parformer'*. Therefore the real meaning of performance is achievement. And the achievement of an investment cannot depend on return and risk alone. This would be a very limited approach. The investor has to think about a third dimension—the meaning.

(*Source:* Xavier de Bayser of Integral Development Asset Management, cited in Bellagio Forum for Sustainable Development and Eurosif, 2006, p 11)

what they share is the incorporation of extra-financial factors into investment decision-making. This includes all manner of asset classes (although listed equity predominates) and applies to all regions. It also has relevance along the investment chain—asset owner, consultant, asset manager, investment researcher, asset—and each of these stages is a potential point of breakthrough or blockage depending on the levels of awareness, incentive, requirements, and opportunities on offer.

We begin by setting out the historical development of SRI and the evolving interests of investors. Pre- and post-investment strategies regarding publicly traded companies and funds are addressed, including the screening methods that are used in assessing a company's products, services, or business practices. We examine how investors are contributing to social and environmental impact through their investment activities and, subsequently, how the role of fund managers is evolving. The provision of alternative investment opportunities is also discussed, including social and environmental venture capital. We look at different geographies and, in relation to the international SRI marketplace, at the investment options that address the unique social, environmental, and economic factors of those regions.

The origins of ethical investment

The principles of socially responsible investing are rooted in the Judaeo-Christian and Islamic traditions, which embrace peace and avoid business practices designed to harm fellow human beings. In the USA, the Religious Society of Friends (also known as the Quakers) is credited with planting the seeds of modern SRI as early as the seventeenth century by following strategies that adhered to their principles of non-violence and human equality. Early Methodist stock market investment strategies purposely avoided companies that were involved with alcohol or gambling and this, in essence, created some of the first 'screens' or frameworks under which investors could evaluate business practices.

Some churches and charities with sufficient capital were able to persuade individual financial institutions to establish ethical funds, eliminating those companies that were engaging in business practices that they perceived as unethical. However, it was not until the mid-1960s that retail funds were available to private investors, with the first such fund being established in Sweden in 1965. The Vietnam War marked another milestone in SRI, when certain investors started screening their investments to identify companies that supported the war; in 1971, the Pax World Fund, which responded to the demand for investment options that excluded companies benefiting from that war, was launched in the USA.

In the 1980s, concerns grew among investors about supporting businesses with operations in South Africa, thereby supporting apartheid and the poor treatment of employees.
Stocks were removed from portfolios, based mainly on ethical or non-financial reasons, and a
divestiture movement in South Africa by US corporations emerged. While the public statement was also significant, there is some evidence that institutional shareholdings increased
when companies divested.[2] Attention also shifted to domestic business practices, including
the use of child labour.

As discussed in Chapter 7, awareness of corporate conduct and responsibility increased
during the 1980s and 1990s. In 1983, the Ethical Investment Research Service (EIRIS) was
established, providing research on company activities and, subsequently, informing the
development and analysis of more investment vehicles for both institutional and private
investors. The first UK ethical fund—the Friends Provident Stewardship Unit Trust—was set
up in 1984, while the US Social Investment Forum conducted the first industry-wide survey
and identified $40 billion of assets managed under SRI principles. Funds addressing concerns
about the environment were also established, including the Merlin Ecology Fund (renamed
the Jupiter Ecology Fund).

In the early 2000s, the end of the equities boom plus a series of major corporate failures
linked to egregious governance practices made pension funds in particular aware of the need
to behave as real owners of companies, and to take a longer-term view of investing (see
Chapter 7). Consequently, traditionally conservative pension funds began to be innovators
in integrating social, environmental, and governance issues into decision-making. In 2001,
FTSE launched the FTSE4Good family of social indices, which will be discussed later in this
chapter (see 'Fund indices', p 233). This sent a strong signal to investors that SRI was indeed
becoming mainstream.

Since 2003, SRI funds and other offerings have emerged to meet the needs and interests
of most investors with offerings in large-cap funds, US domestic equity index funds, international funds, and small-cap offerings. In 2005, the first socially screened exchange traded
funds (ETFs) were launched. New funds are being developed continually, and in 2004, having seen the success of Islamic banks in the Middle East and Indonesia, HSBC launched its
Amanah Pension Fund, which was designed to comply with Shari'ah law, obeying special rules
according to, and avoiding certain investments that are contrary to, Islamic teaching.

At the political level, the year 2000 signalled the mainstreaming of SRI in Europe, and the
beginning of a more international and coordinated approach towards the disclosure of social,
environmental, and ethical practices. The EU heads of state agreed to the Lisbon Agenda,
in which corporate social responsibility and measures promoting sustainability were core
to achieving the agenda's goal of 3 per cent average economic growth and the creation of
20 million jobs by 2010. The first Global Reporting Initiative (GRI) Sustainability Guidelines
were also released, setting out a framework for reporting (see Chapter 8).

In 2001, the European Sustainable and Responsible Investment Forum (Eurosif) was
launched with the support of national European social investment forums and the European
Commission. Also in the UK, the Myners Review of Institutional Investment published its
final report, a short list of non-mandatory principles for investment decision-making that
applied to all pension funds and institutional investors. In the same way as the Cadbury Code
addressed corporate governance (see Chapter 7), the Myners Review addressed investment,
helping to set a new standard advocating shareholder activism.[3] In 2002, at the World Summit

on Sustainable Development in Johannesburg, the 'London Principles' were announced to address how the financial sector, specifically, could contribute to sustainable development (see Box 10.2). Also in that year, a second version of the GRI Guidelines was published.

Box 10.2   The 'London Principles' on the financial sector's role in sustainable development

Economic prosperity

Principle 1   Provide access to finance and risk management products for investment, innovation, and the most efficient use of existing assets.
Principle 2   Promote transparency and high standards of corporate governance in themselves, and in the activities being financed.

Environmental protection

Principle 3   Reflect the cost of environmental and social risks in the pricing of financial and risk management products.
Principle 4   Exercise equity ownership to promote efficient and sustainable asset use, and risk management.
Principle 5   Provide access to finance for the development of environmentally beneficial technologies.

Social development

Principle 6   Exercise equity ownership to promote high standards of corporate social responsibility by the activities being financed.
Principle 7   Provide access to market finance and risk management products to businesses in disadvantaged communities and developing economies.

(*Source:* Adapted from www.environmental-finance.com)

Large-scale global SRI initiatives have continued. In 2004, Kofi Annan, then Secretary-General of the United Nations, issued *Who Cares Wins*, drafted in conjunction with several leading international financial institutions, outlining roles and responsibilities for different groups, including cooperation, working towards the goals of better investment markets, and working towards more sustainable societies. In 2006, the UN Global Compact and United Nations Environment Programme's Finance Initiative (UNEP-FI) coordinated the creation of the Principles for Responsible Investment (see Box 10.3). Initially, twenty mainstream investors worth $2 trillion signed on to the agreement. Within a year, as of June 2007, assets quadrupled to $8 trillion and the number of signatories grew to 183, mostly from Europe and Asia, and it is now worth $20 trillion.[4]

The G8 declaration from the 2007 meeting in Germany highlighted investment decisions, transparency, and sustainable development.[5] The latest iteration of the GRI—called the G3—has been toted as a standard for performance analysis, although the investor-driven Climate Disclosure Project may be more influential. However, it must be remembered that all of these initiatives, including GRI and the Global Compact, are non-binding and voluntary. And while, arguably, significant progress has been made in the last decade, it can be contended that

Box 10.3 UN Principles for Responsible Investment

1 We will incorporate ESG (environmental, social, and corporate governance) issues into investment analysis and decision-making processes.

2 We will be active owners and incorporate ESG issues into our ownership policies and practices.

3 We will seek appropriate disclosure on ESG issues by the entities in which we invest.

4 We will promote acceptance and implementation of the Principles within the investment industry.

5 We will work together to enhance our effectiveness in implementing the Principles.

6 We will each report on our activities and progress towards implementing the Principles.

(*Source:* www.unpri.org)

more is needed. Disturbingly, the *Review of UK Equity Markets and Long-Term Decision Making* (Kay 2012) raised similar points to the Myners Report a decade and one global financial crisis later. Indeed, one of the greatest criticisms of corporate responsibility's effectiveness is that it did nothing to pre-empt, predict, or avert one of the largest corporate failures in capitalism's history when $2 trillion or 25 per cent of the value of a single asset class—mortgages—was wiped out. In the context of this chapter, this raises basic questions about what it would take, or indeed if it is possible, for SRI to become an investment norm. The answers to these questions will be taken up in later sections of the chapter.

Sustainable investing

In the evolution of SRI, one can discern a shift from concerns about tainted money (i.e. capital allocated to unethical or socially and environmentally harmful businesses) to finding ways of deploying capital to address major societal challenges. The most noticeable of these in recent years has been the growth of cleantech investment focused on renewable alternative energy and other technologies suited to the demands of a low-carbon economy; however, issues such as sustainable forestry, water, and natural resource conservation have also attracted investors' attention. Investment specialists with a background in SRI have identified large quantities of what they call 'stranded assets', the value of which would be at risk if climate change and other sustainability issues had the impact that many scientists predict.[6] Important figures within the SRI field are pushing to redefine SRI as 'sustainable investing' (or to preserve the original abbreviation, 'sustainable and responsible investing').

Sustainable investing recognizes the social, environmental, and governance goals of SRI generally, but stresses the need for patterns of finance and investment focused on long-term value creation, sustaining natural as well as financial assets, and a needs-based orientation to financial innovation that would serve the poor. Underlying sustainable investing are two claims: first, that fully incorporating long-term social and environmental trends will deliver superior risk-adjusted returns; second, that global sustainability of the kind discussed in Chapter 3 requires the mobilization and recasting of the world capital markets. For some it is entirely distinct from SRI[7] because, while the behaviour of ethically motivated investors is affected by the societal consequences of business, sustainable investment is built on the premise that sustainably managed enterprises are better able to add value over the long term. The former is highly subjective (i.e. what values are given priority), and taken to its logical conclusion could be an argument for business as usual if one felt (as many do) that 'the business of business is business' was a strong moral position. Values-derived SRI may be profoundly attractive to some for ethical reasons, but it is not underpinned by an encompassing financial discipline or universal logic.[8] Moreover, it is often defensive—the avoidance of certain companies and industries as if to demonstrate that, in defiance of modern portfolio theory, it is possible to build efficient investment portfolios despite excluding parts of the investment universe.

In contrast, it is argued, sustainable investing positively seeks to invest in companies with practices and policies aligned with sustainability goals, not because of ideological reasons, but because the best investments are companies that adhere to long-term drivers of performance, i.e. companies that exhibit superior sustainability. This is a powerful argument (although its persuasiveness hinges in part on an investor's beliefs), and one that gains force from (a) the uncertainty about conventional financial analysis and innovation that is the fall-out from the 2007–2008 financial crisis, and (b) the apparent flood of investment opportunities emerging from addressing climate change (e.g. alternative energy, energy reduction, low-carbon construction, geoengineering). However, as we shall return to later, there is a need for caution, both because of the interpretation and reliability of the historical data produced to support the thesis that sustainable investing outperforms conventional investment, and because the analytical and predictive tools needed to deal with sustainability are only in their infancy. Without a stronger basis for accounting for the past, and for predicting the future, extrapolating too much from a narrow range of companies and industries associated with tackling climate change could be as mistaken as the over-investment that SRI fund managers made in IT and health stocks in the late 1990s, when their funds slumped and underperformed the market.

 Discussion points

This chapter reviews the chronology and spread of SRI initiatives throughout the world, particularly since the 1980s.

- What has driven consumer demand for responsible investment offerings and what are likely drivers for the next decade?
- What are some of the various pre-investment and post-investment SRI strategies?
- What are some of the initiatives that have helped to encourage the international expansion of SRI?

Types of SRI analysis and practice

Box 10.1 summarizes the types of SRI strategy, the main ones of which we review in this section. Screening is the longest established strategy. Religious groups have long limited their investment universe by avoiding industries and activities that offend their moral principles. Screening is a pre-investment stage question that asks if a company is engaging in business practices that support or go against the investor's social, ethical, or environmental principles. Individual and institutional investors take different approaches to answering this question, and to determining which companies are therefore 'socially responsible'. Here, we review the different types of screen that are used, and introduce some of the funds and fund indices that employ screens.

Negative screening

'Negative' screening eliminates from an investment portfolio companies that are engaging in what are perceived to be negative business or environmental practices. In a survey of 201 socially screened funds in the USA, the Social Investment Forum (SIF) found that tobacco is the most commonly applied social screen, affecting more than 88 per cent of the total assets in the socially screened fund universe. Alcohol affects 75 per cent and gambling affects roughly 23 per cent.[9] Other negative screens include weapons, pornography, nuclear energy, poor employment practices, the manufacture of hazardous or ozone-depleting substances, genetic engineering, and animal testing.

The potential risk associated with negative screening is the possibility of biasing the geographic or sector allocation of the investment portfolio. As noted earlier, screened SRI funds appeared to outperform conventional funds in the late 1990s, but this was because they were over-exposed to IT and health stocks which subsequently dropped in value at the turn of the decade. Equally, anti-ethically screened funds such as the Vice Fund (VICEX) have outperformed the S&P for significant periods, but struggled until 2012 to return to their 2005 value following the financial crisis.[10] We discuss performance later in this chapter, but one needs to be cautious about leaping to conclusions on screened fund performance.

'Norms-based' screening is a variation on negative screening, requiring monitoring corporate compliance with internationally accepted norms, such as the Millennium Development Goals, the ILO core conventions, or the UN Global Compact.[11] Like other negative screening it is used to eliminate specific risks to the portfolio, and to communicate with the general public and corporate members on the ethics of the organization. Because the screen itself makes an ethical statement, it might also be used to guard the reputation of the investor.

Positive screening

Unlike negative screening, a particular industry is not excluded from positively screened portfolios. Rather, 'positive' screening is the selection of investments that perform best against corporate governance, social, environmental, or ethical criteria, and which support sustainability. Positive screening is associated with a 'triple-bottom-line' investment approach, ensuring that a company performs well according to financial, social, and environmental criteria. 'Best-in-class' screening, which selects the best-performing companies within a given sector of investments, is one such strategy, while 'pioneer' screening chooses the best-performing company against one specific criterion.

Examples of positive screens might include improvement of health and safety conditions, integration of environmental criteria into the purchasing process, prevention of corruption, elimination of child labour, and promotion of social and economic development.[12] Such screens have the advantage of encouraging companies to improve extra-financial performance irrespective of their industry, but they can be problematic. There is the challenge of how to measure performance in a robust replicable manner, and professional organizations such as the Certified Financial Analysts Institute are only starting to find ways to incorporate this into their certification and career development programmes. More fundamentally, there is the question of whether such screens result in significantly different investment portfolios. Benson et al. (2006) found that SRI mutual funds were virtually no different to mainstream funds, reinforcing Hawken's (2004) conclusion that SRI fund managers were no less likely than conventional managers to put financial returns ahead of trying to combat social injustice or environmental degradation.

In practice, funds may offer a mix of positive and negative screens. BankInvest Global Emerging Markets SRI, an emerging market equity fund, was one of the pioneers. Its negative screen excludes companies that have continuing violations of human rights, the environment, and labour rights, and those that derive more than 10 per cent of turnover from war material, alcoholic beverages, gambling, tobacco, or more than 3 per cent from pornography. The positive screen rewards the best and fastest movers, and companies that have a high score in supporting human rights, labour standards, the environment, and corporate governance. The first investor in this fund was Mistra, the foundation for strategic environmental research that is based in Sweden, which manages its assets in a socially responsible way. Some 80 per cent of its capital of SEK3.6 billion is invested on the basis of environmental and ethical criteria.

 Discussion points

SRI strategies require consideration of ethical, moral, environmental, social, and governance issues.

- How would you go about identifying SRI investment opportunities?
- What are some initiatives that try to ensure that companies are disclosing their social or environmental business practices, so that investors can make an accurate assessment?
- What do investors expect from their SRI investments and how might their expectations differ from those of traditional investments?

Fund indices

One way of addressing the need for reliable performance measurement is the use of specialist fund indices. Three of the major SRI indices are KLD's Domini 400, the Dow Jones Sustainability Group Indexes, and the FTSE4Good Index which is produced jointly by the *Financial Times* and the London Stock Exchange. Each of the indices uses a different weighting system for financial and non-financial performance.

In May 1990, the Domini 400 Social Index (DSI) was launched by Amy Domini, Peter Kinder, Steve Lydenberg, and Lloyd Kurtz. The index removed 200 of the 500 stocks in the S&P 500[13] through the application of social screens and then added another 100 stocks to balance out the new index by sector. The goal of the index was to set a benchmark for SRI fund managers, similar to the S&P 500 but subject to social and environmental screens. Today, approximately 250 DSI companies are S&P 500 companies, 100 are non-S&P 500 companies, and 50 others have been chosen for their 'exemplary' records of environmental, social, and corporate governance practices.

The Dow Jones Sustainability Indexes (DJSIs) were established in 1999 as the first indices to track sustainability-driven companies on a global basis. They were launched together by the Dow Jones Indexes, STOXX Limited (a European index provider), and SAM Group (a pioneer in SRI). There are over $8 billion assets in DJSI-based investment vehicles. The DJSI uses a rules-based methodology and focuses on best-in-class companies. Assessment criteria include corporate governance, risk and crisis management, codes of conduct (including anti-corruption), labour practices, human capital development, sustainability and project finance (for banks), climate strategy (including eco-efficiency and protection of biodiversity), and emerging markets strategy.[14]

The FTSE4Good Index was launched in July 2001 and is derived from the FTSE Global Equity Index Series as an initiative of FTSE, in association with EIRIS and the United Nations Children's Fund (UNICEF). Today, there are two series: a benchmark index and a tradable index. The initial screening process looks at the starting universe—FTSE All-Share Index, FTSE Developed Europe Index, FTSE US Index, and FTSE Developed Index—and screens against tobacco producers, companies providing parts, services, or manufacturing for whole nuclear weapon systems, weapons manufacturers, and owners or operators of nuclear power stations that mine or produce uranium. Positive screens are applied on the subsets of companies, corresponding to each of the original indices, to include companies that are working towards environmental sustainability, have positive relations with stakeholders, and uphold and support universal human rights. The inclusion criteria 'originate from globally recognized codes of conduct such as the UN Global Compact and the Universal Declaration of Human Rights'.[15] Since 2004, FTSE4Good has launched a series of regional indices including ones for Japan, Australia, the USA, South Africa, and emerging economies. New climate change criteria were introduced in 2007, and it also operates an index of European environmental leaders.

Other indices and initiatives

While the KLD's Domini 400, DJSI, and FTSE4Good remain the flagship indices, other initiatives have emerged to address newer dimensions of the SRI market. In 2003, Dutch asset management companies Kempen Capital Management and SNS Asset Management launched an SRI index comprising only smaller companies. USA-based Kenmar hedge firm launched its SRI fund of funds in 2007. SRI indices are also spreading to emerging markets, with the Johannesburg Stock Exchange SRI Index (South Africa) and OWW Consulting's Responsibility Malaysia SRI Index, which applies criteria to the FTSE Bursa 100 Index to determine whether the companies are deemed socially responsible. One of the six groups of criteria in the Malaysian index is community, including Rakyat policies based on Islamic banking principles and Halal accreditation.

Brazil's stock exchange BM&FBOVESPA took the concept one step further by creating a 'social and environmental stock exchange' called Bolsa de Valores Socioambientais (BVSA). It replicates the stock market environment for non-profit organizations.[16] Similar exchanges were subsequently established in Kenya and in South Africa where SASIX (South African Social Investment Exchange) was launched in June 2006 with the support of the Johannesburg

Stock Exchange. In 2013, a social stock exchange (SSE) was launched in the UK. The current focus in Brazil is on educational projects that benefit children between the ages of 7 and 25 who live in poor communities.[17] Education specialists recommend the best NGO projects to the board of BM&FBOVESPA, which then approves a list to become the portfolio of projects presented to investors by BM&FBOVESPA and its 120 brokerage firms. Individuals or organizations can buy 'social shares' in the projects, which are transferred entirely to the listed organizations without commissions, fees, or deductions. As of 2008, almost $5.5 million had been raised for 71 NGOs listed on the SSE.[18]

SSEs are intended to solve the liquidity problem facing investors wanting to allocate capital in social enterprises or societally beneficial projects, but concerned about exiting the investment. However, the concept of a 'social stock exchange' is, arguably, too alien for most investors. When the idea of an SSE was presented to other exchanges in Latin America and Europe, it was met with resistance by those who think that SRI is anathema to shareholder interests.

Engagement

While one set of questions posed by SRI investors arise at the pre-investment stage, another set arises at the post-investment stage: Is the company *continuing* to engage in socially responsible business practices? Engagement is the process by means of which investors become involved with the business to influence its activities, behaviours, and operations. This section discusses some of these engagement strategies, including shareholder activism, proxy voting, policy statements, and engaging at different levels.

Engagement occurs in response to the company's approach to corporate responsibility, or to a change in ethical and social practices. Other issues that might cause concern include the company's overall performance, internal controls, compliance, or general business practices, and responsible investors may raise these matters. Both private and institutional investors may raise the issues, although, typically, it is fund managers who play the largest role in the process. Chatterji and Levine (2006) argue that fund managers are in a position to play an important role in reforming performance metrics of socially responsible funds, enabling firms better to monitor social responsibility and manage shareholder value.

Shareholder activism

Shareholder activism includes activities that are undertaken in the belief that investors and shareholders can work together with management to change course and to improve financial performance over time. These activities can be conducted privately or publicly. Private methods might include letters to other shareholders, or to company management, to raise concerns. Institutional investors might raise issues during their routine meetings with company managers, or communicate their concerns to other investors to build pressure on the company; they might even join forces with other like-minded investors to take subsequent public actions. Public mechanisms for shareholder advocacy include raising questions during annual general meetings, or calling an extraordinary general meeting to propose shareholder resolutions. Investors might also issue press statements, or arrange briefings to make their reservations known to the wider international community of investors.

The mix of public and private facets to shareholder activism means that it is difficult to quantify. There are examples, such as the nuns who threatened a shareholder resolution at a GE AGM about pollution of the Hudson River, where activists have affected corporate behaviour. There are also famous individual and institutional activists such as the pension fund CalPERS (see Snapshot 10.1), Robert Monks, and John Bogle who have fought for more shareholder power, not least in the arena of governance (see Chapter 7). But overall, given the primacy allocated to shareholders by law, company owners have not had the huge influence on extra-financial issues that one might have expected. Even companies with a strong stance on particular social or environmental issues may lack a clear responsible investment policy, although there are signs that this is changing in some markets (e.g. 80 per cent of UK pension funds in one survey now have such a policy[19]). Moreover, public sector pension funds such as CalPERS, the Norwegian Sovereign Wealth Fund, and the Korean National Pension Fund have formed the P8 Group with a focus on getting pension funds to exert leadership in the shift to a low carbon economy.

Proxy voting

There is, though, a surprising lack of shareholder activism overall. One reason often repeated is that many shareholders have the mentality of traders rather than owners, and hence take a short-term view on company performance.[20] Another reason is that institutional investors have to hold shares in certain companies to balance their portfolios, and therefore have limited room to manoeuvre. To understand the relative paucity of shareholder activism, one only needs to look at proxy voting. At a company's annual general meeting, shareholders are given the opportunity to vote on a number of issues on the agenda. Following major corporate scandals such as Enron, Parmalat, and Royal Ahold, more shareholders are beginning to understand the importance and relevance of their voting and active participation. Usually, proxy voting applies to issues of corporate governance and, by voting against the mandatory approval of annual accounts and reports, investors register their protest against company practices. Leading SRI issues that are likely to be the focus of attention include climate change, environmental reporting, sustainability, global labour standards, the HIV/AIDS pandemic, corporate political contributions, and equal employment opportunity.

Voting practices vary from country to country, and Box 10.4 highlights some of the international resources and guidelines available. The Institutional Shareholders' Committee (ISC) Statement of Principles recommends that '*Institutional shareholders and/or agents should vote all shares held directly on behalf of clients wherever practicable to do so*'. It further recommends that institutional shareholders should:

> not automatically support the Board; if they have been unable to reach a satisfactory outcome through active dialogue then they will register an abstention or vote against the resolution. In both instances it is good practice to inform the company in advance of their intention and the reasons why.

(Institutional Shareholders' Committee, 2005, p 20)

Box 10.4   Resources on voting guidelines

Organization	Code
Commissie Tabaksblat (Tabaksblat Commission—The Netherlands)	Concept Code on Corporate Governance (*Concept-Code voor Corporate Governance*)
International Corporate Governance Network (ICGN)	Global Share Voting Principles
Mouvement des Entreprises de France (MEDEF—France)	Bouton Report (*Rapport Bouton*), Promoting Better Governance in Listed Companies
National Association of Pension Funds (NAPF—UK)	Corporate Governance Policy and Voting Guidelines for Investment Companies
Organisation for Economic Co-operation and Development (OECD)	Guide for Multinational Enterprises
Swiss Stock Exchange (SWX—Switzerland)	SWX Code

Quarterly reporting to clients is standard; at this point the fund managers could also report how they voted and any shareholder resolutions. More and more, voting details are made available on fund websites, which could list resolutions, issues, and companies for any given period.

However, a study by Shearman and Sterling (2005) of the hundred largest US publicly traded companies found that nearly one-third did not include any shareholder proposals in their proxy statements during the 2005 proxy season. However, the study did find an increase in shareholder proposals supporting the removal of super-majority voting provisions in its proxy statement and for majority voting in director elections, and a more recent study of UK pension funds found that 90 per cent of those with an SRI policy exercised their voting rights.[21]

 Discussion points

Please review the preceding section on 'Engagement'.

- As a private investor, what are some of the ways in which you might make others aware of your concerns about a company's SRI practices?
- As a fund manager, how might you communicate to the company your concerns about its business practices?
- What are some of the ways in which you think that international investors might better coordinate their engagement efforts, either as institutional members or as members of organizations such as the UN Global Compact?

Snapshot 10.1　CalPERS in Japan: shareholder activism to change corporate governance

CalPERS, or the California Public Employees' Retirements System, provides pensions to nearly 1.5 million active and retired teachers in California. Its fund managers are cited as having revolutionized corporate governance in the USA in the 1980s and 1990s. It was one of the first foreign pension funds to invest in Japan and, in 1992, owned $3.7 billion in Japanese equities. There were three stages to CalPERS' activities in Japan:

1　pursuing activities on its own, voting proxies, using the media, and meeting with company officials;

2　working together with other institutional investors and domestic groups that also wanted to change Japanese corporate governance;

3　withdrawing from large-scale activism and moving towards *'firm-specific efforts based on relational investing'*.

Between 1988 and 1990, CalPERS voted proxies in ways similar to other foreign investors but then wanted to replicate its US proxy voting practices in Japan. CalPERS was particularly concerned with barriers to takeovers and the absence of independent directors, each of which CalPERS had grappled with in the USA. Dividend levels were also an issue of concern and CalPERS wanted so see more cash go to shareholders. Not wanting to be accused of greed or insensitivity to Japanese norms, however, the company was careful to vote against inadequate dividends as well as against excessive dividends.

But proxy voting proved to be an ineffectual way of inducing governance change in Japan and, beginning in the mid-1990s, CalPERS instead applied more 'general principles' of corporate governance. It also engaged in a public relations campaign, championing the virtues of foreign investors. By 1996, it had $5.6 billion invested in Japanese equities. It also found allies, who shared the CalPERS vision, to engage in its second phase of activism, including local partners, and a small group of Japanese businessmen and academics who added legitimacy.

(*Sources:* Sterngold, 1993; Jacoby, 2007; www.calpers.com)

Quick questions

1　How do financial institutions diffuse the US model of corporate governance?

2　What was it about the local Japanese context that brought about a change in strategy?

3　What are the advantages and disadvantages of adopting a partnership strategy to foster change?

Other SRI approaches

One does not need to invest in publicly listed companies to engage in SRI, or indeed trade in stocks (cf. SRI property portfolios). There are a variety of other SRI options, including venture philanthropy, social and environmental venture capital, community investment, and microcredit.

Venture philanthropy

'Venture philanthropy' refers to the application of the venture capital model, principles of entrepreneurial business, and the deployment of private equity to charities and other social purpose organizations. On the heels of the technology boom over the last two decades and the economic success of innovative technology entrepreneurs, there is a broad range of initiatives applying the strategies of venture capital within the social sector. Rather than expect a financial return, venture philanthropists are looking for 'social returns' from the project in receipt of the investment. They recognize that capital is necessary for growth and to cover cash flow difficulties, but this can be difficult for social purpose organizations to access. Grant-makers or banks may be unwilling to provide finance in these situations, creating a space where venture philanthropy alone or co-investing with grant-making trusts offers solutions.

The term venture philanthropy is not new (it was used by John D Rockefeller III as early as 1969), but its use and its definition are evolving and spreading internationally, embodying the following:

1 a long-term investment in organizations;

2 a partnership between the donor and the recipient (usually a charitable or non-profit organization);

3 provision of finance;

4 provision of expertise, skills, and/or resources that add value to the development of the organization and/or entrepreneur (which often includes access to the venture philanthropist's network of partners, who might be able to provide services such as accounting, marketing, or strategic consulting);

5 a view towards maximizing a 'social return on investment', or the bottom line leaning towards outcome-based solutions to the underlying problem;

6 a focus on accountability, because venture philanthropists hope to understand the cause of the social problem in order to develop effective solutions;

7 an exit strategy, making the organization self-sustaining and financially independent after a few years of support.

Much has been written about the pioneering venture philanthropy organizations, largely based in the USA, which embraced these principles to support local social innovation (e.g. Venture Philanthropy Partners, REDF—creator of the 'Social Return on Investment' Index—Accumen Fund, and Social Venture Partners, to name but a few). In the last few years, these principles have been embraced by philanthropists throughout the world to drive social innovation in both industrialized and developing countries, including traditional foundations (e.g. Rockefeller), newer foundations (e.g. Bill and Melinda Gates, Google.org), and individuals charting their own course in the social sector (e.g. the USA's Pierre Omidyar and South Africa's Mark Shuttleworth).

What is called the 'blended value approach' to investing has also been attractive to foundations looking to align the guidelines set in their programmes with their investment strategies. Typically, 95 per cent of a foundation's resources are used to generate income; this is called the asset 'corpus' and normally leaves 5 per cent to support payouts, administration costs, and grant-making activities. But if the asset corpus is invested only to maximize financial return (sometimes without any consideration of the make-up of the portfolio), only 5 per cent of the resources are driving 100 per cent of the social mission of the foundation. An idea put forward by some scholars and foundations is that, if the 95 per cent of the foundation's resources could be used to maximize the financial, social, and environmental impacts—i.e. the 'blended value' approach—the benefits generated by the investments could be exponentially greater than the impact of grants alone.

Environmental venture capital

Concern about sustainability, and in particular the transformation to a low-carbon economy as a response to climate change (see Chapter 3), has created a significant demand for capital in areas such as alternative energy, geoengineering, and green buildings. One aspect of this is 'environmental venture capital', or 'cleantech', which looks at investment opportunities in entrepreneurial environmental projects and companies that will reap financial, social, and environmental rewards for the investors (see Snapshot 10.2). Opportunities for these investments include sustainable energy technologies, such as renewable energy, transportation, and distributed generation of power. The size of some of these initiatives means that much of the capital will have to be raised from conventional financial markets and government-backed bonds. Certainly, some of the immediate investment needs, such as nuclear power and an energy distribution system matched to the specifics of alternative energy, are not suited to venture capital. Nonetheless, in 2012–2013 venture investors put $6.4 billion into the cleantech energy sector in North America, Europe, China, and India, marking year-on-year improvements since 2008.[22] Furthermore, green technology is an important part of the recent economic stimulus packages in some countries. For example, the USA and South Korea, the European Union, and China allocated 81 per cent, 59 per cent, and 31 per cent of their respective stimulus packages to green investment ($31 billion, $23 billion, and $221 billion).[23] However, some investors have lost out by treating clean technology as an asset class in its own right, expecting returns similar to ICT initial public offerings (IPOs) such as Google, rather than as an extension of energy as a whole.[24]

Emerging economies such as China, India, and South Africa are fossil fuel-dependent-nations, and need to take actions to safeguard a reliable stream of fossil fuels, to identify alternative sources of energy, and to pursue greater energy efficiency through technology and innovation. China has already taken significant steps in this regard, although the challenge is enormous (see Case Study 10). India has not attracted the same amount of international scrutiny, but in many ways faces equal challenges, and by some accounts lags far behind where it should be on environmental issues.[25] South Africa, which obtains 95 per cent of its electricity from coal-fired power stations, faces significant difficulties in making the transition to low-carbon energy without jeopardizing political stability and economic growth.

The social significance of climate change and the 'energy revolution' it seems to demand (Chapter 3) has stimulated a lot of debate about green investment. The need for investment in clean technologies, alternative energy, and climate change innovation has led to this revolution being portrayed as a huge investment opportunity. Moreover, this comes at a time when institutional investors in particular are looking for asset classes that can deliver steady inflation-linked income streams that do not imitate the performance or cycles of other classes. By some estimates, $2 trillion of investment is needed a year (equivalent to 2 per cent of GDP) to fund green growth and decarbonization. However, OECD analysis suggests that only half of that sum is being raised at present, and over a third is coming from company balance sheets rather than the financial markets.[26] What is more, the amount of project finance has dropped because of banks pulling out of the project finance market owing to the restrictions placed by Basel III.[27]

The appetite for green investment has also been damaged by a consolidation process in industries such as solar photovoltaic power equipment, which has turned an innovative product into a cheap low-return commodity leading to the high-profile collapse of companies such as Solyndra and retrenchment by others such as Vestas. In addition, institutional investors, who are often highlighted as a potential source of green investment capital, face fiduciary constraints that under the most optimistic scenarios would see them meet less than half of project debt need and a quarter of project equity investment.[28]

 Snapshot 10.2   CANOPUS Foundation—European venture philanthropy

The CANOPUS Foundation, based in Freiburg, Germany:

> promotes private *social investment* and *social enterprise* in order to fight poverty and environmental degradation, and provides business development assistance for social entrepreneurs in developing countries working in the field of clean energy technologies.

It invests only in non-profit organizations that operate in the field of clean energy technologies.

CANOPUS, like many other European venture philanthropy funds, provides several non-financial services in addition to giving grants. A recent study from the Skoll Centre of Entrepreneurship[29] found that many such funds deliver support through both their board members and partnerships. At CANOPUS, business development is built into every project activity. In-house project managers (who are not all fully paid staff) undertake site visits and field trips, and produce reports. In addition to its in-house resources, CANOPUS works with people within its network of cities and local governments to identify those active in sustainable development who are on site, and are willing and able to act as consultants. Specific services are provided through CANOPUS's partners who have provided pro bono services to the foundation, including business plan evaluation, accounting, and writing year-end balance sheets for the portfolio organizations. Fundraising support is also provided to the entrepreneurs. The Foundation is prepared to receive calls, or to go a step further and take part in a meeting with the entrepreneur to speak in support of the project. CANOPUS is also said to be a useful partner in helping the entrepreneur to understand clean energy markets and supply and demand, and to get margins at the lowest price.

(*Sources:* Interview with CANOPUS Foundation; John, 2007)

....

Quick questions

1 Which aspects of the partnership do you feel are most beneficial to the social and/or environmental entrepreneur—funding, business services, strategic advice, etc.?

2 Why does the CANOPUS Foundation refer to itself as a venture philanthropy organization rather than as an environmental venture capitalist or cleantech investor?

3 How might the needs of a social entrepreneur differ from those of a business entrepreneur?

Community development investment funds

Community development investing is defined by the Social Investment Forum as:

> financing that generates resources and opportunities for economically disadvantaged people in urban and rural communities that are under-served by traditional financial institutions.

(SIF, 2001, p 6)

Community development investment funds deploy equity and equity-like investments into small businesses in geographic areas that are traditionally overlooked by traditional venture capital and private equity funds. Typically, the businesses are located in disadvantaged communities and will increase the entrepreneurial capacity of the area and create jobs, resulting in what is termed 'high social impact'. Other development investment funds pool together investors, such as banks, corporations, insurers, foundations, and public pension funds, to provide support that can enable the provision of affordable housing, education, community centres, and small businesses.

Microcredit

'Microcredit' is the making of very small loans (or 'microloans') to individuals. The fundamental idea is to make money available to the poor, based on terms and conditions that are appropriate and reasonable. The concept emerged out of initiatives in the 1970s by organizations, such as Accion International and the Grameen Bank, which wanted to provide economic opportunity to poor people looking to start small businesses. Traditional banks were not interested in making small loans to what were considered 'the unbankable' (i.e. people without collateral), so a system of community banking was set up, under which small informal groups (called 'solidarity groups' within the Grameen Bank) were formed. Their collateral was the social networks that these savers and borrowers formed so that loans were effectively guaranteed by a combination of peer pressure and social cohesion. Women's groups in particular proved successful, and loan repayment far exceeded the normal percentage in traditional banking.

We discuss aspects of microcredit (also called microfinance) elsewhere (Chapters 4 and 12). It has spread rapidly, and not only in developing economies. Originally, the brainchild of NGOs, it is now offered by mainstream banks such as Deutsche Bank and Standard Chartered. However, it is not an unalloyed success. A little money can support the development of a one-person business or the beginnings of a small shop, for example, but scaling up the business to the next level is not always easy when further financial support is needed. If one looks at a country such as Bangladesh, where microcredit is the main form of banking, the signs that it has lifted people out of poverty (e.g. growth in incomes or GDP) are not obvious. This may be due to the entrenched nature of poverty, and microcredit could be as much a strategy for survival as a means of growth. But while the largest bank in Bangladesh is now the microcredit NGO BRAAC, the impact of microcredit on the poor is only starting to be measured systematically (see Chapter 13). In the drive to scale up microcredit, there is evidence from around the world that the solidarity-group-based model has been increasingly bypassed in favour of direct loans to borrowers. Also, interest rates are often very high compared with other formal moneylending. This may make the lending organizations more viable, but it raises questions about the social impact and how microcredit is ultimately different from traditional banks other than the size of their loans.

Impact investing

Impact investing is social investing that actively seeks to have a positive social or environmental impact. It comprises investments for financial return in companies or projects that have social and/or environmental benefit as their core goal. It includes blended value investment which seeks social/environmental and financial returns. Thus, investments that promote energy efficiency, provide credit to rural farmers, or develop drugs that would mainly benefit the poor exemplify blended value.

Impact investments inhabit a space between philanthropy, where no financial return is expected, and pure financial investments, where social considerations are not a factor and financial profit is maximized. Individual examples occupy a spectrum between 'Below Market Financial Return with High Social Return' and 'Full Market Financial Return with Some Social Return' investment philosophies. It is, by definition, a market-based approach to addressing many of the challenges facing the global community and seeks to engage capital in creating sustainable long-term solutions to those same challenges. Such strategies are defined as 'blended value' and not 'double bottom line' because they view the value being created as neither solely economic nor solely social, but a blend of both. This approach recognizes that economic value can create various forms of social and environmental impact and cannot be viewed as a separate component of the value proposition found within any given investment.

Large foundations are amongst the institutional investors that have shown interest in impact investing because it offers a range of investments that provide a blended return and gives foundations the opportunity to vary approaches to risk by choosing the nature of the organization to be supported and the terms of the investment. They can invest through a variety of means including cash, structured notes, securities (debt and equity), funds, and venture capital. They can also invest in a range of sectors where it is possible to measure social impact, including clean technology, microfinance, global health, and SME-oriented job creation in developing economies.

Impact investing is not expected to be a huge part of the investment world. A 2009 report estimated that it could potentially reach $500 billion out of a $50 trillion of managed assets globally.[30] It is estimated that, at present, $10 billion of funds are committed to impact investment, a rise of $1 billion since 2012.[31]

 Discussion points

Most screening techniques are not limited to one screen (e.g. the exclusion of tobacco industries), but consider a variety of factors.

- Pick one of the SRI indices discussed in this chapter and explain its selection criteria.
- If you were to apply an Islamic screen to this SRI index, what companies would you remove and why?
- Pick one of the companies on your screened list and look at recent proxies and/or shareholder resolutions filed. Discuss reasons why corporate governance actions might have been taken.

SRI performance

Although there is a philanthropic type of SRI, most investors want to see a reasonable financial as well as a social or environmental return on their investment, and many want to know how SRI performs compared with traditional full-universe funds. A company may engage in socially, ethically, and environmentally sound business practice, but the financial performance, or potential for return on investment, is undoubtedly an important factor driving the investment decision. As Statman (2000) found, socially responsible investors do not want to sacrifice return for social responsibility. To a degree, this is because of the way some SRI funds have been promoted, promising that they can outperform the mainstream indices in defiance of conventional investor wisdom that screening out part of the investment universe puts investors at a disadvantage.

SRI index performance

One way to compare SRI performance with mainstream investment vehicles is to look at the various indices available. In an analysis of 29 SRI indices (not investment funds), Schröder (2005) found that they did not exhibit a different risk-adjusted return to that of conventional benchmarks. In other words, there was no significant difference between SRI and conventional index performance. However, Schröder did note that many SRI indices have a higher risk relative to the benchmarks.

A closer look at the performance of the KLD DS400, DJSI, and FTSE4Good indices provides a clearer picture of the overall performance of the SRI industry in comparison with overall market performance. Comparing the performance of the KLD's DS400 Index with the S&P 500 (as of May 2007, i.e. prior to the financial crisis), the former outperformed the latter from its inception in 1990 (12.28 per cent compared with 11.71 per cent). Annualized returns over a ten-year period were equal, with 7.78 per cent returns. Looking at the five-year, three-year, and one-year periods, however, the picture is slightly different, showing an underperforming DS400 Index. Equally, analyses of the FTSE4Good indices, conducted over different time periods, found that investors would not necessarily be worse off by investing in a fund that tracks the FTSE4Good index. An important factor to consider is the risk of the market sectors and individual stocks that are included in the index.

Krosinsky's (2008) comparison of different types of SRI with mainstream indices suggests that there is a difference in performance between general SRI funds (values-based ethical investing) and sustainable investing (see Figure 10.1). The former underperform, or at best are comparable to, mainstream indices depending on what time horizon one uses; the latter outperform the mainstream irrespective of the time period being compared. A study of 90 ethical funds over ten years in the UK concluded that annual returns were 0.1 per cent less than the FTSE All Share Index.[32] However, sustainable investing funds have not only outperformed ethical investing funds, but also even the best of the mainstream indices (18.7 per cent versus 17 per cent for 2002–2007). The most recent analysis, covering the 2008 Western stock market crash, shows that sustainable investing funds lost slightly less of their value in 2008, produced net positive returns over the period 2003–2008 (compared with a net loss on the mainstream indices), and outperformed mainstream indices in the first half of 2009 (see Figure 10.2).

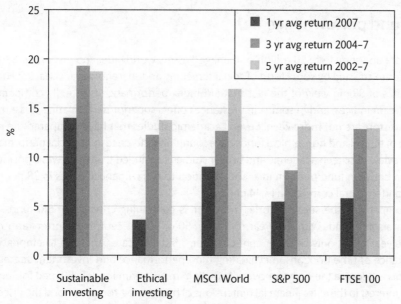

Figure 10.1 SRI returns compared with mainstream indices until 2007

(*Source:* data from Krosinsky, 2008. Reproduced with permission of Taylor & Francis)

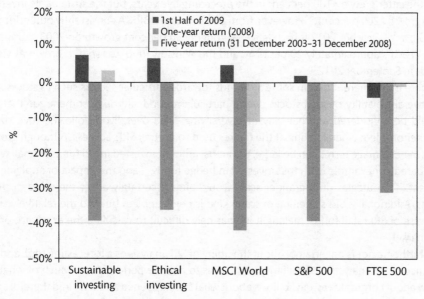

Figure 10.2 Sustainable investing—updated performance analysis

(*Source:* Krosinsky and Robins, 2010, personal communication)

SRI fund performance

There are an estimated $50 trillion of managed assets worldwide, and just under $7 trillion of these are affected by some form of social screening and shareholder advocacy.[33] For some advocates of SRI, in view of the fact that SRI index performance is broadly comparable to mainstream indices, and in some circumstances offers superior performance, it is a mystery why investors are not more keen. Several academic studies that have compared the performance of ethical and non-ethical funds have found no difference in financial performance,[34] and a review of sixteen academic and broker studies concluded that there was a positive correlation between fund performance and attention to extra-financial issues in 38 per cent of cases, and a neutral correlation in 44 per cent.[35]

Accompanying the success stories, however, is continuing criticism of SRI funds. While there are some funds with five-year returns of 50 or 60 per cent, the shorter-term returns for one year might only be 3 per cent or lower.[36] SRI advocates are keen to emphasize the importance of time horizons in evaluating fund performance and investment strategies. In part, this is because the high turnover of stocks in mainstream funds is blamed for investors' lack of interest in the extra-financial dimensions of business performance, and the disconnect between corporations and their owners. But there is also evidence that sustainable investing funds, for example, that have a low turnover (i.e. their portfolios change every three to five years) exhibit stronger performance.[37] However, one needs to be cautious about the period one is considering. For example, a comparison in late 2007 of the Winslow Green Growth Fund (WGGF), a Morningstar five-star rated fund with an aggressive growth policy focused on small-growth companies that have a positive or neutral environmental impact, with Berskhire Hathaway (BRK-A), investment sage Warren Buffett's holding company, would have found that the latter grew by 100 per cent in the preceding five years, but the sustainable investing fund grew by 200 per cent.[38] However, from 2008 onwards, BRK-A consistently outperformed WGGF; as of October 2012 it had delivered roughly 30 per cent growth on 2003, compared with WGGF's approximately 20 per cent, and the Winslow fund was sold to Brown Advisory Funds in September 2012.

There is an inherent bias in some SRI funds towards particular sectors such as stocks, and the overall volatility of such stocks over a particular period, although some argue that this should be considered another way of diversifying one's overall portfolio. Relative size is another problem when looking at the figures used to portray SRI's success. Although growth rates in percentage terms can be large, the actual amount invested in SRI funds is small when compared, for example, with that invested in hedge funds,[39] and the impact of applying the current SRI strategies on a grander scale would almost certainly affect the value of those assets. Additionally, SRI screening of some kind is being applied beyond the relatively small universe of SRI retail funds, making it increasingly difficult to calculate the exact size of the SRI market.

A further factor is uncertainty about the utility of SRI analysis as a forecasting tool, and the absence of, or analysts' unfamiliarity with, tools to analyse performance. Much of what we know about corporate responsibility is about what has happened and why, and therefore falls within the explicative concerns of accounting. Analysis, in contrast, is predictive, so that, for instance, financial analysis—no matter how imperfectly—allows one to forecast future flows in order to obtain the net present value. In the case of sustainable investing, for example, an analyst would want to integrate environmental, social, and governance factors into financial valuation tools, but while, as we have seen throughout this book, there are plenty of ideas about how such factors are material to companies, their incorporation into areas such as risk analysis is not yet commonplace.[40]

Market growth

Throughout the 2000s, the growth of the SRI investment universe has outstripped that of the wider investment market. There is increasing interest in India and China (see Case Study 10), and as described earlier Brazil and South Africa were innovators in establishing social stock exchanges. Nonetheless, the main interest has been in developed economies. Australia has experienced enormous growth, going from practically zero in 2003 to $16.49 billion in 2007. A quarter of Australian managed funds now subscribe to the UN Principles for Responsible Investment.[41] Similarly, SRI funds under management in Canada grew from under $49 billion in 2003 to $472.62 billion by the end of 2007. However, the largest markets are the USA and Europe (see Figure 10.3). In 2005, over 9 per cent of the $24.4 trillion tracked in *Nelson Information's Directory of Investment Managers* were involved in socially responsible investing, equivalent to nearly one out of every ten dollars under professional management in the USA. Mutual funds have been the fastest growing segment of SRI. Between 1995 and 2005, there was a 15-fold increase in assets in SRI mutual funds: $1.5 trillion in assets were in socially screened separate accounts, managed for individual clients ($17.3 billion) and institutional client accounts ($1.49 trillion). This represents 3 per cent of the $5,716.1 billion that is held in separately managed accounts identified by the Money Management Institute.[42] Shareholder advocacy has also become increasingly important. In 2005, institutional investors who filed, or co-filed, resolutions on environmental or social issues controlled nearly $703 billion in assets. Assets in community investing institutions, managed on behalf of institutions and individuals, accounted for $19.6 billion.

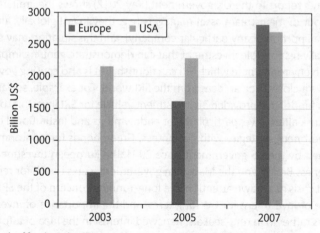

Figure 10.3 Growth of funds under SRI management—comparison of USA and Europe

(*Source:* data from Robins, 2008. Reproduced with permission of Taylor & Francis)

The European SRI market has overtaken the USA to some degree (see Figure 10.3), although there is disagreement about what assets are included. For example, some use the classification 'broad' SRI (including positive and negative screens, engagement by fund managers, and the inclusion by asset managers of corporate governance and social, ethical, or environmental risk into financial analysis),[43] which is a broader definition than that used by SRI investment research company EIRIS, for instance. The assets managed under 'broad' SRI can appear large, but it raises the question of how broad is 'broad'? For example, if companies are screened for little more than pornography or eco-efficiency (one that is largely an illegal activity, and the other a proven business efficiency), SRI may be nothing more than efficient fund management, spurring doubts about the extent to which some of the figures on SRI are useful.

There are a number of developments behind this growth, some of which shed light on the potential of similar trends happening in other markets. One influence was the change in attitude amongst pension funds following the failure of companies such as Enron in the early 2000s (see 'The origins of ethical investment' p 227). Coincidentally or consequently, a group of sustainable investing practitioners emerged (e.g. fund managers and rating agencies) who in turn instigated catalytic initiatives such as the establishment of analytics firms Innovest Strategic Value Advisers, Trucost, and Vigeo. Ethical research organizations such as KLD and EIRIS emerged, alongside which agencies initially focused on corporate governance, such as PIRC, have evolved to include corporate responsibility and sustainability analysis. In other words, in understanding the growth of a market, it is important to look at the enabling infrastructure, and not just the allocation of capital.

Trends in SRI

Whether one is looking at fears about global warming, the opportunities presented by the shift to a low-carbon economy, calls for longer-term investment horizons, the governance lessons from the financial crisis, or the increased interest in products and services for the poor, some long-established concerns of SRI are now higher on political and business agendas than ever before. Kay's report to the UK government (Kay 2012) shows the limitations to changing the behaviour of mainstream asset managers (e.g. they invest globally, and individually only own a small portion of any particular company), and this situation may generate more interest in socially responsible investment that can demonstrate genuine impact. This is not only creating an environment in which SRI can flourish, but is also causing governments and investors to take a closer look at ideas from the SRI world. For example, socially responsible bonds or bond funds have provided an investment vehicle for SRI investors, offering a comparatively low-risk alternative, particularly for endowments and institutional investors looking for safe investment strategies with guarantees. Green bonds for environmental projects have been issued by the US government since 2004, the European Investment Bank issues 'Climate Awareness Bonds' and the Malaysian government issues bonds for reforestation.

The financial crisis has drawn attention to a long-running concern of the SRI community—the importance of investment for the long term, and the importance of investors acting as genuine owners rather than rent-seekers. Renewed interest in the idea of a Tobin tax to limit speculation reflects another well-established concern amongst SRI advocates. As noted earlier, the two main premises behind sustainable investing are that incorporating long-term sustainability-related trends will offer superior risk-adjusted growth, and there needs to be a recasting of the world's capital markets. The first of these is in many ways contingent upon the second, and while some have criticized sustainable investing advocates for appearing to say that nothing can be achieved unless everything is changed, there is a far greater appetite for reform than there was just a few years ago.

However, the question remains as to whether the environment for long-term growth upon which much of SRI's superior performance seems to hinge can be created without further major financial, social, or environmental shocks. While segments of SRI, not least offshoot sustainable investing, are booming, the consistent institutional and legal framework necessary to mobilize capital and bring convergence between SRI issues and financial analysis is scarcely happening. SRI might seem large, but set against the size of the world's capital markets, or indeed the scale of transformation some say is necessary to meet the world's social and environmental challenges, it barely casts a shadow. Moreover, this is unlikely to change if the social and environmental costs of business are not internalized. Furthermore, for all the debate about regulation, and the undeniable fact that at a national level banking is an extremely highly regulated industry, it remains that finance enjoys a privileged status—free, for instance, of the kind of regulation applied to many other sectors. Thus, while pharmaceutical companies will spend years getting regulatory approval for new drugs, financial institutions plough ahead with newer and ever more complex products such as derivatives without any accountability or oversight.

Discussion points

In the light of what we have discussed about SRI's origins and future trends, consider the following.

- What new initiatives are likely to emerge or develop between now and 2020?
- Describe and comment on the Global Reporting Initiative. What are its merits and limitations?
- Which leading social issues are likely to gain attention in your country in relation to corporate governance and why?

Case study 10   China—SRI's rising star or nemesis?

For many years, SRI funds avoided China and took companies to task for labour standards, human rights, lack of transparency, and environmental conditions in that country. While many multinationals argued that avoiding China would be disastrous to their competitiveness, or that transferring best practice from around the world to an isolated autocracy would open new opportunities for democracy, SRI proponents said that foreign investment would inevitably support and legitimize an unacceptable exploitative form of capitalism.

At first glance, China's emergence as the most polluting nation in 2007 seemed to reinforce the SRI position. Its greenhouse gas emissions exceed those of the USA, 700 million of its people (about half of its population) lack access to safe drinking water, it is home to sixteen of the twenty most polluted cities in the world, and 68 per cent of its power comes from coal. Yet, while human rights and democratization have provoked enervation amongst Chinese politicians, the threats of environmental catastrophe have spurred innovation. Since the mid-2000s, there has been a raft of policy and

(continued...)

administrative initiatives such as the Eleventh Five Year Plan for Energy Development (2006–2010), the 2006 Renewable Energy Law, the 2008 amendments to the Energy Conservation Law, and the strengthening of the Ministry of Environmental Protection. The government has promised to reduce the nation's energy consumption as a proportion of GDP by 20 per cent through energy efficiency and new technologies. Stretch targets have been set for an increase in renewable energy and enshrined in law (see table at the Online Resource Centre), and it is expected that by 2020 renewables will make up 16 per cent of total primary energy and 20 per cent of electric power capacity.

The investment opportunities implicit in this redirection of energy policy in what should be one of the world's largest and fastest growing economies has attracted attention from conventional investment funds, but also from SRI funds which have been pioneers of cleantech investing. Some predict that reaching China's renewable energy targets will require investments of $174 billion until 2020, and already venture capital inflows are booming (e.g. $420 million in 2006 with an average deal size of $16.2 million).

China is also home to leading renewable energy companies such as solar panel maker Jiangsu Shunda, and is the largest producer of wind turbines. Thinking about the low-carbon economy is also leading to other innovations such as BYD Auto, producer of electric cars. Its leading green companies such as Goldwind, Shoto, and LDK Solar are listed on foreign exchanges, and the initial public offerings have been profitable.

None of this is to say that there are not any challenges. The growth in solar power is threatened by the dependence on imported silicon for which Chinese firms are paying a premium, and biodiesel distribution has not yet been incorporated into the main petrol station networks. The profitability of wind power still depends on the sale of carbon credits, without which electricity is up to twice the price of that from coal-fired power plants. Moreover, most of the wind power is generated far from the major urban areas, making transmission costly or otherwise unfeasible. A combination of these factors means that many Chinese firms face rising costs and shrinking profit margins on top of an unstable demand—a fact reflected in the share price of companies such as Solarfun Power, JA Solar, and China Sunergy, which have failed to achieve the NASDAQ average since late 2009.

Nonetheless, many SRI funds see China's environmental markets as the ideal opportunity to support positive change in this huge economy. The Taida Environmental Index is the country's first social responsibility index, and Chinese institutions have started to create SRI funds such as the Sustainable Growth Equity Fund and the green private equity fund ZheShang Nuohai Low Carbon Fund. Organizations promoting SRI have emerged, such as the Association of Sustainable and Responsible Investment in Asia (ASrIA). Calvert, a leading SRI house in the USA, was amongst the first partners in the highly profitable cleantech-focused China Environment Fund. For some SRI investors, such as CalPERS, the appeal of environmental investment has meant reversing previous boycott China policies, and led them to wrestle with compromises about the potentially enormous environmental impacts and their principles on human rights and democratic values. Following the argument made by many multinationals, SRI advocates say that the infrastructure for change is being put in place (e.g. an emerging corporate responsibility culture, and new SRI vehicles), and that one cannot bring about change without being active in the country. Their expectation is that a vibrant and indigenous SRI industry will be created, expanding beyond cleantech to other corporate responsibility issues.

(*Sources:* Cheung, 2008; Guo, 2009; www.chinacsr.com)

Questions

1 SRI investors have long been reluctant to invest in China.

   a What are their main objections to investing in China?

   b Do their more recent changes in investment policy reflect an ethical or a business argument?

   c What are the dangers of a narrow focus on environmental industries?

(continued...)

> 2 China's environmental challenges have attracted the attention of SRI investors.
>
>   a Why are companies and the government in China interested in the environment?
>
>   b What investment opportunities are arising as a result of these challenges?
>
>   c Can SRI offer anything to environmental investment that mainstream investors cannot?
>
> 3 'Buyer beware' is an adage often applied to doing business in China.
>
>   a What investment infrastructure needs to be in place to establish a viable indigenous SRI industry?
>
>   b What might be the role of foreign SRI organizations in establishing SRI in China?
>
>   c What are the advantages for Chinese companies of attracting stable long-term investors of the kind identified with SRI?

Summary

In this chapter, we have looked at the development of socially responsible investment and at its appeal to investors as a way in which to maximize financial, social, and environmental returns in the long term. We have looked at both pre-investment and post-investment strategies used to identify SRI opportunities—namely, screening and engagement. In reviewing the comparative performance of SRI and traditional vehicles, we learned that, on the whole, there is no evidence that SRI indices or funds underperform, and that some SRI-related strategies offer better returns, particularly if one takes a longer-term perspective.

While there are those who think that SRI and traditional investment are diametrically opposed, it can be argued that we are in the midst of a convergence. Cleantech, for example, is at the intersection—appealing to both conventional investors and SRI investors. This convergence may continue as reporting mechanisms become more transparent, analytical methods become more sophisticated, established SRI issues become of increasing concern to companies and investors, and SRI offerings continue to grow. But this is not to predict that SRI will radically transform the investment world, and the importance of SRI needs to be considered in the context of the other business, governance, and investment trends that are discussed elsewhere in this book.

Further reading

www.oxfordtextbooks.co.uk/orc/blowfield_murray3e/

Visit the Online Resource Centre that accompanies this book to enrich your understanding of this chapter. Among the resources available are web links, exercises, and additional case studies.

online
resource
centre

Baker, H.K. & Nofsinger, J.R. (eds) 2012, *Socially responsible finance and investing: financial institutions, corporations, investors, and activists*, Wiley, London.

   A far-reaching study of SRI from academics and practitioners.

Bugg-Levine, A. & Emerson, J. 2011, 'Impact investing: transforming how we make money while making a difference', *Innovations*, vol. 6, no. 3, pp 9–18.

   Introduction to impact investing.

Krosinsky, C. & Robins, N. (eds) 2008, *Sustainable investing: the art of long-term performance*, Earthscan, London.

Prominent professionals from the sustainable investment world examine the case for sustainable investing, and how it differs from SRI.

Louche, C. & Lydenberg, S.D. 2011, *Dilemmas in responsible investment*, Greenleaf, Sheffield.

Practical examples of the issues that arise when trying to invest responsibly.

Williams, R. & Elliott, L. 2010, *Crisis and recovery: ethics, economics and justice*, Palgrave Macmillan, Basingstoke.

An economics journalist and the former head of the Church of England revisit finance and capitalism.

Online resources

- Additional materials for use with the chapter's snapshots and case study
- More discussion topics for students
- Suggestions for materials on SRI
- Links to SRI resources

Endnotes

1. This chapter draws heavily on the work of Nick Robins and Cary Krosinsky, and we are especially grateful to Nick for his comments. The first edition version of this chapter was written by Kimberly Ochs. All errors and opinions are the authors' own.
2. Teoh et al., 1995.
3. More detailed information can be found online at www.hm-treasury.gov.uk.
4. Odell, 2007.
5. Keefe, 2007.
6. See, e.g. Gore and Blood, 2012; HSBC, 2012.
7. Krosinsky and Robins, 2008.
8. Global Reporting Initiative, 2007.
9. Social Investment Forum, 2006, pp 6–7.
10. VICEX only began to outperform the Dow Jones Index again in 2012.
11. More information can be found about the Millennium Development Goals online at www.un.org/millenniumgoals and about the ILO core conventions at www.labourstart.org/rights.
12. See extensive lists available at www.eufosif.org.
13. The Standard and Poor's 500 is an index of 500 large-cap companies and is often used as a baseline for comparison. Stocks are chosen using S&P's methodology. Detailed guidelines can be found at www.indices.standardandpoors.com.
14. See www.sustainability-index.com for a summary of indices and screening criteria.
15. www.ftse4good.com.
16. See www.bovespasocial.org.br.
17. Grecco, 2007, p 131.
18. www.newsweek.com/id/139436.
19. UKSIF, 2009.

20. Kay, 2012.

21. UKSIF, 2009.

22. Data from Cleantech Group.

23. Cobb et al., 2005; Collison et al., 2008.

24. blogs.wsj.com/venturecapital/2013/09/13/enertechs-wally-hunter-on-how-clean-tech-investing-has-changed/, accessed 19 October 2013.

25. Reddy, 2008.

26. Kaminker and Stewart, 2012.

27. Basel III is the latest standard on bank capital adequacy, stress testing, and risk.

28. WEF, 2010.

29. John, 2007.

30. Monitor, 2009.

31. JP Morgan figures, www.jpmorgan.com/cm/cs?pagename=JPM_redesign/JPM_Content_C/Generic_Detail_Page_Template&cid=1320509594546&c=JPM_Content_C, accessed 22 October 2013.

32. Jewson Associates, 2008.

33. Monitor, 2009.

34. See, e.g., Kreander et al., 2002; 2005; Gregory et al., 1997; Bauer et al., 2002.

35. UNEP FI, 2007.

36. See historical data on Ave Maria Catholic Values fund, or Calvert Large Cap Growth, as examples of this.

37. Krosinsky, 2008.

38. Krosinsky, 2008.

39. Total money in SRI Funds 2005 = £6.1bn; total money in hedge funds 2006 = $1.786 trillion. Based on figures from EIRIS and HedgeFund.net.

40. Lucas-Leclin and Hahal, 2008.

41. Figures in this section from Robins, 2008.

42. Social Investment Forum, 2006, p 11.

43. European Social Investment Forum, 2006.

Corporate responsibility in smaller enterprises

 Chapter overview

In this chapter, we look at corporate responsibility as an aspect of business theory and management practice as it applies to small and medium-sized enterprises (SMEs). As part of this, we include the field of social entrepreneurship. In particular, we will:

- discuss what is unique about SMEs in the corporate responsibility context;
- explore the distinctions between SMEs, and how these affect their behaviour;
- consider corporate responsibility as an area of opportunity and competitive advantage for SMEs;
- examine how corporate responsibility is being managed in practice;
- discuss those small and medium-sized enterprises that are categorized as social entrepreneurs.

Main topics

The small business 'problem'   255
The meaning and significance of smaller business   255
Local, national, and regional differences between SMEs   258
SMEs as society members   260
SME perspectives on corporate responsibility   261
Responsibility issues for SMEs   263
SMEs and corporate responsibility management   265
Social enterprise   268
Meanings of social enterprise   269
Why now?   272

Key terms

Small and medium-sized enterprises   Lifestyle enterprises

Supply chains   Corporate social opportunity

Social enterprise

The small business 'problem'

For a long time in corporate responsibility literature smaller businesses were considered either irrelevant or problematic. Normative corporate responsibility theory was typically portrayed as something universal with application to all companies, irrespective of their size.[1] Corporate responsibility practice was depicted as something that could be fairly easily transferred from multinational enterprises to smaller companies.[2] However, as the notion of corporate responsibility as a managerial construct gained hold, its application to smaller businesses—not least in developing countries—began to receive more attention.[3] There was increasing recognition that contemporary ideas of corporate responsibility needed special consideration in the small business context, whether because they were seen as irresponsible, or because they were at risk for failing to meet corporate responsibility performance standards.

The role of smaller businesses, particularly entrepreneurs, earned further attention with the rise of new business concepts focused on societal outcomes such as the bottom of the pyramid (see Chapter 4) and social entrepreneurship (see 'Why now?' p 272). Smaller business was no longer just seen as irrelevant or problematic, but was increasingly talked about as having unique contributions to make. Today, there is a significant body of research and innovation built around the theme of corporate responsibility and smaller businesses. This ranges from the types of business involved to the quantity and quality of corporate-responsibility-related activity, the business case, and what constitutes best practice.[4]

In this chapter, we focus primarily on smaller businesses which, for the most part, would not see themselves as having an overt societal mission. We will leave until later in this chapter discussion of social enterprise and those organizations that treat social and environmental outcomes as at least as important as financial results.

The meaning and significance of smaller business

Smaller businesses are typically lumped together under the abbreviation SME—small and medium-sized enterprise. The meaning of SME is explained in the Key Concept box which highlights how firms in this sector are defined primarily by number of workers, size of turnover, and ownership. Although relatively small individually, collectively SMEs are the largest employers worldwide and comprise the vast majority of businesses (90 per cent by some measurements). Moreover, they cannot be defined by quantitative measures alone. As a sector, SMEs exhibit management features that mark them out from larger businesses (e.g. the influence of the entrepreneur/founder/leader, greater informality in management practices, narrower strategic vision, and weak capacity to influence the wider business environment), but it is also a mistake to treat such businesses as homogenous. For example, despite being grouped into the same sector, the owner of rickshaws rented out to 40 drivers in Jogjakarta, Indonesia, is likely to have little in common with a software engineering start-up in Iceland even if the number of workers is about the same. Indeed, SMEs often appear to be defined as much by what they are not (i.e. they are not multinational enterprises) as what they share in common.

Key concept: Small and medium-sized enterprise

SMEs may account for 50–60 per cent of employment worldwide. In countries such as Russia and Kenya they are the major job creators, and even in more developed capitalist economies, such as the UK, they account for nearly half of all jobs. In the EU, an SME has less than 250 workers, an annual turnover of less than €40 million (or a balance sheet not exceeding €27 million), and is an independent enterprise where no more than 25 per cent of capital or voting rights belong to larger enterprises. The World Bank separates out small and medium enterprises, classifying small enterprises as those with 10–50 workers, total assets of $100,000–$3 million, and total sales of $100,000–$3 million. It further defines micro-enterprises as those with less than ten workers, assets of less than $100,000, and annual sales of less than $100,000.

However, as authors such as Jenkins (2006) and Burns (2001) point out, there are many less quantifiable characteristics of SMEs such as less formal management structures, the role of individual personality, and difficulties in diversifying risk. Furthermore, it can be misleading to treat SMEs as homogenous because factors such as industry, ownership, location, and position in the supply chain can all significantly affect how an SME behaves. It is also misleading to treat SMEs as marginal to economic life. In economies such as Italy and Ghana they have always been major sources of employment, and now, with shifting patterns of work in economies such as northern Europe and the USA, the SME sector has grown broader and more complex than ever before.[5]

One reason that SMEs are not homogenous is that they represent different types of entrepreneurship. Much of the excitement about the potential of SMEs in a corporate responsibility context stems from the fact that all innovators start small, and that is true of sustainability innovation and green entrepreneurs. However, these entrepreneurs are a specific type, called variously 'opportunity entrepreneurs' and 'gazelles'.[6] They are often the serial entrepreneurs who derive enormous satisfaction from establishing new businesses, and whom it is hoped will be attracted by the opportunities found in tackling major societal challenges.

Thus, it could be Stephan Schmidheiny, who got out of asbestos, bought Swatch, and now runs the triple-bottom-line conglomerate GrupoNuevo; or it could be Kresse Wesling, the young entrepreneur behind Elvis & Kresse, which creates fashion items from recycled materials.

The opportunities that are arising connected with mega-trends such as demographic change and global warming (see Chapter 14) are already being seized on by such people. It has been argued that they are far more likely to be receptive to ideas and practices associated with corporate responsibility, and therefore should get preferential treatment in the alloca-tion of resources (e.g. government funding to foster corporate responsibility).[7] Even if their products do not have a societal orientation, they will have a growth orientation that provides an added incentive to be aware of their social and environmental footprint, increases the importance of a robust and more complex approach to stakeholder management, and opens the door to new sources of capital (e.g. venture philanthropy). Innocent, the drinks com-pany, and Green & Black's are examples of this type of company that have subsequently been merged into multinational corporations.

However, when we talk about corporate responsibility and SMEs, the gazelles are only one part of the conversation. There are 25 million SMEs in Europe, and most of them are 'lifestyle' businesses, run by people who have chosen to work for themselves or have been left little choice given the changing nature of employment in wealthier economies. They have little desire or indeed potential to grow, and they may regard running an SME not as an exciting springboard to business success, but more as a trade-off between factors such as independence, income, employment, and other lifestyle-related decisions.[8] Most of them serve local markets. They may be heavily engaged in their local communities, and have particular passions such as education or conservation, but they are likely to be unaware or suspicious of terms such as corporate responsibility and sustainability. When Napoleon described England as 'a nation of shopkeepers', he was talking about a nation of lifestyle SMEs. Often it is a lifestyle chosen by immigrants who may lack the education and social networks to enter other strands of economic life, and therefore includes people such as Iranian refugee Kazem Ariaiwand, who owns the Red Polar Bear, the world's most northerly kebab van on Spitsbergen, Sweden, German émigré Frederick Drumpf who ran the Arctic Restaurant serving gold prospectors in late nineteenth century Canada and was to be the grandfather of Donald Trump, and the Bell family from Scotland whose Canadian farm housed the first workshop of telephone inventor Alexander Graham Bell.

Lifestyle SMEs have a different relationship with corporate responsibility than the gazelles as we will discuss. On the one hand, there is a perception that they have poor employment practices akin to Charles Dickens' portrayal of 'Bleak House'.[9] On the other hand, they may feel that they have a closer bond with workers and local communities, and treat formal corporate responsibility requirements on issues from freedom of association to child labour to pesticide management as unwarranted interference. For instance, Ghana's small commercial pineapple growers have identified a list of areas which could be considered part of corporate responsibility practice (e.g. skill transfer, strengthening property claims, job creation, stimulating local economies, investing in local infrastructure) but are not recognized in the corporate responsibility requirements of their overseas buyers.[10]

As part of a shift in ideas of economic development assistance, fostering of entrepreneurship in developing economies has gained increasing attention.[11] There is a tendency in this context to mix up gazelle and lifestyle SMEs, and, as important, to overlook the specific features of what have been called 'necessity entrepreneurs', i.e. small operations (often in the informal economy) where own-account enterprise is the option of last resort, and where the opportunities and incomes are typically worse than in formal employment.[12] Examples include the female small market traders in Nairobi, food hawkers in Jakarta, and the laid-off Detroit car worker who is trying to run his own machine shop. This type of SME presents yet different challenges in a corporate responsibility context; the owners may see the venture as a temporary occupation until something better comes along, there will be little capital to invest in anything that does not show an immediate return, and the very existence of such entrepreneurs may cause tension with local authorities and residents. Moreover, in so far as these enterprises are recognized in a corporate responsibility context, they are more likely to be described as potential recipients of acts of responsibility from larger operations (e.g. preferential contracts, donations) than as actors in their own right.

Discussion points

People have very different motivations for setting up SMEs.

- Why might 'gazelles' be more interested in corporate responsibility than other types of SME?
- Why did necessity entrepreneurs increase in number in North America and Europe in 2008–2009?
- Are SMEs from ethnic minorities likely to have different notions of responsibility than others?

Local, national, and regional differences between SMEs

In addition to the above, there are other differentiators of SMEs relevant in a corporate responsibility context. We have mentioned that immigrants are an important part of the lifestyle SME group. In developed economies these have a particular importance in poorer communities because they often provide a range of services where other businesses are reluctant to go.[13] Interestingly, these are often more growth-oriented than other lifestyle SMEs, notably once the business has been passed on to second or later generations. They are major employers amongst ethnic minorities, and often have a high local multiplier effect as their customers, owners, and workers typically live within a small radius of the business. Furthermore, depending on the ethnic group concerned, there can be a high degree of female ownership of the businesses (e.g. 75 per cent of African and Caribbean businesses in the UK are owned or co-owned by women).[14] Indeed, no matter what sort of SME we are talking about, we should not overlook the importance of women in this sector, whether it be the female traders who are the backbone of West Africa's fish trade, the women's savings groups that were behind the growth of microfinance in Bangladesh, or waste trader Zhang Yin, the richest woman in China.

Figure 11.1 shows the types of social impact that these businesses have, although one needs to be careful not to exaggerate their role in tackling issues such as economic regeneration and social exclusion.[15] In some ways, the close association that such businesses have with local communities is both a strength and a weakness in terms of responsibility. The need to build a strong licence to operate is an important driver of responsible behaviour, but it also means that what constitutes responsibility will be locally determined. Thus, for example, the relationships that SMEs in Tuscany build, involving trade unions, local authorities, and other established stakeholders, are quite different to those that SMEs in Uzbekistan seek to create where 'responsibility' is to a degree defined by Islamic norms of philanthropy and tithing.[16] Equally, these relationships are affected by the sociopolitical context. For example, while much attention has been paid to the role of multinationals such as oil companies in regional conflicts, SMEs can also be a flashpoint. Race riots that periodically erupt in Indonesia are often focused on Chinese-owned SMEs because they are an easy target for unrest. In Nigeria, markets have been flashpoints for ethnic conflict, although conversely they can serve as spaces to bring together conflicting groups. The example of SMEs in Russia (see Snapshot 11.1) highlights the significance of political context.

Figure 11.1 Types of social and environmental impact that SMEs can have

---

⊡ **Snapshot 11.1   SMEs in Russia—unique challenges and common ground**

Many of the private enterprises that have arisen in Russia since the end of communism are SMEs. Their situation is interesting in that they have emerged out of an economy that did not recognize private enterprise, and now exist in one where there is enormous suspicion of business. In the 1990s, American economist Jeffrey Sachs and others encouraged 'shock therapy' to the Russian system which not only left many in greater poverty than before, but through the USA-funded Russian Privatization Center, positioned the private sector as the main engine of economic reform. But instead of allowing a million SME stars to shine, the largest part of the new economic pie seemed to go to a new class of private sector oligarchs including Lisin (steel), Prokhorov (mining), and Abramovich (oil). The way that these people acquired and managed their resources as well as their close relationship with the state has led many locally to feel that big business is detrimental to Russia's interests, and caused others to wonder how business's legitimacy can be improved.

Vladimir Putin, Russia's current president, has initiated efforts to reassure the public that business will be mindful of general welfare, and this has been a driver behind the government's promotion of corporate responsibility, including requirements about corporate responsibility policies and transparency. This has been accepted by many larger companies as the quid pro quo for protecting their assets and independent management. However, SMEs do not have this kind of relationship with the state, and moreover often do not want to be seen as aligned with government. Their concerns are corruption, insecure property rights, arbitrary law enforcement, and bureaucratic inconsistencies.

Thus, there are two tiers of corporate responsibility in Russia: one involving the largest companies concerned about their international reputation and the success of initial public offerings, and the other involving SMEs worried about local sociopolitical conditions and often resentful of the state. The former are often eager to be involved in international initiatives such as the UN Global Compact, but although the Compact advertises advice to SMEs on its Russian website, there is little mention of the issues that smaller businesses want to see addressed, or how to go about tackling them.

(*Sources:* original research; Avtonomov, 2006; Tsalikis and Seaton, 2008; www.undp.ru)

....

Quick questions

In Russia, corporate responsibility is treated as irrelevant by most SMEs.

1   What issues should corporate responsibility practice include to make it of interest to SMEs?

(continued...)

2 Why are SMEs reluctant to be involved in state-backed initiatives?

3 How could the Global Compact's SME guidelines be improved in a Russian context? (downloaded from www.unglobalcompact.org/docs/news_events/8.1/Operational_guide_ME.pdf)

SMEs as society members

It is widely held that SMEs often practice corporate responsibility without knowing it. This is because if they are visible members of local communities, they need to build a strong licence to operate, whether that be through sponsorship of local sports teams, charitable donations, or involvement in community activities. Moreover, as they typically lack the influence over local authorities and other local leaders that bigger companies have, individually or collectively they need to find alternative ways to remain effective. For example, the Rotary and Lions Clubs found around the world are primarily made up of smaller entrepreneurs, and, as well as networking, are used as a means of contributing funds to the local community.

Historically, the need to maintain a licence to operate stems from the particular role entrepreneurs, such as traders, have played in society. Those engaged in trade were often treated with suspicion by local communities concerned about profiteering, and at the same time were relied upon to get the best deal for local products traded with outsiders.[17] It is no coincidence that groups who came to dominate trade were often immigrants or other types of outsider, sometimes differentiated by religion; these were already stigmatized to some degree, and being a trader did not lower their status in the way that it might for indigenous citizens.

Whether it be Arabs in coastal Java, Chinese in Malaysia, or Lebanese in West Africa, suspicion of traders has led them to invest heavily in their own and their adopted communities, often in very visible prestige projects ranging from temples to schools. Some of this suspicion can be explained sociologically, but other perceptions have more to do with business reality. Employment conditions in SMEs are often considered poor, characterized by long hours, low wages, poor working conditions, and few protections. Women working in sweatshop conditions, be it in London or Manila, are emblematic of SME exploitation. Some of the criticism of labour rights in the production of popular apparel is about the conditions amongst second- and third-tier suppliers who are often SMEs. Indeed, to strangers there can appear to be a contradiction between the desire of certain SMEs to retain a respectable external face, and their internal neglect.

Not all SMEs can be tarred with the same brush, and poor working conditions are much less prevalent than they once were in some parts of the world, not least because of greater regulatory oversight and the need to attract good employees.[18] A small hardware store may not be able to compete with the big box stores on price, for instance, but if it has knowledgeable staff it can be a more attractive consumer destination. In industries from tourism to coffee bars, the quality of staff can be essential in wooing customers away from large companies. All of this amounts to a concern with stakeholder management and engagement (see Chapter 9), even if it is done informally and unconsciously. In fact, when SMEs have been approached about corporate responsibility, owners frequently feel that in terms of both issues and approaches, much of what is discussed is what SMEs have historically engaged in.[19]

Box 11.1   SME objections to corporate responsibility

- It is too costly (e.g. the cost of verifying performance)
- Outsiders mistakenly think corporate responsibility strategies from big companies can simply be scaled down for SMEs
- There aren't any real business benefits
- It takes up too many financial and human resources
- There are more immediate concerns to deal with to survive
- SMEs don't have the expertise to manage corporate responsibility
- SMEs typically don't seek external help until late in the day
- It is yet another way that customers can exert power over SMEs

(*Sources:* Quayle, 2003; Grayson and Dodd, 2007; Jenkins, 2009)

SME perspectives on corporate responsibility

Confronted directly with the question 'Should SMEs do corporate responsibility?', the response is often negative. Some typical answers are captured in Box 11.1, and the SME attitudes can be summarized as too hard, too expensive, irrelevant, and unwarranted. Some of these attitudes hardened in the rush to formalize corporate responsibility management practices in the late 1990s, especially in the supply chains of large companies, when SMEs came to be treated as 'little big companies' where practices simply needed scaling down to be effective.[20] As already noted, SMEs are not homogenous, and even if they were they still exhibit quite different managerial, operational, and ownership features to large listed firms.[21] These features tended to be overlooked early on, not least in developing countries where listed firms felt most at risk from the possibility of poor social and environmental performance by SMEs. For example, in Kenya and Zimbabwe, major supermarkets, in collaboration with NGOs and trade unions, sent delegations to encourage SME suppliers to adopt labour codes of practice. This often came across as heavy-handed, especially early on, and was worsened by the seeming lack of coordination between technical staff responsible for the codes of conduct, and supermarket buyers who continued to focus solely on price, quality, and delivery times.[22] In one instance, a supplier in Kenya had its contract terminated despite investing heavily in meeting supermarket J Sainsbury's ethical standards (Dolan and Humphrey, 2004). Such examples reinforced existing tensions in supply chains, and hardened SME attitudes to corporate responsibility which was seen by some as yet another way for large firms to exert control over their suppliers.

That situation has changed over time, not least because multinational companies now see their role less as policing suppliers than aiding them for mutual benefit. Nonetheless, many SMEs still wrestle with corporate responsibility, especially in countries struggling to compete in global markets.[23] One reason is that terms such as corporate social responsibility and sustainability appear vague, too general, and not especially business-related. When the terms are explained or substituted by others, SME managers may start to see managing the business–society relationship not so much as a cost burden but as a source of competitive

> **Box 11.2   Reasons for SMEs to adopt corporate responsibility management practices**
>
> - SMEs are often already 'doing' corporate responsibility even if they don't know it
> - Social and environmental performance is already a common part of supply chain management requirements
> - Provides SMEs with a way to attract and retain good-quality personnel
> - Young people often seem attracted to values-driven organizations
> - The modern networked economy attaches a premium to reputation and relationships, and corporate responsibility is a way of contributing to this
> - Early adoption of corporate responsibility issues helps SMEs anticipate future legislation
> - A growing number of 'lohas' consumers (lifestyles of health and sustainability)
> - Corporate responsibility can be a business opportunity to create new platforms for competitiveness
>
> (*Sources:* Grayson and Dodd, 2007; Morsing and Perrini, 2009)

advantage[24] (see Box 11.2). Furthermore, it has started to be recognized that many SMEs are already 'doing corporate responsibility'; that it is a natural part of running a successful business to engage with local communities, manage stakeholders, create a good working environment, and preserve local natural resources. If this is so, it begs the question whether rather than see SMEs at fault, one should revisit the question 'Should SMEs do corporate responsibility?' Jenkins (2009) argues that it is the corporate responsibility debate that is the problem because it fails to engage SMEs. But this remark in itself treats corporate responsibility as a fixed management approach, and not as a sphere of business concern where the theory (what are the responsibilities of business?) and management practice (how are those responsibilities managed?) are continually evolving as part of the shifting nature of the role of business in society.

One can argue with some of the reasons proposed for SMEs to take corporate responsibility seriously (see Box 11.2). Some, such as attracting good personnel, anticipating legislation, and the growth in 'lohas', are the same reasons given for why large companies should 'adopt corporate responsibility'. Others seem vague or dubious. For instance, are young people more value-driven than in the past, or is it a feature of youth that values play a particular part in decision-making, and if so for how long will values be an advantage to the SME? Equally, how generalizable is the evidence that a premium is being put on relationships and reputation, particularly given the global spread of the debate about SMEs, and the continuing promiscuity of producer–buyer relations at the second and third tier of global supply chains?

The idea that corporate responsibility can be a business opportunity may also seem inexact, but it is one that has attracted considerable attention. Authors such as Grayson and Hodges (2004) and Pedersen (2006) use terms such as 'corporate social opportunity' to describe how companies can look for innovation in non-conventional areas such as those that are a part of the current corporate responsibility agenda. Comparative case studies of European SMEs, such as that by Lamberti and Noci (2012) in Italy, suggest that many smaller firms are well-placed to take advantage of these opportunities, even if it is in a field requiring more investment.[25] (See Box 11.3.)

Box 11.3   SME vantage points on corporate responsibility

Your outlook on corporate responsibility depends on where you sit in the universe of SMEs. Three types of SME viewpoint stand out.

First, there is the 'responsibility innovator', most often seen in social enterprises and amongst entrepreneurs who regard for-profit and not-for-profit private sector mechanisms as an important way of achieving social and environmental benefits. But these innovators are also behind for-profit companies that are trying to balance social, financial, and environmental outcomes, building on the concept of the triple bottom line (Chapter 3). A recent manifestation of this in the USA is B Corporation (where B stands for beneficial), a set of companies that are certified for their social and environmental performance, but it would also include companies such as Seventh Generation, technology firm Linden Lab, and craft seller Etsy.[26]

Second, there are 'supply chain victims'—SMEs that are pressured into adopting certain social and environmental standards as a requirement of doing business with large customers such as retailers. While for some the word 'victim' may describe an early passing disgruntlement that evaporates when the relationship with the customer improves, there are still examples of SMEs that feel that their customers' commitment to corporate responsibility brings little tangible benefit.[27]

Third, there are the 'unconscious agents'—SMEs that in order to maintain their licence to operate, or because of the values of the owner or manager, are already engaging in activities that help manage the company's relationship with society, and are not intended to have a direct impact on the financial bottom line. This accounts for much of the corporate responsibility activity associated with SMEs, but is typically considered informal.

 Discussion points

Corporate responsibility is often portrayed as a burden on SMEs.

- Which do you think are the strongest and weakest reasons for SMEs to take corporate responsibility seriously?
- What are some examples of corporate social opportunity that could be attractive to SMEs?
- Are some SMEs right to see corporate responsibility as an extension of supply chain bullying by larger companies?

Responsibility issues for SMEs

As mentioned earlier, SMEs often practice aspects of corporate responsibility management without recognizing it. Given that many SMEs recruit locally, and produce, buy and sell locally, it would be hard for them to escape the consequences of poor stakeholder engagement. In Tuscany, for instance, SMEs exist within sophisticated networks involving trade unions, competitors, and local authorities, as well as the public, without which they could not operate effectively.[28] In developing economies, the creation of stakeholder partnerships is reckoned by some to be a key element in gaining competitive advantage.[29] Philanthropy and involvement in community development are long-established traditions for many SMEs, reflecting the pragmatic reasoning behind maintaining a licence to operate, or the values-based orientation of an SME owner/manager.

The relatively greater influence an owner's values can have on SME behaviour compared with other types of business has been widely held up as a unique advantage that such companies can have.[30] Because the company is seen as an extension of the owner's sense of self, and because he/she has more control over how to distribute the benefits of the enterprise amongst stakeholders, there may be greater opportunity to use the company as an instrument for realizing personal virtue (see Snapshot 11.2). However, we should not get carried away with this viewpoint as, for various reasons (e.g. inadequate regulatory oversight, struggle for financial survival, lack of transparency, indifference), SMEs may have poor employment practices, inadequate health and safety provisions, and so on. This is evident, for instance, in slave labour on cocoa farms, employer lobbying against maternity and paternity rights in Europe, and the various instances of workers trapped inside blazing sweatshops with locked fire doors. While it may well be true that attention to working conditions is essential to SMEs in skill-intensive sectors where there is a battle for good employees, it would be counter-intuitive to expect the same degree of care to be valued as central to business survival in labour-intensive sectors where there is significant unemployment. Moreover, in the latter case, an SME might have an active external-facing programme to secure its reputation amongst the community, while exploiting its workforce with impunity. For example, in Uzbekistan, as already noted, SMEs abide by religious norms about charity and other matters that enhance their public reputation, but they do not proscribe workplace discrimination and unequal employment opportunities.[31]

Again, it is difficult to generalize about SMEs, even if there is a tendency so to do in some corporate responsibility literature. However, there are other features of employment in SMEs that deserve attention. SMEs can offer opportunities to people who would find it difficult to work in larger companies. This could be because of their educational background, their race or ethnicity, their gender, the need to balance household and income-generating activities, or accommodating physical or mental disorders. While in the worst instance, the willingness of SMEs to be employers of last resort for disadvantaged people can lead to exploitation, in societies where there is sufficient impetus to control abuses an SME's flexibility can benefit those who might otherwise be low down in the employability pecking order.

Snapshot 11.2   Zippos—a responsible circus?

Zippos is a small travelling circus, founded in 1986. It has an international staff of 70, including its owner Martin Burton. It tours Britain from February to November every year, taking the Big Top, the acts, their equipment, and the performing horses and budgerigars from town to town each week.

Circuses may embody family entertainment, but they are also controversial. The word 'circus' conjures up images of poorly treated lions, elephants, and other wild animals. It also brings to mind unsafe facilities, diesel-belching trucks, and unhygienic food. Consequently, over the years, circuses have attracted unwanted attention from local authorities, immigration officials, and animal rights campaigners.

One of the first things one sees at a Zippos show is the red lorries, each with 'fuelled by chip fat' written on the side. The chip fat comes from the food vans at the circus, next to the entrance to the Big Top. The audience are shown to their seats by people in red tunics who a few minutes later turn out to be the high-wire or wheel-of-death stars. Like many SMEs, 'and other jobs as required' is a standard part of everyone's contract of employment. Even the owner appears as one of the clowns.

(continued...)

He is also one of the initiators of the circus industry's code of conduct on animal welfare, and was a pioneer of circuses without wild animals. However, this has not stopped Zippos being the target for animal rights protests or local authority bans, and its one time artistic director, David Hibling, gave evidence in favour of Mary Chipperfield, who was found guilty of twelve counts of animal cruelty when training animals for other circuses.

According to Burton, much of his time is taken up with filling out risk assessments as the industry is held to ever higher health and safety standards. But he is also aware that a good reputation is essential to his company's future, and on the Zippos website there is a page devoted to the various causes it supports, as well as a section on the circus academy that the company has established to train future generations of circus performers.

(*Sources*: www.news.bbc.co.uk/1/hi/uk/259098.stm; www.business.timesonline.co.uk/tol/business/career_and_jobs/ article3707452.ece; www.oxfordmail.co.uk/news/5198052.Big_Top_boss_opposes_plan_for_animal_ban/)

Quick questions

Zippos Circus is an unusual but in many ways very typical example of an SME.

1 Does Zippos have a corporate responsibility strategy?

2 What are the drivers behind Zippos' attention to corporate responsibility?

3 Which of these drivers are typical of SMEs, and which are specific to this company?

SMEs and corporate responsibility management

Introducing corporate responsibility to an SME

There are some who hold that SMEs are by their very nature more responsible than other types of company because of aspects such as their close relationship to communities, long-term family ownership of the enterprise, paternalism towards workers, and less pressure to maximize shareholder value.[32] If this were always true, then it would be relatively straightforward to enhance management performance to improve social and environmental outcomes. To a degree this is what has been tried in initiatives such as People and Profit in Denmark where 12,000 SME personnel were trained to understand corporate responsibility as a way of enhancing competitiveness. However, as the earlier comparison of gazelles and lifestyle enterprises makes clear, not all SMEs are equally responsive to corporate responsibility ideas, from which we can infer that something more sophisticated is required to engage and then enhance the impacts from SMEs.

Grayson and Dodd (2007) highlight five factors that can affect SME receptiveness toward corporate responsibility ideas.

- Using acceptable understandable terminology: a term such as corporare social responsibility could have a very different impact than one such as sustainable enterprise or good citizen.

- Targeting: given the sheer number of SMEs and the fact that some are likely to be more receptive to ideas of corporate responsibility than others, prioritizing which companies are involved in awareness raising and capacity building initiatives seems crucial.

- The messenger: support for improving SME corporate responsibility management may have to come from government, but this does not mean that the public sector is best placed to deliver the message. There is evidence that anything that makes corporate responsibility issues seem part of a political agenda generates indifference or even hostility, and that organizations known and respected by SMEs such as chambers of commerce and trade associations are better conduits.

- An evolutionary journey: in Chapter 6 we explore the idea that corporate responsibility management is an evolutionary journey, and this is as true of SMEs as of other companies. Because of the diverse nature of SMEs and the effect that this has on the company's orientation towards or away from corporate responsibility management, the journey may actually be more complex, but comprehending that 'corporate responsibility' is not a state to achieve but a definitional construct and managerial process is essential to understand direction and progress.

- Think of SMEs as people: following the theory that SMEs are different in character as well as size from larger companies, some argue that they exhibit more 'human' traits. For example, while larger firms value orderliness, formal systems, planning/strategy, and accountability, SMEs might be as comfortable with informality, intuitiveness, and trust. Recognition of such characteristics would in turn affect how SMEs were introduced to corporate responsibility as a concept.

Managing corporate responsibility

Despite the arguments about why corporate responsibility means something different in the SME sector, the advice to SME on corporate responsibility management has much in common with that given to other types of company. The Danish People and Profit programme mentioned previously is one of the most extensive attempts to reach out to SME managers. However, its practical guide to corporate responsibility management, comprehensive though it is in terms of the aspects of management, shares similarities with ones targeted at multinational companies.[33] (The guide can be downloaded at www.csrgov.dk/sw51121. asp.) This is true of the broad areas of suggested managerial activity (see Figure 11.2), and also the more detailed advice on areas from communication to innovation to customer relations. For example, on environmental management the guide recommends the ISO 14001 environmental management system or the EU Eco-management and Audit Scheme (EMAS) as a basis for a systematic approach to planning, implementation, and reporting. It provides a checklist for assessing current performance, and advises the use of a think–plan–do–check model of continual improvement. Such advice may be practical for a Danish SME, but despite the numerous claims made that SMEs are not scaled-down versions of large companies, the advice offered is not significantly different to what might be given to any business.

The same comments are true of guidance about adopting the UN Global Compact, and involvement in poverty alleviation.[34] This would not matter except for the evidence that SMEs are unwilling to manage social and environmental issues because of their specific managerial circumstances and constraints.[35] Even in the area of innovation, highlighted already as an aspect of particular interest to SMEs (or at least to the growth-oriented gazelles), the models proposed rely heavily on conventional consultancy and academic models of innovation (e.g. the Doblin Group (www.doblin.com/); Mullins and Komisar, 2009). If other constraints are not overwhelming, this may not be a bad thing in that framing corporate responsibility issues within established management models could improve their acceptability, but the

Figure 11.2 Areas of SME management where corporate responsibility issues are relevant
(*Source:* adapted from People and Profit, 2007)

limits on transferability of such models set out throughout this chapter do beg questions that current literature does not seem able to answer.

Exceptions to this are work on social enterprises (see next section) and the attention given to the SME dimension to certain aspects of mainstream corporate responsibility management approaches such as stakeholder engagement (Jenkins, 2005; Spence et al. 2003), the distinction between formal and informal aspects of management in SMEs (Russo and Tencati, 2009), and supply chain management, although in the last case most guidance is aimed at multinationals and how to deal with SME suppliers (ETI, 2006; DCCA, 2008; Pedersen, 2009), and the difficulties that can arise (Tencati et al., 2008). Therefore we are left with the sense that although there are unique responsibility dimensions to which SMEs should pay attention, an array of areas where SMEs are already active, and good reasons for some SMEs to consider corporate responsibility issues as part of their competitive advantage, nonetheless the specifics of corporate responsibility as a distinct element of SME management are not well understood.

 Discussion points

SMEs are frequently described as having unique characteristics that affect their attitude to corporate responsibility issues.

- Given the above characteristics, why do you think that a comprehensive body of distinct management approaches has yet to emerge?
- Why have SMEs in supply chains received more attention than most others?
- What role can government play in encouraging corporate responsibility management practices in SMEs?

Social enterprise

One of the most vibrant areas of corporate responsibility in recent years has been in the field of social entrepreneurship. An international phenomenon, social enterprises are being established around the world, applying much of the innovation and management theory associated with entrepreneurship in general to addressing social and environmental challenges. Business schools are now teaching social entrepreneurship, and the emergence of this field of private sector activity is also being studied by disciplines such as international development, anthropology, and environmental studies. Universities such as Oxford, Harvard, and Alberta have centres for social enterprise, and it can be studied in institutes from Argentina and Belgium to Switzerland and Spain. In addition, there are a host of networks and support organizations for social entrepreneurs such as Ashoka (worldwide), NESsT (Latin America and Eastern Europe), and the Skoll Foundation (international). One can call on specialist consultancies such as Bridgespan, and trade bodies such as the Social Enterprise Alliance, and one can one can seek funding from dedicated sources such as EVPA and the Acumen Fund.

By some measures, start-up rates and employment growth in social enterprises are outstripping those in conventional commercial enterprises, and they are having an impact on significant numbers of people; for example, Grameen Bank has 2.4 million microcredit customers in Bangladesh and Afghanistan, and the Bangladesh Rural Advancement Committee is the country's second largest employer after the government.[36] The size of these organizations raises questions about what is meant by social enterprise, and certainly why it is part of a chapter on SMEs. For some, size is not a determining factor, and therefore GE's ecomagination initiative (Chapter 6) or the retail company Wholefoods deserve the label social entrepreneurship as much as Fairtrade's web of small producers or Andrew Mawson's Bromley-by-Bow Centre, a focal centre for enterprise in one London community.[37] Zopa, the peer-to-peer money lending company, is sometimes depicted as a socially oriented enterprise, but is its value proposition of lending out money at competitive rates any more socially oriented than those of other lending institutions? Moreover, as the examples of fraud at A4e, one of the British government's favoured social enterprises, and the death from neglect of five people at Southern Cross's Orchid View rest home demonstrate, social enterprises are at risk from the same ethical and mismanagement pathologies that can affect any firm.

By blurring the definitions of social enterprise, advocates are able to make major claims about its impact. For example, classifying all not-for-profit organizations as social enterprises allows proponents to claim that the sector is worth over a trillion dollars, and subsuming the long-standing credit union sector within social enterprise enables the claim that 25 per cent of the USA population is affected by social enterprise.[38] As noted in other chapters, there is a tendency in certain areas of corporate responsibility for advocates of a particular approach or idea to use self-serving data, but it can lead to the conclusion that almost any business activity that feasibly has a positive social or environmental outcome is worthy of the mantle 'social enterprise', or that any socially or environmentally oriented activity is an enterprise. In other words, it can become harder to identify what a social enterprise is not than what one is.

Meanings of social enterprise

Definition

From the outset, 'social entrepreneurship' has been used to embrace a wide range of entrepreneurial activity. A collection of fourteen academic articles on social enterprise used ten different definitions of the term, including basic disagreements about whether it applied to individual entrepreneurs or to organizations, whether trade and financial objectives were an essential element, or if it were as likely to be found in public and non-profit sectors as the private sector, and whether the defining characteristics are the goals and outcomes (e.g. tackling social problems) or the process (e.g. employing ideas of innovation to create new social value).[39]

In a field where practitioners and theorists can often appear intoxicated by the excitement of their endeavours, it is not surprising that many define social enterprise in terms of its ambition and intent. The Skoll World Forum attracts 1000 attendees each year, and companies such as Selco and Boma Investments describe genuinely innovative business models. The entrepreneurs at such events are called 'disruptive change agents' and 'sectoral iconoclasts', and their enterprises have been described as 'social justice in motion' and world changers. As a social entrepreneur explains:

> ... the real measure of social entrepreneurship should be 'direct action that generates a paradigm shift in the way a societal need is met'. What such people do, in effect, is to identify and attack an 'unsatisfactory equilibrium'. Their endeavors are transformative, not palliative, with the power to catalyze and shape the future.

(Elkington and Hartigan, 2008, p 6)

In what remains an important introduction to the field, Dees (1998) sets out a continuum of social entrepreneurship organizations defined by the way they are funded. On one side are organizations with a social or environmental mission that are run and largely funded by volunteers; at the other end are socially oriented ventures conducted within commercial private sector organizations. In between, lie an array of not-for-profit and for-profit enterprises that are variously funded through grants, capital investments, and revenues. As Leadbeater (1997) points out, these enterprises can be found in the public, private, and civil sectors, and one thing that marks them out is how the competencies associated with one sector are transferred to another. For example, a public sector social enterprise may be marked out by its adoption of business skills to pursue its social and environmental remit; businesses may choose social or environmental returns/outcomes ahead of financial ones; and NGOs may adopt entrepreneurial solutions.

With this in mind, social entrepreneurship could be defined as the innovative use of combinations of resources to build organizations and practices that yield and sustain social and environmental benefits.[40] However, this would still leave us with a large range of only tangentially related initiatives, some of which we have discussed in other chapters (e.g. ecomagination, M-Pesa, and Wholefoods).[41] It would also draw us into a discussion of the roles of government and third-sector welfare provision, both of which largely fall outside the scope of this book. Therefore, Haugh's (2006) definition is broad enough, yet not too inclu-sive, to act as a working definition of social enterprise in this chapter (see Key Concept). It needs to be expanded to explicitly include environmental benefits, but it does emphasize the importance of business-led solutions in pursuit of social (and environmental) outcomes. While some would contest this as too narrow, it fits the purposes of this chapter, and also chimes with an important strand of business-focused (though not necessarily for-profit) social enterprise.[42]

 Key concept: Social enterprise

Social enterprise is a collective term for a range of organizations that trade for a social purpose. They adopt one of a variety of different legal formats but have in common the principles of pursuing business-led solutions to achieve social aims, and the reinvestment of surplus for community benefit. Their objectives focus on socially desired, non-financial goals and their outcomes are the non-financial measures of the implied demand for and supply of services'

(*Source:* Haugh, 2006, p 183)

Social and environmental mission and process

Haugh's definition also helps highlight that even if social enterprises are run at a profit, this is not their primary purpose. For many, what is special about social enterprise is the primacy attached to the social or environmental mission. This means identifying and addressing an unmet need or value creation opportunity. For example, La Fageda in Spain was established to provide meaningful work for the mentally ill, shifting them from pro-ducing ashtrays and trinkets to being the core personnel in a dairy business; the Population and Community Development Association in Thailand exists to tackle overpopulation as a cause of poverty, and does this by funding its birth control programmes from its social business ventures. In such enterprises, financial returns are not an indicator of business performance; rather, they are a means to a non-financial end where what matters is social or environmental impact.

However, measuring this performance is not straightforward, especially as the goods and services produced may be only one form of social enterprise output. For example, in some social ventures, creating employment, engaging community members, empow-ering individuals, attracting government services, and achieving the social integration of marginalized people may be more significant benefits than the actual delivery of tangible products such as potable water, schools, or trading opportunities—a lesson learned from international development (see Chapter 4). These process benefits are widely accepted as being essential to the kinds of sustainable transformational social change that social enterprise aspires to achieve, but they can be difficult to measure and realize, especially compared with more concrete, but perhaps short-term, outcomes such as a wage, a play-ground, or a surgery. The case study of Fairtrade in Chapter 12 highlights this, and in-depth studies of the impact of social enterprise, such as that by Lyon and Moberg (2010), show the complexity of understanding benefits.

Therefore, one finds some who consider social enterprise primarily in terms of the field of social endeavour (e.g. poverty alleviation, health care, education, community development, advocacy), and others who concentrate more on the operational features of the enterprise (e.g. decision-making not based on capital ownership, beneficiaries of the venture are participants not just recipients, limitations on profit distribution, social goals). Neither of these is mutually exclusive, but they might be reflected in the workings of the enterprise. For example, social enterprises are often closely identified with their founders, and the strengths of such single-minded visionaries (e.g. their self-assurance, their emotion, their 'insane ambition' (Elkington and Hartigan, 2008)) can create institutional weaknesses (e.g. unwillingness to delegate or build organizational capacity, reluctance to recognize criticism or fault, inability to think strategically or objectively), and these in turn can prove a barrier to achieving goals such as genuine empowerment, democratization, and indeed the scaling-up of the enterprise.

A further feature is the context within which social enterprises develop. If a social need were being met adequately by other means (e.g. state welfare services), arguably social enterprises would be redundant, and some of the criticisms of social entrepreneurship focus on the extent to which they represent an ideologically motivated privatization of public services rather than a genuine innovation.[43] Emerson (2003) stresses that social entrepreneurs typically work in dysfunctional markets where there might be high transaction costs, a lack of innovation, or no credible information on performance. Enterprises working at what has come to be called the bottom of the pyramid[44] (see Chapter 4) are amongst those working in underserved markets, but the rationale of initiatives such as Hindu Lever's Shakti is to generate a profit by serving poor markets. By contrast, social enterprises are more concerned with the social impact of working in areas of market failure. Moreover, there are examples of 'critical social entrepreneurship' (Nicholls, 2008) that challenge existing institutional structures and aim to build alternatives, and there is a historical continuity between the Rochdale cooperative movement in nineteenth century England and Fairtrade cooperatives set up to counter price monopsony in certain commodity chains.

Examples

There are examples of what might be categorized as social entrepreneurship throughout this book, including Vodafone's M-Pesa (see Case Study 4), Merrill Lynch's investment in Ulu Masen (see Online Resource Centre), Fynsa (see Online Resource Centre), and Fairtrade (see Case Study 12). Another example of the many that have been written about is Witness, a non-profit enterprise that helps human rights activists and others film human rights abuses. It began by giving cameras to victims and witnesses of abuses, and was funded by the Reebok Human Rights Foundation. It then progressed to building better technical and tactical (i.e. advocacy) capabilities, and is now operating in about sixty countries, serving as a watchful eye on public and private sector abuses.

Despite Witness's radical social goals, it is a fairly conventional social organization, relying on grants in the same way as most NGOs have done since the 1960s. Freeplay Foundation is somewhat different. It was born out of Freeplay Energy, a producer of wind-up radios and other electronic devices. Its main markets are in North America and Europe where emergency workers, outdoor enthusiasts, and emergency response teams use the company's torches, radios, generators, and medical instruments. However, profits are used to subsidize the supply of the same robust products to poor nations through the Freeplay Foundation. Thus, Freeplay represents a hybrid of for-profit and non-profit elements, and the founders are keen to emphasize that the company and the foundation are not senior and junior partners in the enterprise, but the Foundation simply represents a more effective way of having a social impact.

This was the situation until 2008 when—a year after winning *Time* magazine's Heroes of the Environment award—Freeplay Energy was bought out by the Narang Group following financial difficulties.[45] The new owners severed links with the Foundation, and the hybrid model ceased. The Foundation continues, and receives funding mostly from philanthropists in the USA, but it is now having to rethink its model of revenue generation, service delivery, and overall strategy.

Recycla Chile deals with electronics in a different way: it tackles end of product life-cycle issues to do with computers, televisions, mobile phones, and other electronic goods. Recycla recognized 'e-waste' as a business opportunity, and employs ex-convicts to dismantle appliances and prepare the parts for export. However, income is reinvested in Recycla's greater social mission—to raise awareness of the need to recycle e-waste, and to create a legislative framework to support this. Within four years, the social enterprise was profitable, and it is now the preferred recycling outlet for many companies.

These examples demonstrate quite different funding and business models. The degree of long-term viability of each example is debatable, as is its scalability, although scale and replication are not defining characteristics of social enterprise. What they have in common is that they seek to serve dysfunctional or underserved markets through innovative ideas, and give primacy to their social/environmental impacts.

Why now?

One effect of the wide variety of definitions of social enterprise is that the term can be applied to all manner of historical examples, including the Quaker family enterprises of Victorian capitalism, the gilded age philanthropy of Andrew Carnegie (see Chapter 1), and the Rochdale cooperative movement. Yet, placing contemporary social entrepreneurship in a long historical tradition goes against some of the claims that it is a new and unique response to a particular set of events and circumstances. For example, it has been portrayed as a response to the market dysfunctions associated with global poverty (see Chapter 4), leveraging the overall rise in global wealth, the spread of capitalist democracies, and the rising crises in health and the environment, income inequality, and inefficient public service delivery.[46] It also complements the 'third way' political paradigm that seeks to balance the free market bias of conventional democratic right-wing parties, and the state-control bias of their left-wing opponents. The third way, which has dominated much European and North American political policy since the early 1990s, treats economic development as an apolitical good that can be achieved through technological development, education, and competitive mechanisms. Entrepreneurship and social inclusion are important parts of this narrative, and social enterprise is often seen as uniquely placed to bridge them.

Social enterprise can also be portrayed as part of a more overt political paradigm where the values of the free market are transferred to arenas that hitherto were the sphere of the public sector. Thus, not only are social entrepreneurs filling roles that in the government agencies of previous decades were the duty of government (even if the entrepreneurs often remain dependent on government funding), the frameworks and language of business come to dominate the poverty alleviation and environmental management discourse. For example, the poor are considered 'dynamic', the 'solutions' to poverty are to be found in 'entrepreneurship' and 'innovation', and even sustainability of the planet is described in terms of natural 'capital'.

As discussed in Chapters 4 and 14, an aspect of corporate responsibility that needs consideration is the extent to which it causes us to translate social and environmental issues into the norms and metaphors of business. However, it is misleading to think of a golden age when government was the sole purveyor of social goods. In some countries during a particular period, as the result of particular social and political upheavals, the state took on a role unprecedented in history. But whether it be mosques and churches, mutual societies and cooperatives, or guilds and masons, there has long been a private social sector that has often been at least as active as government in spawning innovative solutions to meet social and environmental needs.

One new feature of contemporary social enterprise, however, is the widening sources of funding. Our earlier example of Witness shows how conventional grant giving remains important, and Orlando Rincón Bonilla, the Colombian social entrepreneur, is similar in many ways to Carnegie and Rowntree, wealthy businessmen who decided to spend their wealth on tackling social needs. But, as explored further as part of socially responsible investing (see Chapter 10), alternative and increasingly sophisticated capital markets focused on social entrepreneurs are emerging. There are mentor organizations such as UnLtd that provide incremental seed capital as well as advice; there are networks that bring together angel investors and social entrepreneurs; and there are market brokers such as Investing for Good linking investors interested in a blend of social and financial returns on investment with social enterprises. This last group is focused on what is variously called impact investing, programme-related investing, or blended-value investing.[47] These investments inhabit a space between philanthropy (where no financial return is expected) and pure financial investments (where social/environmental considerations are only a factor in so far as they affect profit maximization). The impact investing market is estimated to reach $500 billion by 2020.[48]

Impact

Much of the analysis of the impact of corporate responsibility in Chapter 12 is applicable to the particular field of social enterprise. In general terms, there are a large number of case studies that show social entrepreneurship in action, but these tend to be written by advocates of the field and consequently the cases themselves are weak on objectivity and rigour, and highlight successes rather than the inevitable large number of failures that are typical of entrepreneurship generally.[49] Systematic impact assessment is still at an early stage, even in well-established areas of social entrepreneurship such as fairtrade and microfinance. Moreover, there is a growing body of analysis (again often reliant on individual case studies) that challenges the effectiveness of social entrepreneurship.[50]

It seems likely that a more rigorous approach to understanding impact will be an inevitable consequence of the impact investing market where investors (perhaps unlike philanthropists) will be more concerned with evidence of social returns on investment. Yet, even if a signifi-cant number of social enterprises prosper and have a distinctively strong impact in dysfunc-tional markets, there may be limits on the change they can bring about. Muhammad Yunus, founder of the Grameen Group of social enterprises, says that the *'future of the world lies in the hands of market-based social entrepreneurs. The more we can move in the direction of busi-ness, the better off we are— in the sense that we are free'.*[51] There are echoes in his words of the Hungarian school of business thinkers and economists such as Hayek and Mises (see Chap-ter 2), who interpreted free markets as an escape from dictatorial governments, but there is also an assumption that entrepreneurship is an abundant quality that simply needs to be harnessed. However, most entrepreneurs are 'necessity entrepreneurs' of the kind discussed on ['The meaning and significance of smaller businesses'] p 263 rather than the 'gazelles' that advocates of social entrepreneurship idealize. As one social entrepreneur puts it, *'One does not decide to be an entrepreneur. One is an entrepreneur [from birth]'.*[52] If this is true, then social entrepreneurs may never be sufficient in number to make a significant impact on the social and environmental challenges of the twenty-first century. But if what is meant are the hordes of necessity entrepreneurs who would rather not be entrepreneurs at all, then it seems unlikely that the innovation hoped for from social enterprises will ever be realized.

 Case study 11   SELCO-India—bringing energy to the rural poor

Like many of the largest emerging economies, India is fuelling its economic growth with high-carbon energy plus nuclear power. The country has substantial coal reserves, and in international forums it is at pains to assert its right to exploit these just as OECD countries have done in the past. Yet, according to SELCO founder Harish Hande, coal and nuclear—the backbone of India's electricity grid—are irrelevant to vast sections of the population. Forty-four per cent of Indians lack mains electricity, and for many more the supply is erratic.

Hande established SELCO in 1995. It is based in Bangalore and employs nearly 200 people at its HQ and 21 branch offices across South India. SELCO's purpose is to provide sustainable energy services to photovoltaic (PV) solar home systems for low-income households and businesses. It has served over 150,000 customers, and in the process developed a unique business model that makes solar energy available at an affordable price to underserved markets.

SELCO's success hinges on two types of innovation that are welded together in the company's business model. The first type is technological innovation. SELCO designs and sells photovoltaic energy systems for the home. These are primarily to provide lighting that is cleaner, more reliable, and more affordable than the kerosene lamps found in most rural homes. A typical unit is sufficient to power four 7W compact fluorescent lights, although consumers also use electricity for radios and fans. SELCO's engineers install the systems, which typically comprise a 35W PV module on the roof and a lead–acid battery to store the power inside. Both the cells and the batteries have been specifically designed to meet the needs of their users so that, for example, the batteries can cope with daily discharge in a way that would destabilize conventional car batteries.

Technological innovation is not limited to PV and batteries. SELCO helps customers to modify their homes to get the most use out of their installations. For example, a lamp installed in a corner can serve several rooms if parts of the dividing walls are removed, or bulbs can be moved from one room to another if sufficient wiring and sockets are installed. Whether it be the hardware, the installation, or the subsequent service contract that forms part of the package, SELCO sources as locally as

(continued...)

possible. Its PV modules are made in India, although the success of the Indian solar energy industry has resulted in one supplier ceasing manufacture of the smaller units that SELCO needs. SELCO has developed a network of local installers in what has become a new trade in the areas where the company operates.

Installations typically cost about Rs.18,000: a significant outlay for customers whose daily income could be Rs.400 (under £5) a day. However, energy is a significant outlay for poorer people, and while SELCO's target market could not afford Rs.18,000 in one payment, paying in instalments of about Rs.400 a month over five years is an attractive proposition. Moreover, in many cases the extra productivity resulting from a steady supply of light throughout the day is more than sufficient to pay for the installation and maintenance. PV modules might be too expensive for street traders, but a battery and a fluorescent lamp are within their means, so SELCO has encouraged a network of PV battery-charging businesses. To pay the initial deposit and to organize monthly payments, potential customers can go to the local development banks that India's state-owned banks were compelled to set up in the 1980s. The government also supported SELCO's expansion with 33 per cent subsidies on installations, but this agreement has now ended.

SELCO itself says that its model is sustainable. It has a long-term financing partnership with E+Co, a non-profit organization that provides debt and equity investments in clean energy businesses in developing countries. More recently, it has received support from the Lemelson Foundation (USA) and Good Energies (Switzerland). Amongst its proudest claims is that its success has demonstrated that clean energy need not be expensive, and that a low-carbon economy does not have to deprive poor people of electricity. The next step in innovation will be making better use of the power to which people have access. For example, many women would like to use electric sewing machines, but the PV modules do not generate enough power. However, on further investigation, the problem is that the sewing machines on the market are over-powered for what rural women need them to do, and if a less powerful machine were available it could run off the current modules and still meet the women's aspirations.

(*Sources:* conversation with Harish Hande, Oxford, 29 October 2011; www.ft.com/cms/s/0/cb0b871a-0f98-11de-a8ae-0000779fd2ac.html#axzz1cMJCaiDZ; www.selco-india.com/)

Questions

1 SELCO-India is an example of innovation by a social enterprise.

   a What are the essential elements in the company's success so far?

   b Is the SELCO model replicable in other countries?

   c Is the SELCO model only applicable in rural areas?

2 The company has won various awards for creating a viable business model that addresses social and environmental issues.

   a What are the main sustainability impacts that the company delivers?

   b Could a mainstream energy company adopt a similar approach?

   c What will the company need to do differently in order to increase its impact?

3 SELCO-India is an example of technological and financial innovation.

   a Under what conditions is PV technology more affordable than coal-based energy?

   b How could you develop a similarly innovative approach to a different sustainability challenge, such as clean water?

   c Are there other examples of clean energy being provided to poor communities? How are they similar to and how are they different from SELCO?

Summary

Small and medium-sized enterprises have often been overlooked in discussions of corporate responsibility. For a long time they were viewed as either smaller versions of larger companies, or a threat to large companies because of their perceived poor social and environmental standards in global supply chains. Nowadays, SMEs are more likely to be considered as worthy of special attention. Not just in terms of size, they are fundamentally different from other types of business (e.g. their close relationship to local communities, their resource constraints, their style of management, and their different measures of success).

However, it is misleading to think that SMEs are more naturally responsible, or indeed irresponsible, than other firms. The SME sector is not homogenous, and an SME's attitude towards corporate responsibility is affected by its attitude to growth, the values and goals of the owner/manager, and the reasons why the company was established in the first place. There are SMEs that were established in part to achieve social and/or environmental goals, and for small firms keen on growth 'corporate social opportunity' can help identify profitable openings. However, most SMEs are better seen as 'lifestyle enterprises', or indeed 'necessity enterprises', where the reason for establishing the business is personal preference or lack of other choices. Corporate responsibility is less immediately attractive for these types of SME, and is typically greeted as a burden. Yet often such SMEs are practising corporate responsibility of a kind in order to maintain their licence to operate in their communities, or to achieve business objectives such as attracting and retaining staff.

The difficulty in these instances is that corporate responsibility practices can be too selective (e.g. an emphasis on charitable giving but a failure to attend to working conditions), or they may be ignored (e.g. when a large customer imposes its own standards on SME suppliers irrespective of what they are already doing). For many SMEs, corporate responsibility management is seen as an additional bureaucratic burden or another instance of large companies exerting power over small ones. However, there are examples of companies in the supply chain working together to achieve common corporate responsibility objectives that have demonstrable business benefits. There is also growing private and public sector investment in improving SME corporate responsibility management. What is still missing, though, is a detailed understanding of corporate responsibility management practice as something distinct from the approaches adopted in larger firms.

Further reading

online resource centre

www.oxfordtextbooks.co.uk/orc/blowfield_murray3e/

Visit the Online Resource Centre that accompanies this book to enrich your understanding of this chapter. Among the resources available are web links, exercises, and additional case studies.

Bugg-Levine, A., Kogut, B., and Kulatilaka, N. 2012, 'A new approach to funding social enterprises', *Harvard Business Review*, vol. 90, no. 1/2, pp 118–123.
A look at the problem of social enterprise financing including the challenges of liquidity and exiting.

Business Ethics: a European Review 2009, vol. 18, no. 1, special edition on SMEs.
Series of articles on different aspects of corporate responsibility amongst SMEs including contributions from important thinkers in the field.

Elkington, J. and Hartigan, P. 2008, *The power of unreasonable people: how social entrepreneurs create markets that change the world*, Harvard Business School Press, Boston, MA.
Wide range of examples of social entrepreneurship assembled and discussed by two strong advocates in the field.

Jenkins, H., 2009, 'A "business opportunity" model of corporate social responsibility for small and medium-sized enterprises', *Business Ethics*, vol. 18, no. 1, pp 21–36.
Theoretical framework for understanding when SMEs are most and least likely to overtly address corporate responsibility issues.

Kechiche, A. and Soparnot, R. 2012, 'CSR within SMEs: literature review', *International Business Research*, vol. 5, no. 7 , p 97.
Useful overview of research into corporate responsibility in the SME context.

Southern, A. 2009, *Enterprise and deprivation: small business, social exclusion and sustainable communities*, Routledge, London.
A collection of contributions exploring the complex role that SMEs play in tackling social exclusion and building sustainable communities.

Online resources

- Additional case studies of social enterprise
- Teaching notes
- Exercises and discussion topics for students
- Suggestions for additional materials on SMEs
- Links to other web-based resources

Endnotes

1. See, e.g., Carroll, 1999; Crane and Matten, 2004.
2. See, e.g., Bennett et al., 1999; Hennigfeld et al., 2006.
3. See, e.g., NRET, 1999; Lyon, 2003.
4. See, e.g., Pedersen, 2009; Spence, 2007; Jamali et al., 2009.
5. Sources: Burns, 2001; UNIDO, 2002; Jenkins, 2006.
6. Patricof and Sunderland, 2006; Grayson and Dodd, 2007.
7. Grayson and Dodd, 2007.
8. Jenkins, 2009; Grayson and Dodd, 2007.
9. Jenkins, 2006.
10. Blowfield, 2010.

11. Wilson, 2006; Brainard, 2006; Nelson, 2007.
12. Patricof and Sunderland, 2006.
13. Lyon and Bertotti, 2007.
14. Lyon, personal communication, March 2010.
15. Southern, 2009.
16. Battaglia et al., 2010; Stevens et al., 2008.
17. Evers and Schrader, 1994.
18. Jenkins, 2006.
19. Jenkins, 2006; Perrini et al., 2007; Jamali et al., 2009.
20. Tilley, 2000.
21. See, e.g., Goffee and Scase, 1995; Spence and Rutherfoord, 2000.
22. Blowfield, 2010.
23. See, e.g., Lund-Thomsen and Lindgreen 2013; Lund-Thomsen et al. 2012.
24. Jones and Tilley, 2003.
25. Jenkins, 2009; Murillo and Lozano, 2006.
26. See also Hollender and Breen, 2010.
27. Tencati et al., 2008; Ballinger, 2010.
28. Battaglia et al., 2010.
29. Nelson, 2007.
30. See, e.g., Hammann et al., 2009; Jenkins, 2006; Enderle, 2004.
31. Stevens et al., 2008.
32. Murillo and Lozano, 2006; Grayson and Dodd, 2007; Morsing and Perrini, 2009.
33. Compare People and Profit, 2007 with Hennigfeld et al., 2006 and PR News, 2006.
34. Respectively, UNDP, 2009 (available at www.csrgov.dk/sw51121.asp); Brainard, 2006; Wilson, 2006.
35. Thankappan et al., 2004; Lyon and Vickers, 2009.
36. See Nicholls 2008, p 3.
37. Elkington and Hartigan, 2008; Mawson, 2008.
38. Salamon, 2003; Smallbone et al., 2001 cited in Nicholls, 2008, p 3.
39. See the contributions collected in Mair et al., 2006.
40. Mair and Noboa, 2006.
41. Kanter (1999) provides an overview of social innovation in major companies, and Weiser et al. (2006) offer numerous examples.
42. Dees et al., 2002; Drayton, 2002.
43. Leadbeater, 2004.
44. Prahalad and Hart, 2002; Prahalad, 2005; Hart, 2005; Hammond et al., 2007.
45. The company's debt reached over $13 million on less than $8 million of revenue, apparently due to problems in assimilating an acquisition made in 2006.
46. Nicholls, 2008.
47. See, e.g., Emerson, 2003; Nicholls, 2010.
48. Monitor, 2009.
49. For examples of cases see Elkington and Hartigan (2008), Mawson (2008), and Hollender (2010).
50. See, e.g., Edwards, 2010; Lyon and Moberg, 2010.
51. Elkington and Hartigan, 2008, p 17.
52. Elkington and Hartigan, 2008, p 22.

Part 3

Impact, critics, and future of corporate responsibility

12. The impact of corporate responsibility   281

13. Criticisms of corporate responsibility   312

14. The future of corporate responsibility   334

The impact of corporate responsibility

 Chapter overview

In this chapter, we examine the impact that the practice of corporate responsibility has had. In particular, we will:

- consider the importance of understanding impact;
- look at the ways we learn about impact and the ways it is assessed;
- establish a framework for understanding the different dimensions to impact;
- provide an overview of the impact of corporate responsibility to date;
- discuss the challenges of assessing impact.

 Main topics

Understanding impact   281

Different dimensions of the impact of corporate responsibility   287

The challenges of determining impact   303

Key terms

Impact

Non-financial performance

Corporate responsibility reports

Ratings indices

Corporate responsibility awards

Understanding impact

What does corporate responsibility do? Does it help to make the Earth more sustainable? Does it restore trust in corporations? Does it reduce poverty? Uphold international human rights? Reduce corporate malfeasance? Increase business profitability? Lessen corruption and improve public governance? End illegal activity such as smuggling and human trafficking?

These are some of the areas in which corporate responsibility is intended to have an impact. In this chapter, we look at the evidence to support these claims. In business or any area of life, understanding the impact is essential for making decisions, justifying courses of action, and recognizing the point at which we stand on particular journeys. In the corporate responsibility context, impact is essential if corporate responsibility is to defy its critics and move from being a 'feel-good thing' to being recognized as a 'good thing'. Whether one looks at the theoretical work on corporate social performance in the 1970s and 1980s, or at that on social accountability since the 1990s, the importance of measurement is apparent. Yet, given the emphasis put on *'if you want it to count, count it'*, or the rooting of important corporate responsibility tools and methods in financial accounting, it is surprising how patchy attempts to measure corporate responsibility have been and that we do not know more about the overall impact of corporate responsibility management.

Corporate responsibility embraces big goals, such as contributing to sustainable economic development, improving the lives of workers and their communities, and accelerating progress towards the Millennium Development Goals. Moreover, these contributions are often linked to conventional ones of corporate growth and profitability. Part of this chapter is concerned with finding out what evidence there is to show how far corporate responsibility has met these goals and, as importantly, the extent to which the evidence itself is being gathered. As we shall see, the information is fragmentary and, to make sense of it, we offer a framework that clarifies the different types of impact about which we do know something ('A framework for understanding impact', p 287). We use this framework in an overview of the current state of play in 'Different dimensions of the impact of corporate responsibility' (p 287), and conclude the chapter with a section discussing 'The challenges of determining impact' (p 303) and what might happen in the future.

The meaning of 'impact'

In its most general sense, 'impact' refers to outcomes associated with particular actions. Although this is too simple a definition, it draws attention, first, to the importance of outcomes and, second, to the significance of causality. As examples in this chapter reveal, discussion of impact often confuses 'outputs' with 'outcomes'. But although the two words overlap in some contexts, the former is narrower in meaning, referring to the specific actions that are needed to achieve a larger result, whereas the latter is the larger result itself. (For example, degrees are an *output* of university that have the *outcome* of creating a better educated population.) Thus, in the corporate responsibility context, a corporate responsibility report is an output, not an outcome, if our aim is to enable business to manage its relationship with society better.

However, demonstrating a causal relationship between inputs, outputs, and outcomes is far from straightforward. A company might be clear about what it wants to achieve (e.g. to remove child labour from its supply chain), but even if this happens, can it be sure that the outcome was the result of its own actions rather than, for example, a concerted enforcement effort by the police? Roche (1999) argues that one should not place too much emphasis on causality, defining impact assessment as *'the systematic analysis of lasting or significant changes—**positive or negative**, intended or unintended—in people's lives brought about by an action or series of actions'* (emphasis added). This definition also highlights how, for many, impact refers to the outcomes for people although, as we shall see, the beneficiary of corporate responsibility may also be a company or a particular stakeholder group.

Discussion points

Some people claim that, when we talk about corporate responsibility's 'impact', what we are actually referring to are its 'actions' or 'outputs'.

- What are examples of the distinction between 'actions' and 'outputs', and 'outcomes' and 'impacts'?
- What is the significance of thinking in terms of actions rather than outcomes?
- Taking a real company's corporate responsibility report as the basis, how would you modify it to focus on outcomes?

How we learn about impact and the limits of our knowledge

There are three readily available sources of information relating to the impact of corporate responsibility: corporate responsibility reports (including social, environmental, and sustainability reports); ratings of companies such as FTSE4Good, the Ethibel Sustainability Index, the KLD Indexes, the ARESE social ratings, and the Dow Jones Sustainability Indexes; and case studies of companies undertaken by companies, corporate responsibility organizations, and others.

There are also case studies of companies and industries that are undertaken by a variety of organizations monitoring corporate behaviour (e.g. CorpWatch, Christian Aid, *Stichting Onderzoek Multinationale Ondernemingen* (SOMO)—the Centre for Research on Multinational Corporations). These have been very influential in the overall development of corporate responsibility and, in important ways, have set out benchmarks against which the corporate responsibility practices of firms can be assessed. There are reports documenting the progress of companies within particular partnerships, such as the annual reports on compliance with labour standards by the Ethical Trading Initiative or the Fair Labor Association. There are also publicly available reports about the certification of particular resources in accordance with the criteria of bodies such as the Marine Stewardship Council, or, in some cases, of facilities such as those adopting the ISO 14000 series (although often the information most pertinent for assessing the impact of these is considered proprietary and not in the public domain).

In addition, there are what can be called 'trend-tracking' reports, focused on particular aspects of corporate responsibility (see Box 12.1). There has been a well-documented rise in the number of corporate responsibility reports and, according to the KPMG 2011 International Survey of Corporate Responsibility Reporting, 95 per cent of the 250 largest public companies in the world were issuing reports containing a mix of environmental, social, and governance (ESG) information. The framework of the report, and how that is used over a number of years, is an important factor in showing impact. Seventy-five per cent of the companies in the KPMG survey used the GRI Sustainability Reporting Guidelines described in Chapter 8. Various company reports also refer to the UN Global Compact, the ILO's core labour standards, the UN Declaration on Human Rights, the Kyoto Protocol, and other agreements which, while not binding on business, are often used in defining corporate responsibility performance. As we shall discuss later, a significant area of impact is how corporate responsibility's success has impacted its own behaviour ('The impact of corporate responsibility on itself', p 302), and the adoption of common standards that facilitate comparison between companies is an important aspect of this.

Comparability is a common challenge for anyone trying to measure corporate responsibility performance, and different initiatives often use separate approaches. For instance, the *Business Ethics* list (Box 12.1) reduces numerous components of good citizenship to a single final grade, raising questions about how a strong environmental record, for example, is affected by poor labour relations. In Europe, the People, Planet, Profit framework is often used, which separates out rather than aggregates different aspects of performance.[1]

Box 12.1   Surveys and reports on corporate responsibility performance

- *Business in the Community*'s Corporate Responsibility Index
- *State of Corporate Citizenship*—a biennial annual report highlighting trends and corporate attitudes to corporate responsibility among US companies
- *Business Ethics*' 100 Best Corporate Citizens list
- *Covalence*'s Ethical Ranking—a reputation index of the largest market capitalizations in the Dow Jones Index, based on their contributions to human development
- *Business Week/Climate Group*'s Climate Change Rankings—multinational companies by their total reduction of greenhouse gases
- *Sustainability Reporting Survey* (Germany)—an overview of company reporting
- Fortune 100 *Accountability Rating*—scoring Global 100 companies on how seriously their future decisions will consider non-financial matters
- *GMI*'s Corporate Governance Ratings—3,200 global companies
- Transparency International's *Global Corruption Barometer*—public opinion of corporations
- World Economic Forum's biannual *Trust Poll*

The limitations of the information

Before we look at the types of impact that the above sources of information reveal, it is worth noting some of the comments that have been made, particularly about reports, ratings, and case studies. The 2008 KPMG survey noted that industries with the greatest environmental impact have the highest levels of reporting (e.g. 80 per cent of electronics and computers, utilities, automotive, and oil and gas companies produce reports), although there has been a rapid rise in the financial sector, which is not considered to be an industry with a heavy environmental footprint. The range of topics is increasing so that, now, about two-thirds of reports have sections on corporate governance and 85 per cent mention climate change. Nonetheless, certain issues are seldom reported upon, such as economic impacts (25 per cent of reports), and, in general, environmental impacts are better reported on than social ones. Furthermore, while 40 per cent of reports base their content on GRI guidelines, only 21 per cent employ stakeholder consultation to identify the issues that the reporting company should be addressing.

The use of particular standards, even if well regarded, tells us only so much about impact. As Clarke (2005) shows, corporate responsibility is being undermined by such practices as the falsification of records and the training of workers in how to respond to auditor questioning. The UK consultancy firm Impactt Ltd says that 95 per cent of the factories it visits in China probably falsify records and that managers can buy software to help with this. In response, some have called for stronger independent assurance and, in 2005, 30 per cent of reports were independently assured in some way, mostly by the large accounting firms, even though there are question about the objectivity of such organizations (see Chapter 8). However, in 2002, the *Trust Us* report[2] pointed out that there are major questions about how far such companies had restored public trust in their own integrity, and this remains an area of uncertainty. On the one hand, a company with codes of labour practice, such as Primark, is widely criticized for factory disasters such as that in Bangladesh in 2013, but it can also point out that in part because of its experience of corporate responsibility initiatives it was able to respond by paying affected workers nine months' wages. There is also evidence that competition between firms and the need for credibility has improved the market for standards.[3]

As discussed in Chapter 8, the Association of Chartered Certified Accountants, which for a number of years ran sustainability reporting awards in different parts of the world, identified recurring weaknesses in company reports, and now incorporates sustainability into its professional qualification. The weaknesses are summarized in Box 12.2, but those that particularly stand out are the lack of systemic ecological footprint analysis of the company's impact, the lack of comprehensive maps of stakeholders, and the lack of information on the key impacts that the company's operations and products, or services, have on society and the natural environment.[4]

Box 12.2   Strong and weak areas of corporate responsibility reports

Strengths	Weaknesses
• Comprehensibility; appropriateness of report length	• Lack of a clear and credible articulation of the meaning of sustainable development, consideration of the implications of its pursuit, and any tensions that emerge
• Identification of key social, environmental, and economic impacts and business issues as a basis for credible reporting	• Lack of description of risk identification and management processes, including disclosure of actual risks identified and opportunities resulting from them
• Explanation of the process behind decisions on key impacts and issues for the business and report indicators	• Identification of, and accounting for, social and environmental externalities is rare
• Identification of key stakeholders, including rationale for their selection	• Need for more demonstration that sustainability is integrated into core business strategy
• Explanation of the governance structure in place to manage sustainability performance (e.g. existence of named board director)	• Few reports provide description of how incentives for staff and managers are linked to sustainability performance and achievements of targets

(*Source:* summarized from ACCA, 2008)

Ratings, inasmuch as they derive data from corporate reports, will reflect the above limitations to some degree. The situation is also confused by the heterogeneous methods they use. Schafer (2005) distinguishes between ratings systems that are economically oriented (i.e. those that focus on the economic impact of ethical, environmental, and social criteria on the company) and those that are normatively oriented, within which evaluation criteria are dominated by what he calls 'ethical' motivations. Among the economically oriented systems (which he says predominate), there are four groups:

1 risk assessment approaches (how the company deals with its social or environmental risks);
2 efficiency models (how management strategies relate to sustainability, on the assumption that sustainability offers competitive advantage);
3 industries of the future (identifying the above-average growth companies inside what are considered to be the hot sectors of tomorrow);
4 best-practice corporate responsibility management (identifying companies with the best approaches to corporate responsibility management).

For Margolis and Walsh (2003), this focus on the economic consequences for the company is a basic weakness in our understanding. Echoing some of what we have discussed regarding the business case (see Chapter 6), they say *'if corporate responses to social misery are evaluated only in terms of their instrumental benefits for the firm and its shareholders, we never learn about their impact on society'.*[5] Indeed, they argue that the emphasis on instrumental benefits is so great that there is little attempt to examine when it is permissible or necessary to act on other stakeholders' interests if they are not consistent with those of shareholders.

Work on impact by the UN Development Programme (focusing on developing countries) and the Overseas Development Institute (focusing on tourism) stresses the instrumental benefits of corporate responsibility, and the World Business Council for Sustainable Development's impact assessment framework begins by stating that it was 'built by business for business and thus, begins with the business perspective'.[6] The consequences of an economic orientation in reporting and ratings will become apparent in the next section, when we look at what we do and do not know about the actual impact of corporate responsibility. Moreover, we should not be surprised at this orientation, given the degree to which corporate responsibility has sought legitimacy by rooting important elements of its methods and approaches in the norms and instruments of financial management, accounting, and managerial efficiency. However, anyone looking for a clear correlation between corporate responsibility and financial performance is likely to be disappointed, as even at the most simplistic level of analysis a company's prestige amongst shareholders and amongst non-financial stakeholders can be widely at odds.[7]

Finally, we need to note the limitations of case studies as a way in which to assess impact. These have proved important in terms of drawing attention to particular issues and examples of company behaviour. The best known are probably those of civil society organizations, such as the Clean Clothes Campaign's case study of an Indonesian factory producing for Fila, or SOMO's 2005 investigation of labour rights violations in computer factories (Schipper and de Haan 2005). There are also interesting examples commissioned by companies, such as the 2005 study by Impactt Ltd of overtime in Chinese factories. But by their very nature, case studies tend to use differing methodologies and a meta-analysis of findings is all but impossible. Moreover, as Elliott and Freeman (2003) note, the organizations that produce many of the case studies typically only need to understand the situation on the ground in order to start a campaign; from that point on, the main dynamics happen away from the site of the problem, i.e. through the media, company responses, consumer reaction, and government action.

A framework for understanding impact

If we think about the possible answers to the question posed at the start of this chapter—'What does corporate responsibility do?'—it is readily apparent that 'impact' has a different meaning if we are talking, for example, about helping to make the Earth more sustainable than if we are referring to reducing corporate malfeasance, or to improving business profitability. What is recognized as impact also differs if one is looking at instrumental or normative dimensions of performance.

To help to make sense of these different dimensions, we offer a framework that captures the different ways in which impact is being interpreted. It is based on what others have written about the impact of corporate responsibility and measuring corporate social performance,[8] and also the different aspects of impact included in a selection of award-winning corporate responsibility reports.[9] What emerges are five dimensions on which corporate responsibility practice is held to have an impact.

1 **The social, environmental, and governance 'big picture'** This refers to large social and environmental issues, including global warming, human rights, economic growth, and poverty reduction.

2 **Instrumental benefits** This covers the connection between financial performance and ESG performance, including the impact of making the business case for corporate responsibility.

3 **Business attitudes, awareness, and practices** These refer to the impact that corporate responsibility is having on the way in which companies think about the non-financial aspects of business operations and the way that they operate.

4 **Non-business stakeholders** This refers to the impact of corporate responsibility on other stakeholders, including the critics who advocate for greater ESG responsibility.

5 **The impact of corporate responsibility on itself** This area covers the way in which corporate responsibility's evolution and growth has affected how we think about and practise corporate responsibility today.

We use this framework throughout the following section.

Different dimensions of the impact of corporate responsibility

The impact of corporate responsibility on the 'big picture'

One only has to think of the US$ 65 billion Bernie Madoff scandal, the $13 billion fine paid by JP Morgan for its role in the sub-prime lending crisis, or the Montara oil spill in the Timor Sea to realize that business remains a highly problematic element of society. It would be very unrealistic to expect corporate responsibility to eradicate the abuses and excesses that have always dogged human economic activity. Moreover, one would need an unprecedented belief in industry self-regulation to think that corporate responsibility initiatives could have a fundamental impact on financing, given the disparity that lies between the uniquely high level of regulation applied to banks nationally in the largest economies and the absence of regulation at a global level (see Chapter 10). Nonetheless, corporate responsibility is increasingly being linked to many of the biggest challenges around the world. These include how we:

1   respond to climate change;
2   address the consequences of globalization;
3   increase the effectiveness of internal corporate governance;
4   uphold international human rights;
5   increase justice and equity, especially in the poorest countries;
6   fight corruption and poor governance;
7   achieve stable and sustainable economic growth.

Although some corporate responsibility initiatives have been framed in terms of these big picture issues, it is impossible to show attributable impact at this level. Instead, we can only understand pieces of the mosaic. The GRI Sustainability Reporting Guidelines, the ISO 26000 draft international standard on corporate responsibility, and various other standards used internationally are attempts to break these overarching goals down into addressable pieces.

In this section, we examine what is known about the impact of corporate responsibility on some of these issues. Areas such as corruption are inherently unsuited to measurement of external outcomes, at least in the short term, and have largely been viewed in terms of changes in business attitudes and practices (see 'Impact and the business case', p 293). Therefore, we will look at the broad areas of environmental, social, and economic impact.

Environmental impact

Environmental management has been central to corporate responsibility thinking since the 1980s and it is not surprising that we know more about the impact of corporate responsibility in this area compared with others. The term embraces such aspects as natural resource management, waste management, recycling, marketing of green products, and pollution prevention and control. There are a number of well-developed initiatives that can demonstrate their impact over a period of several years. For example, in 1995, the Forest Stewardship Council had certified less than 5 million hectares of responsibly managed forest, but that figure had grown to over 182 million hectares by 2013.[10]

Many companies, such as Diageo, Procter & Gamble, and Unilever, have successfully reduced their water use. For example, Unilever has lowered its own worldwide usage by 54 per cent over 10 years and has extended this by working with its suppliers so that, for example, tomato growers have reduced their consumption by half.[11] Unilever is often cited as a leader in terms of environmental reporting, and other areas of impact are also worth noting. Before selling on its Birds Eye brand, the company estimated that by 2006 it would source 60 per cent of the fish it sold within Europe from sustainably managed fish stocks; it has increased its paper-based packaging to 83 per cent in Europe; it has reduced diesel fuel usage for transportation; and it has lowered carbon dioxide emissions from its manufacturing operations by 25 per cent since 1995. It demonstrates year-on-year reductions in units per tonne of production in what it recognizes as seven key areas of eco-efficiency, including energy, hazardous waste, and improvements in the management of ozone-depleting gases.

In some instances, companies' management of the environment is basically in compliance with national laws. Therefore it can be difficult to conclude what is an impact of corporate responsibility and what is the result of government regulation. In fact, unlike social impacts, most environmental information seems to concern developed, rather than developing, economies, even though government regulation in the latter seems likely to be weaker.[12] In the USA, however, where federal government was not at the forefront on environmental issues such as global warming, companies such as DuPont, Procter & Gamble, and Coca Cola have adopted targets for reducing greenhouse gas emissions that broadly reflect the spirit of the Kyoto Protocol.

BP, the second-largest oil and gas sector company, positioned itself at the forefront of thinking about how business can contribute to sustainability when, in 1996, it became the first energy firm to withdraw from the Global Climate Change Coalition, which challenged scientific arguments for climate change. It said that it would reduce its greenhouse gas emissions at twice the rate specified in the Kyoto Protocol and met those targets nine years ahead of schedule, reducing emissions by the equivalent of 9.6 million tonnes and bringing operational savings of $250 million.[13] Wal-Mart has now positioned itself in a similar leadership position on the environmental impacts of retail supply chains, achieving, for instance, a 25 per cent reduction in waste in the first three years of its sustainability programme and eliminating 30 per cent of the energy used in stores.[14] Public investment in variations of what Barack Obama calls the Green New Deal will lead to more scrutiny of the impact of corporate environmental actions, and the importance attached to taking environmental issues seriously is evident in companies such as Johnson & Johnson, Pacific Gas and Electric, and Exelon withdrawing from the US Chamber of Commerce because of the latter's policy on climate change.

Figures on individual company performance in important areas of environmental management are available for most major oil and gas companies, automotive companies, utilities, and other industries with high levels of environmental impact. But commentaries on ratings and reporting continue to emphasize that too many companies have not identified what their key sustainability issues are, or how they most affect the environment.[15] The information available is synthesized by ratings organizations, but there has been little attempt to assess the overall impact of corporate responsibility on key areas of environmental management. Furthermore, the data highlight trends (e.g. the year-on-year percentage change in a particular performance area), but do little to show what is the 'right' number, such as the level of carbon dioxide emissions that is ultimately acceptable or the amount of water usage needed to maintain a certain ecosystem. Indeed, companies have tended to shy away from this type of claim. Failure to gauge systemic impact will become a more important issue as certain approaches are accepted as best practice, something that is already evident in the questions being posed about carbon trading.[16]

Discussion points

Companies seem to have made most progress in demonstrating their environmental impact.

- How far do you think the experience with environmental impact is a forerunner for what we will see with social and economic impact? What do you think the possible differences are?
- What are the weaknesses in our understanding of environmental impact at present?
- What is the most important thing that a company can do to have a positive impact on public trust in its environmental performance?

Social impact

Social impact includes such issues as human rights, working conditions, labour rights, the impact on indigenous peoples, and the impact on local communities. As already noted, this is a more recent development than that of environmental management and, not surprisingly, there are fewer data on impact. But the different ways that companies have a social impact are also less well understood, and certainly less comprehensively reported on. In an industry such as horticulture, for example, extended production times, piecework, short-term contracts, and job insecurity have all come to be seen as necessary for competitiveness and, in so far as these are poorly addressed, corporate responsibility protections can appear as a shield for deflecting attention from the most profound social impacts.

Although companies such as Anglo American, with its Socio-Economic Assessment Toolbox (SEAT), have been lauded for developing tools designed to fully understand their social impact, overall there has been a focus on particular aspects, with the adoption of labour standards in supply chains becoming a significant component of corporate responsibility. Vogel's (2005) comprehensive review of the literature concluded that there had been little systematic analysis of the impact on workers and their families, but a study of 800 suppliers in 51 countries concluded that if monitoring of labour conditions were to be accompanied by other interventions (e.g. improved factory management), there would be significant improvements for workers.[17] A multi-country empirical study of the impact of monitoring a voluntary labour standard endorsed by major companies in the UK showed that conditions in some places had improved (especially with regard to health and safety, and child labour), but there had been little effect on wages or freedom of association, and some improvements had even left workers worse off (e.g. a decline in take-home pay because of reduced working hours).[18] However, the study by Nelson et al. (2007) of South African wine producers and Kenyan cut flower producers, in which firms that had adopted voluntary labour codes of practice were compared with those that had not, shows that working conditions and standards of living were higher amongst workers in the former than in the latter. The apparel industry, in particular, has made significant advances in driving out child labour, and the ILO says that child labour fell by 11 per cent during the period 2000–2004. However, there is also evidence that removing children from an export-oriented factory can be a mixed benefit if other opportunities are worse, or if opportunities for education decrease. In fact, the net impact can be that Western consumers have their demand for goods produced by adult labour fulfilled, but there is no change in the numbers of working children.[19]

Exploring labour conditions in Indonesia, Harrison and Scorse (2004) conclude that codes of labour conduct, together with anti-sweatshop campaigns, were responsible for increasing wages in export-oriented factories during the 1990s and, moreover, that this was achieved without reducing employment opportunities. This finding is interesting because of the large dataset with which they had to work, but smaller studies can also be insightful. For example, data from 142 southern Chinese factories audited by Verité in 2002–2003 revealed excessive overtime in 93 per cent of cases, supporting the findings of Impactt Ltd that compliance-focused auditing of labour conditions has had little impact on improving working hours. As ETI remarked in its 2003/2004 report, improved compliance with codes is not necessarily a sign of sustained improvements in labour practice and may only mean that suppliers are becoming better at passing audits. A glance at the most recent ETI report bears this out, stressing as it does the importance of worker training and capacity building amongst suppliers in order for codes of conduct to be effective.[20]

This is probably truer for some aspects of social performance than it is for others. For example, although there may be little sign that workers are receiving true living wages because of corporate responsibility, Vogel (2005) concludes that there are attributable signs of improvements in working conditions, and ETI's annual reports consistently show that the majority of non-compliances detected and addressed relate to workplace health and safety. Although this has been derided for being a simple target in terms of the greater corporate responsibility challenge, when one considers that, in 2005 in China, based only on official figures, there were a quarter of a million workplace accidents and over 126,000 deaths,[21] advances in working conditions are a significant achievement.

But companies are frequently not making data about social impact available. According to Ruggie et al. (2006), only one company—BP—has made public the findings of a human rights impact assessment. Likewise, companies may admit to the need for public reporting on all material aspects of their performance, but this does not mean that they are consistently reporting on the benefits of programmes with potentially significant social impact, such as those in the pharmaceutical industry to combat HIV/AIDS in poor countries.[22] This reinforces the impression noted earlier that many companies are not systematically identifying key issues.

The picture is not necessarily clearer when one examines niche areas of corporate responsibility with explicit social objectives. A series of case studies comparing the social impact of fairtrade, organic farming, and forest certification projects found that they increased livelihood opportunities and income levels for many participants, and provided access to new markets and the opportunity to develop human and social capital.[23] However, the studies also showed that certain groups of people can be excluded, projects can have negative impacts on those not participating in them, and, ultimately, that the most significant long-term determinants of success are factors that are not normally considered to be part of corporate responsibility, such as building the capacity to run a business, overcoming trade barriers, and lowering entry barriers to new markets. Similar findings emerged from a meta-analysis of fairtrade case studies (Nelson and Pound, 2009).[24]

The insights offered by case studies, such as those available on Rio Tinto's website, suggest that individual company programmes are having positive impacts for local communities. However, in areas such as human rights and security, the consequences for local communities of voluntary principles and other corporate responsibility approaches will always be difficult to measure, while the outcomes of actions such as investing or disinvesting, which may even be a consequence of corporate responsibility policies, are not normally being addressed. Moreover, as Rajak's (2008) study of corporate responsibility amongst mining communities reveals, companies may redefine what they mean by corporate responsibility and hence what they consider to be legitimate impacts.

Economic impact

The distinction between social and economic impact is to some degree artificial; after all, what is the economy if it is not part of society, and hence a social institution? Polanyi (1944) argued that a well-functioning society is one where economic activity aligns with that of society, and Ruggie (2003) believes that embedding the economy in this way is something that companies and governments should strive for, not least through corporate responsibility. Nonetheless, corporate responsibility practice and theory still often make a distinction between the social and the economic.[25] There are case studies that seek to test models for defining the meaning of economic impact,[26] and companies such as Unilever and SAB Miller have commissioned studies to examine the economic impact of their operations.[27] Mining companies such as Anglo American and Rio Tinto have also begun to examine the economic impacts of their investments in local communities.[28]

Mainstream companies tend to think of economic impact as the consequences of the conduct of their normal business operations. In contrast, there are alternative business models where the rationale for the operation itself is that it is an effective means for contributing to the social good. Amongst the best-known examples of this are fairtrade and microfinance, as well as a large number of organizations that fall under the social entrepreneurship umbrella (see Chapter 11). Such enterprises are looking further afield than before to raise capital, and new investor interest in knowing about impact has led to the creation of impact analysis tools such as GOODadviser. Nonetheless, social and environmentally focused enterprises are still at the experimental stage of impact assessment. An early overview of microfinance found that to the extent that the impact was known, the poor benefited, but to a limited extent,[29] and according to the latest studies this situation has not changed.[30] Awareness that social goals are not being managed has led to the belated creation of the Imp-Act Consortium to promote social performance measurement in the microfinance community.

The situation is similar with the equally well-established approach called fairtrade. Fairtrade is often held up as a clear example of the kind of economic impact that corporate responsibility has brought, particularly relating to the economic condition of producers in poor countries. In impact assessments, a number of proxies for economic benefit for such producers are used. These include the growth in the volume of fairtrade produce, the increase in the number of producer groups, sales outlets, and importing organizations, and the ability of fairtrade to maintain a floor price that is equivalent to the cost of production.[31] For example, the fairtrade price for coffee in 2003 was $1.26 per pound compared with $0.82 per pound on the world market. However, as the fairtrade company Traidcraft recognizes, sales volume and market growth are not necessarily synonymous with the benefit brought to poor producers, and in its award-winning social accounts it looks at the value of purchases, the sales of goods from developing countries, and the percentage of cost of sales spent in developing countries' volume of sales, revealing, for example, that not only have sales of products from developing countries increased, but that the money spent there has risen from £2 million in 2001 to £3.4 million in 2005.

Case studies of producer groups around the world show that the fairtrade price for farmers can be significantly higher than that available on conventional markets. For example, a study of seven cooperatives found that the price to farmers was twice the world price and three times that paid by local traders, while in Ethiopia fairtrade producers receive 70 per cent of the export price compared with 30 per cent for coffee sold on conventional markets.[32] And even when fairtrade only results in modest increases in per capita incomes, this can be the difference between destitution and survival.[33] However, overall information on the actual impact that fairtrade has on individual producers is scarce,[34] and may be funded by the fairtrade industry.[35] Independent studies have shown that Fairtrade's tag line, 'Guarantees a better deal for third world producers', is hard to substantiate on the ground, with some people excluded and certain types of priority projects for communities not being delivered.[36] Furthermore, the main case study in this chapter draws out some of the difficulties of measuring fairtrade's impact, and how impact on the intended beneficiaries can be overlooked (see Case Study 12). Filling this kind of information gap will be a challenge for corporate responsibility more widely in the coming years.

 Discussion points

Economic impact is something that has started to appear in some corporate responsibility reports.

- What distinguishes 'economic impact' from financial performance?
- What are the ways in which a company has an economic impact?
- Using the Unilever–Oxfam study of impact in Indonesia as a basis (Clay, 2005), how would you develop this into a framework for understanding economic impact in another industry?

Impact and the business case

The majority of impact studies since the 1970s have concentrated on corporate responsibility's relationship with financial performance, and major studies conclude that there is not a strong correlation between doing well financially and doing good for society.[37] But making the business case for corporate responsibility has remained relevant (see Chapter 6), setting corporate responsibility apart from other areas of management[38] even though the rationale for expecting investments in corporate responsibility demonstrably to create shareholder value when other business investments are not held to the same standard is certainly questionable.

This is not the result of any conspiracy by the anti-corporate-responsibility groupings. In fact it as much as anything a result of developments within corporate responsibility. The socially responsible investment movement, in order to distinguish itself from the conventional investment world, has sought to establish a link between wealth creation and the way in which companies address social and environmental issues. SRI performance is discussed in Chapter 10, but overall it is hard to conclude that many firms have been rewarded or punished by investors for their social/environmental performance.[39]

There are other ways of examining corporate responsibility's outcomes from a business case perspective, as we explore in Chapter 6. There is a fair amount of anecdotal evidence that employees and prospective applicants value corporate responsibility and a company's overall image, although there has not yet been a definitive analysis of this. At times, it becomes personal and there is some evidence that employees of companies such as Nike and Dow decided to change attitudes inside their companies after too many taunts about their companies' reputations made over the barbecue grill.[40]

The financial return on corporate responsibility can also be seen, to some degree, in its impact on consumer behaviour. Smith (2003) argues that corporate responsibility has helped companies to avert boycotts of brands and has increased consumer loyalty. We have already mentioned the emergence of corporate responsibility labelling, such as FSC, Rugmark, and Fairtrade, and reputation surveys such as Covalence's EthicalQuote.com demonstrate how companies such as Marks & Spencer can gain global reputation advantages through successful corporate responsibility initiatives.

As described in Chapter 6, the strongest link between financial and non-financial performance is probably the impact of corporate responsibility on environmental management. The often significant improvements in eco-efficiency environmental management that we cited earlier are largely attributed to their neutral or positive impact on the financial bottom line. Company reports provide a wealth of case study material in this area, although, as noted earlier, many companies are not rigorous when it comes to identifying the most material issues for their business and therefore it can be hard to conclude if they are addressing genuine priorities, or simply those that are the most financially advantageous. Wal-Mart is one company that has tried to identify its major environmental impact and develop actions to tangibly reduce them, in the process making considerable savings from waste reduction, less energy consumption, and more efficient management processes. Furthermore, Wal-Mart has had a considerable impact on its supply chain, forcing suppliers to rethink their environmental practices as a condition of continued business.

There is a question as to whether this same kind of positive financial link can be made for areas of social performance. There are numerous individual cases in which companies have stressed that there is money to be made from tackling social needs (e.g. from Vodafone's targeting of the migrant remittance market, valued at $270 billion, to Innocent's growth to become an £80 million business in ethical smoothies, now wholly owned by Coca-Cola).[41] Vogel (2008) says that there are noteworthy examples of US-based companies with a good reputation for corporate responsibility that have fared poorly in leveraging this for improving financial performance (e.g. Starbucks, Gap, Timberland). Collinson has developed and tested a methodology for assessing the business costs of ethical supply chain management, and some consultancy firms, such as Cost Benefit Systems, have product offerings that claim to demonstrate the return on investment of corporate responsibility activities.[42] In general, however, this remains an unexplored area.

While most companies emphasize the financial–ethical win–win outcomes brought by corporate responsibility, Cooperative Financial Services in the UK is exceptional in that it reports on the business opportunities foregone as a result of applying its ethical principles. Although this is widely admired, it might also only be possible because of the organization's cooperative status, and a publicly held company might face legal action if it appeared to be breaking its fiduciary obligations by disclosing this type of business decision.

Discussion points

Margolis and Walsh (2003) say that, because companies are so focused on understanding the instrumental benefits, they may never tackle some of the key impacts they have on society.

- Do you think that this argument is valid?

- Give examples in which society in general might want a company to have an impact, although there may not be a clear business case.

- Under what conditions do you think companies will take action if there is not a business case?

Impact on business attitudes, awareness, and practices

A very important part of the impact of corporate responsibility in recent years has been the way in which it has affected business thinking and practice. Wood (2000) expressed surprise at how quickly corporate responsibility practice had caught up with theory, and Kanter (2009) provides examples supporting her argument that managing social good is now key to future business success. We have already noted the large percentage of the Global Fortune 250 companies reporting on corporate responsibility, and in some countries this growth is also evident amongst small and medium-sized companies.[43]

Although there may be many companies that have still to commit to corporate responsibility, and the uptake is stronger in certain sectors and types of firm (e.g. export-oriented companies, or those with a high public profile),[44] there has been a significant change in awareness and behaviour. It was hard to imagine, as little as five years ago, a company declaring a five-year plan addressing health, working conditions, climate change, waste, and sustainable raw materials, yet this is what UK-based retailer Marks & Spencer did, in 2007, in its Plan A programme. Few major multinational companies with extensive supply chains would now deny that they have a responsibility for the social and environmental performance within those chains—a marked change from the situation in the early 1990s. Not only have they introduced standards for their vendors in areas as diverse as resource management, good agricultural practice, bribery and corruption, human rights, and labour practices, but these have also evolved over time, in terms of both their content and their overall implementation. For example, despite predictions that a large number of labour standards might lead to contentious issues being omitted,[45] in reality competition has largely mitigated against weak standards and to a degree disingenuous monitoring.[46] A similar trend has been observed in the field of forest management standards. Although there is some evidence that companies pick and choose which standard to join based on how stringent or lax it is perceived to be,[47] standards as a form of industry self-regulation have largely been welcomed by non-commercial stakeholders, with examples including the Kimberly Process Certification Scheme (diamonds), the World Gold Council, and the Responsible Jewellery Council. Furthermore, companies that do not participate in credible voluntary standards for their industry can attract criticism in their own right, as has happened to Littlewoods, BHS, and Topshop, which have refused to join initiatives backed by other major UK retailers, and to Boots, which left the Ethical Trading Initiative after it was bought up by the private equity firm KKR.

The successful use of particular corporate responsibility approaches in one industry appears to encourage other industries to become engaged. For example, the model for managing palm oil developed by the Roundtable on Sustainable Palm Oil has been repli-cated in the Roundtable on Sustainable Soy Association and the Better Sugarcane Initiative. Early thinking that corporate responsibility would somehow be part of the comparative advantage of individual firms has largely been displaced by a belief in the greater poten-tial of shared learning and joint initiatives. Thus, for example, leading organizations behind international labour codes of conduct—such as the Workers' Rights Consortium, the Social Accountability International, the Fair Wear Foundation, and the Clean Clothes Campaign—are collaborating in the Joint Initiative on Corporate Accountability and Workers' Rights to develop common guidelines on aspects of monitoring and implementing the provisions of voluntary codes of labour practice. The Equator Principles for managing the social and envi-ronmental dimensions of project financing in developing countries are the result of a part-nership between a range of major financial institutions. There are also a growing number of examples of global framework agreements between international unions and multinational companies.

It is not only that the number of corporate responsibility initiatives has grown, but there are also clear signs of learning, in terms of both how to implement corporate responsi-bility and what issues can, or should, be considered. The Ethical Trading Initiative is an interesting example of how a corporate responsibility initiative can influence companies and change their practices in different ways. ETI's impact on workers is not straightforward (see Snapshot 12.1), but ETI can also claim to have had the following types of impact on company behaviour:

1 improving the knowledge of its member organizations and others about how to monitor labour conditions among suppliers;
2 improving knowledge about what to monitor and what the elements of the chains are (e.g. that there are homeworkers and smallholder farmers, as well as large factories and commercial farms, who are parts of the supply chain);
3 raising member companies' awareness of labour rights issues;
4 influencing legislation (e.g. ETI played an important role in the UK Gangmasters (Licensing) Act 2004);
5 increasing the overall level of monitoring of overseas suppliers;
6 building the capacity of companies and others to implement voluntary labour standards.

Furthermore, there are measurable outcomes in support of some of the above claims, such as changes in buyer behaviour as they integrate labour rights into their business practices, exam-ples of terminating business relations with persistently non-compliant suppliers, increased ability to identify non-compliance in factories, and the integration of labour standards into supplier contracts.

Public commitments to future actions within a certain timeframe are another indication of changing behaviour. While ExxonMobil is said to emit a world-leading 146 million tonnes of carbon dioxide a year, BP set itself the target of reducing emissions in the late 1990s, and is now almost twice as efficient, emitting 261 tonnes of carbon dioxide per million dollars in sales compared with ExxonMobil's 436 tonnes. In 2007, Toyota committed itself to reduc-ing its emission by 20 per cent by 2010, and in its 2012 sustainability report announced

Snapshot 12.1 The impact of ethical trading on workers

In 2002, the Ethical Trading Initiative commissioned a three-year, three-country impact assessment study that is one of the first in-depth empirical studies of how voluntary labour codes affect the lives of workers and their communities. The findings on the impact of the codes at the worker level were mixed, as can be seen from the comparison of workplaces in three countries (see Table 12.1).

Table 12.1 Summary of impacts by ETI Base Code principle at Country Study supply sites

Base Code principle	South Africa (6 worksites)		Vietnam (6 worksites)		India (6 worksites)	
	Mgmt	Mgmt	Wkrs	Mgmt	Wkrs	Wkrs
Freedom of employment	None	None	None	None	None	None
Freedom of association	None	None	None	Minor	None	None
Health and safety	Minor	Minor	Major	Major	Major	Major
Child labour	Minor*	Minor*	Minor*	Minor	Minor	None
Living wage	Minor	None	Minor	Minor	Minor	Minor
Working hours	None	None	Major	Major*	Minor	Minor*
Discrimination	Minor	None	Minor	Minor	Minor	None
Regular employment	None	None	Minor	None	Minor	Minor
Harsh treatment	Minor	None	None	None	Minor	Minor

Mgmt, Management; Wkrs, Workers

*Impacts that were considered negative by some respondents

(*Source:* Adapted from Barrientos, S. and Smith, S. 2007, 'Do workers benefit from ethical trade? Assessing codes of labour practice in global production systems', *Third World Quarterly*, vol. 28, no. 4, pp 713–729. With permission from Taylor & Francis Ltd, www.informaworld.com)

Table 12.1 shows the mix of outcomes. For instance, reduction in working hours or the introduction of health and safety precautions at over half the sites constitutes a major change, whereas the introduction of age documentation or the correct payment of annual leave observed at a few sites is a minor change. In some instances, seemingly positive impacts were viewed as negative by at least some workers (e.g. because a reduction in working hours resulted in a decrease in take-home pay).

Overall, the assessment shows that ETI has brought demonstrable impacts, notably under the provisions on health and safety, and on legal employment entitlements such as the minimum wage, working hours, and deductions for employment benefits such as health insurance and pensions. At

(continued...)

most workplaces, workers' physical and social well-being has been enhanced through health and safety improvements and reductions in working hours. Other improvements may have occurred prior to the study; for instance, the assessment did not discover any child labour. Some improvements were limited to certain types of worker, so that, for example, there was evidence of improvement in the treatment of permanent and regular workers, but contract labour was still poorly treated in most countries.

However, there were other areas where the impact was either mixed or unclear. For example, the ETI has not led to a substantial increase in income in terms of guaranteeing a living wage, and there are workplaces where use of an ETI-based code of conduct has led to a reduction in working hours and a resultant decrease in take-home pay (although this is not necessarily considered a negative outcome if there are other benefits such as more leisure time). Also, ETI has not had an impact on underlying patterns of employment related to gender, ethnicity, caste, and religion, although there is evidence of a connection to certain changes in relation to discrimination in some locations (e.g. employment benefits to women, access to training and promotion). There is an emerging awareness in the ETI that these and other apparently intractable issues ultimately depend on achieving a balance between company power over suppliers, and empowerment of workers to have greater control over their lives. Hence, it is not enough to enforce codes; instead, there is a parallel need to help build the capacity of workers and other local agents to implement a sustainable system of monitoring, enforcement, and remediation.

(*Sources:* Barrientos and Smith 2007; Blowfield, 2007)

Quick questions

1 What are the most important impacts of ETI?

2 What are the major areas of disappointment?

3 How can ETI improve its impact in the future?

that emissions had been reduced by 6,700 tons.[48] The company spends about 14 per cent of its annual capital investment on sustainable options such as alternative fuels and new technologies. Wal-Mart spends notably less (about 3 per cent of capital expenditure), but its public commitment could have a significant impact on the behaviour of consumers and suppliers.[49]

Examples of how corporate responsibility has affected attitudes and behaviour are to be found throughout this book, even if the recent safety scandals affecting BP and Toyota show that positive change in one area may not be repeated in another. What we want to emphasize here is that this is an important element of corporate responsibility's impact. Overall, corporate responsibility has increased awareness of, and spawned initiatives to address, issues as diverse as corruption, international development, labour rights, global warming, human rights, environmental management, and sustainable resourcing (see Snapshot 12.2). It has raised the profile of long-established concerns, such as workplace health and safety, diversity, and discrimination, especially in suppliers' facilities. It has turned these issues into ones of legitimate business interest, even if it has not always found effective ways of addressing them (or, as importantly, has not yet been able to demonstrate its effectiveness). Its impact has been recognized in countries such as China, where corporate responsibility has become

something of a buzzword.[50] In recent years, the appearance in corporate responsibility discussions of corporate taxation, company valuation, responsibilities to women, the role of small producers, the place of local suppliers and small retailers, the terms of trading, and other topics has shown that new issues continue to be recognized, even if it is less clear if and how they can be addressed from within a corporate responsibility framework.

However, it is also important to acknowledge the limits of this impact (see Snapshot 12.2). Some companies are clearly very responsive, others are less so, and some hardly at all. Despite corporate responsibility reporting becoming the norm amongst major companies, the geographical spread is inconsistent, and, as noted, FTSE4Good has expressed concern about the lack of uptake in the USA, other than by its leading multinational companies. The relationship between corporate responsibility as management practice in medium-sized firms remains problematic (see Chapter 11). Equally, most social and environmental standards apply to

 Snapshot 12.2 Levi's and China

Levi Strauss, producer of Levi's jeans and Dockers, sources much of its product from China. In that, it is no different from numerous other global clothing brands such as GAP, Abercrombie & Fitch, or Ralph Lauren. But Levi's relationship with China is more complicated than most, and highlights many of the tensions between competitiveness and responsibility.

In the early 1990s, Levi's was one of several companies exploring the possibility of sourcing from China's emergent garment sector. Low-cost labour, favourable tax and excise regimes, and reliable infrastructure were amongst the attractions. But politically China was a closed country; a single-party state with a poor record on human rights. On issues from freedom of speech to the death penalty to forced pregnancy testing of workers, Chinese practices seemed to jar with Levi's commitment to being a values-centred business. It had a big manufacturing base in the USA where its factories were held to be amongst the best employers in their sector, but the tariffs that helped make domestic production competitive were being phased out.

Levi's went into China hesitantly, making it clear that it expected all suppliers to abide by its Global Sourcing Guidelines that set out how workers should be treated. But by 1993, it was clear that 'pervasive human rights abuses' were taking place, and the company decided to phase out most of its operations. The move was heralded as a victory for values-driven business, but in the following years Levi's looked less of a leader than an isolated figure as its competitors poured ever more investment into China.

In 1998, Levi Strauss announced it would be expanding output in China once again. Company President, Peter Jacobi, said '*Levi Strauss is not in the human rights business*', adding, '*It is clear to us that the environment is getting better there.*' However, the question in labour activists' minds was whether he meant the human rights environment, or the consumer market as Levi's found itself losing out to Lee and Esprit in the battle to win the hearts of China's new middle class.

PS: Levi Strauss closed its last US factory in 2002.

(*Sources:* Beaver, 1995; Landler, 1998; Colwell, 2002)

Quick questions

1 What does Levi's decision tell us about corporate responsibility's impact?

2 Would keeping production in the USA be more 'responsible'?

3 Should companies be in the 'human rights business'?

export-oriented production, and the impact of corporate responsibility on the behaviour of producers for domestic markets (the majority) is unknown. Moreover, it might remain difficult to implement standards effectively, even in export sectors, because auditing capacity is not keeping up with demand[51] and its quality has been criticized, not least by companies.[52]

Companies that are well-ranked in corporate responsibility awards may be open to criticism for particular aspects of their performance. For example, MITIE, a company that has prospered from undermining workers' pay and conditions, was a top category winner in the 2013 Business in the Community responsible business awards, and Citigroup, which was at the heart of funding the sub-prime mortgages that forced many poor people into bankruptcy, won an award for its work on poverty alleviation. Earlier, Fortis NV, Royal Bank of Scotland, Citigroup, and HBOS had been recognized as 'sustainability leaders' but were either out of business or dependent on government bail-outs a year later.[53] BP was long held up as a leader in the area of sustainability because of its work on rethinking energy, but its slogan 'Bringing oil to American shores' took on a very different meaning when the Deepwater Horizon rig caused human and environmental devastation in the Gulf of Mexico.

Such examples raise major questions about analysis of corporate responsibility information, and the usefulness of the data companies provide. Many companies do not make available the information that would help others to assess the degree and effectiveness of their commitment. Similarly, belonging to a partnership means very little if the quality and nature of that partnership is unclear. There is some evidence that partnerships with members from different sectors of society are associated with stronger corporate responsibility performance, compared with those that only involve business, although the latter are still more effective than when companies work on their own. As Chapter 9 explores in more detail, however, it is still uncertain what constitutes a successful partnership and how this can be evaluated.

A standard such as the AA1000 Stakeholder Engagement Standard goes some way towards assessing the process of effectively implementing corporate responsibility, although it has been criticized for not taking power relations seriously. Methodologies used by some of the ratings indices also seek to value the degree to which corporate responsibility is embedded in companies, a question that was also central to a 2007 European study of 200 organizations which concluded that managers were tied to a fairly conservative view of corporate responsibility, focusing on avoiding negative impacts rather than opportunities to have a positive impact.[54]

Overall, therefore, although there have been changes in company behaviour, we are still a long way from understanding, or being able to compare, the relative effectiveness of companies' different approaches. Perhaps this is nowhere more evident than in the extent that success in non-financial performance is a feature of individual performance reviews. Fifty FTSE 100 companies now use a non-financial measure in their annual bonus schemes, but none of them uses more than one measure, and only 7 per cent factor such measures into long-term incentive plans.[55]

Impact on other stakeholders

A further way to look at the impact of corporate responsibility is to look at its outcomes for others in society. For example, we mentioned earlier the growing number of framework agreements between international trade unions and multinational companies that, at least

Discussion points

One area of corporate responsibility in which there appears to have been significant changes is in terms of management awareness and attitude.

- Is it valid to regard these changes as indicators that corporate responsibility is bringing about wider changes?
- Is it more important to understand this type of change in the context of some companies rather than that of others?
- How would you set about measuring and communicating this type of change to external stakeholders?

indirectly, seem to relate to a rising awareness of corporate responsibility. Furthermore, after years of declining union strength, particularly in developed economies, union recognition agreements are part of the criteria used in ratings indices such as FTSE4Good.

There is mixed evidence about the impact that corporate responsibility has had on consumers, with some citing evidence of their willingness to pay higher prices for improved working conditions, while others suggest that attributes unrelated to corporate responsibility, such as customer satisfaction and financial performance, ultimately have more influence on a company's reputation.[56] Environmental and health issues have affected branding, even if there are differences of opinion about what an 'ethical brand' is. A positive relationship between corporate responsibility and purchasing decisions might be expected, but measuring the related benefits seems difficult and a company's reputation can vary greatly from country to country (see Box 12.3). Moreover, when consumers become suspicious

Box 12.3 Country variations in ratings of brand reputation

France	UK
1 Danone	1 Co-op
2 adidas	2 Body Shop
3 Nike	3 Marks & Spencer
4 Nestlé	4 Traidcraft
5 Renault	5 Cafédirect and Ecover
Germany	**USA**
1 adidas	1 Nike
2 Nike	2 PepsiCo
3 Puma	3 Procter and Gamble
4 BMW	4 Prudential Insurance
5 Demeter	5 Sony Playstation

(*Sources:* Werther and Chandler, 2011; Grande, 2007)

about the benefits of ethical consumption, they may change their behaviour, as seems to have happened with the hitherto high-flying sales of organic foods in the UK which fell by 5 per cent in 2008–2009.[57]

Corporate responsibility has an impact on the investment community, as evidenced by the growth in socially responsible investment (see Chapter 10) and the appointment of ESG specialists by banks such as UBS. It has also had some success in persuading students to think more critically about the role of business, rather than simply criticizing companies. For example, NetImpact claims a 15,000 strong network of members, primarily MBA and graduate students seeking to use the power of business to improve the world, and it will be interesting to see if this less aggressive approach will prove more sustainable than, for example, the Workers Rights Consortium, which, despite having used college campuses to affect corporate behaviour, has struggled to maintain more than a handful of its 140 college chapters.[58] Business-oriented web-based resources, such as GreenBiz, and less structured web-based networks, such as the 1300-member CSR Chicks listserv, have also become ways in which corporate responsibility both influences people and is sustained.

The impact of corporate responsibility can also be seen in aspects of government. The UK briefly had a minister for corporate responsibility, and corporate responsibility has been recognized in legislation in both France and the UK. In Brazil, the government officials who have played a major role in that country's relatively effective approach to slowing deforestation often came out of the FSC organization there. Corporate responsibility's impact is felt in the EU Accounts Modernisation Directive, which requires that directors' reports contain a business review including information that is material to the well-being of the environment, communities, and employees.

The impact of corporate responsibility on itself

Over the past few years, there have been significant changes in how we conceive of, and conduct, corporate responsibility and, in any discussion of impact, we should not ignore how the experience of addressing corporate responsibility has affected the evolution of corporate responsibility itself. Earlier, we mentioned an expansion in the range of issues that fall within the, at least theoretical, purview of corporate responsibility. By comparing the initial GRI Guidelines with its two subsequent iterations in 2002 and 2006, we can see how the range of criteria for reporting on sustainability has been extended, the indicators used in measurement have become more sophisticated, and the advice on using the guidelines has expanded (e.g. the guidance on sustainability reporting for small and medium-sized enterprises). Similarly, the AA1000 series relating to stakeholder engagement has been through several modifications since its launch in 1999, incorporating the experiences of its users and others.

Moreover, the experience of one initiative affects others. For example, national social and environment standards, such as those of the Wine Industry Ethical Trade Association in South Africa or the Agricultural Ethics Assurance Association of Zimbabwe, have been strongly influenced by European initiatives. It is interesting to note how what were once contentious issues have been adopted, even to the point of being considered corporate responsibility best practice. There were concerns that codes of labour practice would be more likely to address issues that damaged a company's reputation (e.g. child labour, health and safety) than those that were opposed by management (e.g. freedom of association, collective bargaining), but while some rights have proved easier to address than others, in general the most credible and influential initiatives have proved to be those that set the bar relatively high. This has remained the case even when companies have collaborated to reduce the costs of implementing standards, such as the Global Social Compliance Programme involving Migros, Ikea, Tesco, and others. Even issues that were once regarded as leading edge or contentious, have started to filter into the mainstream. For example, advocates of more local involvement and capacity building in implementing social and environmental standards have seen some of their demands begin to be accommodated, as have groups wanting attention paid to the specific conditions of homeworkers.

This is not to say that there is a virtuous race to the top. Some projects seeking to extend the boundaries of corporate responsibility, such as the Sigma Project in the UK to benchmark sustainability, have failed despite their close links with other corporate responsibility actors and initiatives. The Race to the Top project, coordinated by the International Institute for Environment and Development, brought together NGOs, trade unions, and UK retailers to track what supermarkets are doing to promote a greener and fairer food system, but ended in 2003.[59] Beyond the UK, the Global Alliance for Workers and Communities, established by major US companies and NGOs to help empower workers, also withered away after failing to win long-term support.

The challenges of determining impact

The picture that emerges is that measuring corporate responsibility's impact is as difficult today as it was in the past. There are three main reasons for this, each of which we examine in this section:

1 the practical challenges of assessing impact;
2 the problem of what to measure;
3 the question of in whose interests it is to understand impact.

There are three main sources of information on impact: ratings indices, corporate reports, and case studies of individual companies, industries, or locations. These are self-referential to a large degree in that, for example, researchers compiling ratings will use corporate reports and case studies, in addition to other sources of information, while the report may allude to the company's rating as a performance indicator. A fundamental difficulty is that the basic data needed to assess impact are often lacking because, for example, the company has not properly identified its key issues, or has not reported on them in a clear and consistent fashion. But ratings indices can exacerbate this problem by the a priori assumption that they make about outcomes and causal relations. For example, they assume that the outcome of a blend of stakeholder participation and rigorous social or environmental standards will be better working conditions, sustainable fisheries, etc. Consequently, what is measured is more likely to be the criteria of the standard and indicators for the partnership, rather than an attempt to examine the contribution that such a combination makes towards those bigger goals.

Mattingly and Berman (2006) argue that some ratings indices make incorrect assumptions about associations between different types of social action and that, because they do not properly recognize the context within which actions take place, they end up rewarding actions that appear to be proactive, but are not especially laudable (e.g. those that are easily solved problems or easily achieved targets). In doing so, they overlook those that may appear weak or reactive, but which are actually impressive if the context is understood (e.g. becoming a pioneer in tackling hazardous waste in an otherwise unresponsive industry).

Ratings indices continue to evolve and some of the above limitations may be overcome. For example, the Enhanced Analytics Initiative seeks to redress some of the current information gaps by encouraging quality long-term research, which considers material extra-financial issues that can be used by sell-side analysts. In 2006, the Center for Sustainable Innovation in Vermont, USA, launched Social Footprint to assess the degree to which corporate responsibility contributes to true sustainability. Trucost Ltd, a London financial research firm, has also launched TrueVa (True Valuation) to measure companies' overall value added by subtracting from the firm's operating surplus not only its costs of capital, but also the environmental damage that it imposes elsewhere in the economy.

Nonetheless, ratings indices and other attempts to synthesize company performance are hampered by a strong dependency on case studies, including those from companies, in media stories, and in academic or other reports. There is a tendency for organizations to choose the case study which best tells the story they want to communicate, but even in instances in which that is not true, taken together, case studies do not have the consistency of approach to constitute a systematic body of evidence, or, if taken individually, may not have the necessary depth from which to draw wider conclusions. This is starting to change as impact assessments about particular corporate responsibility approaches and initiatives begin to appear. Two early assessments by business and academics observed that increased incomes alone did not prove that people were better off, and that factors that are harder to measure, such as terms of trade and building strong local institutions, were important. Equally, standards did not adequately capture local people's concerns and priorities.[60] Moreover, even if researchers know what information to gather, there are challenges in obtaining it, either because of the risk of false documents and of respondents who are reluctant to talk honestly or openly, or because of the sheer size of company operations.[61] And when the data are reliable, it can still be difficult to demonstrate whether an action or outcome is the result of corporate responsibility, or of some other event, such as changes in local laws or improved enforcement.[62]

An alternative approach would be to assign a monetary value to particular outcomes such as generating income for the poor. For example, a dollar paid to someone earning just two dollars a day can be predicted to have far greater impact than the same amount paid to someone earning $100 a day. Therefore, one could assign extra value to the dollar paid to the poor person, for example three dollars. Consequently, a million dollars paid to genuinely poor people could be calculated as having a social worth of three million dollars. Such figures could be included in income statements in annual reports, which would then include, in addition to total revenues, total costs, and net income, the value of external benefits, the external costs of greenhouse gas emissions, etc. While this would undoubtedly be controversial, it highlights the importance of the issues raised in Chapter 8 about how we account for corporate responsibility.

Another challenge is how to measure and assess the effectiveness of initiatives that are intended to encourage learning about how to tackle large issues, rather than to have a direct demonstrable impact on those issues themselves. For example, the UN Global Compact highlights how about half of its signatory companies have changed their policies to reflect the Compact's principles and the high level of managers' recognition of the Compact's role as a catalyst for change (see Chapter 5). But relatively few companies have participated in the Compact's learning forums, raising questions about whether participation in the network is responsible for these outcomes.[63]

Ultimately, it could be that companies are producing the wrong kind of data, focusing on outputs and activities when stakeholders want information on outcomes.[64] Yet the type of information that is required depends on knowing who is really interested in corporate responsibility's impact. It is quite possible to argue that it is not in the self-interest of certain stakeholder groups, with a significant influence on corporate responsibility, to gain a more sophisticated understanding of the impact of corporate responsibility practice. Groups such as worker or environmental activists have particular short-term aims when collecting data and may not be motivated to monitor a particular company over the longer term.[65] Professional monitors, on the other hand, have an interest in building a long-term relationship with a company, but are subject to confidentiality agreements and other restraints on how their data are used. Companies, in turn, may have an interest in selecting what they disclose and to whom, especially when reporting is voluntary or the resource implications of proving a company's impact on societal issues may be too great.[66] Whether from companies or multi-stakeholder partnerships, what is disclosed to the public is often a synthesis of a larger and more complex picture that, according to some, too often requires the public to trust the reporters without providing adequate justification for this trust.[67] Arguably, unless there is a change in how investors value companies, real non-instrumental impact in the sense that Margolis and Walsh (2003) intended is not in the interests of the most influential groups that are engaged in corporate responsibility. That kind of impact may only matter to corporate responsibility's stated beneficiaries, whether these are the poor, the natural environment, the victims of human rights abuses, or future generations. Yet the outcomes of corporate responsibility for this type of stakeholder have still not been thoroughly demonstrated, and it remains an open question whether others are prepared to invest in providing this type of information.

 Case study 12   Can corporate responsibility guarantee an impact?— Fairtrade

'Fairtrade guarantees a better deal for third world producers.' That is the promise made for products— coffee, tea, flowers, bananas, cocoa, etc.—that are certified as fairtrade. So confident are fairtrade advocates of the benefits to poor farmers and workers in developing countries that some claim,

(continued...)

'[companies] can meet some corporate responsibility targets just by changing their coffee'. However, neither individual fairtrade organizations such as Cafédirect nor umbrella organizations such as the Fairtrade Foundation systematically monitor the impact on beneficiaries. Consequently, much of what we know about the impact comes from case studies which are notoriously difficult to compare because of the different methodologies used. A 2009 review of 33 case studies, the majority from coffee growing, found that the majority of farmers earned higher returns and had more stable incomes because of fairtrade, but in other areas such as local democracy and labour rights the evidence was less compelling.

According to the above review, part of the problem is that most case studies provide a snapshot in time, and there are few instances of impact being monitored over a long period. An exception is a recent two-year study of smallholder tea farmers in Kenya. Tea is a good example of where fairtrade should help developing country producers. The tea trade in the West is controlled by seven multinationals companies, and in the UK, the third-largest tea importer in the world, the top three packers currently enjoy a 60 per cent share of the tea market. The power of these companies puts pressure on producer countries to cut costs while improving quality, and to remain competitive. Smallholders, who are affected by poor infrastructure (electricity, roads, and water) and resource constraints (land and capital), face declining prices while wage workers on tea estates face low wages, employment insecurity, and long working hours.

There are various ways that fairtrade seeks to redress this situation, but three of the most important are through better farmgate prices, fostering democratic producer-run institutions, and helping marginalized producers to become more secure. More specifically, to gain fairtrade certification farmers must receive a price that is at least equal to the cost of sustainable production, and farmer organizations must also receive a premium from buyers to be reinvested for the benefit of the community. Equally, the organizations should be democratic and transparent, and not discriminate against any individual or social group. In other words, fairtrade's 'better deal' for producers is predicated on better wages, democracy, and inclusion.

Amongst the Kenya smallholders, there is doubt about the reality of this better deal. During the first three years smallholders sold to fairtrade buyers, there was no price guarantee. When a floor price was introduced in 2008, it was well below the actual market price the farmers were receiving, and there is fear that if they demanded more buyers would switch to other fairtrade farmers in Rwanda and South India where the floor price is much lower.

Nonetheless, the farmer organizations are receiving a separate social premium that has been used for projects such as schools, roads, and dispensaries. Over 80 per cent of smallholders acknowledge the contribution that fairtrade has made, although farmers seem to be happier than farm labourers with the choice of projects. This raises questions about the democratic process within the farmer organizations. Several democratic bodies have been set up, but participation is low, and there is evidence that local power relations have a significant influence on decisions. The challenge of creating effective democratic organizations is apparent if one looks at women in the tea-growing community. Women are responsible for much of the on-farm labour, but account for less than 20 per cent of the 12,000 registered farmers because they are far less likely to own land. Only landowners receive the tea registration number that allows them to vote in the main fairtrade bodies. As a result, the majority of people who produce the tea are excluded from the fairtrade democracy.

The fairtrade movement is starting to recognize that there are important gaps in what is known about impact, and believes that 'a new 'wave' of formal, strategic impact studies and participatory monitoring and evaluation is now underway'. As a recent Fairtrade Foundation press release concluded,

(continued...)

There is an inherent tension faced by fairtrade of using simple and positive messaging to inform consumers about fairtrade whilst recognising and being transparent about the complexities involved in any development intervention. There is no easy solution but furthering understanding of how fairtrade has an impact in different contexts based on the perspectives of farmers and workers is a critical first step along the way.

(Blowfield and Dolan, 2010; Bounds, 2009; Nelson and Pound, 2009)

Questions

1. Fairtrade is perhaps the best-known example of social entrepreneurship.

   a Is fairtrade right to claim that it guarantees a better deal for producers?

   b Has the fairtrade movement paid enough attention to the outcomes for producers?

   c Why has it paid more attention to instrumental indicators such as market growth and consumer interest?

2. Measuring fairtrade's impact on producers is likely to be costly and time-consuming.

   a How important is it to demonstrate the benefits for producers?

   b What might be some more affordable and effective ways to assess impact than multi-year studies?

   c What are the risks of not being able to demonstrate impact?

3. Companies such as Cadbury and Starbucks have committed to putting fairtrade certified commodities into important product lines.

   a What impact are these companies hoping to have?

   b Are they at risk from the current situation regarding impact?

   c Will they have a positive or negative long-term impact on fairtrade?

Summary

Many claims are made about how managing corporate responsibility can help business to have a positive impact through its social, environmental, and economic performance. However, the reality is that the data to demonstrate such impact are lacking and, moreover, collecting and collating such data does not appear to be a priority. This is not to deny the numerous case studies of companies addressing important issues, or the efforts of ratings, surveys, and company reports to demonstrate the efficacy of what companies are doing. But there are deficiencies in each of these sources of information.

There are many levels and categories of impact. Most of what we know about relates to the instrumental benefits of corporate responsibility, i.e. how it affects the financial bottom line. This can be considered a sign of progress, in that it creates a link between good business management and corporate responsibility, but it can also be a cause for concern if it precludes companies from considering actions for which the business case is weak.

Also, much of what we know relates more to activities than it does to outcomes. For example, companies may have environmental policies in place, or may be committed to international standards on corruption, but the actual outcome of these actions is often not known. This is less true of environmental issues than it is of those that are social or economic, and the growing sophistication of some companies' environmental management and reporting is a possible harbinger of the future of corporate responsibility more broadly. Even here, however, there is no clear consensus about what acceptable levels of performance look like, or about how to measure impact beyond the level of the individual company.

It remains an open question as to how the current partial understanding of impact will affect corporate responsibility in the future. Critics are using the lack of information to conclude that corporate responsibility is an inadequate response to tackling the social, governance, and environmental consequences of modern business. There is pressure within corporate responsibility for companies to become more rigorous in terms of what they manage and the targets they set themselves. Ultimately, what we know about impact will depend on the demand for information, and the current situation suggests that the various stakeholders are only beginning to understand what it is that they need to know.

Further reading

online
resource
centre

www.oxfordtextbooks.co.uk/orc/blowfield_murray3e/
Visit the Online Resource Centre that accompanies this book to enrich your understanding of this chapter. Among the resources available are web links, exercises, and additional case studies.

Armendáriz, B. & Morduch, J. 2010, *The economics of microfinance*. MIT Press, Cambridge, MA.
Comprehensive overview of microfinance from its beginnings in the 1970s to the present day.

Barrientos, S. and Smith, S. 2007, 'Do workers benefit from ethical trade? Assessing codes of labour practice in global production systems', *Third World Quarterly*, vol. 28, no. 4, pp 713–729.
Detailed case study of the impact of ethical trade, highlighting the possibilities and difficulties of assessing impact.

Heal, G.M. 2008, *When principles pay: corporate social responsibility and the bottom line*, Columbia Business School, New York.
Chapter 11 sets out the challenges and some of the alternatives for measuring the impact of corporate responsibility.

Henriques, A. 2010, *Corporate impact: measuring and managing your social impact*, Earthscan, London.
An exploration of the different ways of measuring a company's extra-financial impact.

KPMG 2008, *KPMG International Survey of Corporate Responsibility Reporting*, KPMG International, Amsterdam.
An overview of companies reporting on corporate responsibility, and insights into the strengths and weaknesses of their reports.

Macdonald, K. & Marshall, S. 2010, *Fair trade, corporate accountability and beyond : experiments in globalizing justice*, Ashgate, Farnham.

Contributions by academics, activists, and corporate responsibility professionals looking at the impact approaches to corporate responsibility management have had around the world.

Margolis, J.D. & Walsh, J.P. 2003, 'Misery loves companies: rethinking social initiatives by business', *Administrative Science Quarterly*, vol. 48, no. 2, pp 268–305.
Widely cited study of impact from a corporate social performance perspective.

Vogel, D. 2005, *The market for virtue: the potential and limits of corporate social responsibility*, Brookings Institution Press, Washington, DC.
Detailed critique of corporate responsibility's effectiveness as a response to social and environmental challenges.

Online resources

- Exercises and discussion topics for students
- Additional case study on the impact of Wal-Mart's environmental programmes
- Links to other web-based resources
- Teaching notes for the chapter case study

Endnotes

1. Mahon and Wartick, 2011.
2. SustainAbility and UNEP, 2002.
3. See, e.g., Elliott and Freeman (2003) on improved labour standards and monitoring.
4. See also Chapter 8. The 2007 ACCA awards also reflect these broad criticisms. Information can be obtained from www.accaglobal.com.
5. Margolis and Walsh, 2003, p 282.
6. www.wbcsd.org/templates/TemplateWBCSD5/layout.asp?type=p&MenuId=MTU3Mw.
7. Mahon and Wartick, 2011.
8. There is a distinction between corporate social performance and corporate responsibility. CSP is an ex post measurement of past performance (e.g. assessing if there is a relationship between social impact and corporate reputation), whereas corporate responsibility can be *ex ante*.
9. The main sources for understanding the impact and measurement of corporate responsibility and corporate social performance were Sethi (1975), Anshen (1980), Wartick and Cochran (1985), Margolis and Walsh (2003), and the discussion in Birch (2003). The company corporate responsibility reports used included the Anglo American 2005 Report, the Unilever 2005 Environmental Report, the Cooperative Financial Services Report 2005, and the Traidcraft Report 2005.
10. ic.fsc.org/facts-figures.19.htm, accessed 24 October 2013.
11. Unilever, 2005.
12. Vogel, 2005, pp 110–111.
13. Vogel, 2005, p 126.
14. corporate.walmart.com/global-responsibility/environment-sustainability, accessed 24 October 2013.
15. Michael Blowfield, personal observation, 15 November 2000.
16. See, e.g. the BBC news broadcast 13 March 2007 headlined 'BA green scheme fails to take off'.
17. Locke et al., 2006.

18. Barrientos and Smith, 2007.

19. Elliott and Freeman, 2003.

20. ETI, 2009.

21. Phylmar Group, 2006.

22. Abbott Laboratories, 2005; www.gsk.com.

23. Vogel, 2005, p 102.

24. NRET, 1999.

25. BSR, 2005; KPMG, 2005.

26. www.economicfootprint.org offers economic impact reports for the agriculture, mining, pharmaceutical, and financial services sectors.

27. Clay, 2005; BER, 2008; Kapstein, 2008.

28. Rio Tinto case studies, and its framework for understanding linkages between its investment in communities and their development, can be found at www.riotinto.com.

29. *The Economist*, 2006.

30. See, e.g., Hermes and Lensink, 2011; Armendáriz and Morduch, 2010; Ansari et al., 2012.

31. See,e.g., Raynolds et al., 2004; IFAT, 2006; Nicholls and Opal, 2005; Nelson and Pound, 2009.

32. Raynolds et al., 2004; Vogel, 2005.

33. Vogel, 2008.

34. Ronchi, 2002.

35. Nelson and Pound, 2009.

36. Berlan and Dolan, 2014; McMichael, 2009; Kuriyan et al., 2012.

37. Margolis and Walsh, 2003; McWilliams and Siegel, 2000.

38. Vogel, 2005.

39. Vogel, 2005, p 73.

40. Vogel, 2005, p 59.

41. UK government data at www.financialdeepening.org; www.innocentdrinks.co.uk.

42. Collinson, 2001; Collinson and Leon, 2000.

43. CCC, 2005c.

44. Vogel, 2005.

45. Varley et al., 1998.

46. Eliott and Freeman, 2003, p 63.

47. Lenox and Nash, 2003.

48. Toyota Motor Corporation, Sustainability Report, 2012.

49. Figures taken from Uren, 2007.

50. McGregor, 2007.

51. Ascoly and Zeldenrust, 2003.

52. ETI, 2006.

53. www.bitc.org.uk, accessed 24 November 2009; SAM-PWC 2008.

54. INSEAD, 2007.

55. www.lapfforum.org.

56. Compare, e.g., Brown (2004) and Elliott and Freeman (2003) with Vogel (2005).

57. Industry data cited in Skapkinker (2009).

58. Kauffman and Chedekel, 2004.

59. Information on Sigma is accessible at www.projectsigma.com. Information on Race to the Top, including an analysis of why it failed, is accessible at www.racetothetop.org.

60. DFID, 2002.

61. DFID, 2002; ETI, 2004.

62. ETI, 2004; Vogel, 2005; Barrientos and Smith, 2007.

63. Vogel, 2005, pp 157–158.

64. Mattingly and Berman, 2006; Mitnick, 2000.

65. Elliott and Freeman, 2003.

66. Weiser and Rochlin, 2004.

67. SustainAbility and UNEP, 2002.

13 Criticisms of corporate responsibility

 Chapter overview

In this chapter, we focus on the most fundamental criticisms of corporate responsibility. In particular, we will:

- discuss why some see corporate responsibility as being anti-business or anti-free markets;

- examine how some regard corporate responsibility as being too pro-business;

- explore why corporate responsibility has been criticized for failing to deal with major areas of the interaction of business with society;

- discuss why some feel that corporate responsibility needs to become more rigorous and tougher in its approach.

 Main topics

Introducing critiques of corporate responsibility	312
'Corporate responsibility is anti-business'	314
'Corporate responsibility is pro-business'	317
'The scope of corporate responsibility is too narrow'	322
'Corporate responsibility fails to achieve its goals'	325

Key terms

Civil society organizations

Corporate accountability

Liberal economics

Self-regulation

Introducing critiques of corporate responsibility

If corporate responsibility came to prominence due to criticisms of business behaviour, in recent years, it has itself become the object of criticism. Fleming and Jones (2013) and Reich (2007) have attacked corporate responsibility from different perspectives, and advocates of social enterprise or impact investing are at pains to distance themselves from what they see as the corporate responsibility movement.[1] To a degree, this reflects the extent to which ideas of corporate responsibility have influenced business thinking, public debate, and public policy in some parts of the world; after all, nobody criticizes what is irrelevant. We have raised some of those criticisms in other chapters (e.g. in Chapter 1, difficulties in defining corporate responsibility; in Chapters 7, 8, and 9, the many challenges of implementing corporate responsibility).

These criticisms are part of an often lively debate within the field about how to carry out corporate responsibility in ways that are efficient, effective, and best able to satisfy the needs of business while recognizing the concerns of other stakeholders. They are largely technical or instrumental in nature, focusing more on 'how to do it' than on 'what it means' and 'why to do it'. For a few, this focus in itself has been the subject of criticism, because it turns corporate responsibility into a pursuit of technical excellence and ignores (or stifles discussion of) more fundamental questions about what the responsibilities of business to twenty-first-century society are.[2] This situation is changing and a scan through mainstream corporate responsibility media such as *Ethical Corporation*, *CSRWire*, and *Ethical Performance* shows that such topics are becoming more widely discussed. But it is debatable how effective new discussions of what constitutes responsibility will be and how desirable they are.

Corporate responsibility theorists and practitioners have raised each of these questions over the past few years. Doubts about effectiveness stem from a sense that the parameters of corporate responsibility have already been set, not least through the ways in which different issues and ideas are assessed and, ultimately, included or excluded. In Chapter 6, we discussed at length the importance of the business case and how this influences corporate responsibility. We also showed how certain tools, techniques, and approaches have come to be regarded as best practice in the ways in which corporate responsibility is managed and implemented; new areas of responsibility are more likely to be accepted if they can be tackled using such established methods.

Doubts about the desirability of extending the realm of corporate responsibility to include a potentially endless array of new issues and expectations stem from a fear that companies will find the demands placed on them overwhelming, and will become more resistant to change. This itself derives from the experiences of academic corporate responsibility theory. As discussed in Chapter 2, there is a rich history of academic debate about what the nature of the corporation's responsibilities should be. But as we also saw, there was frustration, in the past, that academic debate was having little impact on the corporate world and therefore there is now a strong desire not to jeopardize the current enthusiasm among companies for addressing corporate responsibility concerns, even if these concerns are not as broad or their address as thorough as some might have liked.

The urge of some to want to 'protect' corporate responsibility as a discipline for fear of hindering progress ignores the fact that allegations regarding the negative effects of business behaviour continue to emerge from civil society organizations, academics, and legal actions. Most of the criticisms of corporate responsibility discussed so far emanate from within the loose community of corporate responsibility theorists and practitioners. In the rest of this chapter, we want to concentrate on voices that are external to that community—those who, for the most part, either reject corporate responsibility, or are waiting for a different approach before they condone it. We have divided their criticisms into four types of accusation.

1 *'Corporate responsibility stifles the primary purpose of business and, ultimately, hampers the functioning of free markets.'*
2 *'Corporate responsibility favours the interests of business over the legitimate concerns, demands, and expectations of wider society.'*

3 'Corporate responsibility is too narrow in its focus and does nothing to address the key aspects of the business–society relationship today.'

4 'Corporate responsibility is failing to achieve its objectives and needs to adopt new approaches if it is to succeed.'

Before exploring these, it is worth noting that each strand of criticism relates back to the theoretical perspectives outlined in Chapters 1 and 2. The argument that corporate responsibility stifles the primary purpose of business is rooted in liberal economics, whereas the view that it favours the interests of business is a development of the long-standing critique of free enterprise externalizing its costs onto wider society. Similarly, arguments that corporate responsibility is too narrow are part of a wider debate about the role of business in society and contrast with criticisms, rooted in management science, that new approaches are required if corporate responsibility is to succeed.

 Discussion points

The criticisms of corporate responsibility in this chapter are primarily external, i.e. those from outside the world of academics, practitioners, and companies which promote corporate responsibility as a legitimate area of business management. Yet we know from other chapters that there have been internal critiques of corporate responsibility.

● What are the main differences between the internal and external critiques of corporate responsibility?

● To which of the external criticisms should companies respond? Are these the same as those to which they are *likely* to respond?

● Examine the external criticisms made of Berkshire Hathaway's investment in Chinese companies operating in Darfur, Sudan, and Warren Buffet's response, and explain which is strongest, and why.

'Corporate responsibility is anti-business'

In 2005, corporate responsibility was making inroads into management practice. On 20 January of that year, *The Economist* responded with a series of articles that presented corporate responsibility as a threat to the effective functioning of capitalism and free markets, and hence to global prosperity. On the one hand, the articles were a sign that corporate responsibility had come of age, and had entered mainstream business and economic debate; on the other, they offered a sharp rebuke to corporate executives, whom the magazine regarded as being too weak in the face of public criticism and as ignoring their fiduciary duty to shareholders by paying too much attention to the demands of others.

Reflecting a wider sense of anger and unease at the growth of corporate responsibility, the core argument of the articles was as follows. The standard of living in Western industrial democracies is higher today than ever before and is at a level that would have been unimaginable 200 years ago: *'In the West today the poor live better lives than all but the nobility enjoyed throughout the course of modern history before capitalism.'*[3] This is largely due to the

success of free enterprise, yet we have entered an age in which capitalism is deplored, suspected, and feared by a broad cross-section of society, and even by some business leaders.
This anti-capitalist sentiment stems from beliefs that profit has nothing to do with the public
good, and that the pursuit of profit drives companies to put crippling burdens on society and
the environment. These beliefs have given rise to corporate responsibility as a check on business behaviour. Yet they are ill-founded, because they see profit as an unfortunate necessity
that can be controlled and muzzled, whereas it is, in fact, the engine that allows business to
make its phenomenal contributions to the public good, and restrictions on profit or wealth
creation—especially those that come from civil society rather than from governments—will be
more harmful to society than anything else.

The articles repeatedly present corporate responsibility as a victory for the concerns of
NGOs over the traditional priorities of business. But it is not simply that the public is failing
to acknowledge the positive role that business plays that is *The Economist*'s concern; it is also
that the uptake of corporate responsibility by mainstream companies might have a serious
effect on the ability of business to fulfil its role within the capitalist system. An example of this
is that corporate responsibility distracts public company management from its primary purpose of serving the interests of shareholders. This echoes the views of Friedman (1962) and
Jensen (1986), both of whom have argued that corporate responsibility negatively affects the
abilities of company agents to maximize profits for investors (see Chapter 7). *The Economist*
fully accepts that managers must be ethical and that much needs to be done in this area. But
it says that they should never lose sight of the fact they are employees, not owners, and that
it is unethical to put the owners' assets to any use other than maximizing long-term value.
Ideas such as the triple bottom line (see Chapter 1) distract management from this goal and,
by making companies accountable on multiple fronts, threaten to make them accountable
for nothing, because they offer no measurable test of business success.

The articles make clear that none of this is to argue in favour of corporate *irresponsibility*.
On the contrary, there is need for governance reform and, *The Economist* says (although without offering any evidence), *'broken corporate governance and CSR are close relations. You often
see them together'*.[4] In this, however, as in other areas of corporate reform, the articles stress
that it is the role of government to regulate business. As one of the articles says, *'getting the
most out of capitalism requires public intervention of various kinds, and a lot of it: taxes, public
spending, regulation ...'*.[5]

It is important to note that these remarks distinguish *The Economist*'s position from some
free market critics of corporate responsibility who would want much less government intervention in business. These critics argue that it is a priori almost impossible to identify what
interventions cause growth[6] while empirically it is highly apparent that economic success is
associated with free trade and deregulation,[7] whereas *The Economist* claims that intervention
is essential but is the preserve of government, not the wider universe of stakeholders. There
are two reasons for this: first, when managers have to pay attention to too many stakeholder
groups they become distracted. It might be good business practice to take account of multiple stakeholders (see Chapter 9), but that is quite different to being held accountable to them.
And even if, as in Germany, companies are legally required to have non-shareholders on the
board, *The Economist* argues that owner interests should always be the primary concern.

The second reason given is that corporate responsibility is unnecessary because in a
well-functioning free market the marketplace provides consumers with a forum in which to

express their opinions about companies (e.g. by not buying their goods, or by not working for them if they disagree with their policies).

It is ironic that the articles in *The Economist* were not criticized by the kind of free market purists whom Chang (2007) calls 'bad samaritans' because of their strict adherence to a narrow capitalist orthodoxy. Indeed, it is also ironic that such purists have been slow to embrace voluntary corporate responsibility as an answer to managing the business–society relationship in a deregulated environment, in a world where, through Facebook and similar online resources, younger generations can redefine what constitutes a business issue[8] (see Snapshot 13.1).

Instead, pro-business critics of corporate responsibility have more often focused their attention on business's overt critics, arguing that corporate responsibility is an anti-corporate strategy.[9] For example, the website CSRWatch, with the tagline 'Your eye on the anti-business movement', posted information on a range of anti-corporate criticisms. However, it is indicative of the acceptance of corporate responsibility in once critical quarters that CSRWatch is no longer online, and more significant still that in January 2008 *The Economist* itself ran a special feature recognizing the merits of corporate responsibility.

 Snapshot 13.1   The Church takes on Caterpillar over Palestine—giving corporate responsibility muscle

Caterpillar, the world's largest construction machinery company, is a strong advocate of a values-based approach to corporate responsibility and has a worldwide code of business conduct which states that '*our success should also contribute to the quality of life and the prosperity of communities*'. This commitment was challenged in 2004, following claims by a UN Special Rapporteur that the company's equipment was being used to deny Palestinians the right to food by destroying their farmlands. Critics such as War on Want, an NGO, argue that the company sold equipment to the US government knowing that it would be sold on for use in military operations. Some NGOs and watchdog groups have denied this, and the company has retorted that it has neither the capacity nor the legal right to determine how its equipment is used once it has been sold.

For both sides, this has become a test of the ability of corporate responsibility to guide companies in ethical decision-making. The Synod of the Church of England voted to recommend selling the church's shares in the firm. This decision generated criticism of the Church of England itself: whether it was using a stance on corporate responsibility to attack Israeli national policy, and whether disinvestment was more effective than using the Church's holdings to engage with the company. The Church's Ethical Investment Advisory Group advised against selling Caterpillar stock and instead began what it called a '*progressive dialogue*' with the company. Meanwhile, the company said that it did not sell machinery to Israel, and found itself caught in the crossfire of a campaign targeting the policies of the US and Israeli governments.

The Caterpillar case remains controversial, with some arguing that it proves the effectiveness of corporate responsibility approaches, such as a voluntary code of conduct and stakeholder dialogue, and others saying that corporate responsibility has allowed the company to deny any culpability for human rights violations caused by its products. It is also possible to argue that the case is not ultimately about the role of the company, but shows how the public profile of multinational firms makes them a leveraging point in campaigning about wider geopolitical issues.

(*Sources:* War on Want, 2005; *Ethical Performance*, 2006a; Caterpillar code of conduct, online at www.cat.com; UN Commission on Human Rights report on economic, social and cultural rights, January 2005, online at www.ohchr.org)

(continued...)

Quick questions

The Church of England's Ethical Investment Advisory Group says that disinvestment would be too strong at this stage, but that it is looking for change as a result of progressive engagement.

1 What changes do you think Caterpillar might make that would convince its critics that corporate responsibility can make a meaningful difference to company policies?

2 Is the company right to say that it cannot be held responsible for the end use of its products?

3 Is the company right to choose not to sell to the military in certain countries?

 Discussion points

A criticism made by liberal economists is that corporate responsibility hinders company financial performance and poses an obstacle to economic growth.

● What evidence do such economists need to present to substantiate this claim?

● In your experience, is there evidence to support *The Economist*'s claim that *'broken corporate governance and CSR are close relations'*?

● What evidence can corporate responsibility advocates offer to show that it improves company management and makes companies more reliable engines of economic growth?

'Corporate responsibility is pro-business'

Most current criticism of corporate responsibility begins from the position that business is in various ways damaging to the social good, and that neither the theory nor practice developed under the corporate responsibility umbrella has remedied this situation. Critics argue that a key element of corporate responsibility should be to realign business with the values of society and to optimize its contribution, but that companies will not return to their original purpose without reform of the legislative and economic environment surrounding private companies.

This is a broad school of criticism, ranging from those who believe that corporate responsibility is not up to the task of reforming business,[10] to those who regard corporate responsibility as a weak countervailing force,[11] to those who see business interests as being opposed to societal ones.[12] Some highlight the role ownership plays in determining a company's impact, arguing that there is nothing inherent in the legal definition of a company that stops it from having a social purpose, and Kelly (2001) and others point to examples of privately held companies that have just that. But, it is argued, once a company is publicly owned, its purpose can only be to maximize profits. This means that no matter how well intentioned corporate responsibility practice might be, ultimately it will not serve the common good. Arguments, such as those described earlier, that business serves the common good by creating wealth and goods are refuted with examples of companies that have rigged prices, deceived regulators, caused environmental damage, produced harmful products, and otherwise acted in ways that were intended to create shareholder value (and management rewards) at the expense of public well-being. Moreover, some argue, the larger and more powerful some companies become, owing to the opportunities of economic globalization, the greater is the risk that the public good will be jeopardized by what Bakan (2004) calls the 'pathological pursuit of profit'. The Occupy movement which staged long-term protests in major financial capitals adhered to this critique.

It is worth noting that some pro-business thinkers would agree that some of the corporate actions set out above are unethical, and that companies and the public would benefit from better governance, and from greater transparency and disclosure. They might also agree that what is required is better regulation of business, but what they mean by this is only regulations that improve market efficiency. This is in marked contrast to those who are sceptical of business's purpose, who tend to want to see regulation that limits both markets and companies. What both tacitly agree upon, however, is that corporate responsibility is not the best way in which to put right the wrongs of corporate behaviour.

One reason for this is that corporate responsibility is simply too weak for the task at hand. A company such as Unilever, for example, might put in place policies of social and environmental responsibility, but some blame its demand for palm oil for deforestation. Similarly, British Airways might have corporate responsibility policies, but it is part of an industry that is accused of externalizing its enormous environmental costs. This criticism focuses on corporate responsibility as a voluntary approach, something that is already tainted because self-regulation is seen as the corollary of diminished government capacity or unwillingness to regulate private enterprise, and becomes more damaged by examples of how companies have allegedly used voluntary initiatives to dilute their responsibilities to others. A frequently cited example of this is how companies have become signatories to the UN Global Compact—an action which requires them to uphold the Compact's ten responsibility Principles—and yet, according to critics, many such signatories continue to violate UN Principles, knowing that, until very recently, the Compact was without a disciplinary, or even a complaints, mechanism in relation to these transgressions (see Chapter 9). There are many other examples, such as the 2005 Amnesty International report on how the agreement about the Chad–Cameroon oil pipeline, held up as a model of corporate responsibility practice, actually created disincentives for the governments involved to protect human rights by making such rights the responsibility of the private sector, or a study of how voluntary labour standards have failed workers in Vietnam.[13]

As we shall discuss later, such examples are, for some, evidence that corporate responsibility needs to be implemented more effectively; for others, they reveal the fallacy of trying to achieve justice without confronting power. Unless this is recognized, critics claim, engagement with business through corporate responsibility initiatives or similar means leads to co-option by business and fosters an illusion that issues, such as global poverty, can be addressed while continuing to do business as usual.[14] The most obvious recent test of corporate responsibility in practice was the financial crisis of 2007–2008, especially the role of banks. This is the topic of Case Study 13, but the failure of corporate responsibility theory to predict, explain, or resolve the crisis, and the accusations made about banks such as Citigroup and Barclays which have award-winning corporate responsibility programmes, have provided ample ammunition for critics of contemporary corporate responsibility.

Again, there is an irony here: those who see corporate responsibility as anti-business regard it as an imposition of activist agendas onto corporations, while those who see it as pro-business regard it as a co-option and dilution of those agendas by corporate interests. In both cases, corporate responsibility is being criticized for failing to meet particular sets of expectations, yet given the centrality of business in most of the modern world, these expectations embrace all aspects of human welfare and values. As Broad (2002) and others describe, the array of expectations from those who oppose the behaviour of large corporations is diverse and far more sophisticated than is typically portrayed in the media, and in articles such as those in *The Economist* discussed earlier. Consequently, the issues that corporate responsibility is accused of not addressing are equally diverse. For some, it is corporate responsibility's failure to tackle what are seen as aspects of corporate behaviour that pose a threat to the functioning of society and democracy that is at issue. This includes corporate lobbying of government, the avoidance of corporation taxation in developing countries and elsewhere, and the consequences for business and wider society of privatization and liberalization. Others highlight the behaviour of particular companies and industries, such as marketing and smuggling in the tobacco industry, the impact of supermarkets on small farmers, and the conditions of workers in computer manufacturing.[15] And then again, there are goods and services that at one stage are lauded for their social benefits (e.g. sub-prime lending to facilitate house buying for the poor), and end up being derided for being exploitative. As an early pioneer of private equity argues, this now widely criticized financial instrument began with the purpose of freeing up business for the good of workers and investors.[16]

There are a vast number of reports and briefings on these and similar issues, and as we shall see in the next section not everyone sees corporate responsibility as being powerless to address them. In fact, a criticism of corporate responsibility sometimes heard from within the corporate responsibility community is that it has stimulated rather than appeased civil society organizations' demands. This is probably a misplaced sentiment which assumes that there are a finite number of issues in which companies have a role in addressing, or that winning the support of such organizations will end their criticisms of corporate behaviour. Perhaps more significant is to note that, for some, the fact that corporate responsibility does not tackle certain issues is a sign of its inherent weakness, while, for others, it is part of the process of mapping out future challenges and directions.

Some who regard corporate responsibility as inherently weak are not opposed to business, per se, as is evident from their support for fairtrade and other alternative trading companies, and particularly for ethically oriented firms such as nosweatapparel.com. Some also support the new agendas for engaging with companies. But none of this detracts from the repeated call for government intervention and legislative frameworks that prescribe business activity.

Mitchell (2001, 2005) says that corporate responsibility can only succeed if there is a well-developed conceptualization of corporate law that exposes human responsibility and accountability. Arguing that companies are nothing but their individual members, he suggests that the law, companies, and markets need to be structured so as to encourage responsible behaviour and to discourage the irresponsible. He highlights that corporate responsibility has come to the fore at the same time as executive pay has spiralled; corporate governance reforms have too often been about making it easier to conduct mergers and acquisitions, and shareholders—not least, institutional investors—have pressured companies into producing quicker and higher returns. Thus, we see two distinct trends happening: one called 'corporate responsibility', under which companies are reconsidering their duties to society, and the other wherein what critics see as irresponsible behaviour is increasingly considered to be acceptable business practice. Corporate responsibility is not only blamed for failing to mitigate the latter, but also for helping to foster it by putting a gloss on corporate reputations.

A frequently cited example of how corporate responsibility has been hijacked in this way is the tobacco industry (see Snapshot 13.2). For some critics, there are industries, such as tobacco, arms, and gambling, that can never be responsible because of the very nature of their products, and we have already seen how this principle has informed the responsible investment movement (see Chapter 10). There are also those who regard particular companies as egregiously irresponsible, and see it as proof positive of the coercion and co-option of corporate responsibility by business's interests when companies such as Nestlé—long criticized for its marketing of infant milk formula in poor countries—are accepted into high-profile corporate responsibility initiatives such as the UN Global Compact.

 Snapshot 13.2   Tobacco—can bad industries produce responsible companies?

For some corporate responsibility critics, nothing speaks more loudly to its pro-business agenda than the fact that some tobacco firms have positioned themselves as socially responsible. How, they ask, can companies that deliberately hid the addictive nature of nicotine from the public's knowledge be responsible? How can companies that have aggressively marketed their harmful products to the young be responsible? How can companies that knowingly produce something that will kill its consumers in any way claim to be responsible?

Since the 1950s, the industry has continuously been in the crosshairs of governments, consumers, and of course lawyers, but it was only in the 1990s, when state governments alleged that companies had long known about the addictive risk of nicotine and had not only lied about this in public enquiries, but had artificially boosted the nicotine content of cigarettes, that the industry finally agreed to multi-billion-dollar settlements. The settlements were held up as a victory for consumers—but to investors, at least, they were also seen as a victory for the industry and tobacco company stock prices rose.

They also prompted companies to think about corporate responsibility as an approach to managing their societal relations. BAT's endowment to the University of Nottingham to establish the International Centre for Corporate Responsibility prompted protests both on and off campus, and those who seem to embrace companies' commitment to behaving more responsibly, such as the Dow Jones Sustainability Group Index, have themselves been criticized.

Moreover, critics claim that the way in which tobacco companies operate highlights the essential weaknesses of the corporate responsibility approach. For example, the World Health Organization has accused the industry of opportunism by making self-regulation on issues such as marketing to children part of their corporate responsibility programmes, thereby hoping to avoid legislation. Similarly, tobacco companies have been accused of working closely with PR firms to simultaneously promote corporate responsibility and undermine scientific findings about the effects of smoking. But the industry points to the effectiveness of its anti-smoking campaigns on youth consumption. It highlights that smoking is a fact of life and that it is better to have a responsible industry than the one dominated by organized crime that might emerge from prohibition. And they argue that the industry will make most progress when critics engage with it rather than when they attempt to isolate it.

(*Sources:* Palazzo and Richter, 2005; National Conference of State Legislatures, www.ncsl.orgs; WHO Tobacco Free Initiative, 2008)

(*continued...*)

Quick questions

Tobacco is one of a small group of industries the products of which knowingly cause human death or suffering.

1 What are other examples of such industries, and can they ever be considered responsible?

2 What do companies in these industries stand to gain from self-regulation?

3 Are the tobacco industry's critics right to refuse to engage as stakeholders with tobacco companies?

A central question here is whether business is best influenced by engagement (e.g. through stakeholder partnerships) or by confrontation. We have discussed this at length in Chapter 10, and there are many civil society organizations, such as Oxfam and WWF, that engage with companies while keeping up a critique of business in society. For some observers, however, the crucial point is not who takes part in the process of engagement, but rather the norms and conventions that dictate that process, and thereby its possible outcomes. Much of corporate responsibility theory treats the participation or exclusion of particular agents as indicative of corporate responsibility's efficacy (e.g. Kolk et al., 1999). But it is possible to argue that the very nature of business as an element of the capitalist economy excludes certain values and ideals (e.g. Banerjee and Prasad, 2008; Blowfield, 2005a). This raises questions about how particular social systems influence responsibility, and the parameters of what can be achieved by business within the capitalist system. As Alvesson and Willmott (2002) argue in the wider context of organizational theory, the primacy given to prediction and control in all walks of organizational life not only makes it difficult to introduce ideas that do not directly relate to organizational effectiveness, but also reinforces the notion of knowledge as something value-free and empirically derived. What some critics of contemporary corporate responsibility would like to see is business adopting values beyond those justified by an instrumental logic. Therefore the participation of some of the harshest critics of business in a corporate responsibility partnership should not be seen as a sign of success, because the discourse (i.e. the language, mechanisms, tools, agendas, etc.) that governs it has already been settled and, moreover, is that which favours the business's interests. Thus, for example, what can be dealt with or not in a corporate responsibility initiative, the priority given to an issue in terms of time, expertise, and other resources, the array of possible solutions, and even the very language that is used to discuss the issues are all ultimately a reflection of what benefits or causes no harm to business. Moreover, this is something of which the participants themselves may be unaware, because, as Lukes has noted, *'the most effective and insidious use of power is to prevent ... conflict arising in the first place'* (Lukes, 1974, p 23).

The questions of power—who holds it, what form it takes, how it is exhibited, and what it allows or precludes—are an implicit underlying theme in many of the current critiques of corporate responsibility and those that are likely to occupy debates about the field in coming years.[17] In fact, the essential criticism set out in this section is that corporate responsibility (both theory and management practice) is not able to confront corporate power and therefore that alternative approaches are required. Thus, for example, while corporate responsibility has gone some way to challenging both management and neoliberal orthodoxy, it is ultimately an example of how business secures the conditions for the ongoing and long-term accumulation of wealth and power, albeit in more socially and environmentally sensitive ways.[18] However, the critiques outlined in the following sections draw a different conclusion—one

---

 Discussion points

In the influential corporate responsibility book *Walking the talk*, Holliday et al. (2002) argue that sustainability is best achieved through open competitive international markets which promote human progress by encouraging efficiency and innovation.

- Does this claim support or counter the arguments of critics who regard corporate responsibility as being too favourable to business?
- What alternatives to market-based solutions are these critics advocating?
- Are such alternatives plausible in today's world?

---

under which power can be addressed and dominant institutions reformed, even if this has not been achieved as yet.

'The scope of corporate responsibility is too narrow'

We have seen that corporate responsibility is criticized for not addressing what are seen as important areas of corporate behaviour and that, to a degree, those who are supportive of, and sceptical about, the role of business share this view. We have also seen that critics in both camps regard corporate responsibility as not being suited to addressing these larger issues and see government as the proper institution in many cases. This overlooks the fact that, for the time being at least, effective regulatory mechanisms do not exist in many areas of global business activity. Indeed, as pointed out in earlier chapters, corporate responsibility is, at least partly, a response to the limited power of national governments in a global economic system.

Consequently, there are some critics who regard corporate responsibility as desirable, but who feel that the range of issues it currently addresses is too narrow. We have already mentioned corporate lobbying, tax avoidance, and how practices in specific industries to do with marketing, smuggling, and sourcing are said to affect society adversely, especially in poor countries. Some point out that the CEO of Wal-Mart earns more in three hours than a US worker on the minimum wage does in a year,[19] and therefore not only fair wages, but also broader policies concerning wealth distribution, should be part of the corporate responsibility agenda. Women account for just 4 per cent of CEOs in Fortune 500 companies, and there are only two in charge of FTSE 100 companies. Gender in general is largely absent from corporate responsibility theory and practice.[20]

Indeed, employment generally needs to be tackled more comprehensively than at present. For example, corporate responsibility practice does not typically require companies to address the social costs of moving their production to another location, even though the consequences of such actions can be highly beneficial for the company and potentially devastating for the communities left behind. Also, given the worldwide trend for more flex-ible labour arrangements, which are said to aid company competitiveness but make employ-ment less secure than it has been in the past, corporate responsibility is challenged to address the nature of the employment contract by, for example, giving workers stronger protections.

There is a strong national/regional dimension to this because even in countries where there is limited employment protection, the consequences of redundancy are very different; for example, compare the USA (with weak welfare provisions) with Denmark, where dismissed workers can claim state benefits for up to four years. Flexibilization of the workforce is accused of having particular impacts on women. For instance, zero-hour contracts, by which workers must be available for work without being paid, are particularly prevalent in industries with high numbers of female employees, such as retailing and office administration. Moreover, while corporate responsibility has had a significant impact on the way in which companies think about labour conditions in developing countries, issues that are central to labour rela-tions in many developed economies, such as gay and disabled rights, have not been part of the mainstream corporate responsibility debate in places such as China, India, and Latin America.

Outside the workplace, there are expectations that corporate responsibility should do much more to ensure that a company's corporate responsibility policies are not at odds with its policies in other areas. Home Depot, the American DIY chain, has attracted praise from environmental groups because of its timber sourcing policies and, as well as being a major corporate philanthropist, it moved early to provide help to communities affected by the Kat-rina hurricane in 2005. Yet, in marked contrast to its response to civil society organizations, the company garnered a poor reputation for listening to shareholders, exemplified by then CEO Robert Nardelli's refusal not only to answer questions properly at the company's annual meeting, but also even to allow the board to attend the meeting.[21]

Equally, companies that have established strong corporate responsibility credentials are criti-cized for abandoning, or failing to build on, these when they face a crisis. Enron is a widely cited example of a company that had a strong corporate responsibility reputation which did not reveal, but rather masked, the corruption and malfeasance that eventually brought the company down. But tarring corporate responsibility with the Enron brush is probably unfair, given how that company's officers deceived so many institutions. A more illuminating example is Merck, the pharmaceutical company, which had long been held up to be a model of business ethics. That tradition appeared to help the company when, in September 2004, it responded to con-cerns about its pain reliever Vioxx by withdrawing it from sale—at least in the USA. However, it has since been alleged on numerous occasions that, from 2000 on, the company vigorously sought out researchers and physicians who would endorse the drug, and tried to intimidate and stifle those who criticized it.[22] Not that this behaviour was unique to Merck USA, as Goldacre's (2012) comprehensive review of practices in the pharmaceutical industry amply demonstrates.

Another area in which companies have been criticized for inconsistency between their cor-porate responsibility policies and their business practices is in their terms of trading and the way in which some companies use their power in the marketplace to drive out small businesses, or to force producers to adopt management practices which, ultimately, exploit workers, commu-nities, and the natural environment. Just-in-time purchasing practices and promiscuous sourc-ing in search of low costs are examples from the apparel industry of how retailers and major brands are said to exploit their supply chains. These are issues that have started to register in mainstream corporate responsibility, and Tesco, for example, has started to train its buyers in understanding responsibility issues.[23] Yet Tesco is an example of the mixed messages a company can send out: training buyers, supporting research on sustainable consumption, and initiating programmes on carbon labelling, for instance, but also getting embroiled in arguments over animal cruelty and stifling press freedom by using its wealth and questionable litigation.[24]

There are many more examples of aspects of business which critics say that corporate responsibility could be addressing, but which it is not. But a list of issues does nothing to explain why some things have been included and others not. For some corporate responsibility theorists, as touched on in Chapter 2, this is a test of how the nature of business's role in society is defined and hence what we mean by 'corporate citizenship'.[25] A 2005 collection of critical essays from different academic disciplines reveals a number of ways of understanding this inclusion and exclusion.[26] At one level, companies are said to choose the limits of their actions. In some cases, they regard corporate responsibility as being fairly low down in terms of corporate objectives, and it is allocated too few resources and benefits from little push to have the issues taken up by other agents (e.g. by government service agencies). In fact, it is claimed that corporate responsibility can be used to prevent alternative political, economic, and social solutions from being developed—something that has been observed in Nigeria, and also in South Africa, where, critics argue, corporate responsibility has had more to do with helping to erase memories of business's role in apartheid than in seriously tackling today's societal challenges.

Critics argue that corporate responsibility is more likely to include contentious issues if companies are under pressure from governments and civil society, and therefore that we should not view effective corporate responsibility as voluntary. But some take this further and argue that the limits of corporate responsibility may have already been reached. Not only may corporate responsibility be partially to blame for drawing attention away from certain traditional expectations about the role of business (e.g. payment of taxes to fund public policy initiatives), but many of the issues and conflicts that it is now being asked to address are, ultimately, the result of global economic and political systems that cannot be tackled at the company, industry, or other levels at which most corporate responsibility initiatives operate.

Implicit in such criticisms are questionable assumptions about the effectiveness and willingness of even liberal democratic governments to act in the public interest, and especially their acceptance of the need to be accountable and transparent.[27] There is also a tendency to blur the ways business engages with society, failing to distinguish, for instance, between companies as citizens, as governors of citizenship, and as the providers of arenas where stakeholders can interact.[28] Often, those who are most sceptical criticize companies' track-record

---

 Discussion points

A recurring criticism is that corporate responsibility has yet to deliver on its promises and therefore has not proved strong enough to deal with important aspects of the business–society relationship.

● What are the most important areas in which corporate responsibility needs to demonstrate progress in order to win public support?

● How would you structure an effective complaints procedure for use in relation to a voluntary set of principles?

● Is imposing informal sanctions on business through actions such as 'naming and shaming' more likely to influence business behaviour than inter-company learning and peer pressure?

on being citizens, and are fearful of the power they can exert as governors (e.g. influencing government and civil society agendas).

'Corporate responsibility fails to achieve its goals'

For those who see corporate responsibility as a whitewash, greenwash, or bluewash, the fact that corporate responsibility fails to deliver on its promises is no surprise. On numerous email listservs and blogs, corporate responsibility is dismissed as a kind of Faustian pact between business, NGOs, and government that weakens more effective policies. Such criticisms have been levelled at the UK's Business in the Community, which has spoken out against the need for government regulation of corporate responsibility and been criticized for giving its Platinum Performance award to a bank accused of having *a culture of ruthlessness and lies*.[29]

It is often these types of organization, as much as companies, which are the focus of critics who claim that corporate responsibility has not lived up to people's expectations. They are blamed for focusing too much on corporate responsibility's successes and failing to consider its real impact. As of 2013, there are 7,000 corporate signatories to the UN Global Compact out of an estimated 900,000 multinational companies, meaning that little over 1 per cent of MNCs are members. As Bennett and Burley (2005) point out, *'In what realm of life other than the strange world of [corporate responsibility] would a [1 percent] take-up rate be considered to be a success?'*

Moreover, some say that being a signatory to the Global Compact has little effect on corporate behaviour. The 2013 progress report *Global Progress on Corporate Sustainability* (UN Global Compact, 2013) provides a wealth of information on what signatory companies are doing, but is equally noteworthy because (a) less than 25 per cent of 'participants' participated in the report (i.e. submitted information), and (b) of those that did report on their performance, much less than half—especially smaller companies—had reached the implementation stage. In theory, this should leave companies open to peer group and civil society pressure to improve their performance, but in reality the Compact's grievance procedure introduced in 2005 seems to have withered on the vine (it does not appear on the website or in the annual report) and, as already noted, the Compact only agreed a complaints procedure to deal with allegations that signatory companies were breaching its Principles in late 2005. Now, companies that do not respond to complaints can be removed from the signatory list, barred from Compact activities, and forbidden to use its logo. Almost immediately, the NGO Corpwatch lodged complaints against six firms, and in 2008 over 600 companies were delisted. However, since then there has been a hiatus—the Compact's reports and website do not make it clear how to lodge a complaint against a signatory company or how the delisting process works. Furthermore, given the organization's small staff, it is hard to see how a credible process of ensuring members' integrity can be maintained.[30] The Global Compact Critics blog has highlighted how signatories such as GSK, Danone, and BHP have been embroiled in acts that contravene Compact Principles.

Another criticism of the Global Compact is that the high profile granted to a voluntary initiative detracts from broader UN attempts to regulate business behaviour. For example, critics point to the way in which the Compact rose to prominence at the same time as the UN Commission on Human Rights was backtracking on its draft Norms on the Responsibilities of

Transnational Companies and Other Business Enterprises with Regard to Human Rights, following pressure from business and the US government. Since then, John Ruggie, a respected Harvard academic with UN and corporate responsibility experience, has been brought in to assess whether the UN should develop binding norms on human rights for multinational companies, and he made clear at the outset that he felt that the current system of global rule making was imbalanced in favour of markets rather than human rights. His interim conclusion was that the norms so far were too difficult to monitor and enforce, and 'too engulfed by their doctrinal excesses'.[31] But, in a subsequent report, he was optimistic that voluntary human rights initiatives would become the basis for binding standards and that it would be in the interests of business to lobby government for stronger regulations.

Some find it bizarre that the UN sees business as a protector of civil rights, and such criticisms are indicative of wider concerns about what can be achieved through voluntary corporate responsibility. According to Doane (2005), what she refers to as 'CSR' is built on four myths (see Box 13.1). These are a retort to some of the arguments put forward by corporate responsibility thinkers, such as Zadek's work on the competitive advantage of nations, and the many people who have written about the business case. Doane stresses the contradiction between short-term financial returns and long-term societal contributions. This echoes *The Economist*'s view that business serves the public good only when companies focus on 'long-term profitability'. What *The Economist* leaves unexplained is that, as discussed in Chapter 12, in recent years there has been a strong trend in major capital markets towards short-term investment, even among institutional investors, and this is something that is well understood by corporate responsibility theorists. Although some of the challenges of corporate responsibility probably derive, in part, from investor short-termism, it is misleading either to argue that corporate responsibility theory disregards this problem, or to imply that executives feel free to manage companies with a long-term view.[32]

Similarly, it is disingenuous to claim that any worthwhile actions carried out under the banner of corporate responsibility are simply acts of good management. There are elements of good management practice today that were once unknown or unacceptable (e.g. systems for reducing water and energy usage, policies on bribery and corruption) and which might not

Box 13.1   The four myths of corporate responsibility

Myth	Reality
The market can deliver short-term financial returns and long-term societal benefits	This assumes that shareholders are investors with an interest in the company's long-term success; today's investor is more accurately considered an 'extractor', i.e. driven by short-term profit-seeking
Ethical consumers will drive change	In reality, consumers shop in their own narrow financial self-interest and are much more sensitive to price than they are to ethical considerations
Companies will compete in a 'race to the top' over ethics	Although companies may present themselves as socially responsible, there are many areas in which they deliberately pursue acts of social irresponsibility
In the global economy, countries will compete to have the best ethical practices	In reality, voluntary standards in developing nations have brought mixed results, and competition for foreign investment has led such countries to weaken their insistence on strong labour or environmental standards

(*Source:* adapted from Doane, 2005)

have entered into the mainstream but for corporate responsibility initiatives. Nonetheless, as we have seen in Chapter 12, there is surprisingly little information on the impact of corporate responsibility which can be used to defend it against criticisms that it is not achieving its goals.

Utting (2005) makes clear that there has been demonstrable progress in corporate responsibility, although more in some areas than others. For example, as mentioned in Chapter 12, it has had more effect on workplace health than on equal pay, job security, and abusive disciplinary practices. More importantly, however, while corporate responsibility has been successful in increasing the array of issues that companies agree it is legitimate for them to address, the procedures to implement standards often remain weak. He points to the examples of the Global Compact and the Global Reporting Initiative, which tend to rely on dialogue and shared learning between participating companies and other stakeholder groups, rather than on monitoring performance and compliance. He also criticizes current approaches for being too top-down, exclusionary, and technocratic, assigning a minimal role to local organizations. This situation is exacerbated because corporate responsibility tends to categorize people and social formations in ways that are misleading, if not damaging, in certain societies and cultures.[33]

Certainly, some corporate responsibility initiatives reflect a belief that companies will improve their performance by learning from peers, and this has become the basis for the Global Leadership Network and the London Benchmarking Group. Whether this approach is more effective than others is unproven, but it is one that many companies find acceptable, even if, to outsiders, it raises questions about the degree to which business decides by itself what issues to tackle and what constitutes acceptable performance. Equally, it is criticized as a way in which companies can control the speed of progress, allowing them to put the emphasis on process rather than on measurable outcomes in relation to major social and environmental issues.

Frustration with the slow progress of corporate responsibility led a group of international NGOs, including WWF, Oxfam, Friends of the Earth, and Amnesty International, to refuse to participate in the UK government's 'draft international strategy for CSR'. They claimed that the strategy lacked direction and coherence, and that it inadequately analysed the mismatch between company behaviour and society's expectations.[34] As if to confirm the NGOs' scepticism, development of the strategy fizzled out, although this might be used as an argument against government involvement as much as evidence of the slowness of corporate responsibility.

SustainAbility, one of the organizations that also refused to participate, has more recently argued that one reason why corporate responsibility is not achieving its goals is that it has focused on the social and environmental aspects of the triple bottom line, largely overlooking the economic aspect. While fair trade, fair pricing, and fair wages are addressed to some degree, critics argue that there is a need for a broader economic agenda that includes the accountability of companies, the affordability of products, diversity, and equity.[35]

BSR and AccountAbility, two other organizations that are closely associated with corporate responsibility, have developed a framework for including these kinds of economic responsibility.[36] Studies of Unilever's economic impact in Indonesia and South Africa provide similar insights, as does other industry-specific work on tourism.[37] This is part of a wider trend, promoted from both inside and outside corporate responsibility, to expand its scope. Indeed, it is one of the achievements of contemporary corporate responsibility that it has reinvigorated thinking about what society should expect from companies, even if the irony is that it is now criticized for failing to answer some of the questions it has provoked.

For some critics, the answer to these questions is to be found in moving from corporate responsibility to what has been named 'corporate accountability'.[38] The often top-down

Some financial institutions with a strong record of corporate responsibility practice seem to have survived the crisis relatively well—for instance, Standard Chartered and Audur Capital. But institutions like Citigroup, Bank of America, and UBS, all previously acclaimed for their corporate responsibility initiatives, were all embroiled in major controversies during the crisis. Moreover, notions of responsibility seem to have played no part in the ensuing allocation of government bail-outs or the rapid frequently engineered acquisitions. Goldman Sachs, which received $31 billion in US government support, was accused of being *a great vampire squid wrapped around the face of humanity, relentlessly jamming its blood funnel into anything that smells like money*. Having announced it would pay nearly half of that sum in employee bonuses, its CEO Lloyd Blankfein claimed that bankers are *doing God's work* when they raise the capital companies need to grow: *We have a social purpose*, he says. And vice-chair Brian Griffiths rammed the point home, saying that people should *tolerate the inequality as a way to achieve greater prosperity for all*.

Why, then, despite the resurgence of interest in corporate responsibility since the late 1990s, was such a conventional financial crisis allowed to happen? What does it tell us about corporate responsibility today? One perspective is that business cannot be allowed to self-regulate, and as importantly should be reined in from interfering with regulatory governance. In major economies, banking had lobbied for fewer restraints on their behaviour and for light-touch regulation. In some ways, the success of Goldman Sachs and similar institutions was the creation of influential networks that penetrated public policy. In what amounted to 'regulatory capture', they were able to outsmart civil servants and politicians, creating an environment where ill-comprehended and ultimately damaging financial instruments became desirable. While this was taking place, companies such as Citigroup and ABN Amro burnished their reputations by establishing the Equator Principles and supporting other responsible finance initiatives such as the UN Principles for Responsible Investment. In hindsight, critics say that these acts were a smokescreen.

A second perspective is that this was a wake-up call to corporate responsibility thinkers. Perhaps too much attention was being paid to a relatively narrow aspect of investment—i.e. the universe of listed companies—and not enough to banking behaviour (from governance to product offerings). The knowledge of corporate responsibility champions in the financial industry came into question. Were these people at the core of the industry? Did they have any real clout? Why were there so few people like David Pitt-Watson of Hermes with a history of running funds, and why did concerned industry leaders such as Stephen Green and John Bogle have little impact on corporate responsibility thinking?

A third perspective is that, even if much of the heavy lifting to do with financial sector reform is driven by government, corporate responsibility ideas will have an important role. The Tobin tax, which some theorists have discussed in a corporate responsibility framework, is being seriously considered as part of the reform package. Banking bonuses might be something that self-regulation can address. Understanding the social and environmental impact of investments is an area where corporate responsibility practice is starting to develop. Corporate governance is receiving more attention as a specific aspect of corporate responsibility.

Whatever perspective one adopts, the banking crisis raises fundamental questions about how society manages corporate behaviour. Corporate responsibility may not have predicted the crisis, but neither did government regulators despite the fact that banking is probably the most tightly regulated industry, with banks in major markets having to submit daily balance sheets. A different way of looking at the issue is to consider how much can be achieved through banks addressing problems of which they are a part unless some of the experiences and ideas of contemporary corporate responsibility are recognized. Complaints that if one country over-regulates the industry, the main players will migrate elsewhere strike to the heart of the global governance challenge which is central to corporate responsibility. The sense of injustice that bailed-out banks damaged their investors and were spared the consequences is something that might be remediated through genuine stakeholder dialogues as

(continued...)

well as political intervention. Even if the largest questions, such as whether banks that are too big to fail are also too big to exist, may not be addressed through the kind of approaches associated with contemporary corporate responsibility, does this mean that theory and practice have nothing to offer?

(*Sources:* Barrera, 2000; Arlidge, 2009; Hopkins, 2009; Taibbi, 2009; Markopolos, 2010; Lewis, 2011)

Questions

1 The case study points to different perspectives on banks and corporate responsibility.

  a Is it more responsible to allow banks to fail than to bail them out?

  b What aspects of banking did corporate responsibility theorists overlook before the crisis?

  c What aspects should they prioritize now?

2 Many argue that the financial crisis is indicative of contemporary corporate responsibility's weaknesses.

  a What are the main arguments for relying on a regulatory governance solution to banking reform?

  b Are there areas where a non-regulatory approach might be more effective?

  c What do the weaknesses of self-regulation and regulatory governance reveal about the challenges of global governance?

3 Bankers' bonuses have become a lightning rod during the financial crisis.

  a What are the arguments for considering bankers' bonuses to be a corporate responsibility issue?

  b What are the arguments against this?

  c Should bailed-out banks be allowed to pay bonuses?

discussion of impact in Chapter 12, the information does not yet exist to decide what balance of approaches will be optimal.

Summary

Corporate responsibility has come in for increasing criticism, especially from outside the field, perhaps as a reflection of its growing influence on business life. The criticisms fall into four main areas: (a) corporate responsibility is a specific agenda imposed on business by civil society organizations that damages profitability and therefore the ability of business to generate wealth for society; (b) ideas of corporate responsibility are now dominated by business, which is able to shape the agenda in its own narrow interests; (c) the current concerns within corporate responsibility are too narrow and leave out many of the key issues for which the public expects business to take responsibility; (d) to date, corporate responsibility practice has failed to achieve its goals, and needs to be more rigorous and innovative in the future.

The stance taken on these issues is often informed by individuals' responses to two questions. What is the purpose of business? What kind of societal issues can corporate policies rooted in self-regulation, public pressure, and business self-interest adequately address? If one thinks that the primary purpose of business is to make a profit, then corporate responsibility will be criticized if it does not support that end. But if one thinks that the purpose is its social function (e.g. producing useful affordable goods), then corporate responsibility will be assessed on a different set of criteria. Similarly, those who see legislation as a barrier to competitiveness will look at corporate responsibility in terms of its capacity to remove the regulatory burden, while those who are suspicious of market-based self-regulation will want to know whether corporate responsibility is as rigorous and effective as are government interventions.

In consequence, there is neither a dominant critique of corporate responsibility, nor even a common definition of what is meant by the term. But the points raised are often insightful, thought-provoking, and deserving of proper consideration, regardless of whether they are accepted or not.

Further reading

www.oxfordtextbooks.co.uk/orc/blowfield_murray3e/

online
resource
centre

Visit the Online Resource Centre that accompanies this book to enrich your understanding of this chapter. Among the resources available are web links, exercises, and additional case studies.

Banerjee, S.B. 2007, *Corporate social responsibility : the good, the bad and the ugly*, Edward Elgar, Cheltenham.

Critical perspectives on corporate responsibility as practised around the world.

Economist 2005a, 'The good company: the movement for corporate social responsibility has won the battle for ideas', *The Economist*, 20 January, online at www.economist.com.

Economist 2005b, 'The union of concerned executives: CSR as practised means many different things', *The Economist*, 20 January, online at www.economist.com.

Economist, 2005c, 'The world according to CSR: good corporate citizens believe that capitalism is wicked but redeemable', *The Economist*, 20 January, online at www.economist.com.

Economist 2005d, 'Profit and the public good: companies that merely compete and prosper make society better off', *The Economist*, 20 January, online at www.economist.com.

Economist, 2005e, 'The ethics of business: good corporate citizens, and wise governments, should be wary of CSR', *The Economist*, 20 January, online at www.economist.com.

Collection of articles from a special edition of *The Economist*, critiquing corporate responsibility from a liberal economics perspective. However, see also the very different articles on corporate responsibility in the 17 January 2008 edition.

Fleming, P. & Jones, M.T. 2013, *The end of corporate social responsibility: crisis and critique*, SAGE, London.

No holds barred critique of corporate responsibility as an extension of business's domination in a globalized economy.

Moon, J., Crane, A., and Matten, D. 2008, *Corporations and citizenship*, Cambridge University Press, Cambridge.
   A detailed discussion of differing notions of citizenship, the distinct roles business plays as a citizen, and what these reveal about the shortcomings of corporate responsibility.

Utting, P. and Marques, J.C. 2010, *Corporate social responsibility and regulatory governance: towards inclusive development?* Palgrave Macmillan, Basingstoke.
   A collection of articles exploring different aspects of how ideas of corporate responsibility relate to regulatory governance, with a particular focus on developing and emerging economies.

Online resources

- Links to additional material on critiques of corporate responsibility
- Additional snapshots of real-world corporate responsibility criticisms
- Examples of companies under fire for corporate responsibility shortfalls
- Links to other web-based resources

Endnotes

1. See, e.g., Elkington and Hartigan, 2008.
2. See, e.g. Blowfield, 2005a; Levy and Newell, 2002; Strathern, 2000.
3. *The Economist*, 2005c.
4. *The Economist*, 2005a.
5. *The Economist*, 2005c.
6. Harberger, 2003.
7. Friedman, 2000.
8. Ethical Performance, 2007.
9. Manheim, 2004.
10. See, e.g., Reich, 2007.
11. See, e.g., Ballinger, 2010.
12. Ballinger, 2010.
13. Bakan, 2004.
14. Monbiot, 2005.
15. Friends of the Earth (2005) and WWF and Sustain Ability (2005) address lobbying; Christian Aid (2005) examines corporate taxation; WDM et al. (2005) examine privatization and liberalization; Christian Aid et al. (2005) is a study of the tobacco company BAT; Action Aid (2005a,b) are studies of the impact of the retail, food, and agriculture industries on small farmers in developing countries; CAFOD (2005) examines working conditions in the computer industry. An up-to-date source of similar reports is www.corporate-responsibility.org.
16. Brooke and Penrice, 2009.
17. Power in the corporate responsibility context is a central theme in Bendell (2004a), Blowfield (2005b), and Newell (2005).
18. Utting, 2005; Rajak, 2006.
19. Data from www.issproxy.com, accessed 20 June 2006.

20. Radin and Werhane (2003) discuss changing employment contracts; Grosser and Moon (2005) and Barrientos et al. (2001) discuss gender dimensions to corporate responsibility.

21. Nocera, 2006.

22. Ginsberg, 2005; Prakash, 2006.

23. Pamela Robinson, personal communication.

24. For a newspaper perspective on this litigation see Rusbridger (2009).

25. See, e.g., Moon et al., 2005; Wood et al., 2006.

26. Frynas (2005) and Fig (2005) provide case studies of corporate responsibility in Africa; Nielsen (2005) and Newell (2005) provide insights into power in Bangladesh and India; Lund-Thomsen (2005) and Jenkins (2005) explore the wider context within which corporate responsibility operates and its consequences.

27. See, e.g., Brooke, 2010.

28. Crane et al., 2013.

29. Murphy, 2007.

30. There is little mention of UNGC staffing in the academic literature, and the organization's own materials devote more space to the institutional structures than the quantity and qualifications of staff. Most staff seem to be based in New York (about 20 people) with small secretariats in local networks. It is unclear how many staff are full-time employees, and anecdotally a lot of the work seems to be done by unpaid interns.

31. *Ethical Performance*, 2005c; 2006b.

32. Blowfield and Googins, 2007.

33. Dunn, 2004; Tharoor, 2001.

34. *Ethical Performance*, 2004.

35. Elkington and Lee, 2006.

36. Available at www.economicfootprint.org.

37. Unilever publishes various economic development studies at www.unilever.co.uk/sustainability/casestudies/economic-development/, although the South Africa study is no longer available on the website. Information on the economic development of tourism can be found at www.odi.org.uk/programmes/tourism/ and www.icrtourism.org/.

38. Utting, 2005; Bennett and Burley, 2005; Doane, 2005.

14

The future of corporate responsibility

 Chapter overview

In this chapter, we focus on the current trends in corporate responsibility and consider in what directions the field is moving. In particular, we will:

- examine the major trends that will affect what is meant by 'corporate responsibility' over the coming years;
- explore aspects of contemporary corporate responsibility that may be refined or enhanced;
- discuss evolving types of approach to corporate responsibility;
- reflect on what corporate responsibility reveals about the changing role of business in twenty-first-century society.

 Main topics

Where is corporate responsibility heading?   334
Mega-trends affecting corporate responsibility   337
Embedding and integrating corporate responsibility   339
Transition and transformation   345
The role of business in society   349

Key terms

Capital markets

Social and environmental trends

Corporate governance

Business in society

Demographic change

Sustainable consumption and production

Where is corporate responsibility heading?

One of the interesting things about writing a third edition of a book is that one can look back at changes and developments. In our first edition, we began this chapter with a quote from Margolis and Walsh (2003)—'The world cries out for repair'. They were writing not long after the dot.com bubble and the economic downturn that had followed the demise of companies such as Enron and WorldCom. Ten years on, and the cries to repair the world are as strong as ever. In 2013, JP Morgan had to pay a record $13 billion fine to settle investigations into its mortgage-backed securities, HSBC had to pay $4.2 billion for mis-selling financial products, Barclays faced a £50 million fine for a 2008 investment deal that saved it from being taken over by the British government, and UBS paid an $885 million fine for misrepresenting mortgage-backed bonds. Economic growth around the world, including the once vibrant BRICS, has stalled, with many OECD countries struggling to shake off a prolonged recession that came about because of corporate malfeasance. In Brazil, public protest about the government and private sector has become common; in South Africa the killing of 34 protesters at the Marikana mine in 2012 was a stark reminder that the corporate responsibility challenges of the past are still with us.

Yet, as this book shows, business is seen as much as a solution to society's problems as it is a cause of them. For some, corporate responsibility today represents an exciting agenda in which business is increasingly becoming a conscious and accountable agent in delivering non-financial outcomes. Our discussion of social enterprise (see Chapters 4 and 11) demonstrates how a new field has emerged that defines the corporate purpose in terms of societal outcomes. Impact investing (Chapter 11) shows how investor and social criteria are being blended together. Yet there are many who would argue that what cries out for repair is capitalism itself. Corporate responsibility's relatively minor role in addressing the first major economic crisis of the twenty-first century is discussed in Chapter 13, but events such as financial meltdown, recession, and geopolitical shifts all serve as a reminder that, to paraphrase Marx, companies may make their own choices, but they do so in circumstances not of their own choosing. Faced with an array of mega-trends such as decarbonization (see Chapter 3), demographic growth (see Chapter 4), and the emergence of new economic powerhouses (see Chapter 5), companies find themselves operating in new circumstances that present challenges in terms of both what their responsibilities are, and how they can be managed. To return to the definition of corporate responsibility used throughout this book—it is about what the responsibilities of companies are, how they are negotiated and defined, and how they are managed. In other words, there are theoretical and management practice dimensions.

As we look at corporate responsibility's future, both of these spheres are relevant. In 2005, Allen White, one of the people behind GRI, set out three scenarios for corporate responsibility in the next ten years. Now that we are approaching 2015, those scenarios provide an interesting vantage point for viewing yesterday and tomorrow:

1 In Scenario 1, which White calls *'fad and fade'*, he imagines a severe economic downturn that causes companies and governments to concentrate on basic economic survival and recovery, and to discard any thoughts of making corporate responsibility integral to corporate strategy, management, and governance. Companies will still face corporate responsibility challenges, such as transparency, labour standards, human rights, and climate change, but government mandates and regulation, rather than business innovation, will drive their responses.

2 Under Scenario 2 (*'embed and integrate'*), calls for a business case for corporate responsibility have disappeared, because the benefits have already been persuasively demonstrated. Companies of all sizes and types of ownership accept corporate

responsibility as the norm and not only adhere to international standards on good governance, labour practices, and environmental stewardship, but have melded their moral and ethical commitment to corporate responsibility into all facets of their business. In contrast with the fad and fade scenario, corporate responsibility is seen as an integral part of corporate management that will be resilient to economic conditions.

3   Scenario 3 ('*transition and transformation*') describes a wholly different approach, under which frustration with the types of programme discussed in other chapters spurs the formation of a coalition of civil society, labour, and business, pushing for '*corporate redesign*'. For White, this transformation marks an ending of the narrow focus on short-term shareholder value and its replacement by a stakeholder model of the company, within which employees, communities, suppliers, and shareholders are all considered as 'investors' with the right to participate in the firm's governance and to benefit from its surplus.

Parts of the world clearly experienced the kind of downturn envisaged in Scenario 1 in the late 2000s, but it does not seem to have marked the demise of corporate responsibility that Allen speculated upon. The economic recession may have prevented some companies from adopting certain practices, and to cut back in some areas, but there has not been a large abandonment of investment. This is partly because companies from Marks & Spencer to Jones Lang LaSalle to Thomson Reuters are well along the path to embedding and integration (Scenario 2), and corporate responsibility is part of the way they do business. It is also because, although not to the degree that some had hoped, in important jurisdictions such as the European Union companies are required to report on social, environmental, and governance factors material to the firm.

A further reason is that corporate responsibility management has often been implemented without increasing the company's headcount. Predictions that corporate responsibility would require new specialists have come true only to a limited extent. This may differ from country to country, and where corporate responsibility is new as an area of management practice, or where companies are moving beyond philanthropy, the human resource requirements will vary just as they did in the early days at companies such as Rio Tinto, KPMG, and Google.

A final reason is that companies better understand how issues such as demographic change and sustainable development are significant determinants of the environment in which business will be done in the coming years, and corporate responsibility provides useful tools and insights for managing these challenges. A small example of this is that climate change was flagged as a major issue for future corporate responsibility management in the first edition of this book, and now has become one of the main mega-trends affecting the field (see Chapter 3). Likewise, other mega-trends such as developing country poverty have become part of mainstream corporate responsibility (see Chapter 4). Indeed, a weakness of White's scenarios is that, aside from economic downturn, they overlook the wider context within which corporate responsibility evolves. They assume that it is business that decides what it will do, when in reality it is continually renegotiating its relationship with wider society. Therefore, in considering the future, we structure our discussion in terms of both management practice (White's scenarios) and shifts in the business–society relationship that in turn are affected by mega-trends (see Figure 14.1).

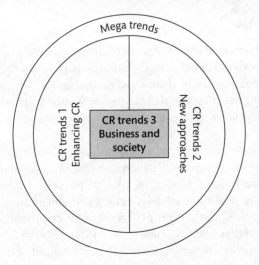

Figure 14.1 A framework for understanding corporate responsibility trends

Mega-trends affecting corporate responsibility

Climate change

By far the most noticeable global issue affecting corporate responsibility has been climate change, and in recent years the term corporate responsibility has started to be used interchangeably with sustainability. Although there has been a resurgence in climate change denial, and there remains a significant amount of public debate about the science, the international scientific community has concluded that there is a 95 per cent certainty that climate change is related to human economic activity.[1] Not surprisingly, many companies are treating this as a serious business issue. We discussed climate change in more detail in Chapter 3, but it is worth remembering that if the consensus of a large part of the international science community is correct, greenhouse gas emissions will need to be reduced by 80–90 per cent by 2050 if we are to avert 'dangerous climate change'.[2] To achieve this equitably, the largest emitters such as the USA would have to reduce their emissions from 25 tons per person to about 5 tons; countries such as Germany, South Africa, and Japan would have to halve their emissions; and while China could raise its emissions slightly, the question remains how it could meet the expectations of an increasingly wealthy population while achieving a low-carbon economy.

This would be challenging enough with a static global population, but by 2050 the population is likely to reach 9.1 billion, compared with 2.5 billion in 1950. Eight billion of these will be living in the poorest countries, within which illiteracy and malnutrition hamper human development. Therefore, while we discuss climate change, the geopolitical shift in economic power, and poverty in other chapters, we need to highlight a further mega-trend—demographic change.

Demographic change

The field of corporate responsibility may provide a framework within which business is able to help to resolve climate change challenges. But there is also a risk that climate change will swamp the corporate responsibility agenda and draw attention away from other major societal changes affecting the relationship of business with society. Demographic change is an example of this that highlights some of the complexities of business's involvement in tackling sustainability.

The world's population has expanded enormously since 1950, but this growth has been unevenly spread in terms of age and location (see Box 14.1). Although the total population is predicted to level off at 9.1 billion by 2050, 95 per cent of growth will be in poorer countries, while that of wealthier nations is expected to remain fairly stable at 1.2 billion. Demographic change will pose all sorts of challenges for companies, including migration (from poor to rich countries, and from rural to urban areas), wealth flows (transfer of remittances from migrant workers to families around the world), health care (as the number and proportion of elderly in developed economies and also in emerging ones, such as China and India, continue to grow), social welfare provision (because of the changing ratio of economically active and inactive people), competition for natural resources (from energy to land to water), and pressure on ecosystems (owing to increased demands for housing, waste disposal, food, etc.).

The upshot of these changes is not known for sure. Malthus's idea that population growth hinders development persists, but some argue that rapid population growth promotes economic prosperity by adding human capital and increasing market size. Perhaps the dominant view today is that population size and growth, in isolation from other factors, have little impact on economic performance. But this perspective ignores a critical variable—the way in which a population is distributed across different age groups and how this affects development. For example, a high proportion of young or old dependants can limit economic growth because of the resources devoted to their care (especially by women). Countries with more people of working age can experience higher growth, because of the higher earnings and savings levels, and less spending on dependants, creating a 'demographic dividend' that developing countries might enjoy just as the US baby boomers did after World War II.[3]

Box 14.1   World demographics at a glance

- Total population has risen from 2.5 billion in 1950 to 6.5 billion today.
- Seventy-six million new inhabitants are added each year because births outnumber deaths by more than 2:1.
- Nearly half the world's population is under the age of 25.
- Population in the least developed countries will triple by 2050 and will change little (it may even decline) in more developed regions.
- Emerging economies, such as China and India, will have increasingly large proportions of elderly people (31 per cent and 21 per cent, respectively, by 2050).

Global geopolitical change

A third trend we are currently witnessing is a fundamental shift in geopolitical power that is recognized within the corporate responsibility context, although at times is misrepresented. In Chapter 4 we highlight how the relationship between business and poverty in developing countries is an important element of corporate responsibility practice. However, in many ways this reflects a historical tradition where many have argued that it is the duty of the rich world to help the poor. This has been the premise behind government to government aid as well as the work of many international NGOs. In addition to this, as we have mentioned earlier (see Chapter 5), there is a tension between corporate responsibility as a means through which values are universalized, and corporate responsibility as something that is constructed and affected by localized cultural and political conditions. This has inspired an interesting body of theoretical work, as well as inter-country studies of corporate responsibility.

However, as became evident in the financial crises of the late 2000s, the rich but heavily indebted developed economies, which have been seen as leaders in corporate responsibility, are now very reliant on loans from emerging economies.[4] In contrast with previous crises in the developed world, emerging economies did not overall suffer a marked downturn. With corporate debt exceeding 100 per cent of GDP in the Eurozone and household debt over 90 per cent in the USA (in the UK corporate debt is 100 per cent and household debt is over 110 per cent), it is emerging market governments and sovereign wealth funds that have prevented economic meltdown. In the seven largest economies, sovereign debt is running at almost 120 per cent of GDP, a figure last seen in the aftermath of World War II. This is only sustainable because emerging economies such as China and Malaysia (and other countries, notably Japan and Germany) are willing to use their reserves to buy sovereign debt. How long that willingness will remain is unknown, but the consequences of this shift in dependency are likely to be lasting and profound.

 Discussion points

Demographic change is likely to be a significant influence on what is considered to be corporate responsibility in the coming years.

- What are the ways in which demographic change might affect business in wealthy democracies?
- What are the scenarios for business in 2050 resulting from demographic change in China, Brazil, or India?
- What can business do to ensure that developing economies better enjoy their 'demographic dividend'?

Embedding and integrating corporate responsibility

What are likely to be the responses within corporate responsibility to the above mega-trends? Based on what is already happening and what is being talked about, two readily discernible types of change are occurring. One is the emergence of 'new types of approach' to corporate responsibility (see 'A new kind of business case' p 345); the other is the enhancement and refinement of some of the well-established responses, and it is to these that we first turn.

The professionalization of corporate responsibility

Perhaps the broadest refinement is likely to be the growing professionalization of corporate responsibility. Among other factors, this is an inevitable outcome of some of the wider trends in corporate governance that we have already noted. Internally, the increased focus on non-financial dimensions of governance generally means that boards want to know that extra-financial risk is being managed effectively, and many companies are emphasizing the internal reporting of such data. Cross-functional teams are being created to manage non-financial risk and compliance agendas, and, as noted in other chapters, new management and report-ing systems are being developed to address corporate responsibility risks (e.g. the ethical and environmental management systems used in the supply chains for Nike and Adidas).

This is part of a trend for internal audit functions to extend their scope of work beyond the financial into areas such as health, safety, and the environment, and responsible supply chain management. There are already many consultancy and certification businesses meeting the demand for outsourcing in these areas. To envisage how this will grow, one needs only to imagine the likely demand for metrics and reporting systems with which to track progress in companies with major commitments to corporate responsibility. For example, Hewlett Packard is one of several companies that discloses its supplier factories, encouraging labour organizations and others to verify conditions. Patagonia provides detailed information on the footprint of its products to help consumers make informed decisions. Companies committed to integrated reporting (i.e. producing joint reports on financial, environmental, and social performance), such as Timberland and BASF, now offer quite sophisticated online resources to help users assess their performance.

The more that these metrics become material to companies, the more impetus there will be for greater professionalization of corporate responsibility. This professionalization will happen in different areas of business. For example, corporate responsibility is likely to become a specific managerial competency, with prospective managers increasingly exposed to the field as an aspect of management practice; corporate responsibility professionals will undergo continual development; and managers, in general, will need to be aware of the issues. Professionalization is also likely to lead professional service firms to build the capacity of accountants, lawyers, and others so that they can offer corporate responsibility services to companies. Equally, if corporate responsibility becomes of more importance to the invest-ment community, analysts, fund managers, trustees, and others will need to meet new stand-ards of professional competence (see Box 14.2).

Beyond ethical sourcing

One driver of professionalization is concern that current services are of insufficient qual-ity. For example, a 2006 report by the US National Labor Committee pointed to numerous labour rights abuses in audited factories, and member companies of the Ethical Trading Initi-ative have been highly critical of the auditing of labour conditions.[5] Such auditing is a key fea-ture of corporate responsibility management in global supply chains, and its poor quality has

Box 14.2 Initiatives aimed at professionalizing corporate responsibility—examples

- Fifty FTSE100 companies have had their non-financial reports externally verified; ten of these verifications have been performed by one of the Big Four accountancy firms
- The Prince of Wales's Accounting for Sustainability project is helping organizations to measure the environmental and social costs of their actions more effectively
- PricewaterhouseCoopers and Ernst & Young are among the sponsors of the AA1000 sustainability assurance standard, which has a professional qualification element
- The International Federation of Accountants (IFA) has issued standards on non-financial assurance engagements.
- The Institute of Chartered Accountants in England and Wales (ICAEW) has started to analyse sustainability from an accountancy perspective

been cited as an indicator of the dysfunctional relationship between brand owners and their suppliers. Companies such as Levi Strauss and Gap have tried to move away from a situation in which they felt that they were policing suppliers through auditing, towards one that was intended to build the capacity of managers and workers. But, even if the auditing were perfect, auditors alone would not improve social or environmental performance. As Utting (2005) points out, there are about 70,000 multinational companies with 700,000 affiliates, served by innumerable millions of smaller companies. Yet no more than 5,000 companies produce corporate responsibility reports, about 700 firms use the GRI's Guidelines, and a similar number have adopted SA8000. Even the most widely used certification scheme, ISO14001 on environmental management, has only been applied in just over 90,000 facilities worldwide.

More ambitious still are efforts to think not only of single issues within the chain, but about what constitutes a sustainable supply chain as a whole, including social, economic, and environmental dimensions. The Sustainable Agriculture Initiative Platform, backed by companies such as Danone, Nestlé, and Unilever, is an example of this, although it is concerned primarily with the environmental aspects of agricultural production. Ongoing work by companies such as Cadbury–Schweppes, as well as initiatives such as the Roundtable on Sustainable Palm Oil, are applying a larger lens that includes issues such as working conditions, land rights, and terms of trading.

Adopting international standards

The desire to use standards in supply chains more effectively is part of a wider debate in corporate responsibility about international standards. For example, in Boston in July 2006, at a meeting of representatives from corporate responsibility organizations such as the International Business Leaders Forum, AccountAbility, Business for Social Responsibility, and the Center for Corporate Citizenship, a United Nations representative proposed that the UN Global Compact and the Global Reporting Initiative's Guidelines be established as global frameworks around which corporate responsibility organizations might align their activities.[6] For some, this is seen as essential for corporate responsibility to reach critical mass and to obtain a broad political legitimacy; it is feared that, without it, the corporate responsibility movement will disintegrate into specialized niches and an incoherent array of commercial applications.

A similar sentiment lies behind other collaborative initiatives, such as Jo-In, under which some of the most prominent ethical sourcing organizations are sharing learning on how to implement voluntary codes of labour practice. Although not made explicit, such collaborations are also an attempt to address complaints by companies that there are simply too many codes and that, if different standards were to be recognized as equivalent, this would reduce the cost of auditing and win more acceptance from suppliers.

There are legitimate concerns that, if those who support corporate responsibility cannot decide meaningful parameters with regard to the meaning and implementation of corporate responsibility, then the so-called movement will fragment. At the same time, it is equally appropriate to be concerned about who is most likely to influence any ultimate consensus and whether what emerges is a genuine agreement, or more the result of coercion. If we look again at the idea of using UNGC and GRI as the basis of a global framework, we see that the organizations involved in this discussion are corporate-funded in some way, whereas a major criticism of corporate responsibility discussed in Chapter 13 is that corporate influence is already undermining its legitimacy.[7] Hence, while alignment around particular definitions and approaches might be desirable, any trend in this direction will ultimately only be sustained if there is an accompanying consensus about what society expects from business (see 'The role of business in society', p 349).

Making corporate responsibility more inclusive

One of the challenges in creating a global vision of corporate responsibility is that norms and values are strongly influenced by cultural factors (see Chapter 5). Moreover, current corporate responsibility practices have been criticized for overlooking, or excluding, the priorities of particular social groups. For example, mirroring the male bias of which business is often accused, codes of labour practice have been criticized for favouring the interests of male workers and ignoring the needs of women.[8] Similarly, some argue that corporate responsibility practice can only be effective when it accommodates the cultural perspectives of the locations in which it is being implemented, while it has also been proposed that non-Western value systems, such as those practised in labour-intensive Indian organizations, are better suited to achieving positive outcomes.[9]

Awareness of the exclusiveness exhibited in some areas of corporate responsibility has been recognized for a number of years and is one of the insights provided by work in developing countries (see Chapter 4). But it is far from certain whether there will be a trend towards tackling the issue in any concerted way over the coming years. On the contrary, there may be a stronger trend towards seeing those who do not fit readily within the company's vision of what constitutes a legitimate stakeholder as hostile adversaries—something that may be inadvertently reinforced by the tools that companies use to manage corporate responsibility.[10]

Responsible consumers

One area of corporate responsibility that is already starting to receive more attention from companies is that of 'product' responsibility. There are different facets to this. In the area of corporate philanthropy, pharmaceutical companies and others are taking product donations more seriously in terms of ensuring that the products are useful and well used. Rather than designing a product and then ensuring that it is made responsibly, companies from Nike to GE to Boots are using external inputs from the outset to think through the meaning of a responsible product—something that is being given a further push by legislation on product life-cycle responsibilities (e.g. the EU Waste Electrical and Electronic Equipment Directive). Media and entertainment corporations, such as Time Warner, are starting to put in place policies relating to how they portray others' products (e.g. the use of cigarettes in films) and, as the discussion of social enterprise shows (see Chapter 11), there is increasing thought going into the responsibility of companies to make products available to the poor.

Uniting each of these examples is a new sense of the company's responsibility towards consumers. This, in turn, reflects a renewed interest in engaging the consumer in corporate responsibility and an awareness that one of the constraints faced by companies in advancing a corporate responsibility agenda is consumer ignorance or indifference. January 2006 saw the high-profile launch of Product Red, a global 'brand' under which major companies, such as American Express, Motorola, and Giorgio Armani, launched product lines, some of the profits of which would go towards fighting HIV/AIDS in Africa.

However, Devinney et al. (2006) say that any belief that consumers are ready to make purchasing decisions based on ethical criteria is not borne out to any significant degree in practice. They point to a marked difference between consumer opinions and purchasing behaviour which suggests that morals stop at the wallet. If, as many corporate responsibility managers seem to believe, the adoption of corporate responsibility as an element of mainstream management practice depends on consumers making decisions based less on price and more on an awareness of what lies behind the price, we might see a variety of initiatives put in place over the coming years.

 Discussion points

Embedding corporate responsibility into mainstream management practice is considered by many to be essential.

- Why are international standards important to integrating corporate responsibility?
- What are the main weaknesses with ethical sourcing at present?
- Why is corporate responsibility sometimes called exclusive?

Engaging financial institutions

The growth of socially responsible investment has been heralded as one of the successes of corporate responsibility (see Chapter 10), but to put that in perspective, the amount invested in SRI funds is less than 1 per cent of that invested in hedge funds.[11] Therefore it is not surprising that many see the future development of corporate responsibility as closely linked to trends in the mainstream financial community. Hope for rapid advances were dashed by the collapse, bailing out, and subsequent destruction of reputation experienced by investment banks (see 'Corporate governance' p 349), but it is notable that, despite these upheavals, the investment community continues to engage in corporate responsibility. Institutions hit by scandal, such as UBS and Merrill Lynch (now part of Bank of America), have continued to have senior personnel focusing on sustainability, and Goldman Sachs has continued to promote its Environmental Policy Framework as a way of linking capital to sustainability.

The figures tend to be presented in ways which suit advocates' beliefs, but there is significant money available for investing on environmental issues. Green stimulus packages that have been part of public economic growth spending are estimated to be $221 billion in China, $112 billion in the USA, and $31 billion in South Korea.[12] Green venture capital is well established, especially in the USA. Proven venture firms, such as Kleiner Perkins Caufield and Byers which has created a $100 million fund for green technology companies, are investing heavily in clean and green innovators. Attracted by trends such as rapid growth in renewable energy and green building materials, roughly 10 per cent of North American venture capital now goes into green technologies, while more than £660 million has been invested in European clean technology since 2001.[13]

Corporate responsibility issues are highly unlikely to be addressed adequately without the engagement of financial markets—but markets only respond when a price is attached to an issue. This has happened with carbon trading, for which London has established itself as the global centre, while New York and Chicago are emerging as competitors as the USA considers national emissions reduction targets.[14] Despite the European carbon market's problems in 2006, over 1 billion tonnes of carbon dioxide were traded in Europe alone, at a value of more than £12 billion. Blue-chip investment houses have been major investors: Goldman Sachs took a 10 per cent stake in London-listed carbon trader Climate Exchange, and as early as 2006 Morgan Stanley promised to invest $3 billion in carbon trading by 2012[15] although it is not obvious from the company's 2012 report if this was fulfilled or not.[16] Moreover, there is little sign that markets will be formed for other issues and limited debate about whether markets for other important issues, such as poverty, could ever be created.

Financial firms, such as Henderson Global Investment, have broadened the abbreviation 'SRI' (see Chapter 10) to mean 'sustainable and responsible investment' and focus on what they consider to be the technologies of the future. Along with initiatives that we have noted in other chapters, such as the emergence of specialist indices from within the conventional investment world (e.g. FTSE4Good and the Dow Jones Sustainability Indexes), these are examples of how corporate responsibility is starting to be integrated into mainstream analysis. In Germany, for example, investors and analysts are demanding increasingly sophisticated information on sector-specific sustainable development key performance indicators.[17] But overall, the investment community is ill equipped to judge the significance of sustainable development actions because it remains focused on assessing financial data and management quality, and the sums of money saved through, for example, eco-efficiency, although large, may not be large enough to attract analysts' attention. Most investors see their role as based on price, rather than on the kind of added value that some feel is achieved by relationship investing and other long-term relationships.[18]

To a degree, progress will depend on distinguishing what Lydenberg (2005) calls 'investable' issues that are material to a company, but not yet factored into the share price (i.e. mispricing), from those that are 'non-investable', for which engagement with investors is unlikely to have any effect. An important theme in future corporate responsibility debates will be how to tackle non-investable issues. Much will depend on the success of the initiatives noted elsewhere in this book in increasing the interest of mainstream analysts (e.g. the Marathon Club, the London Accord, the Enhanced Analytics Initiative, and the UN Principles for Responsible Investment—see Snapshot 14.1).

Snapshot 14.1   UN Principles for Responsible Investment

The UN Principles for Responsible Investment (PRI) is one of several initiatives aiming to persuade investors to think of matters other than the financial bottom line when placing their money. Its backers are investors responsible for 10 per cent of global capital (or more than $4,000bn of assets), including asset owners and investment managers. By signing up to the PRI, these investors commit to integrating environmental, social, and governance (ESG) issues into conventional investment analysis, to being active responsible owners by promoting good corporate practice in these areas, and to reporting transparently on what actions have been taken in this area.

What marks out the PRI is that its supporters are major global institutions that are not known for putting their name to frivolous or marginal initiatives. The initiative's principles make explicit that ESG issues, or extra-financial risks, have an effect on the long-term performance of companies. They mark a step towards learning about measuring companies in ways that do not necessarily fit into the normal accounting framework and, ultimately, towards identifying long-term investment drivers.

(Scott, 2006; www.unpri.org, accessed 1 October 2013; www.greenbiz.com, accessed 1 October 2013)

Quick questions

The PRI has been welcomed as a step towards getting the international investment community to focus on long-term drivers of company value.

1 What is the significance of the PRI?

2 Are its principles genuine ones for responsible investment?

3 How will the PRI influence the development of corporate responsibility?

 Discussion points

Throughout this book, we have looked at the criticisms, strengths, and limitations of corporate responsibility.

● Considering what has been discussed in earlier chapters, which of the trends in this chapter are likely to be most significant?

● Which are those that are likely to be least significant?

● Are there trends that have not been identified?

Transition and transformation

A new kind of business case

The business case for corporate responsibility is discussed in Chapter 6, but the limitations identified there have led some to argue for a different type of case that essentially requires people to look at companies differently. Although the liberal economic critique of corporate responsibility discussed in Chapter 13 argues that corporate responsibility constitutes harmful meddling with the efficiency of free markets, the alternative business case presents corporate responsibility as a way to address market imperfections and failures. As some liberal economists would agree, efficient resource allocation depends on markets yielding prices that reflect true social costs; when they fail to do so, such as when polluters do not have to pay the cost of pollution, the invisible hand can lead one in the wrong direction.[19] Therefore, instead of seeing corporate responsibility as an assault on free markets, it can be argued that it will ultimately make markets, or at least companies, more efficient.

This argument takes three different, if sometimes overlapping, forms. One is that, although there may not be a causal relationship between corporate responsibility and business performance, there can be a correlation between the quality of a company's technical systems and processes and its corporate responsibility practices, and good social and environmental performance can be achieved by companies that perform well financially.[20] If the most important factor with regard to profitability, growth, and future earnings is good management, corporate responsibility may be an indicator of a well-managed company.

The second argument emerges, in part, from the above observation and, more generally, from a belief that there is a need for alternative measures of company performance. For example, some maintain that the current methods of assessing a company's value and performance are flawed because, among other reasons, they do not adequately value the kinds of intangible assets to which corporate responsibility adds value (e.g. reputation, licence to operate). Moreover, conventional methods are poor at predicting long-term business performance, because sell-side analysts, in particular, are primarily concerned with short-term financial performance. A repeated claim made about corporate responsibility is that its true value to business will become apparent once companies focus more on long-term performance, because responsible and sustainable products and strategies are those that are most profitable in the long run.[21] Indeed, according to Goldman Sachs, which has launched an Environmental and Social Index, 60 per cent of company value is determined by long-term returns, and corporate responsibility issues will affect share prices if they come to be seen as affecting those returns. For this to happen, however, proponents claim that there need to be significant changes in the way in which capital markets function, in the types of accounting system used (e.g. the adoption of full-cost accounting of the kind developed at Glasgow University's Centre for Social and Environmental Accounting), and in the other means by which business performance is measured.

There are a number of corporate responsibility thinkers who argue that the strongest element of the business case is the important part that corporate responsibility will play in the successful companies of the future. The growth strategies of the past are portrayed as increasingly less effective, creating a need for new ways to grow. In this scenario, aspects of corporate responsibility are proposed as part of that change, requiring that corporate responsibility be accepted as part of core business strategy (see Chapter 6).[22] Thus, rather than asking how a dimension, such as human rights or eco-efficiency, affects access to capital, the business case hinges more on treating corporate responsibility as a critical link in innovation and learning, or as part of new, more sophisticated approaches to risk management.

This kind of thinking moves us a long way from trying to attach a monetary value to corporate responsibility activities. The alternative business case is already being reflected in the ways in which some large companies are approaching, or at least talking about, corporate responsibility. For example, a group of companies within the World Business Council for Sustainable Development, an early pioneer of eco-efficiency, has tried (in their words) to reunite the interests of business and society by restating the purpose of business as follows: '[The] *fundamental purpose of business is to provide continually improving goods and services for increasing numbers of people at prices they can afford.'[23]* The group holds that tomorrow's leading companies will be those providing goods and services in ways that address major societal challenges, such as poverty, climate change, depletion of natural resources, globalization, and demographic shifts. This is not a major reinterpretation of the role of business, and signatory companies claim that most firms benefit society simply by doing business. But two distinctions separate the group's perspective from those who advocate that 'business is the only business of business'. First, the signatory companies state that, while substantial and sustainable action by business to address pressing societal needs has to be profitable, shareholder value is not an end in itself, but a measure of how successfully companies deliver value to society. Second, the group emphasizes the importance of taking a long-term perspective on company performance and thereby echoes what was noted earlier about the ways in which capital market short-termism undermines the business case. They stress that the purpose of any sustainable company has to be more than generating short-term value for shareholders, yet *'simply by adding the word long-term to shareholder value, we embrace everything necessary for the survival and success of the company'.*[24]

As already noted, any claim that the business case for corporate responsibility can only be made by changing the rules of the game may not strengthen the credibility of corporate responsibility, at least in the short run, because it clearly implies that, in order to make a business case, we first need to redefine the purpose of business. However, it can also be argued that one of the contributions of corporate responsibility is to stimulate thinking about such fundamental issues. As van Tulder (2006) notes, corporate responsibility will need to distance itself from simplistic debates about profit maximization if it is to be more than a fad. He holds that, whether it is Prahalad (2005) arguing for societal issues, such as poverty, to be integrated into company strategies, or Handy advocating for a new type of company scorecard that includes contributions to society and the environment, or de Geus and his belief that companies need to harmonize their values with those of society to survive societal turbulence, leading business theorists have consistently set out the rationale for a different kind of business case. However, he also maintains that this is not a business case for corporate responsibility in the way that notion is typically conceptualized; rather, it is a business rationale for approaching the interface between business and society more efficiently, equitably, and effectively—what he terms *'societal interface management'*. Citing Mintzberg, he argues that companies are social institutions, the existence of which is justified only in so far as they succeed in serving society, in contrast with human beings, for example, who have an inherent right to be. This is a very different perspective to those that underpinned initial thinking about 'doing well by doing good' and the benefits of eco-efficiency, but building (or rebuilding) a societal case for business, rather than what can sometimes appear to be the business case for society, is, for some theorists and also executives, the kind of change that has to occur for the long-term prosperity of global society.[25]

Sustainable consumption and production

Another way of considering transformation is the new types of approach that have entered the corporate responsibility sphere. Social enterprise (see Chapter 11) and some of the poverty-focused initiatives (see Chapter 4) are examples of such approaches. Another that is starting to gain attention is described below.

One of the key challenges of the coming decades for sustainable development theorists is how to decouple certain types of growth, particularly those associated with harmful emissions and unsustainable energy use, from prosperity. This has especially come to the fore as the demands that fast-growing economies, such as India and China, will put on natural resources become apparent, and it has been estimated that for the consumption and production patterns of Canada or the UK to be adopted worldwide would require resources equivalent to those of three Earths—to adopt those of the USA would require those of five.[26]

'Sustainable consumption and production' (SCP) embraces an array of approaches that are aimed at addressing this problem. It refers to the challenge of achieving continuous economic and social progress that respects the limits of the Earth's ecosystems, and meets the needs and aspirations of everyone for a better quality of life, both now and for future generations. SCP requires better alignment between consumption, the natural resources needed for production, and the ecological sinks available to absorb waste.[27] OECD governments have been committed for decades to ensuring that the prices people pay reflect the full social and environmental costs involved, and European governments are committed to SCP through the 2000 Lisbon Agenda. Historically, however, governments have been weak and inconsistent in promoting SCP, for fear that consumers would have to pay higher prices. Moreover, concerns regarding relative national competitiveness have consistently trumped those about sustainable development.

Various principles have emerged for tackling SCP, and centres such as the Tesco-funded Sustainable Consumption Institute are being established to focus on these issues. But, as we have seen with other areas of corporate responsibility, the wider business environment does not always encourage companies to take sustainability-based decisions and may even create disincentives. Moreover, at present, the place of SCP initiatives in the context of corporate responsibility is still uncertain. On the one hand, the core issue—how growth can be achieved while realizing a drastic per capita reduction in the use of resources—is one that is central to corporate responsibility; on the other, much of the current interest has come from government and there is a sense that only government can break the kind of 'I will if you will' impasse that is preventing more business action in this area. But governments are also constrained by not wanting to take action unilaterally for fear that this would sacrifice competitive advantage, while those who view corporate responsibility as voluntary, rather than mandatory, may feel uncomfortable with government-driven SCP for ideological reasons.

 Discussion points

Companies often depend on the behaviour of consumers, investors, and customers to determine how responsible they can be.

- Why is an emphasis on short-term performance seen by some as incompatible with corporate responsibility?
- Should companies drive changes in consumer behaviour?
- Why do you think that an early report on sustainable consumption and production was called 'I will if you will'?

The role of business in society

Today, one does not need to venture far from the mainstream of corporate thinking to hear questions being raised about the effects and efficacy of capitalism. Stephen Green, former CEO of HSBC, had a best-selling book on the value of values and sustainability in business (Green, 2009), and John Bogle, founder of the Vanguard Group with $1 trillion in assets, has railed against Wall Street's greed (Bogle, 2009). Along with recent authors such as Zeitz and Grün (2013) and George Soros (2008), and business thinkers such as Warren Bennis (Bennis et al. 2009) and Rosabeth Moss Kanter (2009), they are part of group of respected individuals from the business status quo who are asking what were hitherto considered radical questions.

What is the role of business?

The roles that business play vary over time (see Chapters 2 and 5), and because of the major shifts that global society is undergoing, the historical roles assigned to business and government are widely held to be outdated. In recent years, corporate responsibility practice has had a mixed record of offering solutions to major aspects of the business–society relationship— providing a range of initiatives on sustainability, poverty, human rights, and climate change, but unprepared for tackling the mis-selling, greed, and deceit that lay behind the 2007–2008 financial crisis. In so far as corporate responsibility is interpreted as an approach to business self-regulation, it is not surprising that it is treated with scepticism by people disenchanted with ideas such as light touch regulation.

The financial crisis also exposed numerous instances of corporate irresponsibility, often in countries with the worst recessions. In addition to instances of corruption, such as Bernard Madoff's investment fraud in the USA and the bribery scandal surrounding Siemens' top management in Greece, there have been various cases where the line between managerial incompetence and abuse has been blurred. Companies with strong corporate responsibility reputations were still exposed by the debt default of Dubai World in 2009, and in hindsight Citigroup's commitment to corporate responsibility could be interpreted as a way of masking its fundamental management problems.

Corporate governance

Such examples show the influence that business can exert over government and the dangers of not getting the regulatory balance right. Robert Monks, corporate governance thinker, has

 Discussion points

Charles Handy (2002) has asked the question 'What's a business for?'

- Is the role of business different today than it was 50 years ago?
- How would you answer Monks' question about the good company's responsibility towards government?
- What is a business for in the twenty-first century?

said that, given the level of distrust about business's influence over government policy, the starting point should be: 'What is the responsibility of the "good company" with respect to government?' His prescriptions that companies disclose relevant information, exercise restraint in trying to influence government, and obey the law are less ambitious than some would want from a comprehensive corporate responsibility agenda, but nonetheless are, in many respects, a significant departure from what is currently on offer.

Huge fines and compensation claims for mis-selling of financial products have further strengthened the call for tighter regulation, although cases such as LloydsTSB's not only mis-selling claims protection insurance but then defrauding victims of those mis-sold products show that there is a long way to go before trust in banks can be restored.[28] Although corporate responsibility theorists can claim little credit in predicting the financial crisis, there is likely to be considerable interplay between new governance ideas and corporate responsibility more generally. The trend towards greater transparency, for example, complements demands that environmental and social issues be incorporated into corporate governance. As noted in other chapters, aspects of sustainable development have also found their way (with mixed results) into governance reform initiatives, such as the UK Company Law Review. In Europe, reporting on aspects of sustainability will increase as a result of the EU Accounts Modernization Directive, which requires that directors' reports contain a business review that includes information about environmental matters, employees, and social and community issues, including information on relevant policies and their effectiveness. This is reflected, for example, in the UK Companies Act 2006 which, for publicly listed companies, requires directors to report on non-financial issues to the extent that is necessary for an understanding of the business (see Chapter 7).

Central to such initiatives is a debate about the duties of corporate officers to those other than shareholders and the idea of enlightened shareholder value. Some legislation regarding directors' liabilities has been strengthened (e.g. the UK Corporate Manslaughter Bill), and recent decisions by the UK and EU courts mean that it is not only in the USA that companies can be held liable for their social and environmental actions abroad. Other regulations relating to sustainability issues have been introduced. For example, the EU's Pollution Prevention and Control Directive raises the bar on controlling industrial pollution across Europe, and its Waste Electrical and Electronic Equipment Directive deals with end-of-life issues for electronic products, which will influence the behaviour of both manufacturers and retailers.

The attention given to the responsibilities of business has increased further since the introduction of the 2007 UK Climate Change Bill, the first attempt to set legally binding targets on greenhouse gas emissions. But it is not legislation alone that is causing companies to act; codes of business practice that include aspects of corporate responsibility can serve to forestall legislation, but equally to meet requirements that companies demonstrate that they have a strong control environment. For example, Basel II (the revised international capital framework) requires major financial institutions to show that they have key risk measuring and monitoring systems and controls in place.

Most large companies now have codes, or sets of principles, that span wide areas of non-financial performance and are underpinned by a framework of policies. Such codes can also help companies to deal with the ethical responsibilities and liabilities that stem from such legislation as the 2010 US financial regulations, the US Sarbanes–Oxley Act 2002, the UK bribery and corruption law, the US Foreign Corrupt Practices Act 1977, and the UK Enterprise Act 2002.

The role of capital markets

The sub-prime mortgage bubble that led to the first major twenty-first century recession brought to the fore some of the structural issues that some believe make capital markets incompatible with responsible corporations. As the global market for capital expands and the costs of trading tumble, investors—even institutional investors—are focused on increasingly shorter time horizons.[29] Furthermore, the logic that owners of public companies are in a strong position to effect change has been challenged by the emergence of private equity firms as an alternative source of capital. Companies engaged in corporate responsibility, such as Aramark, Cadbury, and Boots, have all become privately held, removing them from many of the non-mandatory drivers associated with improved social and environmental performance (e.g. public reporting). This is not to say that publicly held companies are more likely to address corporate responsibility issues than are those that are privately held; Mars is a family-owned company that is widely respected for its work on supply chains and sustainable sourcing, and IKEA, owned by its founder, has invested heavily in sustainable production and retailing. Indeed, in some cases, it may be that, removed from the pressure to meet quarterly earnings targets, some privately held companies may be better placed to take a longer-term perspective than if they were publicly listed. Nonetheless, most large companies are publicly held, and many large private companies, such as Levi Strauss, continue to look to the same capital markets to some degree.

Hence there is a dichotomy that lies at the heart of corporate responsibility's future development: on the one hand, there are many corporate responsibility theorists and practitioners, both inside and outside the business community, who believe that companies that ignore the business–society perspective are putting their long-term prosperity in jeopardy; on the other hand, the short-term culture of the capital markets is affecting, and effectively putting damaging constraints on, how companies address societal issues. If the former viewpoint is true, short-termism is damaging shareholder, as well as stakeholder, value, but this is going unnoticed. Whether this perspective is accurate or not is, at present, more a matter of supposition than demonstrable fact, but the reaction of the capital markets will have a major influence on future trends in corporate responsibility. This is true of the investment community's own decisions, as is already evident, for example, in the way in which climate change is starting to be factored into financial analysis (see Snapshot 14.2). But it is also true in terms of the way in which the investment community affects the decisions of others. For example, it affects the advice that executives follow, so that even a company with a strong corporate responsibility track record might find itself under pressure to make decisions that would undermine its reputation in the name of optimization and efficiency.

The power of multinationals

It is not true that corporate responsibility is only an issue for the world's largest companies (see Chapter 11), but the power of major corporations and how their responsibilities are negotiated and enacted are likely to influence any debate about corporate responsibility as management practice. The power of supermarkets, for example, reflects a wider concern about the power of large companies. Some critics of globalization have turned their attention away from trade legislation, and more towards anti-trust and anti-monopoly

Snapshot 14.2   Tree-huggers at the gate—collaboration of private equity and NGOs over coal-fired power

The acquisition of RJR Nabisco by Kohlberg Kravis Roberts (KKR) in 1989 became infamous as an example of hard-headed, shareholder-value-driven capitalism in Burrough and Helyar's *Barbarians at the Gate* (1990). Two decades on and KKR's record-breaking private equity deal to purchase the energy utility TXU has made headlines for different reasons.

TXU had been under attack from environmental groups because of its plans to build eleven old-technology coal-fired power plants in Texas. The plans became bogged down in a swamp of public outcry, political manoeuvring, and litigation. In what some are holding up as a landmark collaboration between private equity and environmental activists, two environmental NGOs, the Natural Resources Defense Council and Environmental Defense, negotiated a deal whereby, in return for their backing the purchase, KKR agreed to suspend developments of eight of the power plants, pilot a 'clean coal' plant, cut greenhouse gas emissions, invest in alternative energy, and back government climate change legislation.

For the NGOs involved, it is another example of how to collaborate with business to achieve environmental objectives, although this, in turn, has led to criticism from other environmental groups that the KKR–NGO agreement contained too many loopholes. For KKR, the support of these multi-million-dollar NGOs reduces the risk that the purchase might otherwise represent and, it hopes, will strengthen TXU's licence to operate. It also signifies a new development in private equity strategy, under which firms bet on the profits to be made from social and political change.

(*Sources:* Smith and Carlton, 2007; *Economist*, 2007; Paulden, 2009)

Quick questions

The purchase of TXU is one of the first examples in which corporate responsibility issues and partnership with NGOs have overtly played a part in a private equity firm's investment decisions.

1 Although it is portrayed as a 'win–win agreement' between KKR and the NGOs, what do you think were the advantages for the former?

2 What do you think were the risks and potential disadvantages for the NGOs?

3 Do you think that this will be a one-off example, or will it extend to other industries?

activism. For example, there is concern that we inhabit a world dominated by global oligopolies that not only have enormous purchasing power, but are also exercising great political power. Consumers have benefited historically from anti-trust laws that prevent price gouging, but companies such as Wal-Mart and Tesco are today being accused of having such power, even over multinational suppliers such as Procter & Gamble or Rubbermaid, that they can set prices almost at will. They are also suspected of using this muscle to intimidate local governments and to drive through planning applications for new stores, irrespective of local community sentiment. And, of course, this same kind of power can be used against workers, as when McKinsey & Co helped Wal-Mart to prepare a memo on how to cut back employee benefits even though these were already among the lowest in the US retail industry.

The issue of corporate power applies to any industry, not only to that of retail. Suspicion is especially strong in relation to the lobbying of government on legislation, procurement, and spending. Corporate responsibility itself has been a target for lobbyists. For example, the Confederation of British Industry lobbied to have sections of the Company Law Reform Bill altered to limit company accountability to stakeholders and has been accused, more generally, of influencing the government's sustainable development policies. From a different perspective, WWF and SustainAbility (2005) compared corporate responsibility commitments and corporate lobbying activities, and found that, although many companies included discussion of lobbying in corporate responsibility reports, they were reluctant to lobby actively to improve social and environmental frameworks.

One area in which companies have been accused of using their power in ways that might harm the common good is taxation. Worldwide, there has been a trend to cut back corporate taxation, partly based on the argument that this will stimulate growth and generate more total revenues for government programmes. The Tax Justice Network and the Publish What You Pay campaign are examples of civil society responses to the suspicion that companies are not paying their fair share, and even that corporate responsibility is window dressing that is intended to divert attention away from the tax evasion strategies of multinationals. Greider (2006) proposes that corporate taxation could be refashioned, so that tax liabilities might be reduced for those that adhere to higher social or environmental standards. However, parts of the accountancy profession argue that there is insufficient understanding of the true scale of business's taxes, and PricewaterhouseCoopers, for example, has proposed a new framework for reporting a company's total tax contribution, i.e. all of the direct and indirect tax that business pays into the economy.

Transforming the corporate purpose

In previous chapters, we have explained how corporate responsibility relates to debates about new forms of accountability and new ways of valuing the company, and how these, in turn, reflect a resurgence of interest in rethinking the purpose of business. This interest is manifesting itself in different arenas across the spectrum, from theory to practice (see Box 14.3).[30]

Box 14.3   Principles of the redesigned corporation

1 The purpose of the corporation is to harness private interests in the service of the public good.

2 Corporations shall accrue fair profits for shareholders, but not at the expense of the legitimate interests of other stakeholders.

3 Corporations shall operate sustainably to meet the needs of the present generation without compromising the ability of future generations to meet theirs.

4 Corporations shall distribute their wealth equitably among those who contribute to its creation.

5 Corporations shall be governed in a manner that is participatory, transparent, ethical, and accountable.

6 Corporate rights shall not supersede or weaken the rights of natural persons to govern themselves.

(*Source:* White, 2005)

Despite a decade that was marked by two major economic collapses with business at the centre, it is still difficult to detect a widespread appetite for pushing through this kind of radical rethinking of the purpose of business. Indeed, some would argue that elements of corporate responsibility have been used to prevent such change. Nonetheless, we should not ignore the possibility that society is at the threshold of major change. This is certainly the belief of some who see the future of business as closely intertwined with climate change and who hold that this will—in contrast with models of gradual linear change in the past—precipitate dramatic unpredictable non-linear change.

If non-linear theory is true, it could fundamentally affect the way in which we approach the world, causing policy-makers and corporate managers to base their assumptions not on the expectations of gradual predictable growth that justify a focus on efficiency and optimization, but rather on the new realities of unpredictability and vulnerability that, in turn, will make areas such as resilience, sufficiency, and complexity the new focus of management. In such an environment of upheaval, the future directions within corporate responsibility would be hugely influenced by how useful the discipline proved itself to be in relation to the innovative approaches to management practice, technology, and policy that would be required.

Among the criticisms of corporate responsibility is that it only tinkers at the edges of these major societal issues and trends, and has so far lacked the rigour (of theory and practice) to address the most important dimensions of the business–society relationship. With reference to climate change, for example, some of the most demonstrable changes in business practice in recent years relate to eco-efficiency, but these are minor variations on the established models of business that do little to tackle what some argue are the fundamental questions about capitalism's role in ensuring the sustainability of the Earth's carrying capacity. Indeed, it can be argued that the question at the heart of corporate responsibility and its different forms that will surface over the coming years is whether capitalism itself is sustainable. For those who conclude that it is, corporate responsibility may be the discipline that allows them to consider if, and what, changes are needed to the capitalist model; for those who conclude that it is not, it remains to be seen if the frameworks and models within the corporate responsibility umbrella prove to be useful, obstructive, or irrelevant to the new paradigm.[31]

 Case study 14   Google—global struggles and responsibilities

'Don't be evil.' These are the opening words of Google's code of conduct. Founded in 1998, the company behind the world's most used internet search engine has revenues of over US$ 23 billion. It employs nearly 20,000 people, only 250 of whom are at corporate HQ in Mountain View, California.

Google has joined Hoover and Xerox as one of the few brands to become a verb. But as a premier citizen in cyberspace, Google faces unique responsibility challenges. First, there is the conventional problem of market dominance—Google has the world's most used search engine that is the backbone of the advertising business that generates most of the firm's revenue. In this sense, Google shares the same issues of power, responsibility, and reputation that in previous eras faced Standard Oil, De Beers, and the British East India Company. At the same time, Google's rise has been portrayed as a semi-subversive way of undermining the dominance of another information technology giant, Microsoft, and its public acceptance as a brand is evident in places from the blogosphere to The Simpson's cartoons.

(continued...)

Google added to its kudos in some quarters by its stand on information access in China. Since 2005, Google and the Chinese government have tussled over the data that Google's search engine provides. The government has demanded that links it has censored, such as the 1989 Tiananmen Square protest, should not appear on Google, and moreover that Google should hand over information about the sites that alleged dissidents are visiting. Early on Google seemed to comply, but in 2009 it threatened to pull out of the Chinese market after large-scale attempts to hack into messages on the company's Gmail service and to steal proprietary code. The hacking was particularly sensitive because in 2006 Yahoo! had handed over personal data from a Chinese journalist who ended up serving a prison sentence. The US government was increasingly insistent that US companies needed to think about the human rights aspects of their businesses.

Google's stand in China brought protests from the Chinese government, but was well received in many other parts of the world which saw the company as making a stand for freedom of expression despite the business costs. It continued to operate in China, but unlike its main competitors, Baidu and Soso.com, it inserted a warning into searches that the government had censored. However, by 2013 it had removed this function, claiming that it interfered with the users' experience.

Some observers regarded this as unconvincing, especially when seen in the context of other actions by the company. Its Street View service, photographing entire neighbourhoods and making them available on the web, has been criticized as an aid to burglars. The publishing of email accounts on its Buzz social networking service rekindled concerns about the amount of information Google collects and how it is used. The company has also been criticized for its tax avoidance policies which, for instance, saw earnings shifted from its British to its Irish subsidiaries. It has also been embroiled in long-running legal cases about digitizing books in the USA, Germany, and France, and in each case was portrayed as a corporate bully trying to ride roughshod over authors, publishers, and copyright law.

The latest example of Google's seemingly endless struggle to defend its licence to operate is the furore over the role of internet companies in online information accessed by the US security forces. There is no hard evidence that Google or other companies knowingly colluded with the US government in accessing data about phone calls and internet use by millions of private citizens, but at the very least the government seems able to hack in at will to what were once portrayed as secure systems, and there is some evidence that secret trapdoors were deliberately put into software to enable such access. Whatever the truth turns out to be, Google's claim to be empowering people at the expense of the status quo has been weakened, although that has not damaged its share price, which is now over $1000.

(*Sources:* Darnton, 2009; Watts, 2009; Waters, 2010; Wines, 2010; BBC, 2013; Holpuch, 2013)

Questions

1. Google aspires to provide a new model of business.

   a. What are the features of Google's code of conduct, and are they distinct (see investor.google.com/conduct.html)?

   b. What are the challenges for a cyberspace-based company compared, for example, with a conventional retailer or publishing company?

   c. What are the drivers of Google's emphasis on responsibility?

2. Google has developed a strong reputation as a responsible company, but has also been criticized.

   a. What do you think Google is doing that marks it out as a responsible company?

   b. What aspects of the company raise questions about the ethos of 'Don't be evil'?

   c. What should the company do in future to be a corporate responsibility pace-setter?

(continued...)

> **3.** In this chapter, we have set out various future trends and directions in corporate responsibility.
>
>   **a.** What does the case of Google tell us about the role of business in society?
>
>   **b.** What significant contributions is the Google Foundation making to social entrepreneurship and sustainability (see google.org)?
>
>   **c.** What aspects of Google's business have the greatest impact on society and the environment? Is the company addressing these adequately?

Summary

There are many elements to the corporate responsibility universe, as we have seen throughout this book. The indications are that this firmament will grow larger in the coming years for two reasons: first, there are pressing social and environmental issues that represent genuine challenges for both sustainability and global justice; second, there is an increasing expectation from different sectors of society that business will help to meet those challenges.

The future course of corporate responsibility will, to a large extent, be determined by how business's obligations to involve itself in major societal issues, such as climate change, demographic change, and global poverty, are defined and realized. No single institution will dictate how business responds; rather, as with other areas of corporate responsibility, the trends that emerge will be decided in various arenas of conflict, contestation, and collaboration. The growing power of multinational enterprise will be a significant factor in terms of the resources and influence that major corporations possess, and the way in which they act as a pole star for both public protest and aspiration. Moreover, struggles within the corporate world—not least the role of private equity funds as owners of what were hitherto publicly traded companies—will affect how ideas of corporate responsibility evolve.

Government responses to both the mega-trends affecting global society and the changing form of the corporation will also significantly influence what happens in the name of corporate responsibility. In some areas, such as that of flexible labour markets, it would appear that many governments are comfortable encouraging voluntary approaches and relaxing regulations; however, in other areas, notably that of climate change, some governments appear reluctant to rely on non-mandatory solutions. Given this situation, defining corporate responsibility in terms of voluntary actions seems likely to be increasingly less useful. This does not mean that non-mandatory approaches will be unimportant, and there are various ways in which corporate responsibility as management practice may be refined and enhanced over the coming years. Equally, there are strong signs of new types of approach gaining prominence, some of which (e.g. social entrepreneurship) will constitute free market responses to societal needs and others (e.g. sustainable consumption and production) that are likely to require significant government intervention.

However, one of the major trends around corporate responsibility will be less to do with management practice or government intervention, and more about the way in which we consider the role of business itself. Many of the current criticisms of corporate responsibility relate to how the prerogatives of the modern corporation determine its societal role. For some, this severely limits what business can do and, in important instances, causes business to act in ways that are counter to the overall societal good. This will remain the case, it is argued, until the corporate purpose is altered to reflect the rights, duties, and obligations of business as a citizen. There is by no means a consensus that such a radical shift should happen; some argue that this kind of philosophical reflection will divert attention away from the strength of current approaches as pragmatic management responses, while others claim that society should resist the notion of legal entities such as companies being thought of as citizens.

In terms of corporate responsibility as a discipline, there is no right or wrong answer to this type of debate. (Indeed, the weakness of recent corporate responsibility debates may be that thinkers have been too willing to champion either theory or practice as if they are mutually opposed, and their inability to consider reflexively what underlies this division.) Whether we are thinking about the chartered trading companies of the eighteenth and nineteenth centuries, the corporate philanthropists that emerged during the Industrial Revolution, the European cooperative movement, the place of international companies in twentieth-century banana republics, the sense of social obligation that is central to some of the most successful examples of business in Japan, South Korea, and Germany, or the denial of responsibility to anyone other than shareholders that dictated much of corporate strategy in the 1980s and 1990s, we are constantly reminded that, regardless of what we choose to call it, the role of business in society is fundamental to both business and the world at large. This will not change, regardless of what names we choose to assign to the pantheon of issues, practices, and hypotheses that have relevance to the business–society relationship. Future trends in corporate responsibility will not be determined by names, but by the discourse that evolves around the role of business and the relevance of corporate responsibility as a discipline, as a profession, as an antagonist, as a protagonist, or as a commentator in relation to that discourse.

Further reading

www.oxfordtextbooks.co.uk/orc/blowfield_murray3e/
online resource centre

   Visit the Online Resource Centre that accompanies this book to enrich your understanding of this chapter. Among the resources available are web links, exercises, and additional case studies.

Accenture and UN Global Compact 2013, *Architects of a better world*, Accenture and UN Global Compact, New York.
   A thousand CEOs give their impressions of what sustainability means to their business.

Blowfield, M. & Johnson, L. 2013, *Turnaround challenge: business and the city of the future*, Oxford University Press, Oxford.
   A hard look at whether business can succeed given the challenges of global mega-trends.

Branson, R. 2011, *Screw business as usual*, Virgin, London.
   Virgin founder's take on business as an institution for the common good.

Green, S. 2009, *Good value: reflections on money, morality and an uncertain world*, Allen Lane, London.
   HSBC boss reflects on the role of business and the importance of responsibility. Arguments for a radical overhaul of company law.

Henriques, A. 2007, *Corporate truth: the limits to transparency*, Earthscan, London.

An exploration of the limits of transparency in the contemporary corporate world and arguments about how far to push the boundaries.

Hollender, J. & Breen, B. 2010, *The responsibility revolution: how the next generation of businesses will win*, Jossey-Bass, San Francisco, CA.

Popular corporate responsibility entrepreneur provides admittedly US-biased insights into trends in innovation, social entrepreneurship, and investment.

Online resources

- Additional resources on new trends in companies
- Exercises and discussion topics for students
- Teaching ideas on the future of corporate responsibility
- Links to other web-based resources

Endnotes

1. See Fifth Assessment Report of the International Panel on Climate Change, 2013.
2. Fourth Assessment Report of the International Panel on Climate Change, accessible at www.ipcc.ch.
3. Bloom and Canning, 2006.
4. This analysis draws heavily on a series of lectures on the global financial crisis and developing countries given by Valpy FitzGerald at Queen Elizabeth House, Oxford, May 2010.
5. ETI, 2007.
6. Bradley Googins, personal communication, 14 August 2006.
7. Among the organizations receiving corporate funding to a significant degree are the International Business Leaders Forum, Accountability, Business for Social Responsibility, the Center for Corporate Citizenship, the Conference Board, the World Economic Forum, Harvard Kennedy School of Government, and Sustainability.
8. Barrientos and Smith, 2007.
9. Pio, 2005.
10. See, e.g., Hughes and Demetrious, 2006; Blowfield, 2004.
11. Total money in SRI funds (2005), £6.1bn; total money in hedge funds (2006), $1.786 trillion. Based on figures from www.eiris.org and HedgeFund.net.
12. HSBC estimates presented by Nick Robins, London Business School, 27 February 2009.
13. McCarthy, 2006.
14. McCarthy, 2006; Gascoigne, 2007.
15. See also Chapter 11.
16. See Sustainability Report 2012, accessible at www.morganstanley.com.
17. www.altenergystocks.com.
18. Hesse, 2006.
19. Lydenberg, 2005.
20. Bahgwati, cited in Holliday et al., 2002, p 17.
21. Benjamin Heineman in *Wall Street Journal*, 2005; Weiser and Zadek, 2000.

22. Forum for the Future, 2006.

23. Holliday et al., 2002.

24. WBCSD, 2006.

25. WBCSD, 2006, p 9.

26. See, e.g., Dyllick and Hockerts (2002) on the need to move beyond eco-efficiency to 'socio-efficiency' and to factor not only efficiency, but also effectiveness, into social and environmental performance; see also the quotes from executives on the dangers to capitalism of not considering the role of business, cited in Blowfield and Googins (2007).

27. Wackernagel et al., 1996.

28. For coverage of the LloydsTSB case which also involved Deloitte, see for instance www.thetimes.co.uk/tto/news/uk/article3787876.ece, www.theweek.co.uk13/6/13, and www.ft.com/cms/s/0/8d54cec8-d26b-11e2-aac2-00144feab7de.html, all accessed 22 October 2013.

29. See www.lehmanreport.jenner.com/, accessed 29 June 2010.

30. Bogle, 2005.

31. See, e.g., contributions to *Business and Society*; alternative constructs of the corporation on http://www.corporation2020.org/ and the work of authors such as Plender (2003) and Greenfield (2006).

Corporate responsibility information resources

Here are some of the most well-known newsletters, magazines, and web resources offering regular news, analysis, and thinking on corporate responsibility. We have provided dedicated web links where these are available, but you should note that some of these online resources are available only by subscription.

Readers should also check the occasional coverage of corporate responsibility issues in management journals (such as the *Harvard Business Review*), development and economics journals (such as the *Third World Quarterly* and *International Affairs*), and the mainstream media (such as the *Financial Times* and *The Economist*).

Accountability Forum Practitioner-oriented journal, focusing on accountability for sustainable development; published by Greenleaf Publishing.

Brooklyn Bridge-TBLI Group e-newsletter Comprising articles and features on the triple bottom line and sustainability; online at www.tbli.org/index-newsletter.html.

Business and Human Rights Resource Center Web-based resource with links to coverage of discrimination, environment, poverty and development, labour, access to medicines, health and safety, security, and trade; online at www.business-humanrights.org.

Business and Society Academic journal, focusing on social issues and ethics, and their impact and influence on organizations; published by Sage and sponsored by the International Association for Business and Society; online at www.bas.sagepub.com.

Business Ethics Quarterly academic journal debating issues of business ethics; published by Blackwell Publishing.

Business Ethics Magazine Magazine of Corporate Responsibility Officers, a professional association; online at www.business-ethics.com.

Business Ethics Quarterly Academic journal bringing different disciplinary perspectives to bear on the general subject of the application of ethics to the international business community; published by the Society for Business Ethics.

CasePlace Collection of corporate responsibility-related case studies; online at www.caseplace.org.

The Chronicle of Philanthropy Newspaper focusing on corporate philanthropy; online at www.philanthropy.com.

Chronos E-learning tutorial on the business case for sustainable development; online at www.sdchronos2.org.

Corporate Citizenship Briefing Magazine for corporate responsibility news and analysis; published by Corporate Citizenship Company; online at www.ccbriefing.co.uk.

Corporate Governance Academic journal, focusing on international business and society; published by Emerald.

CorporateRegister.com Online collection of corporate responsibility reports; online at www.corporateregister.com.

Corpwatch.com Online information resource monitoring corporate behaviour and malfeasance; online at www.corpwatch.com.

Critical Perspectives on International Business Academic journal, presenting social science perspectives on international business and society; published by Emerald.

CSR and government British government website devoted to CSR information; online at www.societyandbusiness.gov.uk.

CSR Asia Online resource offering information on corporate responsibility in Asia; online at www.csr-asia.com.

CSRWatch Web-based media service offering criticisms of corporate responsibility; online at www.csrwatch.com.

CSRWire Web-based resource featuring corporate responsibility news and press releases from publicly traded corporations; online at www.csrwire.com.

E-Business Ethics.com Online resource offering information on business ethics, corporate citizenship, and organizational compliance; hosted by Colorado State University; online at www.e-businessethics.com.

Eldis Information gateway to web-based resources on globalization and international development, including special section on corporate responsibility; online at www.eldis.org.

Ethical Corporation Monthly magazine featuring corporate responsibility news and analysis in both print and online versions; free email newsletter also available; online at www.ethicalcorp.com.

Ethical Performance Monthly newsletter on corporate responsibility and socially responsible investment; online at www.ethicalperformance.com.

ETHICOMP Journal Journal on computer ethics and social responsibility, connected to the ETHICOMP conference series; online at www.ccsr.cse.dmu.ac.uk/journal/home.html.

Faith in Business Quarterly Journal relating Christian faith and values to the business world; published by the Ridley Hall Foundation and Industrial Christian Fellowship; online at www.fibq.org.

Global Corruption Report Annual report focusing on the consequences of corruption; published by Transparency International; online at www.transparency.org/publications/gcr.

Governancefocus.com Web-based resource offering information on worldwide corporate and board governance issues; online at www.governancefocus.com.

GreenBiz.com Free web-based resource for companies seeking information on environmental business practices; online at www.greenbiz.com.

Green Money Journal Newsletter offering resources and contacts for environmentally and socially responsible investing; online at www.greenmoneyjournal.com.

Greener Management International Management journal focusing on strategic environmental and sustainability issues; published by Greenleaf Publishing.

ID21 Online information service featuring links to research on globalization and international development, plus a series of issues Insights papers; online at www.id21.org.

Journal of Business Ethics Academic journal, covering ethical issues related to business; published by Kluwer Academic Publishers.

Journal of Corporate Citizenship Quarterly academic journal dedicated to corporate responsibility; published by Greenleaf Publishing.

New Academy Review Now defunct quarterly journal that addressed strategic and policy issues related to corporate responsibility; online at www.new-academy-review.com.

Oneworld.net Web-based community and resource focusing on globalization and development; online at www.oneworld.net.

Origo Cross-Sector News News service focusing on the intersection between business and social innovation; online at www.origonews.com.

SD Gateway Online resource offering information from members of the Sustainable Development Communications Network; online at www.sdgateway.net.

SocialFunds.com Web-based resource for individual socially responsible investors; online at www.socialfunds.com.

Socially Responsible Investing Compass Online resource featuring all existing green and ethical retail funds and indices in Europe; online at www.sricompass.org.

Society and Business Review Practitioner-oriented journal, aiming to assist businesses in enhancing their commitment to societal purposes; published by Emerald.

Stanford Social Innovation Review Journal focusing on strategies for non-profit organizations, foundations, and socially responsible businesses; online at www.ssireview.org.

SustainableBusiness.com Online resource offering information and links for environmentally oriented businesses; hosted by Green Dream Jobs, a sustainable business jobs service; online at www.sustainablebusiness.com.

Glossary

accountability The obligation to render an account of one's actions.

auditing The evaluation of an organization in order to establish the validity and reliability of information about that organization. Social auditing relates to the validity and reliability of information about a company's social performance (e.g. its impact on local communities, its relationship with stakeholders); environmental auditing relates to its performance in relation to the environment (e.g. emissions, waste management).

best-in-class screening An approach to positive screening in socially responsible investment that involves selecting the best within a given sector of investments, based on certain criteria.

bottom of the pyramid (also known as base of the pyramid) The potential commercial market provided by the six billion people who live on less than two US dollars a day. Developed by CK Prahalad and Stuart Hart, American business theorists, the concept regards poor people as a seriously underserved market that might be the engine of the next wave of global trade and economic prosperity. Examples include microfinance (the provision of innovative financial services to poor people in ways that help their development), Cemex's affordable housing programme, and Hindustan Lever's marketing of iodized salt to rural communities. Bottom of the pyramid is one of the most discussed areas of social entrepreneurship.

bribery The giving of favour to influence another's action. (*See* corruption.)

Brundtland Commission (formally, the World Commission on Environment and Development) Convened in 1983 by the United Nations and widely known by the name of its chair, Gro Harlem Brundtland, the Commission proved to be a highly influential enquiry into environmental deterioration and the challenge of sustainable development. Its definition of sustainable development—development that meets the needs of the present without compromising the ability of future generations to meet their own needs—is frequently cited in discussions about the role of business in sustainability.

business and society An area of academic enquiry (normally undertaken by social scientists) concerning the relationship between business and wider society. Long established, with its own journals and professional association, the themes of business and society have recently been more widely acknowledged by corporate responsibility scholars and practitioners.

The consultancy firm McKinsey & Co is among those offering services that will help companies to understand business and society issues.

business ethics Typically regarded as a strand of applied ethics, focusing on the ethical issues facing a company and its officers. The US branch of the field, in particular, is primarily concerned with helping individuals to navigate the ethical dilemmas that arise in a commercial context. There is, to a degree, an alternative European approach that is more concerned with the role of business in society, and with the ethical duties and obligations that arise from this. Some would argue that corporate responsibility is a subset of business ethics.

capitalism An economic system under which the means of production are privately owned, and the price of inputs and outputs are determined by markets within which people engage on a free and voluntary basis, and within which goods and services are sold with a view to making a profit. Adam Smith, the eighteenth-century philosopher, was the first to describe comprehensively the free market capitalist system in his books *The Theory of Moral Sentiments* and *The Wealth of Nations*. He recognized that an economic system could not be treated as something separate from society, and hence had implications for the way we live. Issues relating to the moral dimensions of capitalism—such as the responsibilities, duties, and obligations of business—in many ways underlie corporate responsibility.

capital markets The financial markets on which long-term debt and equity securities are traded. The role of these markets in influencing corporate behaviour is an area of debate within corporate responsibility.

change management (also known as transformation management) A systematic approach to managing change within an organization which includes adapting to, controlling, and effecting change. Within management practice, corporate responsibility is often described from a change management perspective.

civil regulation A theory positing that companies are not only regulated by government, but increasingly by the norms and actions of civil society that control a business's licence to operate. This is most evident in the role that civil society organizations play in affecting company behaviour irrespective of legal requirements. In the 1990s, for example, trade unions and non-government organizations were able to pressurize Nike into paying attention to working conditions in its supply chain, despite there having been no government pressure to do so.

civil society Historically, the term has meant private interests that are distinct from those of the state, but in the corporate responsibility context, it tends to refer more specifically to the uncoerced collective action around shared interests, purposes, and values of institutions that are distinct from those of the state and the market (e.g. civil society organizations).

civil society organizations (CSOs) Non-government, non-business organizations with a social function. CSOs include non-government organizations and free trade unions, and are an important constituency both in influencing corporate behaviour (civil regulation) and in conducting partnerships.

climate change Significant change in measures of climate, such as temperature or precipitation, that last for an extended period (i.e. decades or longer). These changes can be the result of natural factors and processes, such as alterations in ocean circulation, or of human activity, such as deforestation and burning fossil fuels. (*See also* global warming.)

code of conduct/practice A set of principles, typically with accompanying criteria, that set out a company's commitment to maintaining a standard in a specific area of its operations. Corporate responsibility codes set standards regarding the natural environment, labour, corporate governance, money laundering, bribery and corruption, human rights, and corporate responsibility reporting principles. While codes may make mention of legal requirements (e.g. minimum wage, toxic emissions), they are themselves voluntary in nature.

corporate accountability A company's moral or legal obligation to account for its actions and performance to its stakeholders. In the corporate responsibility context, it is also often discussed in terms of the capacity of those stakeholders to influence company actions.

corporate citizenship At times used synonymously with corporate responsibility, CSR, etc., but (in the USA, in particular) can specifically refer to discretionary initiatives undertaken by a company, such as employee volunteering and corporate philanthropy.

corporate governance Conventionally refers to the system by which companies are directed and controlled for the benefit of shareholders. In some jurisdictions, the scope of benefit includes multiple stakeholders, and, in recent years, there has been renewed interest in the balance between economic and social goals, and between individual and communal goals as the object of governance, as per the 2002 Cadbury Report.

corporate governance framework The regulatory structure, designed to safeguard investors' assets, within which the rules for the running of companies are outlined.

corporate malfeasance Misconduct by a company or by an officer of a company.

corporate philanthropy Proportion of corporate revenues donated for philanthropic purposes. (In the USA, the amount is typically 1 per cent.) Once associated with somewhat arbitrary donations to worthy causes, there is increasing focus on strategic philanthropy, under which donations are targeted towards areas that are synergistic with the company's interests or competencies.

corporate reporting The act of publicly reporting on a company's performance. In the corporate responsibility context, emphasis has been placed on the publishing of social, environmental, and sustainability reports that, in some cases, form part of the company's annual report to shareholders.

corporate responsibility An umbrella term embracing theories and practices relating to how business manages its relationship with society.

corporate social performance The way in which, and degree to which, a business organization's principles of social responsibility and related processes motivate actions on behalf of a company and deliver outcomes of societal benefit.

corporate social responsiveness The response of companies to the demands that they address their social responsibilities. The term was introduced by scholars in the mid-1970s to denote a greater focus on corporate responsibility as an area of management practice, in contrast with more theoretical debates about the meaning of responsibility that had previously dominated academic thinking.

corruption The misuse of power associated with a public or corporate office for the purpose of personal gain. It includes bribery, which is the giving of favour to influence another's action.

defensive corporate responsibility Actions taken by a company or industry to protect its reputation and to reduce its risk in relation to aspects of its non-financial responsibility.

deterritorialization The detachment of social practices from a specific place, so that the relationship between culture and geographical location is no longer paramount. The phenomenon is a consequence of the social and political processes associated with globalization.

developing country A country with low per capita income relative to the world average. In many developing countries, incomes can be less than two US dollars a day. (*Compare* emerging economy.)

eco-efficiency Achieving efficiencies through the reduced use of natural resources and energy, fewer harmful emissions, greater recycling and reuse, increased lifespan, and the increased use of renewable resources in the design, manufacture, and consumption/use of products.

economic globalization (also referred to as liberal economic globalization) Increased world integration as a result of free trade, and financial, technology, and labour flows. The terms is sometimes treated as synonymous with globalization, but, strictly speaking, refers to only one feature of that phenomenon.

embedded economy Stemming from Polanyi's argument (1944) that a feature of capitalism is the way in which the economy is treated as something separate from society ('*disembedded*'), whereas the interests of justice and prosperity are best served when the economy is interrelated with social, political, and religious institutions ('*embedded*'). Corporate responsibility (theory and practice) can be interpreted as concerned with re-embedding business so that it is more than simply an economic actor.

emerging economy A country that, based on GDP and indicators of human development, is considered to be on a path towards being included among the wealthy/developed nations in the foreseeable future. (*Compare* developing country.)

engagement An approach, used in responsible investment, by which investors become involved with the companies in which they invest in order to influence the activities, behaviours, and operations of those companies.

environmental auditing The evaluation of an organization to ascertain the validity and reliability of information about that organization's claims concerning its performance in relation to the environment (e.g. emissions, waste management).

environmental ethics Enquiry into the ethical relationship of human beings to the environment and non-human entities, and into the value and moral status of these.

environmental impact assessment Assessment of a company or facility's environmental consequences, normally focusing on inputs and outputs within a particular geographical location.

environmental, social, and governance (ESG) Commonly used term that captures the areas of non-financial performance with which corporate responsibility management practice is often concerned.

ethical sourcing A company's recognition of its responsibilities for the social and environmental conditions under which products are manufactured/grown within its supply chain. Typically, this involves the application of a code of practice as a condition of doing business with suppliers, although it may also involve engaging with suppliers to improve their capacity to meet that standard.

ethical theory Theories of what is right and wrong, based on reason. (*Compare* moral theory.)

ethical trade An umbrella term for a variety of approaches under which companies take responsibility for the conditions under which products are manufactured/grown within their supply chains. Includes ethical sourcing, fairtrade, and sourcing from sustainably managed forests and fisheries.

fairtrade A trading partnership established as a contribution to achieving greater equity in international trade through, for example, ensuring a price paid to the producer that is greater than the cost of production, a surplus paid to the producer group (not the individual) for investing in social development activities, and a long-term relationship between producer and buyer. Originally intended to help small producers in developing countries, larger producers are now included, and, for these, the emphasis is on worker rights. Fairtrade takes different forms, but is most widely associated with the Fairtrade label, which certifies that an item has been produced and traded according to the principles set out by the Fairtrade Labelling Organizations International (FLO International).

fair wage (also called a living wage) A wage sufficient to provide the basic needs (food, shelter, education, health care), with some discretionary income, for a worker and his or her immediate dependents within a reasonable working week (typically, not more than forty hours). It is often a provision in codes of labour practice and workers rights, although it is sometimes replaced with a minimum wage, which is a legally defined wage that should reflect a fair wage (although, in practice, it may not).

financing sustainability An emerging facet of corporate responsibility, dealing with the interrelationship between companies' corporate responsibility objectives and the behaviour of the finance community (investors, analysts, fund managers, etc.). At its core is the perceived mismatch between the long-term nature of sustainability and the short-term orientation of much investment activity.

free trade union A type of trade union that is able to operate without interference from employers and government.

global commons Natural assets important to human well-being that are outside national jurisdiction (e.g. the oceans, outer space, the atmosphere).

global governance Historically, governance has referred to the exercise of political, economic, and administrative authority in the management of the affairs of a country or other locality. Globalization and accompanying phenomena, such as deterritorialization, present particular challenges for governance, because important areas of life cannot be managed by the nation state alone. Hence, increasing concern is paid to global governance, including the governing of global commons, such as the atmosphere, and the behaviour of multinational companies. The institutions for addressing such issues are, however, still weak and incomplete for the most part, giving rise to what some see as a governance deficit. The emergence of corporate responsibility as an area of business practice can be seen as a contribution to filling that deficit by making companies pay attention to their global social and environmental performance.

globalization   A term used to refer to the increasing global connectivity, integration, and interdependence in the economic, social, technological, cultural, and political dimensions of existence. It is often used to focus on particular aspects of the phenomenon (e.g. global cultural homogenization, economic globalization, the spread of particular ideas such as democracy and free markets), but what marks it out as historically unique is the interplay of its different facets, which presents all manner of challenges for global governance, justice, and sustainability.

Global Reporting Initiative   The custodian body behind an international effort to create a common framework for the voluntary reporting of the economic, environmental, and social impact of the activities of business and other organizations. This framework is set out in the GRI Guidelines.

global warming   The average increase in atmospheric temperature near the Earth's surface and in the troposphere, which can contribute to changes in global climate patterns. (*See also* climate change).

government   A particular group of legitimate representatives of the state.

health and safety   (also known as occupational health and safety; workplace health and safety) The dimension of corporate responsibility relating to the health and safety of people at work. Some of the most measurable outcomes of corporate responsibility programmes have been in this area.

human rights   Basic entitlements accorded to all human beings. There are significant differences of opinion as to what these rights should be, although the most commonly mentioned ones in a corporate responsibility context concern legal, civil, and political rights, especially those set out in the Universal Declaration of Human Rights.

human rights impact assessment   An assessment of the human rights dimensions of a company's operations, including, for example, issues of the rights of indigenous peoples, intimidation of local communities by company security forces, and the fundamental rights of workers in the workplace.

Industrial Revolution   The historical period, lasting throughout most of the nineteenth century, during which the economies of the USA and many European nations shifted from an agricultural to a manufacturing base, with an accompanying strengthening of the capitalist economic system.

integrated business strategy   In a corporate responsibility context, 'integration' refers to the embedding of corporate responsibility issues into mainstream business practice. The consequence of this is that corporate responsibility becomes a business driver that creates value for the company at the same time as the company creates value for wider society. (*Compare* corporate philanthropy.)

international development   The policies and programmes undertaken by government and non-government agencies in developed and developing economies, with the intention of alleviating poverty and creating sustainable livelihoods for people in developing countries.

liberal economic globalization   *See* economic globalization.

liberal economics   A theory of economics that is rooted in the belief that individuals' economic actions based largely on self-interest ultimately make the greatest contribution to the common good. Some see globalization as synonymous with economic liberalism, particularly its free flow of capital, goods, services, and (more contentiously) labour with minimal government or other non-market interference.

licence to operate   The right granted to a company (or other organization) to carry out its business. In the corporate responsibility context, licence to operate usually refers to the licence granted by a community or other stakeholder group, rather than by a formal regulatory authority.

limited liability   Form of incorporation under which the liability of a partner or investor is limited to the value of his or her shares in the company. The introduction of this legal concept in the nineteenth century greatly affected the role of business, the nature of investment, and the notion of risk.

living wage   *See* fair wage.

microfinance   Financial model that involves making small loans available to help poor people who are denied access through conventional lending channels, typically towards their starting, or expanding, a small business.

Millennium Development Goals (MDGs)   A set of eight targets (including eradicating extreme poverty and hunger, improving maternal health, and ensuring environmental sustainability) that were adopted by all countries represented in the UN General Assembly, and which are to be achieved by 2015. The targets commit countries to a particular vision of international development and are widely used as a framework for measuring development progress.

minimum wage   A legally defined wage that should reflect a fair wage (although, in practice, it may not). (*See also* fair wage.)

moral theory   Theories of right and wrong, based on norms and custom. (*Compare* ethical theory.)

Natural Step An approach to sustainability that is based on four systematic principles, relating to people's capacity to meet their needs, and aspects of the interaction between humanity and the earth. Karl-Henrik Robèrt first proposed the approach in 1989, following the publication of the Report of the Brundtland Commission.

negative screening An approach to socially responsible investment that involves the exclusion of certain companies based on their poor performance against corporate governance, social, environmental, or ethical criteria. (*Compare* positive screening.)

New Deal The legislative and administrative programme, established under US President FD Roosevelt's administration during the 1930s, which was intended to promote economic recovery and social reform following the Great Depression. It marked the end of a period during which the theories of liberal economics had gone largely unquestioned, particularly in the USA.

non-financial performance Aspects of business performance not normally addressed in financial reporting and auditing, including wider environmental, social, and governance indicators.

non-government organization (NGO) A loose term distinguishing a range of organizations that are concerned with particular social and environmental objectives from profit-making organizations and government agencies. Commonly called 'non-governmental organizations', some actually perform a governmental function by way of their role in influencing the process of governing. (*See also* civil regulation).

occupational health and safety *See* health and safety.

offensive corporate responsibility Policies, strategies, and programmes undertaken with the specific intention of addressing societal needs in order to gain commercial advantage. (*Compare* defensive corporate responsibility.)

partnership A collaboration between two or more parties conducted with the intention of realizing mutually acceptable or beneficial outcomes that are greater than those which any single party could achieve. Stakeholder partnership has become an important area of corporate responsibility management practice.

performance standard A code of conduct or similar instrument by means of which achievement is largely measured in terms of specific outcomes, such as workers being paid a fair wage, the eradication of workplace discrimination, etc. Codes of labour practice, organic standards, and good agricultural practice guidelines are examples of this type of standard. (*Compare* process standard.)

pioneer screening An approach to positive screening in socially responsible investment that involves choosing the best-performing company against one specific criterion.

positive screening An approach to socially responsible investment, under which companies are chosen based on their performance against corporate governance, social, environmental, or ethical criteria. Positive screening can be subdivided into best-in-class screening and pioneer screening. Conversely, SRI investors can use negative screening.

process standard A code of conduct or similar instrument by means of which achievement is largely measured in terms of the process that an organization undergoes rather than fixed outcomes. The ISO 14000 series on environmental management and the AA1000 series are examples of this type of standard. (*Compare* performance standard.)

proxy voting A method of voting at a company's annual general meeting on environmental, social, and governance issues.

reporting awards Schemes offering awards for the quality of corporate reports.

reputation management The aspect of management practice that is concerned with understanding perceptions of an organization's reputation, and the actions necessary to protect or enhance it. Reputation management has been identified as a significant driver of defensive corporate responsibility.

rights Powers, privileges, or other entitlements that are assured by custom or law.

Rio Earth Summit A meeting, in Rio de Janeiro in June 1992, of over a hundred heads of state plus representatives of non-government organizations, business, and local government, which was the summit of an international discussion of environmental and development issues of the kind raised by the Brundtland Commission. It was the first time that a multi-sectoral dialogue had been conducted to address these issues, and resulted in leaders signing a number of important agreements, including the United Nations Framework Conventions on Climate Change (UNFCCC) and the Convention on Biological Diversity (CBD), the Rio Declaration on Environment and Development, and Agenda 21 (an international plan of action for achieving a more sustainable pattern of development in the twenty-first century). The meeting is highly significant in the history of contemporary corporate responsibility, because it recognized the importance of business–government–civil society cooperation in achieving sustainable development goals—something that was developed further at the 2002 World Summit on Sustainable Development.

risk management The aspect of management practice that is concerned with understanding and acting upon the degree of risk presented to an organization by political, social, environmental, and economic factors. Risk is often seen as a driver of defensive corporate responsibility and is evident, for example, in the support of food companies for sustainable agriculture and fisheries.

screening A strategy used in socially responsible investment. (*See also* positive screening.)

self-regulation This refers to the practice of a company or other organization voluntarily putting constraints on what it does—e.g. through the adoption of a code of practice or adherence to voluntary guidelines—even though the constrained policy or action might be legal. Some see voluntary self-regulation as a defining feature of corporate responsibility.

shareholder activism Actions taken by shareholders with the intention of improving corporate governance.

small and medium-sized enterprises (SMEs) A classification of company that is normally based on number of employees (or, occasionally, on turnover). In the EU, a small enterprise employs less than 50 people and a medium one, less than 250; in the USA, the figures are higher, but still not more than 100 and 500, respectively. SMEs comprise the vast majority of businesses in the world (99 per cent in the EU) and account for the bulk of private sector employment generation.

social accounting Accounting for the non-financial aspects of corporate reporting.

social and environmental ratings The rating of companies for investment purposes, according to defined criteria for their social and/or environmental performance. Examples include the Domini 400 Social Index, the KLD Climate Change Index, the FTSE4Good Index series, and the Dow Jones Sustainability Indices.

social auditing The evaluation of an organization to ascertain the validity and reliability of information about that organization's claims concerning its social performance.

social contract The implied agreement between members of a society that defines and puts limits on the duties, responsibilities, and obligations of each member. Social contract theory is associated with the ethical theory of John Locke and underpins ideas about the company's licence to operate.

social entrepreneurship An imprecise term used to refer to a wide range of organizations—both profit-making and non-profit—for which the primary purpose is to deliver social and/or environmental value in contrast with financial value.

social impact assessment Assessment of the social consequences of a company or facility, normally focusing on inputs and outputs within a particular geographical location. (*Compare* environmental impact assessment; human rights impact assessment.)

social reporting The reporting of the social and environmental aspects of corporate activity.

socially responsible investment (SRI) An approach to investing that considers the social, environmental, and ethical consequences of investments within the context of financial analysis.

stakeholder An entity with a stake in another organization, by virtue of the fact he, she, or it is affected by, or has influence over, that organization. In corporate responsibility terms, 'stakeholder' usually refers to the stake that an individual or organization has in a company, and includes employees, local communities, shareholders, customers, and clients.

stakeholder dialogue The convening of a discussion between a company and (all, or some of) its stakeholders.

stakeholder engagement The managed process of interaction between a company and its stakeholders.

stakeholder management The application of stakeholder theory to management practice. It includes stakeholder engagement, stakeholder dialogue, and stakeholder partnership.

stakeholder partnership A partnership between a company and its stakeholders, intended to capitalize on their combined capabilities in pursuit of a particular purpose.

state An organized political community, occupying a definite territory and governed by a sovereign government. In some corporate responsibility literature, the term 'state' is used interchangeably with government—but the terms are distinct.

strategic philanthropy A form of corporate philanthropy under which donations are targeted towards areas that are synergistic with the company's interests or competencies.

sustainability Refers to those forms of human economic and cultural activity that can be conducted without long-term degradation of the resources used. The term is often used interchangeably with sustainable development.

sustainable consumption and production Continuous economic and social progress that respects the limits of the Earth's ecosystems, and meets the needs and aspirations of everyone for a better quality of life—now, and for future generations.

sustainable development According to the Brundtland Commission, which is the most widely known definition, this is human development to meet the needs of the present generation without compromising the ability of future generations to meet their own needs.

third-party verification statements Statements made by third parties, verifying the content of corporate reports.

trade union An association of workers in any trade, or allied trades, for the protection and furtherance of their interests with regard to wages, hours, and conditions of labour, and for the provision, from their common funds, of pecuniary assistance to their members during strikes, sickness, unemployment, old age, etc. There is an important distinction between free trade unions and yellow unions. (*Compare* workers' committee.)

transformation management *See* change management.

triple bottom line A framework for measuring company performance and added value in terms of economic, social, and environmental parameters. Triple-bottom-line accounting is an extension of the conventional financial accounting framework to measure these additional areas of performance.

United Nations A supranational organization founded in 1945 with the purposes of: (a) maintaining international peace and security; (b) developing friendly relations among nations; (c) cooperating in solving international economic, social, cultural, and humanitarian problems, and in promoting respect for human rights and fundamental freedoms; (d) acting as a centre through which nations can work jointly to attain those ends. It comprises member states, as well as bodies such as the General Assembly, Security Council, and the International Court of Justice, and it administers programmes to achieve its purpose through agencies such as the UN Development Programme, the UN Environment Programme, and the International Labour Organization.

United Nations Global Compact A UN-convened initiative to promote concrete and sustained action by business participants to align their actions with broad UN social and environmental objectives, the Compact's ten principles, and the international Millennium Development Goals (MDGs). It aims to achieve this through: (a) learning forums to analyse case studies and examples of good practice; (b) global policy dialogues on the challenges of globalization; (c) multi-stakeholder collaborative development projects to further the MDGs; (d) support for new national networks, such as those in India and South Africa.

Universal Declaration of Human Rights A 1948 UN Declaration—signed and ratified by most of the world's countries—that sets out a basic definition of universal human rights. The Declaration is often referred to in human rights and workers' rights codes of conduct.

venture philanthropy Application of the venture capital model of investment and the deployment of private equity to achieve social and environmental outcomes.

Washington Consensus The set of policies that, during the 1980s and 1990s, became a condition of loans to countries from the World Bank. Countries were required to open their domestic markets to foreign competition, to limit state intervention (including income redistribution, public education, and welfare provision), and to establish policies that would promote a favourable business environment. The Consensus encouraged private foreign direct investment and encouraged countries—such as Indonesia and Mexico—to focus on export markets. Some saw it as responsible for creating the exploitative social and environmental conditions that, in turn, led to calls for greater corporate responsibility, especially in relation to multinational corporations.

welfare state A system under which government seeks to provide an economic safety net for the general population (e.g. through unemployment, child, and disability benefits) and the opportunity for individual improvement (e.g. through health care and education). A feature of Communist Bloc countries, it also became widespread in Western Europe (especially after World War II), was mirrored in the US New Deal, and was a feature of many newly independent governments in Africa and Asia. It put a greater tax burden on business, in return for reducing the pressures on companies to take on social responsibilities. Dismantling the welfare state was typically a condition of the Washington Consensus policies adopted by developing countries in the 1980s and 1990s.

workers' committee Sometimes treated as the equivalent of a trade union, but different, in that it brings together employees within a single company (rather than a trade). Some workers' committees are similar to yellow unions.

workplace health and safety *See* health and safety.

World Commission on Environment and Development *See* Brundtland Commission.

yellow union A type of trade union that is tightly controlled by parties other than union members.

Bibliography

Aaronson S.A., Reeves J.T., & National Policy Association (US) 2002, *Corporate responsibility in the global village: the role of public policy*, National Policy Association, Washington, DC.

Abbott Laboratories 2005, *2004 Corporate citizenship report*, Abbott Laboratories, Chicago, IL.

Abrami R. 2003, Worker rights and global trade: the US–Cambodia bilateral textile trade agreement', *Harvard Business School Case Study 703-034*, Harvard Business Publishing, Boston, MA.

ACCA 2005, *ACCA UK awards for sustainability reporting 2005: report of the judges*, Association of Chartered Certified Accountants, London.

ACCA 2008, *ACCA UK awards for sustainability reporting 2008: report of the judges*, Association of Chartered Certified Accountants, London.

ACCA 2013, *What do investors expect from non-financial reporting?*, available online at http://www.accaglobal.com.

Accenture & UN Global Compact 2013, *Architects of a better world: the UN Global Compact–Accenture CEO study on sustainability 2013*, UN Global Compact, New York.

AccountAbility 2002, *AA1000 conversations: lessons from the early years (1999–2001)*, AccountAbility, London.

AccountAbility 2003, *Redefining materiality: practice and public policy for effective corporate reporting*, AccountAbility, London.

AccountAbility 2003, *The state of sustainability assurance*, AccountAbility, London.

AccountAbility 2006, *What assures?*, AccountAbility, London.

Ackerman B.A. 1980, *Social justice in the liberal state*, Yale University Press, New Haven, CT.

Ackerman B.A. & Alstott A. 1999, *The stakeholder society*, Yale University Press, New Haven, CT.

Ackerman R.W. & Bauer R.A. 1976, *Corporate social responsiveness: modern dilemma*, Reston Publishing Co., Reston, VA.

ActionAid 2005a, *Power hungry: six reasons to regulate global food corporations*, ActionAid, London.

ActionAid 2005b, *Rotten fruit*, ActionAid, London.

Adams C. 2004, 'The ethical, social and environmental reporting-performance portrayal gap', *Accounting, Auditing and Accountability Journal*, vol. 17, pp 731–757.

Adams C. & Evans R. 2004, 'Accountability, completeness, credibility and the audit expectations gap', *Journal of Corporate Citizenship*, no. 14, Summer, pp 97–115.

Adegbite E., Amaeshi K., & Nakajima C. 2013, 'Multiple influences on corporate governance practice in Nigeria: agents, strategies and implications', *International Business Review*, vol. 22, no. 3, pp 524–538.

Aguinis H. & Glavas A. 2012, 'What we know and don't know about corporate social responsibility: a review and research agenda', *Journal of Management*, vol. 38, no. 4, pp 932–968.

AICPA 1977, *The measurement of corporate social performance: determining the impact of business actions on areas of social concern*, AICPA, New York.

Aidt T., Tzannatos Z., & World Bank 2002, *Unions and collective bargaining: economic effects in a global environment*, World Bank, Washington, DC.

Akumu W. 2008, 'M-PESA turning into a big virtual bank', *Daily Nation*, Nairobi, 8 April, available online at http://allafrica.com/.

Albareda L. 2008, 'Corporate responsibility, governance and accountability: from self-regulation to co-regulation', *Corporate Governance*, vol. 8, no. 4, pp 430–439.

Alvesson M. & Willmott H. 2002, 'Identity regulation as organizational control: producing the appropriate individual', *Journal of Management Studies*, vol. 39, no. 5, pp 619–644.

Amalric F. & Hauser J. 2005, 'Economic drivers of corporate responsibility activities', *Journal of Corporate Citizenship*, no. 20, Winter, pp 27–38.

Ambachtsheer J. 2005, *SRI: what do investment managers think?*, Mercer Investment Consulting, Toronto.

Amba-Rao S.C. 1993, 'Multinational corporate social responsibility, ethics, interactions and third world governments', *Journal of Business Ethics*, vol. 12, pp 553–572.

Amin S. 1997, *Capitalism in the age of globalization: the management of contemporary society*, Zed Books, London.

Amnesty International 2005, *Contracting out of human rights: the Chad-Cameroon pipeline*, Amnesty International, London, available online at http://www.amnesty.org/.

Anderson R. 2003, 'Ethics ain't rocket science', *Seattle Weekly*, 6 August, available online at www.seattleweekly.com.

Anderson R. 2005, 'From CEO to cipher', *Seattle Weekly*, 9 March, available online at www.seattleweekly.com.

Anderson R.C. 1998, *Mid-course correction: toward a sustainable enterprise: the interface model*, Peregrinzilla Press, Atlanta, GA

Andrews K. 1973, 'Can the best corporations be made moral?', *Harvard Business Review*, Harvard Business Review, vol. 51, no. 3, pp 57–64.

Andriof J. & McIntosh M. 2001, *Perspectives on corporate citizenship*, Greenleaf, Sheffield.

Andriof J., Waddock S., Husted B., & Rahman S.S. 2002, *Unfolding stakeholder thinking*, Vol. 1: *Theory, responsibility and engagement*, Greenleaf, Sheffield.

Andriof J., Waddock S.A., Husted B. & Rahman S.S. 2003, *Unfolding stakeholder thinking*, Vol. 2: *Relationships, communication, reporting and performance*, Greenleaf, Sheffield.

Ansari S., Munir K., & Gregg T. 2012, 'Impact at the "bottom of the pyramid": the role of social capital in capability development and community empowerment', *Journal of Management Studies*, vol. 49, no. 4, pp 813–842.

Anshen M. 1980, *Corporate strategies for social performance*, Macmillan, New York.

Arce A. & Long N. (eds) 2000, *Anthropology, development, and modernities: exploring discourses, counter-tendencies, and violence*, Routledge, Abingdon.

Arlidge J. 2009, 'I'm doing God's work. Meet Mr Goldman Sachs', available online at http://www.thesundaytimes.co.uk/.

Armendáriz B. & Morduch J. 2010, *The economics of microfinance*. MIT Press, Cambridge, MA.

Arnold D.G. 2003, 'Libertarian theories of corporation and global capitalism', *Journal of Business Ethics*, vol. 48, pp 155–173.

Arnold D.G. & Hartman L.P. 2003, 'Moral imagination and the future of sweatshops', *Business and Society Review*, vol. 108, no. 4, pp 425–461.

Ascoly N. & Zeldenrust I. 2003, *Considering complaints mechanisms*, Centre for Research on Multinational Companies (SOMO), Amsterdam.

Ascoly N., Oldenziel J., & Zeldenrust I. 2001, *Overview of recent developments on monitoring and verification in the garment and sportswear industry in Europe*, Centre for Research on Multinational Companies (SOMO), Amsterdam.

Ashridge Centre for Business and Society 2005, *A catalogue of CSR activities*, Ashridge Centre for Business and Society, Berkhamsted.

Asongu J.J. 'The history of corporate social responsibility', *Journal of Business and Public Policy*, vol. 1, no. 2, pp 1–18.

ASSC (Accounting Standards Steering Committee) 1975, *The corporate report*, ICAEW, London.

Attfield R. 1999, *The ethics of the global environment*, Purdue University Press, West Lafayette, IN.

Attfield R. & Wilkins B. 1992, *International justice and the third world: studies in the philosophy of development*, Routledge, London.

Australian Government 2005, *Corporate social responsibility discussion paper*, Australian Government Corporations and Markets Advisory Committee, Canberra.

Avtonomov V. 2006, 'Balancing state, market and social justice: Russian experiences and lessons to learn', *Journal of Business Ethics*, vol. 66, no. 1, pp 3–9.

Ayres C.E. 1946, *The divine right of capital*, Houghton Mifflin, Boston, MA.

Bagehot W. & Marshall A. 1885, *The postulates of English political economy*, Longmans Green, London.

Baird L., Post J.E., & Mahon J.F. 1990, *Management: functions and responsibilities*, Harper & Row, New York.

Bakan J. 2004, *The corporation: the pathological pursuit of profit and power*, Free Press, New York.

Baker H.K. & Nofsinger J.R. 2012, *Socially responsible finance and investing: financial institutions, corporations, investors, and activists*, John Wiley, Hoboken, NJ.

Baker M. 2002, 'The GRI—the will to succeed is not enough', *Corporate Responsibility News and Resources*, www.mallenbaker.net/csr/CSRfiles/GRI.html.

Baker R.W. 2005, *Capitalism's Achilles heel: dirty money and how to renew the free-market system*, John Wiley, Hoboken, NJ.

Bales K. 2004, *Disposable people: new slavery in the global economy* (revised), University of California Press, Berkeley, CA.

Ballinger J. 1992, 'The new free trade heel: Nike's profits jump on the backs of Asian workers', *Harper's Magazine*, vol. 285, pp 46–47.

Ballinger J. 2010, 'The threat posed by "corporate social responsibility" to trade union rights', in MacDonald K. & Marshall S. (eds), *Fairtrade, corporate accountability and beyond*, Ashgate, Farnham.

Ballinger J. & Olsson C. 1997, *Behind the swoosh: the struggle of Indonesians making Nike shoes*, Global Publications Foundation, Uppsala.

Banerjee A.V. & Duflo E. 2011, *Poor economics*, Public Affairs, New York.

Banerjee S.B. 2001, 'Managerial perceptions of corporate environmentalism: interpretations from industry and strategic implications for organizations', *Journal of Management Studies*, vol. 38, no. 4, pp 489–513.

Banerjee S.B. 2007, *Corporate social responsibility: the good, the bad and the ugly*, Edward Elgar, Cheltenham.

Banerjee S.B. & Prasad A. 2008, 'Introduction to the special issue on, "Critical reflections on management and organizations: a postcolonial perspective"', *Critical Perspectives on International Business*, vol. 4, no. 2/3, pp 90–98.

Bannock G., Baxter R.E., & Davis E. 2003, *Dictionary of economics*, Bloomberg Press/Profile Books, Princeton, NJ.

Barmann T.C. 2006, 'Glaxo settles Paxil complaint with 46 states', *Providence Journal*, 29 March, available online at http://www.highbeam.com/doc/1G1-143844591.html.

Barnard C.I. 1938, *The functions of the executive*, Harvard University Press, Cambridge, MA.

Barnett M.L. 2007, 'Stakeholder influence capacity and the variability of financial returns to corporate social responsibility', *Academy of Management Review*, vol. 32, no. 3, pp 794–816.

Barnett M.L. & Salomon R.M. 2006, 'Beyond dichotomy: the curvilinear relationship between social responsibility and financial performance', *Strategic Management Journal*, vol. 27, no. 11, pp 1101–1122.

Barnett M.L. & Salomon R.M. 2012, 'Does it pay to be really good? Addressing the shape of the relationship between social and financial performance', *Strategic Management Journal*, vol. 33, no. 11, pp 1304–1320.

Baron D.P. 2002, *Business and its environment* (4th edn), Prentice Hall, Upper Saddle River, NJ.

Barrera A. 2000, 'Social principles as a framework for ethical analysis (with an application to the Tobin tax)', *Journal of Business Ethics*, vol. 23, no. 4, pp 377–388.

Barrett R. 1998, *Liberating the corporate soul: building a visionary organization*, Butterworth-Heinemann, Boston, MA.

Barrientos S. & Smith S. 2007, 'Do workers benefit from ethical trade? Assessing codes of labour practice in global production systems', *Third World Quarterly*, vol. 28, no. 4, pp 713–729.

Barrientos S., Dolan C., & Tallontire A. 2001, *Gender and ethical trade: a mapping of the issues in African horticulture*, Natural Resources Institute, University of Greenwich, Chatham.

Barrientos S., Dolan C., & Tallontire A. 2003, 'A gendered value chain approach to codes of conduct in African horticulture', *World Development*, vol. 31, no. 9, pp 1511–1527.

Barry B.M. 1989a, *Democracy, power, and justice: essays in political theory*, Clarendon Press, Oxford.

Barry B.M. 1989b, *Theories of justice*, University of California Press, Berkeley, CA.

Barry N.P. 1979, *Hayek's social and economic philosophy*, Macmillan, London.

Bartley T. 2003, 'Certifying forests and factories: states, social movements, and the rise of private regulation in the apparel and forest products fields', *Politics and Society*, vol. 31, no. 3, pp 433–464.

Basu K. & Palazzo G. 2005, 'An inductive typology of corporate social responsibility', in *Proceedings of the Academy of Management Conference, Hawaii, 2005*, available online at http://proceedings.aom.org/content/2005/.

Batstone D.B. 2003, *Saving the corporate soul—and (who knows?) maybe your own: eight principles for creating and preserving integrity and profitability without selling out*, Jossey-Bass, San Francisco, CA.

Battaglia M., Bianchi L., Frey M., & Iraldo F. 2010, 'An innovative model to promote CSR among SMEs operating in industrial clusters: evidence from an EU project', *Corporate Social Responsibility and Environmental Management*, vol. 17, no. 3, pp 133–141.

Bauer R., Koedijk K., & Otten R. 2005, 'International evidence on ethical mutual fund performance and investment style', *Journal of Banking and Finance*, vol. 29, pp 1751–1767.

Bauman Z. 1998, *Globalization: the human consequences*, Columbia University Press, New York.

BBC 2005, ' Costing the earth': the Kenya flower trade, available online at http://www.bbc.co.uk/radio4/science/.

BBC 2013, *Google turns off China censorship warning*, available online at http://www.bbc.co.uk/news/.

Beauchamp T.L., Bowie N.E., & Arnold D. (eds) 2008, *Ethical business and theory* (8th edn), Pearson Education, London.

Beaver W. 1995, 'Levi's is leaving China', *Business Horizons*, vol. 38, no. 2, pp 35–40.

Bebbington J. 2001a, *Sustainability assessment modelling at BP: advances in environmental accounting*, ACCA, London.

Bebbington J. 2001b, 'Sustainable development: a review of the international development, business and accounting literature', *Accounting Forum*, vol. 25, pp 128–157.

Bebbington J. 2009, 'Measuring sustainable development performance: possibilities and issues', *Accounting Forum*, vol. 33, pp 189–193.

Bebbington J., Larrinaga C., & Moneva J.M. 2004, ' Corporate social reporting and reputation risk management ', *Corporate Social Reporting*, pp 337–360.

Beck U. 1992, *Risk society: towards a new modernity*, SAGE, London.

Beck U. 2000, *What is globalization?* Polity Press, Cambridge.

Beck U., Giddens A., & Lash S. 1994, *Reflexive modernization: politics, tradition and aesthetics in the modern social order*, Polity Press, Cambridge.

Belkaoui A. 1976, 'The impact of the disclosure of the environmental effects of organizational behaviour on the market', *Financial Management*, vol. 5, no.4, pp 26–31.

Belkaoui A. & Karpic P.G. 1989, 'Determinants of the corporate decision to disclose social information', *Accounting, Auditing, and Accountability Journal*, vol. 2, no. 1, pp 36–51.

Bellagio Forum for Sustainable Development & Eurosif 2006, *PRIME toolkit primer for responsible investment management of endowments*, Bellagio Forum for Sustainable Development, Osnabrück.

Bendell J. 2000, *Terms of endearment: business, NGOs and sustainable development*, Greenleaf, Sheffield.

Bendell J. 2004a, *Barricades and boardrooms: a contemporary history of the corporate accountability movement*, UN Research Institute for Social Development, Geneva.

Bendell J. 2004b, *Flags of inconvenience? The Global Compact and the future of the United Nations*, International Centre for Corporate Social Responsibility, University of Nottingham.

Bendell J., Collins E., & Roper J. 2010, 'Beyond partnerism: toward a more expansive research agenda on multi-stakeholder collaboration for responsible business', *Business Strategy and the Environment*, vol. 19, no. 6, pp 351–355.

Bennett C. & Burley H. 2005, 'Corporate accountability: an NGO perspective', in Tully S. (ed.), *Research handbook on corporate legal responsibility*, Edward Elgar, Cheltenham, pp 372–394.

Bennett M., James P., & Klinkers L. 1999, *Sustainable measures: evaluation and reporting of environmental and social performance*, Greenleaf, Sheffield.

Bennett M., Rikhardsson P.M., & Schaltegger S. 2003, *Environmental management accounting: purpose and progress*, Kluwer Academic, Dordrecht.

Bennis W.G., Goleman D., & O'Toole J. 2008, *Transparency: how leaders create a culture of candor*, Jossey-Bass, San Francisco, CA.

Benson K.L., Brailsford T.J., & Humphrey J.E. 2006, 'Do socially responsible fund managers really invest differently?', *Journal of Business Ethics*, vol. 65, no. 4, pp 337–357.

Bentham J. 1789, *An introduction to the principles of morals and legislation, etc. MS. notes [by the author]*, T. Payne & Son, London.

BER 2008, *The contribution of South African Breweries Limited to the South African economy*, Bureau for Economic Research, Cape Town.

Beresford D.R. 1973, 'Compilation of social measurement disclosures in Fortune 500 annual reports', Ernst & Ernst, Cleveland, OH.

Beresford D.R. 1975, *Social responsibility disclosure—1974 survey of Fortune 500 annual reports*, Ernst & Ernst, Cleveland, OH.

Beresford D.R. 1976, *Social responsibility disclosure—1975 survey of Fortune 500 annual reports*, Ernst & Ernst, Cleveland, OH.

Berger F.R. 1984, *Happiness, justice, and freedom: the moral and political philosophy of John Stuart Mill*, University of California Press, Berkeley, CA.

Berlan A. & Dolan C. 2014, 'Of red herrings and immutabilities: rethinking fair trade's ethic of relationality among cocoa producers', in Goodman M. & Sage C. (eds), *Food transgressions: making sense of contemporary food politics*, Ashgate, Farnham.

Berle A.A., Means G.C., & Columbia University Council for Research in the Social Sciences 1932, *Modern corporation and private property*, Commerce Clearing House, Loose Leaf Service Division of the Corporation Trust Company, New York.

Bernauer T. & Caduff L., 2004, 'In whose interest? Pressure group politics, economic competition and environmental regulation', *Journal of Public Policy*, vol. 24, no. 1, pp 99–126.

Berns M., Townend A., Khayat Z., et al. 2009, 'The business of sustainability: what it means to managers now', *MIT Sloan Management Review*, vol. 51, no. 1, pp 20–26.

Bernstein P.L. 1996, *Against the gods: the remarkable story of risk*, John Wiley, New York.

Berry A., Capps T., Cooper D., Hopper T., & Lowe E.A. 1985, 'NCB accounts—a mine of disinformation?', *Accountancy*, January, pp 10–12.

Bhagwati J.N. 2004, *In defense of globalization*, Oxford University Press, New York.

Bhattacharya C.B. & Sen S. 2004, 'Doing better at doing good: when, why, and how consumers respond to corporate social initiatives', *California Management Review*, vol. 47, no. 1, pp 9–24.

Birch D. 2001, 'Corporate citizenship: rethinking business beyond corporate social responsibility', in Andriof G. & McIntosh M. (eds), *Perspectives on Corporate Citizenship*, Greenleaf, London, pp 53–65.

Birch D. 2003, 'Corporate social responsibility: some key theoretical issues and concepts for new ways of doing business', *Journal of New Business Ideas and Trends*, vol. 1, no. 1, pp 1–19.

Birkin F. 2000, 'The art of accounting for science: a prerequisite for sustainable development?', *Critical Perspectives on Accounting*, vol. 11, pp 289–309.

Black E. 2001, *IBM and the Holocaust: the strategic alliance between Nazi Germany and America's most powerful corporation*, Crown, New York.

Black J. 2003, *A dictionary of economics* (2nd edn), Oxford University Press, Oxford.

Bladen V.W. 1974, *From Adam Smith to Maynard Keynes: the heritage of political economy*, University of Toronto Press, Toronto.

Blake D.H., Frederick W.C., & Myers M.S. 1976, *Social auditing: evaluating the impact of corporate programs*, Praeger, New York.

Blanchard K.H., O'Connor M.J., & Ballard J. 1997, *Managing by values*, Berrett-Koehler, San Francisco, CA.

Block W. & Barnett W. 2005, 'A positive programme for laissez-faire capitalism', *Journal of Corporate Citizenship*, no. 19, Autumn, pp 31–42.

Bloom D.E. & Canning D. 2006, 'Booms, busts, and echoes', *Finance and Development*, vol. 43 no. 3, pp 8–15.

Blowfield M.E. 1991, *Does Bo know Nike?*, Asian American Free Labor Institute, Jakarta.

Blowfield M.E. 2000a, *A guide to developing agricultural markets and agro-enterprises; fundamentals of ethical trading/sourcing in poorer countries*, World Bank, Washington, DC.

Blowfield M.E. 2000b, 'Ethical sourcing: a contribution to sustainability or a diversion?', *Sustainable Development*, vol. 8, no. 4, pp 191–200.

Blowfield M.E. 2002, 'ETI—a multi-stakeholder approach', in Jenkins R.O., Pearson R. & Seyfang G. (eds), *Corporate responsibility and ethical trade: codes of conduct in the global economy*, Earthscan, London, pp 184–195.

Blowfield M.E. 2003, *Ethical trade: the negotiation of a global ethic*, Doctoral dissertation, University of Sussex.

Blowfield M.E. 2004, 'Implementation deficits of ethical trade systems: lessons from the Indonesian cocoa and timber industries', *Journal of Corporate Citizenship*, no. 13, Spring, pp 77–90.

Blowfield M.E. 2005a, 'Corporate social responsibility—the failing discipline and why it matters for international relations,' *International Relations*, vol. 19, no. 2, pp 173–191.

Blowfield M.E. 2005b, *Does society want business leadership? An overview of attitudes and thinking*, Center for Corporate Citizenship at Boston College, Chestnut Hill, MA.

Blowfield M.E. 2007, 'Reasons to be cheerful? What we know about CSR's impact', *Third World Quarterly*, vol. 28, no. 4, pp 683–695.

Blowfield M.E. 2010, 'Business and poverty reduction', in Utting P. & Marques J.C. (eds), *Corporate social responsibility and regulatory governance: towards inclusive development?*, Palgrave Macmillan, Basingstoke.

Blowfield M.E. 2012, *Business and sustainability*, Oxford University Press, Oxford.

Blowfield M.E. & Dolan C. 2008, 'Stewards of virtue: the ethical dilemma of CSR in Africa', *Development and Change*, vol. 39, no. 1, pp 1–23.

Blowfield M. & Dolan C. 2010, 'Outsourcing governance: fairtrade's message for C21 global governance', *Corporate Governance*, vol. 10, no. 4, pp 484–499.

Blowfield M. & Dolan C. S. 2014, 'Business as a development agent: evidence of possibility and improbability', *Third World Quarterly*, vol. 35, no. 1, pp 22–42.

Blowfield M.E. & Frynas J.G. 2005, 'Setting new agendas: critical perspectives on corporate social responsibility in the developing world', *International Affairs*, vol. 81, no. 3, pp 499–513.

Blowfield M.E. & Googins B. 2007, *Step up: a call for business leadership in society—CEOs examine role of business in the 21st century*, Center for Corporate Citizenship at Boston College, Chestnut Hill, MA.

Blowfield M.E. & Johnson L. 2013, *Turnaround challenge: business and the city of the future*, Oxford University Press, Oxford.

Blyth M. 2002, *Great transformations: economic ideas and institutional change in the twentieth century*, Cambridge University Press, New York.

Bogle J.C. 2005, *The battle for the soul of capitalism*, Yale University Press, New Haven, CT.

Bogle J.C. 2009, *Enough: true measures of money, business, and life*, John Wiley, Hoboken, NJ.

Bond P. 2006, 'Global governance campaigning and MDGs: from top-down to bottom-up anti-poverty work', *Third World Quarterly*, vol. 27, no. 2, pp 339–354.

Bornstein D. 2007, *How to change the world* (updated edn), Oxford University Press, Oxford.

Bounds A. 2009, 'Ethiopian refugees discover benefits of coffee', *Financial Times*, London, 7 May, available online at http://www.ft.com/.

Bowd R., Bowd L., & Harris P. 2006, 'Communicating corporate social responsibility: an exploratory case study of a major UK retail centre', *Journal of Public Affairs*, vol. 6, no. 2, pp 147–155.

Bowen H.R. 1953, *Social responsibilities of the businessman*, Harper, New York.

Bower T. 1988, *Maxwell: the outsider*, Aurum Press, London.

Bower T 1996, *Maxwell: the final verdict*, HarperCollins, London.

Bowman E.H. 1973, 'Corporate social responsibility and the investor', *Journal of Contemporary Business*, Winter, pp 21–43.

Bowman E.H. & Haire M. 1976, 'Social impact disclosure and corporate annual reports', *Accounting, Organizations and Society*, vol. 1, no. 1, pp 11–21.

Bracking S. 2009, *Hiding conflict over industry returns: a stakeholder analysis of the Extractive Industries Transparency Initiative*, Working Paper Series, Brooks World Poverty Institute, University of Manchester.

Brady K. 1984, *Ida Tarbell: portrait of a muckraker*, Seaview/Putnam, New York.

Brainard L. 2006, *Transforming the development landscape: the role of the private sector*, Brookings Institution Press, Washington, DC.

Braithwaite J. & Drahos P. 2000, *Global business regulation*, Cambridge University Press, Cambridge.

Brammer S., Jackson G., & Matten D. 2012, 'Corporate social responsibility and institutional theory: new perspectives on private governance', *Socio-Economic Review*, vol. 10, no. 1, pp 3–28.

Brand S. 1999, *The clock of the long now: time and responsibility*, Basic Books, New York.

Branson R. 2011, *Screw business as usual*, Virgin Books, London.

Broad R. (ed.) 2002, *Global backlash: citizen initiatives for a just world economy*, Rowman & Littlefield, Lanham, MD.

Brooke H. 2010, *The silent state*, Heinemann, London.

Brooke P. A. & Penrice D. 2009, *A vision for venture capital: realizing the promise of global venture capital and private equity*, New Ventures Press/University Press of New England, Lebanon, NH.

Brower M., Leon W., & Union of Concerned Scientists 1999, *The consumer's guide to effective environmental choices: practical advice from the Union of Concerned Scientists*, Three Rivers Press, New York.

Brown C.C. 1979, *Beyond the bottom line*, Macmillan, New York.

Brown D.K. 2004, *Improving working conditions: what works and what doesn't—existing empirical evidence and historical experience*, presented at Globalization and Labor in Developing Countries Conference, Brown University.

Brown T.J. & Dacin P.A. 1997, 'The company and the product: corporate associations and consumer product responses', *Journal of Marketing*, vol. 61, pp 68–84.

Brown W.S., McCabe D., & Primeaux P. 2003, 'Business ethics in transitional economies: introduction', *Journal of Business Ethics*, vol. 47, no. 4, pp 295–297.

Browne J. 2004, 'Beyond Kyoto', *Foreign Affairs*, vol. 83, no. 4, pp 20–32.

Browne M.N. & Haas P.F. 1974, 'Social responsibility: the uncertain hypothesis', *MSU Business Topics*, vol. 22, no. 3, pp 47–51.

Brugmann J. & Prahalad C.K. 2007, 'Cocreating business's new social compact', *Harvard Business Review*, February, pp 80–90.

BSR 2002, *Designing a CSR structure: a step-by-step guide including leadership examples and decision-making tools*, Business for Social Responsibility, San Francisco, CA.

BSR 2005, *Reporting on economic impacts*, Business for Social Responsibility, San Francisco, CA.

BT 2005, *BT social and environmental report*, BT Group, London.

Buchanan A.E. 1985, *Ethics, efficiency, and the market*, Rowman & Allanheld, Totowa, NJ.

Buchanan J.M. & Yoon Y.J. 2002, 'Globalization as framed by the two logics of trade', *Independent Review*, vol. 6, no. 3, pp 399–405.

Buchholz R.A., Marcus A.A., & Post J.E. 1992, *Managing environmental issues: a casebook*, Prentice Hall, Englewood Cliffs, NJ.

Bugg-Levine A. & Emerson J. 2011, 'Impact investing: transforming how we make money while making a difference', *Innovations*, vol. 6, no. 3, pp 9–18.

Bugg-Levine A., Kogut B., & Kulatilaka N. 2012, 'A new approach to funding social enterprises', *Harvard Business Review*, vol. 90, no. 1/2, pp 118–123.

Bulloch G. 2009, *Development collaboration: none of our business?*, Accenture, London.

Bunting M. 2005, 'Africa's flash moment', *Guardian Weekly*, London, 24–30 June, available online at http://www.theguardian.com/.

Burns P. 2001, *Entrepreneurship and small business*, Palgrave, London.

Burrough B. & Helyar J. 1999, *Barbarians at the gate*, Jonathan Cape, London.

Business Week 2005, 'Social issues retailing: can Wal-Mart fit into a white hat?', *Business Week*, 2 October, available online at http://www.businessweek.com/.

Butler E. 1985, *Hayek: his contribution to the political and economic thought of our time*, Universe Books, New York.

Byron N. & Arnold M. 1998, *What futures for the people of the tropical forests?* Centre for International Forestry Research, Bogor, Indonesia.

Cadbury S.A. 1992, *Report of the Committee on the Financial Aspects of Corporate Governance*, London, Gee.

CAFOD 2005, ' *Clean up your computer' progress report*, CAFOD, London.

Cairncross F. 1995, *Green, Inc.: a guide to business and the environment*, Island Press, Washington, DC.

Calabrese A., Costa R., Menichini T., Rosati F., & Sanfelice G. 2013, 'Turning corporate social responsibility-driven opportunities in competitive advantages: a two-dimensional model', *Knowledge and Process Management*, vol. 20, no. 1, pp 50–58.

Callahan D. 2002, *Kindred spirits: Harvard Business School's extraordinary class of 1949 and how they transformed American business*, John Wiley, Hoboken, NJ.

Cannon T. 1994, *Corporate responsibility: a textbook on business ethics, governance, environment: roles and responsibilities*, Pitman, London.

Caplan K. 2003, 'The purist's partnership: debunking the terminology of partnerships', *Partnership Matters*, vol. 1, pp 31–35.

Carnegie A. 1889, *The gospel of wealth*, F. C. Hagen, London.

Carney W.J. 1998, 'Limited liability', *Encyclopedia of Law and Economics*, Edward Elgar, Cheltenham, pp 659–691.

Carroll A.B. 1977, *Managing corporate social responsibility*, Little, Brown, Boston, MA.

Carroll A.B. 1979, 'A three-dimensional conceptual model of corporate performance', *Academy of Management Review*, vol. 4, no. 4, pp 497–505.

Carroll A.B. 1999, 'Corporate social responsibility: evolution of a definitional construct', *Business & Society*, vol. 38, no. 3, pp 268–295.

Carroll A.B. 2000, 'A commentary and an overview of key questions on corporate social performance measurement', *Business & Society*, vol. 39, no. 4, pp 466–478.

Carroll A.B. & Buchholtz A.K. 2006, *Business and society: ethics and stakeholder management* (6th edn), Thomson/South-Western, Mason, OH.

Carroll A.B. & Shabana K.M. 2010, 'The business case for corporate social responsibility: a review of concepts, research and practice', *International Journal of Management Reviews*, vol. 12, no. 1, pp 85–105.

Carroll S.J. & Gannon M.J. 1997, *Ethical dimensions of international management*, SAGE, Thousand Oaks, CA.

Carson R. 1962, *Silent Spring*, Houghton Mifflin, Boston, MA.

Carswell J. 1960, *The South Sea Bubble*, Stanford University Press, Stanford, CA.

Carter D.A., Simkins B.J., & Simpson W.G. 2003, 'Corporate governance, board diversity, and firm value', *Financial Review*, vol. 38, no. 1, pp 33–53.

Caufield C. 1996, *Masters of illusion: the World Bank and the poverty of nations*, Henry Holt, New York.

CCC (Center for Corporate Citizenship) 2005a, *Going global: how US-based multinationals are operationalizing corporate citizenship on a global platform*, Center for Corporate Citizenship, Boston College, Chestnut Hill, MA.

CCC (Center For Corporate Citizenship) 2005b, *Integration: critical link for corporate citizenship*, Center for Corporate Citizenship, Boston College, Chestnut Hill, MA.

CCC (Center For Corporate Citizenship) 2005c, *State of corporate citizenship in the US: business perspectives in 2005*, Center for Corporate Citizenship, Boston College, Chestnut Hill, MA.

CECP 2006, *Giving in numbers 2006*, Committee Encouraging Corporate Philanthropy, New York.

CEP 1997, *SA8000*, Council on Economic Priorities, New York.

CEPAA 1999, *Guidance document for Social Accountability 8000*, New York.

CERES undated, *CERES principles*, Coalition for Environmentally Responsible Economies, Boston, MA.

CFS/CIS 2005, *Sustainability report 2004*, Cooperative Financial Services, Manchester.

Chamberlain N.W. 1973, *The limits of corporate responsibility*, Basic Books, New York.

Chan A. & Siu K. 2007, 'Wal-Mart's CSR and labor standards in China', presented at International Network on Business, Development and Society Workshop, 12–14 September 2007.

Chan C.C.C. & Milne M.J. 1999, 'Investor reactions to corporate environmental saints and sinners: an experimental analysis', *Accounting and Business Research*, vol. 29, no. 4, pp 265–279.

Chandler A.D. & Mazlish B. (eds) 2005, *Leviathans: multinational corporations and the new global history*, Cambridge University Press, Cambridge.

Chang H. 2002, *Kicking away the ladder: development strategy in historical perspective*, Anthem, London.

Chang H. 2007, *Bad Samaritans: rich nations, poor policies, and the threat to the developing world*, Random House Business, London.

Chang H. 2010, *23 things they don't tell you about capitalism*, Allen Lane, London.

Chan Kim W. and Mauborgne R. 2005, *Blue ocean strategy: how to create uncontested market space and make the competition irrelevant*, Harvard Business School, Boston, MA.

Charkham J. 2005, *Keeping better company*, Oxford, Oxford University Press.

Charkham J. 2008, *Keeping better company*, Oxford, Oxford University Press (paperback).

Chatterji A. & Levine D. 2006, 'Breaking down the wall of codes: evaluating non-financial performance measurement', *California Management Review*, vol. 48, no. 2, pp 29–51.

Chenall R.H. & Juchau R. 1977, 'Investor information needs: an Australian study', *Accounting and Business Research*, vol. 7, no. 26, pp 111–119.

Chenoweth J. & Bird J. 2005, *The business of water and sustainable development*, Greenleaf, Sheffield.

Cheung R. 2008, 'China', in Krosinsky C. & Robins N., *Sustainable investing: the art of long-term performance*, Earthscan, London, pp 149–164.

Christian Aid 1997, *Change at the check-out? Supermarkets and ethical business*, Christian Aid, London.

Christian Aid 2004, *Behind the mask: the real face of corporate social responsibility*, Christian Aid, London.

Christian Aid 2005, *The shirts off their backs: how tax policies fleece the poor*, Christian Aid, London.

Christian Aid, ASH, & Friends of the Earth 2005. *BAT in its own words*, Christian Aid, Action on Smoking and Health (ASH), and Friends of the Earth, London.

Chryssides G.D. & Kaler J.H. 1993, *An introduction to business ethics*, Chapman & Hall, London.

Chua W.F. 1986, 'Radical developments in accounting thought', *Accounting Review*, vol. 61, no. 4, pp 601–632.

CIE 2003, *The Global Alliance: benefit–cost framework and application*, Centre for International Economics, Canberra.

Clark J.M. 1939, *Social control of business* (2nd edn), McGraw-Hill, New York.

Clarke E. 2005, *Manufacturing the evidence*, available online at http://www.supplymanagement.com/.

Clarke T. 1993, 'Case study. Robert Maxwell: master of corporate malfeasance', *Corporate Governance*, vol. 1, no, 3, pp 141–151.

Clarkson M.B. 1995, 'A stakeholder framework for analyzing and evaluating corporate social performance', *Academy of Management Review*, vol. 20, no. 1, pp 92–117.

Clay J. 2005, *Exploring the links between international business and poverty reduction: a case study of Unilever in Indonesia*, Oxfam, Oxford.

Coase R. 1937, 'The nature of the firm', *Economica*, vol. 4, no. 16, pp 386–405.

Cobb G., Collison D.J., Power D.M., and Stevenson L.A. 2005, *FTSE4Good: perceptions and performance*, Certified Accountants Educational Trust, London.

Coffee J.C. 2000, *The rise of dispersed ownership: the role of law in the separation of ownership and control*, Columbia Law and Economics Working Paper, Columbia University, New York..

Cogan D. 2004, *Corporate governance and climate change: making the connection*, CERES, Boston, MA.

Coleman J. 2002, 'Gender, power and post-structuralism in corporate citizenship', *Journal of Corporate Citizenship*, no. 5, Spring, pp 17–25.

Collinson C. 2001, *The business costs of ethical supply chain management: Kenya flower industry case study*, Natural Resources Institute, Chatham.

Collinson C. & Leon M. 2000, *Economic viability of ethical cocoa trading in Ecuador*, Natural Resources Institute, Chatham.

Collison D.J., Cobb G., Power D.M., & Stevenson L.A. 2008, 'The financial performance of the FTSE4Good indices', *Corporate Social Responsibility and Environmental Management*, vol. 15, no. 1, pp. 14–28.

Combined Code 1998, *The Combined Code, Principles of Corporate Governance*, Gee, London.

Combined Code 2003, *The Combined Code on Corporate Governance*, Financial Reporting Council, London.

Combined Code 2008, *The Combined Code on Corporate Governance*, Financial Reporting Council, London.

Cone M.H. 2003, 'Corporate citizenship: the role of commercial organisations in an Islamic society', *Journal of Corporate Citizenship*, no. 9, Spring, pp 49–66.

Corcoran T., 2006, 'Just say no to NGOs', *National Post*, 1 April, available online at www.canada.com/nationalpost.

Cornell B. & Shapiro A.C. 1987, 'Corporate stakeholders and corporate finance', *Financial Management*, vol. 16, no. 1, pp 5–14.

Courville S. 2000, *Promoting biological diversity through sustainable certification and fair trade*, Institute for Agriculture and Trade Policy, Minneapolis, MN.

Cowe R. 2002, *No scruples? Managing to be responsible in a turbulent world*, Spiro, London.

Cowen S.S., Ferreri L.B., & Parker L.D. 1987, 'The impact of corporate characteristics on social responsibility disclosure: a typology and frequency based analysis',

Accounting, Organizations and Society, vol. 12, no. 2, pp 111–122.

Cragg W. & McKague K. 2003, *Compendium of ethics codes and instruments of corporate responsibility*, Schulich School of Business, York University.

Cramer J. 2006, *Corporate social responsibility and globalisation: an action plan for business*, Greenleaf, Sheffield.

Crane A. & Matten D. 2004, *Business ethics*, Oxford University Press, Oxford.

Crane A., Matten D., & Moon J. 2008, *Corporations and citizenship*, Cambridge University Press, Cambridge.

Crane A., Matten D., & Spence L.J. 2013, 'Corporate social responsibility in a global context', in Crane A., Matten D., & Spence L.J. (eds), *Corporate Social Responsibility: Readings and Cases in a Global Context* (2nd edn), Routledge, Abingdon.

Crenson M. A. & Ginsberg B. 2002, *Downsizing democracy: how America sidelined its citizens and privatized its public*, Johns Hopkins University Press, Baltimore, MD.

Crowther D. & Caliyurt K.T. 2006, *Globalisation and social responsibility*, Cambridge Scholars Press, Newcastle upon Tyne.

Cummins A. 2004, 'The Marine Stewardship Council: a multi-stakeholder approach to sustainable fishing', *Corporate Social Responsibility and Environmental Management*, vol. 11, no. 2, pp 85–94.

Dallas G. (ed.) 2005, *Governance and risk: an analytical handbook for investors, managers, directors and stakeholders*, McGraw-Hill, New York.

Daly H.E. 1996, *Beyond growth: the economics of sustainable development*, Beacon Press, Boston, MA.

Dando N. & Swift T. 2003, 'Transparency and assurance: minding the credibility gap', *Journal of Business Ethics*, vol. 44, no. 2/3, pp 195–200.

Darnton R. 2009, 'Google and the new digital future', *New York Review of Books*, vol. 56, no. 20.

Daum J.H. 2003, *Intangible assets and value creation*, John Wiley, Chichester.

Davies P.W.F. 1997, *Current issues in business ethics*, Routledge, London.

Davis I. 2005, 'Ian Davis on business and society', *The Economist*, 26 May, available online at www.economist.com.

Davis K. 1960, 'Can business afford to ignore social responsibilities?', *California Management Review*, vol. 2, no. 3, pp 70–76.

Davis K. 1973, 'The case for and against business assumption of social responsibilities', *Academy of Management Review*, vol. 16, no. 2, pp 312–322.

Davis S.M., Lukomnik J., & Pitt-Watson D. 2006, *The new capitalists: how citizen investors are reshaping the corporate agenda*, Harvard Business School Press, Boston, MA.

Davy A. 2004a, 'Companies in conflict situations: a role for partnerships?' in Warner M. & Sullivan R. (eds), *Putting partnerships to work*, Greenleaf, Sheffield, pp 220–229.

Davy A. 2004b, 'Ownership and control of outcomes' in Warner M. & Sullivan R. (eds), Greenleaf, Sheffield, pp 210–219.

DCCA 2008, *Small suppliers in global supply chains: how multinationals can target small and medium-sized suppliers in their global supply chains*, Danish Commerce and Companies Agency/Hewlett Packard, Copenhagen.

de Oliveira J.A.P. 2006, 'Corporate citizenship in Latin America', *Journal of Corporate Citizenship*, no. 21, Spring, pp 17–20.

Deegan C. 2002, The legitimising effect of social and environmental disclosures—a theoretical foundation. *Accounting, Auditing and Accountability Journal*, vol. 15, no. 3, 282–311.

Dees J.G. 1998, *The meaning of 'social entrepreneurship'*, Social Entrepreneurship Funders Working Group, available online at http://www.caseatduke.org/documents/dees_sedef.pdf.

Dees J.G., Emerson J., & Economy P. 2002, *Strategic tools for social entrepreneurs: enhancing the performance of your enterprising nonprofit*, John Wiley, Chichester.

Della Croce R., Kaminker C., & Stewart F. 2011, *The role of pension funds in financing green growth initiatives*, OECD, Paris.

Demirag I. 2005, *Corporate social responsibility, accountability and governance*, Greenleaf, Sheffield.

Department of Trade and Industry 1971, *Report on the affairs of International Learning Systems Corporation Ltd, and Interim Report on the Affairs of Pergamon Press Ltd*, HMSO, London.

Department of Trade and Industry 2001, *Business and society: developing corporate social responsibility in the UK*, Department of Trade and Industry, London.

Derber C. 1998, *Corporation nation: how corporations are taking over our lives and what we can do about it*, St. Martin's Press, New York.

Devinney T.M., Auger P., Eckhardt G., & Birtchnell T. 2006, 'The other CSR', *Stanford Social Innovation Review*, vol. 4, no. 3, pp 30, 32–33, 35–37.

DFID 2002, *The challenges of assessing the poverty impact of ethical trading. What can be learnt from fair trade initiatives and the sustainable livelihoods approach*, Department for International Development, London.

Dicken P. 2003, *Global shift: reshaping the global economic map in the 21st century* (4th edn), SAGE, London.

Dillard J. & Murray A. 2012, 'Deciphering the domain of corporate social responsibility', in Haynes K., Murray A., & Dillard J. (eds), *Corporate social responsibility: a research handbook*. Routledge, Abingdon.

DiLorenzo T.J. 2004, *How capitalism saved America: the untold history of our country, from the Pilgrims to the present*, Crown Forum, New York.

Dion M. 2001, 'Corporate citizenship as an ethic of care, corporate values, codes of ethics and global governance', in Andriof J. & McIntosh M. (eds), *Perspectives on corporate citizenship*, Greenleaf, Sheffield, pp 118–138.

Doane D. 2005, 'The myth of CSR: the problem with assuming that companies can do well while also doing good is that markets don't really work that way', *Stanford Social Innovation Review*, Fall, pp 23–29.

Dobb M.H. 1973, *Theories of value and distribution since Adam Smith; ideology and economic theory*, Cambridge University Press, Cambridge.

Doherty B., Davies I.A., & Tranchell S. 2013, 'Where now for fair trade?', *Business History*, vol. 55, no. 2, pp 161–189.

Dolan C. & Humphrey J. 2004, 'Changing governance patterns in the trade in fresh vegetables between Africa and the United Kingdom', *Environment and Planning A*, vol. 36, no. 3, pp 491–509.

Dolan C.S. & Opondo M. 2005, 'Seeking common ground', *Journal of Corporate Citizenship*, no. 18, Summer, pp 87–98.

Donaldson T. 1989, *The ethics of international business*, Oxford University Press, New York.

Donaldson T. 2003, 'Ethics away from home', in Thomas D.C. (ed.), *Readings and cases in international management: a cross-cultural perspective*, SAGE, Thousand Oaks, CA, pp 133–140.

Donaldson T. & Dunfee T.W. 1999, *Ties that bind: a social contracts approach to business ethics*, Harvard Business School Press, Boston, MA.

Donaldson T. & Gini A. 1996, *Case studies in business ethics* (4th edn), Prentice Hall, Upper Saddle River, NJ.

Donaldson T., Werhane P.H., & Cording M. 2002, *Ethical issues in business: a philosophical approach*, Prentice Hall, Upper Saddle River, NJ.

Donaldson T., Werhane P.H. & Van Zandt J. 2008, *Ethical issues in business: a philosophical approach* (8th edn), Pearson Prentice Hall, Upper Saddle River, NJ.

Doppelt B. 2003, *Leading change towards sustainability: a change-management guide for business, government and civil society*, Greenleaf, Sheffield.

Drayton W. 2002, 'The citizen sector: becoming as entrepreneurial and competitive as business', *California Management Review*, vol. 44, no. 3, pp 120–132.

Drucker P.F. 1946, *Concept of the corporation*, John Day, New York.

DTI 2004, *DTI international CSR strategy consultation*, UK Department for Trade and Industry, London.

Du Cann R. 1993, *The art of the advocate* (revised), Penguin, Harmondsworth.

Dunn E. 2004, 'Standards and person-making in east central Europe', in Ong A. & Collier S.J. (eds), *Global assemblages*, Blackwell, New York.

Durkheim E. & Halls W.D. 1984, *The division of labor in society*, Free Press, New York.

Dyllick T. & Hockerts K. 2002, 'Beyond the business case for corporate sustainability', *Business Strategy and the Environment*, vol. 11, no. 2, pp 130–141.

Easterly W.R. 2006, *The white man's burden: why the West's efforts to aid the rest have done so much ill and so little good*, Oxford University Press, Oxford.

Economist 1999, 'The key to industrial capitalism: limited liability' *The Economist*, 23 December, available on line at http://www.economist.com/node/347323.

Economist, 2004, 'Two-faced capitalism', *The Economist*, 22 January, available online at http://www.economist.com/node/2369912.

Economist 2005a, 'The good company', *The Economist*, 20 January, available online at http://www.economist.com/node/3555212.

Economist 2005b, 'The union of concerned executives', *The Economist*, 20 January, available online at http://www.economist.com/node/3555194.

Economist 2005c, 'The world according to CSR', *The Economist*, 20 January, available online at http://www.economist.com/node/3555272.

Economist 2005d, 'Profit and the public good', *The Economist*, 20 January, available online at http://www.economist.com/node/3555259.

Economist 2005e, 'The ethics of business', *The Economist*, 20 January, available online at http://www.economist.com/node/3555286.

Economist 2006, 'Macro credit: Muhammad Yunus has won the Nobel peace prize for his role in promoting financial services for the poor', *The Economist*, 19 October, available online at http://www.economist.com/node/8049829.

Economist 2007, 'Eco-warriors at the gate', *The Economist*, 3 March, available online at http://www.economist.com/node/8776388.

Economist 2008 'Just good business', *The Economist*, 17 January, available online at http://www.economist.com/node/10491077.

Economy, E. 2004, *The river runs black: the environmental challenge to China's future*, Cornell University Press, Ithaca, NY.

Edwards M. 2010, *Small change: why business won't save the world*, Berrett-Koehler, San Francisco, CA.

Edwards M., Hulme D., & Save the Children Fund (Great Britain) 1995, *Non-governmental organisations: performance and accountability: beyond the magic bullet*, Earthscan, London.

Efstathiou J. 2008, 'Carbon trading can raise billions of dollars to save forests', *Independent*, Dublin, 16 April, available online at http://www.independent.ie/.

Ehrenreich B. 2001, *Nickel and dimed: on (not) getting by in America*, Metropolitan Books, New York.

EITI 2005, *Extractive Industries Transparency Initiative source book*, Extractive Industries Transparency Initiative, London.

EIU 2010, *Global trends in sustainability performance management*, Economist Intelligence Unit, London.

Elfstrom G. 2000, 'The ethical responsibilities of multinational corporations: the case of the North American aluminum companies in Jamaica', in Vallis A. (ed.), *Ethics in international affairs*, Rowman & Littlefield, New York, pp 185–200.

Elkington J. 1998, *Cannibals with forks: the triple bottom line of 21st century business*, New Society, Gabriola Island, BC/Stony Creek, CT.

Elkington J. & Hartigan P. 2008, *The power of unreasonable people: how social entrepreneurs create markets that change the world*, Harvard Business School Press, Boston, MA.

Elkington J. & Lee M. 2006, 'It's the economics stupid. Has the corporate responsibility movement lost sight of the big picture?', *Grist Magazine*, 9 May, available online at http://grist.org/article/lee/.

Elliott K.A. & Freeman R.B. 2003, *Can labor standards improve under globalization?* Institute for International Economics, Washington, DC.

Ellsworth R.R. 2002, *Leading with purpose: the new corporate realities*, Stanford Business Books, Stanford, CA.

Elyachar J. 2012, 'Next practices: knowledge, infrastructure, and public goods at the bottom of the pyramid', *Public Culture*, vol. 24, no. 1 66, pp 109–129.

Emerson J. 2003, 'The blended value proposition: integrating social and financial returns', *California Management Review*, vol. 45, no. 4, pp 35–51.

Enderle G. 2004, 'Global competition and corporate responsibilities of small and medium-sized enterprises', *Business Ethics*, vol. 13, no. 1, pp 50–63.

Engfeldt L.-G. 2002, 'The road from Stockholm to Johannesburg', *UN Chronicle*, vol. 39, no. 3.

Englander E. & Kaufman A. 2004, 'The end of managerial ideology: from corporate social responsibility to corporate social indifference', *Enterprise and Society*, vol. 5, no. 3, pp 404–450.

Ernst & Ernst 1976 et seq., *Social responsibility disclosure*, Ernst & Ernst, Cleveland, OH.

Ernst & Young, KPMG, PWC, & House of Mandrag Morgan 1999, *The Copenhagen charter: a management guide to stakeholder reporting*, House of Mandrag Morgan, Copenhagen.

ESRA 2004, *European Sustainability Reporting Awards 2004: report of the judges*, European Sustainability Reporting Association, Paris.

Estes J. 1976, *Social responsibility disclosure*, John Wiley, New York.

Estes R.W. 1975, 'A comprehensive social reporting model', in Seidler L.J. & Seidler L.L. (eds), *Social accounting: theory, issues and cases*, John Wiley, New York.

Estes R.W. 1976, *Corporate social accounting*, John Wiley, New York.

Estes R.W. 1996, *Tyranny of the bottom line: why corporations make good people do bad things*, Berrett-Koehler, San Francisco, CA.

Ethical Corporation 2005, *The role of the big four in shaping corporate responsibility*, Ethical Corporation, London.

Ethical Corporation 2005, *Why The Economist is wrong about CSR*, Ethical Corporation, London.

Ethical Corporation 2006, *Multi-fibre agreement forum in Bangladesh*, Ethical Corporation, London

Ethical Corporation & Nima Hunter Inc. 2003, *The business of business: managing corporate social responsibility. What business leaders are saying and doing 2002–2007*, Nima Hunter Inc., London.

Ethical Performance 2004, 'Angry critics run boycott over "slow" CSR progress', *Ethical Performance*, July 2004, available online at http://www.ethicalperformance.com/news/article/2783.

Ethical Performance, 2005a, 'Firms put on notice as UN Compact gets teeth', *Ethical Performance*, October.

Ethical Performance, 2005b, 'The United Nations deserves some credit', *Ethical Performance*.

Ethical Performance 2005c, 'Ruggie takes on delicate task of considering UN norms', *Ethical Performance*, October.

Ethical Performance 2006a, 'Caterpillar gets reprieve', *Ethical Performance*, April.

Ethical Performance 2006b, 'Criticisms augur end of "flawed" human rights norms', *Ethical Performance*, April.

Ethical Performance 2006c, 'EC white paper unveils European CSR alliance', *Ethical Performance*, April.

Ethical Performance, 2006d, 'Sliding ingloriously down the pole of excellence', *Ethical Performance*, April.

Ethical Performance 2007, 'Facebook generation puts firms in the dock', *Ethical Performance*, November.

Ethical Performance 2008, 'Presenting case studies of corporate social responsibility', *Ethical Performance Best Practice*, Ethical Performance, London.

ETI 1998, *Purpose, principles, programme, membership information*, Ethical Trading Initiative, London.

ETI 1999, *Learning from doing review: a report on company progress in implementing ethical sourcing policies and practices*, Ethical Trading Initiative, London.

ETI 2001, *From good intentions to good practice: annual report 2003*, Ethical Trading Initiative, London.

ETI 2003, *Raising the stakes: annual report 2003*, Ethical Trading Initiative, London.

ETI 2004, *Putting ethics to work: annual report 2003/2004*, Ethical Trading Initiative, London.

ETI 2005a, *Addressing labour practices on Kenyan flower farms: report of ETI involvement 2002-2004*, Ethical Trading Initiative, London.

ETI 2005b, *ETI smallholder guidelines*, Ethical Trading Initiative, London.

ETI 2005c, *Driving change: annual report 2004-2005*, Ethical Trading Initiative, London.

ETI 2005d, *Managing compliance with labour codes at supplier level. A more sustainable way of improving working conditions?*, Ethical Trading Initiative, London.

ETI 2005e, *Moving production: stalling the race to the bottom*, Ethical Trading Initiative, London.

ETI 2006, *Ethical trade: a comprehensive guide for companies*, Ethical Trading Initiative, London.

ETI 2007, *Getting smarter at auditing: tackling the growing crisis in ethical trade auditing*, Ethical Trading Initiative, London.

ETI 2009, *Marking our first decade: annual review 2007-2008*, Ethical Trading Initiative, London.

Etzion D. & Ferraro F. 2010, 'The role of analogy in the institutionalization of sustainability reporting', *Organization Science*, vol. 21, no. 5, pp 1092-1107.

European Commission 2002, 'Companies face their social responsibilities in Europe and abroad', *Social Agenda No. 3*, Directorate-General for Employment and Social Affairs, European Commission, Brussels.

European Social Investment Forum, 2006, *European SRI Study 2006*, Eurosif, Paris.

Evan W.M. & Freeman R.E. 1988, 'A stakeholder theory of the modern corporation: Kantian capitalism', in Beauchamp T. L. & Bowie N.E. (eds), *Ethical Theory and Business* (3rd edn), Prentice Hall, Upper Saddle River, NJ, pp 97-106.

Evans E.J. 1983, *The forging of the modern state: early industrial Britain 1783-1870*, Pearson Education, London.

Evers H. & Schrader H. 1994, *The moral economy of trade: ethnicity and developing markets*, Routledge, London.

FAO 2003, *Agriculture, food and water*, Food and Agriculture Organisation, Rome.

Farman J.C., Gardiner B.G. & Shanklin J.D. 1985, 'Large losses of total ozone in Antarctica reveal seasonal ClOx/NOx interaction', *Nature*, vol. 315, pp 207-210.

Farmer R.N. & Hogue W.D. 1985, *Corporate social responsibility*, Lexington Books, Lexington, MA.

Feldberg M. 1974, 'Defining social responsibility', *Long Range Planning*, vol. 7, pp 39-44.

Felix D. 1995, *Biography of an idea: John Maynard Keynes and the general theory of employment, interest and money*, Transaction, New Brunswick, NJ.

Ferguson C. 1998, *A review of uk company codes of conduct*, available online at http://www.lancaster.ac.uk/fass/law/intlaw/.

Ferguson C. 1999, *Global social policy principles: human rights and social justice*, available online at http://www.eldis.org/.

Ferguson I. 2003, *Corporate timelines*, available online at www.openDemocracy.net.

Ferguson J. 1990, *The anti-politics machine: 'development', depoliticization, and bureaucratic power in Lesotho*, Cambridge University Press, Cambridge.

Ferguson N. 2003, *Empire: how Britain made the modern world*, Allen Lane, London.

Fig D. 2005, 'Manufacturing amnesia: corporate social responsibility in South Africa', *International Affairs*, vol. 81, no. 3, pp 599-618.

Fig D. 2007, *Corporations and moral purpose: South Africa's Truth and Reconciliation Commission and business responsibility for apartheid*, available online at http://bdsnetwork.cbs.dk/publications/.

Financial Reporting Council 2012, *The UK Corporate Governance Code*, Financial Reporting Council, London.

Fitzpatrick M. 2004, 'Business case for sustainability: finding a new state of equilibrium', Keynote address, Green Chemistry and Engineering Conference, Washington DC, 29 June 2004.

Fleming P. & Jones M.T. 2013, *The end of corporate social responsibility: crisis and critique*, SAGE, London.

Foer F. 2004, *How soccer explains the world: an unlikely theory of globalization*, HarperCollins, New York.

Forum for the Future 2006, *Clean capital: financing clean technology firms in the UK*, Forum for the Future, London.

Foster R.N. & Kaplan S. 2001, *Creative destruction: why companies that are built to last underperform the market, and how to successfully transform them*, Currency/Doubleday, New York.

Fourie A. & Eloff T. 2005, 'The case for collective business action to achieve systems change: exploring the contributions made by the private sector to the social, economic and political transformation process in South Africa', *Journal of Corporate Citizenship*, no. 18, Summer, pp 39–48.

Fowler A. 2000, 'NGDOs as a moment in history: beyond aid to social entrepreneurship or civic innovation?', *Third World Quarterly*, vol. 21, no. 4, pp 637–654.

Fox Gorte J. 2008, 'Investors: a force for sustainability', in Krosinsky C. & Robins N. (eds), *Sustainable investing: the art of long-term performance*, Earthscan, London, pp 31–40.

Fox T. & Prescott D. 2004, 'Exploring the role of development cooperation agencies in corporate responsibility', presented at Conference on Development Cooperation and Corporate Social Responsibility, Stockholm, 22–23 March 2004.

Frank A.G. 1979, *Dependent accumulation and underdevelopment*, Monthly Review Press, New York.

Frederick W.C. 1960, 'The growing concern over business responsibility', *California Management Review*, vol. 2, no. 4, pp 54–61.

Frederick W.C. 1995, *Values, nature, and culture in the American corporation*, Oxford University Press, New York.

Frederick W.C. 2006, *Corporation be good! The story of corporate social responsibility*, Dog Ear Publishing, Indianapolis, IN.

Freeman D. 2003, 'Homeworkers in global supply chains', *Greener Management International*, vol. 43, pp 107–118.

Freeman R.E. 1984, *Strategic management: a stakeholder approach*, Pitman, Boston, MA.

Freeman R.E. 2010, *Strategic management: a stakeholder approach*, Cambridge University Press, New York.

Freeman R.E., Pierce J., & Dodd R. 2000, *Environmentalism and the new logic of business*, Oxford University Press, Oxford.

French P.A. 1984, *Collective and corporate responsibility*, Columbia University Press, New York.

Friedman A.L. & Miles S. 2001, 'Socially responsible investment and corporate social and environmental reporting in the UK: an exploratory study', *British Accounting Review*, vol. 33, pp 523–548.

Friedman M. 1962, *Capitalism and freedom*, University of Chicago Press, Chicago, IL.

Friedman M. & Selden R.T. 1975, *Capitalism and freedom: problems and prospects*, University Press of Virginia, Charlottesville, VA.

Friedman T.L. 2000, *The Lexus and the olive tree* (revised), Farrar, Straus & Giroux, New York.

Friedman T.L. 2005, *The world is flat: a brief history of the globalized world in the twenty-first century*, Allen Lane, London.

Friends of the Earth 2005, *Hidden voices: the CBI, corporate lobbying and sustainability*, Friends of the Earth, London.

Frynas J.G. 2005, 'False promises: evidence from multinational oil companies', *International Affairs*, vol. 81, no. 3, pp 581–598.

FTSE4Good 2005, *Impact of new criteria and future direction: 2004–2005 report*, FTSE, London.

Fukuyama F. 1989, 'The end of history', *National History*, Summer, pp 1–18.

Fussler C., Cramer A., & van der Vegt S. (eds) 2004, *Raising the bar: creating value with the United Nations Global Compact*, Greenleaf, Sheffield.

Gabor A. 1999, *The capitalist philosophers: the geniuses of modern business—their lives, times, and ideas*, Times Business, New York.

Gabriel Y. & Lang T. 1995, *The unmanageable consumer: contemporary consumption and its fragmentation*, SAGE, London.

Galbraith J.K. 1952, *American capitalism: the concept of countervailing power*, Houghton Mifflin, Boston, MA.

Galbraith J.K. 1967, *The new industrial state*, Houghton Mifflin, Boston, MA.

Galbraith J.K. 1972, 'The emerging public corporation', *Business and Society Review*, vol. 1, pp 54–56.

Galea C. 2004, *Teaching business sustainability*, Greenleaf, Sheffield.

Gardner S. 2006, *Pushing business-driven corporate citizenship*. Ethical Corporation, London, pp 8–9.

Gascoigne C. 2007, 'Good for the planet, good for profits', *Sunday Times*, London, 28 January, available online at business.timesonline.co.uk.

GE 2005, *Solving big needs: GE corporate citizenship report 2005*, General Electric, Fairfield, CT.

GEE 2002, *Corporate social responsibility monitor*, GEE, London.

Geertz C. 1963, *Peddlers and princes; social change and economic modernization in two Indonesian towns*, University of Chicago Press, Chicago, IL.

Geisst C.R. 2004, *Wall Street: a history: from its beginnings to the fall of Enron* (revised), Oxford University Press, Oxford.

Gereffi G., Humphrey J., & Sturgeon T. 2005, 'The governance of global value chains', *Review of International Political Economy*, vol. 12, no. 1, pp 78–104.

Germain R.D. 2000, *Globalization and its critics: perspectives from political economy*, Palgrave Macmillan, Basingstoke.

Ghazali B.H. & Simula M. 1996, *Study on the development and formulation and implementation of certification schemes for all internationally traded timber and timber products*, International Timber Trade Organisation, Manila.

Ghemawat P. 2011, *World 3.0: Global prosperity and how to achieve it*, Harvard Business Review Press, Boston, MA.

Gibson K. 2000, 'The moral basis of stakeholder theory', *Journal of Business Ethics*, vol. 26, pp 245–257.

Giddens A. 1990, *The consequences of modernity*, Stanford University Press, Stanford, CA.

Giddens A. 1991, *Modernity and self-identity: self and society in the late modern age*, Stanford University Press, Stanford, CA.

Giddens A. 1994, *Beyond left and right: the future of radical politics*, Polity Press, Cambridge.

Giddens A. 2000, *The third way and its critics*, Polity Press, Cambridge.

Giddens A. & Hutton W. 2000, *On the edge: living with global capitalism*, Jonathan Cape, London.

Gillon R. & Lloyd A. 1994, *Principles of health care ethics*, John Wiley, Chichester.

Gilpin R. & Gilpin J.M. 1987, *The political economy of international relations*, Princeton University Press, Princeton, NJ.

Ginsberg T. 2005, 'Threats to critics of Vioxx alleged', *Philadelphia Inquirer*, 5 June, available online at www.lexis.nexis.com.

Glasbeek H.J. 2002, *Wealth by stealth: corporate crime, corporate law, and the perversion of democracy*, Between the Lines, Toronto.

Gleick P.H. 1999, *The world's water 1998–1999: the biennial report on freshwater resources*, Island Press, Washington, DC.

Global Reporting Initiative, 2007, *The G8 encourage GRI reporting to promote development and support investors*, Press release, 8 June, Amsterdam.

Glover D. 2007, 'Monsanto and smallholder farmers: a case study in CSR', *Third World Quarterly*, vol. 28, no. 4, pp 851–867.

Godfrey A., Huane K., Liying L., Witchalls B., & Yambayamba E. 2005, 'Findings from a learning partnership', *Partnership Matters*, vol. 3, pp 37–39.

Goffee R. & Scase R. 1995, *Corporate realities: the dynamics of large and small organisations*, Thomson Learning EMEA, London.

Goldacre B. 2012, *Bad pharma: how drug companies mislead doctors and harm patients*, Fourth Estate, London.

Goodijk R. 2000, 'Corporate governance and workers' participation', *Corporate Governance*, vol. 8, no. 8, pp 303–310.

Goodpaster K.E. 2002, 'Stakeholder thinking: beyond paradox to practicality', in Andriof J., Waddock S.A., Husted B., & Rahman S.S. (eds), *Unfolding stakeholder thinking: theory, responsibility and engagement*, Greenleaf, Sheffield, pp 43–64.

Gore A. 2006, *An inconvenient truth*, Bloomsbury, London.

Gore A. & Blood D. 2012, 'A manifesto for sustainable capitalism with commentary', *Sustainability*, vol. 5, no. 2, pp 66–69.

Graham D. & Woods N. 2006, 'Making corporate self-regulation effective in developing countries', *World Development*, vol. 34, no. 5, pp 868–883.

Grande C. 2007, 'Ethical consumption makes mark on branding', *Financial Times*, London, 20 February, available online at http://www.ft.com/.

Grappi S., Romani S., & Bagozzi R.P. 2013, 'Consumer response to corporate irresponsible behavior: moral emotions and virtues', *Journal of Business Research*, vol. 66, no. 10, pp 1814–1821.

Gray R. 2001, *Accounting for the environment* (2nd edn), SAGE, London.

Gray R. 2002a, 'The social accounting project and accounting organizations and society. Privileging engagement, imaginings, new accountings and pragmatism over critique?', *Accounting, Organizations and Society*, vol. 27, no. 7, pp 687–708.

Gray R. 2002b, 'Of messines, systems and sustainability: towards a more social and environmental finance and accounting', *British Accounting Review*, vol. 34, no. 4, pp 357–386.

Gray R.H. 2003, *Social and environmental accounting and reporting. From ridicule to revolution? From hope to hubris?*, Centre for Social and Environmental Accounting Research, University of St Andrews.

Gray R.H. 2006a, 'Does sustainability reporting improve corporate behaviour? Wrong question? Right time?', *Accounting and Business Research*, vol. 36, suppl. 1, pp 65–88.

Gray R.H. 2006b, 'Social, environmental and sustainability reporting and organisational value creation. Whose value? Whose creation?', *Accounting, Auditing & Accountability Journal*, vol. 19, no. 6, pp 793–819.

Gray R.H. & Bebbington K.J. 2000, 'Environmental accounting, managerialism and sustainability. Is the planet safe in the hands of business and accounting?', *Advances in Environmental Accounting and Management*, vol. 1, pp 1–44.

Gray R.H., Owen D., and Maunders K. 1987, *Corporate Social Reporting*, Prentice Hall, Upper Saddle River, NJ.

Gray R.H., Kouhy R., & Lavers S. 1995a, 'Constructing a research database of social and environmental reporting by UK companies: a methodological note', *Accounting, Auditing and Accountability Journal*, vol. 8, no. 2, pp 78–101.

Gray R.H., Kouhy R., & Lavers S. 1995b, 'Corporate social and environmental reporting: a review of the literature and a longitudinal study of UK disclosure', *Accounting, Auditing and Accountability Journal*, vol. 8, no. 2, pp 47–77.

Gray R.H., Kouhy R. & Lavers S. 1996a, 'Corporate social and environmental reporting: a review of the literature and a longitudinal study of UK disclosure', *Accounting Auditing and Accountability Journal*, vol. 8, no. 2, pp 47–77.

Gray R.H., Owen D., & Adams C. 1996b, *Accounting & accountability: changes and challenges in corporate social and environmental reporting*, Prentice Hall, London.

Gray R.H., Javad M., Power D.M., & Sinclair C.D. 2001, 'Social and environmental disclosure and corporate characteristics: a research note and extension', *Journal of Business Finance and Accounting*, vol. 28, no. 3–4, pp 327–356.

Gray R.H., Dillard J., & Spence C. 2009, 'Social accounting as if the world matters: towards absurdia and a new postalgia', *Public Management Review*, vol. 11, no. 5, pp 545–573.

Gray R.H., Owen D., & Adams C. 2010, 'Some theories for social accounting? A review essay and a tentative pedagogic categorization of theorizations around social accounting', in Freedman M. & Jaggi B. (eds), *Sustainability, environmental performance and disclosures*, Emerald Group, Bingley.

Grayson D. & Dodd T. 2007, *Small is sustainable (and beautiful!): encouraging European smaller enterprises to be sustainable*, Doughty Centre for Corporate Responsibility, Cranfield.

Grayson D. & Hodges A. 2004, *Corporate social opportunity: seven steps to make corporate social responsibility work for your business*, Greenleaf, Sheffield.

Grayson D. & Nelson J. 2013, *Corporate responsibility coalitions: the past, present, and future of alliances for sustainable capitalism*, Stanford University Press, Stanford, CA.

Grecco C, 2007, 'The Bovespa social stock exchange', in Koch-Weser M. and Jacobs W. (eds), *Financing the future: innovative funding mechanisms at work*, Terra Media Verlag, Berlin.

Green S. 2009, *Good value: reflections on money, morality and an uncertain world*, Allen Lane, London.

Greenbury S.R. 1995. *Directors' remuneration: report of a study group chaired by Sir Richard Greenbury*, Gee, London.

Greenfield K. 2006, *The failure of corporate law: fundamental flaws and progressive possibilities*, University of Chicago Press, Chicago, IL.

Greenfield K. 2008 'Reclaiming corporate law in a new gilded age', *Harvard Law & Policy Review*, vol. 2, pp 1–32.

Gregory A., Matatko J., & Luther R. 1997, 'Ethical unit trust financial performance: small company effects and fund size effects', *Journal of Business Finance & Accounting*, vol. 24, pp 705–725.

Gregory C.A. 1982, *Gifts and commodities*, Academic Press, New York.

Greider W. 1997, *One world, ready or not: the manic logic of global capitalism*, Simon & Schuster, New York.

Greider W. 2003, *The soul of capitalism: opening paths to a moral economy*, Simon & Schuster, New York.

Greider W., 2006, 'The future is now', *The Nation*, 26 June, pp 23–26.

GRI 2002, *Sustainability reporting guidelines*, Global Reporting Initiative, Boston, MA.

Gribben C. & Olsen L. 2004, *An anchor—not the answer: trends in social and sustainable development reporting*, Ashridge Centre for Business and Society, Berkhamsted.

Griesgraber J.M. & Gunter B.G. 1997, *World trade: toward a fair and free trade in the twenty-first century*, Pluto Press, London.

Griffin J.J. & Mahon J.F. 1997, 'The corporate social performance and corporate financial performance debate: twenty-five years of incomparable research', *Business & Society*, vol. 36, no. 1, pp 5–31.

Grinspun R. & Cameron M.A. 1993, *The political economy of North American free trade*, St. Martin's Press, New York.

Grosser K. & Moon J. 2005, 'Gender mainstreaming and corporate social responsibility: reporting workplace issues', *Journal of Business Ethics*, vol. 62, no. 4, pp 327–340.

Grubb M., Thompson K., & Sullivan F. 1993, *The Earth Summit agreements: a guide and assessment*, Earthscan, London.

Gunther M. 2008, 'Merrill Lynch's carbon bet. Why a Wall Street firm wants to save a forest in Sumatra', *Fortune*, 18 April, available online at http://money.cnn.com/

Guo B. 2009, 'Social progress and challenges: building a comprehensive strategy for China's environmental clean-up', *China Currents*, vol. 8, no.2, available online at http://www.chinacenter.net/category/china_currents/8-2/.

Guthrie J. & Parker L.D. 1989, 'Corporate social reporting: a rebuttal of legitimacy theory', *Accounting and Business Research*, vol. 19, pp 343–352.

Habisch A., Jonker J., Wegner M., & Schmidpeter R. (eds) 2005, *Corporate social responsibility across Europe*, Springer, New York.

Hale A. & Shaw L.M. 2001, 'Women workers and the promise of ethical trade in the globalised garment industry: a serious beginning?', *Antipode*, vol. 33, no. 3, pp 510–530.

Hale B. 2009, 'Oxfam is the new Tesco say angry independent bookshops being driven to the wall by charity shop's growth', *Daily Mail*, London, 4 August, available online at http://www.dailymail.co.uk/.

Hamann R. 2004, 'Kelian Equatorial Mining: mine closure', in Warner M. & Sullivan R. (eds) *Putting partnerships to work*, Greenleaf, Sheffield, pp 138–150.

Hamann R. & Boulogne F. 2008, 'Partnerships and cross-sector collaboration', in Hamann R. (ed.), *The business of sustainable development in Africa: human rights, partnerships, alternative business models*, Unisa Press, Pretoria, pp 54–82.

Hamann R., Agbazue T., Kapelus P., & Hein A. 2005, 'Universalizing corporate social responsibility? South African challenges to the international organization for standardization's new social responsibility standard', *Business and Society Review*, vol. 110, no. 1, pp 1–19.

Hamann R., Sinha P., Kapfudzaruwa F., & Schild C. 2009, 'Business and human rights in South Africa: an analysis of antecedents of human rights due diligence', *Journal of Business Ethics*, vol. 87, no. 2, pp 453–473.

Hamann R., Woolman S., & Sprague C. 2009, *The business of sustainable development in Africa: human rights, partnerships, alternative business models*, Unisa Press, Pretoria.

Hammond A.L., Kramer W.J., Katz R.S., Tran J.T., & Walker C. 2007, *The next four billion: market size and business strategy at the base of the pyramid*, International Finance Corporation/World Resources Institute, Washington, DC.

Hampden-Turner C. & Trompenaars A. 1993, *The seven cultures of capitalism: value systems for creating wealth in the United States, Japan, Germany, France, Britain, Sweden, and the Netherlands*, Currency/Doubleday, New York.

Hampel S. R. 1998, *Committee on Corporate Governance: final report*, Gee, London.

Handy C. 2002, 'What's a business for?', *Harvard Business Review*, December, pp 49–55.

Handy C.B. 1998, *The hungry spirit. Beyond capitalism: a quest for purpose in the modern world*, Broadway Books, New York.

Hannerz U. 1996, *Transnational connections: culture, people, places*, Routledge, London.

Hardt M. & Negri A. 2000, *Empire*, Harvard University Press, Cambridge, MA.

Harris D.L. & Twomey D.F. 2010, 'The enterprise perspective: a new mind-set for competitiveness and sustainability', *Competitiveness Review*, vol. 20, no. 3, pp 258–266.

Harrison R. 1964, *Animal machines*, Vincent Stuart, London.

Harrison R., Newholm T., & Shaw D. 2005, *The ethical consumer*, SAGE, London.

Hart S.L. 2005, *Capitalism at the crossroads: the unlimited business opportunities in solving the world's most difficult problems*, Prentice Hall, Upper Saddle River, NJ.

Hart S.L. & Christensen C.M. 2002, 'The great leap: driving innovation from the base of the pyramid', *Sloan Management Review*, vol. 44, no. 1, pp 51–56.

Hartman L.P., Shaw B., & Stevenson R. 2003, 'Exploring the ethics and economics of global labor standards: a challenge to integrated social contract theory', *Business Ethics Quarterly*, vol. 13, no. 2, pp 193–220.

Harvey-Jones J. 1988, *Making it happen: reflections on leadership*, Collins, London.

Harwood I. & Humby S. 2008, 'Embedding corporate responsibility into supply: a snapshot of progress', *European Management Journal*, vol. 26, no. 3, pp 166–174.

Hasseldine J., Salama A.I., & Toms J.S. 2005, 'Quantity versus quality: the impact of environmental disclosures on the reputations of UK PLCs', *British Accounting Review*, vol. 37, no. 2, pp 231–248.

Haugh H. 2006, 'Social enterprise: beyond economic outcomes and individual returns', in Mair J., Robinson J., & Hockerts K. (eds), *Social entrepreneurship*, Palgrave Macmillan, Basingstoke, pp 180–206.

Hawken P. 1993, *The ecology of commerce: a declaration of sustainability*, HarperCollins, New York.

Hawken P. 2004, *Socially responsible investing. How the SRI industry has failed to respond to people who want to invest with conscience and what can be done to change it*, Natural Capital Institute, Sausalito, CA.

Hawken P., Lovins A.B., & Lovins L.H. 1999, *Natural capitalism: creating the next industrial revolution*, Little, Brown, Boston, MA.

Hawkins D. 2006, *Corporate social responsibility: balancing tomorrow's sustainability and today's profitability*, Palgrave Macmillan, Basingstoke.

Headd B. 2000, 'The characteristics of small-business employees', *Monthly Labor Review*, vol. 123, no. 4, pp 13–18.

Heal G.M. 2008, *When principles pay: corporate social responsibility and the bottom line*, Columbia Business School, New York.

Heald M. 1970, *The social responsibilities of business, company, and community, 1900–1960*, Case Western Reserve University Press, Cleveland, OH.

Hebrew Union College–Jewish Institute of Religion 1980, *Ethics and corporate responsibility*, Hebrew Union College-Jewish Institute of Religion, Cincinnati, OH.

Held D. & McGrew A.G. 2003, *The global transformations reader: an introduction to the globalization debate* (2nd edn), Polity Press, Cambridge.

Hemingway C.A. & MacLagan P.W. 2004, 'Managers' personal values as drivers of corporate social responsibility', *Journal of Business Ethics*, vol. 50, no. 1, pp 33–44.

Hemp P. & Stewart T. 2004, 'Leading change when business is good', *Harvard Business Review*, vol. 82, no. 12, pp 61–70.

Henderson D. 2004, *The role of business in the modern world*, Institute of Economic Affairs, London.

Henderson D. & Institute of Economic Affairs 2001, *Misguided virtue: false notions of corporate social responsibility*, Institute of Economic Affairs, London.

Hennigfeld J., Pohl M., & Tolhurst N. 2006, *The ICCA handbook on corporate social responsibility*, John Wiley, Chichester.

Henriques A. 2010, *Corporate impact: measuring and managing your social footprint*, Earthscan, London.

Henriques A. & Richardson J.A. 2004, *The triple bottom line, does it all add up? Assessing the sustainability of business and CSR*, Earthscan, London.

Hermes N. & Lensink R. 2011, 'Microfinance: its impact, outreach, and sustainability', *World Development*, vol. 39, no. 6, pp 875–881.

Herrera M.E. 2012, *Towards strategic CSR: aligning CSR with the business and embedding CSR into the organization (a manual for practitioners)*, Asian Institute of Management, Makati, Philippines.

Hertz N. 2001, *The silent takeover: global capitalism and the death of democracy*, Heinemann, London.

Hesse, A. 2006, *Sustained added value*, Deloitte & German Federal Ministry of the Environment, Bonn.

Higgs D. 2003, *Review of the role and effectiveness of non-executive directors*, DTI, London.

Hill P. 1970, *Studies in rural capitalism in West Africa*, Cambridge University Press, Cambridge.

Hillary R. 2000a, *ISO 14001: case studies and practical experiences*, Greenleaf, Sheffield.

Hillary R. 2000b, *The risk society and beyond: critical issues for social theory*, SAGE, London.

Hinrichsen D. 1987, *Our common future: a reader's guide*, Earthscan, London.

Hirst P.Q. & Thompson G. 1999, *Globalization in question: the international economy and the possibilities of governance*, Polity Press, Cambridge.

Hogner R.H. 1982, 'Corporate social reporting: eight decades of development at US Steel', *Research in Corporate Social Performance and Policy*, vol. 4, pp 243–250.

Hollender J. & Breen B. 2010, *The responsibility revolution: how the next generation of businesses will win*, Jossey-Bass, San Francisco, CA.

Holliday C.O., Schmidheiny S., Watts P., & World Business Council for Sustainable Development 2002, *Walking the talk: the business case for sustainable development*, Greenleaf, Sheffield.

Holliday I. 2005, 'Doing business with rights violating regimes: corporate social responsibility and Myanmar's military junta', *Journal of Business Ethics*, vol. 61, no. 4, pp 329–342.

Holpuch A. 2013, 'Google's Eric Schmidt says government spying is "the nature of our society"', *The Guardian*, London, 13 September, available online at www.theguardian.com.

Hoogvelt A.M.M. 2001, *Globalization and the postcolonial world: the new political economy of development*, Johns Hopkins University Press, Baltimore, MD.

Hopkins K. 2009, ' "Public must learn to tolerate the inequality of bonuses", says Goldman Sachs vice-chairman', *The Guardian*, London, available online at guardian.co.uk edn.

Hopkins M. 2003, *The planetary bargain: corporate social responsibility matters*, Earthscan, London.

House of Commons 1999, *House of Commons Select Committee on Trade and Industry. Sixth report: ethical trading*, House of Commons, London.

HSBC Global Research 2012, *Coal and carbon-stranded assets: assessing the risk*, HSBC, London.

Hudson W.H. 1996, *An introduction to the philosophy of Herbert Spencer*, Routledge/Thoemmes, London.

Hughes N. & Lonie S. 2007, 'M-Pesa: mobile money for the "unbanked"—turning cellphones into 24-hour tellers in Kenya', *Innovations*, vol. 2, no. 1–2, pp 63–81.

Hughes P. & Demetrious K. 2006, 'Engaging with stakeholders or constructing them?', *Journal of Corporate Citizenship*, no. 23, Autumn, pp 93–101.

Humphrey J. & Schmitz H. 2001, 'Governance in global value chains', *IDS Bulletin*, vol. 32, no. 3, pp 19–29.

Huntington S.P. 1996, *The clash of civilizations and the remaking of world order*, Simon & Schuster, New York.

Husted B. 2011, *Corporate social strategy: stakeholder engagement and competitive advantage*, Cambridge University Press, Cambridge.

Hutton W. 1995, *The state we're in*, Jonathan Cape, London.

Hutton W. & Giddens A. 2000, *Global capitalism*, New Press, New York.

Ibrahim S., Jamali D., & Karatas-Ozkan M. 2012, 'Corporate social responsibility (CSR) in small and medium-sized enterprises: a developing country perspective', *Contemporary Issues in Entrepreneurship Research*, vol. 2, pp 167–192.

ICC 2000, *The Business Charter for Sustainable Development*, International Chamber of Commerce, Paris.

ICGN 2009, *ICGN Global Corporate Governance Principles: Revised (2009)*, International Corporate Governance Network, London.

IFAT 2006, *Fair trade in Europe 2005: facts and figures on Fair Trade in 25 European countries*, International Fair Trade Association.

Igalens J. & Gond J. 2005, 'Measuring corporate social performance in France: a critical and empirical analysis of ARESE data', *Journal of Business Ethics*, no. 56, pp 131–148.

ILO 1998, *Declaration on Fundamental Principles and Rights at Work and its Follow-up*, International Labour Organisation, Geneva.

Impactt 2005, *Changing over time: tackling supply chain labour issues through business practice*, Impactt Ltd, London.

Inglis F. 2000, *Clifford Geertz: culture, custom, and ethics*, Polity Press, Cambridge.

Ingram R.W. 1978, 'The investigation of the information content of (certain) social responsibility disclosures', *Journal of Accounting Research*, vol. 16, no. 2, pp 270–285.

Innovest 2005, *Intangible value assessment: Swiss Reinsurance Company*, Innovest Strategic Value Advisors, London.

Innovest & Environment Agency 2004, *Corporate environmental governance: a study into the influence of environmental governance on financial performance*, Environment Agency, London.

INSEAD 2007, *RESPONSE: Understanding and responding to societal demands on corporate responsibility*, INSEAD, Brussels.

Institutional Shareholders' Committee, 2005, *The responsibilities of institutional shareholders and agents—statement of principles*, available online at http://www.ecgi.org/.

International Institute of Tropical Agriculture & International Labour Organisation 2002, *Child labour in the cocoa sector of West Africa*, International Institute of Tropical Agriculture and International Labour Organisation, Ibadan.

Ireland P. & Pillay R. 2007, 'Corporate social responsibility and the new constitutionalism', presented at the Business, Social Policy and Corporate Political Influence in Developing Countries UNRISD Conference, Geneva, 12–13 November 2007.

IPCC, 2007, *Fourth Assessment Report*. WMO/Intergovernmental Panel on Climate Change, Geneva.

IPCC 2013–2014. *Fifth Assessment Report*. WMO/Intergovenmental Panel on Climate Change, Geneva.

ISEA 1999, *Accountability 1000: overview of standard and its applications*, Institute of Social and Ethical Accountability, London.

Ite U.E. 'Multinationals and corporate social responsibility in developing countries: a case study of Nigeria ', *Corporate Social Responsibility and Environmental Management*, vol. 11, no. 1, pp 1–11.

Jacks D.S. 2013, *From boom to bust: a typology of real commodity prices in the long run*, Working Paper 18874, National Bureau of Economic Research, Cambridge, MA.

Jackson I.A. & Nelson J. 2004, *Profits with principles: seven strategies for delivering value with values*, Currency/Doubleday, New York.

Jacoby N.H. 1973, *Corporate power and social responsibility; a blueprint for the future*, Macmillan, New York.

Jacoby S. 2007, 'Principles and agents: CalPERS and corporate governance in Japan', *Corporate Governance*, vol. 15, no. 1, pp 5–15.

Jahdi K.S. & Acikdilli G. 2009, 'Marketing communications and corporate social responsibility (CSR): marriage of convenience or shotgun wedding?', *Journal of Business Ethics*, vol. 88, no. 1, pp 103–113.

Jamali D. & Mirshak R. 2007, 'Corporate social responsibility (CSR): theory and practice in a developing country context', *Journal of Business Ethics*, vol. 72, no. 3, pp 243–262.

Jamali D., Zanhour M. & Keshishian T. 2009, 'Peculiar strengths and relational attributes of SMEs in the context of CSR', *Journal of Business Ethics*, vol. 87, no. 3, pp 355–377.

Jamison L. & Murdoch H. 2004, *Taking the temperature: ethical supply chain management*, Institute of Business Ethics, London.

Jenkins H. 2004, 'A critique of conventional CSR theory: an SME perspective', *Journal of General Management*, vol. 29, pp 37–57.

Jenkins H. 2006, 'Small business champions for corporate social responsibility', *Journal of Business Ethics*, vol. 67, no. 3, pp 241–256.

Jenkins H. 2009, 'A "business opportunity" model of corporate social responsibility for small- and medium-sized enterprises', *Business Ethics*, vol. 18, no. 1, pp 21–36.

Jenkins R.O. 1999, 'The changing relationship between emerging markets and multinational enterprises', in Buckley P.J. & Ghauri P.N. (eds), *Multinational enterprises and emerging markets: managing increasing interdependence*, Pergamon Press, Oxford.

Jenkins R.O. 2001, *Corporate codes of conduct: self-regulation in a global economy*, UNRISD, Geneva.

Jenkins R.O. 2002, 'The political economy of codes of conduct', in Jenkins R.O., Pearson R., & Seyfang G. (eds), *Corporate responsibility and labour rights: codes of conduct in the global economy*, Earthscan, London, pp 13–30.

Jenkins R.O. 2005, 'Globalization, corporate social responsibility and poverty', *International Affairs*, vol. 81, no. 3, pp 525–540.

Jenkins R.O., Pearson R., & Seyfang G. (eds) 2002, *Corporate responsibility and labour rights: codes of conduct in the global economy*, Earthscan, London.

Jensen M.C. 1986, 'Agency costs of free cash flow, corporate finance, and takeovers', *American Economic Review*, vol. 76, no. 2, pp 323–329.

Jensen M.C. 2000, *A theory of the firm: governance, residual claims, and organizational forms*, Harvard University Press, Cambridge, MA.

Jensen M. C. 2001. 'Value maximisation, stakeholder theory, and the corporate objective function', *European Financial Management*, vol. 7, no. 3, pp 297–317.

Jensen M.C. & Meckling W.H. 1976, 'Theory of the firm: managerial behavior, agency costs and ownership structure', *Journal of Financial Economics*, vol. 3, no. 4, pp 305–360.

Jeucken M. 2001, *Sustainable finance and banking: the financial sector and the future of the planet*, Earthscan, London.

Jewson Associates 2008. *The costs of ethical investing*, Jewson Associates, London.

John R. 2007, *Beyond the cheque: how venture philanthropists add value*, interim report for Finance for Change, Skoll World Forum, 29 March, Oxford.

Johnson J. 2004, 'Global trends in employment, productivity and poverty', presented at the Conference on Globalization and Labor in Developing Countries, Watson Institute for International Studies, Brown University, 10–11 December 2004.

Johnston D.C. 2003, *Perfectly legal: the covert campaign to rig our tax system to benefit the super rich—and cheat everybody else*, Portfolio, New York.

Jones K.A. 2004, *Who's afraid of the WTO?* Oxford University Press, Oxford.

Jones L.B. 1995, *Jesus, CEO: using ancient wisdom for visionary leadership*, Hyperion, New York.

Jones O. & Tilley F. 2003, *Competitive advantage in SMEs: organising for innovation and change*, John Wiley, Chichester.

Jonkers J. 2005, 'CSR wonderland: navigating between movement, community and organisation', *Journal of Corporate Citizenship*, no. 20, Winter, pp 19–22.

Kabeer N. 2000, *The power to choose: Bangladeshi women and labour market decisions in London and Dhaka*, Verso, London.

Kakabadse A.P. 2006, 'Management thinking: making CSR work', *Ethical Corporation*, June 20, available online at http://www.ethicalcorp.com/.

Kamara J. 1986, *Socially responsible investment and economic development*, Division of Research, Michigan School of Business, University of Michigan, Ann Arbor, Mich.

Kaminker C. & Stewart F. 2012, *The role of institutional investors in financing clean energy*, OECD, Paris.

Kaminsky J.S. 1995, *Corporate responsibility in the Hebrew Bible*, Sheffield Academic Press, Sheffield.

Kangogo J., Guyo W., Bowen M., & Ragui M. 2013, 'Supply chain disruption in the Kenya floriculture industry: a case study of Equator Flowers', *European Journal of Business and Management*, vol. 5, no. 7, pp 246–253.

Kanter R.M. 1999, 'From spare change to real change: the social sector as beta site for business innovation', *Harvard Business Review*, vol. 77, no. 3, pp 122–132, 210.

Kanter R.M. 2009, *Supercorp: how vanguard companies create innovation, profits, growth, and social good*, Crown Business, New York.

Kaplan R.E.B. & Berenbeim J.M. 2004, *Ethics programs: the role of the board—a global study*, Conference Board, New York.

Kapstein E.B. 2008, *Measuring Unilever's economic footprint: the case of South Africa*, Unilever, London.

Kaptein M. 2004, 'Business codes of multinational firms. what do they say?', *Journal of Business Ethics*, vol. 50, pp 13–31.

Karnani A. 2007, 'The mirage of marketing to the bottom of the pyramid', *California Management Review*, vol. 49, no. 4, pp 90.

Kauffman M. & Chedekel L. 2004, 'As colleges profit, sweatshops worsen', *Hartford Courant*, 12 December, available online at www.courant.com.

Kavlianz P. 2009, *Mattel fined $2.3 million over lead in toys*, www.CNNMoney.com.

Kay J. 2012, *The Kay Review of UK Equity Markets and Long-Term Decision Making', final report (July)*, Department for Business, Innovation and Skills, London.

Kechiche A. & Soparnot R. 2012, 'CSR within SMEs: literature review', *International Business Research*, vol. 5, no. 7, pp 97–104.

Keefe J.F. 2007, 'From socially responsible investing to sustainable investing', *Green Money Journal*, available online at http://archives.greenmoneyjournal.com/article.mpl?newsletterid=41&articleid=544.

Kell G. 2013, '12 years later: reflections on the growth of the UN Global Compact', *Business & Society*, vol. 52, no. 1, pp 31–52.

Kell G. & Levin D. 2003, 'The Global Compact network: an historic experiment in learning and action', *Business & Society Review*, vol. 108, no. 2, pp 151–181.

Kelly M. 2001, *The divine right of capital: dethroning the corporate aristocracy*, Berrett-Koehler, San Francisco, CA.

Kelly P.J. 1990, *Utilitarianism and distributive justice: Jeremy Bentham and the civil law*, Clarendon Press, Oxford.

Kennedy A. 2000, *The end of shareholder value*, Orion Business, London.

Kennedy P.M. 1987, *The rise and fall of the great powers: economic change and military conflict from 1500 to 2000*, Random House, New York.

Khurana R. 2007, *From higher aims to hired hands: the social transformation of American business schools and the unfulfilled promise of management as a profession*, Princeton University Press, Princeton, NJ.

Kiernan M. 2005, 'Sustainable development', in Dallas G. (ed.) *Governance and risk*, McGraw-Hill, New York:

Killick N. 2004, 'BP and others, Azerbaijan: conflict prevention'; in Warner M. & Sullivan R. (eds), *Putting partnerships to work*, Greenleaf, Sheffield, pp 98–107.

King F., Marcus R., & Fabian T. 2000, *Big business, small hands: responsible approaches to child labour*, Save the Children, London.

Klein G.D. 1978, 'Corporate social responsibility: an assessment of the enlightened self-interest model', *Academy of Management Review*, vol. 3, no. 1, pp 32–39.

Klein N. 1999, *No logo: taking aim at the brand bullies*, Picador, New York.

Klein T.A. 1977, *Social costs and benefits of business*, Prentice-Hall, Englewood Cliffs, NJ.

Knights D. & Tinker T. 1997, *Financial institutions and social transformations: international studies of a sector*, St. Martin's Press, New York.

Koch K. 1974, *War and peace in Jalémó: the management of conflict in highland New Guinea*, Harvard University Press, Cambridge, MA.

Kolb R.W. 2008, *Encyclopedia of business ethics and society*, SAGE Publications, Thousand Oaks, CA.

Kolk A. 2003, 'Trends in sustainability reporting by the Fortune Global 250', *Business Strategy and the Environment*, vol. 12, no. 5, pp 279–291.

Kolk A. 2004, 'A decade of sustainability reporting: developments and significance', *International Journal of Environment and Sustainable Development*, vol. 3, no. 1, pp 51–64.

Kolk A. & Pinkse J. 2010, *The climate change-development nexus and tripartite partnerships*, Working Paper 006, University of Amsterdam Business School.

Kolk A. & van Tulder R. 2002, 'Child labor and multinational conduct: a comparison of international business and stakeholder codes', *Journal of Business Ethics*, vol. 36, no. 3, pp 91–301.

Kolk A. & van Tulder R. 2006, 'Poverty alleviation as business strategy? Evaluating commitments of frontrunner multinational corporations', *World Development*, vol. 34, no. 5, pp 542.

Kolk A., van Tulder R., & Welters C. 1999, 'International codes of conduct and corporate social responsibility: can transnational corporations regulate themselves?', *Transnational Corporations*, vol. 8, no. 1, pp 143–180.

Korten D.C. 1995, *When corporations rule the world*, Kumarian Press, Bloomfield, CT/Berrett-Koehler, San Francisco, CA.

Korten D.C. 1999, *The post-corporate world: life after capitalism*, Berrett-Koehler, San Francisco, CA.

Kourula A. & Halme M. 2008, 'Types of corporate responsibility and engagement with NGOs: an exploration of business and societal outcomes', *Corporate Governance*, vol. 8, no. 4, pp 557–570.

KPMG 1993, *International survey of environmental reporting*, KPMG International, Amsterdam.

KPMG 1996, *International survey of environmental reporting*, KPMG International, Amsterdam.

KPMG 1999, *International survey of environmental reporting*, KPMG International, Amsterdam.

KPMG 2002, *International survey of corporate sustainability reporting 2002*, KPMG International, Amsterdam.

KPMG 2005, *International survey of corporate sustainability reporting 2005*, KPMG International, Amsterdam.

KPMG 2008, *International survey of corporate sustainability reporting 2008*, KPMG International, Amsterdam.

KPMG 2011, *International survey of corporate sustainability reporting 2011*, KPMG International, Amsterdam.

Kramer M. & Kania J. 2006, 'Changing the game: leading corporations switch from defense to offense in solving global problems', *Stanford Social Innovation Review*, Spring, pp 20–27.

Kreander N., Gray R., Power D., and Sinclair C. 2002, 'The financial performance of European ethical funds 1996–1998', *Journal of Accounting and Finance*, vol. 1, pp 3–22.

Kreander N., Gray R., Power D., and Sinclair C. 2005, 'Evaluating the performance of ethical and non-ethical funds: a matched pair analysis', *Journal of Business Finance & Accounting*, vol. 32, no. 7–8, pp 1465–1493.

Kreps T.J. & Murphy, K.R. 1940, *Measurement of the social performance of business*, U.S.Government Printing Office, Washington, DC.

Krosinsky C. 2008, 'Sustainable equity investing: the market-beating strategy', in Krosinsky C. & Robins N. (eds), *Sustainable investing: the art of long-term performance*, Earthscan, London, pp 19–30.

Krosinsky C. & Robins N. (eds) 2008, *Sustainable investing: the art of long-term performance*, Earthscan, London.

Krugman P. 1998a, *Why aren't we all Keynesians yet?*, available online at http://web.mit.edu/krugman/.

Krugman P. 1998b, *The accidental theorist: and other dispatches from the dismal science*, Norton, New York.

Krumsiek B. 2004, 'Voluntary codes of conduct for multinational corporations: promises and challenges', *Business and Society Review*, vol. 109, no. 4, pp 583–593.

Kuada J. & Hinson R.E. 2012, 'Corporate social responsibility (CSR) practices of foreign and local companies in Ghana', *Thunderbird International Business Review*, vol. 54, no. 4, pp 521–536.

Kukathas C. 1989, *Hayek and modern liberalism*, Clarendon Press, Oxford.

Kuriyan R., Nafus D., & Mainwaring S. 2012, 'Consumption, technology, and development: the "poor" as "consumer"', *Information Technologies & International Development*, vol. 8, no. 1, pp 1–12.

Kurtenbach E. 2005, 'Chinese sofa factory workers go on strike', available on line at http://www.globallabourrights.org/.

Kwan A. & Frost S. 2002, 'Made in China: rules and regulations versus codes of conduct in the toy sector', in Jenkins R.O., Pearson R., & Seyfang G. (eds) *Corporate responsibility and ethical trade: codes of conduct in the global economy*, Earthscan, London, pp 124–134.

Ladbury S., Young G., & Gibbons S. 2000, *Mid-term review of the ETI: a review of the progress of the Ethical Trading Initiative*, Department for International Development, London.

Ladkin D. 2006, 'When deontology and utilitarianism aren't enough: how Heidegger's notion of "dwelling" might help organisational leaders resolve ethical issues", *Journal of Business Ethics*, vol. 65, no. 1, pp 87–98.

LaFeber W. 2002, *Michael Jordan and the new global capitalism* (new edn), W.W. Norton, New York.

Laffer A.B. & Miles M.A. 1982, *International economics in an integrated world*, Scott, Foresman, Glenview, IL.

Lamberti L. & Noci G. 2012, 'The relationship between CSR and corporate strategy in medium-sized companies: evidence from Italy', *Business Ethics*, vol. 21, no. 4, pp 402–416.

Lash S. 2002, *Critique of information*, SAGE, London.

Laszlo C. 2003, *The sustainable company: how to create lasting value through social and environmental performance*, Island Press, Washington, DC.

Laszlo E. 2006, *The chaos point: the world at the crossroads*, Hampton Roads Publishing, Charlottesville, VA.

Lawrence A.T., Weber J., & Post J.E. 2005, *Business and society: stakeholders, ethics, public policy* (11th edn), McGraw-Hill, New York.

Leadbeater C. 1997, *The rise of the social entrepreneur*, Demos, London.

Leadbeater C. 2004, *Personalisation through participation: a new script for public services*, Demos, London.

Lehman C. 1992, *Accounting's changing roles in social conflict*, London, Paul Chapman.

Leipziger D. 2001, *SA8000: the definitive guide to the new social standard*, Financial Times/Prentice Hall, Harlow.

Leipziger D. 2010, *The corporate responsibility code book* (2nd edn), Greenleaf, Sheffield.

Lenox M.J. & Nash J. 2003, 'Industry self-regulation and adverse selection: a comparison across four trade association programs', *Business Strategy and the Environment*, vol. 12, no. 6, pp 343–356.

Levy D.L. & Newell P. 2002, 'Business strategy and international environmental governance: toward a neo-Gramscian synthesis', *Global Environmental Politics*, vol. 2, no. 4, pp 84–101.

Levy D.L. & Newell P. 2005, *The business of global environmental governance*, MIT Press, Cambridge, MA.

Lewis M. 2011, *The big short: inside the Doomsday Machine*, Penguin, London.

Lewis N., L.D. Parker, & P. Sutcliffe 1984, 'Financial reporting to employees: the pattern of development 1919–1979', *Accounting Organizations and Society*, vol. 9, no. 3–4, pp 275–289.

Light A. & Rolston H. 2003, *Environmental ethics: an anthology*, Blackwell, Malden, MA.

Light A. & Smith J.M. 1997, *Space, place, and environmental ethics*, Rowman & Littlefield, Lanham, MD.

Lim A. & Tsutsui K. 2012, 'Globalization and commitment in corporate social responsibility: cross-national analyses of institutional and political-economy effects', *American Sociological Review*, vol. 77, no. 1, pp 69–98.

Lindblom C.K. 1994, 'The implications of organizational legitimacy for corporate social performance and disclosure', paper presented at the Critical Perspectives on Accounting Conference, New York.

Lindgreen A., Kotler P., & Maon F. 2012, *A stakeholder approach to corporate social responsibility: pressures, conflicts, and reconciliation*, Gower, Farnham.

Lindsay J. 1975, *William Morris: his life and work*, Constable, London.

Lindsey B. 2002, *Against the dead hand: the uncertain struggle for global capitalism*, John Wiley, New York.

Little W.G. 2002, *The waste fix: seizures of the sacred from Upton Sinclair to The Sopranos*, Routledge, New York.

Litvin D.B. 2003, *Empires of profit: commerce, conquest and corporate responsibility*, Texere, New York.

Locke R., Fei Q., & Brause A. 2006, *Does monitoring improve labor standards? Lessons from Nike*, Working Paper 4612-06, MIT Sloan School of Management, Cambridge, MA.

Lodge G.C. 2006, *A corporate solution to global poverty: how multinationals can help the poor and invigorate their own legitimacy*, Princeton University Press, Princeton, NJ.

Loftus P. 2009, 'Merck sees $80 million Vioxx settlement', *Wall Street Journal*, New York, 3 August, http://online.wsj.com/.

Logan D. 1997, *The case for business action on family planning and AIDS prevention in Ghana*, Corporate Citizenship Company, London.

Logsdon J.M. 2004, 'Global business citizenship: applications to environmental issues', *Business and Society Review*, vol. 109, no. 1, pp 67.

London T. & Hart S.L. 2010, *Next generation business strategies for the base of the pyramid: new approaches for building mutual value*, FT Press, Upper Saddle River, NJ.

Long J.C. 2008, 'From cocoa to CSR: finding sustainability in a cup of hot chocolate', *Thunderbird International Business Review*, vol. 50, no. 5, pp 315–320.

Lort-Phillips L, 2006, 'China: one country, two systems', *Corporate Citizenship Briefing*, December/January, available online at www.ccbriefing.co.uk.

Louche C. & Lydenberg S.D. 2011, *Dilemmas in responsible investment*, Greenleaf, Sheffield.

Lucas-Lecin V. & Nahal S. 2008, 'Sustainability analysis', in Krosinsky C. & Robins N. (eds), *Sustainable investing: the art of long-term performance*, Earthscan, London, pp 41–56.

Lukes S, 1974, *Power: a radical view*, London: Macmillan.

Lund-Thomsen P. 2005, 'Corporate accountability in South Africa: the role of community mobilizing in environmental governance', *International Affairs*, vol. 81, no. 3, pp 619–634.

Lund-Thomsen P. & Lindgreen A. 2013, 'Corporate social responsibility in global value chains: where are we now and where are we going?', *Journal of Business Ethics*, July, pp 1–12.

Lund-Thomsen P., Nadvi K., Chan A., Khara N., & Xue H. 2012, 'Labour in global value chains: work conditions in football manufacturing in China, India and Pakistan', *Development and Change*, vol. 43, no. 6, pp 1211–1237.

Lydenberg S.D. 2005, *Corporations and the public interest: guiding the invisible hand*, Berrett-Koehler Publishers, San Francisco, CA.

Lyon F. 2003, 'Community groups and livelihoods in remote rural areas of Ghana: how small-scale farmers sustain collective action', *Community Development Journal*, vol. 38, no. 4, pp 323–331.

Lyon F. & Bertotti M. 2007, 'Measuring the contributions of small firms to reducing poverty and increasing social inclusion in the UK', in Stoner J.A. & Wankel C. (eds), *Innovative approaches to reducing global poverty*, Information Age Publishing, Charlotte, NC.

Lyon S. & Moberg M. (eds) 2010, *Fair trade and social justice: global ethnographies*, NYU Press, New York.

Lyon F. & Vickers I. 2009, 'Challenges of encouraging enterprise in deprived areas', in Southern A. (ed.), *Enterprise and deprivation: small business, social exclusion and sustainable communities*, John Wiley, Basingstoke.

McCarthy R.J. 2006, 'Venture capitalists flock to green stocks', *Inc.*, 28 March, available online at http://www.inc.com/.

McCord N. 1970, *Free trade: theory and practice from Adam Smith to Keynes*, David & Charles, Newton Abbot.

Macdonald K. 2007, *Globalising justice within coffee supply chains? Fair Trade, Starbucks and the transformation of supply chain governance*, Third World Foundation for Social and Economic Studies, London.

Macdonald K. & Marshall S.E. 2010, *Fair trade, corporate accountability and beyond: experiments in globalizing justice*, Ashgate, Farnham.

McDonough W. & Braungart M. 2002, *Cradle to cradle: remaking the way we make things*, North Point Press, New York.

McEwan T. 2001, *Managing values and beliefs in organisations*, Financial Times/Prentice Hall, Harlow.

McGee R.W. 1994, *A trade policy for free societies: the case against protectionism*, Quorum Books, Westport, CT.

MacGillivray A. & Zadek, S. 1995, *Accounting for change: indicators for sustainable development*, New Economics Foundation, London.

McGreal C. 2009, 'Revealed: millions spent by lobby firms fighting Obama health reforms', *The Guardian*, 1 October, available online at http://www.theguardian.com/.

McGregor R. 2007, 'China's good corporate citizens find their voice', *Financial Times*, 25 February, available online at www.ft.com/.

McGuire J.W. 1963, *Business and society*, McGraw-Hill, New York.

McInnes W. 2012, *Culture shock: a handbook for 21st century business*, John Wiley, Hoboken, NJ.

McIntosh A. 2002, *Soil and soul: people versus corporate power*, Aurum, London.

McIntosh M. 2003a, *Living corporate citizenship: strategic routes to socially responsible business*, Financial Times/Prentice Hall, Harlow.

McIntosh M. 2003b, *Raising a ladder to the moon: the complexities of corporate social and environmental responsibility*, Palgrave Macmillan, Basingstoke.

McIntosh M. & Thomas R. 2000, *Global companies in the twentieth century: selected archival histories*, Routledge, Abingdon.

McIntosh M., Leipziger D., Jones K., & Coleman G. 1998, *Corporate citizenship: successful strategies for responsible companies*, Financial Times/Prentice Hall, Harlow.

McIntosh M., Waddock S.A. & Kell G. (eds) 2004, *Learning to talk: corporate citizenship and the development of the UN Global Compact*, Greenleaf, Sheffield.

MacKenzie D.A. 2006, *An engine, not a camera: how financial models shape markets*, MIT Press, Cambridge, MA.

McLean B. & Elkind P. 2003, *The smartest guys in the room: the amazing rise and scandalous fall of Enron*, Portfolio, New York.

MacLean J. 1999, 'Towards a political economy of agency in contemporary international relations', in Shaw M. (ed.), *Politics and globalisation: knowledge, ethics and agency*, Routledge, London.

MacLean J. 2000, 'Philosophical roots of globalization and philosophical roots to globalization', in Germain R.D. (ed.), *Globalization and its critics: perspectives from political economy*, Macmillan, Basingstoke, pp 3–65.

McLellan D. 1972, *Marx's Grundrisse*, Harper & Row, New York.

McMichael P. 2004, *Development and social change: a global perspective* (3rd edn), Pine Forge Press, Thousand Oaks, CA.

McMichael P. 2009, *Contesting development: critical struggles for social change*, Routledge, Abingdon.

McMurtry J. 2002, *Value wars: the global market versus the life economy*, Pluto Press, London.

McPhail K. 2008, 'Contributing to sustainable development through multi-stakeholder processes: practical steps to avoid the "resource curse"', *Corporate Governance*, vol. 8, no. 4, pp 471–481.

McQuaid K. 1977, 'Young, Swope and General Electric's new capitalism: a study in corporate liberalism 1920–33', *American Journal of Economics and Sociology*, vol. 36, no. 3, pp 323–334.

McWilliams A. & Siegel D. 2000, 'Corporate social responsibility and financial performance: correlation or misspecification?', *Strategic Management Journal*, vol. 21, no. 5, pp 603–609.

Mackey J. & Sisodia R. 2013, *Conscious capitalism: liberating the heroic spirit of business*, Harvard Business Review Press, Boston, MA.

Mahapatra S. 1984, 'Investor reaction to corporate social accounting', *Journal of Business Finance and Accounting*, 11(1), 29–40.

Mahon J. & Wartick S.L. 2012, 'Corporate social performance profiling: using multiple stakeholder perceptions to assess a corporate reputation', *Journal of Public Affairs*, vol. 12, no. 1, pp 12–28.

Mair J. & Noboa E. 2006, 'Social entrepreneurship: how intentions to create social venture are formed', in Mair J., Robinson J., & Hockerts K. (eds), *Social entrepreneurship*, Palgrave Macmillan, Basingstoke, pp 121–136.

Mair J., Robinson J. & Hockerts K.E. 2006, 'Introduction', in Mair J., Robinson J., & Hockerts K. (eds), *Social entrepreneurship*, Palgrave Macmillan, Basingstoke, pp 1–14.

Maitland A, 2005, 'Big business starts to scratch the surface', *Financial Times*, 14 September, available online at www.ft.com/.

Maitland A, 2006, 'A responsible balancing act', *Financial Times*, 1 June, available online at www.ft.com/.

Mallen C.A, 2012, *Corporate governance*, Oxford University Press, New York.

Mamic I. 2004, *Implementing codes of conduct: how businesses manage social performance in global supply chains*, Greenleaf, Sheffield, & ILO, Geneva.

Mander J. & Goldsmith E. 1996, *The case against the global economy: and for a turn toward the local*, Sierra Club Books, San Francisco, CA.

Manga J.E., Mirvis P., Rochlin S.A., & Zecchi K. 2005, *Integration: critical link for corporate citizenship. Strategies and stories from eight companies*, Center for Corporate Citizenship at Boston College, Chestnut Hill, MA.

Manheim J.B. 2000, *The death of a thousand cuts: corporate campaigns and the attack on the corporation*, Lawrence Erlbaum, Mahwah, NJ.

Manheim J.B. 2004, *Biz-war and the out-of-power elite: the progressive-left attack on the corporation*, Lawrence Erlbaum, Mahwah, NJ.

Manne H. & Wallich H.C. 1972, *The modern corporation and social responsibility*, American Enterprise Institute for Public Policy Research, Washington, DC.

Margolis J.D. & Walsh J.P. 2001, *People and profits? The search for a link between a company's social and financial performance*, Lawrence Erlbaum, Mahwah, NJ.

Margolis J.D. & Walsh J.P. 2003, 'Misery loves companies: rethinking social initiatives by business', *Administrative Science Quarterly*, vol. 48, no. 2, pp 268–305.

Margolis J.D., Elfenbein H.A., & James P.W. 2008, 'Do well by doing good? Don't count on it', *Harvard Business Review*, vol. 86, no. 1, pp 19.

Markopolos H. 2010, *No one would listen: a true financial thriller*, John Wiley, Hoboken, NJ.

Markopoulos M. 1998, *Impacts of certification on community forest enterprises: a case study of the Lomerio Community Forest Management Project, Bolivia*, Department for International Development, London.

Markopoulos M. 1999, *Community forest enterprise and certification in Mexico: a review of experience*, Oxford University Press, Oxford.

Marland G., Boden T.A., & Andres R.J. 2003, 'Global, regional, and national CO2 emissions,' in *Trends: A Compendium of Data on Global Change*, Carbon Dioxide Information Analysis Center, Oak Ridge National Laboratory, Oak Ridge, TN.

Marling W.H. 2006, *How 'American' is globalization?* Johns Hopkins University Press, Baltimore, MD.

Martin R.L. 2002, 'The virtue matrix: calculating the return on corporate responsibility', *Harvard Business Review*, vol. 80, no. 3, pp 68.

Marx K. 1973, *Grundrisse. Foundations of the critique of political economy*, Vintage Books, New York.

Marx K., Moore S., Aveling E.B., Engels F. & Besant A.W. 1887, *Capital: a critical analysis of capitalist production*, S. Sonnenschein Lowrey & Co, London.

Mason E.S. 1960, *The corporation in modern society*, Harvard University Press, Cambridge, MA.

Mathews M.R., 1993, *Socially responsible accounting*, Chapman & Hall, London.

Mathews M.R. 1996, 'Twenty-five years of social and environmental accounting research. Is there a silver jubilee to celebrate?', *Accounting, Auditing and Accountability Journal*, vol. 10, no. 4, pp 481–531.

Mattar H. 2001, 'Ethical portals as inducers of corporate social responsibility', in Zadek S., Hojensgard N., and Raynard P. (eds), *Perspectives on the new economy of corporate citizenship*, Copenhagen Centre, Copenhagen, pp 113–121.

Matten D. & Crane A. 2005, 'Corporate citizenship: toward an extended theoretical conceptualization', *Academy of Management Review*, vol. 30, no. 1, pp 166–180.

Matten D. & Moon J. 2008, ' "Implicit" and "explicit" CSR: a conceptual framework for a comparative understanding of corporate social responsibility', *Academy of Management Review*, vol. 33, no. 2, pp 404–424.

Mattingly J.E. & Berman S.L. 2006, 'Measurement of corporate social action: discovering taxonomy in the Kinder Lydenberg Domini ratings data', *Business and Society*, vol. 45, no. 1, pp 20–46.

Mawson A. 2008, *The social entrepreneur: making communities work*, Atlantic, London.

Maxwell S. 2005, *The Washington Consensus is dead! Long live the meta-narrative*, Working Paper 243, Overseas Development Institute, London.

May S., Cheney G., & Roper J. 2007, *The debate over corporate social responsibility*, Oxford University Press, New York.

Meadows D., Randers J., & Meadows D.L. 2004, *Limits to growth: the 30-year update*, Earthscan, London.

Meh A. 2004, 'Uneasy partnerships and contradictions: corporate social and environmental responsibility', presented at the 3rd Annual Global Studies Association Conference, Brandeis University.

Melcrum 2005, *How to structure the corporate responsibility function*, Melcrum, London.

Mesure S. 2007, 'Tesco follows M&S with climate change move', *The Independent*, London, 16 January, available online at http://www.independent.co.uk/.

Mill J.S. 1987, *Utilitarianism*, Prometheus Books, Buffalo, NY.

Mill J.S. 2002, *The basic writings of John Stuart Mill*, Modern Library, New York.

Milne M.J. & Chan C.C.C. 1999, 'Narrative corporate social disclosures. How much of a difference do they make to investment decision-making?', *British Accounting Review*, vol. 31, no. 4, pp 439–457.

Mirvis P.H. 2000, 'Transformation at Shell: commerce and citizenship ', *Business and Society Review*, vol. 105, no. 1, pp 63.

Mirvis P. & Googins B.K. 2006, *Stages of corporate citizenship: a developmental framework*, Center for Corporate Citizenship at Boston College, Chestnut Hill, MA.

Mitchell A. & Sikka P. 2004, 'Accountability of the accountancy bodies: the peculiarities of a British accountancy body', *British Accounting Review*, vol. 36, no. 4, pp 395–414.

Mitchell A., Sikka P., Puxty T., and Willmott H. 1991, *Accounting for change: proposals for reform of audit and accounting*, Discussion Paper No. 7, Fabian Society, London.

Mitchell A., Sikka P., Cooper C., Willmott H., and Arnold P. 2001, *The BCCI cover-up*, Association for Accountancy & Business Affairs, Basildon.

Mitchell J., Shankleman J. & Warner M. 2004, 'Measuring the added value of partnerships', in Warner M. & Sullivan R. (eds), *Putting partnerships to work*, Greenleaf, Sheffield, pp 191–200.

Mitchell L.E. 2001, *Corporate irresponsibility: America's newest export*, Yale University Press, New Haven, CT.

Mitchell L.E. 2005, 'Roles and incentives: the core problems of corporate social responsibility', *Ethical Corporation Magazine*, October, pp 46–50.

Mitnick B.M. 2000, 'Commitment, revelation, and the testaments of belief: the metrics of measurement of corporate social performance', *Business and Society*, vol. 39, no. 4, pp 419–465.

Mittelman J.H. 2000, *The globalization syndrome: transformation and resistance*, Princeton University Press, Princeton, NJ.

Monbiot G, 2005, 'Africa's new best friends', *Guardian Weekly*, 5 July, available online at http://www.theguardian.com/.

Monitor 2009, *Investing for social and environmental impact*, Monitor Group, Boston, MA.

Monks R.A.G. & Minow N. 1991, *Power and accountability*, HarperCollins, London.

Moody-Stuart S.M. 2004, 'The role of business in developing countries', *Business Ethics*, vol. 13, no. 1, pp 41–49.

Moon J., Crane A., & Matten D. 2005, 'Can corporations be citizens? Corporate citizenship as a metaphor for business participation in society', *Business Ethics Quarterly*, vol. 15, no. 3, pp 427–451.

Moore B. 1966, *Social origins of dictatorship and democracy; lord and peasant in the making of the modern world*, Beacon Press, Boston, MA.

Moorhead J, 2007, 'Milking it', *The Guardian*, London, 15 May, available online at http://www.theguardian.com/.

Morris C.W. 1999, *The social contract theorists: critical essays on Hobbes, Locke, and Rousseau*, Rowman & Littlefield, Lanham, MD.

Morsing M. & Perrini F. 2009, 'CSR in SMEs: do SMEs matter for the CSR agenda?', *Business Ethics*, vol. 18, no. 1, pp 1–6.

Mosley L. 2011, *Labor rights and multinational production*, Cambridge University Press, New York.

Moss D.A. 2002, *When all else fails: government as the ultimate risk manager*, Harvard University Press, Cambridge, MA.

Mouan L.C. 2010, 'Exploring the potential benefits of Asian participation in the Extractive Industries Transparency Initiative: the case of China', *Business Strategy and the Environment*, vol. 19, no. 6, pp 367–376.

Muirhead S.A. 2006, *Philanthropy and business: the changing agenda*, Conference Board, New York.

Mullins J.W. 2006, *The new business road test: what entrepreneurs and executives should do before writing a business plan* (2nd edn), Financial Times/Prentice Hall, Harlow.

Mullins J.W. & Komisar R. 2009, *Getting to plan B: breaking through to a better business model*, Harvard Business School Press, Boston, MA.

Murillo D. & Lozano J.M. 2006, 'SMEs and CSR: an approach to CSR in their own words', *Journal of Business Ethics*, vol. 67, no. 3, pp 227–240.

Murphy D.Y. & Bendell J. 1999, *Partners in time? Business, NGOs and sustainable development*, UN Resarch Institute for Social Development, Geneva.

Murphy R. 2007, *Platinum performers must shine all the way through*, Ethical Performance, London.

Murray A.S. 2007, *Revolt in the boardroom: the new rules of power in corporate America*, Collins, New York.

Murray A., Sinclair D., Power D., & Gray, R. 2006, 'Do financial markets care about social and environmental disclosure? Further evidence and exploration from the UK', *Accounting, Auditing and Accountability Journal*, vol. 19, no. 2, pp 228–255.

Murray J. 2002, 'Labour rights/corporate responsibilities: the role of ILO labour standards', in Jenkins R.O., Pearson R., & Seyfang G. (eds) *Corporate responsibility and labour rights: codes of conduct in the global economy*, Earthscan, London, pp 31–42.

Muthuri J.N. 2013, 'Corporate social responsibility in Africa', in Lituchi T., Punnett B.J., & Puplampu B.B. (eds), *Management in Africa: macro and micro perspectives*, Routledge, Abingdon, pp 90–111.

Nader R. & Taylor W. 1986, *The big boys: power and position in American business*, Pantheon Books, New York.

Nair C. 2006, 'Eyes wide shut: corporate citizenship in Asia', *Ethical Corporation Magazine*, May, pp 46–47.

Narlikar A. 2005, *The World Trade Organization: a very short introduction*, Oxford University Press, Oxford.

Nash L.L. & Kantrow A.M. 1987, 'Multinational corporations and economic development', in Berger P.L. (ed.), *Capitalism and equality in the Third World*, Rowman & Littlefield, Lanham, MD.

Nelson J. 1996, *Business as partners in development: creating wealth for countries, companies and communities*, Prince of Wales Business Leaders' Forum, London.

Nelson J. 1998, *Building competitiveness and communities: how world class companies are creating shareholder value and societal value*, Prince of Wales Business Leaders' Forum, London.

Nelson J. 2007, *Building linkages for competitive and responsible entrepreneurship*, UNIDO, Vienna, & John F Kennedy School of Government, Harvard University, Cambridge, MA.

Nelson J. & Zadek S. 2000, *Partnership alchemy: new social partnerships in Europe*, The Copenhagen Centre, Copenhagen.

Nelson V. & Galvez M. 2000, *Social impact of ethical and conventional brazil nut trading on forest-dependent people in Peru*, Working Paper, Natural Resources Institute, University of Greenwich, Chatham.

Nelson V. & Pound B. 2009, *The last ten years: a comprehensive review of the literature on the impact of fairtrade*, Working Paper, Natural Resources Institute, University of Greenwich, Chatham.

Nelson V. & Tallontire A. 2002, 'Assessing the benefits of ethical trade schemes in cocoa (Ecuador) and Brazil nuts (Peru) for forest-dependent people and their livelihoods', *International Forestry Review*, vol. 4, no. 2, pp 99–109.

Nelson V., Martin A. & Ewert J. 2007, 'The impacts of codes of practice on worker livelihoods: empirical evidence from the South African wine and Kenyan cut flower industries', *Journal of Corporate Citizenship*, no. 28, Winter, pp 61–72.

Newell P. 2005, 'Citizenship, accountability and community: the limitations of the CSR agenda', *International Affairs*, vol. 81, no. 3, pp 541–558.

Newell P. & Muro A. 2006, 'Corporate social and environmental responsibility in Argentina: the evolution of an agenda', *Journal of Corporate Citizenship*, no. 24, Winter, pp 49–68.

Newman P. & Hotchner A.E. 2003, *Shameless exploitation in pursuit of the common good*, Nan A. Talese, New York.

Newton A. 2005, 'Defining the art of conversation', *Ethical Corporation Magazine*, November, pp 46–47.

Nicholls A. 2008, *Social entrepreneurship: new models of sustainable social change* (2nd edn), Oxford University Press, Oxford.

Nicholls A. 2010, 'The institutionalization of social investment: the interplay of investment logics and investor rationalities', *Journal of Social Entrepreneurship*, vol. 1, no. 1, pp 70–100.

Nicholls A. & Opal C. 2005, *Fair trade: market-driven ethical consumption*, SAGE, London.

Nielsen A.E. & Thomsen C. 2012, 'Corporate social responsibility (CSR) management and marketing communication: research streams and themes', *Hermes—Journal of Language and Communication in Business*, vol. 49, pp 49–65.

Nielsen M.E. 2005, 'Child labour in the Bangladeshi garment industry', *International Affairs*, vol. 81, no. 3, pp 559–580.

Nikoloyuk J., Burns T.R., & de Man R. 2010, 'The promise and limitations of partnered governance: the case of sustainable palm oil', *Corporate Governance*, vol. 10, no. 1, pp 59–72.

Nocera J, 2006, 'The board wore chicken suits', *New York Times*, 27 May, available online at http://www.nytimes.com/.

Novak M. 1982, *Spirit of democratic capitalism*, Simon & Schuster, New York.

Nozick R. 1974, *Anarchy, state, and utopia*, Basic Books, New York.

NRET 1999, 'Ethical trade and sustainable rural livelihoods', in Carney D. (ed.) *Sustainable rural livelihoods. What contribution can we make?*, Department for International Development, London, pp 107–129.

Nussbaum M.C. & Sen A.K. (eds) 1993, *The quality of life*, Clarendon Press, Oxford.

Odell A.M. 2007, 'Principles for responsible investment quadruples assets in first year', *Social Funds*, 1 June, available online at www.socialfunds.com.

O'Dwyer B. & Owen D.L. 2005, 'Assurance statement practice in environmental, social and sustainability reporting: a critical evaluation', *British Accounting Review*, 37, no. 2, pp 205–229.

OECD 1999, *Principles of Corporate Governance*, OECD, Paris.

Okali C. 1983, *Cocoa and kinship in Ghana: the matrilineal Akan of Ghana*, Kegan Paul International, London.

Olsen L. 2004, *Making corporate responsibility work: lessons from real business*, Ashridge Centre for Business and Society/British Quality Forum, Berkhamsted.

Ong A. 1999, *Flexible citizenship: the cultural logics of transnationality*, Duke University Press, Durham, NC.

Onzivu W. 2013, '(Re)invigorating the health protection objective of the Basel Convention on Transboundary Movement of Hazardous Wastes and Their Disposal', *Legal Studies*, vol. 33, no. 4, pp 621–649.

O'Rourke D. 2003, 'Outsourcing regulation: non-governmental systems of labor standards and monitoring ', *Policy Studies Journal*, vol. 31, no. 1, pp 1–29.

O'Rourke D. 2006, 'Multi-stakeholder regulation: privatizing or socializing global labor standards?', *World Development*, vol. 34, no. 5, pp 899–918.

O'Rourke K.H. 2005, *The international trading system, globalization, and history*, Edward Elgar, Cheltenham.

O'Rourke K.H. & Williamson J.G. 1999, *Globalization and history: the evolution of a nineteenth-century Atlantic economy*, MIT Press, Cambridge, MA.

Orr D. 2005, 'The triumph of neo-liberalism but will it really make poverty history?', *The Independent*, London, 25 June, available online at http://www.independent.co.uk/.

Oterberg R. 1993, *Corporate renaissance: business as an adventure in human development*, Paraview, New York.

Owen D. 2003. *Recent developments in European social and environmental reporting and auditing practice—a critical evaluation and tentative prognosis*, ICCSR Research Paper Series, University of Nottingham.

Owen D.L., Swift T.A., Humphrey C., & Bowerman M. 2000, 'The new social audits: accountability, managerial capture or the agenda of social

champions?', *European Accounting Review*, vol. 9, issue 1, pp 81–98.

Paine L., Deshpande R., Margolis J.D., & Bettcher K.E. 2005, 'Up to code: does your company's conduct meet world-class standards?', *Harvard Business Review*, vol. 83, no. 12, pp 122–133, 154.

Palazzo G. & Richter U. 2005, 'CSR business as usual? The case of the tobacco industry', *Journal of Business Ethics*, vol. 61, pp 387–401.

Papista E. & Dimitriadis S. 2012, 'Exploring consumer-brand relationship quality and identification: qualitative evidence from cosmetics brands', *Qualitative Market Research*, vol. 15, no. 1, pp 33–56.

Parker J. 1998, *Citizenship, work, and welfare: searching for the good society*, Macmillan, Basingstoke.

Parket R. & Eilbirt H. 1975, 'The practice of social responsibility: the underlying factors', *Business Horizons*, 18, no. 4, pp 5–10.

Parmar B.L., Freeman R.E., Harrison J.S., Wicks A.C., Purnell L. & De Colle S. 2010, 'Stakeholder theory: the state of the art', *Academy of Management Annals*, vol. 4, no. 1, pp 403–445.

Patricof A. & Sunderland J. 2006, 'Venture capital for development', in Brainard L. (ed.), *Transforming the development landscape: the role of the private sector*, Brookings Institution Press, Washington, DC, pp 74–84.

Paulden P. 2009, *TXU LBO 'disaster' punishes bondholders with offer*, available online at http://www.bloomberg.com/.

Pava M.L. & Krausz J. 1995, *Corporate responsibility and financial performance: the paradox of social cost*, Quorum Books, Westport, CT.

Pearson R. 2007, 'Beyond women workers: gendering CSR', *Third World Quarterly*, vol. 28, no. 4, pp 731–749.

Pearson R. & Seyfang G. 2001, 'New hope or false dawn? Voluntary codes of conduct, labour regulation and social policy in a globalizing world', *Global Social Policy*, vol. 1, no. 1, pp 49–78.

Pedersen E.R. 2005, 'Guiding the invisible hand: the role of development agencies in driving corporate citizenship', *Journal of Corporate Citizenship*, no. 20, Winter, pp 77–91.

Pedersen E.R. 2006, 'Making corporate social responsibility (CSR) operable: how companies translate stakeholder dialogue into practice', *Business and Society Review*, vol. 111, no. 2, pp 137–163.

Pedersen E.R. 2009, 'The many and the few: rounding up the SMEs that manage CSR in the supply chain', *Supply Chain Management*, vol. 14, no. 2, pp 109–116.

Pedersen E.R. & Huniche M. (eds) 2006, *Corporate citizenship in developing countries: new partnership perspectives*, Copenhagen Business School Press, Copenhagen.

Peinado-Vara E. 2006, 'Corporate social responsibility in Latin America', *Journal of Corporate Citizenship*, no. 21, Spring, pp 61–69.

Perkins, R. 2004, 'Sweeter partnerships? An NGO's engagement with the sugar sector', *Partnership Matters*, vol. 2, pp 33–35.

Perrini F., Russo A., & Tencati A. 2007, 'CSR strategies of SMEs and large firms: evidence from Italy', *Journal of Business Ethics*, vol. 74, no. 3, pp 285–300.

Peters G. 1999, *Waltzing with the raptors: a practical roadmap to protecting your company's reputation*, John Wiley, New York.

Peters T.J. 1995, *In search of excellence: lessons from America's best-run companies*, HarperCollins, London.

Phillips K.P. 2002, *Wealth and democracy: a political history of the American rich*, Broadway Books, New York.

Phillips R. 2003, *Stakeholder theory and organizational ethics*, Berrett-Koehler, San Francisco, CA.

Phillips R. & Caldwell C.B. 2005, 'Value chain responsibility: a farewell to arm's length', *Business and Society Review*, vol. 110, no. 4, pp 345–370.

Phillips R., Freeman R.E., & Wicks A.C. 2003, 'What stakeholder theory is not', *Business Ethics Quarterly*, vol. 13, no. 4, pp 479–502.

Phylmar Group 2006, *Phylmar Enews*, February 2006.

Pilger J. 2002, *The new rulers of the world*, Verso, London.

Pinchot G. 1985, *Intrapreneuring: why you don't have to leave the corporation to become an entrepreneur*, Harper & Row, New York.

Pinkse J. & Kolk A. 2009, *International business and global climate change*, Routledge, Abingdon.

Pio E. 2005, 'Eastern karma: perspectives on corporate citizenship', *Journal of Corporate Citizenship*, no. 19, Summer, pp 65–78.

Plender J. 1997, *A stake in the future: the stakeholding solution*, Nicholas Brealey, London.

Plender J. 2003, *Going off the rails: global capital and the crisis of legitimacy*, John Wiley, Chichester.

Polanyi K. 1944, *The great transformation*, Farrar & Rinehart, New York.

Pomeranz K. & Topik S. 2006, *The world that trade created: society, culture, and the world economy, 1400 to present*, M.E. Sharpe, Armonk, NY.

Ponte S., Gibbon P., & Vestergaard J. 2011, 'Governing through standards: an introduction', in Ponte S., Gibbon P., & Vestergaard J. (eds), *Governing through standards: origins, drivers and limitations*, Palgrave MacMillan, Basingstoke, pp 1–23.

Porritt J. 2005, *Capitalism: as if the world matters*, Earthscan, London.

Porter M.E. 1990, *The competitive advantage of nations*, Free Press, New York.

Porter M.E. & Kramer M.R. 2002, 'The competitive advantage of corporate philanthropy', *Harvard Business Review*, vol. 80, no. 12, pp 56–68.

Porter M.E. & Kramer M. 2006, 'Strategy and society: the link between competitive advantage and corporate social responsibility', *Harvard Business Review*, vol. 84, no. 12, pp 78–92.

Porter M.E. & Kramer M. 2011, 'The big idea: creating shared value', *Harvard Business Review*, vol. 89, no. 1–2, pp 62–77.

Porter M.E. & van der Linde C. 1995, 'Green and competitive: ending the stalemate', *Harvard Business Review*, vol. 73, no. 5, pp 120–134.

Posner R.A. 1981, *The economics of justice*, Harvard University Press, Cambridge, MA.

Post J.E. & Altman B.W. 1992, 'Models of corporate greening: how corporate social policy and organizational learning inform leading-edge environmental management', *Research in Corporate Social Performance and Policy*, vol. 13, pp 3–29.

Post J.E., Lawrence A.T., & Weber J. 1999, *Business and society: corporate strategy, public policy, ethics* (9th edn), Irwin/McGraw-Hill, Boston, MA.

Post J.E., Preston L.E., & Sauter-Sachs S. 2002, *Redefining the corporation: stakeholder management and organizational wealth*, Stanford Business Books, Stanford, CA.

Prahalad C.K. 2005, *The fortune at the bottom of the pyramid*, Prentice Hall, Upper Saddle River, NJ.

Prahalad C.K. & Hart S.L. 2002, 'The fortune at the bottom of the pyramid', *Strategy+Business*, no. 26, pp 2–14.

Prakash S. 2006, 'Conflicted safety panel let Vioxx study continue', 8 June, National Public Radio, Washington, DC, available online at http://www.npr.org/.

Preston L.E. & O'Bannon D.P. 1997, 'The corporate social-financial performance relationship: a typology and analysis', *Business & Society*, vol. 36, no. 4, pp 419–428.

Preston L.E. & Post J.E. 1975, *Private management and public policy: the principle of public responsibility*, Prentice-Hall, Englewood Cliffs, NJ.

Preston L.E. & Sapienza H.J. 1990, 'Stakeholder management and corporate performance', *Journal of Behavioral Economics*, vol. 19, no. 4, pp 361–375.

PR News 2006, *Guide to best practices in corporate social responsibility*, available online at http://www.prnewsonline.com/.

Putnam R.D. 2000, *Bowling alone: the collapse and revival of American community*, Simon & Schuster, New York.

PWBLF 1998, *Managing partnerships: tools for managing the public sector, business and civil society as partners in development*, Prince of Wales Business Leaders' Forum, London.

PWC 2006, *Corporate responsibility: strategy, management and value*, PricewaterhouseCoopers, London.

Quayle M. 2003, 'A study of supply chain management practice in UK industrial SMEs', *Supply Chain Management*, vol. 8, no. 1, pp 79–86.

Quinn J. 2009, 'Goldman chairman admits Wall St greed', *Daily Telegraph*, London, 7 April, available online at http://www.telegraph.co.uk/finance/.

Quinn T.K. 1962, *Unconscious public enemies*, Citadel Press, New York.

Rachels J. 1999, *The elements of moral philosophy* (3rd edn), McGraw-Hill, New York.

Radin T.J. & Werhane P.H. 2003, 'Employment-at-will, employee rights, and future directions for employment', *Business Ethics Quarterly*, vol. 13, no. 2, pp 113–130.

Raimbaev A. 2009, 'Corporate social responsibility among SMEs in Uzbekistan', in Aras G. and Crowther D. (eds), *Global Perspectives on Corporate Governance and CSR*, Gower, Farnham, pp 187–196.

Rajak D. 2006, 'The gift of CSR: power and the pursuit of responsibility in the mining industry', in Visser W., McIntosh M., & Middleton C. (eds), *Corporate citizenship in Africa: lessons from the past, paths to the future*, Greenleaf, Sheffield.

Rajak D. 2008, ' "Uplift and empower": the market, the gift and corporate social responsibility on South Africa's platinum belt', *Research in Economic Anthropology*, vol. 28, pp 297–324.

Rajak D. 2011, *In good company: an anatomy of corporate social responsibility*, Stanford University Press, Stanford, CA.

Ramanathan K.V. 1976, 'Towards a theory of corporate social accounting', *Accounting Review*, vol. 52, no. 4, pp 516–528.

Rand A. 1966, *Capitalism, the unknown ideal*, New American Library, New York.

Rangan V.K., Quelch J.A., & Herrero G. (eds) 2007, *Business solutions for the social poor: creating social and economic value*, Jossey-Bass, San Francisco, CA.

Ranganathan J. 1998, *Sustainability rulers: measuring corporate, social, environmental and social performance*, World Resources Institute, Washington, DC.

Ranganathan J. 1999, 'Signs of sustainability: measuring corporate environmental and social performance' in Bennett M. & James P. (eds), *Sustainable measures: evaluation and reporting of environmental and social performance*, Greenleaf, Sheffield, pp 475–495.

Rao K. & Tilt C.A. 2013, 'Corporate governance and corporate social responsibility: a critical review', in Kokubu K., Sawabe N., & Sakaue M. (eds), *Proceedings of the 7th Asia Pacific Interdisciplinary Research in Accounting Conference*, available online at http://www.apira2013.org/proceedings/pdfs/K167.pdf.

Rasche A. 2010, 'The limits of corporate responsibility standards', *Business Ethics*, vol. 19, no. 3, pp 280–291.

Rasche A. & Esser D.E. 2006, 'From stakeholder management to stakeholder accountability: applying Habermasian discourse ethics to accountability research', *Journal of Business Ethics*, no. 65, pp 251–267.

Rasche A. & Kell G. 2010, *The United Nations Global Compact: achievements, trends and challenges*, Cambridge University Press, New York.

Rasche A., De Bakker F.G., & Moon J. 2013a, 'Complete and partial organizing for corporate social responsibility', *Journal of Business Ethics*, vol. 115, no. 4, pp 651–663.

Rasche A., Waddock, S. & McIntosh M. 2013b, 'The United Nations Global Compact: retrospect and prospect', *Business & Society*, vol. 52, no. 1, pp 6–30.

Raufflet E. & Mills A.J. (eds) 2009, *The dark side: critical cases on the downside of business*, Greenleaf, Sheffield.

Rawls J. 1971, *A theory of justice*, Belknap Press, Cambridge, MA.

Raynolds L.T., Murray D., & Taylor P.L. 2004, 'Fair trade coffee: building producer capacity via global networks', *Journal of International Development*, vol. 16, no. 8, pp 1109–1121.

Redclift M.R. 2000, *Sustainability: life chances and livelihoods*, Routledge, Abingdon.

Reddy D. 2008, 'India', in Krosinsky C. & Robins N. (eds), *Sustainable investing: the art of long-term performance*, Earthscan, London, pp 165–176.

Reddy P.L.S. 2002, 'Corporate governance—emerging trends', *Corporate Governance*, vol. 1, no. 1.

Reed M.M. & Neubert M.J. 2012, 'General Electric: ecomagination as a CSR initiative', *Journal of Business Ethics Education*, vol. 8, no. 1, pp 245–254.

Reich R.B. 2007, *Supercapitalism: the transformation of business, democracy, and everyday life*, Alfred A. Knopf, New York.

Rembert T.C. 2005, 'CSR in the crosshairs: a broad counter-attack against corporate reform is growing. (Could that be a sign of progress?)', *Business Ethics*, Spring, pp 30–35.

REWE 2012, *Ensure a successful 'energy transition' in Germany—provide predictability and fair allocation*, REWE, Koln.

Ricardo D. 1817, *On the principles of political economy, and taxation*, J. Murray, London.

Ring P.S., Bigley G.A., D'Aunoo T., & Khanna T. 2005, 'Perspectives on how governments matter', *Academy of Management Review*, vol. 30, no. 2, pp 308–320.

Roberts R.W. 1992, 'Determinants of corporate social responsibility disclosure: An application of stakeholder theory', *Accounting, Organizations and Society*, vol. 17, no. 6, 595–612.

Robertson R. 1992, *Globalization: social theory and global culture*, SAGE, London.

Robins N. 2007, 'The imperious company', *Journal of Corporate Citizenship*, no. 25, Spring, pp 31–42.

Robins N. 2008, 'The emergence of sustainable investing' in Krosinsky C. & Robins N. (eds), *Sustainable investing: the art of long-term performance*, Earthscan, London, pp 3–17.

Robins N. 2012, *The corporation that changed the world. How the East India Company shaped the modern multinational* (2nd edn), Pluto Press, London.

Roche C. 1999, *Impact assessment for development agencies: learning to value change*, Oxfam, Oxford.

Rockoff J. & Kendall B. 2009, 'Pfizer to plead guilty to improper marketing', *Wall Street Journal*, New York, 3 September, available online at http://online.wsj.com/news/.

Roddick A. 2000, *Business as unusual*, Thorsons, London.

Rodrik D. 1997, *Has globalization gone too far?* Institute for International Economics, Washington, DC.

Ronchi L. 2002, *Impact of fair trade on producers and their organisations: a case study with Coocafe in Costa Rica*, Poverty Research Unit, University of Sussex.

Rondinelli D.A. 2002, 'Transnational corporations: international citizens or new sovereigns?', *Business and Society Review*, vol. 107, no. 4, pp 391–413.

Rose C. 2007, 'Does female board representation influence firm performance? The Danish evidence', *Corporate Governance*, vol. 15, pp 404–413.

Rose S. 2007, 'Back in fashion: how we're reviving a British icon (Marks & Spencer)', *Harvard Business Review*, May, pp 51–57.

Rosenberg H. 1999, *A traitor to his class: Robert A.G. Monks and the battle to change corporate America*, John Wiley, New York.

Rosenberg J. 2000, *The follies of globalisation theory: polemical essays*, Verso, London.

Rowledge L.R. 1999, *Mapping the journey: case studies in strategy and action toward sustainable development*, Greenleaf, Sheffield.

Rowley T.J. & Moldoveanu M. 2003, 'When will stakeholder groups act? An interest- and identity-based model of stakeholder group mobilization', *Academy of Management Review*, vol. 28, no. 2, pp 204–219.

Ruggie J.G. 2003, 'Taking embedded liberalism global: the corporate connection', in Held D. & Koenig-Archibugi M. (eds), *Taming globalization: frontiers of governance*, Polity Press, Cambridge.

Ruggie J.G., Wright M., & Lehr A. 2006, *Business recognition of human rights: global patterns, regional and sectoral variations*, UN Human Rights Commission, Geneva.

Rulli M.C., Saviori A., & d'Odorico P. 2013, 'Global land and water grabbing', *Proceedings of the National Academy of Sciences*, vol. 110, no. 3, pp 892–897.

Runciman D. 2003, 'Partnering the state', *Partnership Matters*, vol. 1, pp 12–15.

Runhaar H. & Lafferty H. 2009, 'Governing corporate social responsibility: an assessment of the contribution of the UN Global Compact to CSR strategies in the telecommunications industry', *Journal of Business Ethics*, vol. 84, no. 4, pp 479–495.

Runping Y. 2006, 'Business starts taking social responsibility seriously', *China View*, 17 May, available online at news.xinhuanet.com.

Rusbridger A. 2009, 'A chill on *The Guardian*', *New York Review of Books*, January 15, available online at http://www.nybooks.com/.

Russo A. & Perrini F. 2010, 'Investigating stakeholder theory and social capital: CSR in large firms and SMEs', *Journal of Business Ethics*, vol. 91, no. 2, pp 207–221.

Russo A. & Tencati A. 2009, 'Formal vs. informal CSR strategies: evidence from Italian micro, small, medium-sized, and large firms', *Journal of Business Ethics*, vol. 85, pp 339–353.

Sabapathy J., Swift T., Weiser J. & Polycarpe M. (2002), *Innovation through partnership*, Institute of Social and Ethical Accountability, London.

Saha P. 2005, 'Shopping around: a leaked company document may dampen the Christmas spirit at Asda', *Ethical Corporation Magazine*, December, available online at http://www.ethicalcorp.com/.

Saha P, 2006, 'Doing ethics the Tata way', *Ethical Corporation Magazine*, June, pp 26–28.

SAI 1999, *Guidance document for social accountability 8000*, Social Accountability International, New York.

Saith A. 2006, 'From universal values to millennium development goals: lost in translation', *Development and Change*, vol. 37, no. 6, pp 1167–1199.

Salamon L.M. 2003, *The resilient sector: the state of nonprofit America*, Brookings Institution Press, Washington, DC.

Salzmann O., Ionescu-Somers A., & Steger U. 2005, 'The business case for corporate sustainability: literature review and research options', *European Management Journal*, vol. 23, no. 1, pp 27–36.

Sampson G.P. 2001, *The role of the World Trade Organization in global governance*, United Nations University Press, Tokyo.

Sampson G.P. 2005, *The World Trade Organization and sustainable development*, United Nations University Press, Tokyo.

SAM–PWC 2008, *Sustainability year book 2008*, Sustainable Asset Management, Zurich & PricewaterhouseCoopers, London.

Satre L.J. 2005, *Chocolate on trial: slavery, politics, and the ethics of business*, Ohio University Press, Athens, OH.

Scammell M. 2000, 'The internet and civic engagement: the age of the citizen-consumer', *Political Communication*, vol. 17, no. 4, pp 351–355.

Schafer H. 2005. 'International corporate social responsibility rating systems: conceptual outline and empirical results', *Journal of Corporate Citizenship*, no. 20, Winter, pp 107–120.

Schaltegger S., Burritt R., and Petersen, H. (eds) 2003, *An introduction to corporate environmental management: striving for sustainability*, Greenleaf, Sheffield.

Schaltegger S., Lüdeke-Freund F., & Hansen E.G. 2012, 'Business cases for sustainability: the role of business model innovation for corporate sustainability', *International Journal of Innovation and Sustainable Development*, vol. 6, no. 2, pp 95–119.

Scherer A.G. & Palazzo G. 2007, 'Toward a political conception of corporate responsibility: business and society seen from a Habermasian perspective', *Academy of Management Review*, vol. 32, pp 1096–1120.

Schiller B. 2006, 'Turkish progress: sampling the delights of corporate responsibility', *Ethical Corporation Magazine*, June 2006, available online at http://www.ethicalcorp.com/.

Schipper I. & de Haan E. 2005, *CSR issues in the ICT hardware manufacturing sector*, SOMO, Amsterdam.

Schirato T. & Webb J. 2003, *Understanding globalization*, SAGE, London.

Schmidheiny S. 1992, *Changing course: a global business perspective on development and the environment*, MIT Press, Cambridge, MA.

Schmidheiny S. 2006, 'A view of corporate citizenship in Latin America', *Journal of Corporate Citizenship*, no. 21, Spring, pp 21–24.

Schmidheiny S. & WBCSD 1996, *Financing change: the financial community, eco-efficiency, and sustainable development*, MIT Press, Cambridge, MA.

Schmidheiny S. & Zorraquin F. 1996, *Financing change : the financial community, eco-efficiency, and sustainable development*, MIT Press, Cambridge, MA.

Scholte J.A. 2000, *Globalization: a critical introduction*, St. Martin's Press, New York.

Schouten G. & Glasbergen P. 2011, 'Creating legitimacy in global private governance: rhe case of the roundtable on sustainable palm oil', *Ecological Economics*, vol. 70, no. 11, pp 1891–1899.

Schreck P. 2011, 'Reviewing the business case for corporate social responsibility: new evidence and analysis', *Journal of Business Ethics*, vol. 103, no. 2, pp 167–188.

Schröder M. 2005, *Is there a difference? The performance characteristics of SRI equity indexes*, Working Paper, Centre for European Economic Research (ZEW), Mannheim.

Schwartz M.S. & Carroll A.B. 2003, 'Corporate social responsibility: a three domain approach', *Business Ethics Quarterly*, vol. 13, no. 4, pp 503–530.

Schwartz P. & Gibb B. 1999, *When good companies do bad things: responsibility and risk in an age of globalization*, John Wiley, New York.

Schwittay A. 2011, 'The marketization of poverty', *Current Anthropology*, vol. 52, no. S3, S71–S82.

Scott L. 2005, *Twenty first century leadership*, available online at http://news.walmart.com/.

Scrase H., Wenban-Smith M., & Judd N. 1999, *Certification of forest products for small businesses: improving access—issues and options. Final report*, Department for International Development, London, available online at http://r4d.dfid.gov.uk/.

Searcy C. 2012, 'Corporate sustainability performance measurement systems: a review and research agenda', *Journal of Business Ethics*, vol. 107, no. 3, pp 239–253.

Seeger M.W. & Ulmer R.R. 2001, 'Virtuous responses to organizational crisis: Aaron Feuerstein and Milt Colt', *Journal of Business Ethics*, vol. 31, no. 4, pp 369–376.

Seidman G.W. 2003, 'Monitoring multinationals: lessons from the anti-apartheid era', *Politics & Society*, vol. 31, no. 3, pp 381–406.

Seidman G.W., 2004, 'Deflated citizenship: labor rights in a global era', in Brysk A. and Shafir G. (eds), *People out of place: globalization, human rights, and the citizenship gap*, Routledge, New York, pp 109–129.

Seitanidi M.M. 2010, *The politics of partnerships: a critical examination of nonprofit-business partnerships*, Springer, Dordrecht.

Sen A.K. 2000, *Development as freedom*, Anchor Books, New York.

Senge P.M. 2008, *The necessary revolution: how individuals and organizations are working together to create a sustainable world*, Nicholas Brealey, London.

Sethi S.P. 1975, 'Dimensions of corporate social performance: an analytical framework', *California Management Review*, vol. 17, no. 3, pp 58–65.

Sethi S.P. 2003, *Setting global standards: guidelines for creating codes of conduct in multinational corporations*, John Wiley, Hoboken, NJ.

Sewing T, 2006, 'Mired in the regulation debate', *Ethical Corporation Magazine*, January, pp 13–14.

Shaw M. 2000, *Theory of the global state: globality as unfinished revolution*, Cambridge University Press, Cambridge.

Shaw M. (ed.) 1999, *Politics and globalisation: knowledge, ethics and agency*, Routledge, London.

Shearman & Sterling, 2005, *Trends in the corporate governance practices of the 100 largest US public companies*, available online at www.shearman.com.

Shell 2011, *Signals and signposts: Shell energy scenarios to 2050—an era of volatile transitions*, Shell International BV, Rotterdam.

Shell 2013, *New lens scenarios*, Shell International BV, Rotterdam.

Shleifer A. & Vishney R.W. 1997, 'A survey of corporate governance', *Journal of Finance*, vol. 52, no. 2, pp 737–783.

Sikka P. 2001, 'Regulation of accountancy and the power of capital: some observations', *Critical Perspectives on Accounting*, vol. 12, no. 2, pp 199–211.

Sikka P. & Willmott H. 1995a, 'Illuminating the state-profession relationship: accountants acting as Department of Trade and Industry investigators', *Critical Perspectives on Accounting*, vol. 6, no. 4, pp 341–369.

Sikka P. & Willmott H. 1995b, 'The power of "independence": defending and extending the jurisdiction of accounting in the United Kingdom', *Accounting, Organizations and Society*, vol. 20, no. 6, pp 547–581.

Sikka P., Puxty A., Willmott H., & Cooper C. 1998, 'The impossibility of eliminating the expectations gap: Some theory and evidence', *Critical Perspectives on Accounting*, vol. 9, no. 3, pp 299–330.

Singer N. 2009, 'Judge orders former Bristol-Myers executive to write book', *New York Times*, 8 June, available online at http://www.nytimes.com/.

Singer P. 1972, 'Famine, affluence, and morality', *Philosophy and Public Affairs*, vol. 1, no. 1, pp 229–243.

Skapkinker M. 2009, 'Consumers are savvy about organic food', *Financial Times*, London, 18 May, available online at http://www.ft.com/.

Sklair L. 2002, *Globalization: capitalism and its alternatives*, Oxford University Press, Oxford.

Skocpol T. 2003, *Diminished democracy: from membership to management in American civic life*, University of Oklahoma Press, Norman, OK.

Smart J.J.C. & Williams B.A.O. 1973, *Utilitarianism; for and against*, Cambridge University Press, Cambridge.

Smith A. 1976, *The theory of moral sentiments*, Clarendon Press, Oxford (originally published by A. Millar, London, 1759).

Smith A. 1776, *An inquiry into the nature and causes of the wealth of nations*, Whitestone, Dublin.

Smith N.C. 2003, 'Corporate social responsibility: whether or how?', *California Management Review*, vol. 45, no. 14, pp 52–76.

Smith N.C. & Lenssen G. 2009, *Mainstreaming corporate responsibility*, John Wiley, Chichester.

Smith N.C., Bhattacharya C.B., Vogel D., & Levine D.I. 2010, *Global challenges in responsible business*, Cambridge University Press, New York.

Smith R. 2003, *Audit committees: combined code guidance*, Financial Reporting Council, London.

Smith R. & Carlton J. 2007 'Environmentalist groups feud over terms of the TXU buyout', *Wall Street Journal*, New York, 3 March, A-1, available online at http://online.wsj.com/.

Social Investment Forum, 2006, *2005 Report on socially responsible investing trends in the United States*, Social Investment Forum, Washington, DC.

Solomon J. 2013, *Corporate governance and accountability* (4th edn), John Wiley, Chichester.

Sorell T. & Hendry J. 1994, *Business ethics*, Butterworth-Heinemann, Oxford.

Soros G. 2008, *The new paradigm for financial markets: the credit crisis of 2008 and what it means*, PublicAffairs, New York.

Southern A. 2009, *Enterprise and deprivation: small business, social exclusion and sustainable communities*, Routledge, Abingdon.

Sparkes R. 2002, *Socially responsible investment: a global revolution*, John Wiley, New York.

Spence L.J. 2007, 'CSR and small business in a European policy context: the five C's of CSR and small business research agenda 2007', *Business and Society Review*, vol. 112, no. 4, pp 533–552.

Spence L.J. & Rutherford R. 2001, 'Social responsibility, profit maximisation and the small firm owner-manager', *Journal of Small Business and Enterprise Development*, vol. 8, no. 2, pp 126–139.

Spence L.J., Schmidpeter R., & Habisch A. 2003, 'Assessing social capital: small and medium sized enterprises in Germany and the UK', *Journal of Business Ethics*, vol. 47, no. 1, pp 17–29.

Stacey J. 2003, 'A global partnership with a mining multinational: exploring and realising the capacity for strategic biodiversity conservation', *Partnership Matters*, vol. 1, pp 25–29.

Starbuck W.H., 2005, 'Four great conflicts of the twenty-first century', in Cooper C.L. (ed.), *Leadership and management in the twenty-first century*, Oxford University Press, Oxford, pp 21–55.

Statman M. 2000. 'Socially reponsible mutual funds', *Financial Analysts Journal*, vol. 56, no. 3, pp 30–39.

Steger M.B. 2003, *Globalization: a very short introduction*, Oxford University Press, Oxford.

Steger U. 2004, *The business of sustainability: building industry cases for corporate sustainability*, Palgrave Macmillan, Basingstoke.

Steger U. 2009, *Sustainability partnerships: the manager's handbook*, Palgrave Macmillan, Basingstoke.

Stern N. 2007, *Stern Review on the economics of climate change*, HM Treasury, London.

Stern N.H. 2009, *A blueprint for a safer planet: how to manage climate change and create a new era of progress and prosperity*, Bodley Head, London.

Stern S. 2006, 'Corporate responsibility and the curse of the three-letter acronym', *Financial Times*, 30 May, available online at http://www.ft.com.

Sternberg E. 1996, 'Stakeholder theory exposed', *Economic Affairs*, vol. 16, no. 3, pp 36–38.

Sterngold J, 1993, 'Japanese companies rebuff mighty US pension funds', *New York Times*, 30 June, available online at http://www.nytimes.com/

Stevens D., Kim A., Mukhamedova L., Mukimova M., & Wagner R. 2008, 'How far can CSR travel? Reflections on the applicability of the concept to SMEs in Uzbekistan', in Crowther D. & Capaldi N. (eds), *The Ashgate Research Companion to Corporate Social Responsibility*, Ashgate, Aldershot, pp 319.

Stewart J. & Konieczny K. 1996, 'The voluntary disclosure of environmental information—a comparison of investor and company perceptions', *Accounting Research Journal*, vol. 9, pp 29–39.

Stewart T.A. & Immelt J. 2006, 'Growth as a process', *Harvard Business Review*, June, pp 60–70.

Stiglitz J.E. 2002, *Globalization and its discontents*, W.W. Norton, New York.

Stiglitz J.E. 2005, *Fair trade for all: how trade can promote development*, Oxford University Press, Oxford.

Stopford J.M., Strange S., & Henley J.S. 1991, *Rival states, rival firms: competition for world market shares*, Cambridge University Press, Cambridge.

Stott P.A., Gillett N.P., Hegerl G.C., et al. 2010, 'Detection and attribution of climate change: a regional perspective', *Wiley Interdisciplinary Reviews: Climate Change*, vol. 1, no. 2, pp 192–211.

Strand R. 2013, 'The chief officer of corporate social responsibility: a study of its presence in top management teams', *Journal of Business Ethics*, vol. 112, no. 4, pp 721–734.

Strange S. 1996, *The retreat of the state: the diffusion of power in the world economy*, Cambridge University Press, New York.

Sullivan R. 2003, *Business and human rights: dilemmas and solutions*, Sheffield: Greenleaf.

Sum N.L. 2009, 'Controlling the supply chain through CSR: Wal-Martization in China', in Utting P. & Marques J.C. (eds), *Corporate social responsibility and regulatory governance: towards inclusive development?*, Palgrave Macmillan, Basingstoke.

Suranyi M. 2000, *Blind to sustainability: stock markets and the environment*, Forum for the Future, London.

SustainAbility, IFC, & Ethos, 2002, *Developing value: the business case for sustainability in emerging markets*, SustainAbility, London.

SustainAbility & UNEP 2001, *Buried treasure: uncovering the business case for corporate sustainability*, SustainAbility, London.

SustainAbility & UNEP 2002, *Trust us: the global reporters' 2002 survey of corporate sustainability reporting*, SustainAbility, London.

Sutcliffe H. 2005, 'Finding the CR structure that fits your organization', in *How to structure the corporate responsibility function*, Melcrum, London, pp 6–10.

Svendsen A. & Laberge M. 2005, 'Convening stakeholder networks: a new way of thinking, being and engaging', *Journal of Corporate Citizenship*, no. 19, Autumn, pp 91–104.

Swenson P. 1989, *Fair shares: unions, pay, and politics in Sweden and West Germany*, Cornell University Press, Ithaca, NY.

Taibbi M. 2009, *Inside the great American bubble machine*, Rolling Stone, San Francisco, CA.

Tallontire A. and Blowfield M.E. 2000. 'Will the WTO prevent the growth of ethical trade: implications of the international policy environment for ethical trade schemes', *Journal of International Development*, vol. 12, no. 4, pp 571–584.

Taylor P.L. 2005, 'In the market but not of it: Fairtrade coffee and Forest Stewardship Council Certification as market-based social change', *World Development*, vol 33, no. 1, pp 129–147.

Tencati A., Russo A., & Quaglia V. 2008, 'Unintended consequences of CSR: protectionism and collateral damage in global supply chains—the case of Vietnam', *Corporate Governance*, vol. 8, no. 4, pp 518–531.

Teoh S.H., Welch I., & Wazzah C.P., 1995, *The effect of socially activist investment policies on the financial markets: evidence from South African boycott*, Working paper 222, London Business School Institute of Finance and Accounting, London.

Thankappan S., Hitchens D., & Trainor M. 2004, *Dichotomy between attitudes and environmental performance: a case of European SMEs*, Centre for Business Relationships, Accountability, Sustainability and Society at Cardiff University, Cardiff.

Tharoor S. 2001, 'Are human rights universal?', *New Internationalist*, vol. 332, pp 34–35.

Thornber K. 1999, *An overview of global trends in FSC certification*, International Institute for Environment and Development, London.

Thornber K. 2000, *Impacts of certification on forests, stakeholders and markets. Case study: Bainings ecoforestry project*, International Institute for Environment and Development, London.

Thurow L.C. 1996, *The future of capitalism: how today's economic forces shape tomorrow's world*, W. Morrow, New York.

Tilley F.J. 2000, 'Small firm environmental ethics: how deep do they go?', *Business Ethics*, vol. 9, pp 31–41.

Tinker A.M. & Lowe E.A. 1980, 'Rationale for corporate social reporting: theory, evidence from organizational research', *Journal of Business Finance and Accounting*, vol. 7, no. 1, pp 1–17.

Tinker T. 1985, *Paper prophets: a social critique of accounting*, Praeger, New York.

Tobin R. 1997, 'Encouraging signs. Is the corporate world developing a social vision?' *CHAC Review*, vol. 25, no. 1, pp 19–21.

Toffler A. 1980, *The third wave*, W. Morrow, New York.

Tolba M. & El-Kholy A. 1992, *The world environment 1972-1992: two decades of challenge*, Chapman & Hall, London.

Toms J.S. 2002, 'Firm resources, quality signals and the determinants of corporate environmental reputation: some UK evidence', *British Accounting Review*, vol. 34, no. 3, pp 257–282.

Traidcraft 2005, *Traidcraft social accounts 2004-2005*, Traidcraft, Gateshead.

Tropenbos 1997, *Hierarchical framework for the formulation of sustainable forest management standards: principles, criteria and indicators*, Tropenbos Foundation, Leiden.

Trotman K.T. & Bradley G.W. 1981, 'Association between social responsibility disclosure and characteristics of companies', *Accounting, Organizations and Society*, vol. 6, no. 4, pp 355–362.

Tsalikis J. & Seaton B. 2008, 'Consumer perceptions of business ethical behavior in former Eastern Block countries', *Journal of Business Ethics*, vol. 82, no. 4, pp 919–928.

Tschopp D.J. 2005, 'Corporate social responsibility: a comparison between the United States and the European Union', *Corporate Social Responsibility and Environmental Management*, vol. 12, no. 1, pp 55–59.

Tsoukas H. & Knudsen C. 2003, *The Oxford handbook of organization theory*, Oxford University Press, Oxford.

Tucker R. 2006, 'The next level of corporate responsibility', *Women's Wear Daily*, 16 May, available online at http://www.wwd.com.

Turnbull N. 1999, *Internal control: guidance for directors on the Combined Code*, ICAEW, London.

Turner R.K. 1994, *Environmental economics: an elementary introduction*, Pearson Education, London.

Tyson L. D'A. 2003, *The Tyson Report on the recruitment and development of non-executive directors*, London Business School, London.

UKSIF 2009, *Responsible business: sustainable investment*, UK Social Investment Forum, London.

Ullmann A. 1985, 'Data in search of a theory: a critical examination of the relationship among social performance, social disclosure, and economic performance', *Academy of Management Review*, vol. 10, no. 3, pp 540–557.

UN 2003, *Water for people, water for life: world water development report*, United Nations, New York.

UN 2005, *Business UNusual*, United Nations, New York.

UNDP 2009, *Global Compact--small and medium-sized enterprises on their way towards global responsibility*, UN Development Programme, New York.

UNEP 1987, *Environmental perspectives to the year 2000 and beyond*, UNEP, Nairobi.

UNEP 2005, *Millennium ecosystem assessment—living beyond our means - statement from the Board*, United Nations Foundation, New York.

UNEP 2010, *Africa water atlas*, UNEP, Nairobi.

UNEP 2012, GEO5 *Global environmental outlook: environment for the future we want*, UN Environment Programme.

UNEP, Accountability, & Stakeholder Research Associates 2005, *Stakeholder engagement manual— from words to action.* vol. 1: *The guide to practioners' perspectives on stakeholder engagement*, UN Environmental Programme, Accountability, and Stakeholder Research Associates, New York.

UNEP FI & Mercer 2007, *Demystifying responsible investment performance: a review of key academic and broker research on ESG factors*, UNEP Finance Initiative, Geneva, and Mercer, New York.

UNEP, SustainAbility, and Standard&Poors 2006, *Tomorrow's value: the global reporters 2006 survey of corporate sustainability reporting*, SustainAbility, London.

UN Global Compact 2013, *Global corporate sustainability report 2013*, United Nations, New York.

Unerman J. 2003, 'Enhancing organizational global hegemony with narrative accounting disclosures: an early example', *Accounting Forum*, vol. 27, pp 425–448.

UNIDO 2002, *Corporate social responsibility: implications for small and medium enterprises in developing countries*, UN Industrial Development Organization, Vienna.

Unilever 2005, *Environmental report 2004*, Unilever, London.

Uphoff N.T. 1996, *Learning from Gal Oya: possibilities for participatory development and post-Newtonian social science*, Intermediate Technology Publications, London.

Upton C. & Bass S. 1995, *The forest certification handbook*, Earthscan, London.

Uren S. 2007, 'Hall of shame: which companies are the worst polluters?', *The Guardian*, London, 5 November, available online at http://www.theguardian.com/.

Utting P. 2005, *Rethinking business regulation: from self-regulation to social control*, UN Research Institute for Social Development, Geneva.

Utting P. 2007, *CSR and equality*, Third World Foundation for Social and Economic Studies, London.

Utting P. & Marques J.C. (eds) 2009, *Corporate social responsibility and regulatory governance: towards inclusive development?*, Palgrave Macmillan, Basingstoke.

Utting P. & Marques J.C. (eds) 2010, *Business, politics and public policy: implications for inclusive development*, Palgrave Macmillan, Basingstoke.

Utting P. & Zammit A. 2006, *Beyond pragmatism: appraising UN–business partnerships*, UN Research Institute for Social Development, Geneva.

van Dijk M.P. & Trienekens J.H. 2012, *Global value chains: linking local producers from developing countries to international markets*, Amsterdam University Press, Amsterdam.

van Tulder R. 2006, *International business–society management: linking corporate responsibility and globalization*, Routledge, Abingdon.

van Tulder R., van Tilburg R., Francken M., & da Rosa A. 2013, *Managing the transition to a sustainable enterprise: lessons from frontrunner companies*, Routledge, Abingdon.

Varley P., Mathiasen C., & Voorhes M. 1998, *The sweatshop quandary: corporate responsibility on the global frontier*, Investor Responsibility Research Center, Washington, DC.

Veblen T.B. 1904, *The theory of business enterprise*, Charles Scribner's Sons, New York.

Verhoef P.C., Beckers S.F., & van Doorn J. 2013, 'Understand the perils of co-creation', *Harvard Business Review*, September, available online at http://hbr.org/2013/09/understand-the-perils-of-co-creation/ar/1.

Velasco G. 2005, 'Cross-sector partnership in action: a framework for knowledge management', *Partnership Matters*, vol. 3, pp 10–14.

Verité 2004, *Excessive overtime in Chinese supplier factories: causes, impacts and recommendations for action*, Research Paper, Verité, Amherst, MA.

Vernon P. 2007, 'Saint Stuart—the man who is turning M&S green', *The Observer*, London, 14 April, available online at http://www.theguardian.com/.

Vidal J. 1997, *McLibel: burger culture on trial*, New Press, New York.

Vigar D. 2006, *From challenge to opportunity:the role of business in tomorrow's society*, WBCSD, Geneva.

Virilio P. 2000, *The information bomb*, Verso, New York.

Visser W. 2006, 'Revisiting Carroll's pyramid: an African perspective', in Pedersen E.R. & Huniche M. (eds), *Corporate citizenship in developing countries*, Copenhagen Centre, Copenhagen.

Visser W. & Tolhurst N. (eds) 2010, *The world guide to CSR*, Greenleaf, Sheffield.

Visser W., McIntosh M., & Middleton C. (eds) 2006, *Corporate citizenship in Africa: lessons from the past; paths to the future*, Greenleaf, Sheffield.

Visser W., Matten D., Pohl M., & Tolhurst N. (eds) 2007, *The A to Z of corporate social responsibility: a complete reference guide to concepts, codes and organisations*, John Wiley, Chichester.

Vogel D. 2005, *The market for virtue: the potential and limits of corporate social responsibility*, Brookings Institution Press, Washington, DC.

Vogel D. 2008, *CSR doesn't pay*, Forbes, 16 October, available online at http://www.Forbes.com.

Vogel D. 2012, *The Politics of precaution: regulating health, safety, and environmental risks in Europe and the United States*, Princeton University Press, Princeton, NJ.

von Hayek F.A. 1944, *The road to serfdom*, Routledge, London.

von Hayek F.A. 1960, *The constitution of liberty*, University of Chicago Press, Chicago, IL.

Wackernagel M., Rees W.E., & Testemale P. 1996, *Our ecological footprint: reducing human impact on the Earth*, New Society, Gabriola Island, BC.

Waddell S. 2000, 'New institutions for the practice of corporate citizenship: historical, intersectoral, and developmental perspectives', *Business and Society Review*, vol. 105, no. 1, pp 107–126.

Waddock S. 2001, 'Integrity and mindfulness: foundations of corporate citizenship', *Journal of Corporate Citizenship*, no. 1, Spring, pp 25–37.

Waddock S. 2007, 'Corporate citizenship: the dark-side paradoxes of success', in May S.K., Cheney G., and Roper J. (eds), *The debate over corporate responsibility*, Oxford University Press, New York.

Waddock S.A. 2006, *Leading corporate citizens: vision, values, value-added* (2nd edn), McGraw-Hill, Boston, MA.

Waddock S. & Bodwell C. 2002, 'From TQM to TRM: total responsibility management approaches', *Journal of Corporate Citizenship*, no. 7, Autumn, p 113.

Waddock S.A. & Graves S.B. 1997, 'The corporate social performance–financial performance link', *Strategic Management Journal*, vol. 18, no. 4, pp 303–319.

Walker R.B.J. 1994, 'Social movements/world politics', *Millennium: Journal of International Studies*, vol. 23, no. 3, pp 669–700.

Wall C. 2007, *Kazakh public policy and corporate social responsibility: an analysis of health care provision in an era of CSR and Kazakh nationalism*, Presented at the Conference on Business, Social Policy and Corporate Political Influence in Developing Countries, 12–13 November, 2007, Geneva, Switzerland.

Wall Street Journal 2005, 'Corporate social concerns: are they good citizenship or a rip-off for investors', *Wall Street Journal*, New York, 6 December, available online at http://online.wsj.com/.

Wallerstein I.M. 1974, *The modern world-system*, Academic Press, New York.

Wallerstein I.M. 1978, *The capitalist world-economy*, Cambridge University Press, Cambridge.

Walsh J.P. 2005, 'Book review essay: Taking stock of stakeholder management', *Academy of Management Review*, vol. 30, no. 2, pp 426–452.

War on Want 2005, *Caterpillar: the alternative report*, War on Want, London.

War on Want & GMB 2005, *Asda Wal-Mart: the alternative report*, War on Want, London.

Ward H. 2003, *Legal issues in corporate citizenship*, International Institute for Environment and Development, London.

Warhurst, A. (ed.) 1998, *Mining and the environment: case studies from the Americas*, International Development Research Centre, Ottawa.

Warhurst A. & Noronha L. 2000, *Environmental policy in mining: corporate strategy and planning for closure*, Lewis, Boca Raton, FL.

Warner M. 2004, 'Getting started', in Warner M. & Sullivan R. (eds), *Putting partnerships to work*, Greenleaf, Sheffield, pp 166–181.

Warner M. & Sullivan R. (eds) 2004, *Putting partnerships to work*, Greenleaf, Sheffield.

Wartick S.L. & Cochran P.L., 1985, 'The evolution of the corporate social performance model', *Academy of Management Review*, vol. 10, no. 4, pp 758–769.

Waters M. 2001, *Globalization* (2nd edn), Routledge, Abingdon.

Waters R. 2010, 'Google in fresh retreat on Buzz', *Financial Times*, London, 15 February, available online at http://www.ft.com/.

Watkins K. 1997, *Globalization and liberalization: implications for poverty, distribution and inequality*, UN Development Programme, New York.

Watkins K. & Fowler P. 2005, *Rigged rules and double standards: trade, globalisation and poverty*, Oxfam, Oxford.

Watts R. 2009, 'Google avoids £100m UK tax', *The Sunday Times*, London, 19 April, available online at http://www.thesundaytimes.co.uk/.

WBCSD 2005, *Business for development: business solutions in support of the Millennium Development Goals*, World Business Council for Sustainable Development, Geneva.

WBCSD 2006, *Doing business with the world: the new role of corporate leadership in global development*, World Business Council for Sustainable Development, Geneva.

WBCSD 2007, *Doing business with the world: the new role of corporate leadership in global development*, World Business Council for Sustainable Development, Geneva.

WCED, 1987, *Our common future*, Oxford University Press, Oxford.

WDM, War on Want, NUS, & Friends of the Earth 2005, *2005 and sustainable development*, World Development Movement/War on Want/National Union of Students/ Friends of the Earth, London.

Weber M., Parsons T., & Giddens A. 1992, *The Protestant ethic and the spirit of capitalism*, Routledge, London.

WEF & Accenture 2012, *More with less: scaling sustainable consumption and efficiency*, World Economic Forum, Geneva.

Weinberg A. & Weinberg L.S. 1961, *The muckrakers. The era in journalism that moved America to reform—the most significant magazine articles of 1902-1912*, Simon & Schuster, New York.

Weinstein J.R. 2001, *On Adam Smith*, Thomson Learning, Stamford, CT.

Weiser J. & Rochlin S. 2004, 'Walking in order to run: practical challenges in measuring community and economic development', *AccountAbility Forum*, vol. 1, no. 1, pp 26–32.

Weiser J. & Zadek S. 2000, *Conversations with disbelievers: persuading companies to address social challenges*, BrodyWeiser, New York.

Weiser J., Kahane M., Rochlin S., & Landis J. 2006, *Untapped assets: creating value in underserved markets*, Berrett-Koehler, San Francisco, CA.

Wei-Skillern J. 2004, 'The evolution of Shell's stakeholder approach: a case study', *Business Ethics Quarterly*, vol. 14, no. 4, pp 713–728.

Weiss L. 1998, *The myth of the powerless state*, Cornell University Press, Ithaca, NY.

Welford R. 1995, *Environmental strategy and sustainable development: the corporate challenge for the 21st century*, Routledge, London.

Welford R. 2005, 'Corporate social responsibility in Europe, North America and Asia: 2004 survey results', *Journal of Corporate Citizenship*, no. 17, Spring, pp 33–52.

Werhane P.H. & Freeman R.E. 1997, *The Blackwell encyclopedic dictionary of business ethics*, Blackwell, Oxford.

Werther W.B. & Chandler D. 2011, *Strategic corporate social responsibility: stakeholders in a global environment* (2nd edn), SAGE, Thousand Oaks, CA.

Wettstein F. 2005, 'For causality to capability: toward a new understanding of the multinational corporation's enlarged social responsibilities', *Journal of Corporate Citizenship*, no. 19, Autumn, pp 105–117.

Weybrecht G. 2009, *The sustainable MBA: the manager's guide to green business*, John Wiley, Hoboken, NJ.

Whalley J. 2001, 'World Trade Organization', in Smelser N.J. & Baltes P.B. (eds), *International encyclopedia of the social and behavioral sciences*, Elsevier Science, Oxford, pp 16,613–16,616.

White A. 2005, 'Fade, integrate or transform? The future of CSR', *BSR Newsletter*, August 2005, available online at http://www.jussemper.org/Newsletters/Resources/BSR_Allen-White.pdf.

White C. 2006, 'The spirit of disobedience', *Harpers*, April 2006, pp 31–40.

WHO Tobacco Free Initiative 2008, *Evolution of the tobacco industry positions on addiction to nicotine*, World Health Organization, Geneva.

Wick A. 2001, *Workers' tool or PR ploy? A guide to codes of international labour practice*, Friedrich-Ebert-Stiftung/SÜDWIND Institut für Öknomie und Ökumene, Bonn.

Wiesmann G. & Simensen I. 2007, 'German blue chips ponder switch to SE format', *Financial Times*, London, 12 April, available online at http://www.ft.com/.

Wijnberg N. 2000, 'Normative stakeholder theory and Aristotle: the link between ethics and politics', *Journal of Business Ethics*, vol. 25, no. 4, pp 329–342.

Willard B. 2002, *The sustainability advantage: seven business case benefits of a triple bottom line*, New Society, Gabriola Island, BC.

Williams O.F. 2004, 'The UN Global Compact: the challenge and the promise', *Business Ethics Quarterly*, vol. 14, no. 4, pp 755–774.

Williams R. & Elliott L. 2010, *Crisis and recovery: ethics, economics and justice*, Palgrave Macmillan, Basingstoke.

Willums J., World Business Council for Sustainable Development, UN Environment Programme, Bellagio Forum for Sustainable Development, & Foundation for Business and Sustainable Development. 1998, *The sustainable business challenge: a briefing for tomorrow's business leaders*, Greenleaf, Sheffield.

Wilson C. 2006, *Make poverty business: increase profits and reduce risks by engaging with the poor*, Greenleaf, Sheffield.

Windsor D. 2001, 'Corporate citizenship: evolution and interpretation', in Andriof J. & McIntosh M. (eds), *Perspectives on corporate citizenship*, Greenleaf, Sheffield, pp 39–52.

Wines M. 2010, 'Is Google case a rights bellwether?', *International Herald Tribune*, Paris.

Wohlmeyer H. & Quendler, T. (eds) 2001, *The WTO, agriculture and sustainable development*, Greenleaf, Sheffield.

Woidtke T., Bierman L., & Tuggle C. 2003, 'Reining in activist funds', *Harvard Business Review*, March.

Wolf M. 2004, *Why globalization works*, Yale University Press, New Haven, CT.

Wolff J. 1991, *Robert Nozick: property, justice, and the minimal state*, Stanford University Press, Stanford, CA.

Wood D. 2000, 'Theory and integrity in business and society', *Business and Society*, vol. 39, no. 4, pp 359–378.

Wood D.J. & Logsdon J.M. 2001, 'Theorising business citizenship', in Andriof J. & McIntosh M. (eds), *Perspectives on corporate citizenship*, Greenleaf, Sheffield, pp 83–103.

Wood D.J. & Logsdon J.M. 2002, 'Business citizenship: from individuals to organizations', *Ethics and Entrepreneurship*, vol. 3, pp 59–94.

Wood D.J., Logsdon J.M., Lewellyn P.G., & Davenport P.G. 2006, *Global business citizenship: a transformative framework for ethics and sustainable capitalism*, M.E. Sharpe, Armonk, NY.

Wood E.M. 1995, *Democracy against capitalism: renewing historical materialism*, Cambridge University Press, Cambridge.

World Bank 2003, *Strengthening the implementation of corporate social responsibility in global supply chains*, World Bank, Washington, DC.

World Bank 2005, *World development report 2005. Better investment climate for everyone*, World Bank, Washington, DC.

World Bank 2006, *World development report 2006. Equity and development*, World Bank, Washington, DC.

World Bank Group 2003, *Company codes of conduct and international standards: an analytical comparison*, vol. 1, World Bank Group, Washington, DC.

World Commission on Environment and Development & Brundtland, G.H. 1987, *Our common future*, Oxford University Press, Oxford.

World Economic Forum 2006, *Harnessing private sector capabilities to meet public needs: the potential of partnerships to advance progress on hunger, malaria and basic education*, World Economic Forum, Geneva.

WRI 2002, *Tomorrow's markets: global trends and their implications for business*, World Business Council for Sustainable Development, Washington, DC.

WRI & WBCSD 2004, *The greenhouse gas protocol: a corporate accounting and reporting standard*, World Resources Institute/World Business Council for Sustainable Development, Washington, DC.

Wright C. & Rwabizambuga A. 2006, 'Institutional pressures, corporate reputation, and voluntary codes of conduct: an examination of the Equator Principles', *Business and Society Review*, vol. 111, no. 1, pp 89–117.

Wright S. & Rees S. (eds) 2000, *Human rights, corporate responsibility*, Pluto Press, London.

Wright T. 2007, 'Indonesian proposal: pay us not to chop down our trees', *Wall Street Journal*, New York, 10 August, available online at http://online.wsj.com/.

WWF, 2012, *Living planet report: biodiversity, biocapacity and better choices*, WWF International, Gland, Switzerland.

WWF & SustainAbility 2005, *Influencing power: reviewing the conduct and content of corporate lobbying*, WWF, Gland, Switzerland, and Sustainability, London.

Yunus M. 1998, *Banker to the poor: the autobiography of Muhammad Yunus, founder of the Grameen Bank*, Aurum, London.

Zadek S. 2000, *Doing good and doing well: making the business case for corporate citizenship*, Conference Board, New York.

Zadek S. 2001a, *The civil corporation: the new economy of corporate citizenship*, Earthscan, London.

Zadek S. 2001b, *Third generation corporate citizenship: public policy and business in society*, Foreign Policy Centre/AccountAbility, London.

Zadek S. 2002, *Third generation corporate citizenship*, Foreign Policy Centre/AccountAbility, London.

Zadek S. 2004, 'The path to corporate responsibility', *Harvard Business Review*, vol. 82, no. 12, pp 125–133.

Zadek S., Pruzan P.M., & Evans R. 1997, *Building corporate accountability: emerging practices in social and ethical accounting, auditing and reporting*, Earthscan, London.

Zadek S., Raynard P., & Oliveira C. 2005, *Responsible competitiveness: reshaping global markets through responsible business practices*, AccountAbility, London.

Zadek S., Sabapathy J., Dossing H., & Swift T. 2003, *Responsible competitiveness: corporate responsibility clusters in action*, AccountAbility, London.

Zakhem A.J., Palmer D.E., & Stoll M.L. 2007, *Stakeholder theory: essential readings in ethical leadership and management*, Prometheus Books, Amherst, NY.

Zeitz J. & Grün A. 2013, *The manager and the monk: a discourse on prayer, profit, and principles*, Jossey-Bass, San Francisco, CA.

Zenisek T.J. 1979, 'Corporate social responsibility: a conceptualization based on organizational literature', *Academy of Management Review*, vol. 4, no. 3, pp 359–369.

Zimmerman A., Matthews, R.G., & Hudson, C. 2005, 'Can employers alter hiring policies to cut health costs?', *Wall Street Journal*, New York, 27 October 27, available online at http://online.wsj.com/.

Index

AA1000 205, 210, 300, 302, 341
Abercrombie & Fitch 299
ABN Amro 329
Accenture Development
        Partnerships programme 87
Accion International 89, 242
accountability 9
    boundaries of 79
    corporate accountability 207,
        327, 328
    embedding social
        accountability 205
    ethics 185
    financial products 249
    framework 183
    governance 164, 189
    new forms of 353
    reporting 192
    in SMEs 266
    social accountability 9, 160
    stakeholder 7
    stranded assets 230
    to shareholders 20, 47, 181
    to stakeholders 20, 47, 160, 163,
        170, 180
    UK Company Law Reform
        Bill 353
AccountAbility 158, 207, 224, 327,
        341, 358
Adidas 340
affinity marketing 23
Africa 4, 39, 40, 45, 60, 219, 269,
        333
    cocoa 31, 48-9
    corporate responsibility
        framework 118
    CSR agenda 216
    mining 86
    mobile phones 88
    Probo Koala 41
    relationship with China 105
    voluntary codes 290
    water 60
    women 258
African Institute for Corporate
        Citizenship 220
agency theory 162
Agricultural Ethics Assurance
        Association of
        Zimbabwe 302
agriculture 103, 107, 110, 114, 213,
        219, 310, 332

Amazon 118
Anglo American 290, 292
AP6 *see* Partnership on Clean
        Development and Climate
Apparel Industry Partnership 211
Aravind 88
Asia 45, 63, 219, 229, 250
audit 195, 300
    auditing 164
    auditors 161, 162, 172, 213
    Cadbury Report 166
    Corporate Governance Code 170
    cost of 213, 342
    EMAS scheme 266
    financial 108
    internal 340
    process 161, 214
    quality of 284, 340
    quantity 212
    social 205, 211

B&Q 145
Bank of America 329
Bank of Credit and Commerce
        International (BCCI) 165
Barings Bank 167
Bhopal 58, 59, 190
BHP 36, 325
big business 36
biodiversity 217, 221, 234
BNP Paribas 169
boards of directors 162, 170
Bogle, John 236, 329
bottom of the pyramid (BOP) 23,
        87, 92, 95, 96, 255
Brazil 45, 219, 234, 247, 302,
        335, 339
bribery *see* corruption
BRICS 335
British Airways 318
Brundtland Commission 53, 56,
        61, 62
BT 145
Business Action for Africa 88, 118
business case 9, 15, 60, 61, 64,
        96, 129, 133, 134, 136, 138,
        144-55, 157, 158, 174, 186,
        188, 207, 219, 255, 286, 287,
        288, 293-5, 307, 313, 326,
        335, 340, 345-7
Business in the Community 110,
        284, 300, 325

business ethics 14-16, 46, 323
Business for Social
        Responsibility 341, 358
business and society 37, 347
    concept of 346
    managing 16-17
business-poverty framework 75,
        81-2

Cadbury 307
    boycott 48
    Cadbury Committee 162, 166
    Cadbury Report 166-8
    cocoa partnership 48-9, 114, 115
    ownership of 351
    slavery 31-2, 48-9
    Victorian entrepreneurship 33-4
Cadbury, George 31-2
Cadbury, Sir Adrian 166
Cafédirect 301
California Public Employees'
        Retirements System *see*
        CalPERS
CalPERS 236, 250
    China 250
    governance in Japan 238
CANOPUS Foundation 241
capital market 161
    2007-2008 collapse 169
    emerging economies 172
    implications for corporate
        responsibility 170
    recasting 230, 346
    regulation 175
    role of 351
    short-termism 347
    and social entrepreneurs 273
    and sustainable development
        66-7
capitalism 102, 144, 219, 230, 249,
        314, 331, 349
    Achilles heel 6
    compassionate 48
    different eras of 37
    free market 26
    genius of 35
    historical tradition 272
    history of 34
    post-World War II 37-8
    protectionism 104
    repair of 335
    Rhenish model 16

capitalism (*continued*)
　shareholder 352
　twentieth-century 35–8
carbon emissions 5
　carbon trading 289, 344
carbon trading *see* carbon
　　emissions
Carroll's typology of corporate
　　responsibility 17–24, 47, 118
　discretionary responsibilities
　　23–4
　economic responsibility 18
　ethical responsibility 21–3
　legal responsibility 19–21
Center for Corporate
　　Citizenship 341, 358
Center for Sustainable
　　Innovation 304
Centre for Public-Private
　　Partnership 110
CERES 8, 20, 174, 184, 187, 210
Chad-Cameroon oil pipeline 318
Chernobyl 59, 190
child labour 83, 109, 132, 213, 228,
　　298, 303
　advances in eliminating 290
　alternative views 257
　in cocoa farming 48
　elimination of 232
　impact on reputation 5
　in supply chains 282
　in UN Global Compact 120
China 4, 20, 34, 45, 63, 82, 84, 93,
　　101, 102, 105, 130, 143, 172,
　　211, 217, 218, 219, 240, 247,
　　249–51, 258, 284, 291, 298,
　　299, 323, 337, 338, 339, 344,
　　348, 355
churches 227, 273
　Caterpillar company 316
Citigroup 329
civil society 6, 8, 25, 41–2, 44, 92,
　　93, 108, 109, 110, 111, 112,
　　115, 120, 122, 145, 146, 197,
　　211, 213, 218, 222, 286, 313,
　　315, 319, 321, 323, 324, 325,
　　330, 336, 353
cleantech 226, 230, 240, 250
climate change 4, 5, 21, 22, 24, 55,
　　61–4, 65, 72, 73, 131, 135,
　　154, 158, 179, 180, 200, 230,
　　231, 234, 236, 240, 288, 295,
　　335, 336, 338, 347, 349, 351,
　　352, 354, 355
　and aviation industry 63–4
　BP stance 289
　business implications 42
　in corporate reporting 183
　future threat of 337

government and sustainable
　　energy 72
　human activity 57
　IPCC findings 4, 53
　M&S stance 152–3
　opportunities related to 231
　and prosperity 57
　reporting 284
　Stern Review 57, 65, 66
　UN Framework Convention
　　on 57
co-creation 89
Coca-Cola 294
codes of conduct *see* codes of
　　practice
codes of practice 8, 222
　Ethical Trading Initiative 84, 112,
　　208, 283, 291, 295, 296,
　　297–8, 340
　and investment indexes 234
　labour 261, 296
　as management tool 208
　multi-stakeholder 208, 211, 212
　professional 14
　as self-regulation 118
　voluntary codes 290
collective bargaining 83, 120, 303
Combined Code (2003/2008) 167,
　　168
community development
　　investment funds 242
community investment 23, 24, 49,
　　110, 238
　see also philanthropy
Companies Act (2006) 173–4, 176
competitive advantage 71, 111,
　　141, 154, 215
　European 131
　of low-waged labour 219
　of nations 326
　partnerships 263
　Plan A (M&S) 152–3
　SMEs 261–2, 267
　of sustainability 286
competitive markets 25
competitive practices 27
competitiveness 62, 91, 118, 144,
　　181, 249
　barrier to 331
　of corporate responsibility 265
　corporate responsibility, tensions
　　with 299
　low waged labour 323
conflict
　ethnic 258
　managing 207
　natural resources 86
　and power 321
　regional 258

conflicts of interest between agent
　　and owner 162
consumers 202, 211
　company responsibilities to 223
　consumer advocacy 203
　consumer awareness 221
　consumer behaviour 294
　corporate responsibility's impact
　　on 301
　decisions 340
　engaging with 343
　ethical 302, 326, 343
　product safety 202
　responsible 342–3
　in the West 290
consumption
　ethical 302, 326, 343
　sustainable 347–8
Cooperative Financial Services 294
CORE network 176
corporate citizenship 7, 13, 324
corporate governance 9–10, 329
　audit committees 168
　audit reports 172
　Cadbury Committee 162, 166
　Cadbury Report (1992) 166–8
　Combined Code
　　(2003/2008) 167, 168
　in corporate responsibility
　　indexes 140, 234
　corporate responsibility
　　perspective 25, 172
　development of
　　framework 166–70
　directors 139, 162
　drivers of reform 163
　Economist perspective 315
　future trends 349–50
　Greenbury Report 167
　Hampel Report 167
　Higgs Committee 168
　institutional investors 26, 161,
　　165, 167, 171, 174, 218,
　　226, 228, 232, 235, 236,
　　238, 240, 241, 243, 247,
　　319, 326, 351
　international developments
　　in 22, 171–2
　malfeasance 164
　non-financial dimensions 335,
　　340
　and ownership structure 163–4
　relationship to SRI 124, 226
　Smith Report 168
　and stakeholder engagement 28,
　　174
　theories of 162–3
　trends 317
　Turnbull Committee 167

corporate philanthropy *see* philanthropy
corporate purpose 335
  Nordisk 27
  transforming 353–6
corporate reporting 4, 42, 68, 136, 152
  BP 110
  challenges of 184–5
  comparison with financial reporting 192–3
  definitions 180
  emergence of 185–6
  external verification 194–5
  frameworks 72
  IIRC 175
  integrated reporting 175
  issues for management 193–5
  nature of 182–3
  practice of 188–92
  social accounting 180, 182, 183
  social reporting 190–1, 192
  sustainability reporting 188
  upsurge since 1990s 186–8
  use to investors 189
corporate responsibility reporting *see* corporate reporting
corporate responsibility
  trends 334–7
  beyond ethical sourcing 340–1
  consumers 342
  embedding and integrating 334, 339–45
  financial institutions 343–4
  inclusivity 342
  international standards 341–2
  mega-trends 334, 337–9
  multinationals 351–3
  professionalization 340
  scenarios 335
  sustainable consumption and production 347–8, 356
  transition and transformation 334, 345–8
corporate social performance 6, 52, 149, 151, 282, 287, 309
corporate sustainability 7
  leadership 121
  progress 325
Corporation 2020 174
corruption 5, 15, 19, 20, 41, 58, 90, 104, 110, 120, 145, 210, 211, 218, 219, 232, 234, 259, 281, 288, 295, 298, 308, 323, 326, 349, 350
cradle-to-grave 22, 146
criticism of corporate responsibility 9, 230
  anti-business perspective 314–17

blame for financial crisis 328–30
bottom of the pyramid 23, 87, 92, 95, 96, 255
failure to achieve goals 325–30
globalization 109, 117
labour rights 260
limits of large corporations 135
mixed messages 300
overview 312–14
partnerships 133
pro-business bias 314–17
public relations exercise 23
social entrepreneurs 271
SRI funds 246
stakeholders 207
too narrow scope 322–4
CSR Chicks 302

Danone 139, 301, 325, 341
decarbonization 240, 335
Deepwater Horizon 300
defensive corporate responsibility 81, 133, 134, 142, 231
  differences between 156
  Nike 132
definitions
  changes over time 77
  of corporate governance 162
  of corporate reporting 180
  of corporate responsibility 6–9
  evolution of 141
  of globalization 122
  of social enterprise 272
  of social entrepreneurship 87
  of sustainable development 72
demographic change 356
  trends 337–8
demographics 32
  dividend 338, 339
developing economies 16, 78, 149
  corporate responsibility in 75–97
  demographic dividend 338, 339
  entrepreneurs 257
  and neoliberalism 102
  partnerships 263
  role of government 217, 219
development tool and agent, business as 75, 76–8, 79, 80, 81, 82, 84, 86, 87, 88, 89, 90, 91, 92, 95
directors 139, 162
  as agents 183
  appointment 170
  independence of 238
  legal liability 328, 350
  non-executive 165
  remuneration 165
disclosure *see* transparency

discretionary responsibilities *see* Carroll's typology
discrimination 38, 120, 264, 298
Domini 400 233, 234
Dow Jones Sustainability Indexes 233, 234, 283, 320, 344

eco-efficiency 22, 61, 73, 146, 147, 149, 150, 152, 234, 248, 294, 344, 346, 347, 354, 359
economic crisis 335
economic development 54, 75, 82, 146, 232, 272, 282, 333
economic development assistance 257
economic globalization *see* globalization
economic growth 4, 34, 35, 44, 57, 62, 63, 65, 66, 76, 78, 80, 101, 102, 137, 151, 228, 240, 274, 287, 288, 317, 335, 338, 344
economic impact 285, 288, 290, 292–3, 310
economic reform 259
economic regeneration 258
ecosystems 14, 200, 338, 348
EITI *see* Extraction Industry Transparency Initiative
Elvis & Kresse 256
EMAS scheme 21
emerging economies *see* developing economies
emissions trading scheme 64, 89
  European Emissions Trading Scheme 63
energy
  alternative 42, 230, 231, 240
  consumption 4
  demand 188
  industry 22
  legislation 250
  renewable 22, 226
  and the rural poor 274–5
  and sustainability 72, 140
  unsustainable 348
  Wal-Mart 294
Enhanced Analytics Initiative 304
Enron 25–6, 47, 167, 172, 192, 236, 248, 323, 334
entrepreneurs 22
  and bottom of the pyramid 255
  gazelles 256, 257, 258, 265, 266, 274
  green 256
  hyperbole related to 269
  libertarian 26
  necessity 257, 258, 274, 276, 315

entrepreneurs (*continued*)
serial 256
socially oriented 93
technology 239
theology and philosophy 40
environmental venture capital 240
Equator Principles 110, 145,
214–15, 296, 329
Ernst & Young 341
ethical responsibility 21–3
Ethical Trading Initiative (ETI) 84,
112, 208, 283, 295, 296,
297–8, 340
EU Accounts Modernisation
Directive 302
European Emissions Trading
Scheme 63
Eurosif 189, 227, 228
exchange traded funds (ETFs) 228
exploitation 33, 61, 83, 92, 119,
122, 182, 215, 219, 264
externalities 181, 196, 285
Extraction Industries Transparency
Initiative (EITI) 90, 208, 218
Exxon Valdez 38, 190
ExxonMobil 23, 296

Fair Labor Association (FLA) 84,
115, 210, 283
fair wages 322
fairtrade 49, 84–5, 292–3, 319
case study 305–7
expansion 92
Fairtrade Foundation 305, 306
labelling 22
M&S commitment 153
origins 110
Finance Innovation Laboratory 70
financial crisis (2007-2008) 169–70
Forest Stewardship Council
(FSC) 86, 109, 114, 210,
214, 220, 288
free market 5, 25, 82, 102, 111, 144,
172, 186, 272, 315, 316, 356
freedom of association 79, 120,
257, 290, 303
Freeplay Energy 272
Friedman, Milton 24, 46
FTSE4Good 228, 233, 234, 244, 283,
299, 301, 344
Fynsa 271

Gap 299, 341
General Electric 36, 142, 143
GlaxoSmithKline 27, 28, 140, 325
Global Alliance for Workers and
Communities 303
Global Reporting Initiative (GRI) 8,
68, 184, 212–13, 228, 229,

283, 284, 288, 302, 335,
341, 342
Global Social Compliance 131,
212, 303
global warming *see* climate change
globalization 4, 10, 16, 31, 32,
38–40, 50, 51, 52, 72, 86, 98,
99–100, 101–6, 107, 108,
109–11, 112, 113, 116–17,
118, 119, 120, 121, 122, 123,
168, 201, 202, 203, 208, 288,
318, 347, 351
anti- 102
Goldman Sachs 329
Google 118, 239, 240, 336, 354–6
Grameen
Bank 23, 88, 242, 268
Group 274
Phone 87, 88
GreenBiz 302
Greenbury Report 167
Greenpeace 38, 57, 153, 211
GrupoNuevo 256
GSK *see* GlaxoSmithKline

Hampel Report 167
HealthStore Foundation 88
Henderson Global Investment 344
Higgs Committee 168
HIV/AIDS 27, 85, 86, 236, 291, 343
Home Depot 145, 323

IBM 12, 20, 24, 37, 47, 139,
142, 201
Ikea 145, 303
impact of corporate
responsibility 281–311
dimension of impact 281, 282,
287–303
economic impact 292–3
environmental 9, 21, 66, 69, 142,
144, 146, 187, 196, 197, 198,
214, 226, 227, 240, 243, 246,
250, 259, 270, 272, 284, 289,
290, 294, 328, 329
ethical trade 297–8
limits of knowledge 283–6
producer behaviour 300
social impact 290–2
understanding impact 273,
281–7
impact investing 243, 335
India 4, 37, 39, 45, 49, 51, 58, 63,
77, 89, 93, 101, 102, 105,
143, 219, 220, 240, 247,
274–5, 297, 306, 323, 333,
338, 339, 348, 354
Indonesia 20, 23, 37, 49, 54, 76, 77,
83, 96, 99, 104, 105, 119,

221, 228, 255, 258, 291,
293, 327
Institute of Chartered Accountants
in England and Wales 70,
341
institutional investors 26, 161, 165,
167, 171, 174, 218, 226, 228,
232, 235, 236, 238, 240, 241,
243, 247, 319, 326, 351
International Business Leaders
Forum 341, 358
International Cocoa Initiative 49
International Commission on
Mining and Metals
(ICMM) 112
International Finance
Corporation 110, 214
International Integrated Reporting
Committee (IIRC) 175
International Labour Organization
(ILO) 35, 49, 79, 106, 108
International Organization for
Standardization (ISO) 108
IPCC 4, 53, 54, 62, 63, 73, 74,
172, 199
ISO14001 341

Johnson & Johnson 217, 289
principles 209
Tylenol response 27
Johnson Matthey 148
Joint Initiative on Corporate
Accountability and Workers'
Rights (JOINT) 212
joint initiatives 221, 296

Kenya 88, 94–5, 100, 119, 234,
261, 306
key concepts
business ethics 15
corporate governance 161
external verification
statement 194
international development 78
international governance 108
licence to operate 42
performance (investment) 227
small and medium sized
enterprise 256–7
social accounting 180
social enterprise 270
stakeholder 202
sustainable development 54–5
KPMG 4, 24, 179, 180, 186, 188–92,
194, 195, 199, 283, 284, 308,
310, 336

Latin America 216, 217, 219, 235,
268, 323

legitimacy theory 192
Levi Strauss 138, 211, 299, 341, 351
liberal economics 39, 67, 82, 85,
      101, 102, 106, 123, 161, 203,
      204, 314, 317, 324, 331, 345
liberalization 50, 104, 122, 319, 332
licence to operate 40, 42, 44, 47,
      116, 134, 145, 147, 149,
      192, 258, 263, 269, 276, 346,
      352, 355
limited liability 34, 35, 38, 50
Love Canal 38

M-PESA 88, 90, 94–5
Marikana mine (South Africa) 335
Marx, Karl 335
materiality motivation 12, 16–17
Maxwell, Robert 165
MDGs see Millennium Development
      Goals
Merck 27, 323
microcredit 242–3
Millennium Development Goals
      (MDGs) 85, 121, 232, 282
   relationship to Monterrey
      Consensus 86
Millennium Ecosystem Assessment
      Report 54
MITIE 300
Monks, Robert 236
   governance 349
monster business (Thomas
      Quinn) 36

negative screening 232
neoliberal 64, 79, 86, 102, 321
NetImpact 302
Nike 132, 134, 138, 211, 294, 301,
      340, 343
Northern Rock 169
Novartis 139

OECD see Organisation for
      Economic Co-operation
      and Development
offensive corporate
      responsibility 81, 133, 156
   BP 132
   Nike 132
Organisation for Economic Co-
      operation and Development
      (OECD) 9, 79
   guidelines for MNCs 9
   Principles of Corporate
      Governance 171

P8 Group 236
Partnership on Clean Development
      and Climate 63

Partnership for Quality Medical
      Product Donation 23
partnerships 111–17
   corporate 16, 137
   and globalization 103, 116–17
   as ideology 112–13
   International Cocoa Initiative 49
   and international
      development 93, 111
   multi-stakeholder 108, 111, 113,
      214, 222, 305, 321, 352
      EITI 218
      FSC 214
      RSPO 220–2
      TXU 352
   with other sectors 132
   participation of business
      critics 321
   public-private 111
   PuR 80
   stakeholders 98, 99, 108, 111,
      113, 210, 305, 321
   types 114
      rule-setting 114–15
      unmet challenges 98, 117–19
Patagonia 151, 340
philanthropy 12, 33, 90, 115, 238,
      336, 342
   CANOPUS 241
   and partnership 115
   SMEs 263
   venture philanthropy 238–40,
      241
   Victorian 272
positive screening 232–3
poverty 4, 33, 40, 44, 241, 242, 259,
      300, 318, 344, 347
   alleviation 111, 176
   anti-globalization 102
   aspects of 83
   bias of markets 84
   bottom of the pyramid 88
   business agenda 80
   business' awareness of 77
   business as bystander 82
   business as cause 82–5
   Business as development
      agent 76–7
   business as development
      tool 76–7
   as business opportunity 82, 94–5
   business relationship to 77
   business as solution 86–9
   business as victim 85–6
   business-poverty framework 75,
      81–2
   causes of 79
   child labour 83
   co-creation 89

   and commodized relations 85
   and corruption 83
   and development 93
   effectiveness of interventions 80
   extreme 54, 85
   and famine 60
   footprint 119
   and globalization 86
   and inequality 215
   managing 90–1
   MDGs 85
   microcredit 242
   preferencing 91
   reduction 75, 76, 95
   remaining in 54
   Russia 259
   social enterprise 271, 272, 273
   targeting the poor 88
   wealth and equity 102
   women and 83
      see also women
PricewaterhouseCoopers 341
Principles for Responsible
      Investment 9, 69, 115, 208,
      229, 230, 247
private equity 26, 117, 238, 242,
      250, 295, 319, 351, 352, 356
production, sustainable 347–8
proxy voting 235, 236–7, 238
PUMA, environmental
      reporting 196–8

Quakers 48, 227, 272

Race to the Top project, IIED 303
Ralph Lauren 299
Raytheon 15
Reebok Human Rights
      Foundation 271
religious groups, role in
      investment 231
resource curse 218
responsible investment 35
   engagement in 235–8
   ethical investment 227–30
   growth in the market 225, 247–8
   indexes 225, 228, 233, 243,
      244–5, 246, 251
   negative screening 232
   origins and development 225,
      226–30
   performance 225, 244–5, 246–7,
      293
   positive screening 232–3
   social stock exchange (SSE) 235,
      247
   sustainable investing 225, 230–1,
      245, 252
   trends 225, 248–9

responsible investment (continued)
  types of 225, 231–5
    alternatives 225, 234–5,
      238–43
    UN PRI 69, 115, 208, 229, 230,
      247, 329, 345
return on investment 82, 90, 133
  social return on investment 145,
    239
  Social Return on Investment
    Index 239
Rio Tinto 291, 292, 310, 336
role of business in society 349–53
Roundtable on Sustainable Palm
    Oil (RSPO) 114, 208, 220–2,
    296, 341
RSPO see Roundtable for
    Sustainable Palm Oil
Rugmark 294
Rwanda 306

SA8000 213, 214, 341
Sarbanes-Oxley Act (2002) 167
SELCO-India 274–5
shareholder activism 235–6
Shell 110
  Brent Spar and Nigeria 47
  early reporting 185
Shell Foundation 87
small and medium sized
    enterprise 256–7
  corporate responsibility 261–3
  and corporate responsibility
    management 265–7
  local, national and regional
    differences 258–60
  responsibility issues for 263–6
SME see small and medium sized
    enterprise
Smith, Adam 34, 111
Smith Report 168
social accountability 9, 84, 211,
    282, 296
  embedding 205
  SAI 213
  social accounts 292
social accounting 182, 183, 292
  as key concept 180
  research 195
social conflict 182
social enterprise see social
    entrepreneurship
social entrepreneurship 268, 335
  and the corporate responsibility
    movement 312
  examples 271–2
  impact 273–4
  as key concept 270
  meanings of 269–71

trends 356
why now? 272–3
social investment indexes 225, 228,
    244–5, 252, 281, 300, 301,
    303, 304, 344
social reporting see corporate
    reporting
social return on investment see
    return on investment
socially responsible investment see
    responsible investment
South Africa 27, 39, 76, 77, 83, 85,
    87, 125, 130, 215, 216, 228,
    234, 239, 240, 247, 297, 302,
    324, 327, 333, 335, 337
South African Social Investment
    Exchange (SASIX) 234
SRI see responsible investment
stages of corporate
    responsibility 133–5
stakeholders 7
  accountability to 20, 47, 160,
    163, 170, 180
  business stakeholders 146, 149,
    287
  definitions of 7
  deviance and uniformity 201,
    215–17
  dialogue 205, 207, 316
  engagement 174
    versus management 204–7
  external stakeholders 146, 149,
    181, 182, 186, 194, 301
  impact 300–2
  importance to contemporary
    corporate responsibility 10
  key concept 202
  legitimacy of 342
  legitimate interests of 353
  managing versus
    engagement 204–7
  meaning and origins 201–7
  multi-stakeholder development
    projects 121
  multi-stakeholder
    governance 84, 106–8,
    164, 218
  multi-stakeholder standards 208,
    211, 212
  partnership types 114
  partnerships 98, 99, 108, 111,
    113, 210, 321
  pluralist reponsibility 204
  shift to stakeholder company 47
  SME decision-making 264
  stakeholder analysis 65, 206
  stakeholder theory 47
  tobacco industry 321
standards see codes of practice

Starbucks 23, 84, 85, 118, 294, 307
Stern Review 57, 65, 66
stranded assets 230
strategy
  corporate responsibility as 141–3
  GE 142
  strategic integration of corporate
    responsibility 142
supply chains
  abuse of workers 46
  child labour 282
  environmental performance,
    PUMA 198
  food safety 108
  labour standards 290
  reducing waste in 289
  relationship to 153, 196, 340
  responsibility towards 295
  small producers 87
  SMEs and environmental
    standards 276
  social and environmental
    conditions 131
  social and environmental
    performance 91–2
  trading relations 119
SustainAbility 327, 353, 358
  matrix 149
sustainability leaders, discredited
    companies 300
Sustainable Agriculture Initiative
    Platform 114, 115, 341
sustainable consumption and
    production 347–8, 356
Sustainable Consumption
    Institute 348
sustainable development 54–5
sustainable investing see responsible
    investment

Tata 23, 36, 220
Tesco 19, 138, 303, 323, 348, 352
The Economist 315
  critique of corporate
    responsibility 314
Timberland 137, 294, 340
Tobin tax 248, 329
trade unions 35, 36, 100, 106, 131,
    176, 211, 218, 219, 258, 261,
    263, 296, 300, 303
transparency 5, 13, 20, 134, 146,
    149, 176, 185, 216
  of business operations 176
  as a corporate responsibility
    challenge 335
  EITI 90
  G8 declaration 229
  and governance 216
  level of 194

relationship to
     accountability 195
of share-ownership 164
trends 350
Transparency International 20,
     284
triple bottom line 13, 22, 72, 73,
     118, 134, 145, 146, 315, 327
Trucost 304
Turnbull Committee 167

UBS 302, 329
UK Corporate Governance
     Code 170
Unilever 36, 96, 99, 140, 221, 288,
     292, 293, 309, 318, 333, 341
economic impact 76
Indonesia study 327
Oxfam 104, 119
Shakti 117
website 36
United Nations Development
     Programme 286

United Nations Global Compact 4,
     21, 86, 115, 120–2, 210,
     229, 232, 234, 237, 259,
     266, 283, 305, 318, 320,
     325, 341, 357
United Nations Principles for
     Responsible Investment 69,
     115, 208, 229, 230, 247,
     329, 345
United Nations Universal
     Declaration of Human
     Rights 37

values motivation 12
Venture philanthropy 238–40
Vice Fund (VICEX) 232
Vietnam 227, 297, 318

Wal-Mart 82, 131, 145, 192, 212,
     289, 294, 298, 309, 322, 352
welfare economics 79
   Sen's work on 79
welfare state 37, 271

in developing economies 17
in emerging economies 338
USA versus Denmark 323
Western countries 37
White's scenarios 336
Winslow Green Growth Fund
     (WGGF) 246
women
   gender 83, 91, 322
   gender inequality 85
   gender in labour codes 298
   gender in SMEs 264
   women's rights 38
Workers Rights Consortium 302
World Business Council for
     Sustainable Development
     (WBCSD) 25, 64–5, 96, 186,
     187, 286, 346
World Health Organization 320
WorldCom 167, 172, 334

Zambia 37, 41, 77, 119
Zippos 264–5